In Search of a Nation

EASTERN AFRICAN STUDIES

In Search of a Nation
Histories of Authority & Dissidence
in Tanzania

Edited by
GREGORY H. MADDOX
Professor of History, Texas Southern University

JAMES L. GIBLIN
Professor of History, University of Iowa

James Currey
OXFORD

Kapsel Educational Publications
DAR ES SALAAM

Ohio University Press
ATHENS, OH

James Currey Ltd
73 Botley Road
Oxford
OX2 0BS

Kapsel Educational Publications
PO Box 35013, Dar es Salaam

Ohio University Press
The Ridges, Building 19
Athens, Ohio 45701, USA

1 2 3 4 5 09 08 07 06 05

British Library Cataloguing in Publication Data
In search of a nation : histories of authority & dissidence
   in Tanzania. - (Eastern African studies)
   1. Nationalism - Tanzania - History   2. Tanzania - Politics
   and government
   I. Maddox, Gregory II. Giblin, James
   320.5'4'09678

ISBN 10: 0-85255-488-5 (James Currey Cloth)
ISBN 13: 978-085255-488-3 (James Currey Cloth)
ISBN 10: 0-85255-487-7 (James Currey Paper)
ISBN 13: 979-085255-487-6 (James Currey Paper)

Library of Congress Cataloging-in-Publication Data
available on request

ISBN10: 0-8214-1670-7 (Ohio University Press Cloth)
ISBN13:978-08214-1670-9(Ohio University Press Cloth)
ISBN 10: 0-8214-1671-5(Ohio University Press Paper)
ISBN 13: 978-08214-1671-6(Ohio University Press Paper)

Typeset in 10/10½ pt Baskerville
by Longhouse Publishing Services, Cumbria, UK
Printed and bound in Great Britain
by Woolnough, Irthlingborough

Contents

List of Maps, Figures & Tables   viii

Notes on Contributors   ix

Editors' Preface   xii

1
Introduction
GREGORY H. MADDOX & JAMES L. GIBLIN   1

Part I

POLITICS & KNOWLEDGE

2
On Socially Composed Knowledge
Reconstructing a Shambaa Royal Ritual
STEVEN FEIERMAN   14

3
Kingalu Mwana Shaha & Political Leadership
in Nineteenth-Century Eastern Tazania
EDWARD A. ALPERS   33

Part II

POLITICS, CULTURE & DISSENT
IN COLONIAL TANGANYIKA

4
Colonial Boundaries & African Nationalism
The Case of the Kagera Salient
RALPH A. AUSTEN   57

5
Indirect Rule, the Politics of Neo-Traditionalism
& the Limits of Invention in Tanzania
THOMAS SPEAR   70

Contents

6

Narrating Power in Colonial Ugogo
Mazengo of Mvumi
GREGORY H. MADDOX   86

7

The Tribal Past & the Politics of Nationalism in Mahenge District
1940–60
JAMIE MONSON   103

8

The Landscapes of Memory in Twentieth-Century Africa
E. S. ATIENO ODHIAMBO   114

9

Some Complexities of Family & State in Colonial Njombe
JAMES L. GIBLIN   128

10

Local, Regional & National
South Rukwa in the 1950s
MARCIA WRIGHT   149

Part III

THE NATION & ITS DISSIDENTS

11

Breaking the Chain at its Weakest Link
TANU & the Colonial Office
JOHN ILIFFE   168

12

Censoring the Press in Colonial Zanzibar
An Account of the Seditious Case against *Al-Falaq*
LAWRENCE E. Y. MBOGONI   198

13

An Imagined Generation
Umma Youth in Nationalist Zanzibar
THOMAS BURGESS   216

Contents

14

The Short History of Political Opposition
& Multi-Party Democracy in Tanganyika
1958–64
JAMES R. BRENNAN   250

Part IV

THE NATION RECONSIDERED

15

Engendering & Gendering African Nationalism
Rethinking the Case of Tanganyika (Tanzania)
SUSAN GEIGER   278

16

Between the 'Global' & 'Local' Families
The Missing Link in School History Teaching
in Postcolonial Tanzania
YUSUF Q. LAWI   290

17

Jack-of-All-Arts or Ustadhi?
The Poetics of Cultural Production in Tanzania
KELLY M. ASKEW   304

Index   328

List of Maps, Figures & Tables

Maps

Map of Tanzania   xiv

4.1   Tanzania-Uganda, showing the Kagera Salient   56

Figures

5.1   Arusha Chiefs   75

10.1   Territorial Totals for South Rukwa Groups   152

10.2   South Rukwans in Tanga Province   154

Tables

5.1   Meru Mangi   74

9.1   Marriages of Single and Multiple Wives   138

17.1   A Migrant Ministry: The Tanzanian Culture Division   311

Notes on Contributors

Edward A. Alpers is Professor of History at the University of California, Los Angeles. In 1994 he served as President of the African Studies Association. His major publications include *Ivory and Slaves in East Central Africa* (1975); *Walter Rodney: Revolutionary and Scholar*, co-edited with Pierre-Michel Fontaine (1982); *Africa and the West: A Documentary History from the Slave Trade to Independence*, co-edited with William H. Worger and Nancy Clark (2001); *History, Memory and Identity*, co-edited with Vijayalakshmi Teelock (2001); and *Sidis and Scholars: Essays on African Indians*, co-edited with Amy Catlin-Jairazbhoy (2004).

Kelly M. Askew is Associate Professor in the Department of Anthropology and the Center for Afroamerican and African Studies at the University of Michigan. Her research spans performance theory, ethnomusicology, poetics, cultural politics, nationalism, and media in East Africa. She is the author of *Performing the Nation: Swahili Music and Cultural Politics in Tanzania* (2002) and co-edited with Richard R. Wilk *The Anthropology of Media: A Reader* (2002).

Ralph A. Austen is Professor of African History and Co-Chair of the Committee on African and African-American Studies at the University of Chicago. He is the author of *Northwest Tanzania under German and British Rule* (1969), *African Economic History: Internal Development and External Dependency* (1987); *The Elusive Epic: the Narrative of Jeki la Njambe in the Historical Culture of the Cameroon Coast* (1996); co-author with Jonathan Derrick of *Middlemen of the Cameroon Rivers: the Duala and their Hinterland, ca. 1600-ca. 1960* (1999) and editor of *In Search of Sunjata: the Mande Epic as History, Literature and Performance* (1999).

James R. Brennan is Lecturer in African History at the School of Oriental and African Studies (SOAS), University of London. He received his PhD in History from Northwestern University in 2002. Currently he is writing a monograph on the history of nationalism, race, and identity in Dar es Salaam.

Thomas Burgess is an Assistant Professor at Hampton University. His area of research interest has been the relationships between the Zanzibari Revolution, generation, nationalism and discipline. He lives in Hampton, Virginia and returns to Tanzania almost every summer for additional research.

Steven Feierman was a colleague of Isaria Kimambo's when they were

Ph.D. students together. Feierman is Professor of History and Sociology of Science at the University of Pennsylvania and also Professor of History. He is the author of *Peasant Intellectuals* (1990), and other works.

Susan Geiger was Professor Emeritus of Women's Studies at the University of Minnesota. She earned her Ph.D. from the University of Dar es Salaam. She was the author of over a dozen studies on African women's history including *TANU Women: Gender and Culture in the Making of Tanganyikan Nationalism, 1955–1965* (1997). She also authored articles on the uses of life history in historical research, co-edited three anthologies, and served on the editorial board of *Signs* for four years.

James L. Giblin is a Professor of African History in the Department of History, University of Iowa. Among his publications on Tanzania are *The Politics of Environmental Control in Northeastern Tanzania, 1840–1940* (1992). Another book, a social history of Tanzania's Southern Highlands in the twentieth century entitled *A History of the Excluded: Making Family and Memory a Refuge from State in Twentieth-Century Tanzania*, is forthcoming from James Currey (2005).

John Iliffe is Professor of African History at St John's College, University of Cambridge. Among his many publications are: *A Modern History of Tanganyika* (1979); *The African Poor: A History* (1987); *Africans: The History of a Continent* (1995); and *East African Doctors: A History of the Modern Profession* (1998).

Yusuf Q. Lawi is Senior Lecturer in History at the University of Dar es Salaam. He was Chair of the department from 2000 to 2003. He has published a number of articles locally and internationally in the fields of social and environmental history.

Gregory H. Maddox is Professor of History at Texas Southern University. He has taught in the Department of History at the University of Dar es Salaam. He is the author of several essays on the environmental history of Africa and on the production of history in central Tanzania. He translated and edited Mathais Mnyampala's *The Gogo: History, Customs and Traditions*.

Lawrence E.Y. Mbogoni is a Tanzanian currently teaching at William Paterson University of New Jersey. Previously he has taught at the University of Dar es Salaam, and at Luther College, Iowa. He is the author of *The Cross vs. the Crescent: Religion and Politics in Tanzania* (2004).

Jamie Monson is Associate Professor of History at Carleton College. Her current research interest is the rural development history of the TAZARA railway in Tanzania, and China's development experience in Africa. She is also co-directing a collaborative research project on the Maji Maji rebellion. She has published articles on Maji Maji, on memory and migration, and on agricultural history in southern Tanzania.

Notes on Contributors

E.S. Atieno Odhiambo is Professor of History at Rice University. He is co-author with David William Cohen of: *Siaya: Historical Anthropology of an African Landscape* (1989); *Burying SM: The Politics of Power and the Sociology of Knowledge in Africa* (1992); and *The Risks of Knowledge: Investigations into the Death of Robert Ouko* (2004). He is editor of *African Historians and African Voices* (2001), and co-editor, with John Lonsdale, of *Mau Mau and Nationhood* (2003).

Thomas Spear is Professor of History at the University of Wisconsin and former Director of its African Studies Program and Chair of the History Department. He is the author of *Zwangendaba's Ngoni* (1972), *The Kaya Complex* (1978), *Kenya's Past* (1981), *The Swahili*, with Derek Nurse (1985), and *Mountain Farmers* (1997) and editor of *Being Maasai*, with Richard Waller (1993), *East African Expressions of Christianity*, with Isaria Kimambo (1999), and the *Journal of African History*.

Marcia Wright is Professor of History at Columbia University. She is the author of *German Missions in Tanganyika: Lutherans and Moravians in the Southern Highlands, 1891–1941* (1971), *Strategies of Slaves and Women: Life Stories from East-Central Africa* (1993), 'Maji Maji: Prophecy and Historiography', in *Revealing Prophets: Prophecy in Eastern African History*, ed. D.M. Anderson and D.H. Johnson, (1995), and 'Life and Technology in Everyday Life: Reflections on the Career of Mzee Stefano, Master Smelter in Ufipa, Tanzania', *Journal of African Cultural Studies*, 15, 1 (2002).

Editors' Preface

This volume is first and foremost a tribute to Professor I.N. Kimambo. The quality of the essays contained here reflects the esteem and affection Professor Kimambo has earned over his long years of service to his country, his institution and his profession. Both editors personally have received the benefit of his support and counsel over the years. We would also like to thank Mary and the rest of the Kimambo family for the generosity with which they have shared the professor and the hospitality they have shown our families both in Tanzania and in the United States.

The essays collected here reflect the respect in which Professor Kimambo is held, and the influence which his work has exerted on his fellow historians. The original festschrift that formed the basis of this volume was presented to Professor Kimambo at a meeting of the Historical Association of Tanzania in Dar es Salaam in June 2001. Two essays that formed part of that collection could not be included in this volume. The editors would like to thank Rhonda Gonzalez, Gloria Waite, and Christopher Ehret and Arnold Temu for the contributions and to commend them to readers in their alternatively published forms. The editors would also like to thank the contributors for their patience with the process leading to the publication of this work. Several have held off publication of their essays elsewhere in order to be included. The comments of the reader of the manuscript proved helpful and enlightening. The editors would also like to thank Taylor and Francis (www.tandf.co.uk), the publishers of *Social Identities*, for permission to reprint the article by Susan Geiger from Volume 5, Number 3 (1999) of that journal and the Historical Association of Tanzania for permission to reprint the article by John Iliffe from *Tanzania Zamani*, Volume III, Number 2 (1997) of that journal.

The members and leaders of the historical community in Tanzania played a major role in bringing this project to fruition. Dr N. N. Luanda provided crucial support at the beginning of the project. Dr Y.Q. Lawi and Dr Eginald Mihanjo helped organize the conference that catalyzed the collection. The staff of the History Department at the University of Dar es Salaam and Dr Andrew Burton and the British Institute in East Africa also provided important assistance.

The editors would also like to thank Texas Southern University for its long-time commitment to co-operation with the University of Dar es Salaam. Texas Southern hosted Professor Kimambo as a Fulbright Visiting Scholar in 1991–92 and has underwritten several important initiatives in conjunction with the University of Dar es Salaam. In particular, the editors would like to thank Dr Joseph Jones, Dean of the Graduate School and Associate Provost for Research, for his support. We are also grateful for the assistance of Carol Mitchell of TSU.

Finally, we would like to express our appreciation to our families for both their support and their insight. Kate and Anthony have, as always, kept things lively. Blandina and Sheryl have shaped, and continue to shape, our understanding of the place where, and people with whom, we have come to work. They are our guides even as they follow their own muses.

Map

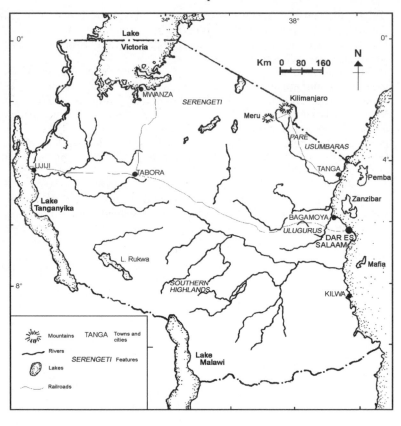

Map of Tanzania

One

~~~~~~~~~~~~~~~~~~~~~~~~~~~~~~~~~~~~

Introduction

GREGORY H. MADDOX
&
JAMES L. GIBLIN

African nationalism has experienced hard going in recent scholarship. Some scholars regard it as an alien, even cancerous presence. Working from a position not far different from Benedict Anderson's depiction of the nation as an 'imagined community,'[1] Basil Davidson has described nationalism as a Western import which prevented Africans from adapting their precolonial heritage of political institutions and ideas to postcolonial conditions.[2] Similarly, Mahmood Mamdani has argued that the nation remains alien to the rural masses who are denied the rights of nationality.[3] Yet, anyone who in October 1999 joined the crowds along the streets of the Tanzanian capital Dar es Salaam or in its National Stadium, as the body of the first President, 'Mwalimu' J.K. Nyerere, was borne through the city to be laid in state, would have difficulty denying that, while the nation may be 'imagined', it is a fundamental reality. Throughout those days, grieving millions could be heard debating the meaning of their nationality.

One year later, the run-up to the second multiparty election in Tanzania,[4] and especially its aftermath, gave ammunition to those who portray African nationalism as a hollow shell. The emphasis of the ruling party, *Chama cha Mapinduzi* (CCM), on peace and unity in the country was used quite explicitly to delegitimize critiques of the government's policies and the state of the economy. Issues including the effects of IMF-imposed economic liberalization, the treatment of Muslims, corruption, and the Union between the Mainland and Zanzibar all became subsumed by CCM's rhetoric about peace and unity. While CCM's rhetoric seemed to have the effect of limiting support for the opposition in some regions of the mainland, on the islands of Zanzibar and especially Pemba continuing tensions over the elections resulted in violent clashes by February 2001.

The double-sided nature of nationalism reflected in these two events – its capacity to inspire expressions of unity on the one hand, and its tendency to narrow political debate on the other – is a manifestation of the

1

history explored in the essays in this book. The narrative of the nation of Tanzania, which was created by the anti-colonist nationalist movement, expanded by the Union after the Zanzibar Revolution, and fused with the ideology of *Ujamaa* by Julius Nyerere, has shaped Tanzanian political discourse for decades, but has not obliterated the great wealth of political discourses and identities which exist within the nation. Some of these identities and discourses have grown out of forms that pre-dated colonial conquest, but were transformed by colonialism, particularly the British policy of Indirect Rule. Others were created by the spread of Christianity and the rise of wage labor and the expansion of urban areas during the colonial period. Many of them, including Muslim religious organizations and networks in particular, have not been recognized as legitimate forms of political expression by either the colonial or postcolonial state

The essays in this volume re-examine the links between politics, culture and knowledge in Tanzania from the nineteenth century up to the present. They place the narrative of nation in a longer history of political authority, control of knowledge, and political dissidence. They suggest that, rather than emerging out of a gradual enlargement of scale of political activity, as an early form of nationalist historiography once had it, the nation formed through contest and debate over state power. Yet, while the nation and national state have never been as hegemonic or as totalizing as both critics and supporters sometimes suggest, they have provided a new context in which older discourses about power and knowledge are transformed and given renewed expression. In this way the nation has become a fundamental part of the lived experience of all Tanzanians, whether they reside in the nation's cities or in its countryside. Much recent scholarly writing on Africa implicitly posits a division between state and community. Authors such as Mamdani, Scott, and Herbst[5] portray states, failed or otherwise, as alien and alienating for the communities over which they rule. In particular, Mamdani argues that, because the postcolonial state draws its legitimacy primarily from urban society and modernity, its rural people remain more subordinated subjects rather than citizens endowed with democratic rights. Yet, in much of Africa, including Tanzania, both urban and rural people possess institutions of modernity – schools, churches, mosques, NGOs, political parties – which provide a multiplicity of networks and a variety of ways of exerting influence on politicians and bureaucrats.[6] While people in both city and countryside may feel alienated from their nation, it remains the frame that encompasses and links the domains of family, locality, and ethnicity with the broader world.

Historicizing Nationalism: an Argument

The double-sided nature of Tanzania's recent experience with nationalism suggests to us that it badly needs to be historicized as both product and cause of historical change. Perhaps the first step in doing so is to explore the relationship between nationalism and the forms of authority and knowledge which pre-dated it, resisted it, and co-existed with it. This is the step taken by the contributions in this volume. Although they address a wide variety of themes and situate themselves in an equally wide variety of localities within Tanzania, they coalesce into the following argument. Precolonial political authority claimed neither omniscience nor monopoly over knowledge. Instead, it sought legitimacy and social cohesion by synthesizing combinations of knowledge, some of which arose in intensely local circumstances, and others which emerged through interrelationships which extended across wide regions. Colonial conquest, however, introduced a new relationship between authority and knowledge. Now, the state claimed the power to control the production and dissemination of knowledge, to classify it in hierarchies which assigned lesser value to some forms of knowledge, and to use knowledge to count, regulate and otherwise administer its population. The colonial state largely denied Africans access to many forms of modern knowledge, leaving them only local bodies of knowledge, which it classified as inferior. Consigned in this way to local spheres of action, however, Africans dissented and questioned authority in a great variety of ways. The resulting crisis of legitimacy forced the state, reluctantly and with much foot-dragging, to begin granting Africans the political liberties which would allow state authority to generate legitimacy and compliance through modern forms of liberal governance. This is a project which, though begun during the last decade of colonial rule, was largely conducted by the postcolonial nationalist state. It was a project, moreover, which placed sharp limits on freedom, particularly by sanctioning political expression only in narrow discursive social fields. Yet, under the postcolonial state dissidents have continuously struggled to efface the boundaries which distinguish legitimate and illegitimate political expression. Let us now look more closely at how the essays in this volume merge into this argument.

Part I of this volume contains two essays about precolonial political authority. Both of them are situated in the portion of Tanzania where documentary sources about its precolonial history are richest – the northeast. The conclusions drawn in these essays by Steven Feierman on Usambara and by Edward Alpers on Uluguru contribute mightily, however, to our understanding of precolonial political structures throughout eastern Africa. Both show how precolonial authority, while demonstrating stunning creativity in the political use of ritual and ideology, sought legitimacy by synthesizing knowledge drawn from different sources. The fascinating aspect of the rituals which followed the death of a Shambaa king and identified his successor, argues Feierman, is that no one could claim possession of all the knowledge needed to complete them. Knowledge about them was divided among numerous individuals and groups, whose co-operation was required if the rituals of royal death and succession were to maintain the continuity of royal authority. Where Feierman stresses creativity in organizing ritual, Alpers emphasizes innovativeness in the political career of the Luguru chief, Kingalu mwana Shaha. The Kingalu, who ruled from the 1850s through to the early 1870s, drew his legitimacy partly from highly localized sources – clan identities and the power of rainmaking. Yet, the surprising twist in Alpers' story is that this Luguru chief was born on the Swahili coast, and derived much of his authority from coastal and Muslim identity as well as coastal connections. These connections, together with his innovativeness in the political use of ritual, tradition and religion, allowed the Kingalu to maintain power in a period when the expansion of trade from Zanzibar was transforming the political landscape of the coastal hinterland.

One reason why resistance to authority, the central theme of the essays in Part II, was such a pervasive aspect of the colonial period is surely because colonial rule discouraged the extraordinary creativity and innovativeness found in these examples from Usambara and Uluguru. Perhaps in a different time and place, a colonizing power might have appreciated political traditions capable of fostering social cohesion and assimilating a great variety of social and religious influences. The forms of authority described by Feierman and Alpers could not easily co-exist, however, with the modernist ambitions of Tanzania's colonial rulers. Like modern states, precolonial rulers depended on knowledge. Yet, because political knowledge was both dispersed and localized, rulers could manipulate it well only by combining competence in intensely local affairs and conditions with participation in social networks which were regional in scope.

By contrast, colonial government claimed near omniscience in the production, preservation and deployment of knowledge. Beginning with the precise demarcation of a field for social intervention through the creation of territorial boundaries, as the essay by Ralph Austen shows, the colonial state claimed the right and obligation to count and classify its population, to define what constituted social improvement, and to intervene in social affairs in order to achieve it. These pretensions demanded hierarchies of authority and knowledge. Colonial hierarchies relentlessly subordinated local knowledge to the rationality of Western knowledge, and at the same time tried to confine African political actors to highly localized fields of action. Unlike precolonial political techniques, they did not encourage integration and cohesion, but caused exclusion, subjugation, and ultimately fierce resentment. Yet, subordinated and confined though it may have been, 'one of the fascinating things about local historical knowledge,' as Feierman reminds us, 'is that we have no way of knowing what its political uses will be'. As many of the essays in Part II show, local historical knowledge took on new meaning as the colonized resisted being confined to the local stage – and resisted being told that their knowledge was inferior, irrational, and lacking in universal applicability. This resistance became probably the strongest political impulse of the colonial period. This impulse continued into the postcolonial era, with members of local communities continuing to try to translate and transform knowledge from the past and to write their way into the future.[7]

Essays by Thomas Spear, Jamie Monson and Gregory Maddox show us that local history provided a crucially important basis for political activity in the period from the mid-1920s through to 1961, when in many areas political life was dominated by chiefs appointed under the British administrative system of Indirect Rule. Although these chapters cover very different regions, the political dynamics discussed within them appear

4

strikingly similar. Spear covers one of the most highly developed areas of the colony – Arusha, the northern region of settler farms and coffee-growers. Monson deals with one of the most isolated areas of the territory – the Kilombero Valley in the south. Maddox studies the central province of Dodoma – a region deeply impoverished, yet closely connected with surrounding regions through trade and labor migration.

Spear focuses on the 'politics of neo-traditionalism'– the reworking of local political knowledge in the new context of Native Authority chiefship. He shows that, to be successful, chiefs had to be resourceful in combining the 'patrimonial politics' of clientship with the bureaucratic politics of the colonial administration. As resentment of European land alienation welled up, however, the Arusha and Meru people combined old ideas of legitimacy and moral economy with new ideas of democracy. Once they found means of putting this combination of ideas into practice within churches and co-operatives, argues Spear, 'neo-traditional politics could no longer contain the tensions emerging within Arusha society'. Spear is careful to point out, however, that the deeply embedded body of ideas which we call 'tradition' was far from inflexible and unchanging. Instead, it was the product of intense debate. Monson and Maddox examine this debate closely. Monson shows that debate about history and ethnic identity in Kilombero became the starting point for opposition to one of the more oppressive chiefly regimes in colonial Tanganyika. It also lit the spark, she shows, that spread nationalism in Kilombero. Maddox describes the very complex political circumstances in which the important Para-mount of Ugogo, Mazengo, operated. Mazengo was regarded as highly dangerous, not only by his British superiors, but also by his subjects. In this context, a great variety of narratives developed, some defending Mazengo's legitimacy and others questioning it, but all trying to explain the source of his frightening, and perhaps malevolent, power.

As Monson points out, the debates which swirled around Native Authority chiefship were situated 'within the contexts of power established by colonial administration'. Similar direct confrontations with chiefly power occurred throughout Tanganyika. They were fed, however, by deeper, subterranean currents which, though not always visible in the narrow venues where political speech and activity were sanctioned by the colonial state, nevertheless nourished dissidence. In part, those currents were generated by an intense drive, reflected in the life course of many members of the colonial generations, to overcome the state regulations which tried to confine them to localized spheres of political and social action. One of the individuals who was most spectacularly successful in breaking out of these confines is described in the chapter by E.S. Atieno Odhiambo. Odhiambo discusses the life of Mohammed Hussein Bayume, a Nubian from Tanga who lived in Germany from 1919 until his death in a German concentration camp in 1943. Yet, the current of dissidence was fed not only by the ambition for mobility, but also by daily life in the most intimate social contexts.

Two essays on the Southern Highlands conclude this section. Marcia Wright shows how the practice of labor migration shaped concepts of community and identity not just in the workplaces of Tanga but also in their home districts around Lake Malawi. She argues that the identities thus formed proved capable of mobilization in the name of a broader anti-colonial nationalism while at the same time preserving room for a locally oriented critique. In his essay on Njombe in the Southern Highlands, James Giblin notes that a highly inflexible concept of tribe and family underlay claims to legitimacy by the district's Native Authority chiefs. While the chiefs pictured themselves as legitimate candidates for chiefly office by virtue of their membership in a rigid hierarchy of patrilineal clans, daily family living encouraged a perception of family as the product of continuous social negotiation and individual effort. Thus chiefly legitimacy was continually undermined, argues Giblin, by the experience of daily life, making the chiefs easy targets once the nationalist movement arose in the Southern Highlands in the late 1950s.

These studies show that, while colonial authority tried to confine Tanganyikans to highly localized spheres of political and economic action, it proved wholly ineffective in drawing legitimacy from local knowledge, political cultures and social relationships. Instead, many kinds of knowledge and many aspects of culture became sources of dissidence. Surely it was the colonial state's lack of legitimacy and its inability to control knowledge and culture which led it, in exceedingly cautious fashion, to expand political liberties during its last decade. Thus the chapters on local political life in the colonial period lead us to argue that the problem faced by the colonial state is that it possessed neither the means to rule through coercion (a point made vividly by John Iliffe's contribution to this volume), nor the means to exercise modern, liberal governance.

The anthropologist David Scott has recently written in very stimulating fashion about the difficulties faced by colonial states that wish to make this transition to modern governance. Drawing heavily on Michel Foucault, Scott argues that modern liberal states exercise control most effectively not through direct physical coercion, but through conceptions of authority, rights and responsibility which 'shape and govern the capacities, competencies, and wills of the governed'. Once such conceptions are 'inscribed into the cognitive-institutional terrain of social and political life,' continues Scott, 'power seeks to operate through the shaping of conduct rather than the shaping of bodies'. Above all, he contends, modern governance seeks to 'promote a *rational* and *responsible* self-conduct'. This modern style of self-conduct, he suggests, limits the social and discursive spheres in which citizens may exercise their political rights. Modern liberal states demand that their citizens confine political activity to very limited public spheres of political action and discourse. Participation in these spheres requires competence in particular forms of discourse. Once modern liberal governance became established, Scott argues, participation by competent actors in state-sanctioned political venues 'would be the only rational and legal way of exercising influence in what now counted as politics'. In short, he argues, the 'political problem' of states such as colonial Tanganyika was 'not merely to contain resistance and encourage accommodation but to seek to ensure that *both* could *only* be defined in relation to the categories

6

and structures of modern political rationalities'.[8] If we accept that the colonial state failed to instill modern political rationalities that would 'contain resistance and encourage accommodation' to itself, then the question remains whether nationalist ideology and the postcolonial state have been more successful.[9]

One aspect of creating modern political rationalities was identifying the areas of social life which would be controlled through liberal governance. An area that seems clearly to have been defined as an object of governance in the 1950s was the complex area that came to be regarded as race relations. The growing significance of race as a matter for government regulation is one of numerous fascinating points which emerge from John Iliffe's rich chapter. As Iliffe shows, safeguarding the rights of minority races through the policy of multi-racialism was an important source of British reluctance to relinquish power to TANU. Of course, Nyerere and TANU ultimately made a more effective appeal to liberal sensibilities than did the British colonial establishment, by arguing that the duty of post-colonial government was to protect the liberties not of racial communities, but of individuals. Nevertheless, once drawn into the discourse of race by its struggle against British multi-racialism, Tanzanian nationalism could not thereafter escape the fact that maintaining equity in matters defined as race relations would remain both a prime concern of government and a measure of effectiveness in governance.

Several chapters which, together with the essay by Iliffe, make up Part III of this volume suggest that the discourse of race obscured the subtleties of political change during the transition from colonial to postcolonial government. Both of our chapters on Zanzibar provide examples of great political and ideological complexity during the 1950s and 1960s. Lawrence Mbogoni's account of a sedition trial in 1954 shows that, among critics of British rule in Zanzibar, identities were shaped by an unstable mixture of ethnicity, language, political ideology and religion. Mbogoni asks us to consider whether, rather than containing racial tension, British tactics may have hastened the polarization of Zanzibar's population around racial identities. Thomas Burgess finds that similar complexity continued to shape radical politics in Zanzibar up to the Revolution of 1964. He argues that, by attributing the tensions that built up in the late 1950s and early 1960s merely to racial antagonisms, historians neglect a variety of factors. These include not only class and religion, but also generational identities, particularly that of the 'youth', and the desire to find access to patronage which animated some political activity among the young. Yet, in spite of these complexities of identity, ideology and political outlook on the ground, the first years of independence witnessed, as James Brennan puts it, an inexorable 'constricting [of the] the meager, late-colonial civil liberties that formed the boundaries of Tanganyika's discursive public sphere'. Brennan's chapter studies two small political parties that opposed TANU after independence, the African National Congress and the All-Muslim National Union of Tanganyika. He shows that, while a wide variety of concerns and interests, including Islam and generational conflict between senior men and young men, brought opponents of TANU into these parties, they trapped themselves within the narrow discursive fields created by the political rationalities which emerged in the last years of colonial rule. The ANC was trapped in talk about race. As Brennan says, it 'phrased ... multi-dimensional grievances in monochromatic racial terms'. Similarly, ANMUT found that the postcolonial state would simply not allow political organizing and political speech based on religious identity.

Brennan's argument – that national identity brought a narrowing of space for political talk and discourse – appears to leave a bleak prospect for the future. Yet grounds for optimism remain. The late Susan Geiger suggests that nationalism restored the dimension of the political culture of precolonial Tanzanian societies that the essays of Feierman and Alpers revealed. This was the way in which precolonial political cultures were made by combinations of knowledge, some produced locally and others obtained through mobility and widely dispersed social networks. Nationalism, she points out, appealed to men and 'women who already lived in multi-ethnic communities and participated in trans-tribal social and economic organizations'. She suggests that nationalism has released the currents of dissidence that remained hidden and subterranean under colonial rule. 'In the tradition of subverting colonial control,' she writes, Tanzanian men and women, 'seek in various ways, including cultural, to resist the authoritarian state.' Only the future can tell us whether Geiger's optimism is warranted. In the essays which conclude this volume, however, Y. Q. Lawi and Kelly Askew teach us a great deal about the practices and discourses which will determine whether the limits of post-colonial freedom will be determined more by currents of dissidence or by state power. Lawi demonstrates the effort made by the postcolonial state to transform the teaching of history into part of the nation-building process. The result, Lawi argues, has been the alienation of local communities from the process of formal historical production, as 'school history' has little relevance for people's lives. Likewise, while discussing musical culture in the 1990s, Askew examines tensions between local performing artists and the agencies of state which attempt to control culture and use it for pedagogical purposes. She leaves us with a very useful way of thinking about the relationship between nationalism, state authority and political dissidence.

The juxtaposition of Geiger's work with Askew's and Lawi's demonstrates a fundamental paradox at the core of the essays in this volume: the way in which nationalism in Tanzania both liberates and represses. While this argument can easily be compressed into a descending narrative emphasizing the betrayal of the emancipatory promise of both nationalism and *Ujamaa*, the history of nationalism in Tanganyika and Tanzania deserves more historicized treatment and the tension remains palatable today. A variety of factors, including the possibility of tribal and nationalist history being combined, the collapse of Indirect Rule legitimacies, the pervasive influence of a Swahili identity, and others outlined in the essays collected here combined to defeat British attempts to promote a tribal alternative to nationalism by the 1950s, leaving the then governor of

Tanganyika to write to his counterpart in Uganda, John Iliffe reports, that he is 'in the happy position of having a number of dissident groups but here every African is a nationalist'. Yet nationalism was more than a temporary alliance. In a passage influenced by Geiger's work, Alexander, McGregor and Ranger argue that people in Matabeleland in Zimbabwe 'feel that the nationalist goals they fought and suffered for were not only valuable in themselves, but remain one of the principal means through which they can hold the state to account'.[10] They note, by way of comparison, that TANU mobilized a diverse alliance of groups across the regions of Tanganyika in a way that was not possible in 'more developed' Rhodesia or more unevenly developed Mozambique.[11] As Brennan's essay notes, there remained little political or rhetorical space for opposition.

Yet Askew's and Lawi's chapters point out the reality of state power which people seek to use both nationalism and locally distinctive bodies of knowledge to resist. Appadurai, in an imaginative essay of local identity, has argued that the nation state:

> ... works by policing its borders, producing its 'people' ..., constructing its citizens, defining its capitals, monuments, cities, waters and soils, and by constructing its locales of memory and commemoration, such as graveyards and cenotaphs, mausoleums and museums. The nation-state conducts on its territories the bizarrely contradictory project of creating a flat, contiguous and homogeneous space of nationness and simultaneously a set of places and spaces (prisons, barracks, airports, radio-stations, secretariats, parks, marching grounds, processional routes) calculated to create the internal distinctions and divisions necessary for state ceremony, surveillance, discipline and mobilization. These latter are also the spaces and places that create and perpetuate the distinctions between rulers and ruled, criminals and officials, crowds and leaders, actors and observers.[12]

While demonstrating some of the ways that the state attempts to control cultural expression, Askew reminds us that, in order to use cultural expression for its own purposes, the state must depend on the creativity and performative ability of artists. In this way she brings us back to a point which runs through all of the contributions in this volume: no matter how energetic political authority may be in imposing its rationalities, people, and not just those the state would label as dissidents, continue to create alternative means, licit and illicit, for critiquing and contesting power.

Conclusion: historians, local histories, and the nation

In June 2001, the Historical Association of Tanzania (HAT) held a conference which, in very unusual fashion, brought academic historians and other scholars from within and outside Tanzania together with Tanzanian secondary school teachers. One of the purposes of the conference was to celebrate – or was it to mourn? – the retirement of the Association's long-serving president, Professor Isaria N. Kimambo, from the Department of History at the University of Dar es Salaam. At the conclusion of the conference, Professor Kimambo received a festschrift consisting of preliminary drafts of the chapters in this book. Professor Kimambo helped to found HAT in the 1960s during the first flowering of Africanist historiography that sought to restore agency to Africans in history. It has endured through several twists and turns in the development of historical study in and about Tanzania. It witnessed the nationalist-influenced concentration on resistance to colonialism, a turn towards Marxist-influenced political economy,[13] and a focus by historians in the 1980s and 1990s on social and environmental change. HAT has also linked scholars at the University of Dar es Salaam with teachers, curriculum developers, and non-professional historians through its publications and periodic conferences. By serving as one of the most important interfaces between the guild historians of the University and the educational professionals of the country,[14] it has played its part in building the Tanzanian nation.

During the conference, one of the secondary school teachers, frustrated with a national curriculum which some might characterize as arcane, as well as with the lack of teaching materials, demanded relevance. 'What,' she demanded, 'can we teach children about history that will help them survive in Tanzania today?' We do not know if any work of scholarly history can answer that question, and the essays in this collection will not try to answer it explicitly. Instead, the question serves as the text for this collection. The question, of course, interrogates not just the historiography of Tanzania but of Africa, and the discipline itself. Bound up in the teacher's question, and the context of its asking, lies one history of Tanzania, as well as the discontents with that history. The question plays off the hegemonic nature of official nationalist history created as Tanzania was created and in some ways pioneered for all Africa at the University of Dar es Salaam. It implicitly draws on the debates at the conference over the validity and importance of local historical knowledge in the face of perceived dramatic change brought about by modernity and globalization. It shifts across the discursive fields generated by colonialism, anti-colonial nationalism, and local resistance to the hegemonic tendencies of that nationalism.

Many of the academic presenters suggested that one way to give history immediacy for students would be to frame it around change in the intimate spheres of everyday life in family and community. Their strategy of studying the relationship between the local and the national, in order to reveal the significance of local historical change for the nation as a whole, took the conference back to what, as Steven Feierman reminds us in his essay, remains a central aspect of Professor Kimambo's scholarship. His work has been marked by a concern with both local and broader arenas; indeed, his long-time fascination with markets in precolonial society betrays a powerful interest in the concrete social institutions that connect localities with wider regions. Professor Kimambo's first book concentrated on highly localized political traditions, but did so in order to make a point of broad significance about them. His second book presented a history of interaction between local communities and the wider regional and international forces that beset them.[15] Yet, he has remained intensely concerned with the problems of building a national polity and a viable national economy. Throughout his career, he has labored to ensure that both the Department of History at UDSM as well as HAT would teach the citizens of Tanzania about the problems of building a cohesive and even prosperous nation. At both an intellectual and institutional level, Professor Kimambo has been at the center of the production of historical knowledge about and from Tanzania. He has remained committed to his profession, his institution and his nation despite at times tremendous hardship. In this volume we see some of the fruits of his labor and at the same time the degree of the struggle that remains. Yet, his steadfastness alone is cause enough to remain optimistic about his project and his country.

Notes

1. Benedict R. O'G. Anderson, *Imagined Communities: Reflections on the Origin and Spread of Nationalism*, 2d edn (New York: Verso, 1991).

2. Basil Davidson, *The Black Man's Burden: Africa and the Curse of the Nation State* (New York: Times Books, 1992).

3. Mahmood Mamdani, *Citizen and Subject: Contemporary Africa and the Legacy of Late Colonialism* (Oxford: James Currey and Princeton, NJ: Princeton University Press, 1996).

4. Tanzania had been a one-party state from the mid-1960s until 1992.

5. Mamdani, *Citizen and Subject*; James Scott, *Seeing Like a State: How Certain Schemes to Improve the Human Condition Have Failed* (New Haven, CT: Yale University Press, 1998); and Jeffrey Herbst, *States and Power in Africa: Comparative Lessons in Authority and Control* (Princeton, NJ: Princeton University Press, 2000).

6. Perhaps no scholar has captured the historicity of the intertwining of nationalism in Tanzania better than the late Susan Geiger in her work with the nationalist leader Bibi Titi Mohamed. See *TANU Women: Gender and Culture in the Making of Tanganyikan Nationalism, 1955-1965* (Oxford: James Currey and Portsmouth, NH: Heinemann, 1997). For a different perspective, see Mohamed Said, *The Life and Times of Abdulwahid Sykes: The Untold Story of the Muslim Struggle against British Colonialism in Tanganyika* (London: Minerva Press, 1998).

7. See the essays in Axel Harneit-Sievers (ed.), *A Place in the World: New Local Historiographies from Africa and South-Asia* (Leiden: Brill, 2002), especially Thomas Geider, 'The Paper Memory East Africa: Ethnohistories and Biographies Written in Swahili', pp. 255–88, and John Lonsdale, 'Contests of Time: Kikuyu Historiographies, Old and New', pp. 201–54.

8. David Scott, *Refashioning Futures: Criticism after Postcoloniality* (Princeton, NJ: Princeton University Press, 1999), pp. 83, 89, 84, 46 and 52 (all emphases in the original).

9. Research that would answer this question is only just beginning. The dissertations currently being written by James Brennan, Ned Bertz and Andrew Ivaska should go far towards addressing this problem.

10. Jocelyn Alexander, JoAnn McGregor, and Terence Ranger, *Violence and Memory: One Hundred Years in the 'Dark Forests' of Matabeleland* (Oxford: James Currey and Portsmouth, NH: Heinemann, 2000), p. 7.

11. *Ibid.*, p. 84.

12. Arjun Appadurai, 'The Production of Locality', in Richard Fardon (ed.), *Counterworks: Managing the Diversity of Knowledge* (New York: Routledge, 1995), p. 213.

13. I. N. Kimambo, *Three Decades of Historical Research at Dar es Salaam* (Dar es Salaam:

GREGORY MADDOX & JAMES L. GIBLIN

University of Dar es Salaam Press, 1993). See also Arnold Temu and Bonaventure Swai, *Historians and Africanist History: A Critique* (London: Zed Books, 1981), pp. 18–60.
14. Y.Q. Lawi, 'Between the Global and Local Families: The Missing Link in the Teaching of History', Paper presented at the Historical Association of Tanzania Conference, June 2001.
15. I.N. Kimambo, *A Political History of the Pare of Tanzania, c. 1500–1900* (Nairobi: East African Publishing House, 1969), and *Penetration and Protest in Tanzania: the Impact of the World Economy on the Pare, 1860–1960* (London: James Currey and Athens, OH: Ohio University Press, 1991).

Part I

Politics & Knowledge

Two

∧∧∧∧∧∧∧∧∧∧∧∧∧∧∧∧∧∧∧

On Socially Composed Knowledge
Reconstructing a Shambaa Royal Ritual

STEVEN FEIERMAN

Social historians of Tanzania, over the years since Isaria Kimambo began to write, have all been subject to the ethnographic impulse – the need to interpret ways of thinking, speaking and acting that are radically different from their own. Whether it was Kimambo himself explaining the spread of the *mshitu* ritual as a political process in South Pare, or Gilbert Gwassa describing the force of Kinjikitile's leadership, whether it was Frederick Kaijage evoking the conceptions of time held by laborers coming to the industrial workplace for the first time, or (more recently) Yusufu Lawi reconstructing precolonial Iraqw ideas about soil and landscape, they have all engaged in the interpretation of cultural practices they themselves do not share.[1] Academic historians who study oral traditions are inevitably subject to the ethnographic impulse because their assumptions about the natural world and about historical causation are very different from those of the men and women who tell traditions.

This essay is about a historical ritual that must be interpreted, or translated – made comprehensible – if it is to become a part of the academic historian's knowledge, but yet is resistant to interpretation. The usual descriptive strategies lead to a form of misrepresentation. The rite in question took place in the nineteenth-century Shambaa kingdom. It began at the moment of a king's death and ended when his successor was acknowledged as king at Vugha, the royal capital, at dawn on the fifth day after the death. The process was an elaborate one, divided into many segments. The heir, who was brought from Bumbuli over a period of two nights, stopped again and again, each time taking part in ritual actions that, taken all together, would make him king. Meanwhile, the old king's body was taken through parallel rites that ended with his burial at just the moment his successor was named king. Each performance – burial and installation – was meant to shadow the other.

It was that most paradoxical of rituals: central to public life, yet unseen and unknown. It was unseen, except for its concluding moments, since it

14

was secret. Even the men who performed it saw only fragments of the total ritual, because its two halves unfolded at the same time, and each one was divided into multiple segments. It was unknown, except in fragments, because each hereditary owner of ceremonial knowledge, and each office holder, knew and performed only a small part of the total rite. Proper performance depended on ritual knowledge, but that knowledge was divided among many men.

One of the jobs of the historian-as-ethnographer is to describe collective knowledge, collective practice, or collective consciousness. But knowledge in this case was not held collectively; each man held a bit of knowledge that was seen as his own, knowledge that circulated only within a limited sphere. Even if the historian were to record many pieces, as I did, these would not add up to collective knowledge, because they would never have been assembled in the same way in the minds of the men who actually owned the knowledge.

A second job of the interpretive historian in relation to ritual is to describe its meaning or significance – the way it works, what it does. A ceremony can be taken as a representation of the values and under-standings people shared at the time. Or it can be taken as a means that people possessed, at that time, for shaping collective emotions among those taking part – bringing the people, for example, to form an affective bond with their king. In this respect, also, the royal ritual of death and accession is resistant to interpretation, because no one ever saw it except in frag-ments. How, then, could it have shaped emotions or represented values?

If we as historians say that the men who owned the ritual knowledge in the late nineteenth century were interested in coherent representation, then we are attempting to speak through those men, much as a spirit speaks through a medium. The role does not suit us.[2] We cannot pretend that the owners of historical and ritual knowledge at the time were interested in making a general picture of collective values. They were, instead, interested in asserting historical claims to political influence. And they were interested – at a moment of the gravest danger and the most violent conflict – in making a king. The separate historical knowledge of each man, each lineage, needed to be mobilized in concert with each of the others if a king were to be made. Knowledge was not collective; it was socially composed.[3] This was at the heart of the political process. The new king could not be installed unless men from diverse lineages, with diverse interests, could be made to assemble their knowledge at the same time in a continuous set of actions.

Oral knowledge that is socially composed is potentially much richer than knowledge that is collectively held and homogeneous. When bits of information are distributed among specialists, or among diverse owners, there is a division of labor in oral transmission. This socially distributed pattern of knowing is well suited to the preservation of a broad range of information. It is, by chance, also suited to providing subject matter for an academic historian. The historian's job, after all, is to compare diverse bits of data so as to reconstruct the probable course of past events. The academic historian and the original owner of the knowledge speak to one another across a great divide. On the one side of the divide, the academic historian pretends to have an encyclopedic intelligence, capable of assembling all the pieces in a single pattern. On the other side, the men who owned the knowledge assembled it through a social negotiation; the transmission of knowledge and the solution of political problems proceeded in a single seamless process. The owners' knowledge of past kings and past installations was, if seen in this way, a usable knowledge.

The subject of usable knowledge brings us back to Isaria Kimambo, because all his work, from the early reconstruction of Pare political history, to his work on regional history, to his analysis of economic history, is meant to create a usable past for contemporary Tanzania.[4] I am suggesting that the history of the Shambaa ritual of royal death and accession ought to be approached as a dialogue between politically and socially situated historians today, with their own sense of a usable past, and the men who actually owned the historical knowledge at the time, who were also socially situated. In addition, a third group of historians enters the picture: the ones who inherited the knowledge and explained it to me, but who were not performing the ritual at that point. If history is written as the product of interactions among the several different kinds of historians, with different social purposes, then the use of oral sources is not a technical exercise, but rather an attempt to reason about fundamental goals and aspirations, now and then.

The process of royal transition began when one king died and ended when another was established as ruler. But a description in these terms, a story in which death and accession frame the totality of the event, and in which the larger event has an agreed beginning, middle, and end, is not in harmony with the narratives told to me. In those, each man began the story at a different moment, and each of those opening moments said something about the socially embedded position from which the teller spoke. Here, for example, is the opening line of Mbwana Mkanka Mghanga: 'The ones who stay awake all night with the king are the Shefaya and the Mshakamai. They sleep in the great house, at the royal court.'[5] The narrative begins with the king seriously ill, but still alive, tended by the Shefaya and Mshakamai. These were not major court officials; they were concerned with the private affairs of the king's household. Mbwana's own position – recognized in private affairs at the court, but not a major official – was a related one. Contrast his statement with the opening words of Ng'wana Aia, senior member of the family of the hereditary chief minister, the Mlughu: 'When the Mlughu sees that the king has died he calls people together – the *wafung'wa* (the major court officials), and the *watawa* (the lesser court officials). He does not beat the drum. He simply calls for them to assemble.'[6] This narrative opens at the moment when the king has already died – later than Mbwana's – and it is told from the Mlughu's viewpoint.

In contrast to the first two narratives, told by men of Vugha, there is the view from among the Nango who live just west of Bumbuli – the place from which the new heir started his journey after the king had already died. Here is the opening of a Nango account, told by Saguti Shekiondo:

16

'The person from Vugha has come to say, "We want your chief; we want him to go to Vugha." We all go together to Bumbuli. The chief comes out of Bumbuli.... The [Nango] chief of Tekwa waits for him at home....[The Zumbe] is given the medicine bag by his mother's brother, [the Nango of Tekwa].'[7] In this account there is no mention of events at Vugha, or of the king's death; the story begins at the moment when Vugha men appear near Bumbuli to start the new king on his journey. And it emphasizes the Nango role as the king's official mother's brothers. The accounts differ not only in their starting points, but also in their center of descriptive gravity – the place where the weight of the narrative is concentrated. For Ng'wana Aia, of the Mlughu's family, it was in the events of the royal court. For Saguti Shekiondo it was in the events of Tekwa. Still others focused elsewhere. Mdoe Loti, who lived near Kihitu, spent most of his time on the segment of the installation that happened at that village. Some of the *wafung'wa* – the major court officials – gave most of their attention to the burial, over which they presided.

We can see, then, that a synthetic version of the ritual as a whole – a description of all the parts in linear order – is not something that would have been produced by its owners, most of whom would have limited themselves to one segment or another. And yet we cannot create a satisfying interpretation of the rite without constructing a summary description, even though the totality proves itself to be less than the sum of its parts. Less, because there are contradictions that must be put to one side. And less for reasons we have already seen – that the ritual was a social negotiation rather than a performance that was controlled by one person, or that followed a predetermined script. The rite that is described here is thus a product of our own need to make history comprehensible – a new thing that serves our own analytical purposes, in a way that is forgivable if it is done with the utmost respect for the people who lived in the kingdom when the rites were performed, and for the people who shared their knowledge with me in the 1960s.

The summary account is based on narratives told by 13 men on 24 occasions between 1966 and 1968. I do not believe that any of these men are still alive today. They include, as we have seen, the hereditary chief minister of the kingdom and a number of senior court officials. They also include men drawn from the Nango clan near Bumbuli, and the last king, Kimweri Mputa Magogo.[8] Some oral accounts overlap with written ones. Mdoe Loti, for example, told me the story of an installation in 1895 under German control, and the colonial officer in charge wrote his own brief account at the time.[9] Other sources on accession include a number written during the German period: two by missionaries, one by a Shambaa convert, and one by a planter. The richest of the early descriptions is by Abdallah bin Hemedi 'lAjjemy, who was educated in the house of the Sultan of Zanzibar, and present in the Shambaa kingdom from about 1867 to 1873, at a time when the Europeans had not yet conquered the region.[10]

Until the last day of the installation, when the new king was greeted publicly, the old king's death was treated as a public secret. It was secret because it was important to preserve the fiction that Vugha never went without a king; it was public because widening circles of people needed to be informed if the transition was to move forward. Everyone was told that the king was alive, but very ill. To preserve the fiction of secrecy, a man lay down in the king's bed with the body, hidden by the covers. He moaned as though in pain, responding in a faint voice to anyone who entered the room. People periodically poured cold water over the king's body, to keep it fresh.

The men who had the greatest control over the transition were the officials of Vugha, who were not themselves members of the royal Kilindi lineage. The Vugha officials included the six *wafung'wa* and the Mlughu.[11] It was they who called the senior royals to Vugha to confer. The representatives of the Kilindi lineage who came were not eligible to rule; they were fathers, grandfathers, or paternal uncles of the possible heirs. Even then, Kilindi did not have the ultimate power to decide. All the descriptions of accession take the position that Kilindi proposed and *wafung'wa* disposed. Kilindi suggested names; the men of Vugha decided among them. This was a universally accepted description of the way things should work, but it was not always the way they did work. At some moments a senior royal had the power to dictate the outcome.[12]

The successor, once summoned by the men of Vugha, came by way of Bumbuli, directly east of the capital. The heir traveled in secret, and mostly at night. He followed the precise paths that had been taken by Mbegha, the hero-hunter who founded the kingdom. The men who described his trip listed streams, particular trees, unusual rocks, and other odd bits of the landscape along the way. The new king took on the charisma of Mbegha, in a sense became Mbegha, by stopping at each of these spots, walking in Mbegha's footsteps. He stopped at Wena, and then again at Tekwa, where his official (or notional) mother's brothers performed an essential ritual, and then went on to Kihitu, a village about two miles east of Vugha.[13]

The new king was installed twice: once in secret, in the middle of the night, and the second time in public, at dawn. The first of the installations took place at Kihitu. That was the spot, according to Mdoe Loti, where the heir to the throne came upon the Mdoe – a modest non-royal village official – sitting upon the stone that represented the impenetrability of the king's strength, and wearing the king's ostrich-feather headdress, the *linga*. The new king and the Mdoe then imitated the original exchange between Mbegha and the ordinary folk, when the hunter king gave meat in exchange for sovereignty. In the ritual re-enactment, the new king passed roasted meat, held between his teeth, to the Mdoe, who later passed back another piece. Then the Mdoe gave away 'his' kingdom: he led the new king to the stone, sat him there, placed the *linga* on his head, and greeted him with the royal praise name, Simba Mwene.

The night-time movements of the new king along the way from Bumbuli, at Tekwa and Kihitu, were shadowed by the movements of the dead king back at Vugha, also at night. The dead king was buried at about the time when the new king took the *linga*. The two sets of actions were described by different sets of participants. The burial at Vugha was described by the *wafung'wa* – the six major officials who, in normal times, represented the king in different parts of his territory. They were responsible for organizing the burial, together with the Mlughu. My own understanding, my own synthesis, is that on the night when the new king entered Kihitu the *wafung'wa*, accompanied by several trusted men, brought the old king's corpse in secret to the royal burial enclosure, where they dug a deep grave. According to some accounts, the man who had been moaning in the dead king's bed came along and lay in the grave before the burial. According to others, this did not happen, but instead a man and woman were made to lie in the grave together.[14] The *wafung'wa* and their men slaughtered a black bull and a black ram at the grave site. They placed the fresh sheepskin at the bottom of the grave and then, at the head, placed and then removed the blade of a hoe, forged that night and covered with carbon. The body of the dead king was lowered into the grave, wrapped in a black cloth, and then covered over with the bull's hide. All this happened during the night-time hours when the Mdoe of Kihitu was installing the new king, giving him the *linga*, and greeting him as Simba Mwene.

The *wafung'wa*, having buried one king, then left Vugha to fetch another. They went to the village of Fune, where they awaited the new king, who was coming from Kihitu, following Mbegha's footsteps across the stone called Kawe Nkajatwa, through the villages of Kigongo and Sakua, and across the Nkozoi stream. When the heir arrived at Fune, the men who came with him killed a bull, built a fire, and began to cook. They laid the king on the ground and covered him with a cloth. After they did this, the *wafung'wa* of Vugha appeared, and began to grab and tear at the meat of the bull. Then, in the words of one of them, 'they stole the king'. They wandered about aimlessly, carrying him. The king was carried across a stream and into Vugha, where he was given control of the ritual houses and ritual objects that belonged to the king.[15] Then he went to the house of one of the *wafung'wa*, the Mdoembazi, where he slept.

When the sky began to redden, the new king was led to the Council Clearing in the royal court. The war drum, *Nenkondo*, was beaten, and then its skin was cut with a knife. The people of Vugha swarmed out in response to the drum, only to find a new king already at the heart of the capital. They knew that it was their turn to act, giving public recognition to the new king, in a performance called *kuikia nkani* – 'to dramatize the tensions' of the relationships between king and commoners, and between king and councillors. The people shouted, 'You are our king, but if you don't treat us properly, we will get rid of you.' 'Give us rain! Give us bananas!' While they were saying this, the king was sitting on one of the stones in the clearing, wearing the *linga*. Then the Mlughu, the chief minister, stood before the crowd, raising a doubled-edged sword in the air and calling out, 'Eh! Eh! Eh! Eh! Eh! Eh!', to which the people responded, '*Mkaa, mkaa, mkaa, mkaa!*' 'The hunter, the hunter, the hunter, the hunter!' The Mlughu handed the sword to the king, and when he called out, the people responded, '*Mbogho, mbogho, mbogho, mbogho!*' 'The buffalo, the buffalo, the buffalo, the buffalo!' The Mlughu and the *wafung'wa* were like hunters who banded together to hunt the dangerous lone buffalo, so that he would not be able to harm them. The ritual drama continued for a period, with additional warnings and set phrases. Once the installation ended, the period of mourning began. For the whole of its duration, the four main paths from Vugha were closed. People did not cut their hair and men did not shave. At least one person was strangled on a path at Kwe Mishihwi, in a ritual murder. Until the mourning period ended no one farmed, and people walked the paths in fear.

The problem with interpreting this ritual is not that its meaning is obscure and impenetrable. It seems to me, if I look at the totality of it, to have a clear, simple, and powerful point. The problem is that no one ever saw the total order. No one organized its parts in the way that they are organized here, as a linear movement of black marks on a white page. Nevertheless, I must go one step further in presenting my synthetic interpretation, before trying to imagine what it might have been like to live with the rite, to practise one part or another of it. And then, even more puzzling, is the problem of why owners of the parts shared their knowledge with me, and why sharing their knowledge might actually not have been equivalent to sharing their power.

It is not just the linear order that is problematic in the rite described above. It is the sense that the burial of the old king and the progress of the new one were shadow rites – each an image of the other, in much the same way that an ancestor was a shadow or a reflection of the living person (a *kizui*, or *kizuli*).[16] With rare exceptions, the men who described the burial did not tell of the new king's progress from Bumbuli, and those who spoke of the heir's movement from east to west, concluding with his installation at Kihitu, did not describe the events at the royal grave site. Neither set of men claimed that their own ritual was half of a larger ritual. Both halves, however, unfolded in cycles lasting four nights. And both ended with the new king's appearance at Vugha, at dawn. The key to my conclusion on the two co-ordinated halves of the ritual was the war drum *Nenkondo*. It called people to the Council Clearing at the end of the burial, and it called them at the arrival of the new king. We know that it was not beaten twice, because in each case it was beaten and then stabbed, only to be given a skin again later, from one of the sacrificial animals. It was only in describing the double use of the drum that senior officials at Vugha acknowledged the co-ordination of the two halves, and then only two officials discussed it: the heir to the position of *Mlughu* – chief minister – and one of the *wafung'wa*, the Mbaruku.[17]

The larger rite, in its totality, was a machine for the suppression of kinglessness. The first moment at which the country's people recognized that the old king was dead was also the moment at which they acknowledged a new king. But it is much too simple to imagine the two halves of the rite as simple movements, one towards burial and the other towards installation. The machine was much more elaborate than that. We must remember that, before he was ever given the kingship at Vugha, the new king had already received the headdress and the title Simba Mwene at

Kihitu, in the night, at the time when his predecessor's body was being lowered into the ground. This happened well before the people of Vugha had public knowledge of the transition, for they had not yet greeted the new king. After the installation at Kihitu, the king was installed again, almost as though the first installation had never happened. It was after the king had been installed at Kihitu that he was laid on the ground at Fune, looking not at all kingly, so that his body could be stolen by the *wafung'wa*, who would then make him king by giving him control of the Great House and the royal medicines at Vugha. Once again, non-royals disposed of their land's sovereignty. Just before the time the king arrived at the Council Clearing, he was given sovereignty for the second time in a night.

The logic of this is clear. It was a way of erasing the interregnum in a society where kingship adhered to the person of the king. As one proverb has it, *zumbe aiho ne kitaa* – wherever the chief is, that is where the court is; another says that for the king, *kubushwa ni kufa* – the only way to abdicate is to die. In the absence of a new king, the absence of a king carried dangerous implications that kingship was dead. At the moment when the old king was buried, the new one was installed at Kihitu so that the land would not be without a king, or without kingship. The new king was then installed, once again, by taking up the regalia at the Great House. When people came to the Council Clearing, they were ostensibly learning for the first time that the king had died. But because the new king had already been installed at Kihitu, and then again at Vugha, the land was neither without a king nor without kingship.

The ritual worked also to impose a rhythmed order on the passage of political time. This is my way of rephrasing the interpretation given by Mdoe Loti who, as we have seen, had been present at the time of the installation of 1895. He explained the installation in terms of lunar imagery. The new king, he said, dies like the moon, only to reappear. The importance of the moon and of rhythmed recurrence in the rites did not originate with Mdoe Loti. It was much older and more general, not an idiosyncratic interpretation. In the precolonial succession rites described by Abdallah bin Hemedi 'lAjjemy, one of the men of Vugha said, *Kumekufa mwezi harang'anyi yaka. Lakini siyo harang'anyi ni mwezi.* 'The moon has died and the morning star has risen. But it is not the morning star; it is the moon.'[18] The king's nocturnal travels were like the moon's, for the king traveled from east to west, as did the moon, and as did the morning star – a lesser heavenly body. Mdoe Loti explained, 'The moon comes from Bumbuli [in the east]. The moon dies and is gone, but it then reappears. [It has not really died;] it has simply been covered over by God.' He went on to try to explain this in terms he thought I would understand: 'If Adam had not eaten the fruit in Eden, we would die like the moon.'[19] Once I thought about this, I saw that the new king's travels followed in the footsteps of Mbegha, the founding king, but the route was simplified, abstracted, so as to resemble the path of the moon. In oral narratives about the kingdom's founding, Mbegha entered the mountains at Ziai in the south, then traveled northeastwards to Bumbuli, and then westwards to Vugha. The new king did not retrace the whole of this route. He did not begin in the south at Ziai, but only traveled from Bumbuli to Vugha, from east to west, like the moon. The men who organized the ritual chose a route that emphasized rhythmed recurrence, not one that re-enacted every detail of the Mbegha story.

Lunar imagery was central also at Fune, at the moment when the men who came with the new king from Bumbuli left him on the ground, where he was found by the *wafung'wa*, and then stolen. The new king was 'covered over' (*-ghubikwa*) with a black cloth; the same word is used to describe what happens to the moon at the time when it disappears from view, the time of the new moon. The new king's body was 'covered over' like the moon; it was not treated as though it were dead. In that case, it would have been 'wrapped' in a cloth (*-gewa shanda*) or in dead banana leaves (*-gewa mashwagho*).[20] The king died like the moon. He was covered over, but then reappeared. He did not die like a person who, once dead, is present only as an ancestral figure.

The marking of a ritual rhythm did not end with the new king's installation. It continued after the accession and through the month of mourning. During that time violence was permitted on the public paths, and people were prohibited from farming, or shaving, or cutting their hair. The purpose was not to avert danger, but to contain it within the formal period of mourning – to bring it under the control of rhythmed ritual time. This way of shaping the popular experience of danger was characteristic also of the ritual called *hande*, which could be practiced at any time when it was needed, not at the time of a king's death.[21] Its purpose was to control epidemics and widespread threats to the crops. The *hande* rite and the burial of the king drew on the same symbolic repertoire, for the objects used in *hande* included a black sheep, a black cloth, and a piece of carbon-covered metal. During the four days of *hande*, as during moon-defined mourning for the king, people were prohibited from farming. *Hande* and mourning for the king both contained danger by marking it off during defined periods. Danger contained was danger managed; uncontained danger could be disastrous. In the 1890s, local people described locusts and an earthquake as consequences of the fact that German conquest had made proper mourning impossible after the deaths of kings.[22] The danger had not been confined by the lunar rhythm of ritual time.

The interpretation of the double rite as a machine for the suppression of kinglessness, as a way of imposing a ritual rhythm on the passage of political time, and as a way of containing danger is, I think, a valid one. The visible texture is my own, but I have tried to build it with structural elements provided by local men and women whose words have entered the historical record. I feel as though I had found the framework of a house – its shape clear – and then added the mud and thatch that would make it habitable.

And yet no one ever saw the rite. No single individual saw the whole of it. Almost no one in Shambaai saw more than a fragment. The fact that the rite was practiced but never seen makes it necessary to think carefully about what people did see – how it is that the subjects of the kingdom experienced this rite. The world of fragments must have been mysterious and frightening. An ordinary farmer in the high mountains near Vugha was likely to hear rumors that the king was dead. These would signal the arrival of a dangerous time. At some point, the king's ritual executioner would appear without warning, and he would seize and strangle a person who happened to be walking along the path. The people knew then that the king was dead and that a period of danger had begun – a period that might lead to warfare and famine. For everyone except the central actors from Tekwa or Wena, Kihitu or Vugha, there was a sense that men from prominent commoner-lineages were acting in secret to shape the kingdom. Strange forces were moving in the night. The people of Shambaai did not experience the coherence of the king dying like the moon, nor did they perceive the symmetrical quality of the double rite, with mirrored actions unfolding in separate places. They knew only that it was a time of rumor, of violence, and of great events that, at unexpected moments, broke through the clouds of secrecy.

The one moment of public release came at the Council Clearing, after *Nenkondo* was beaten, and after the new king had entered Vugha. That was when the people of Vugha would call out, 'You are our king, but if you do not treat us properly, we will get rid of you! Give us rain! Give us bananas!' Even though they continued for a while, this was a brief moment of public release in an extended period characterized either by violence or by secrecy. The secrecy, together with the segmented performance of the rites, meant that ordinary people saw only fleeting fragments of action, or saw nothing and heard only rumor.

One of the fascinating contradictions is that the ritual, at its public moments, declared the importance of secrecy; it announced publicly that secrecy was its theme.[23] It was as though the secret had no weight unless others knew it was secret, and perhaps even knew what the secret was. Here is how Mbwana Mkanka Mghanga described the dissemination of news about the king's death:[24]

> People whisper to one another: 'My friend'. 'Yes'. 'The king is dead, and we have not yet installed a new king.' The young children are the ones who are deceived. Even the women are deceived.... But the grown men all know that the king has died....The whole country is instructed: 'Don't tell! Don't tell!' 'If you say this, and if you are overheard, don't say that it was I who told you.'

The speaker tells us that the king's death was secret and that it was widely known. It was a kind of public fiction of secrecy, and yet the rite would not have had the same quality had the secrecy not been there. This was the point of one of the central declarations that country people made in the great public event at the Council Clearing. The people of Vugha called out, *Nkaviongwa, nkaviongwa, nkaviongwa, nkaviongwa!* 'It is not spoken, it is not spoken, it is not spoken, it is not spoken!' These words were repeated over and over again. Mdoe Loti explained this by saying, 'The things that are done at Vugha are not spoken of because they are insulting. They are cunning acts of domination.'[25] Secrecy and the performance of the ritual at night when powerful but unseen things happen were both expressions of a particular view of power, as grounded in that which is hidden.

We are accustomed to thinking of expressive culture as a reflection of deeper social forces – as a superstructure erected over a base of material relations, as a form in which resistance can be expressed, or as the means in which hegemony is achieved. But in this case, whatever the ritual's role in relation to popular *mentalités*, something much more direct and unmediated was happening. Ritual was not a mask of illusion over the 'real' face of power, but rather a way of constituting power directly. As Bell argues, drawing on the contributions of Geertz, Cannadine, Bloch, and others, ritual is itself a form of power.[26] In the present case, the ritual of burial and accession was not simply a way of creating the illusion of rhythmed recurrence to hide the reality of royal politics; it was a way of making a person king.

Whichever person Vugha's officials sent for, that was the person who became king. It was the performance of the ritual, rather than the application of clear-cut succession rules, that defined who would rule. There were many members of the Kilindi dynasty who might have become king, and usually they were half-brothers to one another. The ideology of kinship – of family relations – within the dynasty would have led them to treat one another as equals, ranked only by age, or perhaps by the seniority of one mother or another, and even then in competition with one another. According to this ideology, every one of the heirs was inferior to Kilindi of the older generation. The only way to separate one Kilindi from all the others and to make him king was through the installation – the trip from Bumbuli, the ceremony at Kihitu, the entry into Vugha, and the transfer of the royal medicines for rain and for war. The senior commoners of Vugha had it in their power to award the office of king, and their instrument for giving it was the installation.

As a form of ritual action, however, it was organized in a radically different way from most rituals in Shambaai. It differed from ordinary people's rites of passage (*mivigha*), because it had only a *kombwe*, and not a *kungwi*. The *kombwe* was the person who had never previously been initiated, the one who was experiencing the ritual for the first time; and the *kungwi* was the person who was bringing the *kombwe* through from the other side – the person who had undergone the passage from one status to the next (from unmarriageable to marriageable young woman, for example), and could serve as an experienced guide. But in the ritual of royal burial and accession, the only possible *kungwi* – the only man who had been through the whole of the accession – was the dead king.

Because of this structural difference, the power dynamics of the ritual of burial and accession were radically different from those of other rites of passage in Shambaai, and different also from the *mshitu* ritual that was so central to Pare history, as described in Kimambo's early work.[27] In Ugweno (in North Pare), for example, there was an entire community of men who had been through the *mshitu* ritual themselves, and the men who controlled initiation were drawn from within this community. The fact that they had earlier been initiated, whether in the royal or the commoner *mshitu*, conferred civic personhood upon them, and their control over the ritual gave them the capacity to confer civic personhood on others. They organized the ritual that defined who would be a publicly recognized member of the political community of adult men. In the Shambaa royal ritual, by contrast, there was no community of initiates. The king was the only person who ever completed the accession. If others had completed it – if there had been a community of initiates – it would have meant that the king was sharing his power and therefore diluting it. Of necessity, the king constituted a political community of one. He was initiated into a political community that had no members, because its only member (the old king) had died. The central problem faced by the men of Vugha was how to control admission to this community of one, when none of them were members of it – none of them had been king, none of them were initiates able to lead the way. The solution to the problem, as we have seen, was to divide the relevant knowledge, and the relevant capacity for legitimate action, among a number of men. Even though they themselves had no experience of kingship, they could install a king if they acted in concert. If they organized the rite together, it could be said that 'the people of Shambaai' or 'the people of Vugha' had given him the kingship.

My argument concerns a particular configuration of power/knowledge, characteristic of the late precolonial period – one very different from its twentieth-century successors. It was a configuration in which power inhered in orally transmitted knowledge, and not in written documents, and in which the particular social process required that bodies of knowledge be kept separate from one another. This interpretation cuts across the grain of several generations of scholarly writing about the historical uses of oral sources. From the start, historians who studied oral traditions were preoccupied with how difficult it is to transmit oral knowledge accurately. The literature focuses on the efforts people make to improve transmission through the technologies of memory, including redundancy, mnemonics, and formal literary structures. The people who depended on oral knowledge found many ways to keep information from getting lost over time.[28]

But if we see power as inhering in the differential possession of knowledge, then the central problem is the opposite one: it is that oral knowledge spreads widely and without boundaries, as did the secret of the king's death. The easy spread of knowledge was dangerous to the social order. Privilege and power could only survive if the flow of knowledge was blocked; if secrets were kept. Seeing the value of blocked knowledge – of knowledge treated in the way today's businessmen treat trade secrets – forces us to think again about a much more recent literature, written by late-twentieth-century scholars concerned with cultural circulation in an age of globalization. The emphasis here is on the ease and informality with which people share cultural practices and knowledge. Snatches of music from pygmies in a central African forest are heard in world-beat music played in Philadelphia; rap music created in American cities takes on Swahili words in Dar es Salaam nightclubs; biblical stories are merged seamlessly into Congolese origin narratives; and even within a single local setting, in one small village in eastern Uganda, people appropriate one another's tales, telling them for amusement, borrowing events, or motifs, or striking punch-lines.[29] So that in the end it is difficult to know who owns knowledge, who is borrowing it, or where it originated. I am not at all denying the validity of this picture, only reflecting on a very different kind of knowledge, so valuable that its owner could make a king, so long as the knowledge did not circulate freely.

But if power grew out of restrictions on the flow of knowledge, then there is no way the owner would ever have told it to me, and yet many owners did, often unstintingly, sometimes even eagerly. Why did they tell me? It is interesting to look, in this respect, at the knowledge that was withheld from me. It may be possible to define the boundary between knowledge that could be shared and knowledge that must be blocked. In May 1967 I went on one of many visits to Kimweri Mputa Magogo, the deposed king, at Mlembule – a cattle camp near Mombo. He was devastated at the loss of the kingship, and also trying to live with dignity. He was always co-operative. The personal chemistry between us was good; perhaps he hoped that my historical writings would lead to a royal restoration. After we had talked for a long time, I asked about rain medicines – the most sensitive of topics – and the conversation turned towards the installation.[30]

SF: What about rain rituals?
KMM: There are rain rituals. But that ritual itself is something people can never talk about. It's heavy. And then there are the kinds that are like medicines.
SF: Are rituals and medicines two different things?
KMM: They're different. Because that ritual, if I can tell you just a bit of it; I won't really talk about it. When the man who had ruled dies, as in the case of the zumbe of Bumbuli, or of Mulungui, or the zumbe out there of Shele [Mlalo], or if it's the person himself, right there at Vugha, [in other words, whether a subordinate chief died, or whether it was the king at Vugha,] there is a body part of his that is taken. Now that body part, that is the ancient ritual itself, all the way. When he dies, when he hasn't been buried yet, there's a thing that is taken, that they take away to dry, so that it becomes desiccated. Now that's the family ritual of rain.
SF: What is it?
KMM: *Nkaviongwa*! It is not spoken! That elder son now, when he takes up the kingship at Vugha, he is shown that secret thing. The elders give it to him. And he too... it is put away by his senior wife. When the land is in need in that way, it is the senior wife who performs the ritual.

Kimweri held back a part of what he knew about rain medicines, the precise part of the dead king's body, but he also told me something that the Mlughu had not told me, and that none of the *wafung'wa* ever told. This was knowledge at the heart of the kingship, and only he had the authority to decide on how far to go. But even then, he never told me enough so that I could actually use it myself.

His statement also raises a question about the role of women in the royal ritual. Several descriptions of the heir's trip from Bumbuli say that his full sister went with him. At the most important moments it was she who made the ululating sound of approval. It is as though a woman's approval was necessary, but only a full sister could be trusted under these conditions of secrecy. If that sister survived her brother, then she had knowledge of the path taken by the new king, but she did not participate in the installation of her brother's successor. Then there is the role of the senior, or great, wife, as discussed by Kimweri. It is something I do not fully understand. It was the great wife who controlled the rain medicine, and it was the great wife whose son was the most likely successor to the throne after her husband's death. This must have given her a very influential role during the transition. And yet the descriptions of the political negotiations leading up to the succession never mention her role. I did not think to discuss the succession with women who had held the role of great wife, so deeply and subconsciously had I accepted the division of gender roles and the appropriateness of hearing about the ritual only from my fellow men.

I think the reason the men who owned the ritual shared their information was that the individual bits of ritual knowledge, taken by themselves, did not have the capacity to constitute power directly. They were necessary but not sufficient for making a king. Oral narratives about succession disputes agree that when the kingship was actively in play, every one of the competitors was able to call on the owners of the ritual to perform their parts. What distinguished the king from all the failed heirs was that the king arrived at Vugha first. Because of the centrality of timing, the most crucial forms of secrecy were the ones governing the actual movement of heirs when the succession was in question. We see evidence of this in the turn-of-the-century description by Karasek, the Shambaa-speaking planter, who wrote about the moment just after the old king's death. The court officials would send messengers to bring selected Kilindi, who would then decide on an heir. Karasek was told that 'If, in earlier times, it happened that an uninvited person heard this information, or was caught eavesdropping, they strangled him'.[31] It is not clear whether this actually happened, or whether this bit of gossip was a way of warning people to keep quiet. In either case, the forbidden behavior had nothing to do with knowledge of the ritual. It had to do with information that would affect the timing of the progress by the competing heirs, as they moved towards Vugha.

In historical narratives about competition for the kingship, there is an image – actually not an image, but a remembered sound – that conveys to the listener the information that a particular Kilindi had failed in his bid. The sound described in the narratives is the drum *Nenkondo*, heard from a distance. The heir is hurrying towards Vugha when he hears the drum sounding, and knows that he has failed. The tardy heir asks, 'Who is entering Vugha?' Once told the name of the new king, he turns and heads for home.

Knowledge of the inherited ritual forms did not give me the capacity to decide who would be in the Council Clearing when the drum sounded, and who would hear it from a distance. My knowledge did not make it possible for me to participate in the 'cunning acts of domination' that were at the heart of the ritual. To do that, I would have had to be able to manipulate the timing of the performance – to make sure that one heir arrives on time, and the other is late. Bourdieu explained the importance of timing when he wrote about the custom of gift exchange; he showed that knowledge of the rules does not by itself bring power. This emerges from control over the strategic flow of information through time.[32] I do not believe that this is only an analytical point, grounded in Bourdieu, and seen by me from the outside. It may well have been a central point for participants, because so much of the rite revolved around bits of knowledge kept separate from one another, and around secret movements in the night, known only to a few important people. Power in this sense had largely been lost in the early colonial period; the rite would have been transformed by this loss even if no word or gesture had changed.

Much later, in 1967 and 1968, at the time when the men of Vugha, and Tekwa, and Wena were speaking to me about the ritual, chiefs had already been removed from office, and the aging *wafung'wa* no longer had a formal political role. The abolition of chiefship, just after independence, was recent enough that it must have felt provisional. Very old men like Ng'wana Aia, of the Mlughu's lineage, had lived through the decline of chiefship under the Germans, its revival under the British, the rise of the nationalist movement, and then the end of colonial rule. From their point of view, it had to have been impossible to know whether chiefship had been lost irretrievably or whether to await yet another change. Men like the *wafung'wa* and Ng'wana Aia had seen, in the 1920s, that white men writing local histories were directly connected to the restoration of royal rule. It was not beyond the realm of imagination in the 1960s that this white man's history would be a part of further changes – desirable ones, seen from the point of view of men linked to the royal court.

It was not my literacy that they needed, so much as my access to centers of power, like the government, vaguely defined, or the University of Dar es Salaam, or the wider world out there. Local men could have written down a description of the ritual without my help. Kimweri Mputa Magogo was literate, and there were others at Vugha who were capable of making a written record. Certainly it would have been difficult for local people to take the necessary time off from farming; the work was arduous. The only explicit justification I offered back then for taking so much of people's time and energy was that over time *mbui za Kishambaa* would be lost ('Shambaa words,' 'Shambaa matters'), as would *mbui za kae* ('old things,' 'old words'). Under the circumstances it would be useful, I argued, to have as rich a record as possible.

My words may have rung with cliché then, but they turned out, of course, to be true. Those men are now dead, and the decline of Kilindi power means that their words have begun to fade in local memory. In the late 1960s, most adult men could tell a rich story about Mbegha, the founding king. In July 2000, when I was staying in the house of a friend near Bumbuli, I asked two of his sons who Mbegha was. Both sons were over twenty; neither had heard of Mbegha, except as the name of a healer who happened to be living in the next village. Thus passes the glory of kings.

Some of the men who told about the ritual in the 1960s were interested in using the written record to establish the prominence of their families. This was certainly the case among the Nango men of Tekwa and Wena. Others were captivated by the expressive possibilities of a richly moving event: the reddening of the dawn and the sounding of the drum, followed by the call of the bushbuck horn – *Ti Pa Ti Paaa!* – and the gathering of the crowd. Family pride and artful expression were not the only motivations among the tellers. For Mdoe Loti, telling me the story was a way for a man with a profoundly philosophical turn of mind to reflect, in concrete terms, on the society in which he lived. But all the men would have been much more hesitant had the political context not been propitious, and that context was set by the fact that the British had used chiefs and their followers as the administrative agents of colonial rule.

That this was the case presents us with a difficult problem, more than 30 years later, when we think about Kimambo's central issue, of how to construct a usable history. Indirect rule – rule through chiefs – was, after all, regressive. It was a way of using local institutions for the purposes of alien domination, and it was deeply grounded in the economic processes by which Tanganyika became underdeveloped.[33] However unfortunate it was that the British appropriated the chiefly aspects of local culture, it does not follow that local cultures and their study ought to be abandoned. Kimambo understood this, even back in the 1960s when the independence battles were still fresh in people's minds.

One of the fascinating things about local historical knowledge is that we have no way of knowing what its political uses will be. The possibilities are almost infinitely variable. In the 1950s and 1960s, the histories of local clan and lineage leaders might have been taken as charters for control by men over women, and by older men over younger men, and for this reason rejected and forgotten. But the same clan histories were invoked by people who wanted to reject royal rule and British rule. In that particular context, they were charters for local autonomy, and for a rejection of oppressive control. Local history is, in this political sense, neither progressive nor regressive. It is simply a rich heritage, and none of us can know all the uses to which it will ultimately be put.

My own interpretation of the ritual was a modernist one – modernist in the stylistic sense of the word: claiming the possibility that one could create a unified narrative out of diverse elements, that the particularity of the local could be penetrated and mastered. At just the same time, Tanzanian society was itself being reorganized on modernist lines.[34] The diverse sweep of local society was being reorganized in uniform units. The economy was administered from the center, by a state that behaved as though it was capable of omniscience, in much the same way that a linear narrative of the ritual can only be written under the pretence of omniscience. The country was being subjected to much more intensive counting and measuring than ever before, and to a sense that the whole of the nation could be seen and understood comprehensively from the center.

In fact, the modernist tendency, whether in the organization of development or in the writing of history, necessarily exists in a tension with a thousand rich things that are irreducibly particular. The challenge, for which Isaria Kimambo's work has been an exemplar, is in constructing a creative synthesis of the particular modernist form of rationality and the rich array of practices, memories, and initiatives that appear on our world's scene without having been imagined at any of the many places that call themselves the center.

Notes

1. Isaria N. Kimambo, *A Political History of the Pare of Tanzania, c. 1500-1900* (Nairobi: East African Publishing House, 1969); C.G.K. Gwassa, 'Kinjikitile and the Ideology of Maji Maji', in T.O. Ranger and I.N. Kimambo (eds), *The Historical Study of African Religion* (London: Heinemann, 1972), pp. 202–17; Frederick Kaijage, 'Peasant Resistance to Proletarianization' (African Studies Center, Boston University, Walter Rodney Seminar, paper 81, Fall, 1983); Yusufu Qwaray Lawi, 'May the Spider Web Blind Witches and Wild Animals: Local Knowledge and the Political Ecology of Natural Resource Use in the Iraqwland, Tanzania, 1900–1985' (Ph.D. diss., Boston University, 2000).

2. For critical writings questioning anthropologists' synthetic writing, see Pierre Bourdieu, *Outline of a Theory of Practice,* translated by Richard Nice (Cambridge: Cambridge University Press, 1977); James Clifford, *The Predicament of Culture: Twentieth-Century Ethnography, Literature, and Art* (Cambridge, MA: Harvard University Press, 1988); George E. Marcus and Michael M.J. Fischer, *Anthropology as Cultural Critique: An Experimental Moment in the Human Sciences* (Chicago: University of Chicago Press, 1986).

3. On the social composition of knowledge, see Jane Guyer and Samuel M. Eno Belinga, 'Wealth in People as Wealth in Knowledge: Accumulation and Composition in Equatorial Africa', *Journal of African History*, 36 (1995), pp. 91-120.

4. For Kimambo's own reflections on these issues, at two very different times, see I.N. Kimambo, 'Historical Research in Mainland Tanzania', in Gwendolen M. Carter and Ann Paden (eds), *Expanding Horizons in African Studies* (Evanston, IL: Northwestern University Press, 1969), and I.N. Kimambo, *Three Decades of Production of Historical Knowledge at Dar es Salaam* (Dar es Salaam: Dar es Salaam University Press, 1993).

5. Mbwana Mkanka Mghanga, 24 January 1968. Transcripts of the original interviews are located in the Feierman Collection in the East Africana section of the library of the University of Dar es Salaam.

6. Ng'wana Aia, 1 April 1967.

7. Saguti Shekiondo, 30 July 1967.

8. Mdoe Loti, Lunguza, Vugha, n.d. April 1967, 29 April 1967, 1 May 1967, n.d. (ca. April 1967); Mbwana Mkanka Mghanga, Mshwai, Vugha, 24 January 1968; Mbaruku Jambia, Kienge, 22 January 1968; Mdoe Barua, 26 January 1968; Mdoe Barua with Ng'wana Aia, Vugha, 18 April 1967; Mdoembazi Kiluwa, Vugha, 10 April 1967; Bakari Kiluwa, Mshihwi, 15 October 1966; Saguti Shekiondo, Nango of Wena, 30 July 1967; Bakari Shekwaho, Nango of Tekwa, 17 July 1967; Kimweri Mputa Magogo, Mombo Mlembule, 24 March 1967; Mdoe Saudimwe Wena, 7 August 1967; Ng'wana Aia, Vugha, 1 April 1967; Kimweri Mputa Magogo and Mbwana Mkanka Mghanga, Vugha, nd; Kimweri Mputa Magogo and Mbwana Mkanka Mghanga, Mombo Mlembule, 19 May 1967; Makao Sangoda, Ziai, 10 May 1967; Mbwana Mkanka Mghanga, Mshwai, 7 May 1967; Mdoe Barua, 14 November 1967; Ng'wana Aia, 19 May 1967; Sylvano Shekaaghe, 27 July 1967; Ng'wana Aia, 7 December 1967; Kimweri Mputa Magogo, Mdoe Barua, and Ng'wana Aia, July 1968; Sylvano Shekaaghe, 27 July 1967.

9. E. Storch, 'Sitten, Gebräuche und Rechtspflege bei den Bewohnern Usambara und Pares', *Mitteilungen aus den Deutschen Schutzgebieten* 8 (1895), pp. 310–31. Mdoe Loti gave his

On Socially Composed Knowledge

description on 10 April 1967.

10. F. LangHeinrich, a Shambaa-speaking missionary who was at Vugha from 1895, reported on the ritual as described by local people at the time, in 'Die Waschambala', in S.R. Steinmetz (ed.), *Rechtsverhältnisse von eingeborenen Völkern in Afrika und Ozeanien* (Berlin: Verlag von Julius Springer, 1903), pp. 218–67. August Karasek was a planter near Bumbuli after the turn of the century. He spoke Shambaa, lived with a Shambaa woman, and spent time in the village of her family, as a relative. His account, drawing on descriptions by local people at the time, is in August Eichhorn (ed.), 'Beiträge zur Kenntnis der Waschambaa', part 4, *Baessler-Archiv*, 8 (1923–24), pp. 19–20. There is a brief account of burial and accession in one of the subordinate chiefdoms written by Marko Kaniki, one of the first literate Shambaa. The rites were similar to those for a king. Marko Kaniki, 'Bestattung der grossem Kilindi', *Nachrichten aus der ostafrikanischen Mission* 17 (1903), pp. 190–91. There are brief comments on accession by P. Wohlrab, a Shambaa-speaking missionary at Mlalo through much of the German period, in 'Das Recht der Schambala', *Archiv für Anthropologie*, 44 (1918), pp. 172, 181. Abdallah bin Hemedi 'lAjjemy's account is in J.W.T. Allen and William Kimweri bin Mbago (eds), *Habari za Wakilindi* (Nairobi: East African Literature Bureau, 1962).

11. The *wafung'wa* included the Mdoembazi, Mdoe, Beeko, Kaoneka, Doekuu, and Mbaruku.

12. In the 1870s, after Shekulwavu's death, the men of Vugha knew that if they chose anyone but the son of Semboja – the most powerful and destructive chief of the time – their new king would be hounded from office or killed. Steven Feierman, *The Shambaa Kingdom: A History* (Madison, WI: University of Wisconsin Press, 1974), chapter 6.

13. The narratives all agree on the route, although they disagree in some details with Abdallah, *Habari za Wakilindi* (Sura 48), and they disagree also on the precise number of nights the heir spent on his way to Vugha.

14. Abdallah, *Habari za Wakilindi* (Sura 27). Marko Kaniki, 'Bestattung'.

15. According to Abdallah, but no other source, the new king invoked the ancestors at the royal burial site. *Habari za Wakilindi* (Sura 60). Abdallah also describes the succession of the second king, Bughe, and says that Bughe's wife sacrificed two bulls at the royal grave site (Suras 27–8).

16. On *kizuli*, see F. LangHeinrich, *Shambala-Wörterbuch*, Abhandlungen des Hamburgischen Kolonialinstituts, vol. 43 (Hamburg: L. Friedrichsen, 1921), p. 171. It refers not only to an ancestor as an image, but also to a reflection in a mirror.

17. Mbaruku Jambia, Kienge, 22 January 1968. Mdoe Barua and Ng'wana Aia, 18 April 1967.

18. *Habari za Wakilindi* (Sura 60).

19. Mdoe Loti, 10 April 1967.

20. On *shanda* during the German period, see Karasek, who was told that Kilindi spirits could be seen at the side of a stream washing their black cloths, while commoner spirits washed white cloths. 'Beiträge zur Kenntnis der Waschambaa', part 1, *Baessler-Archiv*, 1 (1911), p. 193.

21. Mandughu Chai described *hande*, the practice of which was inherited within his own descent group; Bagha, 15 June 1968.

22. Bethel Mission Archives, *Tagebuch Neu Bethel* (15 May 1895); 'Heuschrecken und kein Ende', *Nachrichten aus der ostafrikanischen Mission*, May 1895, pp. 70-73.

23. On secrecy, see Mary H. Nooter, *Secrecy: African Art that Conceals and Reveals* (New York and Munich: Museum for African Art, 1993). Sissela Bok, *Secrets: On the Ethics of Concealment and Revelation* (New York: Vintage Books, 1983).

24. 7 May 1967.

25. 1 May 1967.

26. Catherine Bell, *Ritual Theory, Ritual Practice* (New York: Oxford University Press, 1992), p. 194. Clifford Geertz, *Negara: The Theatre State in Nineteenth Century Bali* (Princeton, NJ: Princeton University Press, 1980). David Cannadine, 'Introduction: Divine Rights of Kings', in *Rituals of Royalty: Power and Ceremonial in Traditional Societies* (Cambridge: Cambridge University Press, 1987).

27. Kimambo, *A Political History of the Pare*, pp. 51–3, 63, 68–71.

28. Jan Vansina, *Oral Tradition: A Study in Historical Methodology*, trans. H.M. Wright (London: Routledge & Kegan Paul, 1961); Jan Vansina, *Oral Tradition as History* (Madison, WI: University of Wisconsin Press, 1985); Walter J. Ong, *Orality and Literacy: The Technologizing of the Word* (London and New York: Routledge, 1982), especially pp. 33–6. Jack Goody and Ian Watt, 'The Consequences of Literacy', in Jack Goody (ed.), *Literacy in Traditional Societies* (Cambridge: Cambridge University Press, 1968) see pp. 28–34. There have, by now, been many critiques of this approach. See, for example, Elizabeth Tonkin, *Narrating Our Pasts: The Social Construction of Oral History* (Cambridge: Cambridge University Press, 1992), chapter 5.

29. Steven Feld, 'Pygmy POP. A Genealogy of Schizophonic Mimesis', *Yearbook for Traditional Music*, 28 (1996), pp.1–35. David William Cohen, 'Doing Social History from *Pim's Doorway*', in Olivier Zunz (ed.), *Reliving the Past: The Worlds of Social History* (Chapel Hill, NC: University of North Carolina Press, 1985). See also Isabel Hofmeyr, '*We Spend Our Years as a Tale That is Told*': Oral Historical Narrative in a South African Chiefdom (Portsmouth, NH, Johannesburg, London: Heinemann, Witwatersrand University Press, James Currey, 1993), and Louise White, *Speaking with Vampires: Rumor and History in Colonial Africa* (Berkeley and Los Angeles: University of California Press, 2000).

30. Kimweri Mputa Magogo and Mbwana Mkanka Mghanga, 19 May 1967.

31. Karasek, 'Beiträge zur Kenntnis der Waschambaa', *Baessler-Archiv*, 8 (1923–4), p. 20.

32. Pierre Bourdieu, *Outline of a Theory of Practice*, trans. Richard Nice (Cambridge: Cambridge University Press, 1977), pp. 4–8 and *passim*.

33. For my own interpretation of indirect rule in these terms, see Steven Feierman, *Peasant Intellectuals: Anthropology and History in Tanzania* (Madison, WI: University of Wisconsin Press, 1990), chapters 5, 6.

34. For a major work on the modernist imagination, see James C. Scott, *Seeing Like a State: How Certain Schemes to Improve the Human Condition Have Failed* (New Haven, CT and London: Yale University Press, 1998). Scott's interpretation of *ujamaa* is weak, but his depiction of the general characteristics of high modernism is valuable.

Three

~~~~~~~~~~~~~~~~~~~~~~~~~~~~~~~~~~~~~~

Kingalu Mwana Shaha & Political Leadership in Nineteenth-Century Eastern Tanzania

EDWARD A. ALPERS[*]

One of the great ironies of African history is the enthusiasm with which European colonial officials, in their determination to identify 'traditional' political authorities, seized upon a variety of innovative nineteenth-century regional political leaders, some of whom had no claim to leadership other than force of arms. This is not a particularly new observation, but it is one well worth remembering. As Jan Vansina has observed for Equatorial Africa during the same period, 'Oral traditions recall it as a time of newcomers and upstarts, for whom might was right, a time of turmoil and brutality'.[1] These big men were usually called 'chiefs' or, in the case of East Africa, 'sultans', regardless of whether or not the society in question was familiar with hierarchical notions of chiefship. Eastern Tanzania was no exception to this rule.

The regional political economy of mid-nineteenth-century eastern Tanzania was characterized by a well integrated commercial network that was dominated by Zanzibar and mediated into the hinterland through the towns of the littoral. International trade in ivory was largely in the hands of coastal merchants and Nyamwezi chiefs, whose caravans moved through the region along well-defined trunk routes that skirted the Uluguru Mountains at their southern and northern extremes. Local authorities fed off the ivory caravans by levying tariffs on those that passed through their domains. By contrast, slave trading, which was mainly in the hands of locals, was based on kidnapping and judicial subterfuge. In general, however, the most active trade within the region was based on agricultural products. On the one hand, local farmers supplied provisions to the long-distance caravans that passed through their lands, flocking to impromptu – but predictable – markets that formed whenever a caravan camped at one of the well-established stages between the coast and the deep interior. On the other hand, small parties of enterprising peasants carried their agricultural products along dozens of less formalized footpaths in quick marches to the daily markets of the principal coastal towns. These locally produced or gathered products were also taxed irregularly by local chiefs and headmen, whenever possible. Several new big men became key players in this regional political economy during the middle and later decades of the nineteenth century. In this essay I address the way in which one of these individuals, Kingalu mwana Shaha, ruler of the Wabena clan of the Luguru-speaking people in eastern Tanzania, changed the regional political landscape so thoroughly that it would have been unrecognizable to any observer at the beginning of the nineteenth century.

The Wabena and the Kingalu

The Wabena were the most important clan politically among the eastern Luguru and Kami people in the nineteenth century, Uluguru designating the mountains and Ukami the plains they inhabited. Their clan head, the Kingalu, also controlled one of three important rain-calling shrines in the Uluguru Mountains. The history of the Kingalu lineage is full of contradictions, but my own research leaves little doubt that the political and economic hegemony that was exercised by Kingalu mwana Shaha in the middle decades of the nineteenth century was quite distinct from the spiritual authority that all the Kingalus enjoyed.[2] In the 1930s Kingalu mwana Shaha's disgruntled grandson, whose claim to the colonial sultanate of Southern Uluguru was rejected by the British in favor of the reigning Kingalu, commented caustically that 'His [the Kingalu's] seat is that of a medicine man (*kiti chake cha uganga*) which his name signifies. All people and Government know about this since a long time ago'.[3] Put less politically, the Kingalu was known for 'the power of rain only, because each clan had its own government', but Kingalu mwana Shaha ruled as Sultan, like a king (*mfalme*). Similarly, yet another source notes, 'Mwana Shaha was our sultan. The first Kingalu was only a medicine man, but Mwana Shaha came from the coast to be sultan of Ukami.'[4] Together with Kisabengo, the Zigua interloper who commanded the plains north of the Uluguru Mountains and who created the town of Morogoro, Kingalu mwana Shaha was a typical representative of the new generation of economically driven and militarily powerful political leaders with whom we are familiar during this period in East Africa's history. What sets Kingalu mwana Shaha apart as an up-country leader, however, is, as his patronymic belies, his natal connection to the Mrima coast and the imaginative manner in which he interwove sources of knowledge and political connections from previously distinct cultural networks to his own political purposes.

Depending on the genealogy one consults, mwana Shaha was either the sixth or seventh holder of the Kingalu title.[5] He was born in about 1788 at Bagamoyo, died in 1872 at Zanzibar, and was buried at Bagamoyo.[6] According to one informant, his precise birthplace was in the *mtaa* (town quarter) of Dunda, where his father resided.[7] His mother was a woman of the ruling lineage of the Wabena clan and a close relative of the Kingalu who held office immediately before mwana Shaha was enstooled or came 'to rule the name (*kutawala jina*)', given the strong matrilineal succession pattern among the Luguru. His father is remembered to have been born near Kaole, at Mbegani, where his grandfather, Mfamawe Shaha, was an important man.[8] According to the incumbent Kingalu in 1972, mwana Shaha's father was a Shomvi (a generic classification for members of the ruling class along the Mrima) whose name was Kijoka.[9] All sources are unanimous that mwana Shaha was the first Kingalu to be Muslim, a religious tradition he inherited from his Shomvi father, while his grandson describes him as 'a big, stout black man'.[10]

The name *Shaha* was actually an inheritable title that was characteristic of the Shomvi subgroup who inhabit the Mrima coast.[11] Perhaps Kingalu mwana Shaha would himself have taken this title had he not been selected to succeed his matrilineal kinsman as Kingalu. Before assuming leadership of the Wabena clan, however, he was known as Shenekambi mwana Shaha. Moreover, according to his grandson, *Shenekambi* was also an inheritable title, since Kingalu mwana Shaha is said to have fought at Kaole with Jumbe Mumbi of *mtaa* Shauri Moyo 'while he held the office of Shenekambi' and when he became Kingalu 'he gave the title of Shenekambi to his first son, Kibwana'.[12] One further indication of links between the Wabena and Bagamoyo comes from Père Anton Horner, who in 1870 visited Kingalu mwana Shaha at Kinole. According to Horner, it was only after extending the limits of his hegemony that mwana Shaha 'took the name of Kingalu. Previously people called him Diwani or Jumbe (chief)', both of which we recognize as Swahili titles.[13]

Wabena Connections to the Mrima

We cannot begin to understand mwana Shaha's history without first undertaking a closer examination of the deeper history of connections between the Wabena and the Mrima. Two important points emerge from this discussion: first, besides being a dynamic personality, mwana Shaha enjoyed the luxury of access to a different tradition of political authority through each of his parents; second, and more significantly, the circumstances of his parentage point to an earlier history of intimate links between Bagamoyo and surrounding settlements and the plains and mountains of Ukami and Uluguru. With respect to the latter, when asked if Shaha went to Ukami to trade or to hunt, informants at Kaole replied, 'He went there only to marry, and he got a Kami wife and produced a child'.[14] At least one son of a Kingalu suggests that Shaha's interests were not only matrimonial, however, when he comments that 'during that time those Wabarawe came to look for slaves at Kingalu's and to marry this Mwana Makuka', which suggests a prior trading relationship between Ukami and the coast.[15] Such an explanation fits well with what we know about the growth of the slave trade in the Mrima hinterland from the early nineteenth century, and helps us to understand stories about two other scions of the Wabena ruling lineage who also had unambiguous ties to Bagamoyo.

The first of these appears as either the fourth or fifth Kingalu in Wabena genealogies and is known as mwana Fimbombili. Although Horner recognizes mwana Fimbombili as a predecessor of mwana Shaha, he also links the name of Fimbombili with that of mwana Shaha, and although there is no confirmation of this notion in the traditions that I collected, one account names both Fimbombili and mwana Shaha as sons of Mwana Makuka.[16] Indeed, mwana Fimbombili is not a name that is usually associated with the Kingalu line on the Mrima, because of the fact that an important nineteenth-century diwani at Bagamoyo whose notoriety coincided with the end of mwana Shaha's reign was also named Fimbombili.[17] As part of a campaign that questioned the British deposition of the Kingalu in 1936 and struggles surrounding the newly combined Sultanship of Uluguru, a group of supporters of the Kingalu (who still held authority within the Wabena lineage) proclaimed to the colonial authorities 'that there was no sultan other than Kingaru Fimbo Mbili of the second generation who went to Sultan Sayid bin Sultan, Zanzibar, to make an agreement. There are many markings made by the Sultan from Kinole to the coast.' They also declared that Sayyid Said and Fimbombili had agreed to divide the country between them, the former taking the coast and the latter the interior, especially the mountains.[18] Frankly, I have my doubts, quite apart from the possible confusion here with stories about Kingalu mwana Shaha. Typical of other genealogical histories, from the alleged founder of the dynasty to mwana Shaha little in detail is recalled about those who held office between these two dominant figures. Rather than delve into the very contradictory evidence about the possible relationship between mwana Fimbombili and mwana Shaha, the key point here is to emphasize that all authorities recognize mwana Fimbombili as a second Kingalu who was born to a Shomvi father at Bagamoyo and who was buried there, as well, although he is not said to have been a Muslim.[19]

The third member of the Wabena ruling lineage who connects the Kami/Luguru to Bagamoyo is Mwana Makuka, who became an integral part of the cultural heritage of Bagamoyo itself. As we have just seen, Mwana Makuka is the name of an important daughter of the Wabena ruling line who married into the ruling class at Bagamoyo. According to one account, her original Luguru name was Masenegeza, but she was given the sobriquet of Mwana Makuka by her husband's people because she moved away from the mountains to settle at the coast. Testimony taken at the Kingalu's enclosure (*mtamba*) indicates, however, that Mwana Makuka may have been another positionally inherited title that dates to the mother of mwana Fimbombili's predecessor as Kingalu, mwana Mkasi.[20]

Before addressing the important structural link that Mwana Makuka represents at Bagamoyo between the Wabena and the rulers of the coastal town, let me try to resolve the question of who exactly she might have been. One Bagamoyo informant suggested that she married Diwani Kizoka of *mtaa* Dunda, the reputed birthplace of mwana Shaha, which confirms the identification at Kinole of Shaha as Kijoka.[21] Another local source claims that this union gave birth to Mwinyi Mkuu, who is remembered as a full brother of Shenikambi.[22] But two different sources, one the first Bagamoyo informant and the other a Luguru, agree that Mwana Makuka was mwana Shaha's full sister, although such an identification cannot be squared with that between mwana Shaha and Shenikambi. Moreover, according to the son of a past Kingalu, Mwana Makuka bore *both* Kingalu Fimbombili and Kingalu mwana Shaha (which would make sense if they were in fact brothers), and possibly also Kingalu mwana Mkasi, the third bearer of the title. The same informant notes, however, that after mwana Mkasi the name of Mwana Makuka was inherited.[23] Despite the many contradictions in the oral evidence, it seems most likely that Mwana Makuka was a positionally inherited title and that the particular woman who was married (presumably for political and economic reasons) into the power structure of Bagamoyo may have been *either* the mother or the sister of mwana Shaha. In fact, both his mother and sister may have borne that title.

The clearest indication of Mwana Makuka's pivotal position as an emblem of Wabena connections to the town elite of Bagamoyo is the fact that her memory has become culturally internalized by its inhabitants. The Kami/Luguru were an especially important component of Bagamoyo's town life because of their specific links to both Dunda and Gongoni *mitaa*, as well as to the Luguru settlement of Migude, one-and-a-half hours' walk to the southwest of Kaole, which was established by Shaha Mkubwa, who came with his brother, Shaha Mdogo, from Kinole, the Wabena seat of authority. In fact, these two brothers had a Kami mother and were *ndugu*, or relatives, of Machupa bin Shenekambi, the grandson of Kingalu mwana Shaha.[24] It is because of these clear, if imprecise, links between the Wabena and Bagamoyo that the possibility exists that the Kami/Luguru were an important counterbalance to the Zaramo, who lived all around Bagamoyo and were, in fact, as much its overlords in the third quarter of the century as the Sultan of Zanzibar.[25]

However problematic this reconstruction may be, the fact remains that in 1973 there was by the side of the old dirt road from Bagamoyo to Kaole, just at about the *mtaa* of Pumbuji, which is one of the pre-Bagamoyo villages to which the Portuguese sources refer in the seventeenth century, a small cemetery that included a tomb without inscription which was said to be that of Mwana Makuka. Abandoned and overgrown with brushwood, it used to be a regular site of *tambiko*, or propitiation, for rain by Bagamoyo Luguru only.[26] The grave was also an important link in the larger regional network of rain shrines, the two most important of which were the one controlled by the Kingalu – thus the link to Mwana Makuka – and that centered on Kolero, in the southern Uluguru Mountains.[27] Further cultural evidence that Mwana Makuka had become fully integrated by the end of the nineteenth century into the larger community consciousness of Swahili Bagamoyo, and not only that of the local Kami/Luguru, is this oath that is cited by Mtoro bin Mwinyi Bakari, whose own mother was Zaramo: 'May Lady Makuka cut my throat if I did it'.[28] The editorial comment on this line states only '"Lady Makuka" – a woman who died in the distant past in Bagamoyo'.[29] Given the short town history of Bagamoyo, as opposed to some of its constituent *mitaa*, such as Pumbuji, and the parallel growth of the Kingalu line, 'the distant past' was almost certainly no earlier than the first quarter of the nineteenth century. If this reconstruction is broadly accurate, it suggests how very rapidly Swahili society could absorb such a clearly non-Swahili figure into its cultural orbit and make her Swahili, as it also demonstrates how tightly integrated coast and interior were in eastern Tanzania.[30]

Kingalu Mwana Shaha's Rise to Power

When mwana Shaha returned to Uluguru to assume the position of Kingalu, the regional political economy dictated that he remain in close communication with the coast. Although there is no available evidence for when mwana Shaha assumed the title of Kingalu, it must have been well before 1857, when Burton recorded Kisabengo's conquest of northern Ukami at the expense of a Muslim *diwani* Kingalu.[31] His apparent age at his death also suggests an accession date some time in the second quarter of the century if one assumes that he was a mature, but not old, man when he became the Kingalu. In 1870 his son-in-law, the Omani Arab Muhammad bin Nasr, was said to have served as his secretary for forty years, which suggests a possible date of around 1830 for his accession.[32] In fact, according to what must be regarded as the official account, there was nothing exceptional about mwana Shaha's succession to leadership of the Wabena. Upon further questioning, however, Wabena elders indicated that he was the grand-nephew (*mjukuu*) of his predecessor, Kingalu mwana Dundaga, rather than the nephew or brother, as would normally be the case.[33]

In theory, the usual rules of positional succession to the position of Kingalu followed the offices of Gungurugwa, Ukumbagu, and Mleke, respectively, or some variation thereof. But Kingalu mwana Dundaga is said to have favored Shenikambi mwana Shaha, even though he was the child of his niece, herself the daughter of his sister. Nor was this a case of there being no eligible males in the generation of mwana Shaha's uncles. Rather, exercising his right to choose his successor, he designated Shenikambi mwana Shaha 'because he loved him greatly ... and because he was the right man to rule the country and as a Swahili even had a little education'.[34] But there is at least one dissenting voice to these familial recollections of an unusual, though constitutional, coming to power by mwana Shaha. According to what Ricklin learned from a remarkable woman named Kulindilo during his trip to Kinole in 1870,

> her father was the brother of Kingalu and reigned over Ukami. Kingalu, sensing that he was the stronger, made war against his brother, defeated him and sold him as a slave with his daughter. The father died in misery and chagrin, and the daughter was sent as a slave to Masqat.[35]

The fact that this version is supported by testimony from two sons of a former Kingalu, who tell us that mwana Shaha fought with his brother and his Wabena allies and seized power from him, suggests that we may be nearer to understanding the actual circumstances of mwana Shaha's gaining of power as the Kingalu.[36] At the very least it suggests that his rise to power may have been accompanied by a certain amount of force that was probably both acceptable under normal circumstances and indicative of the aggressiveness of this ambitious man in those unsettled and rapidly changing times. Horner's characterization of the young mwana Shaha as 'a turbulent neighbor' who carried out 'constant wars' would also seem to support this interpretation.[37]

When Kingalu mwana Shaha finally moved from the coast to the eastern slopes of the Uluguru Mountains, he discovered that the same dual identity that had made him a, if not the, leading candidate to lead the Wabena now posed something of a dilemma for him. At Bagamoyo and Kaole it was easy to be both Kami and Shomvi, since the former did not interfere with his being Muslim. But at Kinole, where his most important role was to make offerings for rain and he could not practise the faith of his father, it was not yet possible to straddle these identities so smoothly. To accommodate this tension, while also building on his strength as a man of the Mrima, Kingalu mwana Shaha first established his residence in the area of Madamu, in the foothills between the heights of the Uluguru Moutains and the Ukami plains, in the neighborhood of the road that runs south from Kingolwira and Kiroka to Mkuyuni. There he could carry out his secular role as head of the Wabena clan, attend to his coastal connections, and be a practicing Muslim. When he was required to make *tambiko* (ancestral propitiation), he simply moved up to Kinole, where his ritual objects of office were kept, to perform his responsibilities.[38] Eventually, apparently stimulated to action by what he saw taking place at Kisabengo's new town of Morogoro, Kingalu mwana Shaha went a step further and built himself a separate stone-walled town at Utondwe, in Mfumbwe, slightly deeper up into the foothills and above the increasingly important caravan stop of Kiroka. Here he not only practiced Islam, he also built a mosque.[39] Utondwe was established as a specifically Muslim town with strong patrilateral connections for Kingalu mwana Shaha, all of whose family were Muslim and whose male children were sent to the coast to be circumcised. In 1870 the local headman of Utondwe was his eldest son, Mustafa, while his elder brother, Makame ya Shani, had his own settlement in the neighborhood of Jaminge.[40]

When the Alsatian Holy Ghost missionary Horner visited Utondwe on the approach to Kinole in 1870, he described it in these terms: 'This village, the former capital of Ukami, is remarkable for the ruins of its stone ramparts, if one can still call a wall two meters high a rampart'.[41] A century later, the ruins of these walls were still visible. They were located in a very large *shamba* (cultivated field) of sorghum millet (*mtama*) that was set deep into a ring of hills to the Kinole side of a peak called Mwene Ubena, which is visible from Mfumbwe. The Mfumbwe River flowed down a deep gorge to one side of the town walls and, in general, the area appeared to be well watered and coursed with smaller streams. The walls themselves ranged from about two-and-a-half to four feet in height and, despite being covered with vegetation, they were in remarkably good condition, neatly coursed and fitted, with mud filling, and approximately two feet thick. Judging by the layout of the walls and corners, it appeared to me at the time that the town was divided into rough *mitaa*, as one would expect for the town of a man of the coast. According to a man who lived near the *shamba*, however, mwana Shaha did not himself live within the walls, but just behind the town, farther back into the circle of hills and near the bank of the Mfumbwe River.[42] Perhaps this decision reflected his recognition that he ought not to risk transgressing the limits on his actions as the Kingalu. The fact that he resided at Kinole in 1870 may also bear witness to his eventual acceptance of the primary importance of the ritual significance of his role as the Kingalu. As for the name of this town, we know that Utondwe is also the name of the coastal settlement north of Bagamoyo that Portuguese sources testify to as being the leading Mrima ivory emporium in the seventeenth century; it may also be that Kingalu mwana Shaha had some family connections there. Certainly, his grandson recalls that he specifically built Utondwe to bring the coast to Uluguru, a sentiment that finds parallels elsewhere in nineteenth-century East Africa.[43]

The emergence of mwana Shaha as the Kingalu apparently raised the stock of the dominant Wabena clan of Uluguru/Ukami; several sources remember that he revived the past glory of the Kingalu line, extending its temporal sway beyond Ngerengere and the generally recognized boundary between Ukami and Ukwere to Wabena stool holders as far east as Kibiki, Sagasa, and Magindu. Indeed, Horner tells us, although the Kami had a reputation as retiring and timid by his time, Kingalu mwana Shaha was 'an intrepid warrior' who greatly extended his domain. During his 1870 visit to Kinole, Horner commented several times upon the numbers of armed troops that the Kingalu seemed to be able to command.[44] His territory was divided into various districts, including those under his direct or close control like Kinole, Utondwe (where his son was chief), and Ponera (where Mamba, an Arab father-in-law of the important coastal merchant Said Magram, was chief); semi-autonomous and eponymous neighboring areas in the mountains under the immediate control of his powerful Wabena kinsmen, like Suwapanga and Kumbaku, both of whom occupied important leadership roles at his court; and those regions in the plains which acknowledged his hegemony. Horner, who like most European observers considered Ukami to be a 'kingdom', fancied that mwana Shaha had 'some three hundred ministers scattered among the different centers of population of the kingdom. These are the village chiefs.' Even if his numbers are reliable, which seems unlikely, Horner clearly had no idea of the way in which local settlements selected their leaders on the basis of founding lineages. Still, he provides an important piece of evidence when he writes, 'The principal ones among them enjoy the privilege of wishing the king good morning. At the palace they each have a special seat: it is a stool made of a single piece of wood.'[45] Eighteen of these stools were still housed in the meeting lodge of the Kingalu's *mtamba* at Kinole in the early 1970s, representing lineage heads as far away as Bagamoyo.[46]

If mwana Shaha constructed his new realm on the twin foundations of his bilateral kinship and his success as a warrior – an interpretation that seems justified on the basis of the evidence about his notoriety at the coast and his accession – then the tales about his hundreds of wives and children suggest strongly that he cemented his reign by making numerous marriage alliances. In doing so he was engaging in a familiar African strategy for establishing relations of patronage and subordination, as James Giblin has argued for the neighboring region of northern Uzigua.[47] Moreover, by the end of the century the notoriety of Kingalu mwana Shaha's marital strategy had already passed into folklore at Bagamoyo, providing still further testimony to the intimate links between coast and interior during this era. In a section of the *Desturi za Waswahili* entitled 'Why the People of the Coast Have Few Children', Mtoro bin Mwenye Bakari recounts this story: 'There was a chief in the Kami country called Shenekambi, who had two hundred children. not by one wife; he had many wives and concubines, and every one of them had ten or more children'.[48] It would seem that while people at Bagamoyo were well aware of mwana Shaha's notoriety as a progenitor, which was part and parcel of his regional political strategy as Kingalu, they remembered him not by that up-country, Kami/Luguru title, but by his Shomvi/Swahili title of Shenekambi.

We have surprisingly little economic evidence specific to mwana Shaha's domination, although the ability to collect tribute and command labor was clearly the basis of his power, as Horner's description of Kinole makes plain. He commanded a significant amount of servile labor at Kinole, as did his principal followers, although there is no evidence with which to determine whether this labor was enslaved, coerced, or some combination thereof. He is said also to have traded slaves and a little ivory to the coast.[49]

Notwithstanding the grand show that mwana Shaha and his retainers put on for the pioneering Holy Ghost envoys who journeyed to Kinole, by 1870 it is clear that both his physical and his political powers were waning. If Burton is correct, this decline dates from the arrival of the Zigua interloper Kisabengo and the building of Zigua hegemony at Morogoro. Indeed, Horner is quite explicit about the threat posed to Ukami by Zigua war bands and the menacing presence of Kisabengo's daughter and successor, Simbamwene, on the northern border of Kingalu mwana Shaha's realm. How was this rivalry resolved, if it was resolved at all? While there are no firm answers, there are stories told that seek both to provide an explanation and to indicate the significant role played by the Sultan of Zanzibar in mediating relationships in the Mrima hinterland.

As an important man of the coast, we should not be surprised that mwana Shaha is reputed to have made many trips over to Zanzibar, although we cannot verify his presence there. Even so, such assertions, which occur frequently in oral traditions about this Kingalu, are quite reasonable. For example, elders at Mdaula, almost halfway from Kinole on the caravan route to Bagamoyo, remember that when he traveled to the coast he was greeted along the way by large crowds of people.[50] What is more problematic, while not beyond the realm of possibility, are stories that mwana Shaha met with Kisabengo in the presence of the Sultan of Zanzibar. Nevertheless, the details of these tales merit recounting, for they tell us about the way in which the regional political economy was taking shape around mid-century.

The official Wabena version of this encounter comes to us through the filter of bitter colonial rivalries for chiefship in Morogoro during the British period. It is recounted as a classic re-reading of the past that turns what external observers characterize as a loss of power, if not an actual defeat, into the generous accommodation of a stranger as a favor to the Sultan of Zanzibar. When Kisabengo came to Morogoro, so the story goes, Kingalu mwana Shaha journeyed to Zanzibar to ask the Sultan who this man was. The Sultan replied that Kisabengo had fought against his brother-in-law in his own country and was now looking for a place to settle. Since mwana Shaha's country was large, the Sultan asked if mwana Shaha would let Kisabengo occupy a part of it. When Kisabengo reached Nguru ya Ndege, a small mountain immediately northwest of the Uluguru Mountains, the local Luguru lineage head, Lukwele, asked him, 'Who are you?' Kisabengo replied by referring them to Kingalu. Lukwele and Wangazi, another local lineage head, went to Kinole to meet Kingalu. 'And here he was given a man to go and show him Bungo Dimwe', the place where he then built Morogoro. In this version, mwana Shaha and Kisabengo were great friends who never fought; moreover, the Wabena lineage elders go even further and state that 'when he came to Morogoro, Kisabengo was like a servant (*mtumishi*) of Kingalu'.[51] In fact, the details of Kisabengo's intrusion were quite different. What interests us here, however, is the linking of this story about local, colonial politics to the role assigned to the Sultan of Zanzibar, who is depicted as a somewhat distant patron for whom an autonomous mwana Shaha was willing to do a favor.

Another version of this encounter duplicates the story up to the Sultan of Zanzibar's request that mwana Shaha allow Kisabengo to settle in his country, but at this point the story takes a different turn.

> Kingalu said that I can't welcome him because if I send him myself people will honor him greatly and will make him like their sultan. I would rather that he come gradually himself with his army. It is then that Kingo came slowly and arrived at Muhale. Then the people found him.[52]

In this version we see that mwana Shaha considered it either unwise or not in his best interests to grant the Sultan's request, but appears to have asked for a kind of face-saving acceptance of the inevitable. As for a meeting that might have taken place between Kisabengo and mwana Shaha, a grandson of Kisabengo claims that they met when the former married a niece of the latter, Kitukila binti Kingalu mwana Shaha, his own mother.[53]

A third variation on this story omits any reference to Kisabengo, which is noteworthy because its source was in 1972 the current Lukwele, but it reveals still more about the possible tensions between mwana Shaha and the Sultan of Zanzibar, who in this instance is identified as Seyyid Barghash (Sultan of Zanzibar Seyyid Barghash ibn Said, r.1870–88).

Listen to the following imagined dialogue, which my source described as 'contrariness (*ubishi*)' between the two men:

Barghash: Bwana Kingalu, what's your ancestral custom (*asili*)?
Kingalu: My ancestral custom is whether on the day I die it will take two or three days for my grave to become visible.
Barghash: I don't believe that.
Kingalu: So, my friend, what's your ancestral custom?
Barghash: My ancestral custom is that on the day I die I will be buried on top of a tree; I won't be buried in the ground.
Kingalu: Ha!! My friend, you will be picked up by carrion crows. But I have important ancestry (*asili*).

About three years later, the story continues, Kingalu died. When the news reached Seyyid Barghash that his friend had passed away, he said now he should be buried. Following three days of *tambiko*, a major rain occurred like those of the Kingalus. The rain made Kingalu's grave disappear, but afterwards a thick forest grew up where there had previously been none, and that is where his grave was located. Only the Kingalu could enter this forest, not even his friend Barghash, who could not find it in Bagamoyo.[54] While the whole story is designed to serve as an illustration of Kingalu mwana Shaha's powers as a rainmaker and the equivalence of his power to that of the Sultan of Zanzibar, I think the dialogue also captures the inherent tension that existed between these two regional political leaders. In any event, taken together these three tales suggest that relations between Kingalu mwana Shaha and the Sultan of Zanzibar were probably both meaningful and problematic. In addition, I read these stories as evidence that the Sultan of Zanzibar had a vested interest in stabilizing relations between mwana Shaha and Kisabengo so that trading caravans could continue to pass unimpeded between the coast and the interior. More substantial evidence to support this interpretation comes from what we know about Kisabengo and the location histories of Kiroka, Kikundi, and Ngerengere.

Because of what I think it reveals about the problems confronting him, I want next to explore the reasons why mwana Shaha, the first Muslim Kingalu, invited the Roman Catholic Holy Ghost Fathers to visit his country in 1870. Thanks to the work of a number of scholars, we know a good deal about the motivations and strategies of the missionaries, as well as their role as political and economic actors in late nineteenth-century eastern Tanzania.[55] With support from Sultan of Zanzibar Seyyid Majid ibn Said (r.1856–70), the Spiritans established themselves in Zanzibar from a base in the French Indian Ocean island colony of La Réunion in 1862; several years later, again with the critical support of the Sultan, they founded their first mission station on the mainland at Bagamoyo in March 1868. Almost at once the mission began to receive invitations from mwana Shaha to visit him at Kinole, an appeal that, despite the uncertainties of penetrating the interior, accorded with the mission's plans to expand its presence in the region. By late November 1868, Horner described the Kami as 'an excellent mountain people' who had helped greatly in clearing and building the new mission station, adding that they 'frequently invite me to visit them' and seeking permission from home to do so. Six months later he spoke about his desire to found a mission in Ukami.[56]

On 17 July 1870 eight sons of the Kingalu, including the trusted Mhamisi, arrived at Bagamoyo while preparations were already being made for the trip up-country. Four days later, the 'King of the Kamis' sent another embassy to the mission to repeat his request that the missionaries come to him. On 24 July a third embassy reached Bagamoyo, this one led by the Arab Muhammad bin Nasr, mwana Shaha's son-in-law and secretary, and two more of his sons, while on the 27th his son Maneno was received there as well. Two days on, a fourth group of emissaries followed in their wake and Muhammad bin Nasr wrote a letter to Kinole 'to announce the imminent departure of the missionaries'. Finally, a few days before they set out on their journey on 13 August, the Kingalu's nephew, whom Horner describes accurately as 'the presumptive heir to the throne' and names as Mwinjuma, arrived at Bagamoyo bearing a very friendly and urgent letter of invitation.[57]

According to Horner, 'What has most greatly impressed the old king is what he has heard said about the medications that we distribute and the music that we make here'. When the Kingalu's heir dined with them at the mission, he too commented favorably on the music, which he seems to have regarded as being a possible complement to the royal musicians of Kinole.[58] In fact, Horner believed, the Holy Ghost missionaries were unusual among Europeans in that their purpose was not to trade, although hope sprang eternal among their African hosts and the Asian traders at Bagamoyo, where they quickly established a reputation for being self-sufficient and dispensing free medical assistance to poor Africans. 'Above all what astonishes them [the Africans] and attaches them to us is the care that we give them when they are ill. This disinterested charity', he continued rather smugly, 'stupefies them. Also, they often repeat: Mzoungou-mêma (the Whites are good).' An Arab up-country trader informed him that their favorable reputation had already reached the interior.[59] How much this was self-promotion cannot be determined, but it strongly suggests that mwana Shaha was less interested in the spiritual message of the Spiritans than he was in their more earthly attractions.

It is also likely that the Kingalu perceived the Holy Ghost fathers to be important new clients of the Sultan of Zanzibar with whom it was important to maintain good relations. The missionaries carried with them three letters from Seyyid Majid, one addressed to the Kingalu, one to Jemadari Sabr bin Muzaffar, the Baluchi representative of the Sultan of Zanzibar at Bagamoyo, and one as a general letter of introduction.[60] The letters read as typical diplomatic letters of introduction couched in the formal language of Islam and although they were issued in the name of Seyyid Majid, each was signed by his son-in-law and *wazir*, Sulaiman bin Ali Mandhry, and dated 7 Rajab 1286 (13 October 1869). Despite the fact that Horner characterizes the first as being addressed to 'his vassal Kingalu, king of Ukami', the published French translation of the letter is addressed from 'Majid bin Said to my friend Kingalu Shenikambi', while the body refers to the missionaries as 'our intimate friends' and requests that they be accorded all honors as 'one knows to treat the friends of the Sultan of Zanzibar in Ukami'.

The letter to Jemadari Sabr adds the important detail that the French priests were being accompanied by Sharif Makaram, better known as Said bin Awadh Magram, an important Hadrami merchant at Bagamoyo, upon whom the Spiritans came to rely for many practical matters over the next two decades, when he became a vigorous supporter of the expanding power of the Sultanate under Seyyid Barghash. Said Magram had conducted business with mwana Shaha for some fifteen years and was able to translate from Kami to Swahili for Horner when necessary. Horner also mentions that Kingalu mwana Shaha was in debt to Said Magram.[61] But Seyyid Majid was already known to be approaching death. On the eve of their departure for Kinole, Horner observed shrewdly:

> The death of the Sultan of Zanzibar, who is the suzerain of that of the Wakami, will lead to complications. Among other things the king [Kingalu mwana Shaha] is very old and infirm. It's important that in his lifetime his subjects get used to a new order for themselves.[62]

When they finally reached Kinole on 22 August, it became clear to the missionaries that mwana Shaha was indeed close to being on his last legs. At eighty-two years of age, he still commanded a considerable court and was able to receive them in great style, although Horner subsequently described Kinole itself as 'a miserable village'.[63] A massive individual, with a reputation for gargantuan eating habits in his youth, he now had white hair and a white beard. As for his health, he had suffered for four years from a hemiplegia that kept him to his bed, although upon their arrival he greeted them seated and was able to extend a warm handshake. At their first meeting he is reported to have welcomed them by stating: 'You are the friends of the Sultan of Zanzibar, this is his country, thus it is also yours. *Simmguéni*, you are not strangers to us'.[64] The following day Horner and his companions made their official visit to mwana Shaha, who received them lying on a *kitanda* or bedstead. When they asked him where would be the best location to establish a mission station, he responded by indicating his own country, provided they received the approval of the Sultan of Zanzibar, 'whose vassal I am'. But mwana Shaha could only guarantee their security in three provinces, the core areas of Kinole, where he was undisputed matrilineal lineage head of the Wabena, plus Utondwe and Ponera, where his patrilateral family – all of whom were Muslims – held sway. It was clear to Horner, at least, that for their practical daily purposes he was by no means lord of Ukami. Still, at Kinole the Kingalu was sovereign and Horner's description of the formal greetings mwana Shaha received from his subordinates, which parallel those reported from among the Swahili of Bagamoyo at the end of the century, reflects the prestige of his position as the Kingalu and are identical to those I witnessed a century later at Kinole.[65]

Before leaving Kinole, Horner also began medical treatment of mwana Shaha, which consisted of some medication provided by the French naval surgeon at Zanzibar and a regimen of vigorous massage. After several days, mwana Shaha appeared to have recovered a little use of one arm and said that his leg also felt better.[66] Discouraged by what they regarded as an unfruitful field for proselytization and reminded of the fragility of Kingalu mwana Shaha's ability to provide security by a fracas with some marauding Zigua near the major caravan stop of Ngerengere, the Spiritans abandoned their plans for Kinole and looked elsewhere in the hinterland to establish a new station.[67] Meanwhile, mwana Shaha was apparently slipping away. According to the mission sources, in 1872 he was transported to Zanzibar to seek relief for his declining health; when the Governor of Zanzibar, to whom he was allegedly in debt, learned of his presence, he ordered mwana Shaha to appear before him and threatened him with imprisonment. He was spared only as a consequence of his ill health and the fact that his son, Mustafa, was able to take his place; soon thereafter he died. His burial at Bagamoyo was celebrated by eight days of festivities. In contrast, according to oral sources, mwana Shaha went to Zanzibar to resolve a dispute with Saad of Kikundi, one of several interlopers in Ukami with strong Busaidi connections, but he contracted smallpox and died at Zanzibar, after which he was buried at Bagamoyo.[68]

It should come as no surprise that there was some dispute over the succession to Kingalu mwana Shaha. In theory, the succession should go through the matrilineal line according to an ordered positional succession. But we have seen in our discussion of mwana Shaha's rise to power that there was a good deal of flexibility, including the use of armed force, in how a successor was finally selected and confirmed as the Kingalu. Despite the realities of lineage politics, over the century 1870–1970 there appears to have been some stability in the principal offices from among which the next Kingalu should be selected, although the order varies according to the source. These were the Gungurugwa, the Kumbagu, the Mleke, and the Zegema.[69] By no later than 1877, it appears that the Kingalu line was occupied by a man who had previously served as the Kumbagu under Kingalu mwana Shaha. When the Spiritans visited Kinole in 1870, Horner described the Kumbagu as being in charge of internal affairs.

> He is chosen from among the closest members of the royal family; he is the counselor and intimate confidant of the king. The current Kumbagu, besides a most amiable man, is leprous. His face is completely scarred by smallpox.[70]

Although they had an evident interest in maintaining reasonably accurate intelligence about the successor to this important 'king', the Holy Ghost understanding of what occurred was not altogether clear. In one place we are told:

> One of the ministers of Kingalu (Waziri) succeeded through intrigues in mounting the throne. But after a little while he was removed and today in his place a leper reigns in Ukami. During our visit he was Kumbagu or second minister and we knew him from the visit that P. Duparquet made to him.

A few pages later, we read that 'he has since usurped the throne of Ukami'.[71] How does this conflicting information compare with oral traditions collected a century later?

The official version from Kinole remarks that, following the death of a Kingalu and before his burial, his successor was chosen from those who were eligible to be considered; once the old Kingalu was buried, the new man was seized and installed as the new Kingalu. Part of the problem in the case of a successor to mwana Shaha may have been his burial at Bagamoyo as a Muslim, which, according to his grandson, upset the normal procedures for selecting his successor and contravened custom.[72] Whether or not this was a complication, mwana Shaha was succeeded by Chawili mwana Kumbang'ombe, a man characterized at Kinole only for not having a good character. Consequently, he was replaced by Kingalu Charamila. Not surprisingly, every recorded version of the authorized Kingalu succession omits Chawili.[73] It is from mwana Shaha's direct patrilineal descendant that we begin to get some clarity.

> After mwana Shaha died his nephew, Kingalu mwana Charamila, governed. But after mwana Shaha died his younger sibling (*mdogo wake*) Chawili was installed as ruler. But because his judgment was not good he released the totems (*alikuwa anaacha miiko*) of Kingalu to the nephew, who carried on the duties of office (*akachukua madaraka*). This nephew was the child of mwana Shaha's sister: same father, same mother. . . . This unworthy Kingalu [i.e. Chawili] was rejected by the elders and ruled for a short time. This man was taking the breasts/nipples of women to suckle them (*Huyu alikuwa anachukua matiti ya wanawake anyonye*). The position of Kingalu was taken away from him and given to Charamila.[74]

What we seem to have here, then, is a straightforward rejection of an unworthy candidate in favor of a more suitable individual from the ruling Wabena lineage. Unfortunately, without information on mwana Shaha's name or title before assuming that of the Kingalu it is impossible to identify him positively with Mwinjuma, 'the presumptive heir to the throne'.

According to one of the Holy Ghost priests who visited Kinole in 1870, however, there may also have been a patrilineal challenge to this succession by Kingalu mwana Shaha's Muslim chief minister, Waziri, who appears in the Shenikambi genealogy as one of Kingalu mwana Shaha's sons.[75] Such a turn of events was perhaps predictable considering the way in which mwana Shaha exercised his personal leadership at Kinole through his sons and affines. That these patrilineal kinsmen and relations by marriage were all Muslims certainly may have influenced their family attitudes towards inheritance, but if there was indeed a challenge by Waziri to the succession, I do not think that it was Islam to which the Wabena elders would have objected; rather it would have been Waziri's threat to the principle of matrilineal descent upon which rested the Kingalu's enduring authority and knowledge as a rainmaker. Although Islam and matrilineality may be uneasy bedfellows, we know from the cases of the Yao and Makua of northern Mozambique that they can and still do co-exist. But in the case of the Wabena, 'the custom of the country does not allow the son of kings to reign, but rather their cousins'.[76] Indeed, mwana Shaha's successors as Kingalu also became Muslims, but they did not challenge the matrilineal descent system by which they gained the position that they still hold. Mwana Shaha's claim to be considered as the Kingalu was legitimate; that of his son was not.

Looked at from another perspective we can see that matrilineal descent prevented Kingalu mwana Shaha from passing his personal power on to his eventual successor. Unquestionably ambitious, mwana Shaha inherited a title that allowed him to claim some limited political authority in the eastern Uluguru Mountains and perhaps the foothills immediately below, as well as considerably greater religious reach across the Ukami plains by virtue of the Kingalu's control of one of the most important rain-calling shrines in the region. Based at Kinole, Kingalu mwana Shaha found himself off the beaten path so far as the two main caravan routes were concerned. But if his geographical dilemma was comparable to that of his Shambaa contemporary, Kimweri ye Nyumbai, who never quite mastered the new, commercially driven political economy, his response was dramatically different. Drawing on both his coastal, patrilateral connections and his matrilineal Wabena power base, he aggressively expanded his religio-political authority by force so that he became a major player in the regional political economy. By the time of his death, Kingalu mwana Shaha had earned a reputation as one of the powerful regional leaders in East Africa.

As an Mbena and a descendant of the previous Kingalu, mwana Shaha legitimately asserted his claim to political leadership among the Kami/Luguru and, thereby, to his ritual leadership over a broader area of eastern Tanzania that looked to the rain shrine controlled by the Wabena for succor in times of need. As a scion of the Mrima political elite with close ties to Bagamoyo and a Muslim, mwana Shaha was able to forge a set of personal political relationships that gave him special links to Zanzibar and the Busaidi sultanate. By combining local and regional, indeed global, sources of legitimacy and authority, Kingalu mwana Shaha succeeded in a political project that anticipated the efforts of modern Tanzanian political leadership, both local and national. That his heirs on both sides did not succeed in institutionalizing his gains reflects both the changing political landscape of late nineteenth-century Africa and the resilience of local custom, while it also reminds us of his own political genius.

Notes

* I am deeply indebted to Isaria Kimambo for enabling me to conduct research in Tanzania in 1972–73. Isaria was at that time Vice-Chancellor of the University of Dar es Salaam and in that capacity he was instrumental in both facilitating my research clearance and securing housing for my family in Morogoro Town. Isaria also urged me to maintain a regional approach to my research at a time when I proposed a narrower focus. It was sound advice. Considering how long I have taken to write up this research, I hope he regards this first essay to be at least partial payment for his collegial

encouragement and support. The present essay has benefited from comments by the anonymous reader of the collection, as also by Gregory Maddox and Steven Feierman. I am also grateful for funding support from the Ford Foundation, the National Endowment for the Humanities, and the Council on Research of the Academic Senate, UCLA.

1. Jan Vansina, 'Upstarts and Newcomers in Equatorial Africa (*c*.1815–1875)', in Philip Curtin et al., *African History*, 2nd edn (London and New York: Longman 1995), p. 377. For brief sketches of some of these leaders in eastern Africa, see Edward A. Alpers, 'The Nineteenth Century: Prelude to Colonialism', in B.A. Ogot (ed.), *Zamani*, new edn (Nairobi: East Africa Publishing House, 1974), pp. 229–48.

2. On this latter point, see James L. Brain, 'Kingalu: A Myth of Origin from Eastern Tanzania', *Anthropos*, 66 (1971), pp. 817–38.

3. Tanzania National Archives, Dar es Salaam (hereafter TNA) Secretariat 19283/II, p. 275, translation of Machupa b. Shenikambi to Chief Secretary, Morogoro, 9 July 1935.

4. Eastern Tanzania Historical Texts (hereafter ETHT) 27/19, Ngerengere Elders, 1 November 1972; Field Notebook (hereafter FN) 3, chance meeting at Kiroka with Ali Zege mwana Mzima of Ngerengere, 22 July 1973. Mzee Ali was one of the elders whom I met with at Ngerengere, so this is not an entirely independent variation.

5. Variants of the Kingalu genealogy are provided by ETHT 18, Kingalu Elders, Kinole, 18 October 1972, and ETHT 47, Amani 'Machupa' Shenikambi, Morogoro, 12 December 1972; L.A. Ricklin, *La Mission Catholique du Zanguebar – Travaux et Voyages du R.P. Horner* (Paris: Gaume, 1880), p. 230; TNA, Secretariat 19283/II, p.325, Sultan Kingalu to Chief Secretary, Dar es Salaam, May 16, 1937; Morogoro District Book (hereafter MDB), 'Tribal History and Legends'; and Roland Young and Henry A. Fosbrooke, *Land and Politics among the Luguru of Tanganyika* (Evanston, IL: Northwestern University Press, 1960), pp. 47-48, Table 4.

6. Ricklin, *Horner*, pp. 208, 232; ETHT 47/4, Machupa Shenikambi, 12 December 1972, who later in this interview contradicts himself by indicating that mwana Shaha was born at Utondwe, on the coast north of Bagamoyo; ETHT 58/5, Ahmed Pazi Pandukizi, Bagamoyo, 22 January 1973.

7. ETHT 56/13, Ramadhani bin Diwani Mwinchuguuni, Bagamoyo, 21 January 1973 and FN 2, entry for 22 January 1973.

8. ETHT 47/5, Machupa Shenikambi, 12 December 1972.

9. ETHT 18/11 and 48/2, Kingalu Elders, Kinole, 18 October and 21 December 1972; Charles Sacleux, *Dictionaire Swahili-Français*, 2 (Paris, Institut d'ethnologie, 1941), p. 843.

10. ETHT 47/7, Machupa Shenikambi, Morogoro, 12 December 1972.

11. See J.W.T. Allen (ed.), *The Customs of the Swahili People: The Desturi za Waswahili of Mtoro bin Mwinyi Bakari and Other Swahili Persons* (Berkeley and Los Angeles: University of California Press, 1981), pp. 216, 267 n.2, 305 n.19; A.H.J. Prins, *The Swahili-speaking Peoples of Zanzibar and the East African Coast*, Ethnographic Survey of Africa, East Central Africa, Part XII (London: International African Institute, 1967), p. 96; Sacleux, *Dictionnaire*, 2, p.827; cf. ETHT 54/5, Kaole Elders, 19 January 1973; FN 2, entry for 22 January 1973 (Ramadhani bin Diwani Mwinchuguuni).

12. ETHT 47/5, Machupa Shenikambi, Morogoro, 12 December 1972; ETHT 54/1, Kaole Elders, 19 January 1973; also FN 2, entry for 22 January 1973 (Ramadhani bin Diwani Mwinchuguuni); cf. ETHT 48/2, Kingalu Elders, Kinole, 21 December 1972, for other evidence of Shenekambi's Bagamoyo struggles. See below, note 57 for another version of the succession to the Shenikambi title.

13. Ricklin, *Horner*, pp. 230–31. Burton mixes up these titles in his garbled version of Kisabengo's conquest of the northern Ukami plains and of the Muslim diwani Ngozi or Kingaru when he claims that Kisabengo appropriated the title of Shenikambi: see Richard F. Burton, 'The Lake Regions of Cntral Equatorial Africa', *Journal of the Royal Geographical Society*, 29 (1859), p. 76. For the two Swahili titles, see Sacleux, *Dictionnaire*, 1, pp. 169, 195.

14. ETHT 54/5, Kaole Elders, 19 January 1973.

15. ETHT 66/2, Salekota Ramadhani Kingalu Akbara, Morogoro, 1 June 1973. Many

Shomvi lineages of the Mrima towns, including Bagamoyo, claim origins from Barawe (Brava) and attach the cognate 'al-Barawa' to their personal names and patronyms. See Walter Thaddeus Brown, 'A pre-colonial history of Bagamoyo: Aspects of the growth of an East African coastal town' (Ph. D. dissertation, Boston University, 1971), pp. 45–80; ETHT 36, Ahmad Muhammad Haji, Sadani, 14 November 1872; Mzee Ahmad identified his father's *kabila* as al-Katani (from Barawa).

16. *Les Missions Catholiques* (hereafter *LMC*), 6 (1874), p. 6; Ricklin, *Horner*, p. 230; ETHT 48/2, Kingalu and Elders, Kinole, 21 December 1972; ETHT 66/2, Salekota Ramadhani Kingalu Akbara, Morogoro, 1 June 1973.

17. See Archives de la Congregation du Saint-Esprit, Paris (hereafter ACSE), 196-B/III, Horner to ?, Bagamoyo, 6 November 1872, and Scheuermann to Baur, Bagamoyo, 3 June 1873; ETHT 54/5, Kaole Elders, 19 January 1973, and 56/14, Ramadhani bin Diwani Mwinchuguuni, Bagamoyo, 21 January 1973, who subsequently noted that Fimbombili was diwani of *mtaa* Pumbuji, for which see FN 2, entry for 22 January 1973.

18. TNA, Secretariat 31347, p. 50, Ukami Club to Chief Secretary, Dar es Salaam, 17 January 1948, the letter being signed by its President, Salim Mohamedi, and p. 49, same to District Commissioner, Morogoro, Eastern Province, Dar es Salaam, 4 December 1947. For the politics of chiefship in Morogoro at this time, see Young and Fosbrooke, *Land and Politics*, pp. 86–7.

19. ETHT 14/13, Lukwele Abdallah, Mbete, 7 October 1972; ETHT 18/11 & 48/3, Kingalu Elders, Kinole, 18 October and 21 December 1972; ETHT 47/4, Machupa Shenikambi, Morogoro, 12 December 1972.

20. ETHT 66/2, Salekota Ramadhani Kingalu Akbara, Morogoro, 1 June 1973; ETHT 18/4, Kingalu Elders, Kinole, 18 October 1972.

21. ETHT 58/5, Ahmed Pazi Pandukizi, Bagamoyo, 22 January 1973.

22. ETHT 56/13, Ramadhani bin Diwani Mwinchuguuni, Bagamoyo, 21 January 1973.

23. ETHT 18/1, Kingalu Elders, Kinole, 18 October 1972.

24. See FN 2, entries for 20 January (Maalim Shani Kissawago, Bagamoyo) and 21, 1973 (Muhina Shomari, Kitopeni), for Kami links to Bagamoyo and Migude.

25. For the Zaramo 'war' of 1875–76, see Brown, 'Pre-Colonial History of Bagamoyo', pp. 270–74.

26. FN 2, entry for 20 January 1973 (Maalim Shani Kissawago, Bagamoyo). See also the description of offerings left at a cemetery by the side of the road from Kaole to Bagamoyo in ACSE, 195-B/II, Horner to Schwindenhammer, Zanzibar, 24–30 December 1863. When I revisited these tombs on 25 June 1994, the road had been diverted slightly inland and they were located behind the Mwana Makuka Primary School, which was clearly built some time after 1973.

27. See G.C.K. Gwassa, 'Kinjikitile and the Ideology of Maji Maji', in T.O. Ranger and I.N. Kimambo (eds), *The Historical Study of African Religions* (London and Berkeley, CA: University of California Press, 1972), p. 207; Marja-Liisa Swantz, *Ritual and Symbol in Transitional Zaramo Society with special reference to women* (Uppsala: Gleerup, 1970), p. 151.

28. Allen, *Customs*, p. 185.

29. *Ibid.*, p. 300 n.7.

30. For the very different history of *makungwi* absorption in Mombasa as a consequence of its slave origins, see Margaret Strobel, *Swahili Women in Mombasa 1890-1975* (New Haven, CT: Yale University Press, 1979), ch. 8, especially pp. 196–202.

31. Burton, 'Lake Regions', p. 76 and see n. 13 above. According to both ETHT 18/11, Kingalu Elders, Kinole, 18 October 1972 and ETHT 10/3, Ali Kambi, Morogoro, 28 September 1972, mwana Shaha was in office before the arrival of Kisabengo at Morogoro, which is usually attributed to some time in the 1840s. *Diwani* was an honorific title at the coast, often signifying a member of the local chief's council: Sacleux, *Dictionnaire*, p. 169.

32. For identification of Muhammad bin Nasr as mwana Shaha's son-in-law (*gendre*), see *LMC*, 5 (1873), p. 624, but cf. *ibid.*, p. 585, where this man's wife, who died on the journey from Bagamoyo to Kinole, is referred to as Kingalu's daughter-in-law (*bru*); see also Ricklin, *Horner*, p. 158, where Muhammad bin Nasr is said to have lived in Ukami

for forty years.

33. Cf. ETHT 18 and 48, Kingalu Elders, Kinole, 18 October and 21 December 1972. Ali Kingalu, the chief spokesperson for the reigning Kingalu bin Sadi Sitembo, was the son of his predecessor and was a leader against terracing during the Uluguru Land Usage Scheme protests in 1955. He was consequently imprisoned for a year and then rusticated to Biharamulo in northwestern Tanzania for another year along with three other individuals. See Young and Fosbrooke, *Land and Politics*, pp. 148, 153, 158–60; but for more complex readings cf. James L. Brain, 'The Uluguru Land Usage Scheme: Success and Failure', *The Journal of Developing Areas*, 14 (1980), pp. 185–88; Pamela Maack, "The Waluguru are not sleeping": Poverty, culture, and social differentiation in Morogoro, Tanzania' (Ph.D. dissertation, Northwestern University, 1992), Ch. 4, especially p. 128, n. 1; and Peter Pels, *Critical Matters: Interactions between Missionaries and Waluguru in Colonial Tanganyika, 1930-1961*, published Ph.D. dissertation, University of Amsterdam, 1993, p. 185, n. 42.

34. ETHT 47/8, Machupa bin Shenikambi, Morogoro, 12 December 1972. For variations on this order of succession, see MDB, Tribal History and Legends; Ricklin, *Horner*, pp. 237–8; ETHT 18/4, Kingalu Elders, Kinole, 18 October 1972.

35. *LMC*, 5 (1873), p. 585; Ricklin, *Horner*, p. 183.

36. ETHT 66, Salekota Ramadhani and Misembe Abdallah Kingalu Akbara, Morogoro, 1 June 1973.

37. Ricklin, *Horner*, p. 212. Horner also attributed the rectangular unplastered houses at Kinole to the need for portability during this phase of mwana Shaha's reign. Young and Fosbrooke, *Land and Politics*, pp. 41–42, claim that the taboo against anything but this style of housing was still in force around Kinole in the 1950s, but offer no explanation for its origin. The indigenous style of housing in Uluguru was a mud and wattle rondavel. The steady encroachment of both Swahili- and European-style rectangular housing in eastern Africa in the 19th and 20th centuries is well known, but the style of housing at Kinole is quite distinct from that of the coast because of the unplastered walls.

38. For Madamu, ETHT 43/4, Msumi bin Ruga, Kalundwa (nchi Kinole), 22 November 1972; for tensions about Islam at Kinole, ETHT 30/5, Kinoro bin Kamba among Kiroka Wazee, 6 November 1972.

39. *Ibid.*; after I visited the ruins of Utondwe, Mzee Kinoro specifically mentioned that Kingalu mwana Shaha only built his walled town after Kisabengo came to Morogoro and built his own walled town there: FN 3, 24 July 1973; ETHT 47/6, Machupa bin Shenikambi, Morogoro, 12 December 1972; ETHT 46/2, Mdungundwa bin Sabu, Kalungwa Village, 5 December 1972; while ETHT 48/3, Kingalu Elders, Kinole, 21 December 1972, emphasize the importance of Islam in mwana Shaha's decision to build Utondwe, they do not mention the mosque.

40. Ricklin, *Horner*, p. 199; ETHT, 47/10, Machupa bin Shenikambi, Morogoro, 12 December 1972; Allen, *Customs*, p. 148 and 295, n. 2. A Makame ya Shani was also the chief of Mdaula, on the route from Uluguru to Bagamoyo, but it is not clear if this is the same person who was apparently a contemporary minor chief at Winde: see ETHT 40/8, Mdaula Elders, 19 November 1972; Bagamoyo District Book, 'Windi–1925'. For the detail about circumcision, see ACSE, 196-B/III, Marcellin to Louis-Stanislaus, Zanzibar, 18 August 1870; for the twentieth-century introduction of circumcision in Uluguru (as opposed to going to the coast), see Pels, *Critical Matters*, pp. 124–30.

41. Ricklin, *Horner*, p. 198. In the original published description of this journey, Horner includes the qualifier 'dry' to his description of the stone walls of Utondwe: *LMC*, 5 (1873), p. 597.

42. FN 3, 24 July 1973.

43. Another new settlement established around Utondwe that replicated a coastal place name was Mbegani, for which see ETHT 48/3, Kingalu Elders, Kinole, 21 December 1972. The phenomenon of naming new up-country settlements after important coastal towns has a long history, e.g. the proliferation of the name Kilwa throughout the interior of East Africa. For making the interior look like the coast, see Yohanna B.

Abdallah, *The Yaos* (London: Cass, 1969; 1st edn, Zomba, 1919), pp. 43–4, 51.

44. *LMC*, 6 (1874), p. 6; Ricklin, *Horner*, pp. 230–31; ETHT 47/12, Machupa Shenikambi, Morogoro, 12 December 1972.

45. *LMC*, 6 (1874), p. 5; Ricklin, *Horner*, pp. 237, 254 (for Mamba).

46. See FN 1, 18 October 1972 (Kinole); cf. Young and Fosbrooke, *Land and Politics*, pp. 56–7 and photograph of lineage stools opposite p. 66.

47. James L. Giblin, *The Politics of Environmental Control in Northeastern Tanzania, 1840–1940* (Philadelphia: University of Pennsylvania Press, 1992), Part II.

48. Allen, *Customs*, pp. 18 and 261 n. 28; the number of 200 children is found also in ACSE, 196-B/III, copy of Marcellin to Louis-Stanislas, 'Voyage des Pères chez les Kamis', Zanzibar, 18 April 1870, and *Bulletin Général de la Congrégation du Saint-Espirit* (herafter *BG*), XIII, 196 (1886), p. 1122; cf. Ricklin, *Horner*, p. 231, for the alleged hundreds of women and children in mwana Shaha's household. According to ETHT 11/12, Ali Selimani Meronge, Morogoro, 28 September 1972, Kingalu mwana Shaha had many wives and 150 children.

49. *LMC*, 5 (1873), pp. 614–15; Ricklin, *Horner*, pp. 203–5, 212–213; ETHT 47/6, Machupa Shenikambi, Morogoro, 12 December 1972; ETHT 10/3, Ali Kambi, Morogoro, 28 September 1972; ETHT 11/8, Ali Selimani Meronge, Morogoro, 28 September 1972.

50. ETHT 40/8, Mdaula Elders, 19 November 1972.

51. ETHT 18/11-12, Kingalu Elders, Kinole, 18 October 1972. In this version, the Sultan of Zanzibar is identified as Seyyid Barghash, which is clearly incorrect. The grandson of Kisabengo agrees that they never fought directly: ETHT 61/4, Muhina Mbugi bin Kingo, Mziha, 14 February 1973. See C.S. Nicholls, *The Swahili Coast: Politics, Diplomacy and Trade on the East African Littoral 1798–1856* (London: George Allen & Unwin Ltd, 1971).

52. ETHT 11/3, Ali Selimani Moronge, Morogoro, 28 September 1972. In this version, the Sultan of Zanzibar is named as Seyyid Khalid, a son of Seyyid Said ibn Sultan who served as regent at Zanzibar and ruled in his father's absences in Masqat, but who predeceased his father in 1854 and never reigned as Sultan. See Nicholls, *Swahili Coast*, p. 275. I should note here that Ali Selimani was a leading supporter of terracing in eastern Uluguru during the 1950s and was on the opposite side of the Uluguru Land Usage Scheme struggle from the Kingalu and his followers, although I cannot say whether this history affected his version of this story. See Young and Fosbrooke, *Land and Politics*, pp. 98–99 (where he is named correctly), 150, 157 (where he is incorrectly called Abdallah).

53. ETHT 61/3, Muhina Mbugi bin Kingo, Mziha, 14 February 1973; cf. ETHT, 47/7, Machupa Shenikambi, Morogoro, 21 December 1972, who remembers her as his grandfather's sister.

54. ETHT 14/13, Lukwele Abdallah, Mbete, 8 October 1972. A meeting with Seyyid Barghash would have been possible but unlikely considering mwana Shaha's failing health, since we know that Barghash assumed power as Sultan in 1870 and mwana Shaha died in 1872. The carrion or Pied crow (*kunguru*) , *Corvus albus*, a large black crow with white back and shoulders, is ubiquitous throughout eastern Africa.

55. See John A.P. Kieran, 'The Holy Ghost Fathers in East Africa, 1863 to 1914' (Ph.D. dissertation, University of London, 1966; Brown, 'Pre-colonial history of Bagamoyo', Ch. 7; Giblin, *Politics*, Ch. 4; Frits Versteijnen, *The Catholic Mission of Bagamoyo* (Bagamoyo, 1991; 1st edn 1968) and 'Zanguebar through Contemporary Records' (cyclostyled, Bagamoyo, 1968); H.G.M. Tullemans, 'Transcripted Letters and Documents of the Bagamoyo Mission during the Arab Revolt 1888–1889', appendix in *Père Étienne Baur en de Arabische Opstand van 1888–1889* (published Ph.D. dissertation, Catholic University of Nijmegen, 1982); Johannes Henschel, *Alles begann in Bagamoyo: 100 Jahre Kirche in Ostafrika* (Aachen, 1983), pp. 10–49.

56. ACSE, 195-B/II, Horner to P. ?, Zanzibar, 29 November 1868; 195/I, Horner to Maupoint, Zanzibar, 15 June 1870; also see ACSE, 196/X, Horner to Propaganda de la Foi, Bagamoyo, 4 March 1869 and 196/XII, Horner to Gaume, Zanzibar, 1 July 1869.

57. Roman Catholic Secretariat, Bishop's House, Morogoro (hereafter RCSM), Bagamoyo Mission Journal, entries for 17, 21, 24, 27, 29 July , and 5 August 1870; ACSE, 195/I, Horner to Maupoint, Bagamoyo, 8 August 1870; Ricklin, *Horner*, p. 158. Kingalu's descendants confirm that such a letter was sent to the missionaries at Bagamoyo: ETHT 18/2–3, Kingalu Elders, Kinole, 18 October 1972. According to MDB, 'Tribal History and Legends', 'Shenikambi's Genealogical Tree (Ukoo Punguji)', a Mwinjuma was the son and first successor to Kingalu mwana Shaha as Shenikambi; but cf. ETHT 47/5, Machupa Shenikambi, Morogoro, 12 December 1972, who names Kibwana as successor to mwana Shaha as Shenikambi.

58. ACSE, 195/I, Horner to Maupoint, Bagamoyo, 8 August 1870. For the attraction and incorporation of Western music in eastern Africa at the end of the century, see T. O. Ranger, *Dance and Society in Eastern Africa* (London, 1975); for the power of *ngoma*, dance and rhythm, in the spread of Christianity in eastern Uluguru, see Pels, *Critical Matters*, Ch. 4.

59. ACSE, 196/X, Horner to Propaganda de la Foi, Bagamoyo, 28 December 1869; Horner's translation into French notwithstanding, *mzungu mwema* is the singular, not the plural, form. See Giblin, *Politics of Environmental Control*, pp. 62–7, 105–7 for the Spiritans as healers in Uzigua during the last decades of the century, and more generally for their comprehensive roles as chiefs and patrons.

60. For Sabr bin Muzaffar, see Brown, 'Pre-Colonial History of Bagamoyo', pp. 259–66.

61. Ricklin, *Horner*, pp. 154–5, 170, 211, 218. For Said Magram's self-identification, see ACSE, 196-B/III, Said bin Awadh Magram to Father Superior, 7 May or 6 June 1873, letter in Arabic script with contemporary French translation. For more on Said Magram, including his support of the Germans at the time of colonial invasion, see Jonathon Glassman, *Feast and Riot: Revelry, Rebellion, and Popular Consciousness on the Swahili Coast, 1856–1888* (Portsmouth, NH: Heinemann, 1995), pp. 205, 211.

62. ACSE, 196-B/III, Horner to P. ?, Bagamoyo, 8 August 1870. One example of this new order would be the removal of Sulaiman bin Ali to Bombay under British protection because of his opposition to Barghash in 1870. For details, see Reginald Coupland, *The Exploitation of East Africa, 1856–1890: The Slave Trade and the Scramble* (Oxford, 1939), pp. 19, 87–8, 91–2; Frederick Cooper, *Plantation Slavery on the East Coast of Africa* (New Haven, CT and London, 1977), pp. 53, 68, 72; Randall L. Pouwels, *Horn and Crescent: Cultural Change and Traditional Islam on the East African Coast, 800–1900* (Cambridge, 1987), pp. 152, 180.

63. ACSE, 196-B/III, Horner to R. ?, Bagamoyo, 6 October 1870. For their reception, see *LMC*, 5 (1873), p. 614; Ricklin, *Horner*, pp. 203–5.

64. *LMC*, 5 (1873), p. 614; Ricklin, *Horner*, p. 208, changes 'us' to 'me'. The phrase '*Simmguéni*' may be garbled and should read either '*Si mgeni*' (singular) or '*Si wageni*' (plural), depending on whether the Kingalu was addressing only Horner or the entire Holy Ghost party.

65. *LMC*, 5 (1873), p. 615; Ricklin, *Horner*, p. 211. I should point out, however, that Horner both ridicules and totally misinterprets the literal meaning of these greetings, rendering *Koutchaméné*, i.e. *Kucha Mwinyi*, as 'lion's paw' rather than 'It dawns, Sir', the implied meaning of *mwinyi* for the Kingalu perhaps being *mwinyimvua*, 'rainmaker, lit. owner of the rain' or simply 'chief'. These greetings and signs of obeisance, which include the laying of one's cap, shoes, and weapons at the feet of the Kingalu, were performed in my presence at the TANU office at Kinole on 18 October 1972 before proceeding farther up the mountain on foot to the Kingalu's *mtamba* and following my formal presentation of official research clearance papers to the local TANU Secretary. They were very clearly intended to impress me and to make the point that, despite the abolition of chiefship in Tanzania, the Kingalu was still chief. Later that afternoon, when I descended back to where we had left the car by the TANU office, a passerby asked if I had removed my shoes inside the *mtamba*, where only the Kingalu was allowed to cover his feet. I had. For an explanation of these greetings, see R.L. Hamdumbavhinu, *Waluguru na Desturi Zao* (Nairobi/Dar es Salaam/Kampala: East African Literature Bureau, 1968), p. 31, and letter from the late James L. Brain to the

53

author, New Paltz, 25 November 1985, neither of which refers to the response Horner attributes to Kingalu, '*Minza!*', for which see Br. Ananias-Denis, *Historia ya Morogoro* (Morogoro, 1964), p. 5, who explains the meaning of '*Mwinza*' (Luguru) as '*nakuamkia*' (Swahili), 'to pay respects to someone'. See also C.J. Mzuanda, *Historia ya Uluguru* (Morogoro, 1958), p. 109, where '*Mwinza*' indicates the ending of one phase of the installation of a lineage title-holder. Pels, *Critical Matters*, p. 28, comments specifically on the persistent manipulation of colonial officials by the Kingalu line, something of which I was well aware and sought to undercut by my interview strategy. For greetings at 1890s Bagamoyo, see Allen, *Customs*, p. 41. This form of greeting was recognized elsewhere in eastern Tanzania, as at an unnamed Doe village a few days' march from Bagamoyo, for which see Étienne Baur and Alexandre Le Roy, *A Travers le Zanguebar – Voyage dans l'Oudoé, l'Ouzigoua, l'Oukwèré, l'Oukami et l'Ousagara* (Tours: Alfred Mame et fils, 1886), p. 29.

66. *LMC*, 5 (1873), pp. 622–3.

67. ACSE, 196-B/III, Horner to R. ?, Bagamoyo, 6 October 1870; Ricklin, *Horner*, pp. 264–7. The Holy Ghost Congregation established its first two up-country stations at Mhonda (1878), in the southern Nguu Mountains, and Mandera (1881), in Ukwere.

68. Ricklin, *Horner*, p. 232; ETHT 28/1-2, Kikundi Elders, 2 November 1972; ETHT 47/7, Machupa Shenikambi, Morogoro, 12 December 1972; ETHT 58/5, Ahmad Pazi Pandukizi, Bagamoyo, 22 January 1973, confirms the detail about smallpox.

69. *LMC*, 6 (1874), p. 6; Ricklin, *Horner*, pp. 237-238; MDB, Tribal History and Legends; ETHT 18/4 and 48, Kingalu Elders, Kinole, 18 October and 21 December 1972; ETHT 47/8, Machupa Shenikambi, Morogoro, 12 December 1972; ETHT 66, Salekota Ramadhani and Misembe Abdallah Kingalu Akbara, Morogoro, 1 June 1973.

70. *LMC*, 6 (1874), p. 6.

71. Ricklin, *Horner*, pp. 232, 238.

72. ETHT 18/5, Kingalu Elders, Kinole, 18 October 1972; ETHT 47/7, Machupa Shenikambi, 12 December 1972.

73. For Chawili, whose name was shared with me only during my second visit to Kinole, see ETHT 48/5, Kingalu Elders, Kinole, 21 December 1972; for the genealogies, see TNA, Secretariat19283/II/325, Sultan Kingalo to Chief Secretary, Dar es Salaam, 16 May 1937; MDB, Tribal History and Legends; Young and Fosbrooke, *Land and Politics*, pp. 47–8; ETHT 18/2, Kingalu Elders, Kinole, 18 October 1972. The versions are lists, rather than genealogies, and there is much variation from list to list on the genealogical relations among the different titleholders, despite their common source within the ruling Wabena lineage.

74. ETHT 47/9, Machupa Shenikambi, Morogoro, 12 December 1972; for another version, see ETHT 66/5-6, Salekota Ramadhani and Misembe Abdallah Kingalu Akbara, Morogoro, 1 June 1973. My thanks to Tom Hinnebusch for help in translating this passage from Kiswahili.

75. ACSE 196-B/III, Marcellin to Louis-Stanislaus, Zanzibar, 18 August 1870; TDB, Tribal History and Legends, 'Shenikambi's Genealogical Tree (Ukoo Punguji)'. Marcellin regarded Waziri as a somewhat unsavory character.

76. ACSE 196-B/III, Marcellin to Louis-Stanislaus, Zanzibar, 18 August 1870. There is no evidence to identify Waziri with Chawili. For the Yao, see Alpers, 'Trade, State and Society among the Yao in the Nineteenth Century', *Journal of African History*, 10 (1969), pp. 405–20, and 'Towards a History of the Expansion of Islam in East Africa: the Matrilineal Peoples of the Southern Interior', in Ranger and Kimambo, *The Historical Study of African Religions*, pp. 171–201. For the challenge of fathers' rights to principles of matrilineal descent in contemporary Uluguru, see Maack, 'The Waluguru are not sleeping', Ch. 7.

Part II

*Politics, Culture & Dissent
in Colonial Tanganyika*

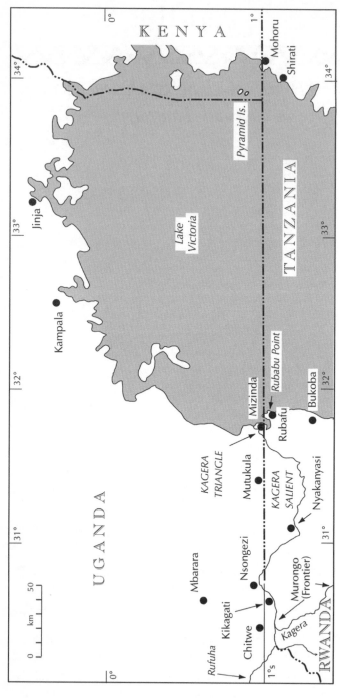

Map 4.1 Tanzania–Uganda, showing the Kagera Salient

Source: Ian Brownlie, *African Boundaries: A Legal and Diplomatic Encyclopedia* (London: C. Hurst, 1979), p. 1012.

Four

∧∧∧∧∧∧∧∧∧∧∧∧∧∧∧∧∧∧∧∧∧∧∧∧∧∧

Colonial Boundaries & African Nationalism
The Case of the Kagera Salient

RALPH A. AUSTEN

The boundaries drawn by Europeans during the Scramble for Africa are at once the bane and the basis for modern African nationalism. The dominant response to this dilemma among Western scholars has been a somewhat pessimistic resignation:

> A paradox is central to the nature of political boundaries in Africa: there is widespread agreement that the boundaries are arbitrary, yet the vast majority of them have remained unchanged since the late 1880's, when they were first demarcated.
>
> ...the present boundary system represents a rational response by both colonialists and post-independence African leaders to the constraints imposed by the demographic and ethnographic structure of the continent.[1]

Although the word 'national' appears in the title of the article from which the preceding statement is cited, such an analysis assumes that the African territorial entities involved are not, in substance, nations or even 'empirical states', but rather legal fictions, maintained in their present form because the global and local risks of altering the admittedly inadequate colonial heritage outweigh the benefits of any imaginable alternative.[2]

A more optimistic, if minority, view is represented by Paul Nugent, who argues that 'the apparently artificial lines forged their own combination of vested interests' so 'that there is much greater coherence to the national project than many people allow'.[3] Nugent supports this contention by noting the degree to which at least the idea of territorial mapping, if not most of the specific colonial boundaries drawn during the Partition, can be found in precolonial African politics.

A third approach, shared in varying ways by some African scholars and several Western current political scientists, is to embrace the weakness or even breakdown of colonial boundaries and even postcolonial states. From such a perspective, the fluid and often violent movements within enclaves and frontier zones not subject to central government control can be seen as exemplars of both continuity with a less bounded precolonial past and the harbingers of a 'post-modern' concept of African political organization.[4]

The issues at stake here are very large and the study of a single disputed African boundary can hardly claim to resolve them. The Kagera Salient, moreover, has never been seen as significant enough to receive serious attention in the sub-field of African boundary studies.[5] Nonetheless, the Kagera case does contain most of the elements which characterize such problems and will thus provide at least a small addition to our understanding of the relationship between boundaries and nationalism.

The Kagera salient (also known as Missenyi) is a small but substantial piece of land (about 660 square miles; 1978 population ca. 50,000) lying north of the Kagera River and south of the international boundary separating Uganda and Tanzania which, between Lake Victoria and Rwanda, is based on the line of one degree south latitude. Because it cuts across both an obvious feature of the natural landscape and a well-recognized province (Buddu) of the precolonial Ganda state, this line has been described as 'a classic example of bad delimitation [that] has resulted in a boundary which is not only anomalous but approaches the absurd'.[6]

The problematic nature of such a border was addressed at various moments in the colonial history of East Africa and gained more dramatic stature in 1978, when Idi Amin sent his armies across the border and 'reclaimed' the Kagera salient for Uganda. It even remains a nuisance worthy of ministerial attention in the present millennium.[7] None of these interventions resulted in any lasting territorial change (although, as will be seen, Amin's initiative did have major international and domestic repercussions), but they at least suggest that colonial cartography might be malleable. Such a suspicion is confirmed if we look more closely at the general history of colonial maps in tropical Africa.

A surprising number (at least in contrast to the consensus expressed by such scholars as Jeffrey Herbst) of African boundary changes did occur between the 1880s and decolonization. The best-known cases involve the former German colonies like Tanganyika, all of which were not only handed over to the victorious World War I allies but also underwent lasting internal territorial alterations.[8] In 1911 German Kamerun was also given a considerable strip of French Central Africa, which was restored after the war; but within the former French Equatorial African Federation many districts were shuffled from one territory (and eventual independent state) to another.[9] British East Africa also witnessed several exchanges of territory, the most notorious being the transfer of the former Eastern Province of Uganda to the East African Protectorate (Kenya) in 1902.[10] Paul Nugent also notes a number of smaller territorial changes which adjusted anomalies in the original partition of West Africa.[11]

Thus, as might be expected, there were several attempts, during both the German and British mandate eras in Tanzania, to rectify the Kagera boundary. All of them failed, largely because the slight territorial advantage which the one degree latitude line gave to German East Africa/Tanganyika came to symbolize a compensation for advantages lost elsewhere.

This is the explanation for the original creation of such an artificial line in the 1890 treaty which first established a border running west of Lake Victoria. Britain and Germany both came to these Berlin negotiations with grand visions of continental realms. The British, seeking a 'Cape-to-Cairo' corridor, hoped to use the historical expansion of Buganda well south of the Kagera river to establish a key territorial link between Lakes Victoria and Tanganyika. The Germans, in a scheme later dubbed 'Mittelafrika', sought to control the territories joining the Indian Ocean with the Congo, with an eventual link to Cameroon. In the end the British appeared to achieve more of their goals, since the Germans gave up all claims to Zanzibar, Uganda (Emin Pasha had signed a treat with Kabaka Mwanga in 1889), and the Lake Nyasa (Malawi)-Lake Tanganyika border with the Congo. The one major concession by the British was to give up the Uganda-Lake Tanganyika link. Once having surrendered their major aim in this region, the British were also prepared to appear generous and offer the Germans a line from Lake Victoria to the Congo which provided them with slightly more territory than the natural Kagera river boundary.[12]

The creation of the Kagera Salient thus typifies the process by which African territory was bartered between European powers without much concern for either ethnography or geography. However, a closer look at the colonial history of this boundary suggests that the European actors were well aware of the regional issues when they drew their arbitrary lines, and that their failure to remedy the anomaly was less a matter of inattention than of an inability to find a fit between the local and global concerns which constantly played off against one another in this small piece of land.

The Ganda state fits well into Nugent's category of precolonial African polities which had fairly precise ideas of boundaries.[13] The *ssaza* (county) of Buddu , which included the Kagera Salient, had been conquered from the neighboring (and less centralized) state of Bunyoro some time in the eighteenth century but for this reason was actually under more direct control by the Kabaka (king) than older, more central areas of Buganda.[14] The Ganda also raided and collected tribute among the Haya communities south of the Kagera during the nineteenth century, but no permanent representatives of the Kabaka were ever stationed there.

At the time of the Partition, British and French missionaries had been present in Buganda for more than two decades and were well acquainted with the political landscape of the region. Indeed, the British claims for a corridor between Lake Victoria and Lake Tanganyika were supported by Church Missionary Society members on the basis of a 'Greater Buganda' which included the tributary areas extending beyond Buddu.[15]

The Germans remained aware that the Kagera constituted a historical boundary between Buganda and the Haya states of Kiziba and Karagwe. They regularly referred to the territory within the Kagera Salient as 'German Buddu'[16] much as the Kamerun authorities referred to the north-eastern portion of their territory as 'German Bornu'. The partitioned areas of Bornu were, however, eventually united under British/Nigerian rule, while the Kagera Salient has remained part of Tanganyika/Tanzania.

The fact that an initial colonial boundary cut off a portion of Buddu is obviously not a sufficient explanation for such persistence.

From the earliest years of colonial administration on the western side of Lake Victoria, the territorial division drawn at the first parallel proved not only arbitrary but inconvenient. Interest in adjusting the boundary was thus expressed from both the British and German sides of the border.[17] In the first decade after 1890, the very physical location of the boundary remained unclear and petty disputes arose quite frequently between the officials on the respective sides over mutual allegations of territorial violations. At this early stage of colonization, the Salient became very much of a lawless border zone where groups equally threatening to British and German rule – criminals, slave traders and rebels – could seek safe refuge.[18] As in the later Amin era, it was particularly rebels against the Uganda government who made use of this zone, although in this case the German authorities co-operated in repressing them.[19]

With the marking of a definite boundary by a 1902–4 joint survey commission, attention was shifted to the possibility of making a systematic adjustment. The frontier could now be more effectively policed, but this practice created hardships for Africans not only in the Kagera Salient but also in the lesser anomalies on both of its flanks: the 'Kagera Triangle'on the Lake Victoria shore which put 15 square miles of the Haya Kiziba state under British rule, and the 'Kagera Loop' which gave the Germans a 240 square mile but thinly populated slice of the Ankole state in western Uganda.

Two obstacles stood in the way of shifting to a more reasonable Kagera river boundary. The first was the value which each of the colonial governments placed upon the territories they would have to give up. The second was the question of what concessions could be made elsewhere to the Germans for conceding an obviously larger piece of territory than the British had to offer on this particular frontier.

Ironically, it was the British who first opposed any exchange on the grounds that their little triangle at the river mouth contained the unique and strategically vital anchorage of Mazinda, which offered a key to control of the entire Kagera Valley.[20] By 1909 this idea had been abandoned; but now the Germans had discovered grounds for a serious interest in the Kagera Salient.[21] A survey of this enclave revealed that it contained forest areas offering supplies of wood seriously needed in this portion of Deutsch Ostafrika. Furthermore, the long-term and much respected Resident of Bukoba, Major Willibald von Stuemer, objected almost hysterically to the effect on local German prestige of any territorial surrender: 'Such an event would place a severe strain upon the obedience and absolute submissiveness of the major sultans in this area.'[22]

From a local perspective, therefore, the problems of an arbitrary border had become manifest, but so had a degree of national interest (in this case the nationalism of European administrators) in the value of specific pieces of territory. At the level of Great Power diplomacy, there was less inhibition about the negotiability of African territory, but problems still arose in deciding what Germany should receive in exchange for surrendering the Kagera Salient (the Kagera Loop was never considered of any significant value). Obviously the minuscule Kagera Triangle would not be enough. As early as 1892 it had been suggested that some form of access from what was then German Ruanda to Lake Albert in southwest Uganda might serve to complete the bargain.[23] By 1905, however, this latter area had become involved in the complex Anglo-German-Belgian negotiations concerning the Lake Kivu-Mfumbiro region and had to be separated from the relatively minor Kagera question.[24] After this the Kagera Salient seems to have been held in reserve by the Germans, to be thrown into the balance for completion of some larger colonial settlement with Britain. Suggestions for such a scheme linked Kagera not only with remoter parts of East Africa, such as the still desirable Nyasa-Tanganyika corridor and Mount Kilimanjaro, but also with Southwest Africa, Togo, and Nigeria. It must be kept in mind that the German Colonial Secretaries of this period, Bernhard Dernburg and Wilhelm Solf, sought to use colonial issues as the basis for a general Anglo-German rapprochement, an effort which ultimately failed, as indicated by the alignments of World War I.[25]

One result of this war was the transfer of the Tanganyika portion of German East Africa into British hands, which would seem to have provided a good basis for rationalizing the boundary running west of Lake Victoria. Indeed, between late 1914, when serious hostilities first broke out in East Africa, and July 1916, when the allies captured Bukoba, the effective line separating Uganda and Deutsch Ostafrika had become the Kagera, a position more easily defended by the inferior German forces than the official boundary.[26] In their immediate administration of the salient as well as their later occupation of the entire Bukoba District, the British used both European and African personnel from their Uganda staff and established a system of rule similar to that in their own territory. The first recorded suggestion that such a policy – and more specifically the needs of uniform tax collection and rinderpest control – could be facilitated by a boundary rectification thus came from a former Uganda district commissioner, D.L. Baines, who was to remain in charge of Bukoba from 1916 to 1923.[27]

The momentum of such integrated administration was broken by the renewed imposition of global political concerns upon the region. A key but also ironic factor here was the greater strategic value placed by Britain upon the former German East Africa as opposed to Cameroon and Togo in West Africa. In the latter colonies, Britain received only small pieces of territory which continued to be administered by the neighboring adminis-trations of, respectively, Nigeria and the Gold Coast. At independence, all or part of these mandate holdings were integrated into the British successor states rather than into the now Francophone heirs to the main German entities. German East Africa was also shared by the British with Belgium, but on the basis of totally separated territories (Ruanda-Urundi vs Tanganyika) and no further supervisory role for Uganda in any part of Tanganyika.[28] It is understandable that, in the initial stages of establishing rule over Tanganyika under League of Nations surveillance, Britain would not want to appear interested in adding territory to its other East African possessions.[29]

By 1925, however, the Kagera Salient was again on the table, this time through African initiative. The Kabaka of Buganda and his ministers used the visit of a Parliamentary East African Commission to air their continuing grievances over the alienation of southern Buddu. The Commission members responded by proposing to bring this matter to the attention of the Council of the League of Nations.[30]

Before such a step could be taken, however, the issue had to be discussed among local colonial officials.[31] Here the attitude of Tanganyika Territory administrators displays remarkable similarities to that of their German predecessors. The Bukoba Senior Commissioner of this period, F.W. Brett, reacted somewhat ambiguously, suggesting that improved relations on the Kagera which might result from the transfer of Missenyi (the formal designation of the Salient) might compensate for the lack of attention given to his region by Dar es Salaam. Forestry officials again noted the value to Tanganyika of the Missenyi timber reserves. Sir Donald Cameron, the Governor, seized upon indications in Brett's report that the inhabitants of Missenyi were not particularly enthusiastic about transfer to Uganda and thus rejected the Kabaka's claim as based solely upon 'the argument of ancient conquest'.

What finally put an end to any serious contemplation of a Kagera boundary adjustment was not so much the Tanganyikan as the Ugandan response to the Parliamentary Commission proposals. The Governor here, Sir William Gowers, welcomed the idea of transferring Missenyi to Tanganyika, along with the less valuable 'Kagera Loop' along the Ankole-Karagwe border. But he linked these measures with a suggestion of his own for annexing the entire Bukoba District to Uganda, on the grounds that it belonged to the same ethnic and geographical Interlacustrine zone as its northern neighbors. Tanganyika officials now refused to consider any further discussion of boundary changes.

The last colonial proposal for alteration of the Kagera boundary came in 1929, when a Colonial Office report on Closer Union in East Africa included a suggestion by Uganda non-officials for again joining Bukoba to Uganda. Given the broader Tanganyika government and missionary lobby objections to regional integration schemes, which were seen as favoring Kenya white settler interests,[32] this proposal had no serious chance of success. Nonetheless, it aroused sufficient concern among the Haya chiefs of Bukoba, who feared any restoration of their earlier subjugation to Buganda, for them to send a petition in 1931 on the subject to the Parliamentary Committee which was investigating Closer Union.[33]

Before looking briefly at the role of the Kagera Salient in postcolonial Tanzania-Uganda relations, it is necessary to consider whether the colonial discourse around the Kagera boundary expresses a form of territorial identity which might foreshadow African nationalism. The continued sense of competition between Uganda and Tanganyika when both were ruled by the same European state might suggest such an interpretation, although, as with much of colonial politics, the conflicts may be as much about controlling bureaucratic turf as an identity with specific territories as 'proto-nations'. The role of Buganda and Haya rulers adds an African voice to these exchanges, thus confirming Nugent's refutation of the 'belief that border peoples were mere spectators in someone else's game'.[34] But the politics in this case hark back more to the earliest stages of colonialism, when Europeans inserted themselves into existing African struggles for power, rather than to nationalism or even late- and postcolonial 'ethnic' issues, since the Ganda and Haya identities involved here do not seem to have been transformed by the colonial process.

Further investigation of the Kabaka Yekka party and more recent Ganda self-representations, which definitely are part of the story of Uganda nationalism and better fit the concept of modernized 'invented tradition', might reveal some significant element of Buddu irredentism; but so far no evidence of this kind has been noted.[35] The most significant legacy of colonial altercations over the Kagera boundary may simply be their recorded existence (rendered conveniently accessible by Thomas' 1959 article) thus allowing their potential incorporation into expressions of nationalism independent of the memories of the populations most immediately involved.

This potential was realized in October 1978 when Ugandan military forces invaded the Kagera Salient and claimed it as their own national territory. The motivation for this action went far beyond disputes over 660 square miles of land, and the eventual restoration of the old border is clearly overshadowed by Tanzania's subsequent invasion of Uganda and overthrow of the Idi Amin regime. Nonetheless, a consideration of the immediate cause of the Tanzania-Uganda war (a foreshadowing of more widespread inter-state military interventions in the 1990s) may shed some light on the role of colonial boundaries in post-independence under-standings of African nationalism.

Most analyses of Idi Amin's decision to invade the Kagera Salient stress the long-term tensions of Tanzania-Uganda relations in the 1970s and the internal dynamics of the military regime in Uganda.[36] From the beginning of Amin's rule in Uganda, Tanzania played host to Milton Obote, the leader who had been ousted in the 1971 coup, and supported his efforts to regain power. Whatever the grounds for this policy – personal loyalty to Obote, socialist ideology, fear of a Uganda-Kenya alliance against Tanzania, or human rights objections to the atrocities perpetrated by Amin – President Julius Nyerere clearly represented a threat to the Uganda regime. Within Uganda, Amin was not always able to manage the various military groups which formed the basis of his power, and in the autumn of 1978 he faced a particular crisis which he apparently sought to resolve by undertaking the adventure of invading the Kagera Salient.

Amin had raised the issue of the Kagera boundary as early as 1971 and undertook minor actions on it in the following years. Ugandan opponents of Amin, following the example of rebels against British colonial rule in the 1890s, used the area as a base for subversion, although without any significant success. It thus came as no complete surprise that Amin eventually sought to annex this territory.

In its official account of the larger conflict, the Tanzanian government stated that

> It is important to note that before Amin seized power there was no border dispute between the two countries and no history of claims or counter-claims against each other's territory. The boundary between the countries was first demarcated by the colonialists in the last century, is well-known and was – until Amin – always respected by the authorities of both states.[37]

In the light of the historical evidence already presented (as well as continuing minor problems on the Kagera border), this statement is not entirely accurate, although none of the previous efforts to change the boundary or informal violations of it took on the seriousness of Amin's early threats and ultimate actions. There is no evidence currently available about whether Amin had ordered research on the earlier history of this boundary, as he clearly did in the case of his 1976 claims against Kenya.[38] In any case, the boundary anomaly was, at best, a secondary cause for Amin's actions. But it does appear to have been at least a necessary cause.

In relation to Amin's immediate goals of securing himself against future threats from Tanzania and assuaging his unruly followers, the nature of the Kagera boundary proved helpful. While Amin did not elaborate on the injustice of the existing border, its anomalous character may have played some role in the unwillingness of the Organization of African Unity, presumably dedicated to maintaining the integrity of colonial boundaries, to act against him.[39] Certainly, if Amin then pursued the broader ambitions he had expressed earlier of conquering territory linking Uganda directly to the Indian Ocean, some action would have been called for, but neither the preparations for the Kagera annexation nor the general condition of Ugandan military resources at this time indicate that such a goal was still actively contemplated.[40]

Amin profited, at least initially, from the logistical geography of the border zone. As in World War I, the initial Ugandan invasion of the Kagera Salient was carried out very easily, as the small Tanzanian forces stationed at this border quickly fell back on the more defensible line of the Kagera River.

All of these advantages were soon lost because of the character of the Ugandan army. In ideological terms, there is no evidence that Ugandans, brutalized by the previous seven years of Amin's rule, cared very much for the small piece of land and the population they had gained. Moreover, any possibility of claiming the sentiments or at least the ethnic identity of the inhabitants of the disputed zone as a justification for Amin's move were immediately lost when the Ugandan troops embarked on an orgy of loot, murder and rape in the region. Most decisively, the Ugandan forces lacked the discipline and technological proficiency to offer any effective resistance to the Tanzanian army, once it had been mobilized in sufficient numbers to counter-attack across the Kagera (and eventually, of course, continue on to Kampala).

The fact that the Kagera boundary was eventually restored suggests that arbitrary colonial borders are more important to African inter-state stability than is the need to adjust them on either geographic or cultural grounds. In the course of the Tanzania-Uganda conflict Julius Nyerere did coin one of the phrases which is often evoked as a critique of this policy, when he accused the OAU of acting 'like a trade union of Heads of State and Government'.[41] However, the context of this utterance is clearly not a critique of colonial boundaries, which Nyerere soon found himself defending, but rather of the unwillingness of other political leaders to countenance his efforts to undermine the atrocious military regime in neighboring Uganda.

Yet we have seen that not only was there a real possibility that the colonial rulers of East Africa might have changed the Kagera boundary, as they did so many others throughout the continent between the 1880s and independence, but also that, even before Idi Amin, the African people on both sides of the border had shown concern about border issues. The gains from a more rational line would, of course, only be minor; by contrast, Amin's attempt to make such a change by force seems to have had a major effect in galvanizing Tanzanian nationalism in a period when there were many grounds for disillusionment with the failures of Nyerere's efforts at 'African socialist' development. Of course Nyerere was a Pan-African as well as a national figure, and one scholar has expressed surprise that 'the Kagera boundary was not changed after 1979' and calls the outcome 'yet another opportunity lost to right a colonial error of judgment'.[42] One small indication that the Tanzanian government consciously sought to play up the nationalist aspect of the Uganda border conflict is the renaming in 1980 of the region containing the Salient from 'West Lake/Ziwa Maghribi' to 'Kagera'.[43]

If, on the other hand, we view the violation of the boundary as only an occasion for carrying out Nyerere's long-standing project of overthrowing Amin, the whole event becomes – like the circumstances which inhibited border adjustments in colonial times – evidence of the limited relevance of territorial boundaries. Nyerere was applauded in the West for putting an end to the horrendous regime in Uganda, but the view of most African scholars is more critical. Okoth, for one, is equally disappointed about the failure of the OAU to intervene in either Uganda's initial territorial seizure or Nyerere's subsequent violation of Ugandan sovereignty.[44] The OAU has not grown more effective since 1978 but recent developments in Somalia, Liberia, Sierra Leone and especially the Congo do suggest that unilateral (or even multilateral) interventions across state boundaries are a serious threat to political order in Africa. Possibly there are still grounds for believing that a strict maintenance of the integrity of colonial boundaries is the most 'rational response ... to the constraints imposed by the demographic and ethnographic structure of the continent'.

One alternative to this minimalist and arbitrary order is represented in the present narrative by Idi Amin. Like the frontier entrepreneurs and warlords privileged, if not fully endorsed, in recent political analysis of Africa, Amin did enjoy some appeal as a leader who dramatically broke with the colonial order and thus opened up new possibilities for African politics.[45] But if we focus just on the Kagera boundary, Amin's actions seem to be arbitrary and opportunistic rather than motivated by any enduring, let alone attractive, vision of African development. In one sense, he and all the more contemporary African figures who traffic in violence in frontier zones have more in common with their colonial predecessors, especially adventurers of the Partition era such as Henry Morton Stanley, Emin Pasha and Karl Peters, than with nation-builders and revolutionaries.

What this brief study perhaps best demonstrates is that colonial boundary-making in Africa was not only arbitrary but also unstable. Thus the prevailing insistence on retaining these boundaries may represent a survival of colonialism rather than an organically African cartography; but efforts to change the borders between the successor states are no less continuous with the patterns of European rule. African nationalism is not easy to develop within lines drawn on the map by outsiders for their own, often not very deeply considered, convenience. However, its sustained emergence depends less on redrawing these lines than on cultivating the conditions for citizenship which are at least possible inside the inherited boundaries.

Notes

1. Jeffrey Herbst, 'The Creation and Maintenance of National Boundaries in Africa' *International Organization*, 43, 4 (1989), pp. 673–92 and *States and Power in Africa: Comparative Lessons in Authority and Control* (Princeton, NJ: Princeton University Press, 2000); for similar views see Christopher Clapham, 'Boundaries and States in the New African Order', in Daniel C. Bach (ed.), *Regionalisation in Africa: Integration and Disintegration* (Oxford: James Currey, 1999), pp. 53–66.
2. Robert H. Jackson and Carl J. Rosberg, 'Sovereignty and Underdevelopment: Juridical Statehood in the African Crisis', *Journal of Modern African Studies*, 24 (1986), pp. 1–31.
3. Paul Nugent, 'Arbitrary Lines and the People's Minds: A Dissenting View on Colonial Boundaries in West Africa' in Paul Nugent and A.I. Asiwaju (eds), *African Boundaries: Barriers, Conduits, and Opportunities* (London: Pinter, 1996), pp. 61, 36.
4. S.A. Asiwaju, 'Borderlands in Africa: a Comparative Research Perspective with Particular Reference to Western Europe', in Nugent and Asiwaju, *African Boundaries*, pp. 253–65 (see references to earlier writings by the same author in this piece); Janet Roitman, 'The Garrison Entrepôt in the Lake Chad Area – Boundaries and Transgression in the Politics of Value', *Cahiers d'Études Africaines*, 38 (1998), pp. 297–329; William Reno, *Warlord Politics and African States* (Boulder, CO: Lynne Rienner Publishers, 1998).
5. It is not cited in Nugent and Asiwaju, *African Boundaries* and is omitted from the list of disputes at the end of Carl Gösta Widstrand (ed.), *African Boundary Problems* (Uppsala: Scandinavian Institute of African Studies, 1969), pp. 183–5. The 'Checklist of Partitioned Areas' in A.I. Asiwaju (ed.) *Partitioned Africans : Ethnic Relations Across Africa's International Boundaries, 1884–1984* (New York : St. Martin's Press, 1985), does contain a reference (p. 258) to the Haya of northwest Tanzania although, as will be seen, the major ethnic issue of the Kagera river frontier involves Ganda people incorporated into Tanzania; there is a brief discussion in Ieuan Griffith, 'The Scramble for Africa: Inherited Political Boundaries', *Geographical Journal*, 152 (1986), pp. 209–10.
6. A. C. McEwen, *International Boundaries of East Africa* (Oxford: Clarendon Press, 1971), p. 265.

7. See references to discussions of this 'long-standing, though low level, boundary dispute' (involving, *inter alia*, markers destroyed in the 1978–79 war) during the summer of 2000 in Faustine Rwambali , 'Uganda, Tanzania in Dispute', *The East African*, 31 July–6 August 2000 (http://www.nationaudio.com/News/EastAfrican/31072000)

8. Tanganyika was separated from the former German East African territories of Rwanda, Burundi and a small enclave along the Rovuma river frontier with Mozambique; Cameroon and Togo were divided for administrative purposes between France and Britain and never restored to their full German extent at independence; Namibia (ex-German Southwest Africa), by contrast, gained control of Walvis Bay from South Africa several years after independence.

9. See map in Ralph A. Austen and Rita Headrick, 'Equatorial Africa under German and French Rule', in David Birmingham and Phyllis Martin (eds), *A History of Central Africa*, vol. 2 (London: Longman, 1983), pp. 27–94; within French West Africa, Upper Volta (now Burkina Faso) was carved out of the former Haut-Senegal Niger (now Mali) in 1919, then re-divided among several surrounding territories in 1932, and reinstated in 1947.

10. For details along with other exchanges of territory between the two colonies up through the 1930s, see McEwen, *International Boundaries*, pp. 249–56. In 1976 Idi Amin also made public statements implying claims on the land lost to Kenya, although they were never acted upon. As an apparent result of this gesture Kenya did, however, co-operate with Israel in the raid which rescued hijacked Jewish air passengers from Entebbe later in the same year; Godfrey F. Okoth, 'Intermittent Tensions in Uganda-Kenya Relations: Historical Perspectives', *Transafrican Journal of History*, 12 (1992), pp. 77–8. A historical irony of this entire episode is that the Kenyan territory which Amin reclaimed had been part of the lands included in the 'Uganda Proposal' through which the British Colonial Office, in 1903, offered to settle European Jews in Africa as an alternative to Palestine; see Robert G. Weisbord, *African Zion; the Attempt to Establish a Jewish Colony in the East Africa Protectorate, 1903–1905* (Philadelphia: Jewish Publication Society of America, 1968), especially pp. 9–11.

11. Nugent, 'Arbitrary Lines', pp. 42–6.

12. On these negotiations see Fritz Ferdinand Muller, *Deutschland-Zanzibar-Ostafrika* (East Berlin, 1959), pp. 459–70; G. N. Sanderson, 'The Anglo-German Agreement of 1890 and the Upper Nile', *English Historical Review*, LXXVII (1963), pp. 49–72.; Wm. Roger Louis, 'The Anglo-German Hinterland Settlement of 1890 and Uganda', *Uganda Journal*, 27 (1963), pp. 71–84; *Die Grosse Politik der europaische Kabinette*, VII, 1676-1685; F. O. 403 (British Foreign Office, Confidential Prints) 141, 142.

13. Nugent, 'Arbitrary Lines', pp. 36–41. On the Ganda state see, *inter alia*, Lloyd A. Fallers (ed.), *The King's Men; Leadership and Status in Buganda on the Eve of Independence* (London: Oxford University Press, 1964).

14. Fallers, *King's Men*, pp. 95–6.

15. See letter of the missionary leader A.M. Mackay, 5 January 1890, cited in H. B. Thomas, 'The Kagera Triangle and the Kagera Salient', *Uganda Journal*, XXIII (1959), p. 76 (Thomas' brief article is the most extensive treatment of the Kagera issue in the period up to World War I; it is well-researched but constitutes somewhat of a partisan plea for Buganda claims).

16. Thomas, p. 78 cites all such references in published sources; the British colonial history of this region also notes the distinction between the true Haya and what was now called the Missenyi chiefdom: Hans Cory, *History of the Bukoba District/Historia ya Wilaya Bukoba* (Mwanza [Tanzania] : Lake Printing Works, n.d. [1959]), pp. 85, 143.

17. Thomas, p. 77; see various pieces of correspondence in F. O. 403/ 210 (1895, #236), 226 (1896, #146), 227 (1896, #6, 128), 228 (1896, #61), 260 (1898, #147).

18. Files A27/3, A28/1, Uganda Secretariat Archives, Entebbe; F. O. 403/194 (1894, #73), 208 (1894, #30), 281 (1899, #121), 283 (1899, #2, 23, 94, 118).

19. F.O. 403/260 (1898, #147), 261 (1898, #151).

20. C. Delmé-Radcliffe Report (London), 31 October 1904, F. O. 2/898, Britain, Public Records Office; F. O. 403/343 (1904. #18), 357 (1905, #144), 358 (1905), #17), 361 (1905, #3).

21. The German side of these negotiations from 1900 to 1909 is documented in Reichs-kolonialamt (German Colonial Office, hereafter RKA) 582-584, Deutsche Zentral-archiv, Berlin (see especially RKA 584: Governor von Götzen to Berlin, 26 May 1905; Herrmann to DSM, 20 June 1905, Colonial Secretary Dernburg to DSM, 6 July 1909).
22. Von Stuemer to Dar es Salaam, 1 January 1905, in DSM to Berlin, 26 May 1905, RKA 584; for von Stuemer's career and the general German presence in this region, see Ralph A. Austen, *Northwest Tanzania under German and British Rule: Colonial Policy and Tribal Politics, 1889–1939* (New Haven, CT: Yale University Press, 1969), pp. 29–118.
23. Bukoba Stationschef Herrmann to DSM, 18 November 1892, RKA 1029; Wm. Roger Louis, *Ruanda-Urundi* (Oxford: Clarendon Press, 1963), pp. 48–49.
24. RKA 584; Louis, *Ruanda-Urundi*, 41–97.
25. Herrmann to DSM, 20 June 1905, Dernburg to DSM, 6 July 1909, RKA 584; Jacques Willequet, *Le Congo Belge et la Weltpolitik* (Brussels: Presses Universitaires de Bruxelles, 1962), pp. 220 ff.
26. W. T. Shorthose, *Sport and Adventure in Africa* (London: Seeley, Service & Co, 1923), pp. 96–101; Charles Hordern, *Military Operations in East Africa* (London: HMSO, 1941), pp. 41–2; Ludwig Boell, *Die Operationen in Ostafrika* (Hamburg: W. Dachert, 1951), pp. 96–9.
27. Bukoba Monthly Report, 8 July 1918, Hans Cory Papers, University of Dar es Salaam Library.
28. William Roger Louis, *Great Britain and Germany's Lost Colonies, 1914–1919* (Oxford: Clarendon Press, 1967), pp. 149–52; Louis notes that in 1919 Britain still sought a Cape-to-Cairo route, Belgium really wanted to exchange Rwanda and Burundi for Portuguese territory at the Congo river mouth, and Portugal wanted a large portion of southern Tanganyika. The compromise included not only the separate British and Belgian mandates, but also the outright cession of the tiny 'Kionga Triangle' south of the Rovuma delta to Portugal.
29. A small but substantial piece of the original (1922) Tanganyika mandate, west of the southern route of the Kagera river, was actually turned over to Belgian control in 1924 on the grounds that it belonged to the traditional kingdom of Rwanda (McEwen, *International Boundaries*, pp. 152, 153–4).
30. *Report of the East African Commission*, Great Britain, Parliamentary Papers (hereafter PP), Cmd. 2387 (1925), pp. 147–8.
31. For the statements cited in this and the next paragraph, see correspondence of July 1925 to October 1926, Secretariat Minute Paper 7791, Tanzania National Archives, Dar es Salaam.
32. Roland Oliver, *The Missionary Factor in East Africa* (London: Longmans, 1952), pp. 247–71; Robert G. Gregory, *Sidney Webb and East Africa* (Berkeley: University of California, 1962), pp. 51–136.
33. Entry of 24 May 1929, Bunona Roman Catholic Mission Diary, Bukoba; *Joint Select Committee on Closer Union in East Africa*, PP, HC 156 (1931), 4823.
34. Nugent, 'Arbitrary Lines', p. 60.
35. Mikael Karlström, private communication. It also appears that 'In postcolonial politics it [Buddu] has often been at odds with the rest of Buganda' because of its domination by the minority Catholic Church; see Christopher Wrigley, *Kingship and State: The Buganda Dynasty* (New York : Cambridge University Press, 1996), p. 219.
36. The major sources here are Tony Avirgan and Martha Honey, *War in Uganda : the Legacy of Idi Amin* (Westport, CT: L. Hill, 1982); Gérard A. Prunier, 'Kuanguka kwa fashisti Idi Amin: Tanzania's Ambiguous Ugandan Victory', *Cultures et Développement*, 16 (1984), pp. 735–56; Amii Omara-Otunnu, *Politics and the Military in Uganda, 1890–1985* (New York: St. Martin's Press, 1987), pp. 140–41; P. Godfrey Okoth, 'The OAU and the Uganda-Tanzania War, 1978–79', *Journal of African Studies*, 14 (Fall 1987), pp. 152–62; M. Rumulika, 'The Development of Tanzanian Foreign Policy' in Taufiq Ahmad Nizami (ed.), *Tanzania and the World* (Delhi : Eastern Media Pub. Co., 1989), 143-60.
37. Government of Tanzania, '*Blue Book* on the War Against Amin's Uganda', 17 July 1979,

reprinted in K. Mathews and S.S. Mushi (eds), *Foreign Policy of Tanzania, 1961–1981: A Reader* (Dar es Salaam: Tanzania Publishing House, 1981) p. 307.

38. Semakula Kiwanuka, *Amin and the Tragedy of Uganda* (Munich: Weltforum Verlag, 1979), pp. 146–52. There seems to be no document on the Kagera Salient comparable to that on 'the Eastern Province', the genesis of which is described by Kiwanuka; however, the Thomas article would have served this purpose, especially since it omits the role of the Kabaka in the last round of colonial efforts to alter the boundary. On the other hand, some accounts (without any supporting documentation either), claim that Amin did not even initiate the 1978 action but rather followed rebellious troops into the Kagera Salient; see Phares Mutibwa, *Uganda since Independence* (Trenton, NJ: Africa World Press, 1992), pp. 113–14.

39. Okoth, 'The OAU' does not pursue this point, and it may be irrelevant but at least worthy of a closer look at the relevant documents than has so far been undertaken.

40. Prunier, 'Kuanguka kwa fashisti', p. 736.

41. Statement justifying Tanzania's boycott of the 1975 OAU Summit in Kampala, *Africa Contemporary Record; Annual Survey and Documents* (New York: Africana Publication Co.,1980-81), p. A69.

42. Griffiths, 'Scramble', pp. 209–10.

43. Adrian Room, *Place-Name Changes 1900–1991* (Metuchen, NJ: Scarecrow Press, 1993), p. 92 (the name had been Swahiliized to Ziwa Maghribi only in 1976).

44. Okoth, 'The OAU;' see Griffith, 'Scramble', pp. 213–15 for a review (and critique) of OAU policies on boundaries.

45. e.g. Ali Mazrui, 'The Resurrection of the Warrior Tradition in African Political Culture', *Journal of Modern African Studies*, 13 (1975), pp. 67–84.

Five

Indirect Rule, the Politics of Neo-Traditionalism & the Limits of Invention in Tanzania *

THOMAS SPEAR

The colonial policy of ruling through traditional authorities, known as indirect rule, has long been an issue in Tanzanian history and historiography. While the British claimed that indirect rule was based on the natural authority of chiefs and the established customs of the people, nationalist critics saw the chiefs as pawns of the colonial state, imposing its dictates on the people. Thus, the nationalist movement focused its attacks on the chiefs, and one of the independent government's first acts was to abolish chiefship.

Historical accounts have taken a similar approach, focusing on the contradictions in colonial theory and practice between the rhetoric of indirect rule and a hierarchical, direct administration; between mediated forms of local politics and a bureaucratic administration; and between the need to maintain traditional authorities and commitment to economic and social reform. As instruments of colonial domination, chiefs were no longer responsible or accountable to the people. Real power rested in colonial hands, while representative local forms of authority atrophied.[1]

More recently, historians elsewhere have focused on the degree to which traditional authorities themselves were not even traditional, but rather invented by colonial administrators as an economical way of establishing colonial hegemony.[2] Chiefs were inventions in two senses: first, the men colonial authorities appointed often lacked traditional legitimacy, and secondly, the positions to which they were appointed were either creations of the colonial administration or had been so corrupted by their incorporation into the colonial administrative hierarchy, with its unpopular demands to collect tax, raise labor, and regulate agriculture, that they no longer represented established patterns of authority at all.

These approaches have been valuable in alerting us to the contradictions in colonial theory and practice and the degree to which tradition was often an artifice, manipulated to facilitate colonial dominance. What they have in common is their focus on the role of ostensibly traditional authorities in the implementation and administration of colonial rule, with power seen as resting exclusively in the hands of colonial authorities. They also accept the colonial polarity between tradition and modernity, as traditional chiefs opposed progressive educated nationalists.

What these views miss, however, is the significance of African participation in the politics of neo-traditionalism[3] that accompanied indirect rule. To the extent that colonial authorities' were forced to depend on local authorities, whether traditional or not, colonial power was limited. For traditional or neo-traditional authorities to be effective, they had to be popularly acceptable and seen as legitimate. Chiefs thus had to respect established local values, such as the responsibility of wealthy and powerful people to ensure the well-being of others, redistribute wealth fairly, and protect others from witchcraft, at the same time as they implemented colonial policies, many of which were seen as unprecedented, corrupt, or immoral. The only way they could do this was to seek to continue to serve local interests at the same time as trying to moderate colonial demands, with colonial authorities often forced to accede.[4]

At the same time, for tradition to be deployed successfully in support of colonial rule, it had to resonate with local values and historical consciousness. Colonial administrators thus had to acknowledge historical precedent and subject themselves to the local discourse of tradition. While tradition was by no means fixed, contrary to colonial assumptions, there were established means for evoking it. People endlessly debated and reinterpreted tradition in support of their own interests, and it was this ongoing debate that colonialists joined, often at their peril. Colonial resort to tradition and traditional authorities was thus as likely to provoke debate and conflict in the ongoing politics of neo-traditionalism as it was to ensure stability.

The Theory and Practice of Indirect Rule in Tanzania

It is thus necessary to re-examine the conception and implementation of indirect rule if we wish to understand its impact on Tanzania. A starting point is the economics of colonial administration. As Sir Donald Cameroon, the governor responsible for the implementation of indirect rule in Tanganyika from 1925 to 1931, readily acknowledged:

> The policy of Native Administration of the indirect character ... is therefore in the first instance a measure of expediency. It is impossible for the Administrative Officer to get in touch with the whole of a primitive people, and it is impossible for financial reasons ... to augment that service.[5]

The colonial administration was thus forced to rely on African auxiliaries to implement its rule, which it then claimed was based on the 'free choice of the people', the 'natural authority' of the chiefs, and the established customs of the people. Anything else, Cameron averred, would be 'vandalism', destroying African 'loyalties to their own institutions... [that] form one of the most valuable possessions which we have inherited.... those loyalties if wisely directed by us make for law and order in the land as nothing else can.'

Furthermore, Cameron warned, nothing could be more disastrous than seeking to invent or subvert such authorities:

> Shun as you would shun evil the make believe 'Indirect Administration' based on nothing that is really true. It is a monster and a very dangerous one at that.[6]
>
> Experience has shown so often that to turn a chief into a placeman of the government, a servant of the government, ... is to destroy his natural authority over his people.... If the chief is ignored or if he becomes a servant of the government, ... his people rapidly lose their respect for him and all he represents in their life founded on their own institutions handed down to them through the ages; his authority gradually dwindles and ultimately perishes.[7]

At the same time, however, Cameron saw the need to employ these sacrosanct institutions to transform and modernize African societies:

> We should make every effort, again, to prevent the old Native constitution – shall we call it? – from becoming frozen-in and thus reactionary. It should be kept as fluid as possible ... so that it may expand and become more liberal under the more liberal doctrines that we preach to them in these more enlightened days.[8]

Native authorities were mandated to levy taxes, recruit labor, enact land-use regulations, impose conservation controls, and support Christian missions and schools, but such innovations could not be allowed to threaten African ways:

> It is our duty to do everything in our power to develop the native along lines which will not Westernize him and turn him into a bad imitation of a European – our whole Education policy is directed to that end. We want to make him a good African.... We must not ... destroy the African atmosphere, the African mind, the whole foundation of his race, and we shall certainly do this if we sweep away all his tribal organizations.[9]

Tradition was thus enlisted both to preserve and to transform African societies, a difficult enough mandate to conceptualize, much less achieve.

Colonial rule rested on the legitimacy, authority, and effectiveness of local chiefs and customs, effectively constraining the unbridled colonial exercise of power and ability to transform African societies. This dilemma has been eloquently captured by Sara Berry as the quest to achieve 'hegemony on a shoe string'. Given scarcity of money and personnel, colonial administrations were dependent on African authorities and customs, and thereby limited in their ability to affect social and political change. At the same time, their attempts to codify and stabilize African practice often produced contradictory results:

In general, the effect of indirect rule was neither to freeze African societies into precolonial molds, nor to restructure them in accordance with British inventions of African tradition, but to generate irresolvable debates for the interpretation of tradition and its meaning for colonial governance and economic activity.[10]

Appeals to tradition thus remained what they had always been – ongoing debates in which people struggled to solve the problems of the present in terms of the lessons of the past. The main difference was that now colonial administrators joined Africans in these debates on an expanding range of topics from traditional marriage to modern agricultural methods, as both old and new practices became subject to the same discourse, as Steven Feierman has insightfully noted. Tradition could be used by Africans or Europeans, women or men, young or old to debate civic responsibilities of wealth and authority, access to land, or obligations young urban migrants owed their families or elders. And since the discourse of tradition was an African discourse, Africans continued to influence the process.[11]

The Politics of Neo-Traditionalism in Arusha and Meru

The experiences of Arusha and Meru societies with colonial rule in northern Tanzania bear out these points. The two peoples had occupied adjacent southern slopes of Mount Meru since the 1820s, when Arusha Maasai settled to the west of pre-existing Meru homesteads and farms. There they slowly adopted the irrigated highland agriculture practised by Meru, combining bananas, cattle, maize, beans, and other crops in a complex intercropped system that produced abundant foodstuffs and milk all the year round.

Neither Meru nor Arusha had strongly centralized political systems. Meru had settled the mountain earlier in small family groups, expanding upwards over time to create contiguous clan territories. All clans were ranked by their order of initial settlement, and those whose forefathers had settled first had certain political or ritual responsibilities. The most senior clan was Kaaya and its most prominent elder became the *primus inter pares*, or *mangi*, among other clan elders.[12]

Arusha, by contrast, also settled in small groups, but they expanded up the mountain as each age-set retired, cleared the forest, and settled together. Age-set spokesmen chosen by their age-mates served as the representatives of local groups in relations with others. Over time, Arusha age-sets also began to raid Meru for women and land, which they used to expand their own settlements and population, so that by the end of the century, Arusha outnumbered Meru and incorporated them in their own age-sets to raid others. As the nineteenth century drew to a close, then, the age-sets and their spokesmen were ascendant, while clan elders exercised only limited powers.[13]

Conquest and the Imposition of German Rule

Colonial conquest ensued after Arusha and Meru warriors killed the first two missionaries who attempted to settle among them in 1896. The inhabitants of Mount Meru had been little affected by the increasing violence accompanying the expansion of trade through the Pangani Valley in the later nineteenth century, but they were well aware of the havoc Germans had wreaked in their conquest of Kilimanjaro, having served there as mercenaries with Chaga chiefs. And so they sought to protect themselves by sacrificing the missionaries, driving off the Germans, and cleansing the land of evil.[14]

The Germans exacted terrible vengeance, as they broke the Meru and Arusha warriors in a prolonged siege and then unleashed their Chaga auxiliaries to loot and kill, burning Arusha and Meru bananas and food stores, confiscating their cattle, and reclaiming women allegedly seized from Kilimanjaro previously. Together with successive bouts of bovine pleuro-pneumonia, rinderpest, locusts, drought, and famine, the mountain economy was destroyed, and Meru and Arusha did not recover until 1907, by which time German rule was firmly established.[15]

Initially, the Germans ruled Mount Meru through local Meru and Arusha leaders. Yet, there were two problems with this. First, while Meru did have a chieftaincy system, albeit a weak one, Arusha had no single leader. Instead, each age-set had its own spokesmen who represented it in communal affairs and disputes. The Germans solved this problem in 1897 by adopting the Meru system for both areas, acknowledging Mangi Lobolu (son of the precolonial leader, Matunda) in Meru and the senior Arusha age-set spokesmen, Rawaito and Maraai, in lower and upper Arusha respectively.

The second problem arose in 1899 after the Germans suspected a combined Chaga, Arusha, Meru and Maasai conspiracy against them; again attacked Mount Meru; arrested and hanged the Meru and Arusha chiefs along with other alleged ringleaders; and constructed a military fort (*boma*) in Arusha town. They then faced the problem of appointing new chiefs. In Meru, they initially chose Lobulu's brother, Masengye, but he

Table 5.1 Meru Mangi

Matunda	1887–96	Kaaya
Lobolu	1896–00	Kaaya, s/o Matunda, hanged
Masengye	1900–01	Kaaya, s/o Matunda, jailed
Nyereu	1901–02	Nasari, jailed
Sambegye	1902–25	Nanyaro
Sante	1925–30	Nanyaro, s/o Sambegye, jailed
Kishili	1931–45	Kaaya, s/o Matunda, deposed
Sante	1945–52	reappointed
Sylvanos	1953–63	Kaaya, ss/o Matunda, elected

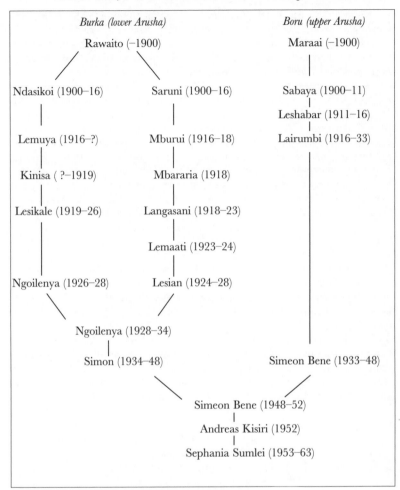

Fig 5.1 Arusha Chiefs

was deposed and imprisoned within a year for murder and replaced with
a non-Kaaya auxiliary, Nyereu, who was also soon deposed and jailed for
neglect of duties and procuring women for German soldiers (see Table
5.1). They eventually found their man, however, in Sambegye, a friend of
the newly re-established German mission, who, together with his son,
Sante, would rule for much of the next fifty years.[16]

Ironically, they had slightly better luck in Arusha, appointing Ndasikoi
(1900–16) and Saruni (1900–16) to the newly split chiefdom in Burka
(lower Arusha) and Sabaya (1900–11), followed by his son, Leshabar
(1911–16), in Boru (upper Arusha) (see Fig 5.1).[17]

While we do not know the degree to which these chiefs benefited the Germans, given the persistence of military rule, the chiefs themselves certainly benefited from their new positions. Throughout the late nineteenth century, Arusha and Meru warriors had been ascendant in both societies. Raiding their neighbors, they became wealthy in cattle and wives, effectively subverting the control over wealth and people previously exercised by elders. Just before the warriors killed the missionaries, the Meru *mangi*, Matunda, and Arusha spokesmen, Rawaito and Masinde, protested to the Germans that they had little control over the warriors, and subsequently the three warned them of the impending attack in vain. Following the warriors subsequent crushing defeat by the Germans, however, their power waned rapidly as they lost many of their cattle and wives together with their ability to fight to replace them. No future Arusha age-set would ever attain such power or fame again, while Meru soon ceased joining Arusha age-sets altogether. At the same time, however, chiefs grew in wealth, influence and power as they became wealthy in cattle, rich in land, and patriarchs of large families. Sambegye had ten wives and Sabaya fourteen. Able to distribute cattle and wives to others, they also became powerful patrons with expanding numbers of clients. As the population grew and land became short due to widespread German land alienation around the base of the mountain, they controlled the allocation of land to those now unable to pioneer elsewhere on their own.[18]

Chiefs walked a fine line between acting as responsible guardians and generous patrons, redistributing their wealth in responsible ways, and as unpopular enforcers of colonial taxes, demands for labor, and alienation of land and water rights. In the process, they could easily lose the support of either their followers or German patrons and be deposed. Masengye and Nyereu were both deposed and imprisoned on suspicious charges by the German authorities, while Leshabar was burned out by Arusha. Chiefs also became increasingly dependent on German support to gain appointment. They thus occupied the uncomfortable position of simultaneously being clients to their German patrons and patrons to their African clients. If they acted as effective colonial administrators, they risked alienating their followers, while if they sought to benefit their clients by redistributing colonial resources or attenuating colonial exploitation, they risked displeasing their German overlords. Adept chiefs managed to strike a balance between the two extremes and grew wealthy and powerful in the process, but inept ones had little influence and some lost office.

British Indirect Rule and the Politics of Neo-Traditionalism

Britain conquered northern Tanganyika in 1916 and acquired formal control over most of German East Africa as a League of Nations mandate in the aftermath of World War I, but it was not able to restore effective administration until the early 1920s. The military and succeeding civilian administrations thus largely continued German colonial policies, maintaining Sambegye in Meru, Lairumbi in Boru, and a succession of weak chiefs in Burka, thus paving the way for the formal establishment of indirect rule in 1926.

Like the Germans before them, British rule depended on the ongoing effectiveness and legitimacy of the chiefs it affirmed or appointed. In Meru, Sambegye (1902–25) and his son Sante (1925–30, 1945–52), together with Kishili (1931–45), ruled for half a century with only occasional disruptions. Similarly, Lairumbi (1916–33) and Simeon Bene (1933–52) proved highly effective in Boru, but lower Arusha remained unstable until both chiefdoms were consolidated under Ngoilenya (1926–34) and Simon (1934–48) and then joined with upper Arusha in a single Arusha chiefdom under Simeon Bene in 1948. Long-serving chiefs not only proved effective colonial administrators, collecting tax, recruiting labor, and adjudicating disputes, however, but they also looked after their own interests and those of their clients, accumulating large herds of cattle, extensive land holdings, acres of coffee, and large families for themselves and granting land, jobs and justice to others. While ultimately accountable to the colonial administration, then, the administration depended on their continuing legitimacy and effectiveness, which chiefs could best maintain by also looking after the interests of their followers, a difficult balance that began to break down after World War II and ultimately collapsed in the early 1950s.[19]

The Limits of Neo-Traditionalism in Arusha

Chiefs were held accountable in different ways by both the colonial authorities and their followers. Colonial officers had a number of sanctions they could employ, from formal reprimand to outright dismissal or imprisonment. Arusha and Meru were more limited, however, as the colonial authorities often saw any popular opposition as a challenge to their authority and dismissed it out of hand. People could, and did, however, challenge a chief's legitimacy through charges of witchcraft, murder or malfeasance – charges to which the colonial authorities were quick to respond. Thus, substantive political disputes frequently involved struggles over legitimacy and rights rather than over policies, as people evoked a discourse of tradition to counter decidedly untraditional colonial practices.

Popular protests were almost always directed against the chiefs, even though the problems were usually caused by the administration. In response to German and British land alienation, for example, Arusha accused the chiefs of selling land to settlers, in spite of the fact that the chiefs themselves were often in the forefront of protests over land. Chiefs were singled out because they were the local manifestation of colonial rule, were accessible, were used to mediate between local and colonial discourses and, most important, were vulnerable to popular pressures.

Thus, in 1925, when the British were consolidating their power and reallocating ex-German estates in the face of increasing Arusha needs for land, Arusha charged all three of their chiefs with extortion and malfeasance. The British dismissed Lesikale and fined and later deposed Lesian, but Lairumbi was deemed too important a chief to lose and was simply reprimanded.[20] Lairumbi was a wealthy cattle trader and nephew of Maraai, one of the original Arusha chiefs hanged by the Germans in 1900, and he initially enjoyed the support of both conservative elders and educated Christians along with that of the British, who viewed him as a forceful and able chief.[21] Popular opposition to him continued, however, and after two men were killed in a dispute over water rights, people charged him with misappropriating cattle, land, and water – charges sure to undercut his popular support – along with favoring certain elements in Arusha society and practising witchcraft and murder – accusations designed to arouse colonial suspicions. Mass meetings of up to one thousand people demanded Lairumbi's dismissal, but his colonial supporters continued to stand firm. When further protests broke out over land and administrative restrictions on coffee growing, however, the authorities finally acknowledged that he had lost his popular support, and in 1933 they persuaded him to resign.[22]

Lairumbi was replaced by Simeon Bene. Simeon rose from poor origins to become one of the first educated Christians in Arusha. He was a close friend of Lazaros Laiser, the leader of the Arusha Christians; married a daughter of Maraai; and served nine years as Lairumbi's clerk.[23] Once chief, Simeon grew wealthy in cattle, land and coffee, and he was soon able to build a modern cement house and later buy a car.[24] He also used his position and wealth to assist others. Unable to marry more than one wife, he enlisted numerous clients and dependants with gifts of cattle and land. He became the patron of Arusha cattlemen establishing large mechanized wheat farms on Mount Monduli as well as of Christian coffee farmers and co-operative members in central Arusha. By the time he retired in 1952, he had become a notable patriarch, with countless clients and dependants and 61 great grandchildren.[25]

The politics of neo-traditionalism, then, combined patrimonial politics, in which wealthy and powerful men redistributed their wealth in order to gain dependants and clients, with the bureaucratic politics of a hierarchical colonial administration committed to exploiting local resources. Given the different goals of each, chiefs had to be skilful to maintain both their popular and their administrative mandates. Over time, however, the two became increasingly intertwined, as newly available administrative resources could be made available to clients or clients could be recruited as workers or political supporters.

Just as chiefs' powers were limited, so too were those of the colonial administration. Dependent on the continued legitimacy and effectiveness of the chiefs, they could not afford to enforce policies that might undercut them. While they often deceived themselves that their demands, such as forced labor to build roads or conservation works, were beneficial, these demands were often seen by Africans as senseless and excessive, and they resisted complying with them. Realizing this, chiefs (sometimes with the connivance of local colonial officers) sought to limit administration demands or deflect them onto weaker members of the community. Thus, in the face of popular opposition to anti-locust work in 1934, Ngoilenya proved reluctant in recruiting conscript labor and was replaced, but the administration was subsequently forced to abandon the project. The politics of neo-traditionalism thus involved continual negotiation and conflict as colonial administrators, chiefs, and ordinary people struggled with one another and among themselves over the interpretation of tradition and the terms of colonial subordination.

As time went on, the number and severity of these struggles both increased markedly, challenging the continued viability of neo-traditional politics. Internal unrest continued in Arusha throughout the 1930s and 1940s over a surtax on land, evictions from Arusha town, land grants by the chief to wealthy Arusha, and the administration's continuing attempts to control the cultivation and marketing of coffee. In the face of the continuing erosion of neo-traditional authority, the administration sought to shore it up by formally drafting a new constitution for the local native authority. The resulting Arusha Constitution of 1948 was the first major attempt by the British to restructure local administration, and it was devised by the government anthropologist, Hans Cory, in a notable example of the invention of tradition.

After conducting a wide-ranging ethnographic study of contemporary Arusha society, Cory sought to rediscover its traditional basis before the German conquest fifty years previously, in an attempt to restore stability and popular unity in the face of subsequent political, social and economic changes. This did not pose the problem it might have done for Cory, however, as he believed that cultures were ultimately racially determined and that he could strip off the historical accretions to reveal the essential genetic core. It was thus important to establish Arusha origins, which he wrongly assumed were Meru and Chaga, not Maasai, and then to differentiate between core Meru institutions and subsequent Maasai influences. In this way, he felt he had discovered the original basis of Arusha chiefship, which he dubbed *olkarsis* (an Arusha term denoting a wealthy big man), that combined Bantu chiefship with subsequent influence from Maasai age and descent systems. He then converted his reconstruction into an elaborate bureaucratic complex, complete with written constitution, that combined a consolidated executive, a legislative council, an advisory council representing local councils, clans, and educated Christians, and a multi-tiered system of civil and criminal courts. These were replicated at the local level, with an appointed headman representing the chief, an advisory council composed of age-set spokesmen, clan elders, and Christians, and local courts. The result was a bureaucratic monstrosity that transformed the mediated patterns of Arusha political life into a static array of formal institutions, each with its own neo-traditional name, rules and procedures, which the colonial authorities then faithfully reproduced as though they were truly authentic and kept the new Assistant District Officer, Charles Meek, running endlessly among 28 councils to try to keep it all going.[26]

While the administration congratulated itself that it had restored legitimacy to traditional institutions, few Arusha considered the newly reformed native authority as either legitimate or traditional. As a result, the multiple councils and courts soon lapsed into disuse as Arusha themselves increasingly utilized a series of new institutions – the Lutheran church, the co-operative, and Arusha Citizens' Union – to mobilize resistance to the native authority and colonial demands.

Land continued to dominate Arusha politics as the administration evicted Arusha who still held land within Arusha town, seized almost 2,000 acres outside town, and threatened to take another 1,000 to expand the town, all the while refusing to provide alternative land elsewhere, as it was legally required to do, or allocate unused and abandoned settler estates to perennially land-short Arusha.[27] At the same time, Arusha squatters began to contest land grants on Monduli made by Chief Simeon to wealthy Arusha cattle-owners that the squatters had then cleared and planted, giving them rights, they claimed, to the land. Other disputes festered as well.[28] Arusha Christians protested that they should not be required to participate in pagan ceremonies initiating new age-sets, but the administration insisted that age-sets were political institutions in which every Arusha had to participate.[29] Coffee and wheat farmers protested that a native authority cess (levy) on all coffee and wheat sold to the newly formed co-operative was discriminatory, and shifted to untaxed maize or sold to private agents instead.[30] And cattle owners refused to comply with new requirements to inoculate cattle, dip them, and provide labor for new conservation schemes in western Arusha.[31]

These disputes, which were routinely rejected by the administration as challenges to its authority, also divided Arusha among themselves, pitting wealthy cattle-owners against small-scale farmers, a Christian chief against the church, the administration against progressive coffee and wheat farmers, and the native authority against a newly formed popular political organization, the Arusha Citizens' Union. These issues came to a head when Chief Simeon retired in 1952 and the government imposed its own candidate, Andreas Kisiri, over the popular Lutheran school inspector, Sephania Sumlei. In response, Arusha protested:

> Why are we called to meetings where we cannot express out views? Why is tax collected when there is no freedom of speech? Why do we dance for the Government but do not receive justice?

Popular protests continued unabated for several months until Andreas was forced to resign and the administration reluctantly allowed a popular election. Sephania easily won and proceeded to appoint Citizens' Union members to the council, replace the selective coffee and wheat cess with a universal head tax, and initiate a widespread social development program.[32]

What was remarkable about these events was the degree to which a once popular and progressive Christian chief, Simeon Bene, was increasingly rejected by Arusha as new centers of power formed around the church, the co-operative and the Citizens' Union and as new political values developed that owed as much to Christian and liberal democratic values as to the responsibilities of wealth. Neo-traditional politics could no longer contain the tensions emerging within Arusha society as local politicians continued to reinterpret tradition in response to changing conditions.[33]

The Politics of Chiefship in Meru

The politics of neo-traditionalism became increasingly disputatious in Meru as well. While Sambegye (1902–25) enjoyed a long and fairly peaceful reign, that of his young son, Sante (1925–30, 1945–52), was initially fraught with controversy, as he was accused of misappropriating funds and consorting with an Indian woman, causing the British to depose and imprison him in 1930.[34] In the spirit of the recently implemented policy of indirect rule, they then sought to return a Kaaya to the chiefship, appointing an illiterate son of Matunda, Kishili (1930–45) over two other Kaaya who were both educated Christian coffee growers.[35] But Kishili finally came under attack as well, as Christians, coffee growers, and supporters of Sante accused him of misappropriating funds, taking bribes, cursing his opponents, and harassing Christians. Faced down by 1,400 people at a public meeting lasting five hours, the British were forced to restore Sante for a second term.[36] Not long after, however, Sante himself came under attack from Christians, coffee growers, and Kaaya over continuing land disputes and attempts by the administration to impose centralized coffee marketing, a cess on coffee sales, and new crop regulations, in the course of which Meru formed the Meru Citizens' Union and boycotted all administrative activities.[37]

As local government ground to a halt, the administration resolved to draft a new traditional constitution, like that recently adopted in Arusha. Again they handed the task to Hans Cory, but this time Cory felt that Meru institutions had been so transformed by Meru adoption of Arusha age-sets in the nineteenth century and Christianity and coffee in the twentieth that he proposed to base representation to the new tribal and parish councils on age-set membership and literacy. Cory was wrong again, however; descent had long been the principal basis of Meru social organization, and Meru had abandoned Arusha age-sets soon after the German conquest – and this time the constitution barely made it beyond the drafting phase.[38] In the face of widespread opposition, Sante and his headmen rushed through their approval, only to have Citizens' Union members boycott the new authority and demand popular elections to replace the chief. Tensions continued to mount, and following protests against a settler seeking to evict long-standing Meru squatters from his land, eleven Meru were arrested and deported from the district, Sante found himself ruling alone, and when the governor visited a year later, a 'small riot' ensued.[39]

While the administration continued to insist that the responsibility lay with 'a small intransigent and fanatical group of Meru' who were 'afflicted by every disease of the mind and the spirit that follows a semi-absorption of Western ideas', their defense of neo-traditional politics proved increasingly in vain, as Meru continued their boycott, appealed to the United Nations against their eviction from land at Engare Nanyuk, negotiated a new constitution based on popular election of the chief and council, and elected a new chief, Sylvanos Kaaya, who was both a Christian and a Kaaya.[40]

The Tradition of Politics and the Politics of Tradition

In both Arusha and Meru, then, new forces had emerged to challenge neo-traditional rule on both traditional and liberal democratic grounds. They condemned chiefs and an administration that did not redistribute wealth, allocate land and new opportunities fairly, provide adequate land for those in need while protecting settlers who had far more than they could use, or allow public expression of views and popular election of chiefs. 'Why,' they asked, 'do we dance for the Government but do not receive justice?'

The administration had sought to harness its rule to the legitimacy of local authorities, but rather than ensuring continuity and stability, tradition itself became the focus of debate as people invoked such values as the responsibility of wealth and protection from witchcraft in challenging chiefly authority or colonial policies. Nor were the British able to contain the influence of new ideas, as dissident Meru and Arusha also framed their protests in terms of freedom of speech, no taxation without representation, justice, and democracy and sought new national and international forums in which to protest.

In the process, the British got both the traditional authorities and those they labeled 'agitators' and 'fanatics' wrong. As Christians and coffee farmers, chiefs also belonged to the church and the co-operative. While ostensibly representing tradition, they also supported the interests of progressive farmers against the restrictions of a supposedly modernist colonial regime. And their opponents combined appeals to the responsibilities of wealth and power with appeals to Christian, capitalist and liberal democratic ideals. Tradition was neither static nor prescriptive, but a dynamic and flexible process, an endless dialogue between the past and the present as people continually employed, debated and reassessed the relevance of past experience for the present on their own terms, as the British realized to their dismay when they sought to reinvent tradition on theirs. Tradition had both deeper roots in the local consciousness, limiting its ability to be manipulated by colonial authorities, and was also more flexible, allowing it to be mobilized by local people in defense of their own interests, than the British thought. If the invention of tradition was limited by the acceptability and legitimacy of local authorities, their acceptability and legitimacy was judged on a variety of grounds, both old and new. The tradition of local politics ensured that the politics of tradition would be hard fought and complex, befitting difficult times.

Notes

* This paper is dedicated to Professor Isaria N. Kimambo, whose innovative historical research, dedicated leadership, and insightful studies of local politics continue to inspire my own work. It draws partly on my book, *Mountain Farmers: Moral Economies of Land and Agricultural Development in Arusha and Meru* (Oxford: James Currey, 1997), and partly on a recent review article, 'Neo-Traditionalism and the Limits of Invention in British Colonial Africa', *Journal of African History* 44 (2003), pp. 1–26. It is based on research conducted in Tanzania in 1988 and 1991 under the auspices of UTAFITI and the Department of History of the University of Dar es Salaam and was supported by grants from the National Endowment for the Humanities and Williams College. Subsequent research and writing were supported by the University of Wisconsin and the John Simon Guggenheim Memorial Foundation. I am grateful to them all and to the many individuals who facilitated my research, including Prof. Abdul Sheriff, Dr N.N. Luanda, Mr Wolfgang Alpelt, Mr Chikote, Mr J. David Simonson, Reverend Mesiaki Kilevo, Reverend Erasto Ngira, and the Arusha and Meru elders who kindly shared their knowledge with me.

1. Contradictions in the thought and practice of indirect rule in Tanzania are explored in Ralph Austen, 'The Official Mind of Indirect Rule: British Policy in Tanganyika, 1919–1939,' in P. Gifford and W.R. Louis (eds), *Britain and Germany in Africa* (New Haven, CT: Yale University Press, 1967), pp. 577–606; *idem, Northwest Tanzania under German and British Rule: Colonial Policy and Tribal Politics* (New Haven, CT: Yale University Press, 1968); Susan Geiger Rogers, 'The Search for Political Focus on Kilimanjaro: A History of Chagga Politics, 1916–1952, with Special Reference to the Cooperative Movement and Indirect Rule' (Ph.D, University of Dar es Salaam, 1972); James Graham, 'Indirect Rule: The Establishment of "Chiefs" and "Tribes" in Cameron's Tanganyika,' *Tanzania Notes and Records*, 77 (1976), pp. 1–9; Walter Rodney, 'The Political Economy of Colonial Tanganyika, 1890–1930,' in M.H.Y. Kaniki (ed.), *Tanzania under Colonial Rule* (London, Longman, 1979), pp. 128–63; and John Iliffe, *A Modern History of Tanganyika* (Cambridge, Cambridge University Press, 1979), pp. 318–41.

2. The classic text is Terence Ranger, 'The Invention of Tradition in Colonial Africa,' in E. Hobsbawm and T. Ranger (eds), *The Invention of Tradition* (Cambridge, Cambridge University Press, 1983), pp. 211–62, but see also, *idem,* 'The Invention of Tradition Revisited: The Case of Africa,' in T. Ranger and O. Vaughan (eds), *Legitimacy and the State in Twentieth Century Africa* (Basingstoke: Macmillan, 1993), pp. 62–111.

3. In an earlier work I used the term 'pseudo-traditionalism', but now think 'neo-traditionalism' better captures a process marked by reinterpretation that was neither spurious nor fake. Spear, *Mountain Farmers*, pp. 194–208.

4. For critical reviews of the literature, see Anthony D. Smith, 'The Nation: Invented, Imagined, Reconstructed?' *Millennium*, 20 (1991), pp. 353–68; Ranger, '"The Invention of Tradition Revisited'; and Spear, 'Neo-Traditionalism and the Limits of Invention'.

5. Donald Cameron, *My Tanganyika Service and Some Nigeria* (London, George Allen & Unwin, 1939), p. 81; *idem,* 'Native Administration in Nigeria and Tanganyika,' *Journal of the Royal African Society* (suppl.), 36 (1937), pp. 5–8.

6. *Ibid.,* pp. 10–11.

7. *Ibid.,* p. 16.

8. *Ibid.,* p. 12.

9. Donald Cameron, 'Native Administration,' 16 July 1925 (Tanzania National Archives [TNA], 7777/20), cited in Iliffe, *Modern History*, p. 321.

10. Sara S. Berry, *No Condition is Permanent: The Social Dynamics of Agrarian Change in Sub-*

Saharan Africa (Madison, WI: Wisconsin University Press, 1993), pp. 22–42.

11. Steven Feierman, *Peasant Intellectuals: Anthropology and History in Tanzania* (Madison, WI: Wisconsin University Press, 1990), pp. 120–23.

12. Spear, *Mountain Farmers*, pp. 17–34.

13. *Ibid.*, pp. 35–57.

14. *Ibid.*, pp. 61–74.

15. *Ibid.*, pp. 75–8.

16. Müller, *Evangelisch-Lutherisches Missionsblatt (ELMB)*, p. 56 (1901), p. 371; Krause, *ELMB*, 57 (1902), pp. 280–81, 59 (1904), pp. 360, 60 (1905), pp. 445–46; Ittamier, *ELMB*, 62 (1907), p. 560; Blumer, *ELMB*, 64 (1909), p. 170; F. Longland in *Arusha District Book* (1931); Hans Cory, 'Tribal Structure of the Meru, T.T.' (University of Dar es Salaam [UDSM]: Hans Cory Papers, nd.); Anton Lukas Kaaya (Meru Historical Traditions [MHT] 1); Rafaeli Mbise (MHT 3); Emanuel Kasengye N'nko (MHT 5).

17. Fokken, *ELMB*, 60(1905), p. 39; Blumer, *ELMB*, 67 (1912), p. 111; C.M. Coke in *Arusha District Book* (1932); Hans Cory, 'Tribal Structure of the Arusha Tribe of Tanganyika,' (UDSM: Cory Papers, 1948), p. 5; Yohanes ole Kauwenara (Arusha Historical Traditions [AHT] 2).

18. P.H. Gulliver, *Social Control in an African Society* (London: Routledge & Kegan Paul, 1963), pp. 154–59; Spear, *Mountain Farmers*, pp. 82–4.

19. Spear, *Mountain Farmers*, p. 111–12.

20. Arusha District (AD), Annual Report, 1925 (TNA: 1733/36); Northern Province (NP), Annual Report, 1925 (TNA: 1733/36).

21. Yohanes ole Kauwenara (AHT 2); NP, Annual Reports, 1927–28 (TNA: 11681).

22. AD, Annual Report, 1929 (TNA, 11681); Blumer to Provincial Commissioner (PC)/NP, 2 Dec. 1929 and reply 4 Dec. 1929: Petition by IlMolelian Elders, 5 Dec. 1929 and 10 Dec. 1929; IlMolelian Elders to Baker-Smith, 9 Dec. 1929; IlMolelian Elders to Asst. Superintendent of Police, 10 Dec. 1929; PC/NP to Chief Secretary (CS)/Dar es Salaam (DSM), 17 Jan. 1930 and reply 24 Jan 1930; PC/NP to District Officer (DO)/AD, 19 March 1930 and reply 27 March 1930; Anon. to Superintendent of Police/Arusha, 31 March 1932 (all in TNA: 69/45/4); NP, Annual Reports, 1931–33 (TNA: 11681); PC/NP to DO/AD, 2 May 1932 and 11 May 1932 (TNA: 69/47/AR/4); PC/NP to CS/DSM, 26 April 1933 and reply 18 May 1933 (TNA: 13368/I).

23. Yohanes ole Kauwenara (AHT 2); S. ole Saibul and R. Carr, *Herd and Spear* (London: Collins and Harvill, 1981), pp. 115–17.

24. DO/AD to Manager/Standard Bank, 2 Sept. 1938; PC/NP to DC/AD, 26 July 1951 (TNA: 69/47/AR/5).

25. AD, Agricultural Annual Report, 1951 (TNA: 472/-); AD, Annual Report, 1953 (TNA: 472/ANR/1); Wheat, c. 1940 (TNA: 9/6/5); Mosingo ole Meipusu (AHT 1); Yohanes ole Kauwenara (AHT 2); Ngole ole Njololoi (AHT 4); Eliyahu Lujas Meiliari (AHT 8); Mesiaki Kilevo, pers. comm.; ole Saibul and Carr, *Herd and Spear*, pp. 114–15; N.N. Luanda, 'European Commercial Farming and its Impact on the Meru and Arusha Peoples of Tanzania, 1920–1955' (Ph.D. diss, Cambridge University, 1986), pp. 165–73.

26. Hans Cory, 'Tribal Structure of the Arusha Tribe of Tanganyika,' 1948 (UDSM: Cory Papers, 201); D.S. Troup, 'Memorandum on the Reorganization ... of the Arusha'; C.I. Meek and D.S. Troup, periodic reports (all in TNA: 472/NA/40); C.I. Meek, 'A Practical Experiment in Local Government' in *Arusha District Book*; Gulliver, *Social Control*, pp. 159–63.

27. Dept. of Agriculture, Annual Report, 1951 (TNA: 472/-); AD, Annual Report, 1952 (TNA: 472/ANR/1); NP, Annual Report, 1952 (TNA:: 19415); P.H. Gulliver, *Report on Land and Population in the Arusha Chiefdom* (Tanganyika Provincial Administration, 1957), pp. 27–30; *idem, Social Control*, pp. 154–63.

28. AD, Annual Reports, 1953–54 (TNA: 472/ANR/1).

29. Lazaros Laiser to Olkarsis Simeon, 1 Sept. 1948; D.S. Troup to Rev. D. Swanson, 9 Sept. 1948; E.R. Danielson to D.S. Troup, 8 Oct. 1948 and reply 23 Oct. 1948; D.S. Troup to Dr. Reusch, 2 Feb. 1949; E.R. Danielson to D.S. Troup, 5 April 1949 (all in

TNA: 472/NA/40).

30. AD, Annual Reports, 1951–52 (TNA: 472/-); Agricultural Officer (AO)/AD, Monthly Reports, Sept.–Nov. 1951 (TNA: 9/24); Comm. for Co-operative Development, 'Notes on Arusha Native Authority Cesses on Produce,' 25 Sept. 1951; Member for Local Government (MLG) to PC/NP, 15 Nov. 1951 and reply 1 Dec. 1951; DC/AD to PC/NP, 7 Feb. 1952 (all in TNA: 32847/1).

31. AO/AD, Monthly Reports, Sept.–Nov. 1951 (TNA: 9/24); Arusha Citizens' Union (ACU) to District Commissioner (DC)/AD, 8 Sept. 1952, and Engiliwata Olosho to DC/AD, 12 Sept. 1952 (TNA: 472/NA/40); AD, Annual Reports, 1951–53 (TNA: 472/- and 472/ANR/1); NP, Annual Report, 1956 (TNA: 471/R.3/2).

32. AD, Annual Reports, 1952–53 (TNA: 472/- & 472/ANR/1); NP, Annual Report, 1952 (TNA: 19415); Arusha Community to CS/DSM, 13 March 1952 (TNA: 32593 & 69/47/AR); Raia wa Arusha nzima to PC/NP, 14 March 1952 (TNA: 69/47/AR & 472/NA/40); Laigwenak Lembalbal to DC/AD, 16 March 1952 and Raiya wako watiifu wa Arusha to DC/AD, 22 March 1952 (TNA: 472/NA/40); Asst. Supt. of Police (CID)/Moshi to Senior Supt. of Police i/c Special Branch, DSM, 4 July 1952 (TNA: 472/NA/40); DC/AD, 'Arrangements for the Installation of Olkarsis Andreas' (TNA: 69/47/AR); ACU, petitions and minutes (TNA: 472/NA/40 & 32593); ACU to Gov., 3 July 1952, 3 Nov. 1952, 18 Nov. 1952; PC/NP to MLG, 13 Aug. 1952; CS/DSM to ACU, 21 Nov. 1952 (all in TNA: 32593); DC/AD to PC/NP, 17 July 1952; DC/AD to Gov., 5 Nov. 1952 (both TNA: 472/NA/40); PC/NP to MLG, 18 Dec. 1952 (TNA: 32593) Olkarsis Zephania to DC/AD, 8 Jan. 1953 and 13 Jan. 1953 (TNA: 472/NA/40).

33. 'The Development of Rural Councils in Arusha' (TNA: 352); Arusha District, Annual Report, 1954 (TNA: 472/ANR/1); NP, Annual Reports, 1955–58 (TNA: 472/R.3/2); P.H. Gulliver and H.L. Smaith, 'Report on the Constitutional Changes in the Local Government of Arusha Chiefdom,' 1957 (UDSM: Cory Papers, 279).

34. Anton Lukas Kaaya (MHT 1); Krause, *ELMB*, 60 (1905), pp. 445–6; Ittameier, *ELMB*, 62 (1907), p. 560; K.R. Gilbert, 'Summary of Events in Chief Sante's Cases,' Sept. 1930; DO/AD to PC/NP, 16 Sept. 1930; Sworn Statements taken by R.A. Pelham, DO/AD, Sept. 1930; PC/NP to CS/DSM, 26 Sept. 1930; Asst. DO/AD to PC/NP, 25 Nov. 1930 (all in TNA: 69/45/9); DO/AD to PC/NP, 11 April 1931 (TNA: 69/47/AR).

35. DO/AD to PC/NP, 11 April 1931 (TNA: 69/47/AR).

36. DO/AD to PC/NP, 9 Feb. 1945 (TNA: 69/47/AR); DO/AD to PC/NP, 1 March 1945; PC/NP to CS/DSM, 7 March 1945, minute by CS/DSM, 12 March 1945, reply 14 March 1945, and further correspondence 7 April 1945 (all in TNA: 69/47/3 & 32893).

37. DC/AD to PC/NP, 4 Nov. 1947 (TNA: 9/NA/1); NP, Annual Reports, 1946–47 (TNA: 19415); H. Mason, 'The Meru Problem,' 1955 (Oxford Colonial Records Project: MSS.Afr.s.1513[r]).

38. H. Cory, 'Proposals for the Adaptation of the Meru Age-Grade System to Modern Requirements' (TNA: 43200); D.S. Troup, 'Memorandum on the New Constitution of the Meru Tribe' in PC/NP to CS/DSM, 17 Aug. 1948; CS/DSM to PC/NP, 22 Sept. 1948; PC/NP to CS/DSM, 6 Oct. 1948; DC/AD to PC/NP, 28 Nov. 1948 (all in TNA: 25369).

39. Minutes, Meeting of District Reps. (TNA: 9/8/1); Mason, 'The Meru Problem'; Luanda, 'European Commercial Farming,' p. 281; Emanuel Kasengye N'nko (MHT 5).

40. Troup, 'Memorandum on the New Constitution'; DC/AD to PC/NP, 28 Nov. 1948 (TNA: 25369); NP, Annual Reports, 1948–49 (TNA: 69/63/A/19 & 69/63/A/29). For an analysis of the Meru Land Case and its aftermath, see Spear, *Mountain Farmers*, pp. 209–35.

Six

∧∧▲▲▲▲▲▲▲▲▲▲∧∧

Narrating Power in Colonial Ugogo
Mazengo of Mvumi

GREGORY H. MADDOX

In 1961, at the celebration of independence for Tanganyika, two 'traditional' chiefs symbolically handed over power to Julius Nyerere. Finding chiefs to perform this task had not been easy for the functionaries of the new government. Many 'Native Authorities' had opposed the Tanganyika African National Union, in no small part because it had promised to abolish the legal authority of chiefs and replace them as local governments with elected ones. While a number of prominent traditional leaders had supported TANU in the drive for independence, many others kept their distance.[1] Eventually, one of the chiefs chosen was the Paramount Chief of the Ugogo Federation of the Central Province (now split between Manyoni and Dodoma Regions) – Mazengo. Mazengo had become a secret member of TANU and patron of the movement's leader in the region during the 1950s. He was also one of the most senior of the recognized chiefs, having been a *jumbe* under the Germans. He had maintained his position as a government chief after the British takeover of the region in 1916. Three generations of British officials regarded him as the most effective Native Authority in the region, and, as they pushed to create a more unified 'tribal' government for the Gogo, had always regarded him as the natural paramount chief. In addition, he had accepted the placement of a Church Missionary Society mission in Mvumi which had become a large complex with a hospital as well as schools.

Oral traditions in their classic form are about power.[2] In the beginnings of modern Africanist historiography, they served as the primary source for political history before the nineteenth century in much of the continent. The debates over their utility have been sharp, and many seemed to have returned to the idea that they provide little concrete information about the distant past.[3] Yet, as Isabel Hofmeyr has argued, the processes that generated oral traditions did not cease with the imposition of colonial hegemony.[4] History, as it had before the imposition of colonial domination, remained the symbolic source of power. As in the

86

past, words operated in the service of guns (or in the eventually more mundane expression of colonial power, the *viboko* whip) in the exercise of power, yet words surrounded them, buffered them, muted them and stood in for them.

Mazengo's power, portrayed as overwhelming in the written sources about him, was always contested. Although he remains something of an iconic presence in Dodoma and Mvumi, people still tell stories about his rise to power that deny that he ever had ritual authority in the *yisi* (country) over which his clan claimed authority, much less over the whole of Ugogo. In stories about Mazengo there is a split between 'official' versions, based on the ideas of legitimate authority embedded in the British system of Indirect Rule and progressive Christianity, as well as nationalist, views of the history of Ugogo, on the one hand, and particular and local versions of power and authority on the other. Stories about Mazengo the usurper reflect the resistance of local communities to domination, which, in some ways, Mazengo came to symbolize.

At the same time, many also spoke of Mazengo as powerful and even malevolent. He was said to be able to stop the rains over those he did not favor, like a true *mtemi*. He was said to have the bodies of his enemies dumped into the stream that flowed through Mvumi. In short, his power was not just as a representative of 'modernity' in Mvumi and Ugogo, but translated and undoubtedly manipulated into a local context.

It is important to preface this discussion of narrative and power in colonial Ugogo by emphasizing that colonialism was first and foremost based on violence and that its first justification was racism. This brutal equation was as true in Ugogo as it was across the continent and as true when Karl Peters marched through Mpwapwa in the 1880s as it was when the colonial state sent the Special Mobile Unit of the police to put down unrest in the region, referred to as 'our own Mau Mau,' in 1954.[5] While the *viboko* (whip) and the boots of soldiers may be more symbolic of German rule in the region, as this chapter will show, violence permeated British colonialism as well; however, the agents of violence were more likely to show an African face. Although, as Mamdani has noted, all colonial regimes relied on African employees, the British policy of Indirect Rule gave a particular cast to the despotism in Ugogo.[6]

Contested versions of histories used to justify Indirect Rule, both the choices of functionaries and the structure of laws, occur in almost every place where the system was imposed.[7] Scholars have long discussed the invention of tradition and tribes in colonial Africa.[8] Sara Berry has particularly focused on the ways that tradition has functioned as a battle ground for control over resources.[9] The widespread acceptance of the 'invented' nature of traditional histories under colonial rule,[10] has generated a response that emphasizes the continuities and contestations of such accounts.[11] Yet, the competing versions of history, and hence of legitimate power, in Ugogo did not just reflect the new source of power in the region during the colonial era; they fought for dominance on the same terrain.[12] Mazengo could stop the rains even though he did not hold the *mabwe gemvula* – rain stones that symbolized control over the rain.

Narratives of power in Ugogo start from a very different premise from that of colonial rule. First, power was expressed in terms of the ability to start and stop the rains.[13] The ritual ability to start or stop the rains was both hereditary and achieved. The *mtemi*[14] held the power to start and stop the rains, a power embodied in phallic-shaped stones used in rituals to call the rain each year. While the *utemi* was hereditary in a particular lineage of a particular clan, the power it wielded was bounded by both spatial and political limits. As clan histories collected by Mnyampala show, the *utemi* could be gained by right of first settlement or conquest of the non-Gogo inhabitants of areas in Ugogo. Yet, Mnyampala's clan histories are replete with instances of the transfer of the authority to new lineages and clans through violence, trickery, and marriage.[15] Such transfers reflect in many cases a greater ability to bring the rains. The power to control the rains was not implicit in the person of the *mtemi*, but instead the *mtemi* had the duty of finding *waganga*, diviners, capable of identifying which forces were stopping the rains when they failed to appear. Yet, as we shall see, a *mtemi* had teeth if necessary; power flowed not just from calling the rains, but also from stopping them.

In further contradiction of the notions of tribe at the heart of Indirect Rule, power in Ugogo had distinct spatial limits. Control of the rains was tied to place. Each *mtemi* controlled the rains only his own *yisi*, or country.[16] People moved, quite often given the arid nature of the region and the repeated droughts it suffers. A *mtemi* successful in bringing the rains gained people for his territory, while an unsuccessful one lost them. This element of mobility, extending to mobility to and from outside the region, contradicted the colonial insistence on the primacy of tribal identity. For colonial administrators the unwieldy 81 separate *watemi* had logically to give way to 34 recognized Native Authority Chiefs. Such a reconfiguration of power created a new arena for contestation in the region.

The emergence of Mazengo as a local power and key intermediary between outsiders and local communities dates to just after the effective establishment of colonial rule. The very earliest mentions of him in the mission archives and in accounts based on German sources name him as the *mtemi* of Mvumi, a relatively well-watered area in what is now Dodoma District, which served as one of the more important stopping points for nineteenth-century caravans between Mpwapwa and Tabora. No sources question his position.

The critical question is, what kind of position did Mazengo hold? The position of *mtemi*, usually glossed as chief, literally controlled the rains in a relatively small region called a *yisi* in Ugogo. The position was held by a clan that claimed the power based on first settler status or conquest. The *mtemi* held rain stones and a three-legged stool (*hegoda*) used in the ceremonies to propitiate the ancestors and bring rain. He had limited executive and judicial power, checked by the heads of households and leaders of age grades (the effective military force of an area).[17] Clan histories are replete with accounts of changes in the clan that holds ritual authority.[18]

In 1905, the Germans began to recognize *Majumbe*, headmen, as local authorities. In most cases in Ugogo they tried to name the legitimate authority, the *mtemi*, as the *jumbe*. Yet their first goal was administrative efficiency, and they often named locally powerful individuals who would be loyal to them. In Ugogo, the dangers of working for the Germans, with possible imprisonment and even death looming, posed a life or death challenge to local conceptions of ritual authority. The *mtemi* controlled the rains. An incapacitated *mtemi* could mean death and destruction for the people of a *yisi*. In many cases, local leaders nominated other members of ritually dominant clans or even 'slaves' to serve as *jumbe*. Colonial administrators, for their part, emphasized efficiency as much as legitimacy and had no compunction about replacing individuals. Colonial sources never doubt the ritual legitimacy of Mazengo, even though some British officers eventually understood full well that often the man they recognized did not hold the rain stones. As one official noted:

> The Watemi withdrew from administrative affairs and devoted themselves to their spiritual functions, rain-making, fertility rites – and they put up their sons or other near relatives to take over executive duties – the so-called jumbes – but as the conception of Indirect Rule has become much clearer and Native Administration took root in the minds of the people the Watemi emerged from their seclusion and came into the open.[19]

Three sources present the official version of Mazengo's claim to authority. First, from 1925 to 1927, British district officials collected local histories in their effort to produce a workable system of Indirect Rule. The text they created and the structure it justified were, of course, broadly determined by the parameters of the ideology of indirect rule. A. V. Hartnoll recorded the following genealogy for the Wanyamzura clan:

His [Mazengo's] family runs as follows:-
Luchinga
Luchingaluasi
Hakamu
Ntyani
Ntigwa
Mtonguchi
Mawala
Chalulu[20]

Hartnoll states that, on Chalula's death, Musonjera inherited the position, and makes no mention of how Mazengo became *mtemi*. This version of the genealogy became the accepted one with Mazengo placed as Chalula's son, despite the fact that Hartnoll does not make the connection explicit. Hartnoll may have known better, but efficiency was more important than legitimacy.

Mnyampala recorded a more detailed version of the history of Mazengo's clan. He wrote:

> The rulers of the country of Mvumi are Wagogo called Wanyamzura of Mnyambwa. Their origin is from the Wahehe, and they came from the country of Wotta (now located in the south of Mpwapwa District). Among the Wahehe their clan is called Wasemwali.[21]

He goes on to state that the English named Mazengo the Native Authority as a result of his position as the son of Chalula, and that 'The country of the Wanyamzura was one greatly feared in Ugogo, as it is said that the Wanyamzura had the power to stop the rains or to give permission for the rains to start again, as they decided.' Mnyampala explicitly states that Mazengo is the son of Chalula and was 'justly' named the Native Authority in 1927. Mnyampala wrote his account under the patronage of the district administration and while serving as an employee of the Native Authority.[22]

The final sources for the 'authorized version' of Mazengo's power come from writings associated with the Church Missionary Society mission. After visiting the area around Mvumi several times in the 1880s, the mission established a post in the area (although about 10 miles from Mazengo's settlement) in 1900. This area became Mvumi Mission, as distinct from Mvumi Ikulu, the home of the *watemi*. The CMS files mention only a 'chief' named Masenha in the earliest accounts. This man could easily have been a *mzengatumbi* (literally 'house builder' – the generally recognized term for a head of settlement) under the *mtemi* of Mvumi.[23] However, later accounts all claim that Mazengo held the position of *mtemi* at the time of the opening of the mission station.[24]

By about 1910, however, Mazengo appears firmly in the record as, first, a *jumbe* appointed by the Germans. From then on he will play a major role in supporting the work of the CMS and as such enhancing his own power by harnessing the resources the mission brought.[25] He first seems to have used the English missionaries as a foil against the Germans. Paul White recorded the following story told him by the Reverend Miki Muloli:

> In the 1914–1918 war, the German District Officer, Herr Sperling,[26] sent a force of Askaris (native soldiers) to capture the Chief, dead or alive. Mazengo got wind of this and hid, simply by living as a humble Mugogo, in an ordinary Mugogo's house. Weeks later news came to the fort that Mazengo was dead. He had fled, they said, to the hills, and, while hiding in a cave, had been killed by a lion. Sperling was dubious, and sent a young lieutenant to view the remains.
>
> The Wagogo had dug a grave, and in it put the carcass of a very dead goat. Under strong protest that it was against their tribal customs to dig up a dead body, they started to disinter the 'dead' Chief. As they dug deeper and deeper, the still, hot air stank vilely of rotting flesh, while the old women kept up a continuous dirge of 'Yaya gwa!' – Oh, my mother! – and the white-bearded Wakombi – old men – stood silently resentful, watching as the hoes of the diggers turned over the soil.
>
> The stench became unbearable, and after seeing a muddy mass of putrid flesh and bones, the lieutenant turned away.
>
> 'That's Mazengo, all right, not a doubt of it,' commented the lieutenant, as he saw a decaying *kanzu* [robe, Kiswahili] come to light. Not a Mugogo batted an eyelid.[27]

Throughout Paul White's memoir, Mazengo is upheld as the paragon of a progressive 'native chief' – not perhaps Christian or literate himself, but surrounded by such men. He writes:

Mazengo is one of the mainstays of our work; he and his family patronize the hospital regularly. Several of his children have been born there, and his influence and enthusiasm were one of the main factors in the building of our base hospital and the extensive C.M.S. Girls Boarding School at Mvumi.[28]

White includes a picture of Mazengo with the Reverend Miki Muloli, calling the pastor Mazengo's constant companion and adviser.[29]

Yet Mazengo was not generally recognized as a true *mtemi*. Within local discourse, the practice of not naming the *mtemi* to a government position led to a firm distinction between *mtemi we mvula* (*mtemi* of the rain) and *mtemi we serikali* (government chief) – one that many often thought the appropriate arrangement.[30] Such stories hung around Mazengo. Ernest Kongola recounts one version of how Mazengo became the *Mtemi*. His account is worth quoting at length because he collected information from his wife and especially his father-in-law who were both members of the Mbukwa Semwali. His father-in-law was a rain-maker, *mganga*. This account follows a long detailed history of the origins of the clan.

Mtemi Mazengo is given the hat by the Germans in Mpwapwa

When the Germans entered this country they built their Boma at Mpwapwa. They built another Boma at Kilimatinde to rule the people of the west. At this time the Boma at Dodoma had not been built.

The Germans passed through the country and asked the people about the countries they lived in. At this time there were clans which had the power to be the leaders in each country. These leaders were called 'Watemi.' Therefore each part of the country which had many people had its own Mtemi. There were many Watemi. There were no Wapembamoto. The name Upembamoto came later.

The Germans passed through the country or region and asked for the leaders, for the person in the area who was brought the elephant tusk? This meant that in the Watemi's area it was the Watemi who had the power over their people including the right to claim the tusk of an elephant killed there. In the region of the Wanyamuzula the man who had the power and the right to rule was of the lineage of Citigwa.

When the Germans issued this announcement all the Watemi in the country who had the most authority to be given the elephant tusk went to Mpwapwa to be given a hat which would make clear that they were the Watemi in their province and they were the ones who would lead the other Watemi.

Then these Watemi had the right to go to Mpwapwa to get a hat. When they arrived in Mpwapwa they were harassed. It was necessary that the Mtemi be hit first hard by hand to see if he was truly a man and then after being hit by hand the hat was placed on him and he was told that 'You are the Mtemi in this area' and others were given the name of Upembamoto.

In Citigwa's lineage at this time Citigwa died. His son was Nghoboce and Nghoboce had begat Nyamayahasi or Mukyu. Nghoboce was supposed to take his child Nyamayahasi (Mukuya) to Mpwapwa to get the hat of the Utemi. Nghoboce did not want to carry his child Mkuya to Mpwapwa to get the hat because his older son Polyasi had died, and his second child Citwecanzoka was about to die after being knifed and cast into the big pool 'Mahato' in the river of 'Ikolonog o lya Mahato' at Mvumi Makulu. So he had only one child left, Nyamayahasi (Mukuya). When he got this announcement, he decided to hide him with his mother's brothers, the Wagonanze. He told them that he was of the lineage of Citongaci. At this time Calula had already died. Musonjela the younger brother of Calula was told to take Mazengo to Mpwapwa to get the hat. (They were of the house of Nghoboce and they said '*Aa lece wawe we nymba ndodo we wabite.*') [He is from the small house].

So those at Mvumi Ikulu when they were required to take Mazengo to Mpwapwa they did it. At this time Mazengo was a youth, still dancing [performing rituals, i.e. before circumcision]. When they received this announcement they prepared Mazengo to go to Mpwapwa. Now because he was afraid of being whipped by the Germans Mazengo took his slave called Cizogolo. So they went. When they arrived at Mpwapwa the Germans said, 'Who is the Mtemi?' Mazengo out of fear pushed the slave Cizogolo forward and said 'Him.' So the slave was hit by hand sharply below and got the hat. He was told he was the Mtemi of that region. Then all the others were made Wapembamoto. They ended they journey and returned home. When they arrived Mazengo grabbed the hat from his slave. He said, 'Bring me the hat, I am the Mtemi.' So this is how Mazengo became Mtemi, and he was a Mtemi with a good reputation.[31]

At the time of the Great War between the Germans and the British Mtemi Mazengo wanted the English to come to rule because he was tired of the harsh rule of the Germans. Therefore every time when the Germans came to find him, he hid. When the people were asked 'Where is your Mtemi?' They answered, 'He is not here; he was eaten by a lion ('*Simba lyamuliye*'). This continued until the English won the war and began to rule.

In 1926 the English called all the Watemi who had been given hats by the Germans. They built baraza courts and made the Watemi collect tax and they had the authority to decide cases about the problems of their people. Mtemi Mazengo because of his reputation was made leader of all the other Watemi.[32]

Kongola's account of Mazengo's rise to power relies on sources from the clan Mbukwa Semwali that lost power and ritual precedence. Yet even those close to Mazengo acknowledge his unorthodox origins. Members of Mazengo's family asked Dr B. Mapunda, an archaeologist at the University of Dar es Salaam, to write a biography of Mazengo in the late 1990s. Mapunda records the transition to Mazengo as follows:

The decision of the Mtemi to leave his great wife and go to his little wife caused great trouble when he died. There was a struggle over the right to inherit the throne of the Mtemi between the children of the great wife and little wife. In the end, the side of the little wife won, and it was Chalulo who was a child of the little wife who was made Mtemi. And since then Mvumi has been known as Mvumi-Makulu, which means the Mvumi of the capital. It is different from Mvumi-Misheni, where the Missionaries put their school, hospital, and church at the beginning of the twentieth century.

When Chalulo died, his heir was Mazengo who was a child of his second wife, Ng'unda. It is remembered that Mazengo was born during the time of famine called Magubike; although his name is not about this famine. The name Mazengo has the meaning of 'building', and it is given to a child who is born during the time of building. The practice of giving names which match the seasons is common among the Wagogo. As a result there are other names of this type, like Matonya, which is given to a child born during the rains, or Malima which means the child was born during the time of cultivation.

When Mtemi Chalula died, Mazengo was still young, having reached the age of about 12 to 15. In the estimation of the customs and traditions of the Wagogo, an age like this is not sufficient to inherit the position of Mtemi; he must be guided by his family. It was necessary to give him a Mzajila, meaning a relative who should give him the opportunity to learn until he is older. And therefore this was done. Msonjela, who was the younger uncle of Chalula ruled in the place of Mazengo.[33]

Mapunda's account, an authorized version, finesses the questions of Mazengo's legitimacy as *mtemi*. Mapunda's sources follow the genealogy found in Hartnoll's account from the 1920s. Where Kongola reports that ritual authority followed from Chitigwa (Ntigwa in Hartnoll's version) to Nghoboce, Mapunda's sources ignore Nghoboce and his descendants. Mapunda, like Hartnoll, reports that Chalula held the position of *mtemi*, which Kongola denies.

The question of whether Mazengo was a true *mtemi* may in some senses be less important than that of why his authority was also suspect. People were divided on the question; many I asked claimed that Mazengo was a true *mtemi*. Particular informants with more detailed knowledge, like the Kongolas, denied it, however. Ingrid Yngstrom's work in the Mvumi area shows how widespread this knowledge was. She argues that Chalula had increased his power as a result of the caravan trade of the nineteenth century, eclipsing the more senior line of Mbukwa Semwali. Her sources from the Mvumi area report consistently, like the Kongolas, that Mazengo was the nephew of Chalula. Hence, he was removed from both ritual precedence and secular power.[34] The process of the emergence of new centers of power and its translation into ritual precedence comes through repeatedly in the clan histories of the region; what is unusual here is the continued memory of the illegitimacy of Mazengo's origins as *mtemi*.

Where power did not follow inheritance, then history must be changed to fit the reality. This applied both within a descent group and across territories. Despite the pretense of consulting elders, the thrust of consolidation was rational administration. Given the conflicts over resources within any locality, this process often resulted in communities that had repeatedly fought with each other combining under the new leadership. Hartnoll, who served several stints in the region up to and during the

1940s, became known as *Makomela*, the 'Mixer', and even the colonial administration did not believe its own fiction. In 1951, R. de Z. Hall wrote of plans to modernize the Native Authorities of the region:

> In the Gogo district there is not a chiefdom of any size which is not artificially created. Even though the creation has the sanction of a quarter of a century of usage, the chiefs are characterized with few exceptions by executive inefficiency which goes down to the sub-chiefs and village headmen, and many have been replaced by direct appointments.[35]

The mixing did not stop with the creation of a hierarchy where none had existed before. From 1927 on, the colonial administration repeatedly replaced *watemi* and *wapembamoto* on a variety of grounds. In several cases either corruption or 'oppression of his people' served as the cause for replacement. In one particularly notable case, one *mtemi* popular with the District Officer 'harassed' the wives of several employees of the Native Authority. He was acquitted on the first charge and the husbands of the victims transferred; however, when the wife of a new Native Authority employee also accused the *mtemi* of sexual assault, he was finally replaced.[36] Yet one cause for removal stands out from the files and I think serves as a metaphor. British officals constantly refer to the 'drunkenness' of Gogo *watemi*. Many of the complaints they make about the inefficiency, venality, and even criminality of the Native Authorities resemble this description of a *Mtemi* in Mpwapwa, who 'embodies all that is worst in the Wagogo. Mental and physical degeneracy, passive insolence, chronic alcoholism and abysmal apathy.'[37]

Beer, of course, played a large part in the social life of people in the region.[38] Hugh Hignell, in a more accusatory tone, outlined its importance.

> Our problem this year is how best to influence the tribe as to the right disposal of excess produce. Last year's harvest filled the bins with a three years' reserve as the women saw to it that no beer was brewed until the future was safe for them and their children. This year – after years of tightened belts – it will do the men no harm to have a few really good beer drinks but we must get the women on our side again to see that this tribal lubrication does not go too far. The women cannot hump heavy loads to a distant township market and they cannot be away from home too long. But if within easy reach there is a market centre with a ready cash sale for their produce and three or four shops with full stocks of cloth, salt, hoes and native finery, most of the surplus grain will find its way to that market. Only a reasonable proportion will be used for pombe [beer] brewing which is a most laborious business for the women. And their share in the actual orgy is usually a sound beating.[39]

Beer played an important role as the offering to the ancestors in *tambiko*, the prayer to them offered at the start of any important endeavor. It had to be poured on the ground to seal the prayer. Likewise, beer served as the means of hiring labor for the fields during the agricultural season. Hartnoll once described the wealthy in Ugogo as 'beef and beer capitalists'. Ernest Kongola describes with relish the role beer played in agriculture:

When someone saw grass was growing in the fields he told his wife to brew beer so that they would get help. The wife brewed the beer. People were invited and with a clean heart they came in large numbers. When they arrived in the morning at the house they were given a little beer. They tasted it there, and then they went to the field. When they arrived in the field the work of cultivating began immediately. After a little while the wife of the field brought a little beer she gave it to them '*Cinola*' they drank it. Later they continued working while singing songs of celebration. They continued for the period of two hours at this. Later the wife again brought more beer, about two or three gourds. This arrive of a little more beer was called '*Lujezo.*' The cultivators sat and drank. By this time some began to be drunk. After the beer then the work of cultivating continued with much singing of songs and women giving many ululations. By this time it was about 1 in the afternoon. The work continued. At about 4 in the afternoon the wife brought some more beer for the return of the cultivators telling them 'Thank you, let's return home.' When they arrived at the house they were given much more beer with a lot of *Jungu* which is maize meal. The women were given their *jungu* and the men were given their *jungu*. The men drank their beer there. But the women divided their beer so they could return home with it. They did not care even if the beer which they brought back was as little as one liter; they did not care. They were happy. After the men had finished their beer they were drunk and sang different songs. Out of respect for the person of the house who had been cultivated they were bade farewell with another large gourd of beer '*Nhowa Magulu*,' which is the beer of saying good bye. After this everyone departed.

But sometimes at 4 in the afternoon when they returned to the house some would decide to return to continue cultivating until the evening at about 7. Then the owner of the shamba would again bring a gourd of beer and a he-goat to give them. They would do this especially if they were youth they would say we are '*Wakwemulima*' we cannot return in the afternoon.

2. *Ngubika Cipeyo*: This is when a elderly lady does not have millet to brew beer. Therefore she invites people to come to help her cultivate but there is no beer, it is *Ngubika cipeyo* I will come to brew beer here when I harvest the new millet which you will cultivate. People with clean intentions will agree. The second day after the invitation men and women come in large numbers. They cultivate the whole day with strength and when they get thirsty they drink only water without a concern. And then they return home at four by custom. They return to their homes without going to bother the elderly lady.

The elderly lady after harvesting the new millet brews beer and goes to call all those who cultivated to come and drink beer. First they are given the gourd for '*Cinola.*' When they finish it they are given '*Lujezo*' which is when they are given '*Sima*' and at the end they are given '*Nhowa Magulu*'. Therefore this is how our grandfathers helped each other. But these days people want to work for payment only. Sometimes they want to be paid their wages before doing the work.

Je! Where did the heart for helping each other like our grandfathers go? Je! We are not like the original Wagogo who have been called to God.[40]

Hence, the consumption of beer was indeed ingrained in the day-to-day life of the region and played a key role in social activities. To call a Gogo a drunk, in one sense, was to call him or her a member of the community. In a symbolic way, drunkenness came to stand in for being too close to the people the Native Authorities governed for the British. The metaphor then extended its influence into local discourses about power under the colonial regime. The case of *Mtemi* Biringi bin Usambo of Dodoma is instructive. He was named *Mtemi* by the British in 1927 of the Dodoma area, excluding the township itself. He governed for them uneasily, with British officers often accusing him of laxity in the collection of taxes and the enforcement of various regulations. For example, in 1931, Biringi went to visit his sons at the government school for the sons of chiefs in Tabora. The sons returned home at the end of term without their father; Biringi had left for a visit with other diviners in the Congo.[41] In 1943, R. W. Varian deposed him for having *kalanga*, honey beer, in his house and being drunk, despite his having served colonial governments since the time of the Germans.[42]

Drunkenness as a metaphor in local discourses about power intersected not just with ideas about resistance to colonial domination, but with resistance to modernity. Modernizers identified with the criticism of things that 'held us back', in Mnyampala's words. They became the people who denounced the chiefs for backwardness and supported some elements of the colonial program for development. At the same time, they became supporters first of Mazengo's dominance in the region and then of the nationalist movement. Yet the discourse of power in the region did not simply constitute a three-way triangle between 'traditionalists,' 'modernizers', and the colonial state. Mazengo, the champion of the CMS mission and of the modernizers was correctly regarded as a dangerous figure by all concerned. Hignell acknowledged Mazengo's anti-colonial side when he reported on a dispute between some of Mazengo's followers and those of *Mtemi* Tupa of Makangwa. He noted that Mazengo calmed the conflict which threatened bloodshed by arguing to his 'young men' that 'Fools! We should not be fighting Tupa but the *serikali*.'[43] Likewise, Mazengo's support for Job Lusinde, TANU and Julius Nyerere in the 1950s resulted in his being asked to symbolically hand over power to Nyerere during the independence ceremonies as a representative of traditional rules giving way to modern.

The irony of a paramount chief of a people who had never had a paramount chief before the British named one for them, handing over power was, of course, compounded by the fact that almost all knew the whispered knowledge discussed by Kongola – that Mazengo was not truly a *Mtemi*. Despite this lack of ritual authority, by 1961 Mazengo certainly exercised what might be called ritual power.

The whispered stories of the illegitimacy of his power matched whispered stories of Mazengo's power to harness supernatural forces. Despite his close association with such seminal figures in the CMS mission as Mika Muloli and Yohana Malecela, despite his position as favorite of the colonial administration, and despite his patronage of Job Lusinde, even

Mathais Mnyampala reported that part of his power came from his ability to stop the rains.[44] Other informants had more prosaic examples of Mazengo's power. Several times in interviews people cited the wealth of Mazengo, claiming that, during food shortages, his stored grain fed many.[45] Others noted that the river running near Mvumi remained, as it had been in the nineteenth century, a place where the bodies of Mazengo's enemies turned up.

In one particularly famous case, a prominent Native Authority clerk found himself falling foul of Mazengo. Jioni, or John, Mbogoni served as a clerk in the Native Authority of Dodoma. During a severe famine in 1942–3, he oversaw the purchase of food from sources within the territory, the distribution of food to villages, and a campaign against rats that were thought a threat to stored food and for which the government paid a bounty for tails. His prominence led many in the region around Dodoma town to remember the famine of 1943 as *Nzala ya Jioni,* John's famine. Yet, late in that year, his rising influence took a serious blow. Mazengo accused him of corruption and the District Officer backed the charge. Mbogoni received a short jail sentence and had sixty cattle confiscated, fourteen 200lb sacks of grain seized, and paid a fine of 1241/65 shillings (over £60).[46] In his appeal, Mbogoni claimed that Mazengo acted 'out of malice for my clan'.[47]

These last two examples bring us back to the interpenetration of active and narrative power. Power flowed from the ability to stop and start the rains, and power flowed from the *viboko* (whip) of the colonial administration. Mazengo lacked the theoretical ritual authority to call or stop the rains, yet his adroit manipulation of the colonial system and of missionaries gave him the power of the *viboko*. People expressed this power of his (and I would venture to guess that he at least encouraged this expression), though in terms that echoed back to older sources of power – the power to stop the rains. Despite the praise of colonial administrators and missionaries in the archives, the popular memory of Mazengo almost always expressed his power in terms of malice, or rains stopped and bodies in the river. Yet even this malevolent vision of power conformed to older ideas of the danger of power. The danger came not just to those around power but to those who sought to exercise it, like John Mbogoni and *Mtemi* Biringi.

Resistance to this sort of despotism was never far from the surface in the region.[48] In the 1950s, resistance resulted in violence directed against those who had benefited from the decades of colonial rule. A famine in 1953–4 in the region has become known as the *Nzala ya Mau Mau,* the Mau Mau famine. The name came not just from the coincidence of the state of emergency in Kenya at the same time but from an outbreak of banditry, particularly in southern and south-western Dodoma. One informant described the situation as follows:

> During the Mau Mau there was much theft due to hunger. Some people would watch the houses of those who had food and when they left home would go in and take their food. People walking around were also often robbed. The targets were almost always those who had food.[49]

As a result of this outbreak of banditry, the administration had to bring in a detachment of the Mobile Company of the territorial police. They set up camp in southern Dodoma District and arrested over fifty men charged with theft.[50]

The memory of this movement expresses both the tensions that existed between the increasingly small minority of wealthy cattle-owners in the region and the growing number of poor and the identification of that minority with the colonial regime. Amos Maloda of Msalato village outside Dodoma recounted:

> The next famine was a bad one in 1953 called *Mau Mau*. It was called that because thieves would come to steal. They would take cows when they went off to graze. They would break into houses and beat everybody up and steal the grain and goats. They would attack people going with their cattle to market or to water, and beat them up and steal their stock. There were both groups and individuals... They tried every way to get food, and they couldn't. So they said, 'Let's go steal it'. They would make a group and go to take whatever they could. The Government tried to stop the thieves. There were many of them around Mwitikira and Nondwa. The government sent a force of police there to fight them. The police made a camp with tents and stayed there until they caught many of them. The thieves would go before a judge and the judge would say, 'Did you steal?' If the thief answered, 'No', the judge would say, 'One year'. He would ask again, and if the thief said,'No', again, he would say, 'Two years'. This would go on until the thief would be in jail for six or seven years. [51]

Several informants associated L. M. Heaney, the Provincial Commissioner at the time, with this story, and he came to acquire the sobriquet of *Bwana Nyuki*, Mister Bee, because seeing him was like stirring up a beehive.[52]

Yet the real challenge to the power of the rains in Dodoma, as in most of Africa, came by the 1940s not from the colonial state, but from a new narrative of power. In 1987, Job Lusinde told me a story about how his grandfather had operated as a *mganga* who brought the rains for the *watemi* of Mvumi. He said he had never heard much from his grandfather, but that some of his cousins had learned a bit from him. They said that while he was a rain-maker, he did not travel much. He had lived in the hills around Mvumi and served the *Mtemi* of Mvumi. He lived in the hills because that is where he could find his medicines. He had a stool and rain stones. He would tell the people that he 'prayed' with the rain stones to bring rain. He told his grandchildren that in fact this was a lie. In order to know when the rains were coming he actually watched mice. He kept these little white mice, and when the rains were coming, these mice would begin to cover the openings to their holes. When this happened, he would call the people together and tell them to start their dances and sacrifices for the rains. He also said that, when there was a bad year and the rains were late, in order to protect himself, he would tell the people to do an impossible task to bring the rains. He would send them off on this task, and they would be gone for one month, two months. When they came back without having fulfilled it, he would tell them their failure was the reason for the bad rains. People also thought that if the rains were bad, it was because someone was stopping them. They still believed this in some places. Only a few years ago some villages had attacked each other because they accused each other of stopping the rains. Sometimes, people from far away would come and ask him to help them, but they had to talk to Mazengo first.[53]

Lusinde presents a rational, modern explanation for both his grandfather's actions and people's beliefs. This new narrative was the challenge for power in the region against both older ideas that expressed the notions of community and the *viboko* of the colonial state. As a coherent narrative alternative to both the discourse of controlling the rains and that of tribal despotism, the modernism that Lusinde expressed found its first coherent expression in Mathais Mnyampala's *Historia, Mila na Desturi za Wagogo*.[54]

Mnyampala's narrative grew out of the juxtaposition of Indirect Rule and emergent nationalism.[55] Both in his social context and in the structuring of his narratives of power, Mnyampala worked the space where nationalism and modernism met.[56] He emphasized the flexibility of Gogo identity, pointing out that almost all people in the region claimed to be relatively recent immigrants. Likewise, he urged his readers 'If we are backward or things hold us back, we should support changes that lead people to progress.'[57] He laments in another place concerning the inheritance of the position of *mtemi* through the female line, 'During this time European rule, which would have been able to rectify the situation, had not begun.'[58]

Mnyampala's narrative, like the political activism of men and women like Lusinde, seems a close parallel with Benedict Anderson's concept of a modular nationalism.[59] For them the project of making the Gogo modern, of winning autonomy, moves easily to the project of liberating Tanganyika from foreign rule and supporting changes which will lead people to progress by throwing off the tribalism that holds them back. It is striking to compare Mnyampala's account of the customs and traditions of his people with those of the government sociologist, Hans Cory. Cory produced a review of Gogo customary law for the district administration with an eye to 'modernizing' its administration. His account is dominated by the rules concerning adultery. Cory based his proposed revision on discussions with a group of senior men brought to Dodoma specially to consult with him. While the extensive discussion of adultery and inheritance no doubt reflects the concerns of senior, undoubtedly wealthy males about control over women and younger males, it also reads as what, in contrast to Mnyampala's narrative, it was – an attempt to divert and trivialize the rapid social changes going on in the region.[60]

As Chatterjee has suggested, for modernizers like Mnyampala and Lusinde, the debate about intimacy was an internal one, one that lived in modern *nyumba* and rural *tembe*, in church and *ikulu*.[61] It was one in which colonial state and tradition were allies. Yet the debate over the realm of the heart was far from over with the triumph of Julius Nyerere's nationalism in the last half of the 1950s. Within that realm the tensions over gender roles and class divisions strained it to breaking point, while the authoritarian experiment of *ujamaa* helped create a continuing need for the local community as a place of refuge.

The continued salience of these stories long after Mazengo and the effective power of Native Authority chiefs have passed into history further reflects the continued struggle for control in local communities. As research by Mapunda and Yngstrom shows, the debate about Mazengo's powers, both secular and supernatural, remains a part of the debate about modernity. The national state and the *Ujamaa* village replaced the Native Authority as the prime mediator of external power for the people. Their authority remained, and remains, one based on force, despite the rhetoric used that emphasizes national solidarity. The alliance between Mazengo the Native Authority and the forces of modernity means that Mazengo's legitimacy remains a critical question.

Notes

1. See the essay by James Brennan in this volume.
2. Jan Vansina, *Oral Tradition as History* (Madison, WI: University of Wisconsin Press, 1985).
3. David Henige, *Oral Historiography* (New York: Longman, 1982).
4. Isabel Hofmeyr, *'We Spend Our Years as a Tale That is Told': Oral Historical Narrative in a South African Chiefdom* (Portsmouth, NH: Heinemann, 1993), p. 41.
5. Erick J. Mann, *Mikono ya Damu: 'Hands of Blood': African Mercenaries and the Politics of Conflict in German East Africa, 1888-1904* (Frankfurt am Main: Peter Lang, 2002), pp. 157–62.
6. Mahmood Mamdani, *Citizen and Subject: Contemporary Africa and the Legacy of Late Colonialism* (Princeton, NJ: Princeton University Press, 1996), pp. 156-61.
7. Martin Chanock, 'A Peculiar Sharpness: An Essay on Property in the History of Customary Law in Colonial Africa,' *Journal of African History* 32, no. 1 (1991), pp. 65–88, and *Law, Custom and Social Order: The Colonial Experience in Malawi and Zambia* (Portsmouth, NH: Heinemann, 1998), pp. 46–49.
8. James D. Graham, 'Indirect Rule: The Establishment of "Chiefs" and "Tribes" in Cameron's Tanganyika', *Tanzania Notes and Records* 77 (1976), pp. 1–9; E. J. Hobsbawm and Terence O. Ranger (eds), *The Invention of Tradition* (Cambridge: Cambridge University Press, 1983).
9. '..."traditions" did not necessarily stop changing when versions of them were written down, nor were debates over custom and social identity resolved, either during the colonial period or afterward. In general, the colonial period in Africa was less a time of transition - from isolation to global incorporation, from social equilibrium to turbulence, from collective solidarity to fragmented alienation – than an era of intensified contestation over custom, power, and property.' Sara Berry, *No Condition is Permanent: The Social Dynamics of Agrarian Change in Sub-Saharan Africa* (Madison, WI: University of Wisconsin Press, 1993), p. 8.
10. Leroy Vail (ed.), *The Creation of Tribalism in Southern Africa* (Berkeley, CA: University of California Press, 1989).
11. Bill Bravman, *Making Ethnic Ways: Communities and Their Transformations in Taita, Kenya 1800-1950* (Portsmouth, NH: Heinemann and Oxford: James Currey, 1998), p. 11; Jamie Monson, 'Memory, Migration and the Authority of History in Southern Tanzania, 1860–1960,' *Journal of African History* 41, 3 (2000), p. 349.
12. Peter Pels, 'The Pidginization of Luguru Politics: Administrative Ethnography and the Paradoxes of Indirect Rule,' *American Ethnologist* 23 (1996), p. 738–61.
13. Steven Feierman, *Peasant Intellectuals: Anthropology and History in Tanzania* (Madison, WI: University of Wisconsin Press, 1990), pp. 16–17; Katherine Ann Snyder, '"Like Water and Honey": Moral Ideology and the Construction of Community Among the Iraqw of

Northern Tanzania (Ph.D. diss., Yale University (1993)), pp. 25–33.

14. Plural *watemi*. The term is used for ruler in other areas of East Africa, including among the Nyamwezi and in the Great Lakes region. See David Schoenbrun, *A Green Place, a Good Place: Agrarian Change, Gender, and Social Identity in the Great Lakes Region to the 15th Century* (Portsmouth, NH: Heinemann, 1998), p. 199.

15. Mathais E. Mnyampala, *The Gogo: History, Customs, and Traditions*, edited and translated by Gregory H. Maddox (Armonk, NY: M.E. Sharpe, 1995), pp. 53–76, 86–94.

16. Rigby glosses the term as 'ritual territory', emphasizing the conditional power of the *mtemi*. See Peter Rigby, *Cattle and Kinship among the Gogo: A Semi-Pastoral People of Central Tanzania* (Ithaca, NY: Cornell University Press, 1969), pp.104–6. The word apparently derives from the same root as the Swahili term, *nchi*, or country.

17. *Ibid.*, pp. 93-104; Mnyampala, *Gogo*, pp. 98–102.

18. Mnyampala, *Gogo*, pp. 53–76, 86–94.

19. TNA 46/41/2 IV Secretary for Native Affairs Safari Notes, 16 December 1927.

20. TNA 41/47 A.V. Hartnoll, September 1926.

21. Mnyampala, *Gogo*, p. 53.

22. Mnyampala, *Gogo*, p. 55.

23. Church Missionary Society Archives, G3 A8 101, John Briggs, 10 August 1900.

24. Elisabeth Knox, *Signal on the Mountain: The Gospel in Africa's Uplands Before the First World War* (Canberra: Acorn Press, 1991), p. 93.

25. Musa Kongola reports that when he met missionaries while a young boy in Handali at some point between 1900 and 1910, they came from 'Mvumi, the country of Jumbe Mazengo.' Mazengo under the German system of administration would technically have been a *jumbe*. Musa may be making a point about Mazengo's real status, but the reference also indicates the close identification of Mazengo with the CMS. See Maddox, "Called to Hear the Word of God: Musa Kongola's Autobiography', in Toyin Falola and Christian Jennings (eds), *Africanizing Knowledge: African Studies Across the Disciplines* (New Brunswick, NJ: Transaction, 2002), pp. 85–102.

26. Sperling had already left the region before the war. John Iliffe, *Tanganyika under German Rule, 1905–1912* (Cambridge: Cambridge University Press, 1969), p. 160.

27. Paul White, *Doctor of Tanganyika* (Sydney: George M. Dash, 1942), p. 77.

28. *Ibid.*, p. 20.

29. *Ibid.*, p. 81.

30. Peter Rigby, 'Politics and Modern Leadership Roles in Ugogo,' in Victor Turner (ed.), *Colonialism in Africa 1870–1960: Volume 3, Profiles in Change: African Society and Colonial Rule* (Cambridge: Cambridge University Press, 1971), pp. 393–438.

31. The story here echoes, but does not directly allege, the often repeated charge that many government chiefs were in fact slaves.

32. Ernest Musa Kongola, *Historia Fupi Ukoo ya 'Wanyamuzula' in Wevunjiliza-Mbukwa Muhindi Nyongeza Kitabu cha Nne* (Dodoma: N.P., 1994) pp. 10–11.

33. Bertram B. B. Mapunda, 'Historia ya Mtemi Daudi Mazengo' (Dar es Salaam: Unpublished paper, 2001). I would like to thank Dr Mapunda for sharing this paper with me.

34. Ingrid Yngstrom, 'Gender, Land and Development in Tanzania: Rural Dodoma, 1920-1996' (Ph.D. diss., Oxford University, 1999), Chapter 5.

35. TNA 12825, R. de Z. Hall to PC, Central Province, 5 September 1851. Hall was the Member of the Executive Council for Local Government, an office formerly called Secretary for Native Affairs, and a former Provincial Commissioner in the Central Province.

36. TNA 40/A2/16 D.V.P. Grant, 12 November 1958.

37. TNA 40/A2/6 C. E. G. Russell to PC, 22 August 1942.

38. Charles Ambler, 'Alcohol, Racial Segregation and Popular Politics in Northern Rhodesia,' *Journal of African History* 31, no. 2 (1990), pp. 295–314; Emmanuel Kwaku Akyeampong, *Drink, Power, and Cultural Change : A Social History of Alcohol in Ghana, c. 1800 to Recent Times* (Portsmouth, NH: Heinemann, 1996).

39. TNA 967.825 *Dodoma District Reports*, H. Hignell, Half Year Report for the Period Ending 30 June 1927.

40. Ernest Musa Kongola, 'Mambo Mbalimbali Muhimu ya Jadi ya Wagogo Miaka ya Nyuma 1885–1989', *Historia Fupi Maisha Yangu, 1922–1988, Kitabu cha Pili* (Dodoma: N.P., 1989), pp. 9–10.
41. For the importance of diviners linked to the Manyema diaspora see Sheryl A. McCurdy, 'Transforming Associations: Fertility, Therapy, and the Manyema Diaspora in Urban Kigoma, Tanzania C. 1850 to 1993' (Ph.D. diss., Columbia University, 2000), p. 196.
42. TNA 40/A2/15 R. W. Varian to P.C., 29 March 1943.
43. TNA 967.828 *Dodoma District Reports,* H. Hignell, Annual Report for 1924.
44. Mnyampala, *Gogo,* p. 55.
45. Gregory H. Maddox, '"Leave, Wagogo! You Have No Food!"': Famine and Survival in Ugogo, Central Tanzania 1916-1961' (Ph.D. diss., Northwestern University, 1988).
46. TNA 13879/83 R. W. Varian to High Court, 17 October 1944.
47. TNA 13879/83 J. Mbogoni to High Court, 2 October 1944.
48. See TNA 46/19/10 Dodoma-Kimehe-Water for an account of a healing movement that spread in the region in 1925. The movement drew on the teachings of a *mganga* in Dar es Salaam and seems to have emphasized cleansing. Its followers included *Watemi.*
49. I/14/12A Meda.
50. TNA 435/R.3/A2 J. T. A. Pearce, Dodoma District Annual Report, 1954.
51. I/21/9C, 27A, 28A Mataya, etc. See also I/30/42B, 43A-45A Kaka, etc.
52. I/30/42B, 43A-45A Kaka, etc.
53. I/46/118A Job Lusinde.
54. Mnyampala, *Gogo.*
55. I have discussed the origin and context of Mnyampala's work in 'The Ironies of Mathais Mnyampala's *Histori, Mila na Desturi za Wagogo*', in Mnyampala, *The Gogo,* pp. 1–34.
56. See Thomas Geider, 'The Paper Memory of East Africa: Ethnohistories and Biographies Written in Swahili', in Axel Harneir-Sievers (ed.), *A Place in the World: New Local Historiographies from Africa and South-Asia* (Leiden: Brill, 2002), pp. 255–88 for a discussion.
57. Mnyampala, *Gogo,* p. 121.
58. *Ibid.,* p. 74.
59. Benedict R. O'G. Anderson, *Imagined Communities: Reflections on the Origin and Spread of Nationalism,* 2d ed. (New York: Verso, 1991).
60. Hans Cory, 'Gogo Law and Custom,' n.d. Hans Cory Papers, Univerisity Library, University of Dar es Salaam.
61. Partha Chatterjee, *The Nation and Its Fragments: Colonial and Postcolonial Histories* (Princeton, NJ: Princeton University Press, 1993), p.74.

Seven

^^^^^^^^^^^^^^^^^^^^^^^^^^^^^^^^^^^^

The Tribal Past
& the Politics of Nationalism
in Mahenge District
1940–60

JAMIE MONSON

Introduction

In the mid-1960s the chairman of the TANU party in Mahenge District, Mohamed Mpapai, compiled a short history of the party. In the first chapter of the small handwritten pamphlet Mpapai described the party's organization and other administrative matters.[1] The second chapter of the pamphlet, written by John Kwalevele, was more interesting. Kwalevele began his history of TANU with a list of the 'original tribes' or *kabila ya asili* of the Kilombero valley. In his view, the origins of TANU could be found in the history of life long ago, or *maisha ya kale*, when people lived peacefully in a democratic society: '*wenyeji waliishi kwa amani bila ugomvi. Waliishi katika demokrasi...*'[2] This peaceful democracy had been disrupted first, not by colonialism, but by the immigration of outsiders or *wageni* who came to rule over the valley. Through TANU, Kwalevele asserted, the local people or *wenyeji* would be able to restore the democracy and freedom that had been lost to them, first under alien chiefship and later under Indirect Rule.

In his chapter, Kwalevele interposed both tribal history and elements of nationalist discourse, thereby making two important claims. First, he established the significance of tribal history for understanding the politics of colonialism and of anti-colonial protest. Second, he made a claim for the locality – the local, indigenous roots – of concepts such as democracy (*demokrasi*), freedom (*uhuru*) and rights (*haki*). In his view, these were principles that had guided the way people lived during 'life long ago' (*maisha ya kale*), before the colonial period. By means of TANU activism, these principles would be restored.[3]

John Kwalevele's chapter was part of a body of historical writing produced by himself and his compatriot, Anton Mwilenga, during the 1950s and 1960s. Kwalevele and Mwilenga were both dissident historians and political activists, and were among the founding members of the

TANU party in Mahenge District. In their struggle for autonomy and self-rule for their communities, they used written history as their primary weapon. Mwilenga, in particular, wrote a large number of historical documents, from small pamphlets to full-length manuscripts. He also wrote an autobiography which was largely a chronology of his political activities.[4] Mwilenga and Kwalevele used their own historical writings together with the writings of others to lay claim to local knowledge, power and authority in the late colonial era. A dominant theme in these works was the reconstruction of the tribal past.

In Kwalevele's history of TANU, he wrote about the distant past in idealized terms that emphasized peaceful co-operation and consensus-based political autonomy. This way of describing the past was nostalgic, looking back to a time when there was no oppressive chiefly hierarchy nor a single dominant lineage. Similar accounts have been recorded from this same period in other regions of Tanzania. In the Usambara mountains, for example, Steven Feierman found that local people used a 'precolonial language of power' when petitioning for self-rule in the nationalist period. Activist members of the Usambara Citizens Union remembered a distant past when elders ruled without chiefship, emphasizing the responsiveness of local authorities to popular opinion.[5] Like Mwilenga and Kwalevele, they understood the timeliness of reconstructing precolonial history during debates about the present and future of local administration in Tanganyika in the 1950s.

Local ethnohistories had been used extensively by the British colonial administration from the mid-1920s through the 1930s, during the establishment of Native Authority chiefship.[6] By writing their own versions of tribal history, Mwilenga and Kwalevele raised questions about the rights of appointed Native Authority chiefs to rule in specific areas. They focused particularly on the history of migration and settlement; inter-group boundaries; and violations of local custom or *mila*. Their tribal history advocated a return to the politics of the precolonial past, while simultaneously appealing to the legitimating ideology of Indirect Rule: their historical arguments were premised on the belief that local government should be reconstructed from local tradition and adherence to custom.[7] At the same time, however, these historians drew on the language of nationalism. They sought a return to what they termed *uhuru* and *demokrasi*, principles that could be located both in the distant past and in the imagined future of an independent nation.

In his short pamphlet on the *mbiru* tax protest in the Pare mountains, Isaria Kimambo wrote in 1971 that it would be foolish to describe rural anti-colonial movements in Tanganyika as embracing either a backward-looking traditionalism or a forward-looking modernism. Protesters were able to utilize the tools they had gained in the colonial era – primarily literacy – while at the same time relying on precolonial strategies for opposing oppressive regimes. Protest against *mbiru* embodied 'a clear combination of traditional methods of resistance against oppressive rulers with modern techniques learned from the colonial period to achieve specific ends'.[8] Like the *mbiru* protesters in the Pare mountains, Mahenge

District historian-activists utilized 'modern' discursive strategies – written tribal histories and the language of nationalism – which they used to reconstruct elements of traditional society that, in their view, had been lost. Thus their politics were both national and tribal, traditional and modern. They situated the origins of nationalist ideals such as democracy and independence in a tribal past that existed long ago, in *maisha ya kale*.

Tribal History

John Kwalevele and Anton Mwilenga were both employed as tailors when they began to write history and to become involved in politics. They had acquired literacy and tailoring skills while they were students at the Kwiro Central School in the Mahenge highlands, a school that contributed substantially to the rise of an educated group of Africans in Mahenge District in the 1940s and 1950s. Mwilenga first used history to challenge colonial authority when he wrote several versions of local history in the 1940s and forwarded them to the District Commissioner. In his historical texts he described in considerable detail the origins of the Ndamba people, elaborating their status as the indigenous people or *wenyeji* of the Kilombero valley. By doing so, he directly challenged the legitimacy of chiefly overrule by Bena chief Towegale Kiwanga. Kiwanga's predecessors had governed the southwestern end of the valley from the late precolonial era, and Bena chiefship had been substantially reinforced first by German and later by British colonial regimes. Mwilenga sought to discredit Towegale Kiwanga's governing authority by showing that Kiwanga was an outsider, without indigenous roots in the valley.[9]

Mwilenga used the genre of tribal history – commonly written in Kiswahili as *historia* or *habari* – because he knew that this genre was central to the establishment of chiefly origins and rights to rule. These works typically combined ethnography and history, and were frequently produced through collaborations between colonial administrators, ethnographers and local informants. The texts followed a conventional format, normally beginning with genealogical information and tribal origins, and then outlining cultural practices including economic pursuits, religion, marriage relations, health and healing, death and burial. Many of these accounts were incorporated into district and regional record books, where they could be easily referenced by colonial officials for guidance during disputes over chiefly succession or territorial boundaries.

The writing of ethnohistory during this period in Tanganyika was therefore a highly politicized project. Colonial ethnographic fieldwork took place in the midst of local and regional debates over group identity and legitimate authority. Because control over the writing of history in this context was essential to the establishment of control over cultural knowledge and local power relationships, chiefly families sought to secure their exclusive right to narrate and disseminate historical texts.[10]

In the Kilombero valley, the primary author of ethnographic history at this time was District Officer A.T. Culwick. Together with his wife,

Culwick produced one of the most widely read ethnographies of southern Tanganyika, *Ubena of the Rivers*, in 1935.[11] Culwick relied heavily on his friendship with the ruling Kiwanga dynasty for his source material, and included an English translation of the royal Manga dynastic history as the second chapter of the volume.[12] Culwick used his authority as ethnographer and local historian repeatedly in the 1930s to campaign for Bena territorial and political rights, particularly during heated border disputes with neighboring Hehe. In one instance, he wrote a 9-page memorandum in defense of Bena rights to lands on the Hehe-Bena boundary.[13]

Thus when Anton Mwilenga began to write his own versions of local history in the Kilombero Valley in the 1940s, he was not only contesting the political authority of Towegale Kiwanga and the Manga Bena lineage. He was also challenging the ethnographic knowledge and authority of A.T. Culwick. Mwilenga's first foray into the politics of history writing involved a small pamphlet of Ndamba history written in 1944. This pamphlet was sent directly to Culwick at the District Office in Kiberege, 'to introduce him to the history of the Ndamba'.[14] Mwilenga went on to write his first book-length history in 1947, followed by a second book some time afterwards. Both of these texts were also sent to the district level, where they were conveniently misplaced. No doubt district officials were reluctant to circulate texts that ran counter to the official versions of history upon which the structures of local government were based. Yet, despite the fact that Mwilenga's manuscripts were lost, Kiwanga was sufficiently threatened by them to request the publication and circulation of some 500–1000 copies of his *Habari za Wabena Wakinamanga* for distribution to primary school children in 1949.[15]

The genre of tribal history that was prevalent in the 1930s during the establishment of Native Authority government had begun to lose its saliency by the 1950s. In the late colonial period the colonial administration in Tanganyika was replacing the Native Authority system with the system of 'local government', which would rely more on representative councils than on hereditary rights to rule. At the same time, however, Governor Twining was developing a new interest in the potential of tribal history to mitigate the rising political influence of a national identity.[16] Twining wanted the government to produce 'popular tribal histories' in order to 'canalize nationalism into local or tribal patriotism'.[17] A government-led effort to produce tribal histories resulted in a number of ethnohistories published by the East African Literature Bureau.[18]

Throughout Tanganyika at this time, therefore, there was a complex and often contradictory relationship between local historical knowledge, colonial control and nationalist politics. In the introduction to his translation of M.E. Mnyampala's *The Gogo*, Gregory Maddox shows how struggles over the control of historical knowledge took on new meaning and significance during the nationalist period. Mnyampala, while writing a local and ostensibly tribal history of the Gogo under the auspices of the colonial administration, was able to produce a text that became an inspiration to the local nationalist movement. Unlike Mwilenga's history of the Ndamba, the version of Gogo history produced by Mnyampala upheld the legitimacy of the Native Authority chiefs. It was not, therefore, a dissident version of history in terms of local and regional claims to power. On another level, however, Mnyampala was able to write a distinctly nationalist version of history – one very different from the type of ethnographic history that would have been written in the 1930s. His text implicitly critiqued not only colonial rule but also native authority chiefship through its use of modernizing language. Mnyampala embraced the authority of the prevailing chiefly lineage, but then went on to show that the traditions of the past – unification of diverse peoples; ability to adapt and change – were signs of the potential of Gogo people to modernize and to seek progress in a new nation.

While Mnyampala used tribal history in an indirect fashion to put forward a vision of modernization, Anton Mwilenga and John Kwalevele were more explicit in their use of nationalist language. These authors combined a tribal with a nationalist vision, but went about it in a different way. In their view, the authority of the ruling Bena chiefs was illegitimate, and thus the historical record that sustained Bena chiefship had to be amended. Their goal was to discredit Bena chiefship by writing an alternative history. Later, after joining TANU, they incorporated nationalist elements into their language and writing.

The Politics of Nationalism

Anton Mwilenga began his challenge to the ruling authority of Bena chiefs in the 1940s, when he started writing historical texts and forwarding them to the district office. He hoped that these written versions of local history would draw attention to the grievances of the Ndamba, while establishing the necessary ethnohistorical documentation through which Ndamba could pursue their claims. In the 1950s, Mwilenga and his fellow dissidents stepped up their political activism when they sent petitions to the colonial administration at the provincial headquarters in Morogoro. In 1955, a delegation of Ndamba leaders paid a visit to the Provincial Commissioner. They argued that the Bena were only recent migrants or '*wageni*,' who were not entitled to rule over the '*wenyeji*' or indigenous inhabitants. They complained about the way they had been treated, comparing their condition to that of slavery: 'To him [Towegale Kiwanga] we are not subjects (*raia*) but slaves (*watumwa*).' The delegates referred to Kiwanga's own text, *Habari za Wabena Wakinamanga*, to support their case against him. Once again, historical texts were introduced as evidence in Ndamba arguments, in this case a text that had been produced by Towegale Kiwanga himself.[19]

The Provincial Commissioner, however, was indifferent to these Ndamba protests. He wrote a letter back to the district office complaining about 'this handful of stupid and stubborn people' who continued to quarrel with him over conditions in Ifema, a place he viewed as 'an insignificant small enclave'. If people did not like living there, he reasoned, they should simply move away to another section of the valley, since there was plenty of fertile land to be had elsewhere.[20] Meanwhile, the Ndamba petitioners resolved to take their case to the next level of colonial administration, and set off for Dar es Salaam. When they reached the coast, they attended a meeting and subsequent rally of the TANU party. Anton Mwilenga and John Kwalevele decided to join the party, and took 54 TANU cards back with them to Malinyi to recruit additional members. At their first meeting after their return to the Mahenge District, over 100 people signed up to join TANU. Many people were eager to join TANU, Kwalevele reflected afterwards, because they believed that 'TANU would help them with their tribal war'. [21]

These Ndamba activists had a long list of specific grievances against Towegale Kiwanga that their petitions to the colonial administration sought to redress. Bena overrule of Ndamba communities had been contentious in the valley since its reinforcement under German colonial rule in the late 1890s and early 1900s. Following the consolidation of Bena political cohesion in the 1930s (under the tutelage of A.T. Culwick), Ndamba opposition was revived. The worst excesses of Towegale Kiwanga, however, occurred in the 1940s and 1950s. During this time, Kiwanga was expanding his economic activities in the fertile alluvial floodplain near Ifema. He used forced labor to work his rice farms, to build a new road and two-storey house and to carve dugout canoes. His rice plantations around Malinyi were up to 35 acres in size, and he expected his Ndamba subjects to weed and harvest them after he had plowed them by tractor. 'Their authority over us [was] bad', remembered one resident of Masagati, 'all the time we had to do work, to do this, to do that for them ... All of us Wandamba moved away, because we feared Kiwanga, because of the *chokochoko* [aggravation] of having to do work, to build roads.'[22] Kiwanga recruited Ndamba carriers to transport him by litter for distances of up to forty miles in difficult terrain, and when they stumbled, they were summoned to his side and beaten. In the 1950s, a European missionary reported that when Kiwanga made his annual tour to Masagati, he appropriated rice, bamboo beer and young maidens (*mwali*) for his own use.[23]

Ndamba representatives were particularly upset in the mid-1950s when Kiwanga required them to list their ethnicity as 'Bena' in government books. Outraged Ndamba petitioners complained to the Provincial Commissioner, 'Now the chief wants us local people of Undamba to join his foreign tribe of Bena. Yet the Bena have no sovereignty here in this valley of Ulanga.'[24] In another petition two months later they wrote, 'Therefore, sir, we are tired of this chief. It is surprising that there is freedom (*uhuru*) in other countries but we here in Ulanga ... who are of the tribe of Ndamba are being completely changed to be called Bena. If you don't like it you are detained or charged a fine.'[25] Those who refused to identify themselves as Bena were in fact fined. Four *jumbes* were fined a total of 500 shillings for calling themselves Ndamba, and 17 persons were arrested. It was indeed a 'tribal war,' in which not only political jurisdiction but also ethnic identity was at stake.

The fundamental question that remained at the heart of the Ndamba petitions was whether Bena had a right to reside and govern in the valley. In Mwilenga's '*Historia*', he addressed this question in great detail. He wrote that, long before the Bena migrated into the Kilombero valley, it had been settled by the ancestors of Ndamba and Pogoro communities that lived in the area. The Pogoro decided to move out of the valley, leaving the Ndamba as the sole residents there. They secured rights to land in the valley, according to Mwilenga, by surveying and demarcating the boundaries of the floodplain (*kupaka nchi*). Mwilenga's ancestor 'mapped' the entire Kilombero valley, claiming it for his lineage. He later secured a verbal treaty with a Bena representative in which the Bena agreed to remain in the mountains and foothills, leaving the valley under the leadership of Ndamba.

Mwilenga's '*Historia*' went on to claim that, during the German period, a Ndamba representative had accompanied Kiwanga to the coast on a journey to meet with the Germans. At the coast both the Ndamba and the Bena leaders were recognized as chiefs, and the boundary between valley (under Ndamba rule) and upland (under Bena rule) was affirmed. Therefore, according to Mwilenga, the Germans acknowledged Ndamba historical rights to governance and to territorial control over the valley.[26] Through these historical precedents, carefully outlined in his handwritten texts, Mwilenga made the case that Ndamba deserved to govern themselves. These historical claims, initially brought forward in Mwilenga's histories, were highlighted in Ndamba petitions to the British authorities in the late 1940s and early 1950s.

The petitions – and the written histories they referred to – framed political grievances in ethnic terms. Once the Ifema activists had affiliated themselves with TANU, however, this strategy began to change. Initially, as John Kwalevele stated, the purpose of the dissidents was to enlist the help of the nationalist party in their 'tribal war.' It was not long, however, before the language and tactics used by the local party leadership reflected their increased exposure to nationalist discourses and organizing strategies. At the same time, Kiwanga and the district office were attempting to dismiss their movement as narrowly parochial. In the middle and late 1950s, therefore, the Ifema leaders responded by replacing their appeals for Ndamba historical rights with a more nationalist political approach.

The Provincial Commissioner may have believed that Ifema was an 'insignificant enclave' when he rejected the petitions of Ndamba activists. But colonial officals became increasingly worried after the first branch of TANU was started there in 1955, and Ifema became the nucleus of anti-colonial political activity in Mahenge District. At the local level, Kiwanga's representatives tried to prevent TANU leaders from establishing an office or holding meetings. Party members were repeatedly harassed and detained, sometimes for extended periods of time, without charges. In 1956 twelve persons were detained and three TANU members put in jail after meetings at Utengule and Malinyi. In one instance, Mwilenga was sentenced to jail for not having planted the requisite acre of cassava.[27] District officials tried unsuccessfully to prevent regional TANU representatives from making visits to the district. When two regional TANU leaders, Lila Mwenyekondo and Mohamed Juma, paid a visit to Utengule in 1956, their canoe was overturned on the Mpanga River. This prompted speculation that Kiwanga had arranged for the canoe accident in order to drown the passengers or have them attacked by crocodiles. When the two visitors returned to Malinyi, they were thrown into jail for distributing envelopes printed with the address of TANU headquarters.

The leadership of Mwilenga and Kwalevele became more difficult for the party to sustain as these incidents of harassment continued. The party members realized that they must distance themselves from the appearance of particularist politics – 'tribalism' – if they were to be successful with their political activity. And tribal politics were closely associated with Mwilenga and Kwalevele, in large part because of their role as ethno-historians. Recognizing that the local TANU party needed new leaders, Anton Mwilenga admitted that 'he who plants a coconut tree does not expect to eat [the fruit] himself'.[28] Mohamed Mpapai was elected TANU chairman in 1958. Although he was the grandson of Anton Mwilenga, he was viewed as less contentious by the district administration. A Ngindo representative was selected to be vice-chairman, to demonstrate that TANU did not exclude anyone on the basis of their ethnicity. Meanwhile, the regional TANU officials also emphasized their opposition to 'factionalism' and to disloyalty to the central and local governments.[29]

Under Mpapai's leadership the TANU party in Mahenge moved away from the issues related to Bena chiefly overrule, and no longer used local history as a political weapon. The party's grievances turned to issues such as taxation, agricultural pricing and transportation. The government was criticized for enforcing taxation when no facilities were provided for getting crops to market. Mpapai wrote a letter to the Mahenge District Commissioner asking how the farmers in the southwestern end of the valley could be expected to come up with tax monies when there were no passable roads or bridges, no working ferry, and no merchants to trade with.[30]

Conclusion

In the politics of the late colonial period in Mahenge District, historian activists constructed new versions of the past in order to make claims to political authority and ethnic autonomy. Anton Mwilenga and John Kwalevele used written histories – especially the reconstruction of the tribal past – to make claims to self-rule in the Kilombero valley. In their histories and their political activism they combined local, tribal history with the discourse of nationalism. The writings and political activities of Mwilenga and Kwalevele illustrate the political relevance of local historical knowledge, colonial control and nationalist politics during the 1940s and 1950s.

Yet dissidents opposed to Bena chiefship were not the only ones in Mahenge District to combine the languages of tribal and nationalist politics during this period. The petitions of a Native Authority chief during the same era further illustrate the complexity of the relationship between tribal history, nationalist discourse and late colonial politics. Johani Mlolere was the chief of the Pogoro chiefdom in Mahenge District. In 1951, popular protest led to the secession of one section of the Pogoro chiefdom, that governed by Mlolere's nephew Mohamed Mlolere. The people in that area had complained about Mohamed's leadership, arguing that they wished to replace him with someone 'who will be chosen by the local people'.[31] In a large public meeting in 1951, the local leaders and their followers voted to remove him from office.[32]

Johani Mlolere responded to this threatened secession by appealing to the colonial government regarding the importance of retaining tribal unity. Like John Kwalevele, Johani Mlolere used the language of nationalism to describe the tribal past. In Mlolere's case, however, he used this language to appeal for the retention of tribal administration under his own chiefship, rather than to campaign for its demise. Mlolere argued that the Pogoro people needed to retain their tribal unity (*umoja wa kabila*) along with the values of brotherhood (*undugu*) and uplift (*maendeleo ya kisasa*). Thus, in his appeal for the retention of tribal administration, Mlolere inserted terms from the discourse of national unity and modernization (*umoja, undugu,* and *maendeleo*). He went on to argue that the preservation of Pogoro chiefship under his leadership would benefit the nationalist cause. Since Africans would sometime in the future be expected to join together and to govern themselves as a single nation, it was important to promote unity rather than divisiveness among groups. He asked, 'If we now begin to be divided within our tribes by the government itself, and to be given thoughts of hatred and of individualism, how will we be able to come together in the future as one nation of Africans?'[33]

Mlolere's appeal illustrates further the way both tribal history and nationalist discourses were used in struggles over local politics during the late colonial period in Mahenge District. During this phase control over local ethno-historical knowledge, once the preserve of colonial administrators and administrative ethnographers, was being contested by the historical writing of Anton Mwilenga and John Kwalevele. At the same time Ndamba dissidents brought forward the chiefly versions of history that were legitimated by ethnographers as evidence in their petitions against Bena chiefly authority. Meanwhile, Pogoro chief Johani Mlolere found that his right to govern was being challenged by popular protest as the structures of Indirect Rule were renegotiated in the local government era. In response, he used the language of nationalism to argue that retaining tribal unity in local government would be a useful preparation for the transition to national independence.

Thus both dissidents and chiefs used tribal history and nationalist discourses as political strategies during the late colonial period in Mahenge District. During this time of change in the power structures of local administration, chiefs and their opponents struggled over the definitions of tribal identity, history and modernity. As they sought to locate precedents in the distant past for their claims and their aspirations, they rewrote history and used colonial ethnohistories in new contexts. As they made claims for the emerging independent nation, they drew on the past to legitimize their claims for the present and future.

Notes

1. Mohamed Mpapai, '*TANU katika Ulanga: Maelezo ya Bwana M. Mpapay*', 1965, unpublished pamphlet.
2. John Kwalevele, *TANU katika Ulanga: Maelezo ya John Kwalevele*, chapter 2 in *ibid*.
3. I use the terms 'tribal' and 'tribal history' here to highlight the centrality of ethnicity in the texts that are under discussion, and in keeping with the emphasis of the writers themselves who consistently refer to '*kabila*'. This genre of historical writing is more commonly described as 'ethnohistory,' a term which I also use below. See, for example, Wim van Binsbergen, *Tears of Rain: Ethnicity and History in Central Western Zambia* (New York, Kegan Paul International, 1992); Gregory Maddox, 'Introduction: The Ironies of *Historia, Mila na Desturi za Wagogo*,' in M.E. Mnyampala, *The Gogo: History, Customs and Traditions*, G.H. Maddox, ed. and translator (New York, M.E. Sharpe, 1995), pp. 1–34; Thomas Geider, 'The Paper Memory of East Africa: Ethnohistories and Biographies Written in Swahili,' in Axel Harneit-Sievers (ed.), *A Place in the World: New Local Historiographies from Africa and South Asia* (London, Boston, Köln, Brill, 2002), pp. 255–87.
4. The extant unpublished works of Anton Ngwawe Mwilenga include a history of the Ndamba people ('*Historia Fupi ya Wandamba*') and at least two versions of his autobiography, '*Habari za Maisha Yangu*', produced between 1950 and 1970. For two previous analyses of this literature, see Jamie Monson, 'Memory, Migration and the Authority of History in Southern Tanzania, 1860–1960', *Journal of African History*, 41 (2000), pp. 347–72; and Monson, 'Claims to History and the Politics of Memory in Southern Tanzania, 1940–1960,' *International Journal of African Historical Studies*, 33,3 (2000), p. 543.
5. Steven Feierman, *Peasant Intellectuals: Anthropology and History in Tanzania* (Madison, WI, University of Wisconsin Press, 1990), p. 207.
6. This topic has been discussed at great length by scholars of Tanzania, most recently by Peter Pels, 'The Pidginization of Luguru Politics: Administrative Ethnography and the Paradoxes of Indirect Rule,' *American Ethnologist*, 23 (1996), pp. 738–61; James Ellison, 'Colonizing Ethnography in Southwest Tanganyika Between the Wars,' paper presented to African Studies Association meeting, November 2000; Jamie Monson, 'Memory, Migration', and 'Claims to History'; and Gregory Maddox, 'Introduction'. See also Geider, 'The Paper Memory', for East Africa more generally.
7. Feierman, *Peasant Intellectuals*.
8. I.N. Kimambo, *Mbiru: Popular Protest in Colonial Tanzania* (Dar es Salaam: East Africa Publishing House, 1971), p. 8.
9. Mwilenga, '*Historia Fupi ya Wandamba*'; and Lorne Larson, 'A History of the Mahenge (Ulanga) District, c. 1860–1957' (Ph.D. diss., University of Dar es Salaam, 1976), pp. 340–5.
10. Jim Ellison spoke with Native Authority chiefs from Mbeya who 'saw writing as essential to the question of appropriate control of cultural and historical knowledge', and sought to ensure that chiefs and chiefly families controlled the dissemination of historical knowledge. (Ellison, 'Colonising Ethnography', p. 3) See also Pels, 'The pidginization of Luguru politics'.
11. The title of this volume exemplified the way the Culwicks conflated place (the Kilombero floodplain) with ethnicity. Thus the river valley itself became 'Ubena', the place of the Bena people and of their political jurisdiction. Subsequent efforts to force Ndamba residents to restate their own ethnicity as Bena are described below.
12. A.T. and G.M. Culwick, *Ubena of the Rivers* (London: George Allen and Unwin, 1935), chapter 2. This text was later published in its Swahili version: Towegale Kiwanga, *Habari*

za Wabenamanga (Dar es Salaam, 1937).

13. Ulanga District Books, Inter-tribal Boundaries, Letter from A.T. Culwick to District Officer Iringa, 26 October 1935; a full description of these exchanges can be found in Monson, 'Memory, Migration and the Authority of History', pp. 366–8.

14. A. Mwilenga, *'Historia ya Maisha Yangu'.*

15. Area Office Files, Mahenge, AOM A.2/7/35, *Mtema* Kiwanga to D.C. Ulanga, July 9, 1949. It is difficult to reconstruct the names of district officials from the district record books, because there were frequent personnel shifts and acting officers during these years. Where names of officers are available in the records they are cited here.

16. Susan Geiger, *TANU Women: Gender and Culture in the Making of Tanganyikan Nationalism, 1955–1965* (Portsmouth, NH: Heinemann; Oxford: James Currey; Nairobi: E.A.E.P.; Dar es Salaam: Mkuki Na Nyota, 1997); Maddox, 'Introduction'.

17. Twining, cited in Geiger, *TANU Women* p. 105.

18. Geider, 'Paper Memory', pp. 268–9; Maddox, 'Introduction', p. xi.

19. *Ibid.*

20. Mahenge District Archive, L.5/19/22, *'Raia wa Kindamba pamoja na Majumbe* 1. Malinyi 2. Lupunga 3. Ngohilanga 4. Nyambira 5. Ihanga 6. Masagati *pamoja na wazee wetu* to P.C. Morogoro,' 7 March 1955; L.5/19/23, Acting P.C. Eastern to D.C. Mahenge, 25 March 1955.

21. Kwaleleve, *'TANU katika Ulanga: Maelezo ya John Kwalevele'.*

22. Interview with Anton Kimamule, Tanganyika Masagati, 6 November 1989.

23. Interview with Peter Mwilenga, Ifakara, 2000; P. Wolfram Burckhardt, *Malinyi Chronicle*, 13/12/70, pp. 1957–8.

24. L.5/19/10, Rashidi Ngula, Donati Lyau, Kambiyana Ligongwe, to P.C. Morogoro, January 1955.

25. L.5/19/22, *'Raia wa Kindamba pamoja na Majumbe'*, to P.C. Morogoro, 7 March 1955.

26. Mwilenga, *'Historia'*, pp. 30–75.

27. Mpapai, *'TANU katika Ulanga'*; Mwilenga, *'Historia ya Maisha Yangu'*; A.6/23/I/161, D.C. (Bullock) to TANU District Secretary, 1958.

28. Mwilenga, *'Historia ya Maisha Yangu'.*

29. TANU headquarters, DSM, 2/A/56/71, Organizing Secretary General TANU (Mhando) to DC Mahenge (Fonseca), 16 October 1956.

30. A.6/23/I/208, TANU District Chairman (M. Mpapai) to D.C. Mahenge, June 1959, Records of Utengule Baraza.

31. L.5/5/2, Raphael Njahiti, *Sauti ya committee na raia wa Mtimbira*, to District Commissioner Mahenge, 15 December 1950.

32. L.5/5/9, Johani Mlolere to Provincial Commissioner, 3 March 1951.

33. *Ibid.*

Eight

∧∧∧∧∧∧∧∧∧∧∧∧∧∧∧∧∧∧

The Landscapes of Memory in Twentieth-Century Africa

E.S. ATIENO ODHIAMBO

Introduction: The Creativity of Power

This essay is dedicated to the life and memory of Mohammed Hussein Bayume of Tanga.[1] Bayume's life has only recently come to scholarly attention, yet this relatively unknown Tanganyikan moved across the world stage of the late nineteenth and first half of the twentieth centuries in ways that both fascinate and prefigure the emergent world of modern Tanzania. Born about 1893 in Tanga township, part of the Pangani valley whose history has interested Professor Isaria Kimambo for the past two decades, Bayume was brought up as a Nubian, a new community in eastern Africa whose origins sprang from the complex Emin Pasha Relief Expedition of the previous decade. Just how his parents found their way to Tanga is unknown; but his early youth straddled the traumas of the German conquest and colonization of Tanganyika, the Bushiri rebellion of 1888 and the subsequent Maji Maji War of 1905–7. The World War I years were crucial to his subsequent career, as Bayume fought on the side of the Germans. At the end of the hostilities he relocated to Germany, and lived the rest of his life there. Between 1921 and 1937 he served as a Kiswahili instructor and language assistant to the great Dietrich Westermann at Humboldt University. Meanwhile he married a German woman and had two or three children by her. With the intensification of Nazism Bayume lost first his post at the university, then his German citizenship, and was subsequently arrested for the offence of having married a German woman. Thus he lost his living and his family. He was taken to various concentration camps and is thought to have perished in one of them around 1943. He remained an 'unknown African' until 1999 when Dr Jan-Georg Deutsch of the Berlin African Studies Association, Dr Achim von Oppen of the Centre for Modern Oriental Studies in Berlin, and Dr Heike Schmidt of the Department of African Studies, Humboldt University in Berlin, jointly revived his memory by hosting the First Bayume Memorial Lecture at Humboldt University.

The opening sentences of *The Seed is Mine,* Charles van Onselen's powerful book on Kas Maine, an unknown South African sharecropper on the northwestern side of the Transvaal whose life bestrode the nineteenth and twentieth centuries, read as follows:

> This is a biography of a man who, if one went by the official record alone, never was. It is the story of a family who have no documentary existence, of a farming folk who have lived out their lives in a part of South Africa few people loved, in a century that the country will always want to forget. The State Archives, supposedly the mainspring of the Union's memory, has but one line referring to Kas Maine. The Register of the Periodic Criminal Court at Makwassie records that on September 8, 1931 a thirty-four-year-old 'labourer' from Kareepoort named 'Kas Tau' appearing before the magistrate for contravening Section Two, Paragraph One of Act 23 of Police District No. 41, was fined five shillings for being unable to produce a dog license. Other than that, we know nothing about the man.[2]

Kas Maine belongs to the 'other' Africans, to 'The Peoples Without History',[3] 'The Unknown Africans',[4] whose agency is all but invisible in the written archives to which modern historiography is accustomed. Historians of Africa have faced this challenge since the 1960s as they have sought to give their peoples a meaningful past derived from oral traditions. Historians of Kenya, in particular, have sought to re-write the Mau Mau war and its freedom fighters into the narrative of an emergent nation-state and to create a nationalist historiography on the Western nation-state model. Likewise, the history of Africa's ordinary peasants under colonialism initially posed a methodological challenge to historians of Kenya, Tanzania, Zimbabwe and South Africa. The emergence of 'peasant studies' as a multidisciplinary field in the 1970s inspired the first efforts at agrarian histories in these regions.[5]

In the past two decades historians of Africa have entered the sub-field of social history, and sought to recapture the voices and the worlds of both rural and urban Africans as free peasants, squatters, the working class, independent sex workers, and the poor underclasses.[6] This effort, carried out largely through oral interviews, has yielded significant narratives regarding the role played by Africans in the unfolding historical events; regarding the dialectics of their own history; and regarding the culturally reflexive accounts of their experiences, their anxieties and their fears.[7]

Kas Maine's biography is the epitome of this restoration. Charles van Onselen succeeds in restoring Kas Maine to the mainstream of African colonial history by excavating the landscapes of memory. That phrase – excavating the landscapes of memory – requires emphasis. It is retained in the thousands of compacts and contracts, transactions, exchanges, fights and hatreds that the inhabitants of northern Transvaal recalled to the researchers about their own personhood and agency. Once again let us underscore that personhood and agency are evident in the making of their long century from the 1870s when diamonds and gold were discovered in South Africa down to 1985 when Kas Maine died. In the process van Onselen constructs a historical figure, namely Kas Maine, who was never far from comprehending his sense of worth, and of the worth of ordinariness – of being just an ordinary person – emphasizing in the process moral equity, moral accountability, even in the ravines of race and class, calling on the common humanity of all South Africans. Mohammed Hussein Bayume belongs to that cluster of the Unknown Africans who serve to remind contemporary historians of our common humanity.

Charles van Onselen, like all guild historians, has been involved in the production of history.[8] The production of history can sometimes take place in the archives. But Kas Maine and Mohammed Hussein Bayume are not accessible in and through the archives. So what is to be done about the rewriting of their stories into our major narratives of Africa?

It is quite evident that African historians have not merely depended on the archives in order to lay a claim on their pasts. They have insisted on rewriting it themselves, re-introducing the African into the world in the twentieth century.[9] Pioneers like Isaria Kimambo and their many students after them have insisted on writing family, group, clan and community histories.[10] From time to time they have insisted on writing national histories, with all the pitfalls that come with this endeavor.[11]

African historical writing, including professional historiography, has tended to make distinctions between collaborators and resisters to colonial conquest. The subject of conflict and collaboration has its own historiography in East Africa. It has had its own periodization, one that relates to the quest for accommodation by some Africans during the period of conquest by the Europeans. But also another that seeks to establish a common narrative that runs to the effect that all Africans were resisters to colonial rule, irrespective of whether they were conscious of their actions or not. This tradition originates from Thomas Hodgkin's populist version of African activism, *Nationalism in Colonial Africa*,[12] where he includes any act of rudeness or being impolite that frustrated the designs of the colonial powers as being acts of nationalism. Later it did have a corrective input from James S. Coleman, Professor of Political Science at UCLA, who argued in *Nigeria: Background to Nationalism*,[13] that not everything that was rude or impolite qualified to be labeled as an act of nationalism. Coleman argued that it is only those acts of African personification and agency that were intended for the attainment of the territorial independence of the African state which should be described as acts of nationalism. In the heyday of 'The Recovery of African Initiative' school of thought in the mid-1960s T. O. Ranger sought to discern the connections between primary resistance, the protest phenomenon of the 1920s and 1930s and the rise of mature African nationalisms in the 1950s in eastern and central Africa.[14]

In the early 1970s younger scholars came onto the scene within the East African region. Informed by a reading of Frantz Fanon's *The Wretched of the Earth*[15] and by a measured amount of radical pessimism arising from the disappointment with the failure of independence to deliver goods to the people in the region, this scholarship questioned the triumphal narrative of nationalism, and the nature of the connections that Ranger had sought to establish. They began debating the whole question of *Conflict and Collaboration*, the title of a book by Edward I. Steinhart.[16] It appeared to this generation that collaborators and resisters were really first cousins; that the options laid open by the collaborators were also the same options laid open to the resisters; that personhood and agency were important; that the decisions that earlier African people made on a day-to-day basis seemed, sixty years down the line, not to have been foreordained or fixed, but that, in terms of the play of personhood, agency and power, these people made day-to-day decisions that sought to maximize on the possibilities of survival and interest, for individuals as well as communities. And therefore on a second look at the list of so-called collaborators in Kenya, Uganda, and Tanzania – Sir Apolo Kagwa and the Baganda Protestant elites, Olonana the Maasai Oloiboni, and Mohammed Hussein Bayume in Tanganyika – what emerges is not just one narrative but a shifting basis of collaboration. A similar gaze at the list of the resisters, a very popular subject of study in the 1960s and 1970s, yields a motley crowd all inspired by varying motives, and willing to shift the basis of their allies in resistance: Bushiri and some cousins of Mohammed Bayume in Tanga and the Pangani valley, Kabaka Mwanga of Buganda, and the *Orkoiyot* Koitalel arap Samoei of the Nandi in Kenya.

Outstanding in scale and intensity is the grand narrative of the Maji Maji war, the study of which John Iliffe, Gilbert Gwassa and the 'Dar es Salaam school' of African history became famous for in the 1960s and '70s. It used to be a narrative of icons and heroes: of Kinjikitile wa Ngwale, Abdalla Mapanda, Omari Kinjala, Kibasila and many others.[17] Fortunately we also have a whole corpus of literature of resistance written by the age-mates of these individuals, written in Luganda, or more immediately for Hussein, in Kiswahili. The *Utendi wa Vita vya Wadachi Kutamalaki Mrima*, a poem written by Hemedi Abdallah bin Said El Buhriy concerning the Arab-Swahili-German war of 1888, portrayed Seyyid Barghash, the Arab Sultan of Zanzibar, as the legitimate ruler to whom the people of Tanga owed loyalty, and the Germans as the usurpers. It was for the Sultan's thriving that El Buhriy wrote:

Mja Wako mjalie	Your servant, enable him
aitulize ezie	to bring peace to his dominions
na adue mshindiye	and defeat any enemy
ambaye amkamia	who threatens him.[18]

Similarly the poetry of Abdul Karim bin Jamaliddini, *Utenzi wa Vita ya Maji Maji*, is centered on the contestation of power between the Germans and the Africans during the Maji Maji war of 1905. 'Who is more powerful, Hongo or the European?' the resisters asked. Their answer was 'Hongo!'[19]

In retrospect, revisiting the question of resistance versus collaboration, we reaffirm an earlier synthesis. A return to these individuals, groups and societies suggests that they were all trying to cope with the contradictions of a newly emergent world, a world of which none of them had full comprehension, a world rather of paradox.[20] Mohammed Bayume was one of those individuals caught in the webs of semi-comprehension and who had to deal with this paradox.

117

Secondly, there is a need to think of him as an agent of African person-hood and agency. A familiar theme, the 'Movement of Ideas' comes in handy in this regard. It is a theme that is familiar to scholars of Tanzanian history, based on an early article by T. O. Ranger in *A History of Tanzania*.[21] Reference to the movement of ideas facilitates thinking about the processes through which people tried to negotiate their lives through-out the new world that emerged; the new world of missionaries like Dr James Rebmann and Ludwig Krapf in the Usambaras and the Kiliman-jaro area at mid-nineteenth century, of footloose European traders and dreamers like Karl Peters in the same neighborhoods, of the chartered companies – the German East Africa Company and the Imperial British East Africa Company; and later of the new world in which European Christian missionaries came looking for souls to save and African children to take to school, and the contexts in which African parents made decisions about which son or daughter to hand over to the missionaries – there 'to get lost forever' – as they thought.

As is now known, within the first two decades of the arrival of the colonialism in Tanganyika and in Kenya, a lot of young people made their own decisions: to go along with the missionaries; to go and work for wages for the European settlers; to go for the lure of travel, marvel and adventure. This lure of things strange, new and foreign very much informed the lives of people like Mohammed Bayume, taking them to far-off lands in eastern Congo, and even to Berlin and Siberia by the end of the nineteenth century.[22]

In the process of trying to create a brave new world for themselves, they entered into contestations within their own families and households, with regard to authenticity, to authority, to obeying one's parents, contestations with regard to interpersonal relations with one's age-mates and peer groups, contestations too about distances to travel. Would the individual have to move to employment close by and remain within the beck and call of family and kin, or was one to travel hundreds of miles away and distance oneself from familial obligations? These 'New Men' – Tanzanian historiographers refer to them as such, and Mohammed Hussein Bayume was certainly one of them – created their new world. It was a world that can be summarized as a world of modernity, another key term in Tan-zanian historiography. It was a world full of inconclusive narratives. They took the gamble to enter into these worlds without necessarily determining that they would know or control the end products or outcomes of their adventures. These people thought of modernity as opportunity; oppor-tunity to travel, to marvel, to adventure, to pursue personal accumulation of wealth, property, novelty, knowledge, secrecy, exoticism and performance.

More mundanely, modernity was also an interface, a terrain for the contestation of tradition. Were a son to say, 'Father, I am not going to listen to you and stay at home as you wish. I am going to Tanga to seek work.' Were he to say further, 'When I get to Tanga I will not come back to marry the local village bride which is part of the tradition of the Pangani Valley; and if I go to Tanga I will come back dressed up as a Mswahili, and speaking Kiswahili; perhaps become a Moslem, and get circumcised in the Koranic tradition', what would be the cultural import of these declarations? What meaning would the autochthonous community in which the son was brought up attach to them? The historiography of this region from which Bayume came, the Mrima coast and the Pangani Valley – next door to the Kenyan coast of Mombasa, and Kwale – is full of these choices that individuals made with indeterminate consequences.[23] The question of Islamic circumcision, for example, re-formulates resistance not just as a remote contest over value systems but as an issue that individuals had to confront as a practice of daily life on a day-to-day basis. Who were the new people, and how were they going to represent tradition or modernity in their attire?[24] These contestations over person-hood and agency continue to be important. They continue to inform the kinds of decisions that people like Mohammed Hussein Bayume made to be a Moslem (we do not know whether he was); to be a Christian (we do not know whether he was); to work at home; to travel.

Bayume and people of his generation in the period between 1890 and 1914 can also be thought of as translators of culture. It is a process with an early ancestry in eastern Africa. Interestingly in East Africa they had the choice to deal with simultaneous processes: being Christian or being Moslem, or being both, while at the same time accommodating the religions of their ancestors. A successful practice of this inculturation came with the rise of the Nomiya Luo Mission church in the period between 1907 and 1912 in western Kenya. It was led by Johana Owalo. Conversion to Christianity, the trajectory officially approved by the Germans and the British, carried its own opportunities – to become a clerk or interpreter like Bayume. Being a Moslem also brought with it new opportunities – to belong to the German administration in Tanganyika before 1916 as an *akida* or *jumbe*. On a wider social plane, it created a new spiritual entity – the Jamaa – a community of the faithful, a global community with local roots in Tanga or Mombasa. It also created an opportunity to assume new identity; one could choose to be a Mswahili rather than a Zigua, Doe or Zaramo in the Pangani valley. It opened doors in very many ambiguous and asymmetric ways within colonial Tanganyika. In summary, the Christian revolution in East Africa between the 1880s and 1920s, plus the equally important Islamic revolution during the same period, offer windows for understanding African initiatives aimed at creating new religious syntheses, new communities and new identities. African peoples did have options during this phase of the colonization of consciousness, and used it in diverse ways.[25]

They came to those options because they exercised individual initiative. And therefore the personhood and agency of these individuals becomes a recurring theme. They were not victims of colonization, not people whose lives just happened to be, but individuals who made choices. To reiterate this refrain is not to romanticize the roles of these individuals. Rather, the point of emphasis is to understand the transitions to modernity in eastern Africa between the 1890s and the 1930s. These people become the subject-matter, the vernacular Christians and Moslems. These are the people without whose efforts there would have been no colonization of consciousness.[26] There would have been no African Christianity without African missionaries to the Taita like George Samuel Okoth, and to the Luo of South Nyanza like Ezekiel Apindi.[27] There would have been no Islam in Mumias and Kendu Bay in Kenya without the actual intellectual efforts of individuals like Mohammed Ongong' and Asuman Ondong', respectively, to translate the new messages into new meanings, into new experiences.

This line of enquiry leads us into thinking about modernity as a form of creativity, *The Creativity of Power*.[28] What is power about for colonized people? Power is about the power of the word. Speaking, and writing and reading German and Kiswahili as well as the Kinubi language, was for Bayume a means of comprehending newness, of understanding new horizons. It is interesting to think about what he was doing alongside many of his age-mates who went into working for the Germans in Tanganyika as *askaris, akidas, liwalis* and *jumbes*. Some of them wrote their memoirs. One of them, Salim bin Abubakari, traveled all the way to Berlin, and from Berlin to Czarist Russia and Siberia between 1893 and 1896, and published his experiences as a narrative, *Safari Yangu Bara Urusi na ya Siberia*.[29] Many of them had traveled from Tanga and Bagamoyo into Eastern Congo with the slave and ivory caravans. This is a very wealthy resource in terms of thinking about how people comprehended and conceptualized the African frontier in the nineteenth century, and how they described and explained it back home. One of them, Sulemani bin Mwenye Chande, wrote one such account, *Safari Yangu Bara ya Africa*.[30] Tippu Tip was the epigone in the autobiographical genre with his *Maisha ya Hamed Bin Mohamed, yaani Tippu Tip*.[31] At the same time, Mutoro bin Mwenye Bakari published the first indigenous orthography of the Mrima coast, *Desturi za Wasuaheli*.[32] The first generation of Western-style intellectuals from the Pangani valley had taken off.

Representations of Modernity

In turn, this leads to the next question, the representation of modernity for the generation of Hussein Mohammed Bayume before he moved away from Tanganyika to Germany in 1919. What did they think of the rapid changes happening around them , and what aspects of these changes did they think of as desirable? Why did Bayume choose to go along with the Germans after their loss of their colony in Tanganyika? This is an intellectual terrain worth exploring in its own right. The succeeding generation in the inter-war years insisted that there was a trajectory towards modernity into which Africa had to gravitate. They called it variously the way of progress, the way of being Christian, the modern way, or more ambiguously, civilization. In Tanzanian historiography they were the 'New Men' who lived through the 'Era of Improvement and Differentiation' in the 1920s and 1930s.[33] That sequencing implied that they were part of the transition pastoral, seeking new identities. Were they going to be known as urban men – *Wa Tanga*, or *Watu wa Mombasa*? Or just as the new people, the *asomi* in Kikamba, the bookmen? Should they be identified as the men in the blanket – the primitive African so much preferred by the colonial settlers – or their alterity, the man in trousers so much loathed by German and British settlers and administrators?

Thinking through this involves debating the colonial project as a whole. On the one hand, it was ostensibly a civilizing mission, and yet the actual products of it – the New Men – were not always immediately accepted as the intended product of that colonizing project. So there is need to think about creativity in the context in which this transition occurred. Hussein and his age-mate Jomo Kenyatta made history, but they did not always make it according to their own will. Their creativity in context then implied what Mahmood Mamdani has recently referred to in his *Citizen and Subject*,[34] they were free to make choices, but they made choices as subjects and not as citizens.

Exile and Alienation

There is a global dimension to this discourse, for that is the context in which Bayume operated from the date of his arrival in Germany in 1919 until his ignominious death in 1943. First, he was a modern Tanganyikan like Ali Migeyo , A. S. Kandoro, Mathais Mnyampala, Kleist Sykes and Leveria Kaaya. Of this galaxy the Sykes family has been the most accessible to historians of Tanganyika, with a recent biography of Abdulwahid Sykes[35] adding to the earlier sketch of Kleist Sykes by his granddaughter Daisy Sykes (now Daisy Buruku) in *Modern Tanzanians*.[36] Mnyampala's work has been the best studied as a genre of literary mapping of the landscape of memory and identity. This is a welcome shift from the nationalist historiography into the trajectory of intellectual history.[37] To their credit, this generation anticipated the rise of modern historiography, and wrote and published in the years following the establishment of the East African Literature Bureau in 1948, among them, for the Arusha, Justin Lemenye in his *Maisha ya Ole Kiwasis, yaani Justin Lemenye* (1956).[38]

In the global context, Bayume was a nobody in Weimar and Nazi Germany. How does his history weave through that silent terrain? At the Versailles Peace Conference in Paris in 1919 there were no African questions tabled on the official agenda for the conference. Although Dr W.E.B. Dubois and the members of the Diaspora Pan African Movement put together a document, *African Questions at the Peace Conference*, the peacemakers refused to read it. President Woodrow Wilson, who had declared that the war had been conducted to make the world safe for democracy, and who won the Nobel Peace Prize that year, refused to read the book or to meet the Africans. So the African agenda lay unattended. Nor, to anticipate, were there any African questions at the founding of the United Nations Organization in San Francisco in 1945, in spite of vigorous efforts by Mboni Ojike of Nigeria for a hearing. 'There is No

New Deal for the Black Man in San Francisco', he desperately screamed to the deaf audience of the victorious Allies through the magazine *West Africa* in London, and in newspapers in the United States.[39]

Nevertheless, these Pan Africanists undertook a series of Pan African conferences and meetings in Paris (1919), Brussels (1921), and London (1923), culminating in the Fifth Pan African Congress in Manchester in 1945. The Africans argued for their own presence and relevance to the West during these inter-war years. They insisted that they had a voice and that they spoke on behalf of those who were unable to speak or who had not spoken. *The African Voice* has been a major concern of African historiography. T. O. Ranger, among others, has continued to popularize this theme.[40] The silencing of that African voice in Germany under the Weimar Republic and the Third Reich explains in part why the strategy has such a contemporary resonance.

Bayume's generation were also interested in the world of learning and the mastery of the Western world, and of Western culture as a means of articulating this African Voice in the metropoles: Jomo Kenyatta in London, Denmark and Moscow, Nnamdi Azikiwe and Kwame Nkrumah in the United States, Leopold Sedar Senghor in Paris alongside Jean-Price Mars and Aimé Césaire, and Bayume in Germany . Like Kenyatta, he married a white woman and had a family, and obtained a job teaching African languages at Humboldt University.

Meanwhile, there were other cultural debates going on in Africa. The British in Tanganyika were involved in the 'Invention of Tradition' of African governance they called Indirect Rule. African historiography has been enriched by Hobsbawn and Ranger's *The Invention of Tradition*,[41] because it has enabled the historians to effectively interrogate the colonial anthropologist's construction of timeless and stagnant African tribes. The British Governor Sir Donald Cameron, having been a disciple of Lord Lugard in Nigeria, invented a whole series of tribes and traditional authorities for such people as the Wagogo, the Bondei, the Wanyakyusa and the Wahehe in the 1920s. The invention of tribes, cultures and native administrations and court systems is familiar terrain both with regard to earlier historiographies of Tanganyika in the 1960s[42] through the 1970s[43] and into the 1990s.[44] This is a crucial fulcrum for understanding how modern Tanganyika came into existence.

The Productions of Knowledge

However, colonial subjects were not involved in the imagining and designing of the colonial state. Bayume was involved in the world of work and the world of survival in a foreign land, as well as in the project currently in vogue as the translation of cultures, specifically the translation of Africa to the Germans. As an instructor in the Kiswahili language, he would be called upon both formally and informally to explain Africa to German society, to the kind of German society he lived in and married into, the details about which remain unknown. His own translation of

African cultures to the Germans was, as a matter of course, contingent on what the Germans wanted to hear.

Certain comparisons become germane at this conjuncture. Kenyatta and Bayume shared many characteristics at this time. They were language instructors, in Kikuyu and Kiswahili respectively, at leading institutions of higher learning in the west – London and Humbolt universities. Both of them were adult students. In the case of Kenyatta, it is known that Malinowski preferred adult students in his classes because they served both as informants and interlocutors in class.[45] Both of them worked under the leading Africanists of the day, Kenyatta for Bronsilaw Malinowski and Bayume for Dietrich Westermann. In terms of intellectual elite aspirations – association with expertise, participation at seminars in the production of knowledge about Africa at the metropolitan centers, and patronage – Bayume and Kenyatta could not have been better placed. But here is the catch: *whose knowledge* were Kenyatta and Bayume propagating? Who was their audience? Between the two students and their renowned patrons, who was the authority on Kikuyu culture and Swahili orthography when it came to relevant knowledge and scholarship about Africa in the West? The *Encyclopedia Britannica* entry on Malinowski mentions Kenyatta as his student.

Malinowski, Bronislaw (Kasper).
Malinowski was active in sponsoring studies of social and cultural change and participated vigorously in educational programs for administrators, missionaries and social workers. In the 1930s he became much interested in Africa; was closely associated with the International African Institute; visited students working among Bemba, Swazi and other tribes in eastern and southern Africa; and wrote the introduction to Jomo Kenyatta's *Facing Mount Kenya* (1938), prepared as a diploma thesis under his supervision.[46]

The entry does not mention that Malinowski's fieldwork on the Kikuyu amounted to a total of six weeks during a flying visit to Southern Africa. So on what authority was he writing the preface to Kenyatta's book? The entry for Westermann mentions that he extended the work of Meinhoff and re-classified the Nilotic and Bantu languages, but is silent about Bayume.

In spite of the silences about their authority in the seminars and outside, one must think of the two men Bayume and Kenyatta as spokesmen, another familiar refrain in Tanzanian historiography. It is assumed that Bayume had occasion to speak to various informal audiences in Germany. Kenyatta certainly did. He traveled often, and spoke much about his people, the Kikuyu, and their stolen lands. One of his period pieces is *My People the Kikuyu and the Life of Chief Wangombe*.[47] He married Dinah Stock, an English woman, and had a son, Peter Magana, named after Kenyatta's grandfather, Kungu wa Magana, a witchdoctor from whom Kenyatta learnt much of the occult sciences including witchcraft. Magana was to provide a link between the two branches of Kenyatta's progeny. In the 1960s he graduated from Cambridge University and later worked for the British Broadcasting Corporation. On the eve of his death, Kenyatta summoned Magana home, together with his mother Dinah, his English wife and his baby son for a final family reunion. Over three generations of the Muigai family are represented in the existing family portrait, both English and Kikuyu. In the case of Bayume it is not known what happened to his families in Tanga and in Berlin.

Restoring the Silenced Voices: Bayume in African Historiography

Arthur Koestler's book, *Darkness at Noon*,[48] is an apt metaphor for Bayume's last days on earth. He lost his German citizenship because of his race. Neither Westermann nor the university bothered to find out what was happening to him. The darkness at noon happened at a time when his life might have taken an absolutely different trajectory, had he been elsewhere other than at Humboldt University, abandoned by his erstwhile mentor Dietrich Westermann and the faculty as a whole. Had he been in London or in Paris, his life-course would have taken a different turn. For this was a season when African intellectuals in those two places were really coming into their own, writing poems on *Negritude* as did Aimé Césaire, Jean-Price Mars, Jacques Rabemananjara and Leopold Sedar Senghor, or authoring *Facing Mount Kenya*, as did Jomo Kenyatta[49] or *The Black Jacobins*, as did C. R. L. James.[50]

Paradoxically they were coming into their own at the very moment of Fascist Italy's invasion and occupation of Abyssinia between 1935 and 1941. In his autobiography, *Ghana* (1957), Kwame Nkrumah, later Ghana's first president, recalls that when, as a graduate student at Lincoln University in the United States he heard the news that the Italians had invaded Abyssinia he felt that all the White world had personally assaulted *him*. Nkrumah could not comprehend how the only independent African kingdom could be so blatantly invaded 'to avenge the defeat of Adowa' way back in 1896.[51] Jomo Kenyatta, George Padmore and T. Ras Makonnen formed the International League for the Defence of Ethiopia in London.[52] Over in the US African-Americans held protest rallies in Harlem, collected funds, and volunteered and served in the Ethiopian resistance.[53] When the Emperor Haile Selassie I arrived at London's Paddington railway station to begin his exile, Kenyatta broke through the cordon and embraced him, man to man. Neither of them forgot that moment of Pan African bonding.

This world was shut off from Bayume by that time. Eventually he disappeared into the gulag. The gulag is an important metaphor. In the closing pages of one of Alexander Solzhenitzyn's novels, a protagonist asks the question: 'What happened to the others?' 'They all disappeared into the gulag', ends the story. So did Mohammed Hussein Bayume. But the survivors of the colonial experience can excavate yet again the landscape of memory to which Mohammed Hussein Bayume belonged.

His life-course can be restored into the history of the Pangani valley and the Mrima coast in his homeland. It can also be written back into the history of resistance and collaboration in Tanganyika, alongside those who collaborated with the Germans and later with the British: Mzee Paulo Njau, the artist Elimo Njau's father, up in Kilimanjaro, and Mzee Mathais Mnyampala among the Gogo, who worked as a tax collector for the colonial regime while developing the perspectives that would later become part of nationalist discourse. It can be rewritten as part of the generation of 'Modern Tanzanians' during the 'Age of Improvement and Differentiation' spearheaded by the 'New Men'. It is part of the African Diaspora in Europe. It is an important exemplar of the trope of the 'Unknown African', alongside Mokgatle and Zula from South Africa. It is also a narrative of the victims of Nazism, colonialism and racism. In Western historiography Bayume's life can be seen through the lenses of freedom and its opposite, slavery, as the sociologist Orlando Patterson has been wont to do. Were he to return, he would write of himself, as Olaudah Equiano anticipated in his own autobiography in 1791, as Mohammed Hussein Bayume, THE AFRICAN.

Notes

1. For Bayume's biography see Jan-Georg Deutsch, 'Bayume Mohammed Hussein', Notes to the author, 22 May 1999.
2. *The Seed Is Mine: The Life of Kas Maine, a South African Sharecropper 1894–1985* (New York: Hill & Wang, Oxford: James Currey and Cape Town: David Philip, 1996), p. 1
3. Eric Wolf, *Europe and the People Without History* (Berkeley, CA: University of California Press, 1982).
4. N. Makgatle, *The Autobiography of An Unknown South African* (Berkeley, CA: University of California Press, 1971).
5. G. Arrighi, *The Political Economy of Rhodesia* (The Hague: Mouton, 1967); E. S. Atieno Odhiambo, 'The Rise and Fall of the Kenya Peasant, 1888–1922', *East Africa Journal*, 5, 2 (1972), pp. 5–11; Colin Bundy, *The Rise and Fall of the South African Peasantry* (Berkeley, CA: University of California Press, 1979).
6. Steven Feierman, *Peasant Intellectuals* (Madison, WI: University of Wisconsin Press, 1990); T. Kanogo, *Squatters and the Roots of Mau Mau* (London: James Currey, 1987); John Iliffe, *The African Poor: A History* (Cambridge: Cambridge University Press, 1987); Luise White, *The Comforts of Home* (Chicago: University of Chicago Press, 1990); and Elias Mandala, *Work and Control in a Peasant Economy* (Madison, WI: University of Wisconsin Press, 1990).
7. Luise White, *Speaking With Vampires: Technology and Rumor in East and Central Africa* (Berkeley, CA: University of California Press, 2000).
8. D. W. Cohen and E. S. Atieno Odhiambo, *Burying SM: The Politics of Knowledge and the Sociology of Power in Africa* (Portsmouth, NH: Heinemann, London: James Currey and Nairobi: EAEP, 1992), p. 20.
9. B. A. Ogot, 'The Reintroduction of the African Man into the World,' *East Africa Journal*, 4, 2 (Dec.1967), pp. 31–6.
10. I. N. Kimambo, *A Political History of the Pare of Tanzania* (Nairobi: East African Publishing House, 1969); and B. Bravman (eds), *Making Ethnic Ways* (Oxford: James Currey, 1998).
11. I. N. Kimambo and A. Temu (eds), *A History of Tanzania* (Nairobi: East African Publishing House, 1972); and John Iliffe, *A Modern History of Tanganyika* (Cambridge: Cambridge University Press. 1979).
12. Thomas L. Hodgkin, *Nationalism in Colonial Africa* (London: Muller, 1956).
13. James S. Coleman, *Nigeria: Background to Nationalism* (Berkeley, CA: University of California Press, 1958).

14. T. O. Ranger, 'Connections between Primary Resistance and Mass Nationalism in East and Central Africa,' *Journal of African History*, ix, 3 (1968) pp. 437–53 and *Journal of African History*, xii, 4 (1968), pp. 631–41.
15. Trans. Constance Farrington (New York : Grove Press, 1963).
16. Edward I. Steinhart, *Conflict and Collaboration : The Kingdoms of Western Uganda, 1890–1907* (Princeton, NJ: Princeton University Press, 1977).
17. Iliffe, *Modern History*.
18. Hemedi bin Abdallah bin Said bin Adballah bin Masudi el Buhriy, *Utenzi wa vita vya Wadachi kutamalaki Mrima, 1307 A. H.* 'The German conquest of the Swahili coast, 1891 AD', with translation and notes by J. W. T. Allen, 2nd edn (Dar es Salaam: East African Literature Bureau, 1960).
19. Abdul Karim bin Jamaliddini, *Utenzi wa Vita vya Maji Maji*. trans. W. H. Whiteley, Supplement to *Journal of the East African Swahili Committee*, 27 (1957).
20. E. S. Atieno Odhiambo, *The Paradox of Collaboration* (Nairobi: East African Literature Bureau, 1974).
21. T. O. Ranger, 'The Movement of Ideas, 1850–1939', in Kimambo and Temu, *History of Tanzania*, pp. 161–88; and E. S. Atieno Odhiambo, 'The Movement of Ideas', in B. A. Ogot (ed.), *Hadith 6: History and Social Change in East Africa* (Nairobi: East African Literature Bureau, 1976), pp. 165–85.
22. Sulemani bin Mwenye Chande 'Safari Yangu ya Bara Africa', collected by Carl Velten, in L. Harries, *Swahili Prose Texts* (London: Oxford University Press, 1965 [1896]), pp. 92–121; and Salim bin Abubakari, *Safari Yangu Bara Urusi na ya Siberia*, collected by Carl Velten, in *Swahili Prose Texts* (orig. 1896), pp. 122–50.
23. J. Willis, *Mombasa, the Swahili and the Making of the Mijikenda* (Oxford: Clarendon Press, 1993); and J. Glassman, *Feasts and Riot: Revelry, Rebellion, and Popular Consciousness on the Swahili Coast, 1856–1888* (Portsmouth, NH: Heinemann, 1995).
24. E. S. Atieno Odhiambo, 'From Warriors to Jonanga: The Struggle Over Nakedness in Western Kenya, 1900-1945', in Werner Graebner (ed.), *Sokomoko: Popular Culture in East Africa* (Atlanta, GA: Editions Rodopi, 1992), pp. 11–26.
25. Jean Comaroff and John Comaroff, *Of Revelation and Revolution*, vol. I and vol. 2 (Chicago: University of Chicago Press, 1991 and 1997).
26. *Ibid.*; and Paul S. Landau, *The Realm of the Word: Language, Gender, and Christianity in a Southern African Kingdom* (Portsmouth, NH: Heinemann, 1995).
27. P. A. Indaru, *Man With a Lion Heart: Biography of Canon Ezekiel Apindi* (Achimota, Ghana: African Christian Press, 1974).
28. W. Arens and Ivan Karp (eds), *Creativity of Power: Cosmology and Action in African Societies* (Washington, DC: Smithsonian Institution Press, 1989).
29. Abubakari, *Safari Yangu*, in Velten, *Swahili Prose Texts*, pp. 122–50.
30. Chande, *Safari Yangu*, in Velten, *Swahili Prose Texts*, pp. 99–121.
31. Tippu Tip, *Maisha Ya Hamed bin Muhammed El Murjebi, Yaani Tippu Tip, Kwa Maneno Yake Mwenyewe* (Kampala: East African Literature Bureau, 1974).
32. Mtoro bin Mwinyi Bakari, *The Customs of the Swahili People: The Desturi Za Waswahili of Mtoro Bin Mwinyi Bakari and Other Swahili Persons*, ed. and trans. J.W.T. Allen (Berkeley, CA: University of California Press, 1981).
33. John Iliffe, 'The Age of Improvement and Differentiation (1907–45)', in Kimambo and Temu (eds), *History of Tanzania*, pp. 123–60.
34. Mahmood Mamdani, *Citizen and Subject: Contemporary Africa and the Legacy of Late Colonialism* (Princeton, NJ: Princeton University Press, Kampala: Fountain, Cape Town: David Philip and Oxford: James Currey, 1996).
35. Mohammed Said, *The Life and Times of Abdulwahid Sykes* (London: Minerva Press, 1998).
36. John Iliffe (ed.), *Modern Tanzanians: A Volume of Biographies* (Dar es Salaam; East African Publishing House, 1973).
37. Mathais Mnyampala, *Mathias E. Mnyampala's The Gogo: History, Customs and Traditions*, trans. Gregory H. Maddox (New York: M. E. Sharpe, 1995); Gregory H. Maddox, 'Tribal Histories and the Meta-Narrative of Nationalism: Some Examples from Eastern Africa,' *Tanzania Zamani* , III, 1 (1997), pp.1–15 and 'Christianity and Cigogo: Father

Stephen Mlundi', in Thomas Spear and I. N. Kimambo (eds), *East African Expressions of Christianity* (Oxford: James Currey, 1999), pp. 150–66.

38. Justin Lemenye, *Maisha ya Ole Kivasis, yaani Justin Lemenye* (Nairobi: East African Literature Bureau, 1956).

39. Marika Sherwood, ' "There Is No New Deal For The Black Man in San Francisco": African Attempts To Influence The Founding Conference of the United Nations, July–October 1945,' *The International Journal of African Historical Studies* 29, 1 (1996), pp.71–94.

40. T. O. Ranger, *Are We Not Also Men? The Samkange Family and African Politics in Zimbabwe* (London: James Currey and Portsmouth, NH: Heinemann, 1995) and *The African Voice* (London: Heinemann, 1970).

41. Eric Hobsbawm and Terence Ranger (eds), *The Invention of Tradition* (Cambridge: Cambridge University Press, 1983).

42. Ralph Austen, *Northwest Tanzania Under German and British Rule* (New Haven, CT: Yale University Press, 1968).

43. Iliffe, *Modern History*.

44. J. Willis 'The Makings of a Tribe: Bondei Identities and Histories,' *The Journal of African History* 33, 2 (1992), pp. 191–208; I. N. Kimambo, *Penetration and Protest in Tanzania: The Impact of the World Economy on the Pare, 1860–1960* (London: James Currey, 1991); and Feierman, *Peasant Intellectuals*.

45. A. Kuper, *Among the Anthropologists* (London: Athlone Press, 1999).

46. 15th edn (Chicago: Encyclopedia Britannica, 1995).

47. Jomo Kenyatta, *My People of Kikuyu and the Life of Chief Wangombe* (Nairobi: Oxford University Press, 1966).

48. Arthur Koestler, *Darkness at Noon*, trans. Daphne Hardy (New York: Modern Library, 1941).

49. Jomo Kenyatta, *Facing Mount Kenya: The Tribal Life of the Gikuyu* (London: Secker and Warburg, 1948).

50. C. L. R. James, *The Black Jacobins; Toussaint l'Ouverture and the San Domingo Revolution*, 2d edn, rev. (New York: Vintage Books, 1963).

51. Kwame Nkrumah, *Ghana: The Autobiography of Kwame Nkrumah* (New York: Nelson, 1957).

52. T. Ras Makonnen, *Pan Africanism from Within* (Nairobi: Oxford University Press, 1971).

53. J. E. Harris, *African-American Reaction to War in Ethiopia, 1936–1941* (Baton Rouge, LA: Louisiana State University Press, 1994).

Nine

~~~~~~

Some Complexities of Family & State in Colonial Njombe

JAMES L. GIBLIN

An Argument about Family and Nation

This essay explores the space between ideological representations of family and the experience of living in families. To do so, it draws upon material from Bena-speaking communities of Njombe District and adjacent areas of southern Tanzania. Much talk about family tends to be normative. It dwells on what people take to be the normal state of affairs, the way things ought to be. It suggests that there is a normative form of descent, for example, which in the case of the Bena is patrilineal. It tends also to suggest that authority is normally exercised by older males within clans. The normal condition of women and younger men, this talk suggests, is to live under the authority of older males in their own or their husbands' clans.

Talk of this sort which emphasizes normative tradition has exerted a strong influence on historians and anthropologists in Africa. It has contributed to the great confidence which scholars have shown in classifying African societies as matrilineal or patrilineal. To the extent that such classification simplifies deeper complexity, it might be said to have contributed to creating an excessively simplistic discourse about the African family. For, obscured by the talk of norm-governed family relations, is another sphere in which people create and experience their own family relations in their day-to-day lives. Whereas normative talk of family stresses rules, particularly rules of descent, and individual adherence to them, the sphere of daily family existence involves contingency and negotiation by individuals. Individuals can be said to negotiate their day-to-day family lives in two senses. They negotiate in the sense that the terrain of relationships which they traverse in their family life is dangerously potholed. For while some family members are benign and supportive, others may be neglectful or exploitive. They also negotiate with other members of their families to reach understandings about the nature and extent of the obligations involved in their relationships. By comparison with normative family talk, which provides a way of generalizing and theorizing about relations of kinship, the sphere of family interaction is dominated by the particularities of one-to-one relationships, contingent actions and negotiated practices. For this reason, it is less easily accessible to scholars.

African political authority has probably long sought to control and exploit the legitimizing potential of normative talk about family. The political importance of such talk became particularly acute, however, under twentieth-century colonialism. Faced with the problem of administering immense territories with small numbers of European personnel, colonial governments in Tanganyika and elsewhere resorted to creating hierarchies of chiefs who would serve the state as administrators and tax collectors in rural regions. As appointees of the colonial state, these chiefs often had scant legitimacy in the eyes of their subjects. Hence both chiefs and their European superiors cast about for sources of legitimization. They came to rely heavily upon representations of chiefly authority as an extension or elaboration of the authority normally exercised by senior men over their families.

Scholarly views of African family which are based primarily on normative talk might be expected to lead to the conclusion that family and kinship provided a highly effective source of legitimization. If you believe that family life was characterized primarily by compliance with the rules and strictures emphasized by this talk of norms, you would also expect that a chief who represented his relations with subjects as kinship would readily obtain the submission of his subjects. If you were to find that patriarchal authority was unchallengeable, rules of descent and conceptions of obligation immutable, and adherence to them rigid, you would likely assume that any chief who could represent his power as the extension of kinship would be little troubled by dissent.

This chapter takes a very different position. It argues that scholarly views often overlook the disjuncture between, on the one hand, the ideological view of family relations expressed in talk of norms and, on the other hand, the experience of individual negotiation through daily family life. Furthermore, it suggests that this disjuncture was the fatal weakness in attempts to legitimize chiefly rule by making it appear as an extension of kinship. This weakness helps to explain why the chiefs' elaborate efforts to develop kinship-based forms of legitimization collapsed swiftly when they were challenged by nationalist activists in the 1950s. It also explains why nationalists were able to turn the chiefs' talk of family-based legitimacy back against them.

Bena villagers of the colonial period were surrounded by talk which represented chiefs as the most powerful of their fathers. This form of representation described the chiefs as standing at the apex of a hierarchy of clans, by virtue of the fact that they headed the most senior or most politically important clans. I suggest, however, that when it reached the ears of most commoners, such talk had a distinctly unauthentic ring. It did not seem authentic because the normative view of family on which it was founded did not reflect their own experience. Talk which depicted the Bena as living in a hierarchy of strictly patrilineal clans did not reflect the reality of men and women who constantly struggled to assemble from both their matrilineal as well as patrilineal relationships the groups of kin which were their family. The very experience of daily living in family undermined the chiefs' efforts to win legitimacy through talk about family and kinship, for it made such talk appear as artifice and invention. I think that this is one of the reasons why the experience of family life predisposed commoners to listen attentively when, in the late 1950s, nationalist activists began to articulate a subversive interpretation of kinship in the regime of the chiefs.

I also think that there was a second reason why daily family life predisposed many commoners to be open-minded and willing to listen to TANU activists. The chiefs' position was never hegemonic. Instead, it co-existed alongside alternative ways of talking about family relations. Unlike the normative talk of the chiefs, however, these alternative forms of talk about family grew out of lived experience of family. This chapter discusses one of these alternative discourses of family – talk about Christian improvement. Many Christians believed that their faith improved marital relations by reducing polygyny and increasing individual choice of spouses. In emphasizing individual choice it reflected the lived experience of individual negotiation within family. In another sense, however, this discourse was just as ideological as the normative talk of the chiefs. For just as the chiefs created conceptions of family which bore little relation to the lived reality of family, so too the form of change which was regarded as the marker of Christian improvement – decline in polygyny – probably did not occur in the colonial period.

Family in the Ethnography of the Wabena

Evidence from colonial Njombe and adjacent areas includes both ideological representations of family and descriptions of the negotiated experience of life in family. The form of ideological representation which was most important in efforts to legitimize the rule of colonial chiefs was stories of patrilineal clans. Whereas these stories took collective agents – the clans – as their subjects, descriptions of family life are found in narratives whose subjects are individuals living in groups. These include both stories which the elderly of Njombe tell about themselves, their parents and grandparents, and also in genealogies. The life histories of individual men and women very often describe their struggles to assemble around them the groups of kin which we would call their families. More surprisingly, genealogies are also individual-centered. We often think that genealogies are about groups, and that their function is to enumerate the members of a descent group, but for Njombe's elderly genealogies were about individuals. They explained an individual's relationships with an array of kin who were drawn together as much by chance, proximity, common interests and routine as by descent.[1]

Life histories and genealogies are expressions of the individual-centered discourse about family which was dominant in daily life. The discourse which dominated in political life, however, spoke of family as enduring corporate groups sharing collective interests and performing collective action. This public discourse supported the political agenda of the chiefs, who worked with British officials to construct a political order dominated by a handful of ruling clans. In their effort to make clan identity the basis of political organization, they composed histories of their clans and united behind clan identities in competition for chiefly offices.

Thus different ways of speaking about kinship co-existed. The tendency to speak of corporate clans was more common in the virtually all-male world of Native Authority politics. The tendency to speak of family-building individuals was more common among the subjects of chiefs and in social settings, such as homes, where women had influence. The former tendency spoke about hierarchy, power and subordination, the latter about individual initiative outside the sphere of chiefly politics. These forms of talk about family were perpetuated by political authority and daily social life. Chiefly rule reinforced the tendency to think of family as corporate clans. Life within households and circles of kin reinforced the tendency to think of family as groups constantly created and transformed by individuals. Thus in speaking of co-existing discourses, we are describing not only speech and thought, but also action, habit and daily social interaction which continually subverted colonial ideology. For while colonial authority emphasized ascribed, collective identities in patrilineal clans, in daily life individuals shaped self-identity by creating inclusive families of both matrilineal and patrilineal kin.

Signs of these different discourses and the disjuncture between ideological representation and lived experience are found in the major works of colonial anthropology on Bena-Hehe culture. (Although this chapter concentrates on the Bena communities of Njombe, the Hehe communities of nearby Iringa are virtually indistinguishable, both linguistically and culturally, from the Bena.) Two important studies, one on the Bena communities of Ulanga, the other on the Hehe of Iringa, were conducted in the early 1930s. Both studies found a particularly prominent disjuncture in the difference between talk about clans and their role in social action. Both studies found that, while clans were much talked about, clan members did not seem to act collectively. The Hehe study was conducted by Gordon Brown, an anthropologist, and Bruce Hutt, a district officer. They concluded that the much talked-about 'clan', which they defined as a group comprising 'all people counting direct patrilineal descent from some common male ancestor,' was neither 'a functional unit,' nor 'a unit of great social significance'.[2]

A.T. and G.M. Culwick came to a similar conclusion about Bena-speaking communities in the Kilombero River valley, where A.T. Culwick served as a district officer. 'Since the clan,' they wrote, 'is normally the key-stone of Bantu social organization, the writers naturally expected to find it occupying that position in Ubena of the Rivers, and spent a considerable time hunting about for the usual manifestations of the clan system.' They found, however, that,

> the family tree which usually provides the fundamental data on which clanship is based had gone... It is very common to find men and women who have no idea to what clan they belong... with the exception of members of the leading families of the more important clans, it is unusual for an Mbena to have any accurate knowledge of his antecedents, and in many cases it is not the father's line or clan which is remembered at all.[3]

We must consider very carefully the exception which the Culwicks made for 'leading families'. This was a critically important observation. It reveals that there was disjuncture between the manner in which Bena chiefs spoke about family, and the manner in which commoners experienced family.

The Culwicks thought that patrilineal clan identities had formerly been important throughout Bena society, but were now disappearing among commoners. They survived, thought the Culwicks, primarily among the 'leading families' which had most to gain by retaining them. Yet, they probably misunderstood what was happening. For rather than struggling to preserve a dying knowledge of clans, the 'leading families' were probably discovering new reasons to insist upon an idealized vision of the past. They insisted that images of patrilineal, territorially discrete clans represented not only how the ancestors had lived, but how the Bena actually organized their families in the present. They would have been particularly intent on driving home this point in meetings with district officers such as A.T. Culwick.

In this way, Culwick heard from them talk about family which did not match his own observations of social routine. Culwick explained this divergence between chiefly talk and daily life by saying that a formerly clean-cut system of patrilineal descent was breaking down as the Bena assimilated matrilineal people. Yet, what was happening was almost the reverse. The change which so worried the Culwicks was not taking place among the commoners, and did not involve the disappearance of clan lore. Instead, the chiefs were talking more about hierarchies of patrilineal clans. They used this talk to influence Culwick and other district officers.

Culwick was too closely involved in the process of change to see it clearly, for the chiefs were responding to the very method of colonial administration, 'Indirect Rule', which Culwick and other district officers were charged with implementing. Indirect Rule required that district officials first identify the clans which had been dominant in precolonial society, then choose chiefs, subchiefs and village headmen from among them. It gave the chiefs enormous reason to persuade their district officers that their society had always been organized in a hierarchy of clearly defined clans. In this way, Indirect Rule opened up a gap between the talk of chiefs and the realities of family life.

While chiefs spoke of clans as being sharply bounded by patrilineal descent and arrayed in a hierarchy, different talk prevailed outside the sphere of chiefly politics. There, villagers spoke less about hierarchy and boundaries, and more about opportunities for forging relationships and widening social networks. At the center of this manner of speaking about family was not collective identity, but individuality exercised within social networks.

The Culwicks, who were perceptive observers and thorough anthropologists, heard this inclusive talk among commoners. Their anxiety about the decline of patrilineal tradition led them to call it a 'slack modern way of talking'.[4] To them it showed that the Bantu norm of patriliny had been corrupted by the assimilation of slaves and matrilineal newcomers.[5] While the Culwicks may have been mistaken about the origin of this style of speaking, they were nevertheless perceptive in seeing its ego-centeredness, or the way in which it situated individuals at the center of social networks. They themselves used this ego-centeredness in describing the 'characteristic group of Bena society.' As their point of reference they began with the male individual. His family, they wrote, included 'all his blood relatives, both maternal and paternal, his and their connections by marriage, those with whom he has sworn blood-brotherhood, and lastly any particular friends on whom he may rely for help in time of need, and who will similarly look to him for aid'.[6] Curiously, while the Culwicks preferred patriliny as a norm, when they wished to describe family life they turned to a more inclusive idiom.

The Culwicks were forced into this inclusive way of speaking by their realization that matrilineal relationships were always part of households and families, and that marriages were very often matrilocal.[7] In Uhehe, Brown and Hutt formed similar views. The 'closeness of the bond with the mother's family,' they wrote, 'is fully as intimate as that with the father's family.' A contemporary of both the Culwicks and Brown and Hutt, the educator W. Bryant Mumford, advanced a similar view about the circumstances of a married woman in Bena-Hehe culture. 'As a member of her own family,' he wrote,

> she has behind her the strength of the whole group of relatives through her father; it is their business to see that she is happy and properly treated and it is to them that she goes if she is in trouble or for illness or child-birth... she can, and does, hold property of all and any kind in her own right and takes her share in inheritance of her father's property.[8]

The Culwicks found a major difference between the chiefly discourse of patrilineal clans and the daily practice of family living among commoners. While the chiefly discourse generalized and theorized, the experience of constant negotiation through daily family life did not lend itself to generalization. This fact frustrated the Culwicks and led them to speak of it in a condescending manner. Despite their tone, however, their observation remains important. The Bena, they wrote, 'cannot visualize the system [of family and kinship] as a whole but are preoccupied with the peculiarities of particular cases. The changes and compromises are therefore the work of individuals who do not generalize and cannot apprehend the principles involved'.[9] Speaking elsewhere of the great diversity of conditions and circumstances encountered in marital and sexual relations, they elaborated on this point,

It is doubtless unnecessary to point out that the Wabena have no idea why these things are so and, moreover, that they think of all these diverse cases singly and independently, each in its immediate context and not grouped ... as a series of similar customs. The do not perceive that these examples have anything in common.

As for most aspects of their social life, continued the Culwicks, the Wabena, 'have never thought [them] out, analyzed, speculated or philosophized.'[10] It is not true, of course, that these Bena communities were incapable of generalization and classification. The Culwicks themselves qualified their point by saying that the 'only classification of custom the Wabena know is that which groups their practices round special events or occupations...'.[11] What frustrated the Culwicks is that they sought in vain for classification and systemization in a sphere of daily social practice where what counted was prudent and nimble judgment, discretion, and the ability to make fine judgments. This was no place to find rules, codification, classification and generalization.

Despite their skills as ethnographers, the Culwicks could not come to terms with the disjuncture between chiefly talk of norms and the daily social practices whose great diversity of circumstances and outcomes bewildered them. The divergence between normative talk and daily family living they explained by speaking of the degradation of patrilineal tradition and Bena inability to classify and analyze. Their inability to get beyond this position stemmed from their political program, which required that they uphold patrilineal tradition. As a district officer, A.T. Culwick's primary task was to establish a robust system of chiefly administration. As a source of legitimacy, Culwick and his chiefs depended on an idealized image of Bena society as a hierarchy of patrilineal clans at whose head stood the paramount chief. The importance of patrilineal tradition in the establishment of a chiefly regime can be illustrated by looking briefly at similar events in Njombe District.

A contemporary and fellow district officer of A.T. Culwick at Njombe, F.J. Lake, received his chance to establish a lasting chiefly regime when the paramount of the Ubena chiefdom died in 1931. Lake wished to place the paramountcy in the hands of what he believed to be the most influential and powerful clan in Ubena. He denied the claims of the deceased paramount's family, and handed the paramountcy to Pangamahuti Mbeyela, a member of a rival clan. He justified his action by comparing not the virtues of rival candidates, but rather the history and prospects of the rival clans. Whereas 'Kiswaga's ancestors were merely cultivators of the soil,' reported Lake, Pangamahuti's father had been 'the most powerful man in Ubena in his day.' Lake's choice of Pangamahuti established clan identity as the primary factor to be considered in the selection of paramounts.[12]

As paramount chief of Ubena, Pangamahuti consolidated the political dominance of his clan, the Mkongwa. They were not yet dominant in 1936, when a district officer reported that Pangamahuti exercised influence in only a small portion of Ubena. The 'Wabena do not look to him as paramount over their Sub-Chiefs', he stated.[13] Yet, Pangamahuti was busily establishing the primacy of his clan. Aside from appointing numerous members of the Mkongwa clan as village headmen, he oversaw the installation of a brother, Mtenzi, and a brother's son, Mtaki, as two of the five subchiefs of Ubena. By 1939, a district administrator recognized that Pangamahuti had 'consolidated his position to such an extent' that Mkongwa control of the paramountcy would henceforth be 'unassailable'.[14]

When Pangamahuti died in 1942, the Mkongwa officeholders united in support of his brother, Mtenzi. Their control of numerous Native Authority offices enabled them to give British officials the impression that 'support for Mtenzi was general whereas the support for [rival candidates] was local only'. Thus despite Mtenzi's involvement a few years earlier in a bribery scandal, the district officer did not hesitate in selecting him as paramount. The district officer cited the overriding importance of keeping the paramountcy under the control of a dominant clan. 'With the present choice,' he wrote, 'the chieftainship will and should become more or less crystallized in one family or the other, so as to avoid the recurring claims of rival candidates, with its consequent unsettlement of the tribe.'[15]

By 1949, when Joseph Mbeyela became paramount following the death of Mtenzi, administrators were unwilling to consider any candidates from outside the Mkongwa clan. They worried only about how to select a paramount chief among several candidates from within the clan. For by now the Mkongwa clan, having taken advantage of the opportunities for schooling provided to families of chiefs, included not only village headmen, but also an important subchief, Mtaki of Igominyi, several teachers, government employees and craftsmen, and the influential town headman at Njombe. Despite initial disagreement, when the administration made clear its preference for Joseph, the youthful, cautious and comparatively well educated son of Pangamahuti, the clan united behind him.[16] Clan identity was a crucial factor in the selection not only of paramounts, but also of subchiefs and village heads. When death vacated subchieftaincies, administrators insisted that village leaders and other senior male electors begin by voting not for individual candidates, but for the clan from which they preferred to see a successor chosen.[17]

An Alternative Representation of Family as the Site of Christian Improvement

We have now seen that the creation of the chiefly regime of Indirect Rule encouraged a particular representation of family. It encouraged chiefs to describe their society as a hierarchy of patrilineal clans dominated by senior males. Despite the fact that this vision was propagated by the most powerful political figures in rural Tanganyika during the 1930s – the chiefs and district officers – this view of family and kinship could not exclude alternative visions.

During this same period, as chiefs like Pangamahuti Mbeyela and district officers like Culwick and Lake were seeking to legitimize the new regime of chiefs, Christianity was spreading fast throughout Njombe. In this period much of southern Njombe became Catholic, while northern Njombe became predominantly Lutheran. Among young, first-generation Bena converts there prevailed a spirit of devout religiosity.[18] In the neighborhoods around the important Lutheran mission of Ilembula, for example, the very landscape became biblical as villages adopted names such as Kanani [Canaan] and Korinto [Corinth]. Villagers learned about Christianity at so-called 'bush' schools run by Bena evangelists. The lives of Christian youths revolved around a weekly schedule of devotion and instruction.[19] In those years, said one elder, 'Christianity was very strict, it really had a hold [on us]... There was much more devotion at that time than there is now. All night long we would sing, at weddings we sang and sang. If I'd died in those days, even I would have gone to Heaven. I was pleasing to Almighty God because we were real Christians then.'[20]

Among these young Christians, new ideas of marriage and family developed. They began to envision themselves as a vanguard bringing about social improvement by abandoning 'pagan' practices in favor of more enlightened Christian ways. In particular, they sought to replace the arrangement of marriages among parents with voluntary agreements between spouses, and to substitute church weddings presided over by clerics for the 'pagan' wedding celebrations which had featured night-long dancing and drinking along with sexual instruction for the bridal couple. The major change associated with Christian improvement, however, was renunciation of polygyny and commitment to monogamy. One woman whose own marital experience typified this change was Tulalumba Kawogo of Palangawanu, one of the villages near Ilembula where Lutheran devotion spread fast in the 1930s. When she first married in the late 1920s, she said, she learned that she had been found a husband only when 'I saw a hoe inside the house.'[21]

> They simply said, 'Some man is looking for you.' They would call you, and you'd come in and be told, 'A certain man is looking for you, are you willing?' If you were willing you'd say, 'Yes,' and you'd take the hoe. If you weren't willing you'd say, 'No, no, I don't like him.' There was no agreeing between the two of you, he'd just be brought there... That's how it was in the past, we didn't come to an agreement between ourselves.

At that time, she said, villagers were still unfamiliar with church weddings. A wedding itself was a simple affair: 'The parents would make *pombe* [beer], then the relatives would come get you.' Kawogo's first wedding was undoubtedly quite similar to those described by one of her neighbors. The wedding day was spent drinking *pombe*, he said, and the evening devoted to instructing the couple about married life:

> A lot of instruction was given ... the girl's grandmother would come, and the boy's grandmother would come, so that the marriage could be completed that night... In the morning they would have questions and

would see how things were ... to see whether the boy was mature enough to marry.

After the death of her first husband, Kawogo was married for a second time. By now it was the late 1930s, and the spirit of Christian improvement had taken hold among Palangawanu's young. 'We decided for ourselves to be Christians', said Kawogo. 'There were many of us who decided to do this because [Christianity] was attractive'. Thus her second marriage occurred in this atmosphere of Christian devotion. Rather than allowing marriage to be arranged by parents, a procedure which Christians were now beginning to regard as 'pagan,' Kawogo's new husband,

> came from Wanging'ombe with a letter [of introduction] and the purpose of finding a wife, and they introduced me to him. We agreed between ourselves [to marry], and we had a wedding, for by this time we all followed the Word of God. There were none of the *maungo* [the grandmothers' instruction in sexuality], *ngadule* [a dance done throughout the night by unmarried girls], or *mbeneha*... All these things were bad... The meaning of *mbeneha* is instruction when you are pregnant... They would also instruct you when you had given birth to a boy... and you'd have your hair cut after giving birth... before hearing the Word of God we were really sunk in these bad things.

These young Christians of the 1930s were Njombe's elderly in the 1990s. Looking back in old age, they believed that they had witnessed great change in marriage. They believed that not only had the young gained greater choice of spouses, but that during their lifetimes monogamy had become the predominant form of marriage. Certainly this change was the goal of Lutheran missionaries. From the moment of their arrival in Njombe in 1898, Lutheran evangelists of the Berlin Missionary Society labored to eradicate marriage to multiple wives, which they regarded as the primary obstacle to Christianization among the Bena. They denied polygynists the right to live on their land.[22] The missionaries reported great resistance to their attempts to end polygyny, however, and frequently complained of backsliding Christians and catechumens who bowed to family pressures by taking second wives.[23]

Yet, it is not clear that the colonial generation actually experienced a marked decline in polygyny. As Table 9.1 indicates, several small-scale surveys showed that the proportion of married women in polygynous marriages varied during the 1930s between 26 and 60 per cent, and in the 1970s between 33 and 40 per cent. The proportion of married men who had multiple spouses ranged between 14 and 39 per cent in the 1930s, and remained in the range of 23 to 33 per cent in the 1970s.

Not only do ideas of Christian improvement appear to have brought about no more than a modest decline in polygyny, but they may have made less impact on the freedom to choose spouses than the colonial generation supposed. In the 1930s, women exercised choice and couples made their own matches, even outside the areas which witnessed a dramatic expansion of Christianity.[24] The colonial generation may have

Table 9.1 Marriages of Single and Multiple Wives

	Ulanga		Uhehe		Njombe District							
					Uwemba		Mdandu		Entire district			
	1930s		1933		1939		1939		1970		1977	
Married Men & Women:	M	W	M	W	M	W	M	W	M	W	M	W
Number in sample	10,784	12,617	3028	1881	455	607	249	386	217	278	214	–
Married women per married men		1.16		1.53		1.33		1.55		1.28		–
% in marriages of:												
1 wife	86	73.5	62	40	74	55	61	40				
2 wives	12	20.2	28	36	21	32	28	36	18	29	–	–
3 wives	1.5	3.9		7	14	4	9	6	11	4	10	–
4 or more wives	0.5	2.4	3	10	1	4	5	13	1	1	–	–
% in polygynous marriage	14	26.5	38	60	26	45	39	60	23	40	33	–

Sources: Ulanga data from A.T. and G.M. Culwick, 'A Study of Population in Ulanga, Tanganyika Territory', *The Sociological Review* 30 (1938), p. 377; Uhehe data from Brown and Hutt, *Anthropology in Action*, p. 107; Uwemba and Mdandu data from General Land Report, Njombe District, Southern Highland Province, Report Number I (April, 1939), Appendix A, pp. 3–4, TNA 28/19; Njombe District data from H. Järvinen, E. Bakke, C. Branner Jespersen and A.A. Moody, 'Southern Highlands Socio-Economic Study: Final Report' (Typescript: Mbeya, 1971), p. 30; Oddvar Jakobsen, 'Economic and Geographical Factors Influencing Child Malnutrition: A Study From the Southern Highlands, Tanzania', BRALUP Research Paper no. 52 (University of Dar es Salaam, Bureau of Resource Assessment and Land Use Planning, 1978), pp. 50 and 78.

exaggerated change in marriage because they spoke about the past with didactic purposes. Just as they had learned about marriage in prior generations from parents who wished to impart moral lessons, so too they told stories which, whether intended to stress improvement or degeneration, emphasized differences between past and present. One way of emphasizing difference was to present norms as the way things really were in the past.

The true impact of ideas of Christian improvement may not have been to change actions so much as to provide a new idiom in which men and women claimed personal autonomy. The ideas which they articulated in it, however, were not necessarily new. In using it to assert their right to choose spouses, for example, young women were preferably renewing a battle against parental authority fought in earlier generations. Similarly, the men and women who now took up this idiom to oppose polygyny were probably expressing older concerns. In precolonial generations, women had presumably weighed their reluctance to enter the households of co-wives against their duty to accept the wishes of parents. Men had weighed the burden of multiple wives against the urgings of parents who desired many grandchildren. Christian teaching offered a new language in which individuals could think about situations which had always posed moral and practical dilemmas.[25] Christianity provided an alternative field of moral concepts which helped men and women to articulate their preference for monogamy. Yet, while Christian improvement supported individual choice, it also imposed upon individuals extremely rigid injunctions against divorce. One elderly woman who had been treated brutally by a husband explained that, even for victims of spousal abuse, Christian marriage put divorce out of the question. 'If it had all happened these days,' she said of the abuse inflicted by her husband, 'I wouldn't have stood for it. But at that time we held firmly to the Christian laws of marriage... I was afraid to go to the government [for a divorce].'

Critiques of Ruling Clans and the Beginnings of Rural Nationalism

Whatever legitimacy the chiefs may have gained by representing themselves as the patriarchal heads of a hierarchy of clans dissipated quickly once they began to face the challenge of nationalism. TANU became active in Njombe in 1956, though the chiefs had begun to face the winds of change some years earlier. The weakening of their position began in the years after World War II, when a wave of European land alienation climaxed in the expropriation of a huge parcel in central Njombe District for a Colonial Development Co-operation wattle scheme. The government required that the chiefs throw their authority behind the forced removal of thousands of householders from their land. Many villagers bitterly resented the chiefs' role in forced resettlement. Moreover, progressive individuals with an eye on the future feared that land alienation would leave Njombe impoverished and its men without hope of finding any alternative to long-distance labor migration. The animosity created by the chiefs' collaboration with government in land alienation ensured that, after the government instituted a system of district and tribal councils in the early 1950s, a group of relatively well-educated and business-oriented young men would use these venues to make increasingly forceful criticisms of the chiefs.

Thus, even before branches of TANU began springing up, the chiefs felt themselves to be increasingly on the defensive. They reacted by trying to portray themselves as the senior fathers of the Bena tribe. They did this in numerous ways. In part, they asserted patriarchal authority by trying, though with virtually no success, to regulate a variety of domestic and marital matters. These included attempts to fix the manner and amount of bridewealth, to define the circumstances under which a woman had the right to marry, to determine guidelines for mediating conflicting claims of fathers and husbands to authority over women, and to regulate inheritance. Virtually all their attempts were unsuccessful. The role which the chiefs hoped to play in such matters was to codify and systemize rules and customs. But these were precisely the aspects of family life which resisted codification because they demanded discerning judgment of specific circumstances.

The chiefs also tried to shore up their position by greatly elaborating on the image of the Bena tribe as a hierarchy of clans at whose peak stood the chiefs themselves. They invoked both history and rituals of ancestor veneration in this attempt. As we have seen, the Mkongwa clan gained control of the paramountcy of Ubena in 1931, and over the next two decades captured a number of sub-chieftaincies and other positions. The Mkongwa clan embellished both theory and history to reinforce the idea that traditionally their society had been a hierarchy of ruling and commoner clans. Underpinning their theories was the belief that in the past, society had been composed of clans ruled by firm patriarchal authority. 'At that time', explained a son of Paramount Pangamahuti, alluding to the precolonial past,

> Each clan ['*ukoo*'] had its ruler... each person [speaking here exclusively of men] had his own homestead ['*kaya*']... Authority ['*utawala*'] meant that you were the leaders, and all others were under you.[26]

Their theories influenced British officials, including the District Commissioner who in 1949 described Bena society as a rigid hierarchy of clans:

> The Bena have always been ruled by autocratic *Watwa* [chiefs] belonging to a few traditional ruling families. The *Watwa* have the deciding vote in the choice of Jumbes, the Jumbes choose their own local unpaid headmen (*ruga ruga*) so the impulse of local rule runs from the top downwards.[27]

These theories generated at least two explanations of the process by which chiefly clans had achieved dominance. One theory held that a country's original clan deserved to rule. In the Upangwa chiefdom of southern Njombe, for example, chiefly theorists argued that theirs was the oldest Pangwa clan. 'From the beginning', wrote a son of the paramount of Upangwa,

> each country has found its customs, its roots – the young shoots of the country from which spring its lineages, customs and laws – in the tribe or its major clan ['*ukoo mkuu*']... All countries are rightfully held by those who have inherited this legacy from their grandfathers...[28]

'Eventually,' he continued, alluding to the institution of Indirect Rule in 1926, 'those who possessed these ancient rights were recognized.' In Ubena, chiefly theorists took a different approach. They held that the Mkongwa clan had become dominant by using force to impose unity. The Mkongwa chiefs added substance to such claims by tracing descent from a legendary leader of the past, Kahemele. They claimed that Kahemele fathered both their ancestor, Mbeyela Mkongwa, as well as the founder of a rival clan. Kahemele, they said, offered both sons the choice of a spear or an *ungo*, a tray for sifting flour. When Mbeyela Mkongwa chose the spear, Kahemele said, 'the holder of the spear will... rule'.[29]

Chiefly clans also sought legitimacy by asserting a leading role in rites of ancestor veneration [*matambiko*]. They did so, moreover, in a way which offered an implicit rebuttal to their role in land expropriation and forced resettlement. At two different sites, chiefs struggled during the 1950s to maintain control over the wooded sites where *matambiko* were performed. The ancestors venerated at these sites were not merely the ancestors of particular families, but were believed to have the power to bring rain and generally protect the welfare of communities across large areas.

One of these episodes involved the forest of Iditima in Lupembe, in the far east of Njombe District. When the government's Department of Forests decided to create a forest reserve at Iditima in the early 1950s, the sub-chief of Lupembe intervened aggressively. He had good reason to build an image of himself as the protector of the site where rituals which contributed to the welfare of his community took place. His own position was exceedingly shaky, for at least three reasons. First, he himself did not belong to a local family (indeed, his father had been installed as the chief of Lupembe by the colonial government). Second, he had been involved in the alienation of land to Europeans. And third, he faced the challenge of a group of educated, progressive and entrepreneurial young villagers – the products of Lupembe's mission school and growing coffee business. The chief argued that he and his clan would be more effective in preserving the forest than would the Forest Department, whose employees were notorious for their inefficiency and corruption. Despite his conservationist arguments, however, and after several years of controversy, the government eventually made Iditima a reserve.[30]

Although the chief of Lupembe failed to retain control of Iditima, the Paramount of Ubena, Joseph Mbeyela, successfully preserved a site of ancestor veneration at Nyumbanitu. Today, Nyumbanitu is a densely overgrown rectangle of a couple of acres. Neighbors say that it remains thick in trees and undergrowth because no one would risk the wrath of the ancestral spirits who inhabit these woods by cutting wood or collecting firewood. Nor would they dream of making a meal from its population of free-running chickens. Visitors frequently bring black sheep for sacrifice as part of the *matambiko* which implore the blessings of the ancestors. They come not merely from Ubena, but also Usangu and elsewhere in the Southern Highlands, for the spirits of Nyumbanitu are renowned across a large region.

The spirits of Nyumbanitu are now believed to be the ancestors of the Mkongwa clan of Paramount Mbeyela. Yet, both the origin of the grove and how it came to be associated with the Mkongwa clan are not entirely clear. The reputation of Nyumbanitu as a place of spiritual and historical importance probably owes less to the wooded grove than to caves located about a kilometer away. Presumably the name Nyumbanitu, or 'dark house', refers to the caves. Like the grove, the caves also witness ancestor veneration. The reputation which Nyumbanitu enjoys throughout the Southern Highlands as both a location of important *matambiko*, and as a point of dispersal from which various peoples scattered to settle in Usangu and elsewhere in the region, would seem more likely to have grown up around the unusual caves than around a commonplace grove.[31] This view seems all the more probable considering that the grove has not always been there. 'There was no forest there', said Joseph Mbeyela. 'But after people had lived there for a long time', he continued rather vaguely, 'as was often the case *matambiko* began to be performed there'. Thus the renown of the grove and its *matambiko* seems to have derived partly from its proximity to the caves of Nyumbanitu.

The association of the grove with the Mkongwa clan of the Bena paramounts is similarly tenuous. It is widely acknowledged that the family of Mbeyela Mkongwa, the grandfather of Joseph Mbeyela, neither buried their dead nor practised *matambiko* at Nyumbanitu. Even members of the Mkongwa clan such as Joseph Mbeyela say that the site was originally the veneration place of the ancestors of Kiswaga, the first Paramount of Ubena.[32] A son of Paramount Kiswaga claimed that the site initially became famous because it was associated with Paramount Kiswaga's father, who possessed a medicine which protected crops from locusts.[33] Apparently the grove at Nyumbanitu became associated with the Mkongwa ancestors after the paramountcy passed from Kiswaga to the son of Mbeyela Mkongwa in 1931. In linking their clan with a prestigious *tambiko* site known throughout Njombe and the Southern Highlands, the Mkongwa chiefs were, of course, elaborating their vision of clan hierarchy.

Perhaps the most striking aspect of the grove is the contrast which it makes with its surroundings. On one side the grove faces a motor road. On its other three sides, the wildly overgrown rectangle is surrounded by neatly cleared, precisely aligned rows of wattle belonging to the Tanganyika Wattle Company, the successor to the CDC. How the grove was spared, while all the surrounding land was planted in wattle, is the subject of many stories. These stories all say that Europeans attempted to clear the grove for wattle, only to abandon their efforts when they confronted mysterious forces more powerful than their bulldozers. Trees felled one day would be found standing the next, bulldozers stalled and could not be restarted, Europeans wandered into the grove and disappeared, never to be seen again.[34]

Yet, it would seem not unlikely, as some residents of Njombe suspect,[35] that more prosaic political considerations may have also played a part in the preservation of the sacred grove. 'I'm sure', said one of Njombe's most prominent political figures of the 1950s and 1960s, 'that the leaders conferred with the CDC so that [Nyumbanitu] wouldn't be destroyed. I think there was an agreement. It's not that the tractors were unable to clear the area.'[36] The eviction of villagers from the CDC land took place just as Joseph Mbeyela was taking office following the death of Paramount Mtenzi.

Initially, Nyumbanitu was a potential source of vulnerability for the new paramount. Descendants of the first paramount, Kiswaga, claimed that Ubena could not prosper so long as the paramount and leader of the Nyumbanitu *tambiko* were not members of their lineage.[37] Mbeyela needed to convert Nyumbanitu from a liability into a source of authority. As an educated Christian, he would not lead the *matambiko* personally, but he stood to gain prestige if he could show that he had saved the grove from the CDC bulldozers. Nyumbanitu also represented a political opportunity because it was very widely known. It offered the opportunity to create a symbol of Bena tribal identity by making Nyumbanitu a 'tribal' *tambiko* shrine recognized by all Wabena. Mbeyela welcomed such opportunities because he worried constantly about the feebleness of Bena tribal feeling.[38]

Government and the CDC shared Mbeyela's interest in bolstering tribal identity, because it was the primary source of legitimacy for the paramount on whom they relied to persuade thousands of villagers to vacate their homes and farms. For all these reasons, when one sees how the riotously overgrown grove remains surrounded by precisely aligned rows of neatly tended wattle, one cannot help but think that the government and the CDC perhaps spared the grove to reinforce Mbeyela's legitimacy. The CDC would not have been unhappy to contribute to the impression that the paramount commanded mysterious forces which saved the sacred grove.

The chiefs intended to bolster their own position by enlisting both history and the ancestors to show that they headed clans which had long been politically and ritually predominant. Nevertheless, the very clan identities which the chiefs tried to burnish became the target of their critics. Some critics began saying that Mkongwa control of multiple chiefly offices was clear evidence of their nepotism. Others blamed them for monopolizing all opportunities for schooling, saying that they made sure that only their fellow clan members would be granted places in schools.

One elderly man whose resentment of the chiefs led him into TANU, Reuben Mlenga, would recall that in the 1930s and 1940s, when he had been young, 'it was very difficult to go to school. It was very hard in the past. You know, the sub-chiefs didn't want the children of ordinary people. The only ones who went to school were children of chiefs, sub-chiefs and village headmen.'[39] Another veteran of pre-independence TANU organizing termed the chiefs 'great misers', because they hoarded all opportunities for schooling.[40] TANU critics focused in particular on the inefficiency and mismanagement which, they claimed, stemmed from the dominance of a single clan. They argued that a paramount such as Joseph Mbeyela would not dare discipline those of his subordinates who were his kin. For this reason, said the critics, corruption, malfeasance and laziness prevailed among sub-chiefs, village headmen and officials of local courts.

By the mid-1950s, some fearless villagers were willing to make such charges in the presence of Paramount Mbeyela. In 1955, for example, one commoner criticized to his face Mbeyela's choice of a relative as a village headman. 'He told the Paramount that he had no right to do this and was simply favoring his own children.'[41] Such open and direct criticism of the ruling clans was somewhat more common in the district and tribal councils where nationalists were gaining increasing influence. TANU activists blamed the ruling clans for denying positions to well qualified and educated individuals, protecting unqualified office-holders, preventing appeals against the decisions of chiefs' courts, and perpetuating inefficiency and corruption. 'The *majumbe* [village heads] who belong to the ruling clan do not satisfy their citizens', stated one TANU organizer. 'This is why citizens often say that the chiefs should not be chosen from the ruling clan so that their work can be performed in an energetic and beneficial manner.'[42] Officials who owed their office to nepotism were insufficiently educated and unable to understand matters brought before them, argued the Njombe branch of the TANU Youth League. In a submission to the District Commissioner in 1960, the TYL argued that because many members of the tribal and district councils had gained their seats by virtue of clan identity, they felt no accountability to the citizenry and made no effort to inform villagers of issues before the councils. In the view of the TYL, domination by chiefly clans excluded most citizens from any role in the councils' affairs.[43] On another occasion, a critic of the chiefs stated that, 'representatives failed to speak the truth in the [District] Council because of the kinship ties in the leadership ['*undugu katika utawala*']'.[44]

British officials eventually realized that Mkongwa identity had ceased to serve as a source of legitimacy. Following the retirement of Mtaki, the Mkongwa sub-chief of Igominyi, the British, who were anxious to deny TANU grounds for criticizing the colonial government, declared that his successor need not be an Mkongwa. Anyone, they declared, was entitled to stand as candidate before the tribal and district councils which would elect the new sub-chief.[45] Many people in Igominyi supported the candidacy of Edward Mwenda, who was educated and was not a Mkongwa. But, while the change in the British position signaled the declining effectiveness of clan identity as a source of popular legitimacy, the Mkongwa office holders remained a cohesive political force. Mkongwa chiefs tried to divide their opponents by choosing as their candidate a clan member named Benedict Mkongwa, who was both an educated employee of Njombe's government hospital and a member of TANU. At the decisive meeting of the District Council, the opponents of Benedict Mkongwa found that 'kinship [*undugu*]' remained 'the law in the Bena Tribal Council'. For while non-chiefly representatives from Igominyi argued that the people of Igominyi should be entitled to elect their own sub-chief – an argument which made Paramount Mbeyela 'exceedingly angry' – the chiefly majority on the council elected the Mkongwa candidate. The victory of the Mkongwa chiefs in this instance was pyrrhic. It cast the whole council system into disrepute, made the chiefs appear as enemies of democracy, and showed TANU to be the defenders of the democratic rights of commoners.

In the 1990s, when veterans of pre-independence TANU organizing reflected on their past, these conflicts and rhetoric remained very much on their minds. Speaking of the headman of his own village, who, like Paramount Mbeyela, was a member of the Mkongwa clan, Reuben Mlenga said that, in selecting officers, 'they followed the same clan as that of Mbeyela, that's how they chose someone to rule as a headman'. Listening to Mlenga was his brother, Eliasi, who now broke in to say, 'Yes, they traded offices back and forth to each other within the clan'. And Mlenga continued, 'They would insult us by saying, "you'll never get freedom, and as for chiefship, until the day you die you'll never be able to rule".' To which Eliasi added, 'They were very arrogant'.[46] In Mlenga's view, the chiefs were deeply committed to maintaining the dominance of their clan. Had the postcolonial government not intervened to abolish chiefship, he argued, they would have prevented all forms of democracy. 'They would have continued to keep the power to rule among themselves', he said. 'First of all, they didn't like the idea of rule by someone who did not belong to the clan of the chiefs. They didn't like it, it made them very angry, they detested it. When TANU came and changed the form of government, they hated it, hated it very much.'[47] And in his village, said Mlenga, when the government abolished chiefship after Independence, the villagers decided to get rid of their old headman, the member of the Mkongwa clan. 'So we chose someone', said Mlenga, 'who was not a member of the chiefs' clan [*ukoo wa kichifu*].[48]

Conclusion

When we look at family and kinship during the colonial period, we find hidden and perhaps unexpected complexity. Ethnographers of the colonial period found among chiefs a discourse which imagined society as a hierarchy of clans and stressed patriarchal authority. Chiefs, district officers and ethnographers all expected this discourse to provide an effective form of legitimization for the regime of chiefs which was created by the British policy of Indirect Rule in the 1920s and 1930s. Yet, it failed to do so. It failed because the daily experience of living in family continually exposed its artificiality. Experience made evident the dissonance between its images of neatly ordered hierarchy and unfailing compliance with patriarchal authority, on the one hand, and the contingent, negotiated quality of daily family life, on the other. Signs of this dissonance could be found even within the highly ideological tellings of clan history which the chiefs used to legitimize their position. The story of the Mkongwa clan explained how the clan had claimed political power, for example, by describing a rivalry between brothers which led to the division of a patrilineal clan. The chiefly telling of this story avoids discussion of this division, although the process which it describes is precisely the fissioning which resulted constantly from the everyday negotiation of family relationships.

Everyday experience of family living also generated forms of talk about family which stood as alternatives to the chiefly images of patriarchal clan hierarchy. One of those alternatives was a discourse of Christian improvement in marriage and family. Like the chiefly talk of clan hierarchy, talk of Christian improvement also became important in the 1930s. The discourse of Christian improvement was no less ideological than that of clan hierarchy. It departed from the reality of family life in assuming that Christianity brought at least two kinds of change – decline of polygyny and increased opportunity for individuals to choose their spouses. Yet, it is not clear that the colonial period witnessed either of these changes. Talk of Christian improvement was similar to that of clan hierarchy in that neither of them accurately reflected the lived experience of family. Instead, both were intended to serve ideological purposes. Those who talked of clan hierarchy often wished to legitimize the chiefs. Those who talked of Christian improvement had two purposes. The first was to articulate an aspiration for the individual autonomy that was needed if one were to negotiate the treacherous ground of kinship relations profitably. The second purpose of talk about Christian improvement was didactic. By creating a sharp contrast between the 'pagan' past and Christian present, it taught the lesson that to fail to adhere to Christian morality meant slipping back into a state of paganism.

While the representations of family found in talk of Christian improvement were no less ideological than those found in talk of clan hierarchy, the Christian language of family does show that alternatives to the elite language of authority and hierarchy existed. Many authors have suggested that chiefs held great power within colonial systems of Indirect Rule, at least during the period of high colonialism before the emergence of nationalism. They have suggested that chiefly power must have been awesome, because it combined the political authority emanating from their position in the colonial bureaucracy with the patriarchal authority stemming from the belief that chiefship was an extension of kinship. The material from Njombe, however, shows that chiefs never achieved either political or ideological hegemony. All their efforts in the 1940s and 1950s to retell history and assert control over relations with ancestors could not make their representation of kinship hegemonic. Indeed, when TANU organizers became active in Njombe in the 1950s, they directly attacked the concept that authority should be vested in particular clans. They did so because they recognized that, while clan identities could indeed unify chiefly office holders in defense of privilege, among common villagers ideas of clan hierarchy were foreign. Outside the tight circle of chiefs who controlled offices and opportunities for schooling, they failed to persuade anyone that the British-appointed chiefs possessed the right to rule.

Notes

1. This style of genealogy is described in W. Bryant Mumford, 'The Hehe-Bena-Sangu Peoples of East Africa', *American Anthropologist* 36 (1934), p. 209.
2. G. Gordon Brown and A. McD. Bruce Hutt, *Anthropology in Action: An Experiment in the Iringa District of the Iringa Province, Tanganyika Territory* (London: Oxford University Press, 1935), pp. 93–4.
3. A.T. and G. M. Culwick, *Ubena of the Rivers* (London: George Allen and Unwin, 1935), p. 179.
4. *Ibid.*, pp. 186 and 187–9.
5. *Ibid.*, pp. 179 and 184–6.
6. *Ibid.*, pp. 186–7.
7. *Ibid.*, pp. 299 and 316–19.
8. Mumford, p. 207.
9. A.T. and G.M. Culwick, 'The Functions of Bride-Wealth in Ubena of the Rivers', *Africa* 7,2 (1934), p. 141.
10. Culwicks, *Ubena of the Rivers*, pp. 382–3.
11. *Ibid.*, p.383.

12. F.J. Lake (Acting District Officer, Njombe) to Provincial Commissioner (Iringa), 24 November 1931, Tanzania National Archives [hereafter TNA] 77/26/6.

13. N.F. Burt (District Officer, Njombe) to Provincial Commissioner (Iringa), 10 December 1936, TNA 77/26/6.

14. W.B. Tripe (Acting District Officer, Njombe), 'Memorandum on the Claim of the Late Chief Kiswaga's Sons to Office Under or in the Native Administration of Ubena' (n.d., but 1939), TNA 77/26/6.

15. District Officer (Njombe) to Provincial Commissioner (Mbeya), 2 April 1942, TNA Secretariat File 29148.

16. J.W.L. Makinda, 'Succession Ubena Chieftainship' (8 June 1949), Njombe District Book, vol. 1. Tanzania National Archives, Regional and District Books (Dar es Salaam: University College Library Microfilm, 1968).

17. 'Tribal History, Wabena', Njombe District Book, vol. 1; Solomoni Mkalumoto Mwanjali, 'Kuugombea Utwa wa Eneo ya Lupembe' (n.d.), Mtwa Mbeyela to Lupembe Baraza, Watu Wote wa Lupembe (16 September 1959), and District Commissioner (Njombe) to Provincial Commissioner (Mbeya), 14 October 1959, TNA 535/A.2/26.

18. Marcia Wright, *German Missions in Tanganyika, 1891–1941: Lutherans and Moravians in the Southern Highlands* (Oxford: Clarendon Press, 1971), pp. 189 and 190–1; A.L. Sakafu, 'The Pastor: Yohane Nyagava', in John Iliffe (ed.), *Modern Tanzanians: A Volume of Biographies*, (Dar es Salaam: East African Publishing House, 1973), pp. 198–9.

19. Tumwendage Mtalulowo Kaduma, Palangawanu, 7 July 1994.

20. Reuben Mlenga, Palangawanu, 20 July 1992.

21. Tulalumba Kawogo, Matowo, 5 July 1994. This section also draws on conversations with Mlelwa Mwajuma Kilowoko (Makambako, 22 June 1992), Mama Kapwani (Makambako, May 19, 1992), Dzituvene Mgaiwa Mnyalape (Lupembe, 10 July 1994), Tulahigwa Sahwi (Matowo, 6 July 1994), Ero Muhanje (Makambako, 4 May 1992) and Tumwivukage Mlawa (Matowo, 6 July 1994).

22. Report of Bezirkschef (Iringa), 14 March 1912, TNA G9/14; District Officer (Njombe), 'Tour Report no. 20' (4–16 December 1928), TNA 28/21.

23. For example, see 'Nachrichten aus Deutsch-Ostafrika', *Berliner Missionsberichte* (January 1901), pp. 50–60; Alexander Merensky, 'Deutsch-Ostafrika', *Berliner Missionsberichte* (1903), pp. 243–61; and Alexander Merensky, 'Nachrichten aus der Kondesynode', *Berliner Missionsberichte* (1905), pp. 413–27.

24. G. Gordon Brown, 'Bride-Wealth Among the Hehe', *Africa* 5, 2 (1932), pp. 146 and 151; A.T. and G.M. Culwick, 'The Functions of Bride-Wealth', pp. 142–3 and 156.

25. Among those who gave accounts of their own struggles to reconcile conflicts between their non-Christian elders, who wished them to marry multiple wives, and their own desire to remain monogamous, were Jimu Kilima (Palangawanu, 19 July 1992) and Lujabiko Mwamgongolwa (Palangawanu, 21 July 1994).

26. Maynard Pangamahuti, Utengule, 15 November 1997.

27. District Commissioner (Njombe), 'Memorandum on Proposed Native Authority' (20 July 1949), TNA 178/A.2/5.

28. Donald Makamba to the District Commissioner (Njombe), 2 November 1956, TNA 178/A.2/2/iii. Linguistic evidence suggests that in Njombe such arguments are at least 1500 years old: Christopher Ehret, *An African Classical Age: Eastern and Southern Africa in World History, 1000 B.C. to A.D. 400* (Charlottesville: University Press of Virginia and Oxford: James Currey, 1998), p. 250.

29. Donald Maynard, Joseph and Charles Pangamahuti to District Commissioner (Njombe), 8 August 1949, TNA 178/A.2/5; Chief Joseph Pangamahuti Mbeyella II, Mdandu, 29 June 1994; Lutengano Fute and Vangamere Msigwa, Nyumbanitu, 24 July 1994.

30. Discussion of the Iditima dispute is based on John A. Mhaville, Njombe, 20 November 20, 1997, Senior Agricultural Officer (Soil Conservation) to Director of Agriculture (Dar es Salaam), 16 July 1951, TNA Secretariat 40899/2, Mtwa Mkuu Mbeyela (Mdandu) to District Commissioner (Njombe), April 10, 1957, TNA 535/L.5/23, Minutes of meetings of Bena Tribal Council, 3–6 August 1954, 4 April, and 15–18 August 1955, and Minutes of meetings of Njombe African District Council, 5–7 October 1954, 5–7

May and 25–27 October 1955, and 6–8 June 1956, TNA 465/L.5/8. The difficulties encountered by the Forest Department in protecting forest reserves during this period are described in Forestry: Annual and Monthly Reports, TNA 77/12/18, particularly D.P. Webb, 'Report for September–October 1952 of Southern Highlands Forest Division'.

31. For the reputation of Nyumbanitu outside Njombe as a point of dispersal, see Seth Ismael Nyagava, 'A History of the Bena to 1908' (Ph.D. dissertation, University of Dar es Salaam, 1988), pp. 69–70 and 85–7 and *A History of the Bena to 1914* (Peramiho: Peramiho Press, 2000), pp. 39, 45–6, 48. Traditions in the Southern Highlands of dispersal from Ubena are mentioned in Monica Wilson, 'The Peoples of the Nyasa-Tanganyika Corridor' (University of Cape Town, Communications from the School of African Studies, N.S. no. 29, 1958), p. 48.
32. Michael Asangile Mkongwa and Samligo Josepha Mapugila, Igominyi, 9 July 1994; Chief Joseph Pangamahuti Mbeyella II, Mdandu, 29 June 1994.
33. Daniel Kiswaga, 'Habari za Inchi ya Ubena Hapo Kale' (1933), Mss. Afr. S. 2047, Rhodes House Library. My thanks to Jamie Monson for providing me with a copy.
34. Lupumuko Pandisha (Ero P.) Lugalla, Dar es Salaam, 20 August 1997; Michael Asangile Mkongwa and Samligo Josepha Mapugila, Igominyi, 9 July 1994; Leknard Matola and Ferdinand Jacob Matola, Luponde, 13 November 1997; Lutengano Fute and Vangamere Msigwa, Nyumbanitu, 24 July 1994.
35. Andreas Mlowezi Mwalongo, Ihalulu, 8 November 1997.
36. John A. Mhaville, Njombe, 20 November 1997.
37. '*Raiya wako Tulio huku Mapolini*' to District Commissioner (Njombe), 21 September 1959, TNA 178/A.2/2/a.
38. See his comments in '*Safari ya Mtwa Mkuu Mbeyela II huko Dar es Salaam*', *Twende Pamoja* (Njombe) 12 (December 1955), p. 158.
39. Reuben Mlenga, Palangawanu, 20 July 1992.
40. Mikidadi Alliy Mlingisingo, Njombe 23 November 2000.
41. Mwalimu P.M. Kiswaga, '*Kuweka* Jumbe *Mpya Igawilo (Igominyi)*', *Twende Pamoja* (Njombe), no. 11 (November 1955), pp. 146–7.
42. Minutes of meeting of Bena Tribal Council, 15–17 July, 1959, TNA 465/L.5/8.
43. Chairman, TANU Youth League (Njombe) to District Commissioner (Njombe), 16 February 1960, TNA 576/A.6/30.
44. Tasili M. Mgoda, '*Union Yabashiriwa Njombe*', *Twende Pamoja* (Njombe), no. 79 (May 1962), p. 7.
45. This paragraph is based on Mwalimu Franz C. Mwalongo, Uwemba, 10 November 1997, who is quoted.
46. Reuben Mlenga and Eliasi Mlenga Mpindo, Palangawanu, 22 July 1994.
47. Reuben Mlenga, Palangawanu, 22 July 1994.
48. Reuben Mlenga, Palangawanu, 20 July 1992.

Ten

Λ/\/\/\/\/\/\/\/\/\/\/\/\/\/\/\/\/\/\Λ

Local, Regional & National
South Rukwa in the 1950s*

MARCIA WRIGHT

National sentiment in Tanzania at the end of the twentieth century was strong, based on shared experiences of intensified commercial integration from the mid-nineteenth century, a common language in Kiswahili, and the homogenizing administrative and governmental apparatus of colonialism. A mounting opposition to colonial rule had been channeled by a highly successful nationalist movement whose leader Julius Nyerere laid stress upon generic qualities of family and community co-operation and the necessity to supplant the artifices of colonial local government by invoking the capacity of commoners for democratic participation. The post-independence experience of Tanganyika and Tanzania has certainly deepened national sentiment by the spread of education with its powerful nation-building litanies and practice in orienting the youth. Yet debates over the stamp of *Ujamaa* on the mainland and persisting questions about the benefits of the union between mainland and islands further pose the question, who is a real Tanzanian?

This chapter treats a set of issues that test the history of national sentiment in what may be one of its weaker locations, on international boundaries among people supplying migrant labor, with a degree of choice as to national identity. The intention is to widen the horizons of thinking about the era of late colonialism and nationalist mobilization, paying attention to the fluidity of ethnic consciousness, localism, nationalism, and trans-nationalism in the South Rukwa region straddling Tanzania and Zambia.

When new generations come to treat the 1950s, they will continue to learn of a time of epic nationalist mobilization against controlled decolonization. How can it be otherwise as schoolchildren learn civics and their future teachers prepare in the university and teacher training colleges to instruct them? Yet the 1950s also witnessed the peak of migrant labor. Migrant labor, such a key experience for legions of African men and a few women in eastern and southern Africa in the colonial period, is likely to fade into the historiographical as well as the social background. To relegate it to the status of a mere distortion would be a regrettable reification. Migrancy is only one factor among many contributing both to regional history and to national sentiment, and while this facet is favored for present purposes, it will become evident that the brew of heightened consciousness in the 1950s contained numerous other elements, including the politics of local government, degrees of nationalist party activity, and rural economic conditions ranging from subsistence crisis to expanding markets for peasant produce, not to speak of demands for witch cleansing and millennial expectations.

The interest of this study and its perspective may be summarized in four ways. First, it poses and accepts the challenge to consider national sentiment as built through processes not necessarily heralded and embodied in political parties or kindred organizations. It is allowed that national sentiment may even be expressed as disaffection. Next, the chapter advocates the adoption of region as a conceivable whole containing differences that lend texture and open the way to a fuller appreciation of local and personal histories. As a methodological feature, ethnic identification within the region, and on the part of sisal workers coming from it, is queried in the light of census data for 1948, 1957 and 1967. The final aspect, joined to general conclusions, opens up for further study questions of the salience of the migrant experience for nationalist manifestations in home areas and in the South Rukwa region as a whole.

Region is a spatial concept. While it has been used to designate a politically circumscribed unit, it is far better deployed to analyze an unbounded area of economic activity and social interaction among heterogeneous people. The notion of region in the latter sense is elusive in that it calls for an appreciation of a core of interactivity that has no specific outer limits. In his discussion of environmental control and hunger, Isaria Kimambo took up local histories within northeastern Tanzania. While assuredly not confined to the tribalist straitjacket of Indirect Rule, his treatment nevertheless reflects the actuality that social identities and ownership of land and resources have continued to be passionately linked. Yet, turning his analysis from the local to the regional arena, Kimambo wrote of complementarities that propelled wider exchanges. For him, therefore,

> an internal focus is incomplete because it does not include the relationships between ... communities themselves and their neighbors.... [E]xchange was necessitated not only by drought, but also by uneven distribution of natural resources such as iron, clay and salt.

A little later, he continues

> All over the Pangani Valley, the caravan trade required alliances with leaders on the plains and mountains. As the caravans became larger (perhaps for defence as well as for economic reasons), the provisioning business, as well as slave and ivory trading, became part of the economic endeavours of all these communities.[1]

Many features of this scenario resonate in South Rukwa, for, as in the Pangani Valley, the late precolonial period brought opportunity amidst danger. Caravan traffic entailed demands for provisions that stimulated agricultural and artisanal production. In terms of the iron age horizon, South Rukwa also has an archaeologically and linguistically certified history of shared material culture and communication.[2] The juxtaposition of highlands and lowlands, with their different seasonalities, rainfall, resources and craft production undergirds long-standing production practices. Iron smelting is not least among the comparable activities that figured in northeastern and southwestern Tanzania.[3] For all their parallels, the difference between the two regions in the twentieth century is that they were at opposite ends of poles of migrant circulation. For South Rukwans, 'Tanga' was a source of experience that became bound up with national sentiment. 'Tanga' helped to configure the nation, as its earlier regional character was overtaken by its economic modernity. If 'Tanga' was a region at the end of the twentieth century, it was because the railway, Tanga town and port, and the ever spreading sisal plantations of the Pangani Valley had made it so. Historians liken the region to a magnet, aptly.[4] The newly mechanized region of capitalist colonial enterprise gathered momentum before World War I with the proliferation of sisal plantations. Migrant laborers came from greater and greater distances to the sisal plantations to work in the fields, deliver cut leaves to the mills, and handle the processed fiber. South Rukwans entered this work force beginning in 1907, their numbers increasing up to late 1914 and the dislocation brought on by World War I.[5] Such labor was genuinely industrial in being continuous through the year, requiring a regular and continuous inflow of leaves to feed the mills.

By contrast, South Rukwa seemed old-fashioned to many urban Tanzanians and, indeed, the natural environment and long-standing agricultural practices continued to shape daily life. Lake Rukwa introduces a physical dimension with deep demographic implications. Being shallow and without an outlet, it has expanded and contracted for millennia, registering cycles of higher and lower rainfall in its watershed. From the standpoint of modern South Rukwa inhabitants, these fluctuations demanded social elasticity. When the lake was high, the abundant wildlife of the plains encroached on villages and damaged cultivated areas. On the other hand, hunters thrived on this easy quarry and game meat was available. A low lake expanded grazing for domestic and wild animals alike. Good grazing in the late 1930s and 1940s supported a larger number of cattle. When drought persisted, however, streams from the escarpment and even the major river Momba stopped running, river fishing suffered, and cattle overgrazed. Following generations-long practices, people from the parched valley climbed the escarpment to get food. Notwithstanding certain ethnic concentrations and modes of segregation, social mobility over the long term and in modern times alike resulted in a markedly interspersed population. Local and regional history has remained entwined in practice, if not always at the level of consciousness.

Indirect Rule over the period since World War I, by sustaining the position of chiefs and their councilors, had become part of a local reality. In the 1950s, local government was a site of contradiction. Native Authorities carried institutional weight not only through the entrenchment of Indirect Rule, but also from the resolve on the part of Governor Twining in Tanganyika to court chiefs and warn them against nationalists as their natural enemies.[6] Yet the program of political devolution called for increasing numbers of representatives to be elected to local councils that would supersede the old Native Authorities. When gathered in 1951 to discuss the prospective reforms, the chiefs of South Rukwa were among those who rejected the 'tribal' definition of citizenship and insisted on geographical units. So decided were they that the colonial report dubbed them 'Pan-African'.[7]

The censuses of 1948, 1957 and 1967 which frame this section of the chapter are used to establish the patterns of distribution for the population groups of the South Rukwa, the Fipa, Nyamwanga, Nyika, and Mambwe, listed here in order from largest to smallest in number.[8] While these three censuses have been much improved upon in subsequent enumerations and share with all such instruments certain weaknesses, they represented a major increase in inclusiveness. As documents punctuating the period under discussion, they conveniently mark respectively the threshold of a new wave of recruitment for the sisal plantations, the apogee of this labor system, and the onset of post-migrant conditions premised upon a stabilized workforce and the retention and absorption of labor in home communities.

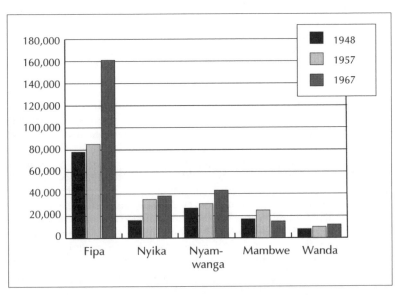

Fig. 10.1 Territorial Total for South Rukwa Groups

The most dramatic changes recorded in these censuses include an increase in the total numbers of Nyika of 130 per cent between 1948 and 1957, an increase of Fipa between 1957 and 1967 of 88 per cent, and an increase of Mambwe between 1947 and 1957 of 60 per cent followed by a decrease of 56 per cent in 1967, leaving them less in number than in 1948. Figure 10.1 displays these data.

The *Census Report* in 1957 did not remark specifically upon this level of fluctuation, confining its comments to anomalies such as the marked short-fall of men in national totals. External migration, it suggested, followed from the attractions of mine employment, especially the attractions of the Northern Rhodesian Copperbelt or South Africa. It concluded with reference to mobility within and outward: 'Finally, the question of migration constitutes the most difficult of all problems of Tanganyika demography'.[9] From the regional perspective, whether persons ultimately belonged to one nation or another could not be fixed by the census. In using it as one source for understanding the times and popular orientations, however, it is vital to take note of several specific features of demography and enumeration. The boundary people, the Mambwe and Nyamwanga, were counted as domestic to Tanganyika even though many came from south of the border.[10] Their movement, whether they happened to be in Tanga or southwestern Tanzania, was of two kinds, reflecting the relocation of persons through the in-marriage of women and resettlement of whole families across the border or the jumping of migrants to Tanga or elsewhere to work. Enumeration was improved in 1957 over 1948 by a supplementary check asking whether the person came from a specific district or neighboring districts. The Nyika were expected to come from Ufipa and the Nyiha from Mbeya. Certain Nyika in western Mbeya nevertheless resolutely insisted upon being counted as Nyika rather than Nyiha. In short, by the 1950s, consciousness was no more easily contained than it ever was by colonial rubrics.

While the commentary on the 1957 census had remarked on an outflow of men, its details for South Rukwan groups indicated an inflow. The 1967 census reflects a reversal of movement with a steep recession in the numbers of Mambwe in Tanzania. Figure 10.2, contrasting the numbers in Tanga at a peak in 1957 and in 1967 after stabilization of the sisal plantation workforce, demands further consideration. Still increasing numbers of Fipa and Nyika in Tanga suggest tenacity on the part of groups residing mainly away from the border, and withdrawal by those that straddled it.

The male–female ratios in Tanga had become less extremely skewed by 1967, as was to be expected given the longer contracts beginning in 1959, increased wages and benefits, and the liquidation in 1965 of SILABU, the Sisal Industry Labor Bureau.[11] The disparity in 1957 had been reduced by over 50 per cent for all groups, the Nyamwanga and the Nyika ratios improving by about 60 per cent and 62 per cent respectively. But the disparity was still 113 males to 1 female for the Nyamwanga and 115–1 for the Nyika.

The benchmark 1957 Census in respect of the Tanganyikan portions of South Rukwa found the Mambwe to be most numerous in two of ten

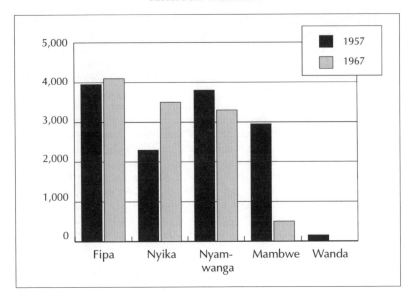

Fig. 10.2 South Rukwans in Tanga Province

census areas, the Fipa in five, the Nyika in two, and the Nyamwanga and Wanda in one each. Dispersed most widely were the Nyika, dwelling in all ten areas, followed by the Nyamwanga and Fipa in nine, the Mambwe in eight and the Wanda in two only. Only the Wanda lived in one ecological zone, the Rukwa Valley. To put it briefly, no jurisdiction of local government was homogeneous and in certain cases the 'tribal authority' presided over ethnics that outnumbered the putative tribe. Every group had been sending young people to the sisal estates for more than one generation, but during the time of intensified recruitment in the 1950s the most marked increase was registered among the Nyika.

The history of sisal migrant labor opened a new chapter with the ending of World War II. From conscription justified by the war effort, attention turned to the absorption of returning military personnel and the routinization of labor supply without overt coercion. Managers of the Labour, Manpower, Civil Reabsorption and Training Departments, combined in the Labour Department, described the necessity of imposing order:

> The chaotic condition into which recruiting had descended last year (1944), due to the inadequacy of sections ... of the Master and Native Servant Ordinance to control 'Touting' by native estate headmen, was remedied.... It was laid down that no person could undertake any form of recruiting without a licence and 'recruiting' was properly defined. This had an immediate effect for the better, but at the same time it prohibited the system of forwarding voluntary unattested labour that was desirous of proceeding to specified places of employment, a system which had long

been in force and was operated through the medium of so-called 'forwarding agents' who were usually Indian shop keepers.... It was recognized that it was well nigh impossible to control the activities of native employees going home on leave and returning in due course with fellow tribesmen (which action in theory would be tantamount to 'recruiting') and so it was laid down as a basis of policy that when these employees returned ... to their original place of employment accompanied by friends, they should all be regarded as volunteers, proceeding independently and not as recruited labour, and so would be exempt from the need of being attested on written contracts of service, if they so desired.

This system has been to some extent vitiated by various sisal estates issuing pro-forma letters of authority indiscriminately to each and every employee returning home.... Steps have been taken ... to control the issue of these letters....[12]

Given that the majority of migrants to the sisal plantations from South Rukwa had been and continued to be 'volunteers', the described practices capture an ongoing process of building ethnic cohorts which traveled and lived together at their workplaces and plugged into networks already in place in Tanga. Employers rewarded the bringers of 'friends' and also encouraged the experienced workers to renew their own engagements. The 'forwarding agents' identified in the 1945 *Bulletin* as Indian could also be African notables. Probably the most eminent, if indirect in manner, was Mwene Kapere, the Chief of Nkansi in Ufipa from 1932 to his death in 1957.[13] For the entire country in the first half of 1946, from all directions, 8,494 workers were formally recruited for sisal. A further 1,977 volunteers, 'forwarded by employers' organizations' were accompanied by 711 dependants, a pattern that may help to explain the numbers of South Rukwan women in the Tanga Province.[14]

With the inauguration of the Sisal Industry Labour Bureau (SILABU), the first targets were Lake Province where the Sukuma had a high reputation as workers.[15] The areas of Western Mbeya and Ufipa District of concern to us were reached with regular recruiting infrastructures in 1948, intensifying in Ufipa in 1951.[16] SILABU established three camps where people assembled for transport to the main depot at Mbeya, from which they were dispatched to specific plantations. Two camps situated in the Rukwa valley were at Mbao, a main junction on the road from Mbeya via Vwawa to Ivuna, the site of commercial salt-making, and at Mkulwe, on the Momba River some twelve miles west of Mbao. After SILABU lorries in June 1948 made three trips a week over the rough track to Mkulwe at great risk to the vehicles, they contracted with the White Fathers to build a passable road.[17] The third camp, at Mosi (alternatively Mozi), was near the boundary with Northern Rhodesia, approached by way of the all-season road passing through Northern Rhodesia from Tunduma for a distance of a hundred miles before turning north, back into Tanganyika. Mbao recruits tended to enroll as Nyamwanga, Mkulwe recruits as Fipa or Nyika. Mosi's social hinterland contained about equal numbers of Mambwe, Fipa and Nyika, who probably signed on as such.

Two of the five groups, the Nyamwanga and the Fipa, had relatively strong dynastic chiefships. At the other extreme, the Nyika were at certain times denied the status of 'tribe' because they had no specific territory or recognized tribal authority.[18] Some of the Mambwe and the Wanda lived under their own tribal authorities, but many did not. The Mambwe aggressively routinized their migrant careers and retained their identity as Mambwe. The Wanda dropped their tribal identity and passed as Nyamwanga ethnics in Tanga. Each of these identity groups will receive separate treatment below, but always with the caveat that the characteristic patterns of behavior do not touch all the variability amongst people of an ethnic category.

The Nyamwanga and Fipa, as peoples, have each been highly assimilative, distinguishing themselves as extremely 'open' societies. Many a 'Fipa' of the mid-twentieth century would have owned a Mambwe, Nyamwanga or other forebear. An extreme diversity of recalled antecedents is given by Owen Sichone in his study of the Zambian Nyamwanga, where he mentioned 73 'patriclans' in Tanzania and 104 in Zambia, making the point that Nyamwanga culture welcomed incomers. Among the 52 most common names, the believed origins included twelve that were putatively Mambwe and seven Fipa. Only eight counted as autochthonous Nyamwanga/Iwa. Sichone reported a funeral practice whereby people were buried facing in the direction from which their clan name founder came, and concluded that those who 'lived as Winamwanga, in death became Nyika, Mambwe and Fipa again'.[19] This curious post-mortem secession had nothing to do with the local rights of descendants. It certainly exaggerated the patrilineality of the Nyamwanga and erases the extent to which mothers' families have also been recognized in Nyamwanga, Wanda and Fipa culture. The important point is that Nyamwanga and Fipa readily absorbed and acculturated strangers. When the Wanda assumed the migrant identity of Nyamwanga, they thus affirmed their cultural and social ties with a larger, and by predisposition inclusive, contingent in the sisal labor force.

The Nyika

The census-takers in 1948 denied the Nyika group of South Rukwa the status of tribe, since, as already mentioned, they had no recognized tribal authority oe assigned homeland. To satisfy the intrinsic tribalism of Indirect Rule, they were lumped with the Nyiha of Mbozi from whom they had allegedly wandered as hunters in the centuries before colonialism. The following sketch of the Nyika underscores their complex place in the regional history of South Rukwa, agreeing that they were not a tribe but became an ethnic group, beginning in the later nineteenth century at the very least. By the 1950s, joined in a full range of contemporary economic activities, they retained a separate identity, well aware of Fipa stereotypes of their inferiority. The Nyika indeed figure in the imagination of the Fipa, who regard them collectively as 'wild' and 'of the bush' in contrast to themselves, whose stable village life was civilized.

This binary opposition looms large in the work of Roy Willis as an anthropologist and folklorist in research and publication spanning the mid-1960s to the mid-1980s.[20] The compendium of colonial knowledge, *The Handbook of Tanganyika*, published in 1958, suggests that they were reclusive and backward: 'the Wanyika live scattered all over the district in the more inaccessible places, e.g. the mountain valleys, the plateau and the Rukwa valley plain'.[21] Without Tribal Authorities, the Nyika lived as subjects of the Fipa rulers of Lyangalile and Nkansi, and the Mambwe chiefs of Koswe and Nyanda. One obstreperous Nyika line of headmen had tried to claim ethnic-territorial recognition in a part of Koswe, but never succeeded.[22] Politically, then, the Nyika before the 1950s were indeed recessive. But they were hardly inert. They had figured as an important factor in the affairs of the Fipa principalities, where they were exempt from tribute or military service but could be crucial allies against aggressive or oppressive outsiders, including the brigand-ivory hunter Kimalaunga. In 1905, the Lyangalile chief was executed by the Germans because he could not deliver the Nyika for tax labor and shared their defiant attitude.[23] The Nyika proved themselves as independent-minded workers, self-employed or for wages, long before they made their strong showing in the 1957 census in Tanga.

The stereotype of Nyika as hunters is one that they themselves indulged. A Nyika headman in the early twentieth century fully embraced the role of Nyika hunters as temporary consorts of the royal women who usurped the prior rulers of Ufipa.[24] Some Nyika continued to define themselves as hunters. In the later 1930s, when game was depleted on the plateau, they moved in numbers to the Rukwa Valley to stalk wildlife which, conveniently for them, had been pushed out of their normal havens and the official Game Reserve by the extremely high waters in the lake.[25]

The Nyika were also skillful and successful cultivators. In 1906, the Nyika headman near Mwazye struck an alliance with the Father Superior of the recently established Catholic Mission, allowing the missionaries to obtain substantial provisions. The Nyika also gravitated to Mwazye where they formed a discrete moiety living in their own ward.[26] This proximity meant that certain Nyika increasingly shared in the material culture of the Mambwe and Fipa. With deforestation, they joined in the grassland type of agricultural production, hoeing up the green manure mounds that distinguished the fields of the plateau savanna. By 1937, officials describing the mound system referred to the practices as those of the Wafipa and Wanyika.[27] There was comparatively little waged employment in agriculture in the region. The most flourishing settler farm in the inter-war and postwar period was at Malonje, the promontory near the Rukwa escarpment east of Sumbawanga. The Damm family ran a dairy, bought cattle for sale to Northern Rhodesia, and served as contractors for commodity foods which they purchased from surrounding cultivators, and also as labor forwarding agents. The little hub they formed was nothing if not a school for economic engagement. They hired Nyika exclusively.

In the course of their integration into the general economy of the region, Nyika became noted among the smelters and iron workers. These crafts were never closed and they contributed to livelihoods in Ufipa until well after World War II. An auspicious moment for the Nyika ironworkers came with the construction of the Roman Catholic mission at Pito. Around 1940, Andrea Monela was among the Nyika master smelters who resettled in this new community and attracted other Nyika to work and live there.[28]

The Depression of the 1930s had important country-wide ramifications, demoralizing marginal market-oriented production and putting the sisal plantations on a retrenched production schedule. Many migrant workers went home and new recruitment was at a standstill. This situation precipitated a crisis in South Rukwa, even though the rush to the alluvial gold fields at the Lupa, just northeast of Lake Rukwa, increased demands for both labor and provisions. The passage of Bemba work-seekers marked a reversal of orientation from the copper mines of Northern Rhodesia to the speculative and seasonal Lupa zone. The renewal of recruiting for both the Copperbelt mines and Tanga sisal in 1937 drew migrants away again, to better paid, more distant destinations. For the history of the Nyika group, this sequence in all probability coincided with greater willingness to allow young men to spend time in the sisal plantations.

To what degree was the remarkable inter-census increase of Nyika natural as well as a manifestation of consciousness? In respect to fertility, child survival, and cultural attitudes towards reproduction and upbringing, the Nyika seem to have been set apart from their neighbors. They were known for their scrupulous attention to children. One royal informant in Nkansi spoke of his own fostering by a Nyika couple, as well as the fame of Nyika doctors as specialists in treating infertility.[29] The district census consistently recorded a higher ratio of men to women among Nyika than for their neighbors, a retention that supported the convention that newly married girls were to be kept secluded until they became pregnant. The Nyika household was more strictly patriarchical than the Fipa or Mambwe, whose collective, reciprocating female fieldwork was thought to cause a certain inattention to infants and small children. Modern Fipa women looked upon marriage with Nyika men as hard and subordinating.[30] From the standpoint of child survival, however, the Nyika culture was favorable, at least until male absenteeism in migrant labor escalated after 1948.

The cohesion of the Nyika survived their modernization and may have been underscored by the more zealous tax collection targeted at their villages in 1951 and carried out by the Lyangalile 'Fipa' chiefs. The Nyika villages of Lyangalile supported TANU from 1956 onwards, whereas the Fipa were at best tepid toward the party.[31] That a number of Nyika found it expedient at last to become finally assimilated Fipa is suggested by the very low increase in their numbers from 1957 to 1967.

The Mambwe

The Mambwe had distinguished themselves as porters across the Nyasa-Tanganyika plateau organized in the later nineteenth century in the employ of the African Lakes Company. They remained alive to all ensuing opportunities and became known especially through William Watson's book, *Tribal Cohesion in a Money Economy*. Watson's research was carried out in 1952 and 1953, mostly among the grassland communities in Northern Rhodesia, just south of the Tanganyika border. At precisely that time, the Mambwe of Northern Rhodesia experienced aggressive colonial implementation of land and forest conservation measures. Simultaneously, nationalist resistance to the dictated incorporation of the colony into the Central African Federation was fully registered in Mambwe country. After an insurrection in the last months of 1952 and early 1953, the senior Chief Nsokolo was deposed.[32] These events took place in the rainy season, December to February, at a time when most men were at home. They customarily departed for migrant work in March and April, after the main cultivation was complete and when the crops were ripening.[33] In any event, local/nationalist politics were unlikely to have swayed the decisions of migrants, given the degree of integration between wage-earning and rural life at the time.

Watson disputed the received opinion that the absence of migrant men led to rural demoralization. Mambwe men, he found, were indeed in 'ceaseless movement' to the Copperbelt mining towns, but they continually returned home and reinvested the proceeds of their work. Village censuses conducted for this study revealed that, in 1952 and 1953, young people conventionally began their migrant careers with a stint on the sisal plantations of Tanganyika. In six Mambwe villages in Zambia, the majority of them from grassland areas close to the border, but several also from the more wooded areas with the ash-bed system of cultivation, Watson undertook a census that provided details of different age groups. He summarized the life stages for males as follows. Between the ages of 7 and 14, the boy herded; if his father owned cattle, he might be assigned to a joint herd for two days a week, rotating with herd boys supplied by other owners. Between 14 and 18, he looked forward to the start of migrant labor, even seeking tax registration while still under age (18) in order to obtain a registration card, a prerequisite for employment on the Copperbelt. A youth without the card might try for work in Tanganyika, where employers and officials were not very vigilant in this regard.

Volunteers certainly received less scrutiny. Since 1946, the Tanganyika Labour Department had distinguished the age category of children under 15 from 'young people' aged 15 to 18 who were eligible to work even though they were not taxpaying adults, 18 or over.[34] Those in the work-entry age group, 15 to 24, made their inaugural journey to the sisal plantations. This apprenticeship in labor in the early 1950s had lengthened from nine months to a year or more, in part owing to the incentive of free return transport for those who worked for at least a year.[35] In a way, this experience was taken as a seasoning, sisal work being disciplined but less arduous and skilled than jobs in the copper mines. The social milieu was less tough, as well. Once their apprenticeship in sisal ended, young men returned with enough money to marry. When they set forth once again, it was likely to be towards the Copperbelt, which offered higher wages. Many a 'distance' worker, having established himself in the Copperbelt, called for his wife to follow.[36] Mambwe men built up a position in their rural villages and not only remitted wages but took their turn in the fields when at home between episodes of migrant work. Watson estimated that, up to the age of forty, men might still choose to go south again. Afterwards, they retired from distant migrancy.[37]

That the decision to go for a second tour in Tanga was neither inconceivable nor always the result of employers' inducements is illustrated by the instance of a Northern Rhodesian Mambwe to whom William Watson gives the name Driver. After he returned from his inaugural contract, he was persuaded to go again in order to accompany three inexperienced youths. They were volunteers, not SILABU recruits, although they probably availed themselves of free transport on the SILABU bus. Driver and his three companions worked for a year in the sisal estates and systematically saved, both in cash and by buying things to take home. Each month they locked these savings away in a wooden chest bought with their first month's wages. At the end of the year, they each returned home with not less that £4.10s and many gifts in the form of clothing, cloth, and blankets.[38]

In 1953 in the six villages he surveyed, Watson established that 40 per cent of the men were in the sisal plantations.[39] This number suggests that sisal may have been a more continuous career than was stated in his model. Other conditions escaped his attention. The dynamics of cross-border movement, for example, have been highlighted in a post-migrant period restudy of the Mambwe by Johan Pottier. Pottier's invaluable work can be fruitfully read alongside the 1967 Tanzania census, which registers the steep decline in Mambwe in Tanga. Many Mambwe discovered that they were more definitively Zambians and oriented their work-seeking to the Copperbelt, even though they confronted stabilization of the workforce there as well.[40]

The Wanda-Nyamwanga

Joseph Mullen concludes that the Wanda yielded more migrants relative to their population than did the Nyamwanga and the Fipa.[41] The virtual absence of Wanda from the census at migrant destinations is indeed frustrating, although it induces added curiosity about who the Wanda in fact were. The matter was complicated by the non-recognition of a Wanda chief as a subordinate authority in Lyangalile, although they were a compact majority in the Sakalilo area north of the Momba River in the Rukwa Valley.[42]

A youth departing for his initiation into migrant labor as a sisal worker would have been very little involved or interested in these affairs of local government. Coming back, especially in the post-World War II era, he was likely to want to establish himself as a worldly person adept in the latest ballroom dances, ready to marry and establish a household. Only gradually, after deciding not to go off again as a migrant, would he begin to engage with the burning issues in local politics, tribal and/or nationalist. The following discussion starts from an ex-migrant's (CK) rather skeletal narrative and wraps around it a loose commentary on the circumstances in the Rukwa Valley at the time of his departure for Tanga in 1954, during his absence, and upon his return in 1959:

I wrote down my name at Silabu in Mbao in 1954, then I was taken by bus to Mbeya with a number of other local men. At Mbeya we were distributed among the varius plantations and I opted for the plantation of Kwamdola near Korogwe. I was given a blanket and four shillings with which to buy rations for the journey. The second day of our journey we stayed overnight at Iringa and then we travelled the following day to Kilosa. On the fourth day we entered Korogwe and we were driven to our various estates. On arrival at the estate, we were allocated to a house where there were four or five of us together, all from the same area. Then we were given jobs, jobs for adults – cutting sisal, and tasks for children – weeding, etc. The task for cutting was 70 bundles of 30 leaves per day, if you cannot complete your task then you lost a full day's work, if you were ill the day was not counted. I described myself as Mnyamwanga instead of Mwanda because I was afraid that I might be sent back to work on the Locust Control of Rukwa.

I left home to get away from the old people, when I got my freedom I enjoyed it so I continued to stay at the coast. It was not until 1959 that the elders followed me to the coast to fetch me back to Uwanda. Then I returned home, I brought 100/- and clothes with me, it was sufficient to become engaged and also to distribute some among the elders and my family. Later I was married and settled down at home.

Before going to the coast I thought that Europeans were something out of this world but on the plantations they cheated us, disallowing us days work which they took for their own benefit. Because of malpractices we went on strike.[43]

The Rukwa Valley, not least in the southeast where the Wanda lived, sustained repeated punishment by the weather, drought and occasional flood, beginning in 1947. The harvests in 1948 were poor and in 1949 worse, causing that year to be recalled locally as the time of the Great Famine. Some relief came in 1950 to 1952 but rainfall fell again in 1953 and 1954. The River Momba failed to flood and the staple of fish became unavailable. Wanda complained of fishing by 'foreign' Nyakyusa in the residual waters of southern Lake Rukwa.[44] Cattle had to be sold to pay for food trucked in from Mbeya. Women continued to dig *ndago*, wild grasses with root nodules that, with care, could be cleansed of their poison in order to be ground and prepared as a substitute for millet and sorghum.[45] In early 1954, a witch cleansing movement caught fire in Uwanda.[46] All of these matters were on the minds of the elders from whom CK sought freedom.

In the Rukwa Valley, where its experiments and control operations were focused, the International Red Locust Control Service (IRLCS) was in the early 1950s for all practical purposes the sole employer of unskilled labor, to develop and maintain roads in the valley and down the escarpment and in the actual work of scouting and controlling locusts. Finding it unusually difficult to attract labor, the IRLCS in 1953 turned to the government for help but did not specify what it meant exactly when the officials 'proved sympathetic' to appeals for workers.[47] Coercion at this time in the region was indirect, for example through explaining to old men seeking exemptions from tax that they would get them only if the young men were added to the rolls.[48]

SILABU contracts, at a wage of 42 to 60 shillings per month, made the 27 shillings offered by the IRLCS seem poor, even with the added offer of full rations if requested and a blanket to be owned after three successive months on the job. In times of extreme dearth, with the doubling of prices for millet, maize and groundnuts on the market, such conditions might have attracted a married man. But a single youth like CK went to Mbao and escaped.

CK traveled and lived with acquaintances, all of whom were now called Nyamwanga. Philip Gulliver in 1954 reported that the Nyamwanga men as a whole avoided tough industrial and urban sites, preferred to work in Tanganyika, and appreciated the free transport supplied by SILABU. The normal migrant career had been two trips, but he foresaw a tendency to add a third, between the ages of 18 and 35. Only 11 per cent of Nyawanga men had never been away. From eighteen months of work in Tanga, migrants usually returned with 100–150 shillings in cash and clothing.[49] Did they also bring back a new attitude? In Tanga, this group was judged by a Catholic priest to be very difficult and testing of authority. Such a manner was not, however, merely the result of experience on the plantations. The progressives just south of the border, who had formed the Mwenzo Welfare Association before World War I, figure as founding fathers of Zambian nationalism. Isoka district officials in Northern Rhodesia from World War I on repeatedly noted an especially critical frame of mind among the educated elite of the Nyamwanga, who sometimes even reproved white officials for slack standards in government. At the chief's village, Msangano, in 1956 Tanganyika colonial officials noted that the people were 'fully alert, asking what they got for their taxes'. Such a challenge came as a surprise, as the Mbeya District officers usually dismissed the Nyamwanga/Wanda areas as 'backward'. There was no direct connection between the 'old nationalists' in the south and the leadership of TANU in Uwanda, but the TANU mobilizer was a Protestant Nyamwanga from Msangano, whose kin in Zambia came from a new class of traders and radical younger nationalists who later co-ordinated with members of the TANU Youth League. Over the longer term militancy subsided, although political manners among the Nyamwanga still called for respect, given, and even more important, claimed. The intricacies of traditions of resistance and accommodation, modernity and traditionalism, have yet to be rendered in light of a history that fostered complex sentiments of belonging to any nation.

After five years, CK was fetched home in 1959 – a veteran of the recent sisal strikes, aware of the litany of union grievances, and critical of white bosses. The savings from his pay, 100 shillings and clothing, seem to have been typical for returning migrants whether from short or long stints away. The cash portion of bridewealth since 1954 had increased by about 20 per cent to 220 shillings, while the number of expected cattle varied between four and six.[50] As his cash savings permitted him only to begin a protracted process of gathering the means to complete the payment and thus the marriage, he needed to be on good terms with relations who would subscribe.

In his absence, Uwanda had moved from witch-cleansing to support for TANU. In brief, an accelerant had been friction between the quite authoritarian White Fathers of Mkulwe parish and their African workers and neighbors. Squatters had taken over mission lands, employees went on strike, and community leaders opposed the mission's access to communal clay deposits to make tiles. The Mission had banned ballroom dancing by mixed couples.[51] As Mullen says, Uwanda was ripe for TANU. Yet colonial officials were surprised:

> In the area of Kamsamba, TANU membership has risen from approximately 700 to 1652 in a period of five months only. The cold facts are that without the rabble-rousing speeches of Mbutta MILANDO (Provincial Secretary of TANU), without a single visit by a TANU personality, without a large scale distribution of 'Mwafrika' (TANU vernacular newspaper) or the poison of Cairo Radio, without any trade union activity, TANU in this very backward area is stronger than in Mbeya (the Provincial capital).[52]

CK returned to a highly politicized Uwanda, with many TANU initiatives under way, crowned by a set of TAPA (Tanganyika African Parents' Association) schools and agitation for free clinics under secular rather than church management.

For all the support provided by the surrounding communities in Tanga at the time of the strikes, which Tambila regards as nationalist, it is most likely that CK had learned to express economic and work-place demands, not the broader political challenges, especially as TANU had been banned in Korogwe from 1957 to 1959.[53] It is also worth recalling Steven Feierman's observations about what activated the Shambaa politically:

> The peasant resistance movement established a tight bond with the nationalist movement, but not with the sisal workers, even though many of the peasant men themselves worked on sisal plantations. The sisal unions were cut off also from nationalist politics. Their isolation in this period is in fact of fundamental importance for the later shape of Tanzanian socialism, yet it is rarely noted in the historical literature.[54]

This view skirts the issues surrounding national sentiment raised here with respect to South Rukwa, seen as an outcome of tolerance of pluralism in the vernacular region, the experience of distant workplaces, and the permeation of values associated with the Swahili-speaking nation.

Conclusion

Local, regional and national sentiments in the case of Tanzanian South Rukwa have been elastic. This chapter asks readers to be open to permeation. Elements of national sentiment inflect local sentiment. Ultimately, it is the functioning, vernacular region that gathers the least sentiment or explicit awareness. Perhaps the region persists – within and beyond the nation – as an arena in which women circulate in disregard of boundaries, either owing to marriage or quiet inter-household exchanges. From the perspective of the South Rukwa region, neither ethnicity nor nationalism is unproblematic. Migrant workers belonged to a projection of capitalism and dualistic development whose time was up, just as TANU in Tanzania assumed the reins of power. The discussion of migrant consciousness and identities in this chapter downplays but does not dismiss the nationalist sentiments of migrants. How could they not be at least latent nationalists, given their experience of the world beyond their localities of birth? The synergies that made up the environment for anti-colonial activism in rural areas include all that generations of previous migrants had brought back with them, as well.

National sentiment positively embraces a common membership in a society that prospers and suffers together. Consciousness of this co-prosperity and collective destiny can be fostered by historical narratives stressing both the progress of the nation as a whole and the existence of parallel conditions in varied localities where concurrent identities flourish. Yet another ingredient of national consciousness in a now bygone era was the actual sojourning of people in migrant destinations and the existence of this other arena in the imagination and practical affairs of the migrants, their families, and communities from which they emanated. National sentiment thus existed even where nationalist party affiliation or activism in the 1950s was slight. Local conditions could also ignite fervent, programmatic nationalism. To trace nationalist politics exclusively, however, is inadequate for a full plotting of the history of the nation.

Notes

* Leander Schneider is to be thanked for his critical reading and technical support in the production of this essay.
1. Isaria Kimambo, 'Environmental Control and Hunger in the Mountains and Plains of Northeastern Tanzania' in Gregory Maddox, James Giblin and Isaria Kimambo (eds), *Custodians of the Land: Ecology and Culture in the History of Tanzania* (Oxford: James Currey and Athens, OH: Ohio University Press, 1996), pp. 81, 92.
2. Monica Wilson pioneered a regional analysis in her survey, 'The Peoples of the Nyasa-Tanganyika Corridor' (University of Cape Town, Communications from the School of African Studies, N.S. No. 29, 1958). The archaeology springs mainly from the major excavations at Kalambo Falls. See J.D. Clark (ed.), *Kalambo Falls Prehistoric Site*, vol. 2 (Cambridge: Cambridge University Press, 1969).
3. M. Wright, 'A Life and Technology in Everyday Life: Reflections on the Career of Mzee Stefano, Master Smelter in Ufipa, Tanzania', *Journal of African Cultural Studies*, 15, 1 (2002)
4. Kapepwa Tambila, 'A Plantation Labour Magnet: The Tanga Case', in Walter Rodney, Kapepwa Tambila and Laurent Sago (eds), *Migrant Labour in Tanzania during the Colonial Period: Case Studies of Recruitment and Conditions of Labour in the Sisal Industry* (Hamburg: Institut für Afrika-Kunde, 1983).
5. Anselm [Kapepwa] Tambila, 'A History of the Rukwa Region (Tanzania) ca

1870–1940: Aspects of Economic and Social Change from Pre-Colonial to Colonial Times' (Ph.D. diss., Hamburg University, 1981), pp. 183ff.

6. Even though this maneuver is well known to historians, the actual considerations on the part of tribal politicians at this juncture deserve much more attention, commensurate with the recent work on the calculations of the Colonial Office. See John Iliffe, 'Nationalism: Breaking the Imperialist Chain at its Weakest Link', *Tanzania Zamani* 3, 2 (1997).

7. The Place and Development of African Councils in Local Government – Progress Reports, Mbeya District Office, File L5/2, TNA Acc. 327.

8. The Lungu who lived near the shores of Lake Tanganyika and did not participate significantly in sisal migrancy have been excluded for present purposes.

9. *Tanganyika Census Report* (1957), p. 93.

10. Sizable numbers of sisal workers were 'extra-territorial'. One of the best discussions of these is to be found in Walter Rodney, 'Migrant Labour and the Colonial Economy' in Rodney *et al.*, *Migrant Labour*, pp. 22–5.

11. East African Statistical Department. *Tanganyika General African Census, 1957: Tribal Analysis*, Part I, p. 15 and *1967 Population Census*, vol. 3, table 217, pp. 464–5. See also Adolpho C. Mascarenhas, 'Resistance and Change in the Sisal Plantation System of Tanzania' (Ph.D. diss., UCLA, 1970).

12. Labour Department. *Quarterly Bulletin* (January to September 1945). TNA 63/L1/2.

13. As a young ruler at the turn of the century, Kapere had readily taken to the role of labor broker. See Otto Schloifer, *Bwana Ulaia* (Berlin, 1938). In contrast to the Tutsi chiefs of Buha as described by Sago, he was less despotic and corrupt. Sago, 'Labour Reservoir', in Rodney *et al.*, *Migrant Labour*, pp. 69-70.

14. Labour Department, *Quarterly Bulletin* (April to June 1946). TNA 63/L1/2. Caution is warranted, for the ethnic identity of the head of household was simply assigned to all in it.

15. Labour Department, *Report 1946*. TNA 63/L1/2.

16. *Sumbawanga Safari Report* (4–21 September 1951) TNA Acc. 159.

17. J. E. Mullen, 'Church and State in the Development of Uwanda, Tanzania, 1920–1975' (PhD. diss., Edinburgh University, 1978), p. 239.

18. J. P. Moffett (ed.), *Handbook of Tanganyika*, 2nd edn (Dar es Salaam: Government Printer, 1958), p. 297.

19. Owen Sichone, 'Labour Migration, Peasant Farming and Rural Development in Uwinamwanga' (Ph.D. diss., Cambridge University, 1991), p. 54.

20. Roy G. Willis, *A State in the Making: Myth, History, and Social Transformation in Pre-Colonial Ufipa* (Bloomington, IN: University of Indiana Press, 1981).

21. J. P. Moffett, *Handbook of Tanganyika*, p. 297.

22. Tribal Notes: 'Mambwe Nkoswe', Sumbawanga District Note Book (hereafter DNB).

23. J. Lamb, 'History', 1927, Sumbawanga DNB.

24. A. Wyckaert, 'Watwaki et Wanyika: Pages de leur histoire', *Les Missions Catholiques*, October 1919. Wyckaert built on interviews with Kasea, 'Chief of the Wanyika Tribe', the leader of the Nyika in the Mwazye parish of Lyangalile and a convert.

25. See M. Wright, 'Nature and Development: The International Red Locust Control Service 1949–1957 and its Legacies in the History of South Rukwa, East Central Africa', (St Antony's College, Oxford, conference paper 1999). Locust control personnel took a global view of the Rukwa plains and waters and worked closely with the Game Department.

26. See M. Wright, 'The First Generation of Catholics at Mwazye' (New College, Edinburgh University, seminar paper, 1990).

27. R. Tripe, 'Cultivation of Land Ufipa', 28 May 1937.

28. Interview with Andrea Monela, 26 October 1982.

29. Mwene Kapere's recollection, embedded in Lamb, 'History'.

30. Mary Tazaro, personal communication.

31. A study of Nyika politics from the 1950s to the 1980s in Lyangalile would entail a biography of C.E. Mzindakaya, a politician of Nyika background who rose to be a junior

minister in the 1970s.

32. M. Wright, 'An Old Nationalist in New Nationalist Times: Donald Siwale and the State in Zambia, 1948-1963', *JSAS*, 23, 2 (1997).
33. William Watson, *Tribal Cohesion in a Money Economy: A Study of the Mambwe People of Northern Rhodesia* (Manchester: Manchester University Press, 1958), p. 67.
34. Labour Department. *Quarterly Bulletin* to September 1946, referring to the Employment of Women and Young Persons (Amendment) Ordinance No. 10 of 1946.
35. Watson, *Tribal Cohesion*, pp. 52, 67.
36. *Ibid.*, pp. 44–6.
37. *Ibid.*, p. 70.
38. *Ibid.*, 117–19.
39. *Ibid.*, p. 61.
40. Johan Pottier, *Migrants No More: Settlement and Survival in Mambwe Villages, Zambia* (Bloomington, IN: University of Indiana Press, 1988).
41. Mullen, 'Church and State', p. 221
42. See Sumbawanga DNB and Safari Reports for agitation for recognition of a Wanda chief.
43. Mullen, 'Church and State', p. 241.
44. *Mbeya District Report*, 1954. TNA Acc. 327.
45. *Ufipa Safari Report*, 20 June 1953. TNA Acc. 159.
46. Mullen, 'Church and State', p. 295.
47. International Red Locust Control Service, *Annual Report of the Director*, 1952–53.
48. *Ufipa Safari Report*, 4–21 September 1951. TNA Acc. 159.
49. P.H. Gulliver, 'A Report on the Migration of African Workers to the South from the Southern Highlands Province, with Special Reference to the Nyakyusa of Rungwe District', mimeo. Feb. 1955, Part C, Mbeya.
50. Mullen, 'Church and State', pp. 55–6.
51. Mullen, 'Church and State', Appendix II, 'Marriage Dowry in Uwanda, 1934–1973'.
52. Tanganyika intelligence summary, April 1958. Public Record Office (PRO) London, CO822/1362.
53. Tambila, 'Plantation ... Magnet', in Rodney. W., Tambila, K. and Sago, L. (eds), *Migrant Labour*, pp. 55–6.
54. Steven Feierman, *Peasant Intellectuals: Anthropology and History in Tanzania* (Madison, WI: University of Wisconsin Press, 1999), p.199.

Part III

The Nation & its Dissidents

Eleven

Breaking the Chain at its Weakest Link
TANU & the Colonial Office

JOHN ILIFFE

This chapter tries to summarize the evidence available in British Government records about the winning of independence in Tanganyika (mainland Tanzania).[1] Such documents generally become available to the historians thirty years after the events described. The most important documents may eventually be published as part of a project covering the entire British colonial empire,[2] but a short, interim account may be of interest. However, this chapter is not a history of nationalism and decolonization in Tanganyika. That would require study of the Tanganyika African National Union archives in Dodoma, the private papers and recollections of TANU members, and the records of the British Government of Tanganyika (presumably in the National Archives in Dar es Salaam). This chapter is purely about the thinking of British policymakers.

The records of decolonization already published show that the British Government expected that all its major colonies would eventually become self-governing within the Commonwealth. Moreover, by the end of World War II the broad principle of British colonial policy was to prepare these territories for self-government.[3] This preparation, however, was expected to take much longer in some colonies than others, while the character of the subsequent independent states would also vary. In particular, West African colonies were thought more developed – educationally, economically, and politically – than those of East and Central Africa, whose European settler communities seemed to dictate a multi-racial rather than a purely nationalist future.[4] Even when active decolonization in West Africa began in response to disturbances in the Gold Coast (Ghana) in 1948, the British Colonial Office did not see it as a model for East Africa. Rather, although guided by the overall expectation of ultimate self-government, decolonization normally consisted in practice of unplanned, erratic, defensive, and minimal responses to nationalist challenges in one part of the empire after another.

The Colonial Office records show this to have been especially true of Tanganyika, partly because its Governor from 1949 to 1958, Sir Edward Twining, responded to nationalism with breathtaking fluctuations of policy, but more profoundly because Tanganyika was the least developed of the British East African territories and might logically have been the last to gain independence, but was in fact the first. There were four main reasons for this. One was that the weakness of political organizations in Tanganyika in the late 1940s allowed Twining to devise an electoral system – the tripartite voting system – which proved to be (from the British viewpoint) a disastrous error: instead of returning a moderate, multi-racial leadership, as intended, it gave the African nationalist movement, TANU, a sweeping victory in the territory's first elections in 1958–9. This victory introduced the second reason for Tanganyika's unpredictably early independence, for the constitutional procedures which the British had devised to control decolonization did not work where there was a single dominant party with no effective opposition. TANU's strength, which drove liberation forward, owed much to Tanganyika's earlier history and to the skill of the party's leaders, but it was also aided by the territory's lack of development, which meant that almost all existing political ambitions could find space within a single party. The same lack of development underlay the other two reasons for rapid independence: that the security forces available were too weak to repress a nationalist movement, and that to develop Tanganyika to a level at which the British might have thought it fit for independence would have taken so long and cost so much as to be politically inconceivable, so that there was little point in trying to delay independence for this purpose.

Thus, whereas in West Africa the first British colony to gain independence was the most developed, Ghana, in East Africa it was the least developed, Tanganyika. The chain of imperialism in East Africa broke at its weakest link. And once broken there, imperial control unravelled throughout the region. Discussions of decolonization in East and Central Africa have often argued that British policy there was transformed from October 1959 when a new Colonial Secretary, Iain Macleod, took office and initiated a hasty retreat from empire. This was not so. The decisive breakthrough was TANU's electoral victory of 1958–9, roughly a year before Macleod took office. It faced him with an untenable situation which he tried and failed to stabilize before recognizing that in Tanganyika there was no realistic alternative to rapid independence. And once that was conceded in one territory, there was neither hope nor reason to resist it elsewhere in the region. The key to the rapid liberation of East Africa from colonial rule was the Tanganyikan election of 1958–9 and the voting system under which it was conducted.

The origins of this voting system lay in November 1949, shortly after Twining became Governor. Hitherto Tanganyika had not experienced the postwar constitutional changes which stimulated nationalist politics elsewhere in British Africa. The first two Africans were appointed to the unofficial side of Tanganyika's Legislative Council in 1945 and two more were added by 1948, joining three Asian and seven European representatives.[5] But the African and Asian councillors twice refused the offer of an unofficial majority in the Legislative Council – the key to British plans for constitutional development in tropical Africa at this time – because they feared domination by their European colleagues.[6] Moreover, no African as yet sat on the Executive Council, nor was there any electoral system, for neither the European settler community nor the African elite of townsmen and civil servants grouped into the Tanganyika African Association who called for elections were considered numerous enough to warrant them.[7] This at least had the advantage that neither separate racial electorates (as in Kenya) nor ethnic electorates (as in Nigeria) were institutionalized in Tanganyika.

Rather, Twining's constitutional initiative in November 1949[8] – his 'cock-shy', as he called it – was designed to create a political basis for the inter-racial co-operation which he believed was the only way of achieving his main goal of developing Tanganyika economically. He proposed that the reluctant unofficial members of the Legislative Council should all form a committee to produce a plan for constitutional reform. This might include partly elected and multi-racial provincial councils which, 'within a relatively short time', would each elect one African and one non-African to the Legislative Council, although the body would retain its official majority. This was a radical proposal to come from a colonial governor, for in Kenya at this time it was the Europeans who enjoyed parity with the other two races combined. Settlers protested furiously when Twining's proposals were leaked to the press.

After fifteen months collecting and considering evidence, the Constitutional Development Committee proposed a different, compromise formula: a Legislative Council with an official majority, 21 unofficial seats shared equally by Europeans, Asians, and Africans, and (at European insistence) the introduction of elections at some imprecisely defined date in the future.[9] The Colonial Office enthusiastically welcomed this version of racial parity, but the Conservative Government which took office in Britain later in 1951 accepted it only grudgingly and instructed Twining to begin by reforming local government and to avoid giving a date for the constitution of the new Legislative Council.[10] Twining was in no hurry. Although the Constitutional Development Committee had proposed elections for all races, it had rejected his suggestion that provincial councils should be the electing bodies. He proposed instead that an expert commissioner should devise an electoral system. It was not until 1953 that the commissioner's proposals were published. When the new Legislative Council first met in 1955, with 30 unofficial members drawn equally from the three races, all were still appointed by the Governor.[11]

In the meantime a major change was taking place in African politics. The Constitutional Development Committee's rejection of parity between Africans and non-Africans in favour of parity between each of the three races had alarmed the more politicized members of the Tanganyika African Association, whose Mwanza Branch complained in 1951 'that the settlers' voice has managed to turn to nothing the proposed constitutional changes'.[12] During the next three years such up-country branches in the

Lake and Northern Provinces, radicalized by agrarian grievances, reinforced the Association's traditional nucleus of teachers, civil servants, and townsmen in Dar es Salaam. In 1953 the Association elected a new president, Julius Nyerere, who as a student in Britain had recognized racial parity as 'a principle which in spite of its deceptive name assumes the principle of racial superiority'.[13] At the meeting in July 1954 which converted the Association into TANU, tripartite representation was rejected in favour of a demand that African representatives should outnumber those of all other races combined.[14]

The Special Branch gave Twining an accurate record of TANU's inaugural meeting and the Governor – well-intentioned but reactionary, authoritarian, and blustering – sent the Colonial Office a dismissive account of the new organization: 'Its useful purpose, if it is to have one, is likely to be that of providing a foil for the establishment of a party better able to represent moderate African opinion.'[15] Officials in London were better attuned to African nationalism and noted Nyerere's initial assurances of moderation. 'He seems', one observed, 'just the sort of "pen-is-mightier-than-the-sword" African who could do his country, and us, a lot of good – if patiently handled and allowed to work off steam.'[16] The Colonial Office records confirm but add nothing to accounts of TANU's growth and social composition derived from its own records.[17] What the records do reveal is Twining's extraordinary fluctuations of attitude towards the party, which bewildered his political masters and prevented them from formulating a coherent response. After his initial dismissive account, the Governor was prejudiced further against TANU by the attention paid to it by the United Nations Mission which visited Tanganyika in August 1954 and criticized his multi-racial strategy. 'They thought our constitutional development was far too slow,' he complained; 'regretted our attitude about elections and thought that TANU was the finest thing in Tanganyika and that Julius Nyerere and Kirilo Japhet were the prophets. They considered that they should be given every assistance to lead the country to its proper destiny (sic).'[18]

Twining and his officials held that by confining its membership to Africans and insisting that Tanganyika was primarily an African country, TANU displayed a black racialism which threatened Britain's multi-racial strategy for East and Central Africa. As Nyerere reminded the Member for Local Government after an interview in December 1954,

> With the greatest emphasis you said, Sir, that Government can never entertain the idea that this country is primarily African; that the only sense in which this country can be regarded as African is the sense that it is on the African Continent. When I pointed out that the Africans are in an overwhelming majority you retorted, 'so what!' and, I must own, I was so over-awed by the retort that I did not attempt to reply.[19]

As his anger grew, Twining came to see TANU as the tool of a malign conspiracy by all the anti-British forces he detested:

> the people ... are, at best, apathetic and are anxious to pursue political developments step by step, but we are faced with a challenge, and what I

171

regard as a very dangerous challenge, for the introduction of universal suffrage. This has been initiated by India and I believe, has some support from the United States. It was put fairly and squarely to us by Julius Nyerere who, undoubtedly, had been primed by Jaipal, the Indian Delegate to the Trusteeship Council's Visiting Mission, and, we think, by the American Consulate in Dar es Salaam.[20]

Eventually Twining convinced himself than even TANU's constitution had been drafted in the American Consulate at the initiative of a visiting Afro-American.[21]

Despite the Governor's fulminations and much local conflict with the administration in Lake Province, TANU's aim to *prepare* Tanganyika for independence remained quite modest during its first year of existence, and its relations with the authorities were relatively harmonious. As the Chief Secretary told officials in September 1955, racial parity was not open to negotiation, but 'African nationalism is a fact of life to be treated with understanding and, in so far as its energies are directed to African advancement with the regard [sic] to the obligations thereby incurred, with encouragement. Grievances which are genuine and removable must be removed, and those which are imaginary patiently and persistently explained away.'[22] Shortly afterwards, however, the government announced its intention to introduce the promised Legislative Council elections in 1958. Knowledge of this encouraged the Council's more liberal European members to plan a multi-racial United Tanganyika Party (UTP) to contest the elections, with Twining's strong encouragement. 'I should have liked to have carried Julius Nyerere and the Union along with us,' he told the Colonial Secretary, Alan Lennox-Boyd, in October 1955, 'but there are serious difficulties in the way... What they are after is Africa for the Africans, universal suffrage and the toppling over of the present constitution in 1958.' Instead, therefore, 'We are taking steps to discredit the Union whenever there is cause to do so' and seeking 'to canalize nationalism into local or tribal patriotism'. Most important,

> We are fostering the idea of another political party. When I make my first reference to elections, probably at the end of November, Ivor Bayldon, who is the leader of the Unofficials, intends to invite people to form a political party to be ready in time to fight the elections in 1958. ... A certain amount of lobbying has already been done and it is hoped to get strong financial support from the sisal industry, the mining industry, commerce, the Northern Province and Southern Highlands Province European farmers, the coffee industry and various other powerful and wealthy bodies... It is then intended to call a convention and get agreement on a platform which will probably be the acceptance of a multiracial society with the present constitution as being the most suitable one for some time to come... It will, in fact, be a Conservative Party with a liberal pro-gramme. The difficulty will be to get it really popular support, but with a strong organization, good financial backing and the right man to run the party, I think it will receive support from a good solid conservative and 50% Muslim population which runs from north to south through the

center of the territory. This must, of course, be very carefully handled, but it is worth making a bid of such a nature.[23]

'All strength to your elbow!' replied Lennox-Boyd, who had been prejudiced by Twining's contempt for Nyerere and believed passionately that multi-racialism was the only policy by which East and Central Africa could avoid violent conflict between black and white.[24] His Permanent Secretary, similarly, found Twining's scheme 'most stimulating and encouraging...The views expressed may prove in time to have been in parts over-optimistic, but the determination which Sir Edward Twining continues to show is certainly a welcome contrast to present attitudes in both Kenya and Uganda.'[25] The Governor himself now came to see the UTP's success as central to his policy. 'The 1958 elections will be the first real test,' he wrote in May 1956:

> If U.T.P. succeeds, TANU will probably collapse and be replaced by a variety of new parties with more extreme and probably left-wing tendencies springing from Trade Unions, the Co-operatives and other similar movements. If U.T.P. is defeated at the polls, African nationalism will have won. The non-Africans will begin to leave the territory; outside capital will dry up; progress will be retarded and this will lead to frustration, disillusionment, disorder and chaos.[26]

To avert that apocalyptic scenario, 'the need is to sustain multi-racialism, in the short run for the economic development of the territory, and in the long run for the retention of the territory within the Commonwealth.'[27] The timetable he envisaged at this time provided for Legislative Council elections in four constituencies in 1958, elections in all constituencies in 1964, and self-government possibly in the late 1970s.[28]

Four months later, in September 1956, Nyerere paid his first visit to the Colonial Office. He told W.A.C. Mathieson, who had charge of Tanganyikan affairs, that TANU wanted Britain to declare Tanganyika to be primarily an African country which would follow West African patterns of constitutional advance, rather than a plural society like Kenya or Central Africa where 'Africans were on the losing side'. He also insisted that Tanganyika should have universal adult suffrage on a common roll, and he warned that, if most voters in the 1958 elections were to be Europeans and Asians, TANU would boycott the elections. Mathieson replied 'that we believed that in Tanganyika the possibility of evolving a successful multi-racial society was greater than anywhere else and we must succeed,'[29] but Nyerere nevertheless impressed him. 'I confess,' Mathieson told his superiors, 'that I feel that there is something to be said for the view that since the future of Tanganyika is so manifestly an African country we might as well say so if it will induce confidence in our intentions amongst 8 million Africans.' He added, however, that the potential impact on opinion in Kenya and Central Africa might make such a declaration impossible, [30] and that was the view of his superiors, Gorell Barnes and Macpherson, who ruled out the suggestion and insisted on maintaining the policy of multi-racial parity.[31] Nyerere was anxious to meet the Colonial

Secretary. Lennox-Boyd eventually agreed to see him, despite Twining's strong opposition, but assured the Governor after the interview that he had given nothing away.[32]

It was therefore with consternation that in November 1956 the Colonial Office received Twining's proposal for a drastic change of course. The Governor's motive was disillusionment with the UTP, which had gained only 1,200 members and merely demonstrated the bankruptcy of European leadership in a territory with virtually no committed settler population. Of the Asian communities, the Muslims were apolitical and the Hindus hostile to British rule. From this, Twining concluded, 'It will already be obvious to you that with European leadership virtually defunct, and Asian leadership no more acceptable to the Africans than it would be to us, the transition to African leadership had best be made as soon as practicable.' He considered TANU 'a disgraceful mess' in imminent danger of fragmentation. But its emotional appeal was powerful, its threat to boycott the coming elections would probably abort them, Nyerere was the most influential African available, and 'it is very strongly in our interests that we should try to gather him into the fold, although this might mean making some concessions'. If that proved impossible, 'there would still be some good if less sophisticated Africans through whom we could work and make the leaders for the time being, if not for longer'. The crux, however, was to retain the initiative: 'The important thing in all these constitutional matters is to keep moving and let it be seen that we are so doing.' Twining therefore proposed to announce that after the 1958 elections a committee of Legislative Councilors would consider further constitutional change, including the future of racial parity, the franchise, and the introduction of a ministerial system.[33] 'This is indeed a volte face', Gorell Barnes noted,[34] but he and other officials positively welcomed the proposal to accelerate constitutional change by a decade. The Permanent Secretary, Sir John Macpherson, had previously been Governor-General of Nigeria and seized the opportunity to shift Tanganyika's course in a more West African direction:

> I have been leaning over backwards to understand and support the policy now in force for constitutional advance in East and Central Africa – where the conditions, because of white settlement, are so different from those in West Africa. And this notwithstanding the fact that, by comparison with West African nationals, the demands of people like Julius Nyerere strike me as very reasonable in content and moderate in tone... When you asked me if I thought our policy in East and Central Africa was wrong I said that I did not think so. I agreed with it. But I felt that we ought not to be taken by surprise if the build-up of an African nationalism made it necessary for us to travel rather faster than we had planned.
>
> If Tanganyika (and Nyasaland) were isolated from territories like Kenya and Northern Rhodesia I would unhesitatingly have favoured or advocated the change of direction and pace now suggested by Sir E. Twining.[35]

Lennox-Boyd, however, was about to leave for the officially multi-racial but actually white-dominated Central African Federation, and he knew that Tanganyika could not be isolated. He refused to be committed to Twining's 'very strange change of view'.[36] The Governor was told that his proposals were too drastic for immediate acceptance, but that he could prepare to create ministries headed by unofficials – perhaps telling Nyerere that he might be offered the Education portfolio if he won a seat in the 1958 election – and might thereafter reconsider the parity voting formula.[37] When Nyerere met Macpherson on 18 January 1957, all was moderation:

> He [Nyerere] said all the right things – about eliminating fear on the part of any of the communities in Tanganyika, and about the Africans behaving in such a way as not to cause apprehension among the other two communities ... he thought that an organization like TANU could be a sort of 'bridge' between the 'orthodox' situation, as in West Africa, and the situation where there was a plural society consisting of different races. He said that he himself was the 'agitator' in Tanganyika and he suggested – with a cheerful grin – that Tanganyika might have had something much worse! He wanted to 'mop up' African discontent before it became dangerous ... Provided the direction of the advance had been shaped he could satisfy his people... He hoped that the step to be taken next year i.e. the election and its aftermath would be sufficient to 'shape the direction'.[38]

The honeymoon collapsed as soon as Nyerere regained Dar es Salaam. On 27 January 1957, as reported by the Special Branch, he told a crowd estimated at 30,000 that it was only where European settlers existed that Africans had difficulty in gaining independence:

> In Tanganyika, Government intended to rule on multi-racial lines, but this was a myth. Multi-racialism meant government for the good of Europeans and Indians and eventually only for Europeans. There were only 3000 European settlers in Tanganyika, but they intended to rule the country and exhorted all the inhabitants to live quietly together... In the end TANU would succeed in this matter and Government would find that they could not prevent it... In the old days the Germans might have prevented it with guns, but this was not 1700 and right, not might, would prevail.[39]

Even as reported, the speech seems remarkably innocuous; the European press commented that it 'could in no way be interpreted as some fiery, political outburst intended to play on the less rational emotions of his listeners.'[40] But its direct targeting of Europeans alarmed the administration. Claiming that 'much of the danger ... lies in the emphasis, intonations and sneering way the speech is delivered', [41] A.J. Grattan-Bellew, the Chief Secretary who was administering the government in Twining's absence, appears to have seized the opportunity for a decisive confrontation with Nyerere:

> He has made it absolutely clear that he is virulently opposed to this Government and all its works...I must make it clear that you should not underestimate the effect of Nyerere's speech on all shades of opinion in Tanganyika, though it is now generally recognised that TANU is an evil

thing...It will be necessary to take urgent, stringent and robust measures to contain TANU's activities, and it may, later on, be necessary to proscribe it altogether. But all such measures would be purely negative and of no avail unless we have a positive alternative policy. I am working on this and will inform you as soon as I have some proposals to make which are like to be based principally on fostering the emergent moderate African leadership which is available and which is likely to be acceptable to the mass of African opinion in the Territory.[42]

In March 1957 A.J. Grattan-Bellew explained his belief that a confrontation with TANU was to be welcomed, 'particularly if it had the effect, which I am sure it would have, of persuading the 99% of the African population (who are not at present members of TANU) to gently and clearly come over in favour of Government, and also possibly the effect of causing a new African political party with a new leader to emerge':

> If we are to follow our policy of non-racialism and of developing the territory for the benefit of all the inhabitants and progressively leading the people towards self-government, we will be able to do so not, I am sorry to say, because the people are willing to follow the guidance we can give on account of their trust and affection, but because they are made to realize our strength and determination and that our policy is in their best interests. This has to be done against the background which is now being created by TANU and which has come to mean to the gullible and idle (and unfortunately these two terms apply to the majority of Africans) that TANU means the denial of law and order and that self-government, as represented by TANU, is the negative of any respect for authority.[43]

Nyerere was banned from public speaking. The Societies Ordinance requiring police permission for public meetings was rigorously enforced. By March 1958 ten TANU branches had been closed, often for challenging native authorities or attempting to exercise powers considered to belong properly to government.

Although the Colonial Office accepted in March 1957 that the 'attempt to bring Nyerere into the fold...should now be abandoned',[44] the officials were alarmed by the Tanganyika Government's fluctuations of policy. Macpherson, who believed that the government had over-reacted to Nyerere's speech in January 1957,[45] accepted the need to find African allies against extreme nationalism, but wished 'that it had been possible to carry this out in a steadier way, without being pressed by events to act on the grounds of expediency ... and without "tacking"'.[46] When Twining, with characteristic over-enthusiasm, adopted Grattan-Bellew's view and proposed in April 1957 to seek the agreement of his Executive Council that he might if necessary pre-empt the likelihood of eventual bloodshed and 'declare TANU throughout the territory to be unlawful', Lennox-Boyd warned him firmly to close only branches against which convictions had been obtained in the courts, for a total proscription of the party 'would obviously be a very serious step and I would need to be supplied with a strong case in defense'.[47] 'Maintenance of blanket ban on public meetings held by TANU will be difficult to sustain indefinitely', the Governor was warned a month later when he planned to prohibit a meeting in the capital.[48] But Twining's passion was still rising. On 29 May 1957 he wrote his most vitriolic denunciation of TANU:

> The point which needs to be stressed is the debt which TANU owes for its growth, finances and guidance to outside influences…TANU's efforts are now aimed at making a nationalist issue out of every one of Government's policies. Whether it be wages or education or elections, the picture they seek to create is one of a united nation struggling for freedom and justice against an oppressive foreign rule. *A priori* the falsity of this picture is glaring. Tanganyika does not exist because of any natural unity, but only by the accident of events over which its peoples have exercised no control, and there is no special reason why the hard-won loyalties of European nation-states should repeat themselves here. There is no language nor tradition nor interest in common, except what has been lightly overlaid by little more than half a century of alien authority. All that there really is in common is the blackness of the African skin and that is why TANU's appeal is now becoming fundamentally racialist and not nationalist… To sum up, we are dealing at present with a thoroughly spurious organization. It is no longer a political party in the ordinary sense of the word, but a racialist movement, which, if not contained, can do immense harm. The leadership is mean and corrupt, actuated by malice and self-interest. They are efficiently advised by people of ill-will and by others of small understanding both within and without Tanganyika. The permanent rank and file of the movement are the detribalised Africans of the towns and those for whom modern education or progress has destroyed the traditional peasant way of living. And there is always temporary access of strength available when there is a local grievance to be exploited or even, among the mass of the population for short periods, when some instance of colour discrimination may be invoked as a rallying call.[49]

A month later Twining visited the Colonial Office and repeated his views at length to the officials.[50]

And then the storm ceased. On his return to Tanganyika in July 1957 Twining offered Nyerere a seat in the Legislative Council, in the hope of 'taming him by letting him see at first hand the problems with which Government has to deal',[51] and was surprised when Nyerere accepted it, despite considerable opposition within TANU. 'He is very moderate and co-operative', the Governor reported.[52] At later meetings, according to Twining, Nyerere 'agreed that a period of five or ten years of political stability is very desirable and he indicated that he would say so in public'.[53] The Governor attributed Nyerere's accommodating attitude to the disastrous condition of TANU's organization and finances. But Twining gave no reason for his own reversal of policy. The records do not suggest that Lennox-Boyd laid down the law while the Governor was in London.

One intervention came from Sir Andrew Cohen, who had pioneered Britain's decolonization strategy in tropical Africa at the end of the war and was now its permanent representative to the United Nations

Trusteeship Council. Cohen was finding the ban on Nyerere's speeches impossible to defend. In June 1957 he met Nyerere in New York and told Twining, 'He struck me as able and very intelligent and I imagine that he is likely to have a leading position for a long time ahead. He also struck me as essentially a moderate in politics... The impression I formed of Nyerere had made me wonder whether even now it is too late to get him into the fold.' Cohen suggested that Nyerere might be appointed to the Legislative Council.[54] Twining's dislike of Cohen was notorious, but, for whatever reason, he made the appointment. He may also have reflected that a new United Nations Mission was to visit Tanganyika shortly and the government was dangerously exposed.

Yet the chief reason for conciliation on both sides was probably the evolving and complex situation surrounding the coming elections. Responsibility for devising a procedure for electing the unofficial members of Legislative Council – with equal representation for each race – had been entrusted in 1952 to Professor W.J.M. Mackenzie of Manchester University.[55] He proposed to divide the territory into constituencies, each returning one member of each race. Initially most African members and some of other races would be appointed or elected indirectly, but at least in Dar es Salaam and possibly in Tanga Province it would be possible at an early stage to hold direct elections for all three races. In these constituencies, instead of voters choosing only a candidate of their own race, as was the practice in Kenya, inter-racial co-operation would be fostered by placing all voters on a common roll. Voters would have three votes and could cast all or some of them for any candidate, save that they could not give any one candidate more than one vote. Since there would be little point in supporting more than one candidate of the same race, voters could, if they wished, vote for one candidate of each race. Candidates would therefore need to emphasize their moderation in racial matters.

Mackenzie emphasized that this ingenious system would work only if three conditions were met. First, candidates must be nominated by a substantial number of voters of their own race, for otherwise that race might not be effectively represented. Second, inter-racial voting must be voluntary, for 'compulsion would certainly defeat its own ends'.[56] Third, a constituency must have a roughly equal number of voters of each race, for if one race was numerically predominant it could choose the successful candidates for all three races; in Tanganyikan circumstances, this meant setting the franchise qualifications (in terms of income, property, and education) relatively high in order to restrict African voters to about the numbers of the immigrant races, but even with this restriction there would at first be only a few constituencies where direct tripartite elections would be possible, while in most of the country they must be ruled out 'for a long time to come'.[57]

Although the Tanganyika Government accepted these proposals in principle, its anxiety to defeat nationalism and legitimate multi-racialism led it to ignore the conditions which Mackenzie had seen as vital to the system's success. After much discussion, in May 1955 the government proposed franchise qualifications designed not to equalize the voters of the different races but 'to avoid universal suffrage on the one hand and a vote confined to the so-called intelligentsia on the other. Particularly do we want to bring into play the territory-wide body of traditionally middle-of-the-road African opinion which is formed by the men and women of substance who are and must continue for some time to be the natural leaders of their people.' In addition, the government argued, against Mackenzie, that every voter *must* cast three votes, one for each race, for otherwise few if any Africans would vote for a European or Asian candidate, thus discrediting the elections and exacerbating rather than ameliorating racial divisions. At this stage the government planned to hold elections in 1958 in only the Tanga and Northern Provinces,[58] but as time passed it became eager to conduct them in as many constituencies as possible, despite Mackenzie's warning that few were yet suitable.

The potential danger of this system was immediately perceived by the Colonial Office staff concerned. The junior official responsible minuted:

> We are not happy about the proposal…that each voter should be forced to throw one vote for a candidate of each race. Such compulsion appears to be unnatural let alone undemocratic and might well bring cross voting into disrepute. If at first cross voting is only limited in extent, this does not seem to matter very much. The very existence of a marginal cross vote may be expected to induce candidates to stand on a multi-racial platform, and as cross voting develops this tendency will increase.
>
> We do seem to need a more careful assessment of the effect which cross voting will have in weighting the voting power of the three races. This is the problem which Mr Grattan-Bellew raised with us informally in April [1955]. It was pointed out that unless the racial voting power was roughly equalized (a state of affairs which it would be difficult to attain and even more difficult to preserve) you would get a situation where the election of the European candidate would be largely determined by the African vote.[59]

Clearly as this danger was perceived, it was almost immediately lost to sight again, with vital consequences for East Africa's future. Three days later Gorell Barnes put the problem to Twining, and it promptly became confused:

> I gained the impression that Sir E. Twining would not be surprised if we pressed for the abandonment of the proposal that each voter should be forced to throw one vote for a candidate of each race and that he would withdraw his proposal if we did so… We cannot possibly insist that voting strength should be roughly equal and we must rely, to avoid the sort of trouble Mr Kisch has in mind, on the provision that each candidate must have a certain minimum backing from members of his own race.[60]

A minimum backing, of course, would not decide the election. Yet Mathieson, the next to comment, saw the danger differently:

> The crucial question is clearly the pitch of the franchise. I do not agree with Mr. Kisch that decisions on this matter should be governed by a statistical assessment of the likely number of voters. In gauging the effects of any decision it would be useful for the Tanganyika Government and for us to

have an estimate of the likely statistical effect of the qualifications suggested; but these must, I think, be considered fundamentally on their merits...

On compulsory voting I agree with previous minutes. I am sure it would reduce the attraction of this system for Africans if they felt they were to be obliged to vote for an Asian. Such an obligation might in fact, under the influence of African political parties, lead to a boycott of elections and it is essential to demonstrate that any system adopted has the willing support of the population.[61]

As discussions between Tanganyikan officials and the Colonial Office continued during mid-1955, the issue which came to predominate was not that African voters might decide the entire election but that Africans must be forced to legitimate the multi-racial constitution by voting for all three races if they wanted to vote at all. The Colonial Office found this thoroughly distasteful. As W.A.C. Mathieson put it, 'It can easily be pointed to as an illustration of the unreality of our contention – or at least our lack of faith in it – that there is a genuine spirit of inter-racial co-operation in Tanganyika effectively reflected by parity in the legislature. If TANU, for example, wanted to get Africans to boycott the elections this feature of the arrangements would be a good talking point.'[62] Nevertheless, at a meeting of officials on 30 August 1955 (beneath a mulberry tree in the garden of Queens' College, Cambridge), *'It was agreed* that in the circumstances it was desirable to put to the public in Tanganyika the proposal that each voter exercising his right to vote, must cast one vote in respect of each vacancy and to see what their reactions were. If there was strong opposition to the idea then, the Meeting thought, it should be dropped.'[63]

Twining announced the proposal in April 1956, but by then the possibility that a majority of African voters might elect all the members, regardless of race, had been further obscured by the formation of the UTP, whose multi-racial character was designed to match a franchise based on racial parity. Mathieson, for example, had convinced himself by July 1956, on no grounds at all, that 'So long as the three-member constituency is a feature of the electoral system, two out of the three members will almost inevitably be U.T.P.'[64] Hopes of the UTP and misunderstanding of the electoral system may also have led the government, which had from the beginning expected Africans to be the largest group of voters, to accept in November 1956 recommendations from a Franchise Committee which put it beyond doubt that African voters would outnumber Europeans and Asians combined.[65] The despatch covering this report described compulsory tripartite voting as agreed policy.[66]

Nyerere appears initially to have shared the widespread misunderstanding of the electoral system. In discussion with Mathieson in September 1956, 'He said that under the government proposals the electorate in any constituency would be composed of a majority of immigrant races and for any party to put up candidates before such an electorate would be a mockery. TANU candidates would not stand if the electorate were largely non-African.'[67] Shortly afterwards, he told a press conference that TANU would boycott such elections. This remained the party's position during its intense conflict with the government in the first half of 1957.[68] In January 1957, however, as UTP's failure to win popular support became evident, the authorities decided to publicize the fact that Africans would be a majority of voters, in the hope of preventing an electoral fiasco. By May the scheme was under attack not only by nationalists who rejected multi-racialism but by non-African politicians and officials. In June the government assured the United Nations that Africans would predominate and Nyerere replied that TANU wished to participate in elections if they were truly free.[69]

The United Nations Visiting Mission in August 1957 reported that there was no support whatever for the tripartite voting plan, except among some UTP leaders. This was the moment when Nyerere accepted a Legislative Council seat, ostensibly with the intention of changing the electoral proposals, as opinion within TANU demanded.[70] But by now Nyerere had clearly realized that, however uncongenial a parity election might be, the African majority offered a good chance of winning it. His goal, he told a reporter in August 1957, was that alongside the fifteen members elected under parity provisions, another fifteen should be chosen by single-seat constituencies.[71] Several meetings with him during the following weeks left the Minister for Constitutional Affairs with the impression that Nyerere did not wish to boycott the elections but was unsure of his ability to carry TANU with him.[72] Meanwhile few Africans registered to vote, but in August 1957 TANU ordered its officers to encourage registration and Nyerere told a public meeting early in September that TANU would fight the elections.[73]

In October 1957 Lennox-Boyd paid his first visit to Tanganyika as Colonial Secretary. By now the Government of Tanganyika was itself firmly opposed to compulsory tripartite voting and urged him to make it optional, warning that compulsion would give TANU an excuse to boycott the elections and reduce them to a farce.[74] TANU, from the other side, pressed its plan for parity between Africans and the other races combined, with elections in single-member constituencies. Nyerere told Lennox-Boyd at a meeting that TANU would like to participate in the elections, but that it depended on the circumstances.[75] However, the Colonial Secretary was committed to both multi-racialism and a qualified franchise as his general policy for East and Central Africa.[76] He ruled that it was too late to change Tanganyika's electoral plans, which

> would undoubtedly be interpreted by responsible people of all races as a retreat by Government in the face of irresponsible African pressure.
>
> Before leaving Tanganyika I accordingly intend to make it clear that the present plan (which includes the provision [for tripartite voting] and which has already been incorporated in legislation) will be adhered to.
>
> African nationalism here, though spreading, is at present somewhat *jejune* and lacking in organisation and clear purpose. On the other hand, Europeans, Asians and responsible Africans are beginning to get demoralised by fear that Government may be in retreat in the face of African nationalism. I accordingly intend to take every opportunity to reiterate

that lawlessness will not be tolerated and that H.M.G.[77] do not regard themselves as fighting a rearguard action and have no intention of abandoning their trust or of handing it over to irresponsible people, or, indeed, to any Government under which responsible people of all races in Tanganyika would not feel secure. It is, indeed, clear to me that constitutional development here is in danger of being too rapid rather than too slow and that H.M.G. will need to remain in charge for many, many years to come.[78]

Lennox-Boyd's decision forced Nyerere back to his second line of action: to persuade TANU to fight and win the election under the tripartite voting rules. After displaying his intransigence by resigning in protest from the Legislative Council during December, Nyerere faced perhaps the most critical meeting of his career when TANU's annual conference assembled at Tabora in January 1958. This meeting has been described elsewhere.[79] The party was deeply divided by a resolution from the Mwanza delegation denouncing tripartite voting as *haramu* (forbidden). The debate swayed back and forth before Nyerere summed up in favour of participation. He won the vote, concentrated his subsequent speeches on threats of civil disobedience if *madaraka* (responsible government) was not granted during 1959, and launched a campaign to encourage electoral registration, strengthen party organization, and expand membership. At the time of the conference he estimated that some 250,000 people had at some point paid TANU's entrance fee; by early 1960 that figure had reached perhaps 1,000,000.[80] By February 1958 Twining was anticipating a TANU victory,[81] and the election in five of the territory's ten constituencies in September proved him right. TANU not only won all five African seats, but by throwing its 68 per cent of the vote behind the most sympathetic European and Asian candidates, it won eight of their ten seats as well, the other two successful candidates being unopposed Europeans.[82] Against all its intentions, the parity formula had put real constitutional power into African hands for the first time in East and Central Africa since the colonial invasion.

Twining, however, had already left, and it was his successor, Sir Richard Turnbull, who had to come to terms with African power. He experienced it first in its popular form, for shortly after his arrival in July 1958 a local crisis occurred in the Geita District of Lake Province, where discontent at refusal to register a TANU branch merged with hostility to a new multi-racial district council whose Asian members were seen by activists as a threat to the local co-operative society. 'Ringleaders' were arrested, demonstrators outside the provincial office in Mwanza were dispersed with batons and teargas, and Turnbull found it impossible to address the people.[83] Between 1 April and 24 December 1958 the authorities in Lake Province recorded 8 forcible releases from custody, 69 illegal meetings and assemblies, 14 unlawful courts and attempts to impose fines, and 30 cases of intimidation and besetting.[84] Twining had contemplated meeting such civil disobedience 'with a little resolute handling'.[85]

Turnbull, who had suppressed Mau Mau in Nairobi and had been appointed to Tanganyika by the Colonial Secretary as 'the toughest guy I knew in East Africa',[86] quickly recognized that Tanganyika's security forces were too weak to repress civil disobedience, and, unlike his predecessor, his judgment did not thereafter waver. Three days after the police action in Mwanza and before the September 1958 elections, Turnbull put his first political recommendations to the Colonial Office. Parity, he explained, was dead, as was Twining's notion of multi-racialism. Instead TANU's propaganda had created widespread expectation that 1959 would see *madaraka*, which ambiguously embraced both responsible government and self-government but was interpreted by Nyerere to mean elected majorities in both the Legislative and Executive Councils. The current British position, as stated by Lennox-Boyd, was that no further constitutional change was possible until elections had been completed in the five remaining constituencies during 1959 and a Post-Elections Committee had then considered the next stage of constitutional advance.

Turnbull proposed instead to regain the initiative by announcing that multi-racialism meant no more than security for non-Africans, and by bringing forward the second stage of elections to February 1959 so that the Post-Elections Committee could consider *madaraka* as soon as possible.[87] Initially this proposal delighted the Colonial Office. It 'warms my heart', Macpherson commented, 'and to me gives proof, if proof were needed, of the rightness of his selection as Governor. I am sure that this is the sort of direction the Territory has been waiting for.'[88] The officials approved Turnbull's proposals and encouraged him to prepare for the appointment of elected ministers.[89] Three weeks later, in September 1958, the Governor went further and sought permission to announce that Tanganyika's government at independence would be largely African, as Nyerere had long demanded, and that in July 1959 five elected ministers – three Africans, one Asian, and one European – would be appointed, thereby abandoning any form of parity.[90] This time, however, Lennox-Boyd stopped him in his tracks. 'This raises very big issues' for the entire region, he wrote, and after discussion he approved the statement about Tanganyika's future but ordered that an announcement regarding ministers must wait until after the elections planned for March 1959.[91]

By now TANU had won the first round of elections decisively and was pressing harder for *madaraka* in 1959, Nyerere was talking of independence by the mid-1960s,[92] the security situation in Lake Province was deteriorating, and Turnbull was contemplating a crisis in 1959 unless he could offer some dramatic constitutional advance. 'The major struggle,' he speculated in December 1958,

> may take place at the end of 1959 or early in 1960. It will depend on whether Nyerere gets enough from the Post-Elections Committee to satisfy him and his followers; and if it comes it will be between the Government and the whole of TANU under the leadership of Nyerere. He has announced that what he expects from the Committee is an elected majority in the Legislative Council and a majority of elected unofficial

ministers (including Europeans and Asians as well as Africans) in the Council of Ministers; if he does not get what he wants it is probable that he will withdraw his co-operation (such as it is) and embark on a Territory-wide campaign of resistance to Government.[93]

It was now the Colonial Office's turn to come to terms with African power. Turnbull's letter struck Gorell Barnes as 'extremely alarming', suggesting that Tanganyika might well become independent by 1965. 'The time has arrived,' he warned Macpherson on 31 December 1958,

> when the Secretary of State will either have to put his foot down and insist, possibly or even probably at the cost of disturbances in Tanganyika, that advance shall continue to be step by step and at a reasonable pace, or to resign himself to our being out of East Africa within five to ten years. It seems to us that, if Tanganyika rushes over the precipice, Uganda could not fail to follow – for, although Sir F. Crawford (the Governor) has said that it needs another twenty-one years and that we can perhaps hope for fifteen, it is more advanced and more predominantly African than Tanga-nyika – and Kenya, surrounded by the two of them and Somalia and Ethiopia, could hardly survive for long afterwards.[94]

With Lennox-Boyd's approval, Turnbull received a sharp rejoinder:

> The Secretary of State is quite certain in his own mind that the bringing of Elected Ministers into your Government and some adjustment on the representative side of Legislative Council in favour of Africans are about the only major constitutional steps in Tanganyika that he can contemplate for some time to come... We believe that it would be a complete abdication of responsibility to retreat in the face of Nyerere's sweet reason and acquiesce in the establishment of an unofficial majority as the essential end product of the Post-Elections Committee, let alone the establishment of a government with a majority of unofficial Ministers in 1960 or pretty soon thereafter. We are quite sure that you could not hold out for more than a few years after that and that it would be a disastrous decision not only for Tanganyika but also for her neighbours. We take this view in the full realisation that this will probably lead to very serious trouble in the country – perhaps from the middle of 1959 onwards; but if we cannot convince Nyerere that what we are doing is in the best interests of the people of Tanganyika and thus get him to co-operate in a policy of gradual progress, then we had better have the showdown at the outset rather than a year or two later.[95]

The Governor was asked for a security assessment of the implications of this decision. The letter crossed an even more alarming despatch in which he had advocated the announcement of a constitutional timetable which would have granted a majority of unofficial ministers during 1960 in the hope of then deferring full independence, the alternative being civil disturbances which would be more difficult to contain than Mau Mau, for 'TANU would have a 90 per cent following', there would be no loyalists, Tanganyika's security forces were weak, the world would back TANU, and the country would be ruined. 'I don't deceive myself that the move would not be premature', Turnbull added; 'but these chaps will be little more ready for self-government in fifty years time than they will be in fifteen, and it may be better to take the chance of going ahead too fast than to risk a wholesale insurrection.'[96]

Thus Turnbull was coming to see Tanganyika's very lack of development as a reason for accelerated decolonization. When he received the Colonial Office's instructions, he accepted that an official majority must remain, but he insisted that the ministerial system must concede enough to attract TANU to accept office, and he warned that the Colonial Office timetable would demand at least a doubling of his security forces. 'If there is to be an open breach with TANU – and I recognise that this may be inevitable – I am anxious that it should not happen until we are better prepared for the disturbances that will follow... At present there is scarcely a strand of barbed wire or a spare vehicle or wireless-set in the Territory.'[97]

The Colonial Office now realized that TANU's electoral victory threatened Britain's entire position in East and Central Africa. Explaining this in January 1959 to a Cabinet committee reconsidering colonial policy, the Colonial Office stressed that

> much depends on decisions which will have to be taken very shortly by Ministers on the handling of the situation in Tanganyika. It is certain that, when the remaining half of the seats on the representative side of Legislative Council are filled by the elections due to be held next March, the results will be similar to the results of last September's elections... The position of the Tanganyika African National Union will then be very strong and it is known that Mr Nyerere will demand an early move forward to an unofficial majority both in Legislative Council and in Executive Council. If that demand is conceded, it would seem that the last possibility of stopping the momentum toward early independence will have been lost, and that it will be difficult to prevent the territory from becoming independent by about 1965. On the other hand, the territory will certainly not have the human and material resources to support independence for many years to come and in those circumstances it would not be consistent with our declared policies for East Africa to go forward at such a rapid pace.

If Tanganyika moved rapidly towards independence, the memorandum warned, Uganda and then Kenya would inevitably follow. 'The alternative to following the line of least resistance would be to state quite clearly that H.M.G. intend to remain in ultimate control of all the East African territories for a considerable period,' perhaps fifteen to twenty years, and this was the policy favoured by the Colonial Office.[98] It was motivated not only by fear of the domino effect of concessions in Tanganyika, but also by a sense of duty to ensure that when the territory gained independence it would have the civil servants, legislators, and economic capacity to run its affairs. 'Even if Tanganyika were an island in the Pacific,' Macpherson wrote at this time, 'I do not believe for a moment that we would contemplate the possibility of giving it independence by 1965.'[99]

Turnbull had already challenged this thinking, but it broadly prevailed when Lennox-Boyd and his officials met the East African governors at a hastily summoned conference at Chequers (the Prime Minister's country house) in January 1959. No record of this meeting has yet come to light, but it appears that, while Turnbull alarmed those present by describing the weakness of his security forces, even he believed that Tanganyika's independence could be delayed for seven or eight years, while the other governors insisted that they needed far more time to resolve their territories' political problems. Eventually it was decided that internal self-government in Tanganyika must be delayed until 1969.[100] On 19 March 1959 the Minister of State for the Colonies told the Cabinet of the Central African Federation that 'a halt is being called to the rapid advance of colonial territories to independence. For Tanganyika, for example, we are proposing a long-term programme.'[101]

In fact this strategy was already collapsing when Turnbull returned from Chequers to Tanganyika, so that he came to see the advice he had given as 'utterly unrealistic'.[102] Since the Tabora Conference of January 1958 TANU had demanded *madaraka* in 1959 and Turnbull's intelligence services had reported preparations for a general strike and civil disobedience campaign if the demand was not met.[103] On 7 February 1959 Nyerere – strengthened at this time by TANU's capture of all fifteen seats in the second round of elections – told Turnbull that, when the Governor made a promised constitutional statement on 17 March, he would be expected to announce that responsible government (a majority of elected members and ministers) would be granted during 1959.[104] Turnbull feared that if he did not satisfy TANU's demand there might be unrest so widespread that he might need to bring in security forces from outside the territory, an especially grave step at this time because a parallel emergency was taking place in Central Africa.[105] Yet in accordance with the decisions at Chequers, all Turnbull was authorized to say on 17 March was that a minority of four unofficial ministers would be appointed and that he hoped to announce in January 1960 when unofficial majorities would be introduced.[106] On 12 March Nyerere warned Turnbull that unless his announcement promised a majority of elected ministers there would be trouble. Turnbull refused.[107] Two days later TANU leaders told him that they would be able to explain the refusal of an elected majority if they were granted a fifth elected minister alongside the seven official ministers.[108] Turnbull had deliberately held this possibility in reserve as a bargaining counter,[109] agreed to consider it, secured Lennox-Boyd's instant agreement and congratulations, and made the announcement, to general satisfaction.[110]

From Lennox-Boyd's viewpoint, Turnbull had successfully resisted TANU's pressure for unofficial majorities and thereby bought time to reconsider the entire future of East Africa. On 10 April 1959 Lennox-Boyd submitted a major policy paper to the Cabinet's Colonial Policy Committee.[111] He pointed out that hitherto the official majorities in East Africa's Legislative and Executive Councils had secured Britain's major interests in the region, which he defined as a positive defence interest in overflying and staging rights, the use of ports, and a base (in Kenya) for Britain's forward reserve for use in the Middle East, Central Africa, and the Far East; a negative defence interest in ensuring that East Africa remained friendly to the West in Cold War terms; and a general need 'to do everything we reasonably can to ensure that people of all races, who have made their homes in these territories with the encouragement of successive British Governments, will be able to continue to live there in security and to contribute to the development and prosperity of the area.' However,

> The time is approaching, certainly in Tanganyika and Uganda, when future constitutional advance will start the process in earnest of tipping the balance of power in favour of unofficials. So long as the territories are not allowed to advance beyond the stage of internal self-government H.M.G.'s control in the vital matters…will remain more or less unimpaired. But the experience elsewhere suggests (*a*) that once the balance moves in favour of the unofficials rapid progress to internal self-government is difficult to check and (*b*) that thereafter it is not likely that the state of internal self-government itself can be maintained 'intact' for more than a very few years.
>
> For these reasons, it is important now, *i.e.*, before full official control begins to be eroded, to consider the general policy that should be adopted in East Africa.

The erosion had gone furthest in Tanganyika, where

> the Tanganyika African National Union … dominates the political scene. It commands the support of the great mass of the Africans and its influence is apparent through the length and breadth of the country. There is no effective opposition either from moderate Africans or from the non-African communities. A country-wide campaign initiated by Nyerere led, early in 1958, to the widespread acceptance of the notion that Tanganyika should be 'free' in 1959, and that all members of TANU would be expected to take part in a campaign of 'positive action' if freedom were not, in fact, achieved. Nyerere soon found that the wave of nationalist hysteria he had set in motion was beyond his ability to control, and it is doubtful whether he has made any whole-hearted attempt to check it. Nyerere himself has been at pains to explain that he was misunderstood and that all he had in mind was 'reasonable government', by which he meant that the official majorities in the Executive and Legislative Councils would give way to unofficial elected majorities. He has made it clear that he expects this changeover to be implemented within the next year or two and, more recently, he has been reported as stating his intention of working for independence by 1963. The internal security forces are weak and will require at least two years to be put on a sound footing. Steps are being taken to expand the Police force with all possible speed. Meanwhile the Tanganyika Government could not engage in a real show of force with Nyerere without invoking military assistance, with all the consequences this would be likely to involve.

Faced with this situation, so Lennox-Boyd held, Britain had three alternatives. It could withdraw rapidly from East Africa, say by 1965, but would thereby sacrifice its defence interests, probably leave behind violence in Kenya, transfer power to incompetent governments, and create 'a most dangerous political vacuum in a large area of Africa of which our enemies would be quick to take advantage and which would seriously prejudice the British position further south in Central Africa'. Alternatively, Britain could declare its intention to retain control for the foreseeable future, but could do so only by force, thereby isolating itself 'from even moderate world opinion' and eventually leaving behind bitterness and hostility. Or, as Lennox-Boyd himself advocated, Britain could adopt 'The Policy of "Gradualness"':

> This, in effect, means the continuation of our policy of step-by-step constitutional progress with the aim of meeting the legitimate aspirations of the Africans while at the same time (i) securing sufficient time for the countries to be more adequately equipped for the responsibilities of ultimate self-government; (ii) drawing out the period during which H.M.G. can retain control in vital matters.

The gradual policy implied that advance in Tanganyika and Uganda should be controlled to permit a ten-year period before predominantly elected Councils of Ministers would have effective control of internal affairs. The key points would come when each Council of Ministers first had an unofficial majority. In March 1959 Turnbull had persuaded TANU to defer such a majority, but only by undertaking 'to consider the question of further constitutional advances, to promise a statement on these and to include in that statement a forecast of when (if there is no untoward developments [sic]) it may be expected that unofficial majorities will be introduced into the Council of Ministers and into the Legislative Council'. This statement must be made by the end of 1959, so that 'Tanganyika can ... be regarded as the key to the situation in the sense that decisions announced for Tanganyika at the end of the year will largely determine the pace of development for Uganda and elsewhere in East Africa.' The Colonial Secretary proposed that late in 1959 Turnbull should announce that in 1961 the unofficial members of the Council of Ministers should be increased to seven, giving them parity with the seven official ministers. This situation would continue until 1965, when the ratio would change to seven unofficials and five officials, a balance to be preserved until 1969, beyond which nothing could be promised except substantial (but not complete) self-government. Lennox-Boyd warned that such an announcement late in 1959 might provoke violent opposition, but if so it must be repressed. The Colonial Policy Committee approved this programme on behalf of the Cabinet. In effect, having failed to delay the appointment of a large minority of elected ministers, the British intended to reduce Tanganyika's further constitutional development to glacial pace. Officials outside the Colonial Office already doubted the feasibility of this policy.[112]

So, very soon, did Turnbull, for he had now begun to feel the second form of power which TANU as a party had gained through its near-monopoly of electoral representation. First, Nyerere refused to be incorporated into British plans by accepting a ministry, believing that it would compromise him and split the party. Next, the TANU majority on the Post-Elections Committee, which met in mid-1959 to consider future electoral arrangements, went beyond their terms of reference to give broad endorsement, as one alternative, to TANU's own proposals for a rapid expansion of the franchise, and an unofficial majority of Legislative Councillors elected from fifty open (i.e. overwhelmingly African), eleven Asian, and ten European constituencies. Then TANU's legislative councillors resisted British plans to expand and re-equip the police.[113] Urged by Lennox-Boyd in May 1959 to hold firm to the new policy, Turnbull replied, 'I did not foresee that T.E.M.O. [the Tanganyika Elected Members Organisation, i.e. the TANU parliamentary caucus] would develop into the monolithic, strictly disciplined structure that it has become', adding that it was, ironically, exactly what British policy in Tanganyika professed to encourage – 'a non-racial body of Tanganyikans, every member of which is dedicated to the development of a non-racial society'. Faced with such party discipline, he explained, he could not hope to resist demands for a majority of unofficial ministers during 1960, rather than parity between unofficials and officials in 1961, for if he did so the existing ministers would all resign and precipitate a major crisis.[114]

Macpherson saw the point immediately: 'The situation in Tanganyika is unique in my experience, in that the Governor has no one, except his officials, opposing the head-long rush to "Uhuru"…In no other Colonial territory that I know of (even all-African territories) has such a situation occurred.'[115] When Governor Crawford protested that Tanganyika's speed of constitutional advance might precipitate civil war and economic disaster in Uganda,[116] Turnbull wrote a devastating reply:

> Nothing would please me more than to be able to announce that we proposed to defer all constitutional advance until we had in the country a sufficient number of Africans of experience, ability and integrity to fill posts in the public service, and in commerce and industry. But I cannot see that happy position being achieved in less than twenty years. And what would happen in those twenty years? There would be at least two major insurrections; the first in 1960 or 1961, working up from a series of strikes, boycotts and campaigns of positive action; and the second in 1970 by which time the nationalists would have profited from their earlier experiences and would have laid on something that we should not have a chance of holding; it would be a combination of Mau Mau and the Maji Maji rebellion, with all the support of modern techniques in guerilla warfare, sabotage and fifth column activities. You, I know, are in the happy position of having a number of dissident groups; but here every African is a nationalist and we should be faced with a situation very much like that in Cyprus but without the Turks. I cannot imagine that H.M.G. would be willing to see all the East African Forces and the Middle East Strategic Reserve deployed in Tanganyika to look after sisal estates and Greek tobacco plantations…

We are, after all, under an obligation to make Tanganyika self-governing, and it would be better to reach that consummation too early with the people on our side than after a campaign with the people irrevocably against us. Our first interest must surely be to maintain peaceful conditions and public confidence so that the solutions to political problems can be sought in a tranquil atmosphere, and so that when the final change comes about, Tanganyika will look to us and not to the Soviet bloc to keep the country supplied with technicians and as a source of manufactured articles...

It is essential for us to use Nyerere whilst he is still powerful; if we wait too long, he will be ousted by the extremists; and with him will go all hopes of an enduring European influence in Tanganyika. Indeed, 1960 may present the last chance we shall have to prevent Tanganyika from becoming a purely African state. If we got into a shooting match here, Nyerere would quickly be displaced as a leader, and instead of him we should have a group of hairy men demanding 'Africa for the Africans'.[117]

Twenty years later Turnbull reflected, 'It was a question of how slowly we dared go, not how fast we dared go.'[118]

Nevertheless, even in the face of this ruthless logic, the Colonial Office temporized through the middle of 1959 as the Conservative Government neared the end of its term of office and the despondent Lennox-Boyd's multi-racial policy disintegrated in the face of an emergency in Nyasaland and the Hola tragedy in Kenya.[119] What was at issue in Tanganyika was TANU's demand – backed by threats of ministerial resignations – for a statement during 1959 that after new elections in 1960 there would be an elected majority of ministers. Turnbull believed that this could not be resisted, but that, if it was granted, further significant constitutional progress could be suspended until the next election in 1964.[120] In other words, he proposed to defer the moment of confrontation one stage further than the colonial Policy Committee had approved, and he was encouraged by Nyerere,[121] whose strategy of combining insistence on immediate concessions with vague assurances of future gradualism was winning him an unjustified reputation for moderation. When Nyerere put his demand to Lennox-Boyd at the Colonial Office in June 1959, it was rejected. A month later he returned to the charge, with Turnbull's endorsement but no greater success.[122] 'At this rate we shall end by giving Tanganyika self-government yesterday!' the Parliamentary Secretary complained, while Lennox-Boyd insisted that the Cabinet had found even the existing policy hard to swallow and could not be persuaded to abandon it before Britain's imminent general election, which provided a perfect excuse for delay.[123]

The British election of October 1959, which returned a younger and more progressive Conservative Party to power, is generally thought to have precipitated the final decolonization of East and Central Africa.[124] Prime Minister Macmillan, it is said, was determined to rid Britain of the remnants of an empire which had ceased to be profitable and had become during 1959 a major political liability. His agent as Colonial Secretary, Iain Macleod, was an able, progressive, courageous, and utterly ruthless politician who saw the colonies purely as a problem to be solved rather than a responsibility to be shouldered. Macleod made no secret of his intention to take a radical line in winding up the empire. After leaving office he would stress how much he had accelerated decolonization.[125]

He did, indeed, bring a new urgency to colonial policy and his indifference to European settlers was a dramatic break with the past, but for the most part, like Turnbull, he responded to the momentum of a situation which was already beyond British control. His main initial dilemmas were Kenya and Nyasaland, but his first important decision concerned Tanganyika, the pace-setter where the British position was weakest. On 16 November 1959 Macleod told his officials and Turnbull that he intended a rapid and substantial step forward in Tanganyika. The step, approved by the Cabinet ten days later, was in fact chiefly the acceptance of Turnbull's long-standing proposal to announce in December 1959 that, after elections in 1960, the Council of Ministers would have an unofficial majority. The details were to be worked out at a conference with Nyerere during the first half of 1960, but the Cabinet agreed that they might include an unofficial majority of nine to three, appointing Nyerere Chief Minister if that was the only way of bringing him into the Council, and, on the other hand, an electorate significantly narrower than that proposed by the Post-Elections Committee lest it should be a dangerous precedent for nationalist demands in Central Africa.[126] Significantly, as also in Nyasaland at this time,[127] Macleod was still speaking of stabilization rather than rapid withdrawal and his step forward was still in the spirit of Lennox-Boyd's strategy, for he professed to hope for four years of government with some official ministers and another four without, before a final move to independence in 1968. 'We are bound to be pressed from about 1960 onwards to telescope the time-table,' he wrote, 'but I think that we should have every justification in digging our toes in... Moreover the grant of the major responsibility in the administration to elected members may very well bring to the surface the latent jealousies, fears and clash of interests that at the moment are concealed within the "monolith" of T.E.M.O.'[128] He was trying to defer the moment of confrontation one last time.

Yet, like so many earlier attempts at stabilization, Macleod's was rapidly swept away. In October 1959 Oscar Kambona, who had been TANU's first Organizing Secretary General, returned to Tanganyika from studies in London, resumed his former post, took command of the radical wing of TANU's leadership, and increased the pressure on Nyerere. Rather than being satisfied with the promise of an elected majority, when Nyerere met Macleod in London in March 1960 he put forward the radical proposal that after the election a Chief Minister should preside over the Council of Ministers, nominate its members, and control the provincial administration and (through another minister) the police.[129] Macleod insisted that the governor must preside and appoint ministers on the Chief Minister's advice; it was agreed that the Chief Minister should hold a portfolio of provincial affairs; and, in a characteristic finesse, Macleod insisted that a council would be established to administer the police, Nyerere (to satisfy his colleagues) would protest, the Chief Minister would then be made its chairman, but operational control of the police would remain with the Governor.[130] Nyerere was warned that if his colleagues reneged on this deal, so would Macleod's, while Turnbull was firmly told that he must control the police whether he liked it or not.[131]

Yet the idea of a long pause between responsible government and independence was becoming patently unrealistic. In May 1960 TANU's National Executive Committee first demanded independence during 1961 and Macleod, who thought Nyerere 'probably the wisest and best of the African leaders that we have, at least in East and Central Africa', ducked Britain's last opportunity for confrontation, abandoned his attempt at stabilization, adopted Turnbull's belief that it was safer to move quickly than slowly, and told the United Nations that a conference in 1961 might arrange independence in 1962 or 1963.[132] 'I am not too concerned with the inconsistency between now and last November,' he told his officials in July 1960. 'The wind has been gathering force since then.'[133] The officials, less brutal, justified the abandonment of their long-held principles by the need to satisfy TANU's radicals, the impact of decolonization in francophone Africa, and their helplessness in the face of Tanganyika's very lack of development:

> If...Ministers feel that it is not practical politics...to try and arrest for more than a short period the pace of 'emancipation' on the grounds of administrative maturity there is everything to be said for [independence in 1962]...Tanganyika will not be significantly more 'ripe' for independence in 1963 than in 1962 and it is not worth H.M.G.'s while needlessly to incur odium by arguing for 1963 rather than 1962, once the decision has been taken that we cannot hold the position until Tanganyika's native resources are sufficient to the needs of an independent state.[134]

In the election of September 1960 TANU won every seat save one. On 3 October Nyerere formed his first ministry.

The final steps to independence were confused by the possibility of delaying them so that Tanganyika could federate with the other East African territories. In November 1958 Nyerere was reported to have said that he did not intend to let this issue interfere with Tanganyika's achievement of independence,[135] but federation was certainly a goal and in June 1960 he wrote a private paper suggesting that Tanganyika might delay independence in order to facilitate it. When, by error, this became public, TANU hastened to support it, despite misgivings, and Nyerere stated his willingness to delay independence until 1962 provided the British could bring Kenya and Uganda to full self-government by that date, doubtless hoping thereby to accelerate the process.[136] East African federation was a long-standing British goal and Macleod welcomed this 'wonderful prize' by which 'many of the problems, including the racial and tribal ones in Kenya and the troubles in Uganda, could fall into place in the wider setting of a federation'.[137] In November 1960 he agreed with Nyerere that a constitutional conference in March 1961 should fix an independence date for Tanganyika but provide that if constitutional progress in Kenya and Uganda went smoothly a federation conference in October 1961 should take precedence over the Tanganyikan decision. In fact progress was not smooth and by February 1961 Nyerere had decided that Tanganyikan independence must have priority.[138]

Macleod went to the constitutional conference in Dar es Salaam in March 1961 hoping to delay independence until 1962, but willing if necessary to concede an earlier date if it would strengthen Nyerere's position, for 'His continuance in power is vital to us in East Africa'.[139] The British also hoped that Tanganyika would join the Commonwealth, accept a Governor-General appointed by the Queen for at least the first three years in order to reassure expatriate civil servants, and enact constitutional safeguards to prevent a dictatorship such as was thought to be taking shape in Ghana. The safeguards included an executive Public Service Commission to keep the appointment and control of civil servants out of the hands of politicians, a Police Service Commission for the same purpose, provision for dual citizenship, and a bill of rights. TANU, by contrast, wanted to gain independence during 1961 and as a republic, desired the Public Service Commission to be advisory to the Prime Minister, opposed dual citizenship, and rejected a bill of rights as an unnecessary incitement to legal quibbles. As usual, Macleod struck a deal, accepting independence in December 1961 in return for agreement to a short-term Governor-General and an executive Public Service Commission (with the proviso that the Prime Minister would choose Permanent Secretaries), while dual citizenship and the bill of rights were abandoned.[140] These were the terms on which Tanganyika became an independent state. The chain of imperialism in East Africa had broken at its weakest link.

Notes

1. These documents in the Public Record Office, London, are cited as CAB (Cabinet), CO (Colonial Office), and PREM (Prime Minister's Office). UDL signifies the University of Dar es Salaam Library.
2. This is the British Documents of the End of Empire Project. The volumes so far published and relevant to this paper are: Ronald Hyam (ed.), *The Labour Government and the End of Empire, 1945–1951* (4 vols, London: HMSO, 1992); David Goldsworthy (ed.), *The Conservative Government and the End of Empire, 1951–1957* (3 vols, London: HMSO, 1994); Richard Rathbone (ed.), *Ghana* (2 vols, London: HMSO, 1992).
3. The best survey of British policy is the introduction to Hyam, *Labour Government*, vol. 1.
4. *Ibid.*, vol. 1, pp. xxxvii, 338; vol. 4, p. 256.
5. J. Clagett Taylor, *The Political Development of Tanganyika* (Stanford, CA: Stanford University Press, 1963), p. 78.
6. Cohen to Twining, 1 November 1949, Hall Papers, UDL (a volume of papers on constitutional development apparently belonging to R. de Z. Hall).
7. Cohen, 'Tanganyika constitutional questions,' 10 September 1946, CO 691/192.
8. Twining to Cohen, 11 October 1949, and Government memorandum to Legislative Councillors, 18 November 1949, Hall Papers, UDL.
9. Tanganyika, *Report of the Committee on Constitutional Development 1951* (Dar es Salaam: Government Printer, 1952), pp. 19–20, 36.
10. Cohen to Twining, 13 March 1951, CO 537/7196/2; Gorell Barnes to Twining, 19 February 1952, CO 822/606/63.

11. Taylor, *Political Development*, p. 92.
12. 'Petition from the Tanganyika African Association, Mwanza Branch, concerning Tanganyika,' United Nations Trusteeship Council document T/PET.2/103, 1 October 1951.
13. Julius K. Nyerere, 'The Race Problem in East Africa' (1952), in his *Freedom and Unity* (Dar es Salaam: Oxford University Press, 1966), p. 26.
14. Saadani Abdul Kandoro, *Mwito wa Uhuru* (Dar es Salaam: Thakers, 1961), p. 76.
15. Twining to Lennox-Boyd, 8 September 1954, CO 822/859/1.
16. Barton, minute, 10 January 1955, CO 822/859.
17. See John Iliffe, *A Modern History of Tanganyika* (Cambridge: Cambridge University Press, 1979), pp. 513–20, 523–73; Maguire, *Toward 'Uhuru' in Tanzania*.
18. Twining to Gorell Barnes, 22 September 1954, CO 822/859/3. Kirilo Japhet was the Meru spokesman in their land case against the government.
19. Nyerere to Member for Local Government, 24 December 1954, CO 822/859/6.
20. Twining to Gorell Barnes, 26 May 1955, CO 822/925/2.
21. Twining to Lennox-Boyd, 29 May 1957, CO 822/1591/1.
22. Stapledon, circular, 16 September 1955, CO 822/859/33.
23. Twining to Lennox-Boyd, 31 October 1955, CO 822/859/33.
24. Lennox-Boyd to Twining, 7 December 1955. CO 822/859/36. For his views, see Viscount Boyd of Merton, 'Opening Address,' in A.H.M. Kirk-Greene (ed.), *The Transfer of Power: The Colonial Administrator in the Age of Decolonisation* (Oxford: Inter-Faculty Committee for African Studies, University of Oxford, 1979), pp. 2–14.
25. Lloyd to Lennox-Boyd, minute, 3 December 1955, CO 822/859.
26. Twining to Gorell Barnes, 14 May 1956, CO 822/1143/1.
27. Twining to Lennox-Boyd, 2 May 1956, CO 822/1143/1.
28. Twining to Gorell Barnes, 14 May 1956. CO 822/1143/1.
29. Mathieson, 'Note of conversation with Mr Julius Nyerere,' 7 September 1956, CO 822/859/76.
30. Mathieson to Gorell Barnes, minute, 7 September 1956, CO 822/859.
31. Gorell Barnes to Macpherson, minute, 12 September 1956, and Macpherson to Minister of State, minute, 17 September 1956, CO 822/859.
32. Lennox-Boyd, minute, 27 September 1956, CO 822/859; Lennox-Boyd to Twining, 10 October 1956, CO 822/859/107.
33. Twining to Gorell Barnes, 12 November 1956, CO 822/912/26. This is reprinted (with the succeeding minutes) in Goldsworthy, *Conservative Government*, vol. 2, pp. 264–81.
34. Gorell Barnes to Macpherson, minute, 29 November 1956, CO 822/912.
35. Macpherson to Gorell Barnes, minute, 4 December 1956, CO 822/912.
36. Lennox-Boyd, minute, 25 December 1956, CO 822/912.
37. Mathieson to Twining, 28 December 1956, CO 822/912/30.
38. 'Note by Sir John Macpherson of conversation with Mr Julius Nyerere,' 18 January 1957, CO 822/1361/1.
39. Connolly, 'Tanganyika African National Union, Dar es Salaam,' 27 January 1957, CO 822/1361/4.
40. *Tanganyika Standard*, 29 January 1957.
41. Grattan-Bellew to Mathieson, 18 March 1957, CO 822/1361/29.
42. Grattan-Bellew to Macpherson, 5 February 1957, CO 822/1361/2.
43. Grattan-Bellew to Mathieson, 18 March 1957, CO 822/1361/29.
44. Lennox-Boyd to Twining, 11 February 1957, CO 822/1361/3.
45. Macpherson, minute, 13 June 1957, CO 822/1361.
46. Macpherson, minute, 22 March 1957, CO 822/1446.
47. Twining to Gorell Barnes, 3 April 1957, CO 822/1361/37; Lennox-Boyd to Twining, 12 April 1957, CO 822/1361/42.
48. Lennox-Boyd to Twining, 16 May 1957, CO 822/1361/62.
49. Twining to Lennox-Boyd, 29 May 1957, CO 822/1591/1.
50. 'Note of discussion on political situation in Tanganyika,' 26 June 1957, CO 822/1446/70.

51. Twining to Gorell Barnes, 9 August 1957, CO 822/1361/137.
52. Twining to Lennox-Boyd, 31 July 1957, CO 822/1361/125. For TANU reactions, see 'Extract from Tanganyika intelligence summary for July 1957,' CO 822/1361/129.
53. Twining to Lennox-Boyd, 2 August 1957, CO 822/1361/122.
54. Cohen to Twining, 28 June 1957, CO 822/1361/107.
55. See Government of Tanganyika, *Report of the Special Commissioner appointed to examine matters arising out of the Report of the Committee on Constitutional Development* (Dar es Salaam: Government Printer, 1953).
56. *Ibid.*, p.70.
57. *Ibid.*, p. 73.
58. Stapledon to Gorell Barnes, 27 May 1955, CO 822/925/1.
59. Kisch to Mathieson, minute, 3 June 1955, CO 822/925.
60. Gorell Barnes to Mathieson, minute, 6 June 1955, CO 822/925.
61. Mathieson to Gorell Barnes, minute, 10 June 1955, CO 822/925.
62. Mathieson to Gorell Barnes, minute, 17 August 1955, CO 822/925.
63. 'Minutes of a meeting held at Queens' College, Cambridge,' 30 August 1955, CO 822/925/18.
64. Mathieson, 'Brief for the Secretary of State', 23 July 1956, CO 822/1143/5.
65. Twining to Gorell Barnes, 12 November 1956, CO 822/912/26.
66. Fletcher-Cooke, 'Tripartite voting,' 30 September 1957, CO 822/1446/81. This is the best account of the issue.
67. Mathieson, 'Note of conversation with Mr Julius Nyerere,' 7 September 1956, CO 822/859/76.
68. Colonial Office to Governor, 28 September 1956, CO 822/859/90; 'Extract from Tanganyika intelligence summary for April 1957,' CO 822/1361/70.
69. United Nations Trusteeship Council record, 12 June 1957, p. 106, and 18 June 1957, p. 147.
70. Fletcher-Cooke, 'Tripartite voting,' 30 September 1957, CO 822/1446/81.
71. *Tanganyika Standard*, 3 August 1957.
72. Fletcher-Cooke, 'Tripartite voting,' 30 September 1957, CO 822/1446/81.
73. 'Extract from Tanganyika intelligence summary for August, 1957,' CO 822/1361/135; E.B.M. Barongo, *Mkiki mkiki wa siasa Tanganyika* (Dar es Salaam: East African Literature Bureau, 1966), p. 100.
74. Fletcher-Cooke, 'Tripartite voting,' 30 September 1957, CO 822/1446/81.
75. 'Extract from Tanganyika intelligence summary for October 1957,' CO 822/1362/159; 'Record of interview granted by the Secretary of State for the Colonies to Mr Julius Nyerere,' 21 October 1957, CO 822/1446/79.
76. Colonial Policy (Ministerial) Committee (C.A. (55) 5th Meeting) 10 November 1955, CAB 134/1201.
77. Her Majesty's Government.
78. Lennox-Boyd to Macpherson, 28 October 1957, CO 822/1320/E7/19.
79. See Iliffe, *Modern History*, pp. 556–7 and the references therein.
80. 'Extract from Tanganyika intelligence summary for January 1958,' CO 822/1362/195; 'Historia ya TANU,' pp. 103-5 (an untitled, duplicated history by the TANU Research Division, c.1964, in TANU Archives).
81. Twining to Lennox-Boyd, 17 February 1958, CO 822/1591/4.
82. G.W.Y. Hucks, 'Report on the first elections of members to the Legislative Council of Tanganyika,' duplicated, 1959. (I owe this reference to Dr S.R. Walji.)
83. Maguire, *Toward 'Uhuru' in Tanzania*, chap. 7.
84. 'Diary of political disturbances in the Lake Province from 1 April 1958 to 24 December 1958,' CO 822/1299/49.
85. Twining to Lennox-Boyd, 7 April 1958, CO 822/1362/200.
86. Lennox-Boyd, transcript of oral memoirs, p. 155, Lennox-Boyd Papers, Bodleian Library, Oxford, MS. Eng. c. 3433.
87. Turnbull to Gorell Barnes, 28 July 1958, CO 822/1447/95.
88. Macpherson, minute, 7 August 1958, CO 822/1447.

89. Colonial Office to Turnbull, 19 August 1958, CO 822/1447/108.
90. Turnbull to Gorell Barnes, 2 September 1958 and 11 September 1958, CO 822/1447/116 and 120; Gorell Barnes to Macpherson, minute, 11 September 1958, CO 822/1447.
91. Lennox-Boyd, minute, dated 15 October 1958 but actually 15 September 1958, CO 822/1447; Webber to Gorell Barnes, minute, 17 Septermber 1958, CO 822/1447.
92. Turnbull to Lennox-Boyd, 2 October 1958, CO 822/1362/227.
93. Turnbull to Gorell Barnes, 23 December 1958, CO 822/1460/8.
94. Gorell Barnes to Macpherson, minute, 31 December 1958, CO 822/1460.
95. Gorell Barnes to Turnbull, 6 January 1959, CO 822/1448/165.
96. Turnbull to Gorell Barnes, 13 January 1959, CO 822/1448/166.
97. Turnbull to Gorell Barnes, 13 January 1959, CO 822/1448/167.
98. Colonial Office, 'Prospects for the African territories for which the Colonial Office is responsible,' January 1959, Africa (Official) Committee paper A.F. (59) 5, CAB 134/1353.
99. Macpherson to Lennox-Boyd, minute, 2 January 1959, CO 822/1460/10.
100. Lennox-Boyd, transcript of oral memoirs, p. 156, Lennox-Boyd Papers, Bodleian Library, Oxford, MS. Eng. c. 3433; Lennox-Boyd, minute, 7 May 1959, CO 822/1449.
101. Sir Roy Welensky, *Welensky's 4000 days* (London: Collins, 1964), p. 139.
102. Lennox-Boyd, transcript of oral memoirs, p. 156, Lennox-Boyd Papers, Bodleian Library, Oxford, MS. Eng. c. 3433.
103. 'Extract from Tanganyika intelligence report – 11 November–10 December 1958,' CO 822/1363/237.
104. Turnbull, 'Note by the Governor,' 7 February 1959, CO 822/1448/170.
105. Turnbull to Webber, 14 February 1959, CO 822/1322/1; Colin Baker, *State of Emergency: Crisis in Central Africa, Nyasaland, 1959–1960* (London: Tauris, 1997).
106. Lennox-Boyd, 'Possibility of disturbances in East Africa,' 12 March 1959, Cabinet Paper C. (59) 56, CAB 129/97.
107. Turnbull to Gorell Barnes, 13 March 1959, CO 822/1448/201.
108. Turnbull to Gorell Barnes, 14 March 1959, CO 822/1448/203.
109. Turnbull to Gorell Barnes, 24 December 1958, CO 822/1460/9.
110. Lennox-Boyd to Turnbull, 15 March 1959, CO 822/1448/205; Turnbull to Governor of Kenya, 17 March 1959, CO 822/1322/18.
111. Lennox-Boyd, 'Future Policy in East Africa,' 10 April 1959, Colonial Policy Committee paper C.P.C. (59) 2, CAB 134/1558.
112. Africa (official) Committee (A.F. 59 (7th Meeting)) 6 March 1959, CAB 134/1353.
113. Turnbull, 'Note by the Governor,' 31 March 1959, CO 822/1464/2; Government of Tanganyika, *Report of the Post Elections Committee 1959* (Dar es Salaam: Government Printer, 1959), p. 19; Turnbull to Gorell Barnes, 3 July 1959, CO 822/1450/240.
114. Turnbull to Gorell Barnes, 12 May 1959, CO 822/1449/229.
115. Macpherson, minute, 15 June 1959, CO 822/1449.
116. Crawford to Turnbull, 25 June 1959, CO 822/1449/237.
117. Turnbull to Crawford, 9 July 1959, CO 822/1450/245.
118. Comment recorded in Kirk-Greene, *Transfer of Power*, p. 56.
119. David Goldsworthy, *Colonial Issues in British Politics 1945–1961* (Oxford: Oxford University Press, 1971), pp. 33–4.
120. Turnbull to Lennox-Boyd, 10 May 1959, CO 822/1449/227.
121. Fletcher-Cooke to Webber, 6 July 1959 CO 822/1450/243.
122. 'Note of the Secretary of State's discussion with Mr Nyerere,' 29 June 1959, CO 822/1449/238; Webber to Fletcher-Cooke, 21 August 1959, CO 822/1450/255A.
123. Amery to Monson, minute, 23 August 1959, CO 822/1450/257; Monson to Martin, minute, 4 September 1959, CO 822/1450; Perth, minute, 18 September 1959, CO 822/1450.
124. Goldsworthy, *Colonial Issues*, pp. 365-6.
125. Robert Shepherd, *Iain Macleod* (London: Hutchinson, 1994), p. 161; Iain Macleod, 'Trouble in Africa,' *The Spectator*, 31 January 1964.

126. 'Note of a meeting in the Secretary of State's room,' 16 November 1959, CO 822/1451/308; Cabinet Conclusions (C.C. (59) 60 (8)) 26 November 1959, CAB 128/33.
127. Macleod to Macmillan, 29 December 1959, PREM 11/2586/2.
128. Macleod, 'Constitutional development in Tanganyika,' 12 November 1959, Colonial Policy Committee paper C.P.C. (59) 20, CAB 134/1558.
129. Nyerere, 'Memorandum on the executive,' 14 January 1960, CO 822/2304/4.
130. Webber to Turnbull, 22 March 1960 CO 822/2304/30.
131. Macleod to Turnbull, 1 and 14 April 1960, CO 822/2304/42 and 51.
132. Cohen to Eastwood, 22 June 1960, CO 822/2299/2; Macleod to Macmillan, 22 November 1960, CO 822/2300/109.
133. Macleod, minute, 28 July 1960, CO 822/2299.
134. Manson to Martin, minute, 21 July 1960, CO 822/2299.
135. 'Substance of Mr Mason Sears' conversation with Mr Julius Nyerere during the former's visit to Dar es Salaam, November, 1958,' CO 822/1362/231.
136. Nyerere, 'The federation of East African States,' June 1960, and Wright to Foreign Office, 20 June 1960, CO 822/2040/29; *Tanganyika Standard*, 22 June 1960; *Sunday Times*, 30 October 1960.
137. Macleod to Macmillan, 22 November 1960, CO 822/2300/109.
138. 'Note of Secretary of State's discussion with Mr Nyerere,' 18 November 1960, CO 822/2300/94; Monson to Turnbull, 24 February 1961, CO 822/2414/4.
139. Macleod, 'Independence of Tanganyika,' 27 February 1961, Colonial Policy committee paper C.P.C. (61) 5, CAB 134/1560.
140. Macleod to Perth, 28 and 30 March 1961, CO 822/2413/56 and 61; minutes of Constitutional Conference, 27–29 March 1961, CO 822/2415/E46/1; 'Tanganyika pre-independence discussions: summary record of the fourth plenary session,' 28 June 1961, CO 822/2322/5.

Twelve

$\bigwedge\!\!\bigwedge\!\!\bigwedge\!\!\bigwedge\!\!\bigwedge\!\!\bigwedge\!\!\bigwedge\!\!\bigwedge\!\!\bigwedge\!\!\bigwedge\!\!\bigwedge\!\!\bigwedge$

Censoring the Press in Colonial Zanzibar
An Account of the Seditious Case
against Al-Falaq

LAWRENCE E.Y. MBOGONI

Introduction

When Zanzibar became a British Protectorate in 1890, it was already being ruled by an Omani Arab dynasty. The Arabs began arriving in Zanzibar in significant numbers during the ninth century AD. They enjoyed a relatively peaceful co-existence with the local natives, the Hadimu. However, the development of the plantation economy in the early nineteenth century necessitated the importation of slave labor from the mainland. Seyyid Said, the first resident Omani Sultan of Zanzibar, invited Indian merchants to Zanzibar in order to facilitate the financing of slave caravans into the interior of Africa. By the mid-1950s the Arabs comprised about 17 per cent of Zanzibar's nearly 300,000 inhabitants. Three-quarters of the population was black African, the bulk being descendants of freed slaves. The rest were mainly Indians, Goans and people from the Comoro Islands.

The Arabs in Zanzibar therefore constituted a minority whose political dominance was symbolized in the person of the Sultan. As a British protectorate, Zanzibar came to bear a double yoke of colonial domination. While the majority of Zanzibaris were Muslims, the population was not homogeneous. Wealth and status reflected the racial stratification of Zanzibari society: a wealthy Arab landowning class at the top, a wealthy Indian merchant class, and African squatter tenants on Arab-owned clove and coconut plantations.

As Zanzibar took tentative steps toward self-government during the 1950s, class and ethnic differences played a significant part in the politics of divisiveness. Indeed, the very physical outlay of Zanzibar city reflected these ethnic and class differences especially between Arabs and Africans. The majority of Arabs lived in the Stone Town while the majority of Africans lived in Ng'ambo. According to the 1948 census, there was a total of just under 200,000 Africans, 51,000 of whom considered themselves as

198

'mainlanders'. Of this 51,000, 37,404 lived on Zanzibar Island. The Arab population numbered 44,560, 13,977 of them on Zanzibar Island. The Asian population numbered 15,892, with 13,705 of them on Zanzibar Island. Ng'ambo, where the majority of 'mainland' Africans and members of the African Association lived, was one big slum area. In comparison, the Stone Town where the wealthier Arabs and Indians lived was cleaner and, as the name suggested, made of stone-built residences.

Conditions in Ng'ambo were so bad that the editor of *Mwongozi* in a front-page edition of 8 March 1957 questioned why Ng'ambo should suffer the most. What he said is worth quoting at length:

> Is poverty a crime? It seems so the way the poorer section of our town is treated or not treated, for neglect has been the hallmark which distinguishes Ng'ambo Trans-Creek, Omdurman of Zanzibar, from what is normally known as the Stone Town. This sprawling habitation of wattle, daub and thatch of thousands of Zanzibaris is a disgrace to society. While large sums of money are being spent on building bitumen macadamised roads to the remotest villages in both Zanzibar and Pemba, Ng'ambo remains largely without anything that may, by any stretch of the imagination, be termed a road... Mounds of rubbish in various stages of decomposition abound everywhere giving off stench and forming ideal breeding ground for flies. Unless you are armed with a torch you risk your neck trying to venture outside your hut at night, for street lights are conspicuously rare, probably for the very good reasons that Ng'ambo has no streets.[1]

The editor of *Mwongozi* blamed Ng'ambo's squalor on a haphazard, ill-planned slum clearing scheme 'under an amateur architect and a retired motor-mechanic who had qualified being put in charge of this expensive town-planning scheme by building a cottage for himself in England!'[2] The connection between the poverty of the residents of Ng'ambo and the fact that they were predominantly African eluded the editor of *Mwongozi*.

Historical background

During World War II the demand for news in Zanzibar greatly increased, and both private publishers and the government made efforts to satisfy it. On 3 September 1939, the British administration established an Information Office whose major function was the dissemination of government policies and to inform Zanzibaris about the progress of the war. The government financed the publication, by the Information Office, of three periodicals:[3] the *Daily News Bulletin*, a Swahili-language evening paper, *Habari za Wiki*, a mimeographed weekly, and a *Monthly Newsletter*. Of the three probably the *Daily News Bulletin* had the widest reach as it was distributed to coffee shops, social clubs, reading rooms, and district offices in rural areas.

At the same time the government also started what may qualify as the predecessor of Radio Zanzibar. As in Dar-es-Salaam, the Information

Office used a public address system mounted on a van. The van was mainly used to read news of the war to audiences in Zanzibar town and in the rural areas. Another public address system was installed in the Sultan's palace, Beit Al-Ajaib, in Zanzibar town. The Beit Al-Ajaib system was strategically located on the seafront popularly known as Forodhani, an area used by one and all for evening recreation. Similar systems to the Beit Al-Ajaib one were installed in other areas such as Kiembe Samaki.

The following private publications were started during the war.[4] *The Zanzibari*, a weekly Swahili paper, was started in 1939.[5] Its editor was Khalil Ali Khalil. *Mwongozi*, also a weekly, was first published on 3 February 1941, and was edited by Ahmed S. Kharusi and Masoud M. Riami.[6] The *Zanzibar Times*, another weekly, started publication in 1945 and was owned by the Indian Muslim Association.[7] Besides these new papers, there were old ones like the fortnightly *Al-Falaq* which started in 1929,[8] *The Zanzibar Voice* started in 1922, and the *Samachar*. These also carried news of the war and other information.

The emergence of private publishers during the war prompted the Zanzibar Government to adopt and strengthen legal controls over the dissemination of information. In 1954, *Al Falaq*, the voice of the Arab Association, became the first victim of the government's laws against sedition. Following in its footsteps was *Adal Insaf*, which was suspended for a few weeks in 1960 when its owner was arrested and accused of sedition.[9] In both cases, the charges of sedition were based on the Zanzibar Newspaper Decree of 1938, which prevented the publication of anti-government material. The Decree facilitated the official monitoring of locally published newspapers by requiring that a copy of every published newspaper and news sheet be delivered to the government free of charge.

It should be noted that the application of sedition in the colonies was different from its application in England. As Ronald Brown aptly puts it:

> In the Colonies a person may be convicted of sedition even though the words complained of by the prosecution did not contain any incitement to violence and were not likely to cause any breach of the peace or public disorder. Irrespective of any question of public order, certain forms of political expression are criminal.[10]

Also, in England newspaper owners could not be prosecuted for something published in their newspapers, provided they did not authorize or consent to the publication and provided their conduct was not negligent.[11] In the colonies, however, owners could be prosecuted for sedition regardless of whether they were aware of such publication. Indeed, this happened to be the case in Zanzibar.

The censorship of news and other information in colonial Zanzibar limited the freedom of the press as well as the right of Zanzibaris to be informed by independent sources. Such censorship, however, was in the colonial administration's interest. The uninformed Zanzibaris were rendered passive and susceptible to political manipulation, both of which were intended to make them feel powerless against the colonial forces around them. To inform the colonized of the evils of British colonialism, as

Al-Falaq tried to do, enabled some Zanzibaris to assess their colonial experience for themselves.

Since the case against *Al-Falaq* was the first seditious case to be brought against a newspaper in colonial Zanzibar, it is surprising that historians have not paid due attention to its historic importance, in particular how it subsequently affected the dynamics of Zanzibar 'nationalist' politics. One of the seditious charges was that *Al-Falaq* had called for a *jihad* against the British administration. What was the significance of the Muslim faith in Zanzibar 'nationalism'? To the British, why did the introduction of the notion of the Muslim faith into Zanzibar 'nationalism' constitute sedition?

According to some sources, the word *jihad* 'can denote any effort towards a subjectively praiseworthy aim, which need not necessarily have anything to do with religion'.[12] In this regard, it has been used to denote class struggle or the struggle between old and new. When used in a religious context, it may mean an inner struggle against one's evil inclinations or a spiritual struggle for the betterment of Islamic society. However, due to Western stereotypes *jihad* has come to be regarded as the battle cry of bloodthirsty Muslim 'fanatics' and 'terrorists' in pursuit of religious and political agendas.[13]

The stereotypical view of Islam (as intolerant) and Muslims (as inimical towards persons of a different faith) was part of the psychological baggage that Europeans carried with them to the colonies. Such stereotypes made British officials in Zanzibar suspicious that behind the outward appearance of Muslim submissiveness lurked a spirit of rebelliousness, nourished by the idea of *jihad* and waiting for the opportunity to manifest itself.[14] Thus, on reading the call for a *jihad* which appeared in the *Al-Falaq* edition of 10 March 1954, British officials in Zanzibar assumed that religion was being used to incite Muslim Zanzibaris to rise up against the infidel British masters.

Moreover, *Al-Falaq*'s call for a *jihad* in 1954 may have reminded Zanzibar officials of what had happened in 1951. In that year the British administration had to deal with riots, popularly known as *Vita vya Ng'ombe*, which had been incited by cries of '*Jihad*'. Nineteen villagers at Kiembe Samaki had refused to have their cattle inoculated against anthrax. They were arrested, tried, found guilty and sentenced to imprisonment. According to Lofchie, their sentence provoked an instantaneous reaction: 'Cries of *Jihad* rang out and transformed an angry crowd into a riotous mob'.[15]

When *Al-Falaq* started in 1929, it was published in Arabic and English. The choice of editorial language was not accidental but was rather influenced by the class interests of the owners. The newspaper was owned by the Arab Association and was used to propagate the interests of Arab landowners.[16] Initially *Al-Falaq* was not openly critical of the British administration in Zanzibar. However, its stance changed when postwar political developments threatened to jeopardize Arab interests.

Arab political rumblings first caught the government's attention in 1948. In that year the British administration proposed that the unofficial members of the Legislative Council (eight in all) should be elected instead of being nominated by the government. The proposals included a clause which sought to bestow on Zanzibar Indians the status of 'British Protected Persons' and thereby enable them to elect their own representatives. The Arab Association vehemently objected to the enfranchisement of Indians in Zanzibar; it wanted the franchise to be restricted to Zanzibar nationals only. The Arabs feared that such a privilege would give the Indians more clout than they already had commercially.[17]

The roots of Indian commercial predominance in Zanzibar stretched back to the early nineteenth century. When Seyyid Said moved his capital from Muscat to Zanzibar in 1832 a new chapter in Zanzibar history was about to begin. Seyyid Said not only encouraged the expansion of the clove and coconut plantation economy in Zanzibar, he also invited Indian merchants to act as financiers of what came to be known as the long-distance trade, which brought slaves and ivory from the mainland to Zanzibar. What enabled the Indian merchants to achieve this commercial leverage was the absence of a viable and properly managed credit system.[18]

Subsequently, the Indians became a well-organized group of merchant profiteers and money lenders with a firm grip on Zanzibar's economy. It was this influence which the Association detested and probably sought to undermine by denying the Indians any political privileges. Three years of clandestine negotiations on this issue between the Arab Association and the government produced no agreement. The Arab Association was adamant that Zanzibar possessed a separate and constitutionally autonomous national identity which precluded the privileging of non-nationals.[19]

Besides the enfranchisement of Indians another sensitive issue was the 1951 Government proposals for a new Zanzibar Constitution. The proposed constitutional changes, also known as the Rankine Plan, after the then British Resident Sir John Rankine, sought to enlarge the membership of the Legislative Council to include four ex-official members who were also members of the Executive Council, nine official members, and twelve unofficial members, under the chairmanship of the British Resident. Initially the Arab Association opposed the proposals but later, after reconsideration, it supported the constitutional changes. Apparently, Ahmed Mohamed Nassor Al-Lemki, the editor of *Al-Falaq*, was not very happy about the Arab Association's support for the Rankine Plan. He therefore embarked on an editorial campaign against the British administration in Zanzibar using *Al-Falaq* as his forum. Lemki's use of the press against British hegemony was obviously effective because of the charges of sedition against *Al-Falaq*.

Historically, therefore, it may be true to say that *Al-Falaq* helped to spark the 'nationalist' impulse in Zanzibar. But is the term 'nationalist' really applicable to political developments in Zanzibar during the early 1950s? In the case of colonial Zanzibar, the difference between a sense of nationhood and the desire to be free of foreign domination is of great significance. The sense of nationality, and who was a Zanzibari, played a crucial role in the way different segments of colonial Zanzibari society perceived the future of an independent Zanzibar.

According to Wole Soyinka, 'the lineage system in [colonial] Zanzibar did permit people to continue to be Arab or Persian generations after their Arab or Persian forebears'.[20] Soyinka raises a pertinent question when he asks, what choice, within this permissive lineage usage, did Arabs make? And we may add, how did that choice affect the dynamics of Zanzibar 'nationalist' politics? Soyinka suggests that Zanzibar Arabs chose to remain Arab rather than become African.

Whether Arab identity in colonial Zanzibar was self-perceived or historically based,[21] as a constitutive element of Zanzibar 'nationalism' it was a divisive factor. Within the Arab Association there was a rift between those who put emphasis on the primacy of Arab identity and those who advocated 'multi-racialism'. The older generation were orthodox, reserved, conservative and as long as they were comfortable and secure they wanted to continue with a social hierarchy that privileged the Arabs.[22] The younger generation, who understood the machinations of British colonialism and its racial implications, wanted a multi-racial Zanzibar which, however, would remain under an Arab Sultan after independence. Thus, despite these inter-generational differences, the Arabs in Zanzibar aspired to replace British hegemony with Arab hegemony.[23]

Since the Arab elite considered Zanzibar to be an Arab state, their sense of 'nationalism' differed from that of the Africans who saw Zanzibar as an African country and wished to rid Zanzibar of both British and Arab domination.[24] In the early 1950s African sentiments against the British administration and the Arab elite were voiced by *Afrika Kwetu*, which was founded by Mtoro Rehani Kingo in 1948.[25] The alien nature of both British and Arab hegemony was clearly voiced in the *Afrika Kwetu* issue of 25 September 1952:

> Our interests have for long been represented by the alien races and the result is... the alien races have become the masters and the real natives of the island and we the Africans in these islands have become the alien races denied of all justice and all the rights that a native should have.[26]

Moreover, the view that Zanzibar was an African country was expressed in the *Afrika Kwetu* issue of 5 May 1955 as follows:

> We wish to assure all the so-called Zanzibaries (sic) ... that anything short of an African state will never be accepted when self-government is achieved in this protectorate... We are also opposed to multiracial government in these islands.[27]

Evidently Mtoro Rehani Kingo did not subscribe to versions of Zanzibar history which sought to portray the Sultanate as a homegrown and legitimate sovereignty. Given Zanzibar's racial dynamics, there was little chance that the end of colonial rule would be reached smoothly. As Lucy Mair aptly put it, the Arabs like other minorities in East Africa who had made Africa their home envisaged a very different balance of power in a self-governing Zanzibar from that to which African leaders looked forward.[28]

In the ideological tug-of-war that ensued between Africans and Arabs, what Jonathan Glassman calls 'Sorting Out the Tribes',[29] one of the defining features of the dialogue was the power of narrative. On the power of narrative, Chinua Achebe observes:

> There is such a thing as absolute power over narrative. Those who secure this privilege for themselves can arrange stories about others pretty much where, and as, they like.[30]

What Achebe says in this regard is very pertinent to the newspaper wars and politics of nationalism in Zanzibar during the early 1950s. The more intellectually grounded editors of *Al-Falaq* and *Mwongozi* not only emphasized the moral inferiority of Africans but presented the cause of Arab nationalism in ways that made the less intellectual editor of *Afrika Kwetu* appear to represent racist African attitudes towards Arabs.

The Seditious Case Against Al-Falaq

On 8 and 9 June 1954, a case was heard in Zanzibar in which nine committee members of the Arab Association and the editor of *Al-Falaq* stood accused of sedition against the Government of Zanzibar. Legally the case of sedition against *Al-Falaq* is unique because people who had nothing to do with editing the newspaper were charged for allegedly publishing seditious material. The case is also interesting as a historic melodrama which was full of turns and twists.

Prior to the hearings, the first turn in the case came about when the British Resident, Sir John Rankine, was made to believe that not all members of the Arab Association committee exercised control over what the editor printed; that not all sympathized with what was published; that some committee members had proposed to remove the editor. In a recent interview Sheikh Ali Muhsin Al-Barwani, one of the accused, corroborated some of Rankine's suspicions:

> Two people were assigned to vet his articles. Ali Muhsin and Amour Zahor Al-Ismaili, a retired CID officer with 30 years of service, were assigned to oversee that the articles went to the brink, but did not break the law. The vetting was sometimes not effectively done. Ahmed [Al-Lemki – the editor] was unpredictable...[31]

Another twist in the case was when Sir John Rankine made it known to some of the accused, who he believed were respectable members of the Arab community, that he did not desire to humiliate them with a trial if it could be avoided. Apparently, Rankine was ready to influence the prosecution to drop the charges if the accused were ready to make a sufficient apology. He went to great personal trouble up to the end of his term on 1 June 1954, to arrive at a compromise which the government could 'properly' accept.[32] However, the committee could not bring itself to make such apologies. The government was, therefore, forced to proceed with the trial.

According to Ali Muhsin Al-Barwani, 'the committee refused to apologize because they did not want to be turned into perpetual political pawns by the administration'.[33] Sheikh Abdallah Al-Harthy, undoubtedly one of the 'respectable members of the community', was afraid of being imprisoned but Ali Muhsin made it understood by all committee members that it would be better to be imprisoned if it would serve to expose the machinations of the British colonialists internationally.[34] Supposedly, the colonial government got wind of this intent and was therefore forced not to consider imprisonment as an alternative to fines.

Before the issue of summonses, a warrant was obtained authorizing the search of the premises of the Arab Association, part of the ground floor of which was used as a printing press and the editor's office of *Al-Falaq*. A search of the editor's office produced, 'communist propaganda, consisting of two (copies) of the *Africa Newsletter*, published by the Africa Committee of the (British) Communist party ... and a copy of *21ˢᵗ February, 1954*, a "special newspaper" published by the World Federation of Democratic Youth in Budapest'.[35] According to Ali Muhsin Al-Barwani 'the papers found during the search used to be sent out everywhere by communists; the *Mwongozi* offices used to receive the papers, as did *Al-Falaq* and possibly others too'.[36] Al-Barwani further contends that during the trial 'the prosecutor was questioning the *Mwongozi* articles more than the *Al-Falaq* article and kept insinuating and insisting that Ahmed Al-Lemki, Ahmed Seif Al-Kharusi, and Ali Muhsin were all communists and Mau Mau'.[37]

The discovery of communist propaganda in the offices of *Al-Falaq* was followed by prompt orders of the Acting Resident under Section 47 of the Zanzibar Penal Decree which prohibited the importation of the *Africa Newsletter*. He also ordered the immediate arrest of all ten members of the executive committee of the Arab Association: Abdulla Suleiman Al-Harthi, Seif Hamoud bin Feisal, Hamoud Salum Al-Ruwehi, Sultan Khamis Al-Mugheiri, Ahmed Mohamed Nassor Lemki, Abdulla Hamoud Al-Harthi, Ali Muhsin Al-Barwani, Ahmed Seif Al-Kharusi, Amour Zahor Al-Ismaili, and Salum Ahmed Al-Busaidi, and charged them with sedition. Eventually, the case against Sultan Khamis Al-Mugheiri was withdrawn following a letter of apology to the British Resident.

The particulars of the eight charges of sedition brought against the nine defendants merit a closer analysis for two reasons. On the one hand, the charges highlighted British concerns for 'law and order' in Zanzibar. On the other hand, the charges are evidence of how the colonized thought and felt about their British colonial masters. The particulars of the eight charges were as follows.[38]

First count. That the nine accused, on 12 May 1954, published an article entitled 'The Margate Conferences and the Colonies', in the newspaper *Al-Falaq*, containing the following seditious words:

> Mr Lyttelton, whose policies and actions have resulted in the two years he has been at the Colonial Office, in the mass killing of Nigerians, Gold Coasters, Malayans and other colonial people and in the destruction of elementary civil rights of millions, had the effrontery to say that he was carrying on a grim and stern task unflinchingly in order to continue the life and liberty of ordinary men and women in the colonial territories.

Oliver Lyttelton, a Conservative, was the Secretary of State for the Colonies from 1951 to 1954. During his tenure as well as that of his successor, Alan Lennox-Boyd, the British Government's colonial policy was one of 'rigid paternalism'.[39] Any reference to self-government was in terms of a period of not less than 25 years. Due to such rigid paternalism nationalist leaders such as Kwame Nkrumah, Hastings Kamuzu Banda and Jomo Kenyatta were considered rabble-rousers and thrown into jail. In this period almost every colony experienced rioting and civil disturbances, the suppression of which led to significant numbers of casualties.

In any case, it is questionable, on the above account, that the British administration was solely and geuinely concerned for law and order in Zanzibar. Its major concern was probably the increasing momentum of the struggle for independence in the region. The above account also indicates that colonial intimidation was comparable around the colonies.

Second count. That the nine accused, on 3 February 1954, published an article entitled 'Imperialism' in *Al-Falaq*, containing the following seditious words:

> We should not, however, pay much attention to the rumours we hear about the superiority of the white people in their special mission of promoting civilization to the backward nations to help them reproduce wealth from their agricultural and metal resources; for these rumours cannot face the bitter facts which portray to us the truth or the material germ of imperialism, for they are at once destroyed by the well-known facts about the subjecting, domineering, not to say tyrannising [sic] methods on which all imperialists, without exception, depend.

The tone of the article is strikingly similar to the anti-imperialist criticism emanating from Cairo Radio ('The Voice of the Arabs') which at the time could be heard in Zanzibar.[40] However, similar sentiments were echoed all over the colonies from India to West Africa, Egypt and Syria.[41]

Third count. That the nine accused on 10 March published an article entitled 'Freedom and Democracy in Kenya' in the newspaper *Al-Falaq*, containing the following seditious words:

> Freedom, to the Kenya Government, means frustration and threatening. Freedom in Kenya is obviously the freedom of the Government to revenge, to confiscate others' freedom, to check the freedom of thought and freedom of the press – aye, freedom in Kenya tends to kill the very germ of freedom – Democracy is a hollow word – it has neither economical history nor social establishment: it is in fact, a word without any principle. This is the system of Government in that democratic Kenya. This is the system that embodies the whole meaning of authority and slavery....

The editor of *Al-Falaq* was evidently referring to the ongoing Mau Mau crisis and the state of emergency in Kenya.

Fourth count. That the nine accused on 10 March published the following seditious words in the Arabic language in *Al-Falaq*, which translated as:

> Wisdom of the Week. Oh, my brother, the oppressors have exceeded the bounds. It is right that we should wage Jehad [sic], it is right that we should redeem ourselves. Why?

This 'seditious' passage in Arabic, according to Ali Muhsin Al-Barwani, happened to be a quotation from a song by Abdulwahab, a renowned Egyptian musician. Here was a cultural difference. While the intended audience understood that the quote was from Abdulwahab's song, the British either did not know that or if they did, they ignored or hid the fact in order to make political mileage out of it.[42]

The call for *jihad* raises interesting questions about the role of Islam in Zanzibar 'nationalist' politics. Who did the editor of *Al-Falaq* expect to answer the call for *jihad*? Who did he think needed redemption? Part of the answer is to be found in colonial Zanzibar's demographic composition. In 1948 about 97 per cent of the population of Zanzibar was Muslim; the non-Muslim 3 per cent were Hindus, Christians, Parsees and Buddhists.[43] The call for *jihad* and the appeal for redemption were targeted mostly at Muslim Zanzibaris.

Much like other societies and ideologies, Islamic ideology provides alternatives to resolve conflicts between people and between countries. Conflicts and disagreements including those over politics and religious matters can be resolved either through diplomacy or by force.[44] It is probable that the editor of *Al-Falaq* made the call for *jihad* in order to mobilize the Muslim population, to justify the nationalist struggle, and to identify the non-Muslim British as the enemy rather than the Arab sultanate. However, despite Islam being the common religion of the majority of Zanzibaris, the call for a *jihad* did not appear to have been taken seriously. Indeed, there is reason to believe that, while Islam in Zanzibar brought people together, it failed to unite them.[45] Support and lack of support for the defendants in the seditious case against *Al-Falaq* clearly reflected cleavages in Zanzibar's body politic along class and ethnic lines. Since Zanzibar newspapers tended to cater to sectarian interests,[46] the case against *Al-Falaq* was made to appear to be a case against the Arab Association with which Africans and Indians had little empathy.[47] Indeed, the ethnic and class nature of *Al-Falaq*'s constituency emerges clearly in its edition of 22 April 1954:

> Legal safeguards for the protectorate's most important community [i.e. Arabs – author] are being entirely overlooked which in turn puts the inhabitants in the worst position. Those whom we refer to are the agriculturalists who have time and again been subjected to discriminatory legislation apparently for the 'yes man'. Many decrees have been passed in the Legislative Council (legco) concerning labour which give workers an advantage in the absence of legal provisions to safeguard the employers' interests. The most recent of such discriminatory legislation is one providing for the compensation to workers injured in the cause of employment. Agriculture being the most contributory force in the development of our country, it is surely a disappointment to those engaged in that pursuit to find such lack of cooperation from the government whuch (sic) is more concerned with the workers interests than the development of the protectorate's economy.[48]

It is likely that the editor of *Al-Falaq* believed that diplomacy would not succeed in securing Arab interests in the proposed constitutional changes which would guide Zanzibar towards independence. However, it is uncertain why the editor of *Al-Falaq* thought that what was good for Arabs was also good for Africans in Zanzibar. It is tempting, however, to think that he was alluding to some common identity based on the allegiance of all Muslims in Zanzibar to the Islamic faith. Yet, one of the grievances being given expression by pro-Arab newspapers was a sense of loss of Arab sovereignty under the British. A *Mwongozi* editorial of 6 January 1956 reads:

> Loyalty to the country and throne as the symbol of the indivisibility of the state, must come first before everything, and that to preach communalism as is being done by even those who have taken oath to serve his Highness the Sultan as his councilors, is tantamount to undermining the natural loyalty that the people feel for their sovereign.[49]

Al-Falaq's call for a *jihad* was an attempt to give the struggle for Zanzibar nationalism 'an almost holy status as a sacred obligation'.[50] It was especially a call for all Arabs in Zanzibar, regardless of their station in life, to reject British hegemony. It was, presumably, intended to jolt Arabs out of their passiveness and submission to an infidel nation.[51] In this regard, the call for a *jihad* questioned Britain's moral authority as well as its right, as an infidel nation, to rule Zanzibar. What *Al-Falaq* and the Arab Association did not question was Arab superiority and dominance over the African majority.

Fifth count. That the nine accused on 20 May, without lawful excuse, had in their possession a seditious publication, an article entitled 'The Margate Conferences and the Colonies', in a publication entitled *Africa Newsletter* dated November 1953, containing the same seditious words as in the first count. It is not clear from the charge whether the Arab Association or individual members subscribed to *Africa Newsletter*. Also uncertain is whether the Arab Association maintained any clandestine relationship with the British Communist Party, the publishers of *Africa Newsletter*. Whatever the case, it is ironic that the British administration in Zanzibar found the reference to the Margate Conferences seditious, while the Home Government did not charge the British Communist Party with sedition over the same reference.

Sixth count. That the nine accused on 20 May, without lawful excuse, had in their possession a seditious publication entitled *Africa Newsletter* dated February and March 1954, containing the following seditious words:

> Over a hundred years ago the Chartist leader, Ernest Jones spoke of the British Empire in the following words: On its Colonies the sun never sets, but the blood never dries. The Chartist declaration of 1846 could equally be applied to the British workers of today in relation to Kenya and Malaya: they, your masters, will take the land – they will fill all the higher situations [sic], civil and military of the new colonies – your share will be the slaughter of the combat and the cost of winning and retaining the conquest.

Needless to say, this was a serious indictment against colonial rule under which economic, social, racial and other inequities were created or exacerbated.

Seventh count. That the nine accused on 20 May 1954, at Zanzibar, without lawful excuse, had in their possession a seditious publication, illustrated matter in a publication entitled *Twenty-First February 1954* containing the following seditious words:

> Colonialism is misery, oppression, war, but the youth and the people of the world demand an end to this modern form of slavery.

Why this constituted sedition is unclear. First, other than the Legislative Council, there was no other democratic avenue for airing criticism of British imperialism. Second, the above statement reflected a global concern and trend against European colonialism, and the 'seditious' words were not from *Al-Falaq* but from *Twenty-First February*.

Eighth count. That the nine accused on 12 May, 1954, at Zanzibar, published the newspaper *Al-Falaq* without adding or printing at the foot of the last page of each copy thereof, the true and real name and place of abode of the printer and publisher, and the true and real description of the place of printing and of publication of this newspaper.

From the administration's viewpoint, the above charges contained statements which 'were unjustified and untrue'.[52] While the administration considered the charges to be serious offences, it was felt that some if not most of the accused were probably 'ignorant of the seriously seditious nature of what was being printed in their paper'.[53] In other words, the government believed the committee members had been used, hoodwinked, or even coerced into supporting the militant stance of *Al-Falaq* and its editor, whose displeasure at the proposed constitutional changes was no secret. It appears that this possibility was not far-fetched. But then why was the entire executive committee of the Arab Association arrested? Although Ali Muhsin Al-Barwani believes the committee had legal responsibility,[54] it is also possible that such action was taken to set an example to others.[55]

Lofchie attributes a lot of *Al-Falaq*'s militancy to Lemki's own communist background.[56] However, the administration suspected that Ali Muhsin Al-Barwani was behind the new militancy of *Al-Falaq*. Evidence at the trial suggested that he had been receiving copies of the Communist *Africa Newsletter* for the previous three years, and had also from time to time received communist literature from East European countries including the special newspaper *Twenty-First February 1954*. Lemki, the editor, stated in evidence that he had received only three copies of the *Africa Newsletter*, two of which were seized by the police, and it is probable, despite what he stated in evidence, that Ali Muhsin Al-Barwani was passing his copies of the *Africa Newsletter* to Lemki for publication.

According to the Zanzibar Protectorate Intelligence Report of June 1954, Ali-Muhsin Barwani and Ahmed Seif Kharusi, the joint editors of *Mwongozi*, were the first to come forward at the end of the trial and insist that the Arab Association should promptly pay Lemki's fines. Lemki was fined a total of 11,100 shillings or 43 months' imprisonment with hard labor in default and was placed on a bond of 5,000 shillings for two years with two sureties in the same amount. The fines were promptly paid. The above intelligence report also observed that:

Lemki is a young man who has suffered since childhood from apoplectic fits and in giving evidence did not strike one as particularly intelligent, whilst on the other hand, ALI MUHSIN BARWANI is an extremely intelligent but highly dangerous individual and it would be typical of his technique to use LEMKI, a known communist, as his tool.[57]

Following the trial Ali Muhsin Al-Barwani was said to be in a 'thoroughly disaffected and impassioned frame of mind' against the government.[58]

Intelligence reports also suggest that Al-Barwani and other young militant Arabs expected that the government would bring charges of sedition against *Al-Falaq* and frustrated every attempt to reach a compromise and prevent the case coming to court. They intended to exploit the sedition trial for political purposes, and preparations were under way to mobilize Arab support in Zanzibar, Pemba, Dar-es-Salaam, and Mombasa. Lemki and Amour Zahor, another of the accused, visited Dar-es-Salaam before the trial to meet with their counsel, Mr Fraser-Murray, and also approached the President of the Baluchi community in Dar-es-Salaam for its support.[59]

In the meantime, Sir Said bin Ali Al-Mugheiri and Sheikh Suleiman Abdulla Kiyyumi, the leader of the Pemba branch of the Arab Association, visited Zanzibar. Their purpose was to dissuade the committee of the Arab Association from sending a delegation to Pemba to mobilize anti-government feelings there. Their advice was ignored and Sheikh Abdulla Suleiman Al-Harthi, Ahmed Seif Kharusi and Mohamed Nassor Lemki (father of Ahmed Lemki and a known anti-British Arab leader) visited Pemba and held a meeting at the Wete Mosque attended, it was alleged, by 8,000 Arabs.[60]

The Arab Association in Zanzibar also tried to obtain the support of the Hadhramout Arabs in Mombasa. Sheikh Abdulla Shirigdin, the Secretary of the Central Arab Association in Mombasa, visited Zanzibar at the time of the trial with a view to obtaining a fuller picture of the situation. He stayed with a Hadhramout Arab and is reported to have left unimpressed with the Arab Association case, but he promised financial support in view of his own association's commitment in the East African Arab Union.[61]

Meanwhile in Zanzibar itself preparations were under way, as the date of the trial drew nearer, to mobilize mass Arab support. The Arab Association called upon the Arab community to congregate in numbers at the Court on the day of the trial. Although the Arab leaders emphasized the need to preserve order, there were rumors of impending trouble, especially from Omani Arabs.[62] The government feared a repeat of the 1936 riot when mostly 'Manga' Arabs from the rural districts protested violently against the government regulation of copra prices.[63] Considerable precautions were therefore taken for the preservation of order during the trial. The Tanganyika Government and the Army General Headquarters in Nairobi were warned that it might be necessary to ask for reinforcements for the Zanzibar police, the two government ships were kept in the harbor, the Special Constables were mobilized, and a large body of police in riot gear were posted near the Court.

Since the administration suspected that it would not be possible to prevent a large crowd from assembling outside the Court, steps were taken to encourage the exhibition of patience and orderliness by the provision of benches and by ensuring that refreshments were available. These somewhat unusual measures, and also the tactful handling of the crowd by the police on duty, probably contributed to the complete absence of incident throughout the proceedings, although the crowd of onlookers on the first day of the trial numbered nearly a thousand. There was a smaller gathering on the second day of the trial, which was completed on that day. The nine accused were convicted by the Resident Magistrate, W.M. Mackenzie, on 19 June 1954, on three counts of possessing seditious matter, four counts of publishing seditious literature and one count under the Newspaper Decree of 1938. All were bound over in the sum of 5,000 shillings to keep the peace and be of good behavior for two years. An order was also made for the confiscation of the *Al-Falaq* printing press and for the banning of *Al-Falaq* for one year. The accused appealed against the sentence in the Zanzibar High Court, and in all respects the appeal was dismissed.

The immediate consequence of the trial and the guilty verdict was the resignation, on instructions from the Arab Association, of Arabs from the Legislative Council and all statutory and government boards.[64] Most if not all of these appointments were made from lists of persons recommended by the Arab Association. It would appear as though the Arab Association was emulating Mahatma Gandhi's tactic of passive non-co-operation with the government.

Ali Muhsin Al-Barwani was one of the Arab members of the Legislative Council who resigned.[65] The reason he gave for his resignation was the 'unco-operative' attitude of the government. In their joint message to the Sultan, the Arab Association used the same expression, instancing (a) the Resident's refusal to accept an invitation from the Arab Association to attend their annual reception at the festival of Id-el-Fitr;[66] (b) the publication of Immigration Control Regulations in which the special treatment afforded at the time to natives of Southern Arabia was not provided for;[67] and (c) the Government's refusal to impose a special levy on cloves for the sole purpose of raising the price to the overseas buyer and paying it back to the grower.[68] According to the British Resident, none of these reasons was 'to a responsible person, a "good and sufficient reason" for permitting a member to resign his seat as required by the Council's Decree'.

Prior to the trial efforts were made to affect the unity of the Arab community. After the trial a special committee was set up to investigate the activities of certain Arabs during the trial with the intention of showing them up as traitors. The investigation escalated into a 'witch-hunt' against Arabs who might at any time have been seen in conversation with members of the Special Branch. However, the main target was Sultan Ahmed Al-Mugheiri, a Legislative Council representative for Pemba. He was especially singled out for ostracism by the Arab community and the words 'Sultan Ahmed – Traitor' could be seen chalked up on walls all over Zanzibar town. When he refused to resign from the Legislative Council he was promptly murdered.[69] It is ironic that on the day the trial of Mugheiri's murderer began in March 1955, two other Arab members of the Legislative Council announced that they would resume attending the Council meetings.[70]

Another consequence of the case which was of historical importance was the emergence of Ali Muhsin Al-Barwani as an influential figure in Zanzibar politics. By the end of 1955, he had emerged as the principal leader of Arab nationalism. His views on Zanzibar's sovereignty have already been alluded to. His leadership of Hizbu l'Wattan l'Riaia Sultan Zanzibar provided him with a multi-racial platform and the opportunity to try and win wide popular support for Arab nationalism. Subsequently, Hizbu, whose origins and stronghold were the peasantry, was transformed into the Zanzibar Nationalist Party (ZNP) and an Arab-dominated urban nationalist movement. The motto of the ZNP was national unity regardless of tribal and traditional differences. However, as Lofchie succinctly puts it, 'The terms of this mystique made any articulation of the glaring economic differences between the various racial groups a basic violation of national-istic political norms.'[71] It is not surprising, therefore, that most African members of the ZNP eventually became suspicious of its Arab leadership, and began to look elsewhere for political leadership.[72]

In the aftermath of the seditious case against *Al-Falaq* the Arab boycott of the Legislative Council was mainly supported by the Arabs.[73] According to Ali Muhsin Al-Barwani, he and Ibuni Saleh (a prominent Comorian) appealed to the two African Legislative Council representatives in Zanzi-bar to join the boycott.[74] Rashid Hamad, the representative of Shirazi origin in Zanzibar, listened sympathetically but Ameri Tajo was not supportive.[75] The Arab Association also sent a delegation to Pemba to canvass support from Arab and Shirazi leaders. In Pemba the delegation met with Ali Shariff Moosa, the African/Shirazi Legislative Council representative for Pemba, and Ali Muhsin Al-Barwani pleaded for the support of the boycott 'but Ali Shariff Moosa did not agree up front, demanding that the Arab members should first return to LegCo and then they would see from there'.[76]

Conclusion

During the 1950s, a period of rising anti-colonial sentiments, the press in Zanzibar was the main outlet for the frustrations and resentments of the educated urban elite. It was also a decade of increasing official concern abuot communist-inspired subversion in the colonial world. The British administration in Zanzibar endeavored to control both the constitutional changes necessary for self-government and public access to news from the outside world, especially to prevent the infiltration of communist 'propa-ganda'. Editorials and news which administrators felt constituted 'reckless statements or misinformation' were subject to penal sanctions.

The controversy over the Rankine Plan of 1951 provided the editor of *Al-Falaq* with the opportunity to write scathing editorials against British rule in Zanzibar and elsewhere. The British administrators were unable or unwilling to suffer quietly the printed criticisms of their policies. In early June 1954 the entire committee of the Arab Association, the owners of *Al-Falaq*, was arrested and charged with sedition. The case of sedition against *Al-Falaq* to some extent united the Arab community against the British administration. However, the majority of Africans, due in part to racial and class differences, did not sympathize with the defendants in the case. The African reaction to the case was the first sign of the polarization of Zanzibar nationalist politics along racial lines, despite the predominance of Muslims in Zanzibar's population.

Notes

1. 'Why should Ng'ambo suffer the most?', *Mwongozi*, 8 March 1957, p. 1.
2. *Ibid.*
3. Martin Sturmer, 'The Media History of Tanzania' (PhD diss., University of Vienna, 1998), p. 279.
4. For a short history of newspapers in Zanzibar see: Mariam M. A. Hamdani, 'Zanzibar Newspapers, 1902–1974' (Diploma Thesis, Tanzania School of Journalism, 1981).
5. It sold at 10 cents a copy and had a circulation of 1,000 copies. It ceased publication in the late 1940s partly due to the death of its editor and partly due to financial problems.
6. Published in English, Swahili and Arabic. It sold at 30 cents a copy; 100 copies were printed daily. According to Hamdani, its readership was mainly Arab and its tenor was in favor of the Arab Association and later the Zanzibar Nationalist Party. See Hamdani, 'Zanzibar Newspapers,' p. 28.
7. It was published in English and Gujerati, and had a circulation of 500. It sold at 30 cents a copy. It ceased publication in the 1950s due to financial problems.
8. It is not certain if the name was symbolically derived from one of the ships, *Al-Falaq*, under the command of Seif bin Sultan who 'liberated' Zanzibar from the Portuguese in 1652. According to Khatib M. Rajab, *Al-Falaq* was the largest ship and carried eighty guns. See: http://victorian.fortunecity.com/portfolio/543/crusades.
9. There was also the case of *Al Nahadha* whose editor was arrested and fined several times for his 'inflammatory' editorials against the Administration.
10. Ronald Brown, 'Sedition in the Colonies', *Mwongozi*, 29 March 1957, p. 1.
11. *Ibid.*, p. 1.
12. Rudolph Peters, *Islam and Colonialism: the Doctrine of Jihad in Modern History* (The Hague: Mouton, 1979), p. 3.
13. James P. Piscatori, *Islam in a World of Nation-States* (Cambridge: Cambridge University Press, 1986), p. 96.
14. See Peters, *Islam and Colonialism*, p. 3, for a similar argument about the larger Muslim world under imperialism.
15. Michael F. Lofchie, *Zanzibar: Background to Revolution* (Princeton, NJ: Princeton University Press, 1965), p.149.
16. Sturmer, 'Media History', p. 278.
17. Albion Ross, 'Bazaar is Found Ruling in Zanzibar', *New York Times*, 8 June 1954, p. 7.
18. *Ibid*
19. After Zanzibar became a British Protectorate in 1890, a constitutional government was established in 1891 with a British Representative as First Minister. Although the government was administered by the British Representative, also known as Resident, important questions of policy were referred to an Executive Council over which the Sultan presided in person.
20. Wole Soyinka, 'Response to Ali's Millennial "Conclusion"', *West African Review* (2000), at http://www.westafricareview.com/war/vol1.2/soyinka2.html
21. Abdulaziz Y. Lodhi, 'National Language, Culture and Identity: the role of Kiswahili in

the context of Zanzibar'. Paper presented at an International Conference on the History and Culture of Zanzibar, Zanzibar, 14-16 December 1992, p. 1.

22. Issa Nasser, interviewed by Saada Al-Ghafry on behalf of the author, at Muscat, Oman, 27 September 2000.

23. It was envisaged that an independent Zanzibar would be ruled by an Arab constitutional monarchy.

24. According to Khatib M. Rajab Al-Zinjibari, the Omani Sultanate in Zanzibar was neither imperialist nor colonialist. Supposedly the local people had requested help from the Omanis to get rid of the Portuguese. After being 'liberated' from the Portuguese the local ruling dynasty under Queen Mwana wa Mwema 'then pledged allegiance to the Sultan of Omani for protection and friendship.' Zinjibari at:
. http://victorian.fortunecity.com/portfolio/543/crusade_in_znz

25. It came out on Thursdays and was published in English and Swahili. It had a circulation of 800 and was sold at 25 cents a copy.

26. Quoted by Hamdani, 'Zanzibar Newspapers,' p. 33.

27. *Ibid.*

28. Lucy P. Mair, 'East Africa', *Political Quarterly* 29, 3 (July-September, 1958), pp. 278–88.

29. Jonathan Glassman, 'Sorting Out the Tribes: The creation of racial identities in colonial Zanzibar's newspaper wars,' *Journal of African History*, 41 (2000), pp. 395–428.

30. Chinua Achebe, *Home and Exile* (Oxford: Oxford University Press, 2000), p. 24.

31. Ali Muhsin Al-Barwani, interviewed by Saada Al-Ghafry on behalf of the author, Muscat, Oman, 19 September 2000.

32. P(ublic) R(ecord) O(ffice), CO 822/840, British Resident, Zanzibar to Secretary of State, confidential telegram dated 7 June, 1954.

33. Ali Muhsin Al-Barwani, interview, 19 September 2000.

34. *Ibid.*

35. PRO, CO 822/840, Acting British Resident to Secretary of State, confidential telegram dated 17 June 1954.

36. Ali Muhsin Al-Barwani, interview, 19 September 2000.

37. *Ibid.*

38. PRO, CO 822/840, Acting British Resident to Secretary of State, telegram dated 19 June, 1954.

39. Charles Allen (ed.) *Tales from the Dark Continent* (London: André Deutsch, 1979), p. 139.

40. In July 1954 Radio Cairo introduced a Swahili program for audiences in East Africa. Before then broadcasts to sub-Saharan Africa were in Arabic.

41. Ali Muhsin Al-Barwani, interview, 19 September 2000.

42. I am grateful to Saada Al-Ghafry for this observation.

43. Lodhi, 'National Language', p. 1.

44. Actually this is not unique to Islam. Every society and ideology has at one time or another resorted to diplomacy or war in conflicts with neighbors.

45. Brian D. Bowles,'The Struggle for Independence, 1946–1963,' in Abdul Sheriff and Ed Ferguson (eds), *Zanzibar Under Colonial Rule* (London: James Currey, 1991), p. 94.

46. Hamdani, 'Zanzibar Newspapers', p. 7.

47. The Arab Association was founded in the 1920s. According to Ali Muhsin Al-Barwani it was initiated as a result of a court case against one Sheikh Mohamed Said Al-Barwani, the owner of a big farm. At the time, there was a *virukia* (parasitic plants) infestation. The government ordered farmers to clean up all parasitic plants from their clove plantations or face fines. When parasitic plants were found on Sheikh Mohamed's farm he was taken to court and fined. When he wanted to go home to fetch the money he was refused permission, and the fine was kindly paid by Saleh Gangji, an Ismaili Indian. Subsequently, a meeting was convened at the now Istiqama mosque to discuss the case and to form a farmers' association to protect their interests. Among those who attended were Bihar Lal, a Banian Indian editor of *Zanzibar Voice*, and other Indians and Comorians. The association initially dealt with farming interests or immigration issues. Later the farmers' association became the Arab Association.

48. Quoted by Hamdani, 'Zanzibar Newspapers,' pp. 21–2.

49. *Ibid.*, p. 28.
50. Lofchie, *Zanzibar*, p. 129.
51. Conformity and submission are conceived from the Qur'anic injunctions to 'obey God, the Prophet, and those in authority among you' (Qur'an, 4:59). Nonconformity and activism are also construed from Qur'anic injunctions which call for believers to combat evil with good (Qur'an, 13:22, 41:34) and do justice (Qur'an, 16:90).
52. PRO, CO 822/840, Acting British Resident to Secretary of State, confidential telegram dated 17 June 1954.
53. *Ibid.*
54. Ali Muhsin Al-Barwani, interview, 19 September, 2000.
55. Issa Nasser, interview, 27 September, 2000.
56. Lofchie, *Zanzibar*, pp. 140–44.
57. PRO, CO 822/840, 'Extract from Zanzibar Protectorate Intelligence Report – June, 1954'.
58. *Ibid.*
59. PRO, CO 822/840, 'Intelligence Report – June, 1954'.
60. *Ibid.*
61. *Ibid.*
62. Ali Muhsin Al-Barwani suggests that the rumors were unfounded; that there was no intention of making trouble as this would have defeated the Arab Association's purpose of exploiting the case for political gain.
63. Zanzibar Protectorate, Report of the Commission of Enquiry Concerning the Riot in Zanzibar on the 7ᵗʰ of February, 1936 (Zanzibar, 1936).
64. Ali Muhsin Al-Barwani disputes this. In his view the boycott was not the consequence of the case but of the Resident's refusal to attend the Eid Baraza, and also because the committee was on trial.
65. Two others of the accused who also resigned from the Legislative Council were Abdulla Suleiman Al-Harthi and Hamoud Salum Al-Ruwehi.
66. It was customary for the British Resident to attend this reception, but the Acting Resident felt unable as Her Majesty's representative to do so when the Arabs through their newspaper had cast what were considered to be gross aspersions on the Secretary of State.
67. In the new Regulations the government redefined the concept of 'alien' in the previous provision with a view to excluding Omani Arabs from the new coverage. However, the Regulations, which had been published for information, had not yet been in force.
68. PRO, CO 822/840, Acting Resident to Secretary of State, confidential telegram dated 7 June 1954.
69. His assassin was Mohamed Hamoud Barwani. His son, Hamoud Mohamed, assassinated Abeid A. Karume, the President of Zanzibar, on 7 April 1972. Mohamed Hamoud Barwani was sentenced to death but his sentence was later commuted by the Sultan to a penal servitude of ten years. According to the Afro-Shirazi Party, the commuted sentence was intended to placate and please the Arabs. See: Afro-Shirazi Party, *The History of Zanzibar Africans and the Formation of the Afro-Shirazi Party* (Dar-es-Salaam: Dar-es-Salaam Printers, n.d.), p. 3.
70. Leonard Ingalls, 'Zanzibar takes self-rule step', *The New York Times*, 21 June 1956.
71. Lofchie, *Zanzibar*, p. 155.
72. *Ibid.*, p. 156.
73. The African members of the Legislative Council continued to attend its meetings.
74. Ali Muhsin Al-Barwani, interview, 19 September 2000.
75. *Ibid.*
76. *Ibid.*

Thirteen

⋀⋁⋀⋁⋀⋁⋀⋁⋀⋁⋀⋁⋀⋁⋀⋁⋀⋁⋀⋁⋀⋁⋀⋁⋀

An Imagined Generation
Umma Youth in Nationalist Zanzibar

THOMAS BURGESS

The Zanzibari Revolution of 1964 ended a century and a half of Arab political and economic pre-eminence in Zanzibar, claiming the lives and property, and sending into permanent exile much of the population of the Arab community, especially on Unguja Island. In the following weeks and months, Zanzibar rapidly assumed the status of East Africa's most radical regime. The Revolution put into positions of power a number of young socialist intellectuals anxious to implement wide-reaching social and economic reforms based on models provided by socialist nations of the North. It also offered a violent solution to racial and economic inequalities not limited in East Africa to the islands of Zanzibar. Such developments convinced many African and Western observers that Zanzibar was quickly becoming the 'Cuba' of East Africa, and would soon attempt to export its revolutionary ideas to the mainland.[1] And at least some Zanzibari politicians were convinced that this was indeed revolutionary Zanzibar's role in the region. Abdulrahman Mohammed 'Babu', the Zanzibari Minister of External Affairs just after the Revolution, said in April 1964, 'East Africa is a powderkeg, and Zanzibar is the fuse'.[2]

Throughout early 1964, regular discussions between Western and East African officials focused on what could be done to put out that fuse. Julius Nyerere eventually put pressure on Zanzibar's President Abeid Karume to accept a union of their two nations, in order to limit Zanzibar's regional influence, and to strengthen Karume's position within his own government, which was perceived to be threatened by the rising power of the socialists. Although after the announcement of the federation agreement on 22 April 1964, the island government was supposed to accept the non-aligned foreign policy of the new union government of Tanzania, Zanzibar continued to run its internal affairs without union interference.

This meant that in the 1960s and 1970s the revolutionary Zanzibari government enjoyed a free hand in instituting policies designed to establish a socialist paradise in the islands. During these years Zanzibar adopted a form of socialism centered on government control of the wholesale and retail trades, as well as the overseas marketing of its cash crops of cloves and coconuts. Karume's regime redistributed urban and rural property, and embarked on an ambitious housing construction scheme. Urban housing was just one of a series of public works projects that included schools, roads, and state-owned farms which depended on the forced labor of Zanzibari citizens. Participation in 'voluntary' labor projects was a recognized means by which citizens could demonstrate their loyalty and service to the revolutionary state. Citizens also endured food rationing and chronic shortages of basic household commodities, as well as periods of service in labor camps in the countryside. The goal was to establish a modern, economically developed society free of race and class inequalities.

The Zanzibari one-party state managed to extend its powers of intervention in the lives of ordinary citizens through the development of institutions altogether new to Zanzibari society. A standing army, an East German-trained department of 'security' officials and informants, and a pervasive nation-wide Youth League organization, including such departments as the Young Pioneers and the feared Green Guards, all made their appearance shortly after the Revolution. All assumed the responsibility of making sure that citizens strove to 'build the nation' (*kujenga taifa*) and to defend the Revolution from its enemies both foreign and domestic. The accent in these years, in official rhetoric and public policy, was on production over leisure and consumption. Citizenship in Zanzibar became synonymous with revolutionary notions of discipline, sacrifice and vigilance; values considered necessary in order to construct the new socialist Zanzibari state.

Zanzibari socialists emerged as a generation that reached political maturity in the early 1960s and helped establish their government's revolutionary policies during the rest of that and the following decade. Zanzibari socialists were both African and Arab in racial identity;[3] as a whole they did not emerge from any single class or ethnic group within Zanzibari society, nor were they from any particular rural district or urban neighborhood. They were, on the other hand, representatives of a generation of Zanzibaris uniquely exposed to foreign cultural and intellectual influences in the post-World War II era that encouraged faith in socialist precepts. For socialist youth, generational identity as a result had considerable explanatory value. They considered themselves members of a vanguard generation, prepared through their unusual access to Western education and travel, to lead Zanzibar out of an era of colonial backwardness and capitalist exploitation.

Elsewhere I have discussed the emergence of a youth identity within the Afro-Shirazi Party (ASP) during Zanzibar's nationalist struggle for independence.[4] In the present essay, however, I shall examine the construction, beginning in the 1950s, of a socialist generational identity within the Zanzibar Nationalist Party (ZNP). The ZNP's most concentrated electoral strength lay in Pemba and in the heavily Arab and Asian neighborhoods of the capital collectively known as 'Stone Town'. The party in fact depended heavily on the services of Arabs living in the capital city, individuals with access in Zanzibari society to wealth and/or education.

Despite its reliance on Arab leadership and financial support, the ZNP managed to somewhat transcend the stigma of being the party of the islands' Arab minority by attracting to its fold thousands of African supporters. Many of these came after 1959 when the ZNP succeeded in exploiting serious differences within the ASP leadership and African voting majority in Zanzibar to form an alliance with a third, breakaway, party, the Zanzibar and Pemba People's Party (ZPPP). The creation of the ZPPP represented long-standing cultural differences between Africans of longer and shorter residence in the islands, known respectively as Shirazis[5] and mainlanders. The Shirazis who gave their support to the ZPPP and its ZNP allies regarded mainlanders as more of a threat to their economic interests and cultural identity than Arabs with whom they had long-established affinal ties. The ZNP also attracted significant support through its doctrines of Islamic non-racialism, anti-colonialism, and Zanzibari nationalism. The party's excellent grassroots organizational efforts were also decisive in winning a series of electoral victories in the early 1960s which guaranteed that the ZNP-ZPPP alliance would inherit power from the British at independence in December 1963.[6]

As the ZNP gained strength in the early 1960s, its younger party members believed, however, that it was not prepared after independence to address the islands' serious racial and economic inequalities. A socialist identity gradually emerged among ZNP youth in Zanzibar Town increasingly critical of the policies not only of the British colonial regime, but also of their own party. They were convinced that the realization of their vision of Zanzibar as a viable independent state could come about only through efforts to encourage unity between the islands' racial communities – unity based not so much on appeals to Islamic universalism as on principles of socialist development. Eventually in mid-1963 young ZNP socialists seceded from their party to form the Umma Party. Led by Babu, the Umma Party was conceived as a mass movement of island youth towards socialism. As a result of its socialist rhetoric, Umma was altogether an urban phenomenon, with virtually no support in the countryside. Its outspoken opposition to the ZNP-ZPPP government in late 1963, however, brought the new party into a working alliance with the ASP – a co-operative relationship that was strengthened by the events of the Revolution in 1964. Although the Zanzibari Revolution was conceived, organized and executed by the Youth League of the ASP (ASPYL), Umma partisans played a significant role in the revolutionary events in the capital city.[7]

The close relationship between Umma and the ASP in the Revolution was formalized during the '100 days of the People's Republic of Zanzibar', when Umma officially merged with the ASP. With the prohibition at the same time of the ZNP and the ZPPP, the ASP one-party state in Zanzibar was born. Within that one-party state, Umma socialists continued as a faction and generational cohort; they helped shape revolutionary policies, as Babu assumed a position of power in the islands second only to that of Karume himself. The prominence of Babu and his young supporters within the revolutionary government in 1964, and the perception that their influence would continue to grow until they either overthrew or sidelined the more moderate Karume, caused great anxiety among Western observers. American representatives considered Babu to be personally at the epicenter of the 'communist virus' in East Africa. The Tanganyika-Zanzibar federation agreement should be, and has been, considered, then, as an attempt to neutralize the socialists within the ASP government, in particular Babu and others of Umma political ancestry.[8]

With such a background in mind, it is possible to introduce the main themes of this chapter. It will begin with a discussion of the social and political environment after World War II that encouraged ZNP youth to imagine their generation as uniquely endowed by historical circumstances to play a major role in the nationalist struggle for independence. The chapter will then describe the origins of the Umma Party. I shall then reconstruct the role of Umma youth in the 1964 Zanzibari Revolution and in the months immediately thereafter, when Umma 'cadres' enjoyed their greatest influence in shaping revolutionary policies. The purpose of the chapter will therefore be to retrace the history of the Umma Party as an important thread in the intellectual history of the Zanzibari 1964 Revolution and the subsequent period of socialism and nation building.

Class, Race and Generation

I also intend, however, to encourage a debate about the relationship between identities of class, race and generation. Scholars employing Marxist interpretive lenses, for example, have in the past not been fully willing to recognize the importance of either generational or ethnic identities in the formation of movements supportive or not of 'progressive' social and political change. Examples emerge from within Zanzibar's own historiography of writing that permits only Western scripted readings of the identity of historical actors, ignoring how locals themselves understood their own fundamental alliances and political coalitions. In an essay published in 1991 B.D. Bowles characterized the ASP as 'a petty-bourgeois party'.[9] Bowles then argued that

> the understanding and analysis of Zanzibar history depends on thinking of workers as they actually were, that is, workers, rather than mainlanders or Africans, and to think of employers as employers and not as Zanzibaris or Arabs and Asians. To do otherwise is to write the history of images.[10]

Thus despite the fact that the ASP literally stood for the 'Afro-Shirazi Party', such identities should, according to Bowles, be ignored in favor of those based solely on what are perceived to be Zanzibaris' clashing material interests. Not to do so would apparently be to descend to the 'false consciousness' of those Africans whose history is under examination. Evidently locals have no explanations to offer about why they instigated the Zanzibari Revolution, because they think in 'images' not recognized by Marxist scholars. In this chapter I oppose such an approach, suggesting that generational identities have considerable explanatory value for scholars seeking to understand the conflicts within Zanzibari society which culminated in the Zanzibari Revolution.

Indeed, the architects of the Umma Party considered their movement to be the voice not necessarily of a revolutionary class, but of a vanguard generation. Umma members were uniquely informed by their *times*, and not necessarily their heterogeneous racial or class origins *per se*, to lead the socialist cause in Zanzibar. For this reason Umma intellectuals imagined their generation, despite the demographic imprecision and theoretical impoverishment of that term, as occupying a position on the front line of historical progress. Rather than asserting the demographic reality of a generation unified by shared views, historical experiences, and a common political vocabulary, I intend to focus simply on how and to what extent generational identities emerged in Zanzibar during the nationalist struggle, and the manner in which individuals assuming a youth identity played a revolutionary role in the islands.

Jonathan Glassman has more recently contributed another assessment of the intellectual origins of the Zanzibari Revolution.[11] He describes how Zanzibari newspaper propagandists indulged in the politics of race to such an extent that by 1957 'the idea of exclusionary ethnic nationalism had become an unquestioned "given" across the entire spectrum of Zanzibari intellectual discourse'.[12] My essay suggests that after 1957 Babu and other Umma intellectuals made concerted efforts to resist ethnic nationalism in Zanzibar, by promoting socialism as a 'cure' for racism. But because they came to identify with a set of political doctrines of at least partial foreign ancestry that did not organically emerge from the kind of nationalist debates Glassman describes, their appeal was limited to a relatively small number of young people who gravitated towards Zanzibar Town, and who participated in the currents of socialist discourse that Babu and his colleagues attempted to foster there. Umma youth who participated in the 1964 Zanzibari Revolution did so as a form of protest against a ZNP-ZPPP government they were convinced would not tolerate political opposition or do anything to address the economic grievances of the poor. After the Zanzibari Revolution Umma intellectuals worked closely with those from the ASP to disseminate socialist ideas widely and to implement a socialist nation-building strategy.

Scholarly attention to the relationship between race, class and generational identities in nationalist or revolutionary movements is certainly warranted in consideration of the wealth of 'images' through which locals understand history. The world's leading revolutionary tradition of the twentieth century contains considerable ambiguity over the issue of exactly what exactly constitutes a vanguard. Lenin did not always share Marx's convictions regarding the revolutionary potential of workers. In *What is To Be Done?* he laboriously distinguishes between true socialist revolutionary consciousness and what he regards as trade unionism's reformist, 'spontaneous' character.[13]

The potential of 'spontaneous' trade unionism to initiate revolutionary struggle helps to explain Lenin's conception of a vanguard party drawing strength not only from workers, but also from the intelligentsia, many of whom like Marx and Engels were 'the educated representatives of the propertied classes'. His concept of a vanguard party also permitted him to consider young people, particularly students, as potential recruits. His writings in fact betray pragmatic interest for over two decades in mobilizing youth for revolution, and in canalizing into his revolutionary cause the 'spontaneous' student protest that, in the last decades of Tsarist rule, had become a repetitive feature of the political landscape.[14] In an essay 'The Tasks of Revolutionary Youth' published in 1903, Lenin argued that students were 'the most responsive section of the intelligentsia'.[15] A Bolshevik general congress declared that the party 'welcomes the growing revolutionary initiative among the student youth and calls upon all organisations of the Party to give them every possible assistance in their efforts to organise'.[16] In 1905 Lenin wrote in a letter:

> We need young forces. I am for shooting on the spot anyone who presumes to say that there are no people to be had. The people in Russia are legion; all we have to do is to recruit young people more widely and boldly, more boldly and widely, and again more widely and again more boldly, *without fearing them*. This is a time of war. The youth – the students, and still more so the young workers – will decide the issue of the whole struggle.[17]

The following year, in 'The Crisis of Menshevism' he quoted Engels, who wrote:

> Is it not natural that youth should predominate in our Party, the revolutionary party? We are the party of the future, and the future belongs to the youth. We are a party of innovators, and it is always the youth that most eagerly follows the innovators. We are a party that is waging a self-sacrificing struggle against the old rottenness, and youth is always the first to undertake a self-sacrificing struggle.[18]

Lenin was thus well aware of the prominent role played by students in the turbulent last years of Tsarist Russia, and it was therefore expedient for the Social Democrats to establish specific institutions for their mass recruitment. Socialist youth mobilization, then, evolved within Leninist revolutionary tradition rather than Marxist theory. Lenin's views on youth were not derived from any theoretical text but appear to have emerged instead out of tactical necessity and his own reading of the 'concrete' political circumstances of the time.[19]

After seizing power, the Bolshevik interest in youth mobilization became codified in the establishment of the Young Communist League, or *Komsomol*, in 1918. In his address to the Third Congress of the Komsomol in 1920, Lenin traveled through several themes, calling for electricity supply, literacy, and economic recovery. He concluded with the following prediction of the future:

> The generation of people who are now at the age of fifty cannot expect to see a communist society. This generation will be gone before then. But the generation of those who are now fifteen will see a communist society, and will itself build this society. This generation should know that the entire purpose of their lives is to build a communist society. ... We must organise

all labour, no matter how toilsome or messy it may be, in such a way that every worker and peasant will be able to say: I am part of the great army of free labour, and shall be able to build up my life without the landowners and capitalists, able to help establish a communist system. The Young Communist League should teach all young people to engage in conscious and disciplined labour form an early age. In this way we can be confident that the problems now confronting us will be solved.[20]

What did come true was that within a few decades youth leagues based upon the *Komsomol* model gained a transnational currency, as nationalist parties, revolutionary movements, and ruling parties adopted socialist techniques of youth mobilization. The emergence of the Umma Party in Zanzibar in the early 1960s, therefore, may be placed within an international socialist revolutionary tradition that actively sought to mobilize youth for the task of establishing a workers' and peasants' paradise. Complicating the picture somewhat in Zanzibar was the dominance of ethnic nationalism which meant that young people were not only supposed to serve workers and peasants but also the African poor, despite their own heterogeneous racial identities or class origins.

Schools and scholarships

The origins of youth as a political identity within the ZNP may be traced to the rapid expansion of educational opportunities in Zanzibar in the post-World War II era. As late as 1939 60 per cent of all adult males were literate in Swahili written in Arabic script, while only 2 per cent were literate in the Roman script.[21] Enrollment in Qur'anic schools in 1939 was three times that of colonial schools.[22] Then in the 1940s the British introduced Qur'anic education into their school curriculum, and in so doing gained for the first time the interest and support of Zanzibari parents. Numbers of students multiplied, especially through the capital. By 1959 35 per cent of the boys and 22 per cent of girls in the islands were studying in colonial primary schools, learning the Roman alphabet and English as a second language.[23] Furthermore, between 1955 and 1961 secondary school enrollment in the colony rose from 442 to 984 for boys and from 185 to 526 for girls.[24]

Among Zanzibaris, Arabs were educationally privileged. While Arabs comprised 16.8 per cent of the total population, by the late 1950s they received 32.1 per cent of places available in government secondary schools.[25] Of these places, most were allocated to male Arabs living in Zanzibar Town, since rural and female education lagged behind.[26] It was normally prohibitively expensive for rural parents, most of them African, to send their children to board at a secondary school in town. Arab townsmen were only outnumbered in the schools by more urbanized Asians. Asians, comprising only 5.8 per cent of the total population, were 94 per cent urbanized, and received 41.4 per cent of the places in government secondary schools.[27]

Graduates of Zanzibari secondary schools were able in the 1950s to go on as never before to higher education overseas. As late as 1949 there were only 21 Zanzibari students overseas; by 1963 approximately 300 were living and studying in Britain.[28] These numbers indicate the extent to which the British became interested in the post-war era in preparing Zanzibaris, Arabs in particular, for careers in their islands' civil service. After World War II government positions in Zanzibar underwent rapid Arabization.[29]

Meanwhile, beginning in 1958 the ZNP also organized hundreds of overseas scholarships, for the purposes of youth mobilization and recruitment. The ZNP in fact could not find enough qualified students to accept all the scholarships offered by countries such as Egypt, China, and East Germany, which were intent on gaining influence among a generation of Zanzibari leaders reaching maturity during the height of the Cold War. Such politically-inspired patronage gave Zanzibari youth able to meet minimum educational requirements far more concentrated access to universities than any other community in East Africa. Such access meant that the days of illiteracy in the Roman script were rapidly coming to an end. And rather than only a small number of youth from elite Zanzibari families attending colleges, hundreds of students were each year exposed to a thoroughly secular foreign education.

It is no exaggeration to suggest that in the 1950s travel represented a new form of pilgrimage, this time to learn the secular skills necessary for inclusion in an emerging literate generation back in Zanzibar. As the first cohort in large numbers with access to bilingual fluency and Western education, some students began to attach a deep significance to their youth. In an era of widely discussed nationalist heroes and colonial departures, young people imagined themselves uniquely endowed by their education to grasp the meaning of contemporary events and to understand their times. This emerging historical sense may be seen in an editorial exchange in the ZNP-affiliated newspaper *Al-Falaq* in April 1956. An elderly reader submitted an 'Open Letter to Students' suggesting that young people, with all their new 'book learning', were forgetting respect and deference towards their elders. He warned urban youth that they (you) were 'forgetting that it was "old fools" who made you what you imagine you are.... Your parents are complaining that you are loose in manners, impolite in speech ... unaffected by public opinion and having no respect for your elders.'[30]

Such a letter suggests the concern among some elders about the unprecedented cultural influence that school life exerted over young people, as well as the degree to which youth in the 1950s had become associated in Zanzibar Town with autonomous social conduct, even bad manners. Taking these allegations seriously, the editors of *Al-Falaq* published a front-page editorial, entitled 'Zanzibar in Transition'. Their response illustrates that what they might have considered merely a mundane complaint about disrespectful youth was instead indicative of larger developments that were beginning to divide the generations. The editors wrote that rapid change like the spread of Western education could

223

'be dangerous because it breeds fear, suspicion and conflict' between the generations. However,

> It is no good for the die-hards to shut their eyes to the inevitable, come it will .... The life of our girls as well as boys is rapidly undergoing a change. They do things which were simply 'not done' twenty years ago. And rather than fight against the tide the old should adopt an intelligent approach and do their best to guide them....
>
> This is not peculiar; every country in the world has passed or will pass this stage. We therefore advise our old friends to observe these changes not with abhorrence or indifference but with an understanding eye....

The editors thus counseled the elders to show tolerance towards the new generation, and to recognize that these changes were *historically inevitable* and had political implications. They warned the elders that they faced political obsolescence if they continued to live in the past, or, as they put it, with 'yesterday's timid and undeveloped consciousness.' In an era of colonial withdrawals and unprecedented opportunities for a nationalist elite to emerge, they rebuked the author of the 'Open Letter' in the following terms:

> unless you wish to be trampled into insignificance, [we] should again advise you to march with the time.
>
> We full realize that only a few understand the importance of the situation but then the mass has always been guided by the few. And we take it as their responsibility to educate the less fortunate ones....
>
> There is thirst for progress and no amount of 'bado kidogo' [not quite yet] will quench it.[31]

In other words, in the minds of the editors of *Al Falaq*, the elders lacked education and the knowledge of contemporary events necessary for political insight and leadership. The editors implied that they considered themselves as among 'the few' who possessed an enlightened perspective on Zanzibar's historic stages, knowledge of which gave them a 'thirst for progress' and a responsibility to educate their 'less fortunate' elders.

Constructing youth, 1957–63

Schools and scholarships were not alone in encouraging generational consciousness. Beginning in 1957 party elites in Zanzibar exploited generational identities for purposes of political mobilization. This happened first within the Zanzibar Nationalist Party, which came to enjoy almost universal support among Arabs and Asians in Zanzibar Town.[32] And considering the overwhelming advantages of these communities in the realm of education, it is no accident that the vast majority of Zanzibari high school graduates and those overseas also came to affiliate themselves with the ZNP. One of the earliest to be recruited by the ZNP was Babu, who in 1957 was an Arab-African university student in London in his early thirties and active in the British Labour Party. Babu was a leading figure in London among a growing circle of Zanzibaris pursuing higher education and low-wage employment. He had frequent discussions and intense debates with other Zanzibaris, including Ali Sultan Issa and Khamis Abdullah Ameir, about the need to struggle against colonialism, and the merits of various political philosophies. All three in these years came to identify themselves as socialists.[33]

On his return to Zanzibar in 1957 Babu found a home in the ZNP as then the only expressly multi-racial, anti-colonial party in Zanzibar. He was appointed the party's Secretary General., and almost immediately set about recruiting young people into the party, hoping thereby to eventually provoke a mass movement of the islands' youth towards socialism. He was among the founders of the Youth's Own Union (YOU). On 27 July 1957, Babu urged all ZNP members to 'get their sons and daughters to register as members of the Youth Movement and to spread the news to other youths,' regardless of race or religion, between the ages of 15 and 25. The first official YOU meeting took place two days later.[34]

Within a year the YOU was firmly established in Zanzibar Town. It started a newspaper in 1958, *Sauti ya Vijana* (Voice of Youth), that deliberately targeted youth, and which continued publishing until the Revolution, one of at least ten newspapers affiliated with the ZNP during the nationalist period.[35] The YOU opened a bookshop in the ZNP party headquarters in Darajani, displaying party newspapers and various political tracts, many of which were donated by the Chinese. It also established three different 'societies', for education, drama, and debate.[36] Such efforts were apparently effective in recruiting young people and convincing many of their special role in the political contests of the period. An anonymous youth filing a report to YOU leaders about a series of YOU debates held during Ramadhan in 1960 claimed that these events were

> more important than dances and other things because they train us to be people who can stand anywhere and speak for our country. We are supposed to be the leaders and defenders of our country in the future, so let us learn how to play that role from now....
>
> The elders fight for our political rights and we should work side by side with them. But how many things should the elders do for us? It is our responsibility, we youths, to do things which are beneficial to us, our elders, our brothers and sisters and our country. We should always remember the word 'ORGANIZE'.[37]

When young people attended a YOU lecture series, or came together at night to debate such motions as 'Democracy is the best form of government' or 'Self-government in poverty is preferable to servitude in plenty', they were participating in YOU forums clearly designed to encourage awareness of the key issues of their times. They were learning how to 'stand anywhere and speak for our country'. Mass demonstrations served the same purpose of providing lessons on contemporary history, by putting young people on the streets to perform ritualized demands for more secondary schools or an end to racial discrimination, for example.[38] YOU demonstrations went further than debates, however, by physically inserting young people, specifically organized as a vanguard generation, into the struggle against colonialism not only in Zanzibar but elsewhere in Africa. In 1958 the YOU held protests against Belgian colonial policies in the Congo, and in support of the Algerian liberation struggle against the French.[39]

YOU members could also frequently be seen parading in red and white uniforms, drilling in a small 'Guard of Honor', or performing in their own traveling brass band. Some indication of the impact that such spectacles had in Zanzibar can be seen from the opposition they aroused. The ASP was for good reasons infuriated by the presence of the YOU brass band at various official functions presided over by the Sultan, who was supposed to have remained non-partisan. In 1959 the colonial state passed the Public Order Bill, which banned all YOU members from wearing their uniforms at public meetings, claiming such actions were needlessly provocative in an atmosphere of escalating racial and partisan tension. One British police officer later recollected that YOU members were 'strutting around' in red berets, 'so I had to sit on them pretty smartly'.[40]

The YOU, finally, also played an indispensable role in various ZNP welfare projects intended to increase the party's stature and patronage powers among Zanzibari voters. It organized drives for blood donors and operated its own ambulance unit, conveying the sick or injured in the rural areas to the hospital in the capital. Probably its most ambitious project was a massive literacy campaign, that reportedly reached several thousand pupils in 120 branch schools throughout the islands; these schools were open to all but were mainly patronized by ZNP members.[41] Plans in 1958 to establish with Egyptian funding a ZNP secondary school in Zanzibar Town were, however, quashed by the colonial government, which feared this would only lead to further expansion of YOU 'communist' influence among the younger generation.[42] The British closely monitored the YOU, considering it 'an attempt, and a successful one, to attract to its ranks the youths of Zanzibar'.[43] It was 'clearly following the pattern of militant youth movements that caused such trouble in other parts of the world'.[44]

Michael Lofchie in 1965 offered another perspective on YOU activities:

> The most impressive structural feature of the ZNP was its administration of numerous philanthropic and benevolent operations.... Its programs of charity and welfare work, medical care and adult education were so extensive as to place the ZNP in competition with the government itself as a dispenser of social services. These activities furnished the party with a superb medium for the recruitment of new members.[45]

YOU activism also earned praise in an editorial in the ZNP-affiliated newspaper *Mwongozi*, whose propagandists sought in 1958 to explain these developments in terms of general historical patterns. In an editorial entitled, 'The Youth of Zanzibar', the editors effused:

> It is remarkable that whenever a country is in a transition to political maturity its youths tend to get more and more militant. Political parties with

more progressive platforms invariably attract larger numbers of the younger element, who in turn adorn the older parties with their youthful spirit.

It is an established fact that the older people … are notoriously sceptical about independence … at least they [the youth] are more realistic than the older generation which faces the future with its head permanently turned to the past.[46]

British intelligence reports in 1958 put YOU membership at around 800; two-thirds of these were regarded as Arab youth, the remainder mostly African.[47] YOU membership expanded further in the early 1960s. Ali Sultan Issa estimated that one-third of the YOU membership was female.[48] The activities of the YOU foregrounded youth in the political struggles of the time; a seemingly endless succession of fundraisers, rallies, debates, demonstrations, performances and service projects encouraged many young people to imagine themselves a vanguard generation in the history of their islands. Such shared events encouraged a sense that theirs was a generation 'moving [together] onward through calendrical time'.[49]

Although literature from the socialist world was freely distributed at the YOU bookshop, Babu does not appear to have used YOU gatherings to openly spread socialist belief. Nevertheless, according to his personal statements, it was his intention that YOU exercises would ultimately encourage young people to grasp that the ZNP's claimed adherence to non-racialism should be defined not only by Islamic principle but also by socialist commitment. Babu wanted young people to turn towards socialism as a means of transcending the intense racial conflicts of their islands, and as a model for nation-building. He believed that they could more easily than other elements of society perceive the need to organize social conflict so that it targeted the real class enemies of the workers and peasants – colonialists, feudalists, and capitalists – rather than specific racial communities.[50] Babu thus seems to have shared Lenin's 1903 enthusiasm for students as 'the most responsive section of the intelligentsia'.[51] The British correctly placed his work among Zanzibari youth within the Leninist revolutionary tradition. In his own writings Babu held fast to the concept of a vanguard generation through to the early 1990s.[52]

To advance the ZNP's patronage powers further and to promote the education of party youth, ZNP leader Ali Muhsin obtained hundreds of scholarships from Egypt. Beginning in 1958, Colonel Nasser provided the ZNP with a hostel in Cairo to house the approximately 800 ZNP primary, secondary and college students who studied there prior to the Zanzibari Revolution.[53] Such patronage was part of Nasser's general interest in making Cairo the international capital of African anti-colonial movements, by providing their representatives with free office space, salaries, unlimited air travel, and scholarships. By 1964 there were in all about 2,000 African students in Cairo.[54]

It was probably among students overseas that socialist ideas first emerged among ZNP youth, as a set of private beliefs held by individuals within a party that was not officially socialist. In Cairo signs emerged as early as 1960 of the ideological divide within the ZNP that would lead to the formation of the Umma Party. A serious split developed among students over the question of whether or not Arab economic privileges back in Zanzibar should be preserved. Inspired by the 1952 Egyptian Revolution, a minority argued for the overthrow of the Sultan and land redistribution to poor African peasants. In this context, the 28-year old Ali Sultan Issa, a close friend of Babu and a fellow socialist since their years in London, arrived as the ZNP's Chief Representative in Cairo, appointed to end the 'open rebellion among some students'.[55] Ali Sultan took advantage of the presence of socialist embassies in Cairo to arrange still more scholarships for ZNP youth. He was able to send the 'rebellious' 'republican' students on to Eastern European and Chinese universities as part of a strategy to encourage their growing interest in socialism.[56]

Babu had initiated efforts to obtain such scholarships back in 1959 during extended visits to Beijing, Prague, Moscow and East Germany.[57] By 1962 he and Ali Sultan had managed to place an estimated 116 students in socialist universities, far fewer than the actual number of scholarships offered. Most of these were in Eastern Europe; but 18 were in China.[58] Africa was perceived by the Chinese to be a weak link in the imperialist chain, and they hosted several official ZNP delegations on month-long tours of China. They also provided Babu and the ZNP, in addition to the scholarships, with considerable financial support, communist literature, and duplicating equipment.[59] Through repeated extended visits to China in these years both Babu and Ali Sultan came to be deeply influenced by Maoist thought and revolutionary praxis.[60] In Zanzibar Babu started his own newspaper, *ZANEWS*, which relied upon both Chinese funding and news sources. In Cairo, meanwhile, Ali Sultan also founded a ZNP newspaper, *Dawn in Zanzibar*. He also established ZNP offices in both London and Havana, sending to Cuba three young men carefully selected for their socialist views.[61]

At this juncture the editors of *ZANEWS* claimed that the international prestige of the ZNP was

> rising daily, thanks to the devoted services of our young representatives in all our foreign offices. These young lads have left their countries and all those who are dear to them in order to serve their people in presenting to the rest of the world the true picture of Zanzibar.[62]

While visiting Cuba in 1962, Ali Sultan arranged for twenty scholarships for ZNP youth to study 'trade unionism' in Cuba, which really meant military training, alongside recruits from Algeria, South Africa and the Congo. Ali Sultan and Raul Castro agreed upon this number after discussing Zanzibar's limited security arrangements; they were convinced that twenty recruits were sufficient to overthrow the government in Zanzibar.[63] Among the 18 who actually arrived in Cuba, two remember being impressed by the lack of racial discrimination they were able to observe in Cuban society, as well as by some of the early effects of the Cuban revolution: land redistribution, the nationalization of urban housing, free education and medical attention.[64] The parallels between Cuba and

Zanzibar were not lost on the trainees. Such impressions were of course the anticipated result; Ali Sultan remarked to the author that

> The old were a spent force, they were cold blooded. Where could we go except the youth?[65]
>
> I wanted them to go everywhere; wherever it was open for us, we would send them. Listen, there's a dictum of Mao: 'let a hundred flowers blossom, and school of thoughts contend'. Whatever education you have, whether western oriented or eastern-oriented, at the end of the day you come back here [to Zanzibar].[66]

Whether in Cuba, Egypt, China or Eastern Europe, the Zanzibari students overseas nurtured a sense of their own importance in the political struggles back home. In 1962 the YOU in Cairo published a statement declaring: 'The Zanzibar youths under the leadership of the Youths Own Union shall always be in the forefront in the struggle to oust British colonialism and neo-colonialism in Zanzibar.'[67] The conference resolutions of the All Zanzibar Students Association meeting in Prague in September 1963, expressed the same sense of self-importance:

> We, as true sons of our people, feel that we have a great role to play in the present developments that are unfolding in our country. We have always been at the forefront of our people's struggles against colonialism and imperialism. We will continue with this good tradition of ours until all the forces of oppression, reaction and capital are wiped out completely from the face of our motherland.[68]

Thus by the early 1960s Babu and Ali Sultan, who were still in their thirties, and who had only preceded the flood of student travelers by a few years when they themselves arrived in London in the early 1950s, were now patrons and 'elders' over their own growing network of scholarship routes for party youth. This was especially disturbing to the British and the ZNP conservatives, since, regardless of where the students enrolled and what sort of politics they absorbed overseas, return flights always deposited them back in Zanzibar Town, where they commonly came to associate with Babu's faction within the ZNP, depending often on where they had studied. Babu's success marked him in the eyes of the British Resident in Zanzibar as having a dominant 'hold over the frustrated, unemployed youth of the ZNP'.[69] He observed 'the building up within the country of a measurable body of young people, who, even if they do not become card-carrying Communists, at least become so imbued with the doctrines of Communist subversion that they must constitute a threat to future security'.[70]

In the early 1960s 'youth' thus emerged as a political identity commonly employed by ZNP nationalists, colonial officials, and young people in reference to the unprecedented mobilization of the young in a new era of mass politics. 'Youth' possessed most currency in the physical and intellectual context of Zanzibar Town, where young people in the ZNP had most access to all of the shared events that together combined to encourage generational identity in the nationalist period: parades and demonstrations, debates and party volunteer work, schools and scholarships. In

Zanzibar Town over twenty newspapers reported on events from the outside world that described the global retreat of colonialism. In *Admiring Silence* Abdulrazak Gurnah remembers that as a young student in the early 1960s

> Politics was what everyone did and talked about: in the streets, at the café, at school, at home.... We kept track of colonial departures like keeping score in a game: Ghana, Nigeria, Somalia, the Congo, Senegal, Mali.... Heroic leaders indiscriminately filled the imagination: Kwame Nkrumah, Ahmed Sekou Touré, Patrice Lumumba, Jomo Kenyatta. There were new maps to be studied, new names, new countries that seemed to surface with incredible solidity out of the featureless mass that had previously been Africa.[71]

As a peculiar facet of the 1950s and 1960s, these events provoked discussion among young people about the content and meaning of independence, and the role they were to play in the years ahead. Students nurtured fantasies over their own roles in contemporary history. Youth emerged as an imagined generation comparable to and in rhetorical relationship with elders, workers, women, and racial terms employed in the partisan discourse of the time. Youth was neither a class nor an ethnic community, but a rhetorical construct with unusual meaning for young people in Zanzibar Town.

The ZNP was not officially a socialist party, although the socialist tradition informed the party's critique of colonialism, its techniques of mobilization, and, among some party members, its vision of the future. Socialist doctrines had penetrated currents of party discourse, but only a minority of members identified themselves as socialists. The ZNP, despite its heterogeneous nature, had managed to preserve party unity. The 'open rebellion' among students in Cairo was something of an anomaly, since ZNP intellectuals, whatever their private inclinations, considered the British and the ASP their primary enemies. The following will discuss how ZNP unity collapsed with the secession from the party of leftist students, youth and workers, who then formed a new party that publicly espoused socialism and conceived of itself as a movement of vanguard youth.

The emergence of generational dissent

After experiencing severe defeat in the 1957 elections, the ZNP was able to emerge from almost complete political insignificance to win remarkable electoral victories in 1961. These came as the result of an alliance with the ZPPP and the intense organizational efforts of the ZNP and its youth wing. The British in fact considered Babu, as the ZNP's Secretary General, as the architect of these victories.[72] British Chief Secretary P.A.P. Robertson remarked that, although there were many youth who

> went to Cuba and places like that and then came back and threw themselves about, but none of them had quite the same sort of effective sustained capacity for planning and action and doing things and Babu you see traveled widely....[73]

With their electoral triumphs the ZNP-ZPPP alliance reconsidered the direction the coalition was taking, and its fundamental doctrines. With the potential that the alliance might obtain power suddenly real, came worry among both ZNP-ZPPP conservatives and the British that Babu's emerging faction would in the future be in a position to exert actual political influence. The 1961 elections thus had the effect of bringing more into the open the contradictions within a party dependent on the financial support of the Chinese and wealthy Arab plantation owners and responsible for introducing socialist vocabulary into local discourse while at the same time promoting Islamic universalism and its own version of 'exclusionary ethnic nationalism'. Clearly by 1961 two factions were coalescing within the ZNP around the personalities and ideas of Babu and Ali Muhsin, one of the 'progressive' youth, the other of the conservative 'old guard'.[74] The former was most established in the party's foreign missions, among students, the YOU, and trade unions affiliated with the ZNP and organized under an umbrella organization, the Federation of Progressive Trade Unions (FPTU). The latter was supported throughout the party's extensive network of local branch leaders and by the rural rank and file.

The British Resident, Sir George Mooring, noted for the first time in July 1961 a growing friction between Babu and party leader Ali Muhsin. Not surprisingly, the immediate issue between Babu and Muhsin was the distribution of scholarships to communist countries.[75] Another apparent factor was the colonial state's increasing pressure on Muhsin, who was informed, according to oral sources, that the ZNP would not inherit power from the British if Babu remained in the party leadership.[76] Mooring considered Babu a 'menace to the peaceful development of Zanzibar',[77] while Robertson regarded Babu not just as 'a thorn in the flesh' but as 'the most sinister man in Zanzibar ... an evil genius.'[78] Muhsin appears to have been compromised in 1961–3 between desires to maintain ZNP unity and keeping Babu on his side, while demonstrating to the British and his conservative base that the ZNP was not a socialist party intent on overthrowing the Sultan or becoming a communist satellite state in East Africa.

Legal actions taken against Babu by the colonial government, however, postponed a major confrontation between Babu and Muhsin. These were the result of Mooring's profound distrust of Babu, and of plans formulated by him even before the elections to remove Babu from politics.[79] At the beginning of 1962 the British charged Babu with sedition over the inflammatory contents of articles published in *ZANEWS*. Babu was convicted and fined; then in early May the colonial government brought additional charges of arson against him, and against leading members of the YOU. Although the police found no evidence of arson,[80] Babu nevertheless stood trial the next month for sedition. News of these events provoked a series of published statements from ZNP student associations overseas. That of the YOU office in Cairo is representative:

> The Youths Own Union demands the immediate and unconditional release of the detainees ... and the eradication of British colonialism in

231

Zanzibar, the presence of which is a curse and insult to the youths and people of Zanzibar in particular and the world in general.[81]

The trial opening attracted 300 young protesters, shouting slogans, refusing to disperse until the police mounted a baton charge.[82] Babu was nevertheless sentenced to 15 months imprisonment for sedition, a crime for which he previously had only been asked to pay a fine.[83]

Babu's imprisonment infuriated Ali Sultan, who not only believed the sentence to be unjust, but that Muhsin and the conservative 'old guard' had at the very least acquiesced, if not conspired, in the imprisonment of their Secretary General. Ali Sultan returned immediately from Cuba and publicly denounced the ZNP leadership both in Cairo and in Zanzibar Town, describing their motivations and citing circumstantial evidence to prove his case.[84] Ali Sultan's remarks earned him expulsion from the ZNP's Executive Committee in June 1962.

In response, he convened a press conference where he read a statement with the Castroesque title, 'Condemn me now but history will absolve me'. His statement opened with an historical commentary characteristic of his generation's unique secular analysis of the 'objective realities' shaping their contemporary times, in this case informed by socialist theory.

All students of history both contemporary and medieval will not fail to recall that what is taking place now in our country has taken place elsewhere on earth.

What is taking place now in Zanzibar has not surprised me at all but confirms the belief I have always held since I have started to think and use my intelligence, to differentiate right and wrong, just and unjust....

[The ZNP] is a liberation movement. It is a mass movement comprising different sections and strata of the people. This is an objective reality and anyone who tries to deny this is just fooling himself.

Concretely, we have within the ZNP the following main features, a section which cherishes capitalism and abhors socialism, the capitalist class and the landlords who prosper and grow fat by exploiting the working people. They live like parasites while others toil and sweat. And a section of proletariats, peasants, small farmers, small shopkeepers, individuals who through their own labour manage to make the two ends meet. We have also the professional, the intelligentsia, the students, the youths and the women....

After citing the social and class divisions within the ZNP, he deplored the recent takeover of what was once a genuine liberation movement by the 'reactionary' and 'opportunist' allies of Ali Muhsin. He charged that, because of Muhsin's continuing belief that 'Africans in Zanzibar would come to appreciate how many benefits the Arabs had brought them and would in the end prefer enlightened Arab guidance', he was a 'racialist and [yet] posing as a leader of a non-racial organization – ZNP'. Ali Sultan closed his statement with the following predictions:

I say this openly that it will be either the progressives who will lead the ZNP and so achieve real independence or I shall not support the reactionaries who I know are ready to sell the interests of our people and for that I shall oppose them to the end.

I am confident that we shall win in the end, and by we I mean the progressives not only in Zanzibar but throughout the world. VENCE-REMOS, VENCEREMOS, VENCEREMOS.[85]

Towards the end of 1962 Ali Sultan made attempts to start an independent youth movement, the 'Zanzibar and Pemba Youths' and Students' United Front'. This was an effort to unite ZNP youth with like-minded ASP intellectuals like Kassim Hanga and Hassan Nasser Moyo, each of whom had made extended sojourns in the Soviet Union and were in the early 1960s prominent trade union leaders in Zanzibar Town. Ali Sultan sought to form an alliance of Africans and Arabs with a common socialist identity in preparation for the eventual release from prison of Babu, who, he believed, would provide crucial leadership.[86] Although these efforts yielded no immediate fruit, they anticipated the future socialist coalition that would shape Zanzibari society after the Revolution.

It was nonetheless evident that Babu's imprisonment and Ali Sultan's expulsion alienated many young people, students and trade unionists in the ZNP. A minority of ZNP youth were no longer satisfied with remaining subordinate to party elders whom they now distrusted, and whom they accused of 'selling out' to the British. In August 1962, a speech delivered at a YOU meeting deplored Babu's imprisonment and called the ZNP ministers 'stooges', who drove nice motor cars, while forgetting the working people of the islands.[87] The FPTU refused to expel Ali Sultan from its leadership, and the ZNP office in Havana came out in open hostility to Muhsin.[88] And yet the absence of Babu and Ali Sultan also allowed Muhsin to consolidate his support within the party among hundreds of local branch leaders for whom socialism remained a set of wholly foreign doctrines. Mooring wrote happily that Muhsin was becoming less tolerant of communists in the ZNP, saying this was the result of 'British coaching'.[89] However, the ZNP leadership were reportedly still 'not strong enough to expel' the young socialists.[90]

Nor was Muhsin willing to abandon all hope of preserving ZNP unity. In August 1962, he gave a speech at the YOU's fifth anniversary celebrations. During seven hours of songs, fireworks, dances, plays and speeches, Muhsin reiterated that 'the future of Zanzibar depended on the struggle of the Zanzibar youth. Mr Muhsin exhorted the young boys and girls who assembled there to be firmly united, and they should not be confused and be deviated from their aim of fighting for freedom.'[91] As the months went by, Muhsin agonized over Babu's state of mind while in prison. He sent messages to Babu, claiming that the party was preparing itself for a 48-hour fast to obtain his release.[92] Other messages from Muhsin requesting Babu's co-operation after his release did not obtain any positive response. During a private meeting with Mooring in January 1963, Muhsin tried to get the British Resident to grant YOU members permission to wear uniforms once again and perform as a traveling band. After Mooring's refusal, Muhsin 'became personally abusive and finally left the meeting in tears of frustration and anger ... worried about his failure to secure the support of radical youth'.[93]

Upon his release from prison in early 1963, Babu received a hero's welcome organized by the YOU. He decided that, at a ZNP conference in June 1963, convened in order to approve parliamentary candidates for the final elections before independence, he would make demands that, if not met, would result in his resignation from the party. At the conference Babu proposed a list of three candidates he wanted the party to nominate to safe seats in ZNP strongholds. Babu was working in conjunction with a parallel move made by Hanga and Moyo in the ASP's own conference convened in preparation for the 1963 elections. In both parties these candidates were known 'progressives' who, once elected, would form a multi-racial socialist bloc within parliament that would hold the balance of power between the ZNP and ASP after independence.[94] At the conference, however, Babu identified his nominees not as progressives but as Shirazi candidates, whom he said he wanted to stand for election in largely Arab and Asian constituencies in the capital. In doing so, Babu argued that the ZNP would prove its authentic commitment to multi-racialism.[95]

The *putsch* failed in both parties, however. An assembly of over 300 ZNP branch leaders rejected Babu's proposal, arguing that local party leaders and not Babu had the authority to nominate candidates.[96] Babu resigned, claiming the ZNP had become too racist, and that Muhsin had been responsible for his long imprisonment. Muhsin denied this charge. A member of the 'progressive youth' faction named Kadiria Mnyeji then stood up to say that the party should support Babu's proposals because they nominated young people who could win the election. He closed by saying, 'the elders have already done their work. Now is the time of the youth.' This infuriated the branch leaders. In the midst of such acrimony Babu and some of his young supporters walked out of the meeting.[97] None of the 300 branch leaders followed him, indicating the strength of support in the rural areas for Muhsin and the conservative 'old guard'.[98]

The circumstances of Babu's resignation also demonstrate the extent to which Zanzibari politics by 1963 were not simply a contest between the interests of competing racial communities. Indeed, the very confusion and dissimulation over the identity of Babu's list of candidates suggests the widespread conflation of racial, political and generational identities in pre-revolutionary Zanzibar. They were, at various times and according to different accounts, either Shirazi, 'youth' or 'progressives'. Babu felt it tactically necessary to disguise his 'young progressives' as Shirazi candidates. When this failed, Babu was free to make the public allegation of racism (which he did in the newspapers immediately afterwards), a charge that commanded far more popular resonance than if he had accused the ZNP of conservative ideology. It was simply wiser politically to test the ZNP's commitment to non-racialism than to socialism. ZNP leaders meanwhile fumed over Babu's allegations of racism, and over Kadiria Mnyeji's infuriating reference to an imagined, unified generation of youth ready to lead the ZNP to power.

Umma Youth

The day of his resignation from the ZNP Babu and about thirty supporters met in Darajani, Zanzibar Town. Although they were convinced that the ZNP would win the elections and inherit power from the British, they decided to form a new party anyway.[99] Babu claimed in *ZANEWS* that his resignation was on behalf 'of the people and youth of Zanzibar'.[100] He and his associates founded the Umma party, which soon developed into a well-organized party far more influential than its relative size might immediately suggest.[101] In its six-months existence Umma signed up approximately 3,000 members;[102] almost all these were young people in the capital, many former members of the YOU. Babu wrote in the early 1990s:

> The youth of all parties who were beginning to be demoralised and disenchanted with the political atmosphere were immediately charged with new enthusiasm. The first mass rally of the new party on the second day of its formation attracted several thousand young people, especially young workers from all political parties. The first week of the party's existence saw the registration of masses of youth as card-carrying members. The three major parties were shaken by the event because they were rapidly losing their youth support to the new party.[103]

Despite such reports of the emergence of a politically unified generation in Zanzibar Town, Umma was formed too late to have any discernible impact on the 1963 elections, won again by the ZNP-ZPPP alliance which combined to win 18 of 31 contested parliamentary seats. The ASP, however, in winning 13 seats, rolled up much larger majorities, attracting in total over 54 per cent of the popular vote.[104] While these results ensured that the ZNP-ZPPP alliance would inherit power from the British upon their final departure in December 1963, they also encouraged the view within Umma and the ASP that the electoral process had failed and that the ZNP-ZPPP government was illegitimate.

In the last months of 1963 Umma sought to organize its own base of popular support. Despite consistent efforts it found virtually no support among the old, in the rural areas of Zanzibar, or anywhere in Pemba. Umma broadsheets were distributed in the countryside, with little effect. According to Umma's former Secretary General, the ZNP and ASP outside of Zanzibar Town were too 'strong', and 'the youth didn't know'. Furthermore, there was not enough time before independence to 'awaken the people'.[105] As the progeny of a new era of mobility and secular influences, Umma was thoroughly associated with the capital. The party evoked hostility among Zanzibaris for whom Umma members were atheists, communists, and infidels.[106]

Umma partisans almost immediately set about replicating the structure of the ZNP by, for example, rapidly establishing, a youth wing. The party also sought to define itself through a series of printed manifestos as the friend of the poor African majority. 'A People's Programme' defined colonialism as 'an obnoxious system which has so far degraded the people of Zanzibar bodily and mentally to a sub-human condition'. Umma sought to replace colonialism with socialism, the only system, the tract argued, that could ensure the 'dignity' of the individual. In this task, the new party was 'a conscious vanguard of the oppressed people of Zanzibar. It represents the broad interests of the African people who today are bearing the brunt of economic oppression'. As participants in a vanguard movement, it was necessary for each member of Umma 'to be strictly disciplined' and 'to endeavor to raise the level of his consciousness and to understand the fundamentals of socialism and the theory of African revolution'.[107]

In 'A Programme of People's Youth', Umma propagandists described the youth wing as 'a serious and conscious youth movement', and 'a forefront in the battle of the oppressed and exploited masses of the African youth of Zanzibar....' Its object was 'to win the young generation for the democratic and socialist regeneration ... [when] the younger generation's mental and physical development will enjoy boundless opportunity.' Open to all people aged 14 to 30, it was the duty of members to read the party newspapers, take part in local branches, and serve 'the people and youth' by working among them and getting to know their problems.[108] Umma youth were to be characterized by their discipline and selflessness. Umma leaders warned that all forms of 'spinelessness [have] no place among our ranks and personal suffering can never deter us from the pursuit of our ultimate objective, namely socialism. The Umma Party cannot tolerate the existence of opportunists, self-seekers among its ranks, and it must be vigilant against the infiltration of such destructive elements.'[109] Instead, Umma youth were to live according to codes of secular discipline imagined worthy of cities like Havana or Beijing.

Such tracts suggest that by late 1963 Umma intellectuals had decided that the struggle against colonialism was no longer the primary contradiction. They indicate the degree to which Umma youth had come to associate class oppression with racial inequalities in Zanzibar. The socialist struggle against feudalists and capitalists, they declared, was an 'African revolution'. Such claims came from a party whose leading intellectuals (Babu, Ali Sultan, Khamis Abdallah Ameir, Salim Ahmed Salim, Ali Mafoudh, Ahmed Abubakar Quallatein) and a significant number of its members were of at least partial Arab ancestry. For such youth, however, socialist theory exercised a greater pull on their loyalties than the strong racial solidarity of Zanzibar's Arab community.

In the capital, boarding schools were major Umma recruiting grounds. Umma vehicles arrived at dusk on school grounds to ask secondary school boys to hand out hundreds of copies of *Sauti ya Umma* (Voice of the People) daily.[110] Members of school debating societies were quick to join the new party, in part because Umma youth were thought of as intellectuals. Students gathered after school at the Umma bookshop on Creek Road to read and discuss imported Marxist literature.[111] They also read *ZANEWS*, which published news stories from Vietnam, Cuba and Algeria supplied by Chinese news agencies. These narratives repeatedly condemned both capitalism and colonialism, and encouraged a growing community of opinion hostile to both the British and Arab 'feudalism'.[112] Umma branch meetings were scenes of frequent debates over the meaning of both local and international events. *ZANEWS* reports were often the inspiration for heated discussions over the nature of imperialism and freedom.[113]

Rashid Khamis Rashid remembered that

> Umma was educating the youth in their branches ... they were not communist, just secular in their approach towards political, economic and national affairs. They taught English and typing ... and we didn't tell our parents because they would have opposed us, branded us as 'commies'. Umma had new ideas, and was very scientific.[114]

For some, their affiliation with Umma caused them problems. Politics penetrated family relations, distorting them as it had those of the plantation, workplace, marketplace, mosque, and playing field. Parents came under pressure from the ZNP to disown their sons, forcing them to seek shelter with other Umma party members.[115] As an openly secular youth movement Umma was briefly the talk of the town, the subject of accusations. British intelligence considered Umma a dangerous 'social evil', 'whose agents infiltrate homes and try to attract young people of both sexes by money and immorality under the guise of freedom of thought and action against religious and customs inhibitions'.[116] Muhsin claimed that Umma partisans used all manner of vices 'to ensnare the young and the gullible'.[117] Such reports were perhaps inevitable, considering the extent to which ZNP rhetoric had for years fused religion and politics. Scandalous reports of Umma members' lifestyles nonetheless inhibited the spread of Umma beyond the outer limits of the capital. Only in town was there an atmosphere conducive to a youth movement that projected its own standards of morality and discipline. In the pages of *ZANEWS* Umma propagandists claimed that 'certain politicians are fanning the flames of fanaticism under the guise of "save religion". It is all too familiar that reactionaries will resort to all forms of slander to vilify genuine patriots.'[118]

Umma also attracted support from both the YOU and the FPTU, the leadership of which went over to Umma virtually en masse. Umma also had definite appeal among ASP youth in the capital, who in late 1963 saw their party leadership, following their latest electoral defeat, paralyzed by factional disputes. Umma journalists freely attacked the government, and the new party was perceived to be genuinely sympathetic to African grievances. Robertson recalled that Babu 'definitely did get the support of young Africans and others who previously would have been ASP'.[119] The partnership imagined by Ali Sultan with ASP socialists like Moyo and Hanga also began to materialize at this time. Umma-affiliated trade unions co-operated openly with Moyo's Zanzibar People's Federation of Labor (ZPFL). Meanwhile Babu and Abeid Karume, the chairman of the ASP, publicly co-ordinated efforts in their opposition to the ZNP-ZPPP government. Although ASP youth in Zanzibar Town joined the new party, more would have joined had Umma not been identified by many as another 'Arab' party, despite its claims otherwise.[120]

The Umma's growing significance in late 1963 was testimony to the emergence of youth as a distinct political identity and to the effectiveness of socialist techniques of youth mobilization. Its initial core of support came from disaffected ZNP young people; as relatively privileged members of society, however, they would perhaps have been regarded by Marx somewhat ambivalently as bourgeois intellectuals, unstable and undependable in their political loyalties. Reflective of this, only a minority were ever convinced that socialism was the doctrine most appropriate to their status as 'intellectuals', and perhaps the only means of transcending racial inequalities in Zanzibar. For only a minority did socialism's wider frame of historical reference possess all the authority of a science, powerful enough to dismiss Zanzibar's 'exclusionary ethnic nationalism' as merely the regrettable affairs of the older generation, or the lumpen proletariat, for example. Youth in Zanzibar Town never became a separate class or a cohesive group with like characteristics and interests. Some young people gravitated towards Umma not so much out of an identification with socialism but as a system of patronage alternative to that of other parties. Some were interested in education and jobs and saw Babu as most in a position to help.

Nevertheless the idea of a vanguard generation motivated Umma intellectuals to recruit urban youth. Whether illiterate or educated overseas, whether fluent or not in a socialist vocabulary, many young people gravitated towards Umma because they identified a common race and class enemy: the ZNP-ZPPP government. Thus Umma's rank-and-file members were neither wholly African nor Arab, neither poor nor rich, but they were young, and they supported propaganda that criticized colonialism, feudalism, and capitalism. Umma was able to establish co-operative networks among young people that crossed racial, political and neighborhood frontiers. Such networks provided the basis for co-operation between Africans and radical Arabs in the Zanzibari Revolution, and afterwards during the '100 days' of the People's Republic of Zanzibar. They also suggested that by 1964 a significant number of Zanzibari intellectuals had come to accept socialism as a set of defining principles, despite their alien origins and international points of reference.

The Zanzibari Revolution

After the ASP defeat in the 1963 elections, ASP Youth League (ASPYL) leaders such as Chairman Seif Bakhari, Abdalla Said Natepe, and Yusuf Himidi began to consider violence a more serious option.[121] Probably around November, 1963, as a result of personal networks and friendships, discussions began between Umma 'comrades' and ASPYL leaders about the possibility of insurrection. The leadership of the Umma party was indirectly drawn into these discussions. Despite Umma's public espousal of 'African Revolution', the small party lacked the mass popular confidence to mount a revolution of its own. Although it promised its support in the event of an ASPYL uprising, the meetings were otherwise unproductive, as a result of mutual distrust.[122]

In the following weeks, Zanzibar celebrated its independence from the

British, and then in the first week of January, 1964, the ZNP-ZPPP government banned the Umma Party, confiscated its property, and forced its leaders into exile.[123] Perceived to be a lesser threat, the ASP continued to function publicly as a loyal opposition party; meanwhile the ASP Youth League proceeded with its plans for insurrection, eventually launched on the night of 11–12 January 1964. Hundreds of young people recruited and organized through the structure of the ASPYL captured two key government armories without serious resistance. By first light on the 12th Umma youth had joined the growing revolutionary crowd in the capital and participated in the capture of key buildings and installations.[124] In the following days, Umma 'comrades' took on various responsibilities around the capital; they were recognized by their black arm bands, and their slogan *Mwenge!* (Torch!)[125] Their radio broadcasts of Cuban revolutionary songs, their popularization of Castro-style beards and the Spanish phrase *Venceremos!* (We shall conquer) even encouraged rumors among some Western observers that the revolution was the work of Cuban agents.[126]

Umma memories bring to the fore their attempts to restore order in a city given over to looting and widespread violence against people, especially Arabs, identified as supporters of the former regime. While the predominantly Asian and Arab neighborhoods of Stone Town were ironically spared the worst violence during this period,[127] houses outside of Stone Town belonging to ZNP supporters were usually easily identified by the party symbols painted onto their exterior walls. To protect such residents from arrest or execution Umma youth distributed small posters of Babu, originally printed in mass quantities in East Germany. Displaying Babu's photograph might serve as a convincing symbol of the occupants' sympathy towards Africans.[128] Umma youth also participated, however, in the rough, spontaneous and cruel system of revolutionary justice that emerged in those weeks. During the round-up of ZNP-ZPPP members hiding in their homes or in the bush, Umma youth sometimes provided testimony on their character and personal history. Those they considered to have been most prejudiced or abusive towards Africans faced the severest punishment.[129] Ali Sultan, appointed a District Commissioner in Pemba just after his return from China in February 1964, recalled that he regularly prescribed public canings as a punishment for individuals accused of various offenses, rather than imprisonment. He remarked:

> In that period in Pemba there was a sort of spirit of revenge, which was wrong I think... The court was there, but they would not take their case to the court. There was a breakdown of law and order; it was a revolution, and it was like any revolution in the world. We tried to tell people to work together and to forget the past, that they were one people after all. But still there was a day of reckoning. The arrogant ones suffered after the Revolution. There were certain repercussions, depending on how you treated your fellow human beings. It was chaos almost.[130]

Such distancing from the worst excesses of the Zanzibari Revolution remains a repetitive feature of Umma memories. Umma youth regarded themselves as a distinct faction within the emerging ruling establishment, possessing the 'new political ideas' necessary to give socialist meaning to the insurrection. 'For us, we joined the Revolution because we thought they had manpower but no idea about how to organize and develop,'[131] is a representative comment. The common distinction drawn in these memories is between young vanguard intellectuals, whether African or Arab, who exercised restraint and who spoke the modern language of socialism, and the lumpen 'proletariat of the ASP', without such a vocabulary, for whom the Revolution had a very different meaning. Such Leninist distinctions appear in Babu's writing, even in the very title of his essay 'The 1964 Revolution: Lumpen or Vanguard?'[132]

The prominence and activity of Umma youth during the '100 days' of the People's Republic of Zanzibar represented the temporary realization of Babu's theories of a vanguard generation bringing about socialist development. Umma merged with the ASP, and Umma youth came to occupy influential positions in the new army and bureaucracy, as officers and junior ministers. Their overseas training and education were essential to a new government absolutely serious about replacing as soon as possible a colonial civil service overwhelmingly staffed by British expatriates, Arabs and Asians. Ali Sultan recalled that 'we had to get our [Umma] boys in the administration, depending on their qualifications … if you get a chance to put someone in you are pushing your ideas as well. Mind you, the idea was to revolutionize the mind'.[133] Unity among Umma comrades in the new government dramatically enhanced their capacity to shape public policy and encourage the growing socialist orientation of the revolutionary regime.

As Minister of External Affairs and Trade, Babu had a prominent voice in cabinet discussions. Initially the cabinet was, with the exception of Babu, merely a 'who's who' of leading ASP politicians from before the Zanzibari Revolution, with Karume in theoretical command as the new President. None of these individuals played any role in the planning of the uprising, and most in fact spent the first days of the Zanzibari Revolution in hiding. Appointed, however, to positions of power by ASP revolutionaries who, with the exception of John Okello, considered themselves unfit to assume the highest positions of political authority in the islands, Karume and the new ministers assumed posts in a government deeply divided by personal and ideological disputes. Babu made strenuous efforts to influence revolutionary decrees, to increase his power and to have his enemies purged. First to go in early March was Okello, who was not a member of the cabinet but who regarded himself as the 'Field Marshal'. Next to go were two moderate mininsters, Othman Shariff and Hasnu Makame, assigned two weeks later to overseas diplomatic posts. Their replacement by Hassan Nasser Moyo and Abdul Aziz Twala, both outspoken ASP socialists, meant the moderate elderly Karume was now encircled by a ring of young socialist ministers, of whom Babu emerged by March as the leading spokesmen.[134] While Western observers nervously witnessed the emergence of a socialist consensus among Zanzibari political elites, Julius Nyerere initially regarded these developments with some favor. American Ambassador William Leonhart quoted Nyerere as saying:

Karume had mass support but for him the fact that the African revolution had been successful was enough. Left to himself he would merely replace Arabs with Africans in same feudal structure. This is not enough. If real social reform did not come, Communists would take over. Babu had ideas necessary for thoroughgoing social reform. Zanzibar had to be modernized and no regime there could remain in power unless social change was rapid and effective.[135]

In March and much of April it appeared that Karume was gradually losing control of events. Babu, socialist ASP ministers, and Umma youth worked together to radicalize the new regime. While they labored to gain Karume's trust, his ministers issued orders without his consent and worked behind the scenes to shape policies. Scores of foreign experts from China, the USSR and East Germany arrived to replace British government servants, and to initiate various aid-based nation-building projects intended to make Zanzibar a regional showcase for socialism. Repeated demonstrations and newspaper attacks against America also made Western and East African observers increasingly concerned that Zanzibar was drifting from African non-alignment into the ranks of communist satellite nations. Babu was pinpointed as the mastermind of this drift. As American Vice Consul, Don Petterson attended a public rally on 8 March where Ali Mafoudh, 'dressed as usual in his Cuban combat fatigues', introduced Babu, who then presented Karume to the 10,000 assembled Zanzibaris. Karume announced to the crowd the nationalization of all land, the closure of exclusive racial clubs, and, within a few months, 'a better way of life' for all islanders.[136] A State Department guidance of 15 April, stated that China, the GDR and USSR were Zanzibar's 'principal benefactors', and that Babu had emerged as the 'dominant political figure with [his] own security force and own lieutenants in key GOZ positions'.[137]

Nyerere suddenly became alarmed in April over the arms build-up in Zanzibar, and rumours of an Arab counter-revolutionary army training somewhere in the Middle East. Nyerere pressured Karume to accept a federation agreement, using the possible withdrawal of 300 Tanganyikan police from the island as leverage.[138] Apparently racial and partisan heritage were important, after all. The federation agreement gave Karume's authority in the islands the full backing of police and army forces from the mainland. With such military support Babu and several leading Umma figures and army officers were safely transferred to positions in the new Union government and forced into relative exile from Zanzibar.[139] Despite such developments, Leonhart reported in August 1964 that 'UMMA types have built themselves into second echelon all strategic ministries and organizations and will not be dislodged without fight'.'[140] The CIA reported the following month:

> What constructive work is going on in the islands, whether in road-building, agricultural development, or the training of security forces, is all directed by foreign communists. The ruling authorities listen only to Communist advisors, exclude Westerners from contact with the people or with themselves, and systematically attack Western interests. Babu and his

colleagues have brought Zanzibar further under Communist influence, or at least for the time being, than has been the case in any other African country.[141]

Karume in later years was nevertheless able to tighten his control gradually over the island regime. Zanzibari revolutionary policies, although strongly influenced by, and even imitative of, overseas socialist practices and institutions, had Karume's unmistakable imprimatur. By the end of the 1960s many Umma observers in Tanzania, still retaining their own networks of 'comrades', were increasingly frustrated over what they considered to be Karume's betrayal of the principles of the Revolution. In 1972 they launched a failed coup attempt that resulted in Karume's assassination and the imprisonment of approximately seventy of their own number, including Babu and Ali Sultan.[142] Their years of imprisonment, and their individual diasporas following release, seriously eroded the political influence of Umma networks in Zanzibar. Even in prison in the mid-1970s, however, Babu continued to theorize about the relationship between class, generation, and power in Africa. He dedicated his volume of essays, *African Socialism or Socialist Africa?*, to the workers and youth of Africa.[143] As recently as 1991 the vanguard imagined by Babu was still generational. After a lengthy description of the untrustworthiness of the petty bourgeoisie as a class in Zanzibar in the early 1960s, and the difficulties involved at the time in recruiting both workers and peasants to a genuine liberation movement, Babu concludes his essay on the Zanzibari Revolution with a clear enunciation of what was to him the fundamental lesson. It:

> brought about an atmosphere of revolt in which the revolutionary potential of the Zanzibar youth revealed itself with a dramatic impact... As new revolutionary experiences [in the 1990s] continue to unfold in Africa, as the youth of Africa are everywhere increasingly spearheading the current revolutionary struggle against neocolonialism and imperialism with all its agents, the lessons of the Zanzibari Revolution, its ups and downs, its betrayals and heroism, will no doubt contribute enormously towards enriching and strengthening the struggles.[144]

Notes

* The author wishes to thank the US Department of Education for a Fulbright-Hays fellowship which provided the financial means for this research to take place. He also wishes to thank Kathleen Smythe for inviting him to present an earlier version of this paper at the annual African Studies Association conference in Columbus, Ohio, in November 1997, as part of a panel entitled 'Reconsidering Childhood and Youth in Africa'.

1. A. Wilson, *US Foreign Policy and Revolution: The Creation of Tanzania* (London: Pluto Press, 1989); D. Petterson, *Revolution in Zanzibar: An American's Cold War Tale* (Boulder, CO: Westview Press, 2002).
2. Telegram, Leonhart to Secretary of State, 4/6/64, Zanzibar Cables and Memos, Vol. II, 2/64-4/64, National Security File, Country File; Africa – Zanzibar, Box 103,

Lyndon Baines Johnson Library, Austin, Texas (hereafter LBJ Library).

3 . I recognize the changing local construction in Zanzibar of such racial identities as 'African' and 'Arab', at least a significant minority of the latter in this period were of mixed Arab-African descent.

4. T. Burgess, 'Remembering Youth: Generation in Revolutionary Zanzibar', *Africa Today*, 46, 2, (Spring, 1999).

5. Shirazis claimed status as indigenes with the longest historic residence in Zanzibar. A majority of Zanzibar's population identified themselves as Shirazi prior to the Revolution; see Michael F. Lofchie, *Zanzibar: Background to Revolution* (Princeton, NJ: Princeton University Press, 1965), p. 250. Shirazi identity has attracted considerable scholarly attention. See for example, D. Amory, *The Politics of Identity on Zanzibar* (Stanford, CA: Stanford University Press, 1994); F. Cooper, *From Slaves to Squatters* (New Haven, CT: Yale University Press, 1987); Laura Fair, 'Pastimes and Politics: a Social History of Zanzibar's Ng'ambo Community 1890–1950' (Ph.D. diss., University of Minnesota, 1994); Jonathan Glassman, 'Sorting Out the Tribes. The Ceation of Racial Identities in Colonial Zanzibari Newspaper Wars', *Journal of African History*, 41 (2000), pp.401ff.

6. See M. Lofchie, 'The Plural Society in Zanzibar', in L. Kuper and M. Smith (eds), *Pluralism in Africa* (Berkeley, CA: University of California Press, 1969) p. 314.

7. Despite the Revolution's long shadow, who was actually responsible for its planning and execution remains a matter of controversy. See A.M. Babu, 'The 1964 Revolution: Lumpen or Vanguard?' in A. Sheriff and E. Ferguson (eds), *Zanzibar Under Colonial Rule* (London: James Currey and Athens, OH: Ohio University Press, 1991) and H. Mapuri, *The 1964 Zanzibar Revolution: Achievements and Prospects*, (Dar es Salaam: Temu Publishers, 1996). While these two authors both give credit to the ASPYL, they disagree regarding the contribution of the Umma Party in the execution of the Revolution. My own research suggests that members of the Umma Party played a significant role in revolutionary events, but only in Zanzibar Town, and only after the key initial seizure of weapons by the ASPYL was already complete. Thomas Burgess, 'Youth and the Revolution: Mobility and Discipline in Zanzibar, 1950–80' (Ph.D. diss., Indiana University, 2001).

8. See Wilson, *US Foreign Policy*; Petterson, *Revolution in Zanzibar*, p. 207; D. McHenry, *Limited Choices: The Political Struggle for Socialism in Tanzania* (Boulder, CO: Lynne Rienner, 1994), pp. 190–4.

9. B.D. Bowles, 'The Struggle for Independence', in Sheriff and Ferguson, *Zanzibar Under Colonial Rule*, p. 100.

10. *Ibid.*

11. Glassman, 'Sorting Out the Tribes'.

12. *Ibid.*, p. 427.

13. V.I. Lenin, *What is To Be Done?*, Joe Fineberg and George Hanna (trans.) (New York: Penguin, 1962).

14. For the best collection of Lenin's essays, speeches and letters that feature discussion of youth, see V. I. Lenin, *On Youth* (Moscow, 1970).

15. *Ibid.*, p. 89.

16. *Ibid.*, p. 85.

17. *Ibid.*, p. 122.

18. *Ibid.*, p. 148.

19.. Soviet scholars in the 1970s regarded Lenin as a great deal less pragmatic, asserting that 'Lenin's approach to youth was always class-oriented'. V. Desyaterik and A. Latyshev, *Lenin: Youth and the Future* (Moscow: Progress Publishers, 1977) p. 8. See also Joel Kotek, *Students and the Cold War*, Ralph Blumenau (trans.) (Oxford: St Martin's Press, 1996), p.vii.

20. Lenin, *On Youth*, p. 247.

21. F.B. Wilson, 'A Note on Adult Literacy amongst the Rural Population of the Zanzibar Protectorate', (Zanzibar, 1939), as cited in N. Bennett, *A History of the Arab State in Zanzibar* (Cambridge: Methuen and Co., 1978), p. 229; also Fair, 'Pastimes and Politics', p.239.

22. J. Cameron and W. Dodd, *Society, Schools and Progress in Tanzania* (Oxford: Pergamon Press, 1970) p. 76.
23. Bennett, *History of the Arab State*, p. 244.
24. Cameron and Dodd, *Society, Schools and Progress*, p. 129.
25. See E. Batson, 'The Social Survey of Zanzibar' (unpublished study by the University of Cape Town, under the direction of the Zanzibar Government), vol. 10, n.d., as cited by Lofchie, *Zanzibar*, pp. 71, 92.
26. For example, in these same years 63 per cent of urban children attended primary school in Zanzibar, compared to only 35 per cent of rural children. Cameron and Dodd, *Society, Schools and Progress*, p. 130; see also A.Y. Mzee, 'Basic Education in Zanzibar: Progress, Problems and Issues' (University of Alberta, 1994), pp. 17–20.
27. Although Africans represented 75.7 per cent of the population, only 19 per cent lived in the capital; they accounted for only 19 per cent of secondary school enrollment. See J.Middleton and J. Campbell, *Zanzibar, Its Society and Politics* (Oxford: Oxford University Press, 1965), pp. 13, 14.
28. Zanzibar National Archives (hereafter ZNA) AD 32/27, 'List of Zanzibar Students Studying Abroad, 1956–63'.
29. See Rhodes House Library, Oxford (hereafter RHL), Mss. Afr. s. 2250, Zanzibar symposium; RHL, Mss. Afr. s. 2249, interview of J. R. Naish, Oxford, 16 Oct. 1971, by J. Tawney; see also Middleton and Campbell, *Zanzibar*, pp. 44–5, 53; Cooper, *From Slaves to Squatters*, pp. 138, 168; Lofchie, *Zanzibar*, pp. 63, 77, 90.
30. *Al Falaq*, 4 April 1956.
31. *Al Falaq*, 18 April 1956.
32. See Lofchie, *Zanzibar*, pp. 202, 218.
33. See RHL Mss.Brit.Emp.s.390, Buxton Papers 1958–63, Box 3, 'Commission of Inquiry into Civil Disturbances', Babu testimony, 5 Oct. 1961; Petterson, *Revolution in Zanzibar*, p.108; see also Ali Sultan Issa's forthcoming 'Walk on Two Legs: A Revolutionary's Memoir of Zanzibar', edited by the author.
34. Public Records Office (herafter PRO) CO 822, 1377, British intelligence report, July 1957; the British identified Babu, Jamal Ramadhan Nasibu, Ahmed Nassor Lemki and Ahmed Said el Kharusi as 'the adults most concerned with YOU' in 1957. PRO CO 822, 1377, General Intelligence Report on ZNP.
35. Unfortunately copies of this newspaper were unavailable to me. The Zanzibar National Archives houses an extensive but incomplete collection of some of these pre-Revolution newspapers. See M. M. A. Hamdani, 'Zanzibari Newspapers, 1902 to 1974' (Diploma thesis, Tanzania School of Journalism, 1981), pp. 42–45, 51.
36. Interview, Haji Uthman Haji, Zanzibar Town, 3 July 1996.
37. ZNA, AB 12/184, YOU, 1960-62.
38. PRO CO 822, 1377, British intelligence report, November 1957.
39. PRO CO 822, 1377, British intelligence reports, March–June 1958. According to Babu the ZNP also developed a 'clear-cut international stand' against apartheid in South Africa, against French torture in Algeria, for the Palestinian liberation struggle, for the People's Republic of China's admission to the United Nations, and for the unification of Korea and Vietnam. See Babu, 'The 1964 Revolution', p. 227.
40. RHL, MSS.Afr.s.1446; R.H.V. Biles interview, 11 Dec. 1971; despite YOU protest marches, the prohibition on uniforms remained in place until 1963. PRO CO 822, 1377, British intelligence reports, October 1958 to March 1959.
41. RHL, MSS. Brit. Emp. s. 390., Clarence Buxton papers, Box 5, 'Commission of Inquiry into Civil Disturbances', Ali Muhsin testimony, 10/6/61; Dawn in Zanzibar, 3, July–August 1961, p. 19.
42. PRO CO 822, 1382, Potter to Governors of Kenya, Uganda, Tanganyika, 12 May 1958.
43. PRO CO 822, 1377, General intelligence report on ZNP.
44. PRO CO 822, 1377, British Resident to Secretary of State of Colonies, 29 March 1959.
45. Lofchie, *Zanzibar*, pp. 225–6.
46. Mwongozi, 11 April 1958.

47. PRO CO 822, 1382, British intelligence report, November, 1958.
48. Interview, Ali Sultan Issa, Zanzibar Town, 13 July 2001.
49. B. Anderson, *Imagined Communities: Reflections on the Origin and Spread of Nationalism*, rev.edn (London: Verso, 1991), p. 27.
50. Interview, Abdulrahman Mohammed Babu, Dar es Salaam, 24 August 1995.
51. Lenin, *On Youth*, p. 89.
52. See his prison essays of the mid-1970s, in which generational and class identities as instruments of analysis appear alongside one another: Abdulrahman Mohammed Babu, *African Socialism or Socialist Africa?* (Dar es Salaam: Tanzania Publishing House, 1981). See also his 1991 essay, 'The 1964 Revolution'.
53. Interview, Ali Sultan Issa, Zanzibar Town, 4 July 1996; A. M. Barwani, 'Conflict and Harmony in Zanzibar', (unpublished memoirs), pp. 98–105; PRO CO 822 1378, British intelligence report, May 1959; PRO CO 822, 1382, British intelligence report, October 1958; Bennett, Arab State, pp. 194–5.
54. P. Mansfield, *Nasser's Egypt* (Baltimore: Penguin Books, 1965), pp. 100–1.
55. Barwani, 'Conflict and Harmony', p. 110. Petterson, American Vice Consul in Zanzibar from 1963 to 1965, wrote about Ali Sultani: 'In 1964, there was no more zealous Marxist in the whole of Zanzibar'. Petterson, *Revolution in Zanzibar*, p. 182.
56. Interviews, Ali Sultan Issa, Zanzibar Town, 2 July 1996, 4 July 1996, 13 July 1996, 21 August 1996; Shafi Adam Shafi, Dar es Salaam, 26 June 1996; anonymous, Zanzibar Town, 8 July 1996; anonymous, Dar es Salaam, 21 May 1998; in his memoirs Barwani harshly criticized such efforts, stating that some of the students in Cairo were 'lured' by 'Comrade Ali Sultan Issa to various Eastern Bloc countries.... Many became the ragtag and bobtail followers of Babu to be disillusioned when Babu and Ali Sultani came to power and discarded them;' 'Conflict and Harmony', p. 142.
57. PRO CO 822, 2166, Secret File on Babu.
58. PRO CO 822 2070, E56ii, Appreciation of Zanzibar Central Intelligence Committee report, July, 1962. See A. Ogunsanwo, *China's Policy in Africa, 1958–71* (Cambridge: Cambridge University Press, 1974), p. 85; E. Hevi, *An African Student in China* (New York: Praeger, 1963), pp. 115–43, 162–3, 195. Hevi describes the reasons for discontent among African students in China, which after a series of public incidents compelled nearly all the Zanzibari students to return home early. Eastern European universities were far more popular, but here also, the students encountered racism that sometimes turned violent.
59. See Adal Insaf, 'No One Starving or Jobless in China', 13 September 1960. For a discussion of overall Chinese objectives in seeking influence in Africa in the early 1960s, see B. Larkin, *China and Africa, 1949–1970* (Berkeley, CA: California University Press, 1971), pp. 44–5. For China's specific interest in and aid to Zanzibar, see also Petterson, *Revolution in Zanzibar*.
60. Interview, Ali Sultan Issa, *Zanzibar Town*, 27 July 2001.
61. These were Salim Ahmed Salim, Ali Mahfoud, and Muhammed Ali Foum, who established in Havana yet another ZNP-affiliated newspaper, *Sauti ya Jogoo*; interview, Ali Sultan Issa, 12 July 2001.
62. *ZANEWS*, 20 October 1961.
63. Interview, Ali Sultan Issa, Zanzibar Town, 13 July 2001.
64. Interview, Haji Uthman Haji, Zanzibar Town, 3 July 1996, 2 August 2001; anonymous, Zanzibar Town, 15 July 1996, 12 July 2001. For a brief account of the experiences of ZNP youth in Cuba, see Moore, *Castro, the Blacks, and Africa* (Los Angeles: CAAS, 1988), pp. 159–60. Although Moore asserts that the Cubans treated the Zanzibaris in a racist manner, he remarks that they continued to strongly identify with Castroism after their return to Zanzibar in late 1963. See also P. Gleijeses, *Conflicting Missions: Havana, Washington and Africa 1959–1976* (Chapel Hill, NC: University of North Carolina Press, 2002), pp. 57–60.
65. Interview, Ali Sultan Issa, Zanzibar Town, 12 July 2001.
66. Interview, Ali Sultan Issa, Zanzibar Town, 14 July 2001.
67. PRO CO 822, 2132, Robertson to Morgan, Colonial Office, London.

68. *ZANEWS*, 17 and 26 September 1963.
69. PRO CO 822, 2047, British Resident to Secretary of State, Zanzibar security situation, 23 June 1962.
70. PRO CO 822 2070, British Resident to Colonial Office, 6 October 1962.
71. Abdulrazak Gurnah, *Admiring Silence* (New York: The New Press, 1996), pp. 65–6.
72. PRO CO 822 2132, British Resident to Secretary of State, 15 June 1962.
73. RHL, Mss. Afr. s. 2250, interview by Alison Smith with P.A.P. Robertson, Oxford, 16 October 1971.
74. Petterson describes Muhsin as an 'ardent nationalist, a fervent Muslim, and a friend of Egypt's Gamal Abdul Nasser', who 'typified Arabs' self-confidence'. Petterson, *Revolution in Zanzibar*, 28.
75. PRO CO 822 2046, British Resident to Secretary of State, 13 July 1961.
76. Interviews, Hussein Kombo, Zanzibar Town, 7 July 1996; Ali Sultan Issa, Zanzibar Town, 4 July 1996; Muhammed Abdullah Baramia, Zanzibar Town, 22 Aug. 1996; Shafi Adam Shafi, Dar es Salaam, 26 June 1996; Khamis Abdallah Ameir, Zanzibar Town, 15 May 1998. Pressure may also have come from Mohammed Shamte and other conservative ZPPP leaders. Babu claims that they required 'the ZNP to purge its radical and socialist elements' as a precondition for agreeing in 1961 to a political alliance. See Babu, 'The 1964 Revolution' p. 233.
77. PRO CO 822, 2166, Secret file on Babu; RHL, MSS.Afr.S.1446; R.H.V. Biles interview.
78. RHL, East Africa, MSS.Afr.S.2250, 'Zanzibar Symposium', tape recording of interview at Oxford University by Alison Smith, 16 October 1971.
79. Telegrams, King to Secretary of State, 29 December 1960, and 18 January, 1961, File 745T.00/1-1560, Central Decimal File, 1960–63, General Records of the Department of State, Box 1709, National Archives, College Park (hereafter NACP).
80. PRO CO 822 2132, British Resident to Secretary of State, 11 May 1962; interview, Wolfango Dourado, Zanzibar Town, 21 August 98; for a list of names of those detained, see *Dawn in Zanzibar* (May–June, 1962); they included the leaders of a YOU group known as the 'Action Group', apparently organized to take more 'positive action' in the struggle against colonialism.
81. PRO CO 822, 2132, Robertson to Morgan, Colonial Office, London.
82. PRO CO 822 2132, British Resident to Secretary of State, 15 June 1962.
83. PRO CO 822 2166, Supplement to Zanzibar intelligence summary; PRO CO 822 2132, Robertson to Morgan, Colonial Office, London; interview, Wolfango Dourado, Zanzibar Town, 21 Aug. 1998; *Dawn in Zanzibar* (September–October, 1962).
84. That, for example, Juma Aley, the Vice President of the ZNP, refused to testify in Babu's defense, that Muhsin remained in Morocco during Babu's trial, as well as the existence of 'bar' rumors and threats of an agreement to sacrifice Babu. Recalling his return to Zanzibar, Ali Sultani told the author, 'I could not remain silent about Babu's imprisonment. I blew up as I finished my speech. I related the whole story, and all the past conversations that together made it very clear that it was the intention of Muhsin and [Chief Minister Muhammed] Shamte to get Babu out of the way and put him inside'. Interview, Ali Sultan Issa, Zanzibar Town, 13 July 2001. This theory is still vigorously asserted by many former Babu supporters. Muhsin has meanwhile strenuously denied these allegations. See Barwani, 'Conflict and Harmony', pp. 176–7.
85. Photocopy of Ali Sultan Issa's original, in author's possession.
86. PRO CO 822 2132, British Resident to Secretary of State, 31 May 1962. Interview, Ali Sultan Issa, Zanzibar Town, 12 July 2001. Hanga had obtained a degree from Moscow's Lumumba University. Moyo, as a trade union representative, had made multiple visits to the Soviet Union.
87. PRO CO 822 2046, E60ii and E60iii, British intelligence summary, August 1962.
88. PRO CO 822, 2132, #299 and 300, British Resident to Secretary of State, 30 August and 6 September 1962.
89. PRO CO 822, 2046, E56, British Resident to Secretary of State, 4 August 1962.
90. PRO CO 822, 2046, E63, 31 November 1962.

91. 'Youth's Own Union Marks 5th Anniversary', *Dawn in Zanzibar* (July–August 1962).
92. PRO CO 822, 2070, E/i/66, Supplement to Intelligence Summary, November 1962.
93. Telegram, Picard to Secretary of State, #67, 17 January 1963, Central Decimal File 1960-3, Box 1709, NACP; PRO CO 822 2046, E56, British Resident to Secretary of State, 8 April 1962.
94. Interviews, Abdul Razak Mussa Simai, Paje, 23 July 1996; Ali Sultan Issa, Zanzibar Town, 21 August 1996; Babu, 'The 1964 Revolution' p. 237; A. Fairoz, *Ukweli ni Huu* (Dubai, 1995) p. 61; ZNA AK 31/15, Urban district intelligence meeting, 19 June 1963; RHL, Mss. Afr. s. 2250, interview by Alison Smith with P.A.P. Robertson, Oxford, 16 October 1971.
95. See Lofchie, *Zanzibar*, 259; *Samachar*, 3 June 1963.
96. See Fairoz, *Ukweli ni Huu*, pp. 53–8.
97. *Ibid.*, pp. 59–60; Fairoz was an eye-witness of these events.
98. *Samachar*, 3 June 1963; Lofchie, *Zanzibar*, p. 228.
99. Interview, anonymous, Zanzibar Town, 2 August 2001.
100. *ZANEWS*, 26 June 1963.
101. See Lofchie, *Zanzibar*, p. 262.
102. Interviews, Saed Baes, Zanzibar Town, 8 July 1996; Ali Sultan, Zanzibar Town, 13 July 1996; anonymous, Zanzibar Town, 8 July 1996.
103. Babu, 'The 1964 Revolution', pp. 237–8.
104. Lofchie, *Zanzibar*, 218.
105. Interview, Abdul Razak Mussa Simai, Paje, 23 July 1996. This informant was also one of those nominated by Babu in the 1963 ZNP party conference.
106. Interviews, anonymous, Zanzibar Town, 7 August 1996; anonymous, Zanzibar Town, 24 July 2001.
107. RHL, Mss. Brit. Emp. s. 390, Clarence Buxton Papers, Box 3, 'A People's Programme'.
108. RHL, Mss. Brit. Emp. s. 390, Clarence Buxton Papers, Box 3, 'A Programme for People's Youth'.
109. *ZANEWS*, 18 July 1963.
110. Interviews, Haji Uthman Haji, Zanzibar Town, 3 July 1996; anonymous, Zanzibar Town, 25 Aug. 1996; A. Clayton, *The Zanzibar Revolution and its Aftermath* (London: C. Hurst & Co., 1981) p. 62.
111. Interviews, Shafi Adam Shafi, Dar es Salaam, 26 June 1996; ; Khamis Abdallah Ameir, Zanzibar Town, 15 May 1998; ZNA AK 31/15, British intelligence report, 18 November 1963.
112. See ZNA for *ZANEWS* issues from the early 1960s.
113. Interview, anonymous, Zanzibar Town, 2 August 2001.
114. Interview, Rashid Khamis Rashid, Zanzibar Town, 12 July 1996.
115. Interviews, Shafi Adam Shafi, Dar es Salaam, 26 June 1996; Hussein Kombo, Zanzibar Town, 7 July 1996; anonymous, Zanzibar Town, 25 August 1996; Ali Sultan Issa, Zanzibar Town, 2 July 1996, Khamis Abdallah Ameir, Zanzibar Town, 15 May 1998; anonymous, Dar es Salaam, 28 August 1996.
116. ZNA AK 31/15, Urban District intelligence meeting, 16 August 1963.
117. Airgram, Povenmire to Department of State, #A-46, no date, Central Foreign Political Files, 1963, NACP.
118. *ZANEWS*, 30 July 1963.
119. RHL, East Africa, MSS. Afr. s. 2250, 'Zanzibar Symposium', interview by Alison Smith with P.A.P. Robertson, 16 October 1971; Hank Chase, 'The Zanzibar Treason Trial', *Review of African Political Economy*, 6 (May–Aug. 1976), pp. 16–17; Lofchie, *Zanzibar*, pp. 260–5; Clayton, *The Zanzibar Revolution*, pp. 59–61; Bennett, *History of the Arab State*, p.264.
120. Lofchie, *Zanzibar*, pp. 260–5; Clayton, *The Zanzibar Revolution*, pp. 59–61; Bennett, *History of the Arab State*, p.264.
121. Interviews, Seif Bakhari, Dodoma, 1 May 1995; Alex Karigo Msangi, Zanzibar Town, 6 August 1997; Ali Mwinyigogo, Zanzibar Town, 16–17 July 1996; Muhammed Khatibu Suleiman Reja, Zanzibar Town, 27 August 1997; Wolfango Dourado,

Zanzibar Town, 21 Aug. 1998.

122. Interviews, Mohammed Abdallah Baramia, Zanzibar Town, 24 August 1996; anonymous, Dar es Salaam, 28 August 1996; anonymous, Zanzibar Town, 25 July 1996; Haji Uthman Haji, Zanzibar Town, 3 July 1996, 22 August 2001. Haji Uthman lists several Umma youth who participated in these discussions, including himself, Hamed Hilal Mohammed, Said Salum Kiazi, Ali Khatib Chwaya, Abeid Salim Hankil, and Salim Saleh.

123. Petterson, *Revolution in Zanzibar*, pp. 31, 40. Babu stayed in Dar es Salaam, whereas Ali Sultani, for example, had weeks earlier joined his family in Beijing.

124. In many cases Umma young people had several days' prior knowledge of the timing of the insurrection. Interviews, Hussein Kombo, Zanzibar Town, 17 July 1996; anonymous, Zanzibar Town, 8 July 1996; Haji Uthman Haji, Zanzibar Town, 3 July 1996; anonymous, Zanzibar Town, 21 August 1996.

125. Interviews, Enzi Talib, Zanzibar Town, 5 August 1997; Haji Uthman Haji, Zanzibar Town, 3 July 1996, 17 July 1996; Mohammed Abdullah Baramia, Zanzibar Town, 24 August 1996; anonymous, Zanzibar Town, 28 August 1996; anonymous, Zanzibar Town, 8 July 1996.

126. See K. Kyle, 'The Zanzibar Coup', *The Spectator*, 24 January 1964; 'How it Happened', *The Spectator*, 14 February 1964. Petterson records his wife speaking with a Cuban-trained revolutionary in Spanish on the 12th, one source of the rumors of Cuban involvement. Petterson, *Revolution in Zanzibar*, p. 73.

127. Mostly because revolutionaries feared entering the narrow streets with multiple balconies overhead. RHL, Mss. Afr. s. 2250, 'Zanzibar Symposium', interview by Alison Smith with A.H. Hawker, Oxford, 16 October 1971; interviews, Abdul Razak Mussa Simai, Paje, 23 July 1996; anonymous, Zanzibar Town, 19 August 1996; Haji Uthman Haji, Zanzibar Town, 17 July 1996; anonymous, 17 August 1996; anonymous, Zanzibar Town, 25 August 1996; anonymous, Dar es Salaam, 28 August 1996; Wolfango Dourado, Zanzibar Town, 21 August 1998.

128. Interviews, Ali Sultan Issa, Zanzibar Town, 14 July 2001; Haji Uthman Haji, Zanzibar Town, 3 August 2001.

129. Interviews, Enzi Talib, Zanzibar Town, 5 August 1997; Haji Uthman Haji, Zanzibar Town, 3 July 1996, 17 July 1996; Mohammed Abdullah Baramia, Zanzibar Town, 24 August 1996; anonymous, Zanzibar Town, 28 August 1996; anonymous, Zanzibar Town, 8 July 1996.

130. Interview, Ali Sultan Issa, Zanzibar Town, 26 July 2001.

131. Interview, anonymous, Zanzibar Town, 8 July 1996.

132. See Babu, 'The 1964 Revolution', pp. 240ff; also Wilson, *US Foreign Policy*, pp. 12–13.

133. Interview, Ali Sultan Issa, 18 July 2001.

134. These ministers were Babu, Hanga, Moyo, Twala, Aboud Jumbe, Saleh Saadalla, and Idris Abdul Wakil. Babu, Hanga, Twala and Saadalla, by the end of the decade, were all by Karume's order either executed or exiled from Zanzibar. The more moderate Jumbe and Wakil survived to become Presidents of Zanzibar in the 1970s and 1980s. A reliable source on power shifts in Zanzibar in 1964, and US worries over growing socialist influence in the islands, is Petterson's memoir, *Revolution in Zanzibar*. Petterson shares the view of virtually all observers about Babu's growing power in February–April 1964.

135. Telegram, Leonhart to Secretary of State, 1/20/64, #6, National Security File, Country File, Africa – Zanzibar, Box 103, Zanzibar Cables and Memos, Vol. I, 1/64, LBJ Library.

136. Petterson, *Revolution in Zanzibar*, p. 178.

137. *Ibid.*, p. 204.

138. See files in the LBJ Library, such as Zanzibar Cables and Memos, Vol. II, 2/64-4/64, National Security File, Country File: Africa – Zanzibar, Box 103. For a discussion of Nyerere's complete about-face in April, 1964, and his motivations for orchestrating the union see Burgess, 'Youth and the Revolution', pp. 269–77. Also see Petterson, *Revolution in Zanzibar*; McHenry, *Limited Choices*, pp. 190ff; Wilson, *US Foreign Policy*,

Wilson's conclusions might have been different had she had access to the full range of recently declassifed files. Nyerer's interests coincided with those of the United States, but he was not a puppet of the Americans, as Wilson contends.

139. McHenry discusses the extent of Zanzibari socialists' influence in Nyerere's union government in the 1960s: McHenry, *Limited Choices*, pp. 201–10.

140. Telegram, Leonhart to Secretary of State, 8/6/64, #52, United Republic of Tanganyika/Zanzibar, Zanzibar Cables, Vol. I, 4/64-1/65 [1 of 2], National Security File, Country File, Africa–Tanganyika, Box 100, LBJ Library.

141. CIA memorandum, 9/29/64, URT-Zanzibar memos, Vol. I, 4/64-1/65, National Security File, Africa–Tanganyika, Box 100, LBJ Library.

142. See, for example, H. Chase, 'The Zanzibar Treason Trial', *Review of African Political Economy*, 6 May 1976.

143. Babu, *African Socialism*, pp. ix, xvi.

144. Babu, 'The 1964 Revolution', p. 245.

Fourteen

The Short History of Political Opposition
& Multi-Party Democracy
in Tanganyika
1958–64

JAMES R. BRENNAN

Introduction:
Political Opposition and the Public Sphere

By any measure, political opposition to TANU during Tanganyika's brief period of multi-party democracy was a failure. TANU resoundingly defeated its competitors in three national elections between 1958 and 1962, and was nearly as overwhelming in local elections. The three major opposition parties, the United Tanganyika Party (UTP), the African National Congress (ANC), and the All-Muslim National Union of Tanganyika (AMNUT), were all poorly conceived and poorly organized, gaining only marginal popular support during their brief careers. Although the UTP was the most successful electorally, its support of multi-racialism rendered it a political anachronism by 1959. Few outside observers lamented its passing, and even fewer lamented the banning of ANC in 1963 or the disappearance of the AMNUT by 1965. The British High Commissioner in Dar es Salaam observed the following after the ANC's registration was terminated: 'I don't think we should be wise to waste any pity on the A.N.C. as such. Its politics were viciously racialist and its performance as an "Opposition" was absurd'.[1] Academic observers were no less damning. Judith Listowel described Congress as a 'small, violent racialist group' whose president led 'ridiculously unsuccessful efforts to oppose Nyerere'.[2] Julius Nyerere met little internal or external resistance when he declared Tanganyika a one-party state in January 1963.

Yet as Tanzania returns to a multi-party political system,[3] a consideration of past political opposition can illuminate the nature of Tanzanian nationalism, the contours of nationalist discourse and its recurring polemical devices, and the viability of ideology-driven political organization. This chapter will focus on the career of the African National Congress, a splinter group from TANU that had far greater potential than the 'multi-racial' UTP because it was led by Africans and took up political issues that resounded among voters. The major studies on this period dismiss the ANC as an aberration and accept TANU's claim that it represented the entire country, centering their analyses on TANU itself and its important if ill-defined internal divisions.[4] The ANC deserves our attention not simply because the political sentiments that its leaders sought to raise remain powerful today, but more importantly because the party succeeded to the extent that it responded to broader public dissatisfaction with a TANU-led government. The ANC failed not only because of TANU's growing discursive controls, but also because it lacked TANU's organizational and clientelist capacities.

By tracing the trajectory of Tanzania's African National Congress, this chapter also explores the development and contours of Tanzania's public sphere. Except for the even weaker AMNUT, ANC was the only organization positioned to channel discontent with TANU into a public sphere dominated by bureaucratic discourse. During 1954–8, TANU came up against numerous tools that the state utilized to limit direct criticism and general critical thought, such as libel laws, press censorship, and public assembly regulations. By 1959, however, the colonial state realized that TANU would soon succeed it, and grew more tolerant of its increasingly nominal opponent. This interdependence and limited comity between nationalist party and colonial state on the eve of independence – a point often understated or ignored in the academic literature – emerged in part from the shared discursive backgrounds of British officials and African bureaucrats, who, as Steven Feierman has argued, became TANU's dominant figures at the expense of chiefs, peasants, labor and religious leaders.[5] ANC opposition leaders were also bureaucrats, but their success depended on their ability to transcend social boundaries in order to exploit the emerging resentments that these latter groups held towards TANU bureaucrats taking power. Their failure to do so reveals in part the limitations of their bureaucratic background, but more importantly the emerging discursive injunctions of TANU that forcibly limited such appeals during the transition to independence. This triumph of bureaucratic discourse in the public sphere undermined the legitimacy of alternative discourses and constricted public dissent to the rarefied realms of development and socialist theory, debates far removed from the daily concerns of Tanzanians.

The success of Tanzanian nationalism and the country's relative political stability owe a great deal to the paradoxical talent of TANU in co-opting dissent while pursuing authoritarian techniques to ensure its containment. Though it had flatly opposed the UTP, TANU alternately confronted and incorporated subsequent African political opponents and much of their rhetoric. Confrontation was surprisingly simple and effective in quelling opposition as TANU gained access to the tools of the colonial state after its victories in the 1958/59 elections.[6] But TANU's president Julius Nyerere was initially uneasy with authoritarian tactics, and philosophically unable to accept that African society was sufficiently fundamentally divided to warrant political opposition. He reasoned that all disagreements could be resolved within TANU, tolerating seditious behavior by some colleagues so long as they remained in the party.[7] The ideal of one-party democracy reflects the genuine sentiments of Nyerere, but its enactment limited the nation's range of political debate and action. Following TANU's ascent to power, unco-opted co-operatives, ex-chiefs, trade unions, and opposition parties took up the shrinking discursive freedoms of the nation's public sphere. These freedoms ended decisively with the January 1964 army mutiny, which exposed the precarious position of the postcolonial state and forced Nyerere to utilize the full power of party and state to eliminate organized dissent.

The (Tanganyika) African National Congress

TANU's annual delegate conference held in January 1958 at Tabora is recognized as a critical moment in Tanganyika's history. After having built a viable, nation-wide political organization over the preceding three and a half years, the party was faced with the choice either to compete in national elections that weighted two-thirds of elected representation to the non-African population, or to boycott the elections and protest through mass non-co-operation or possibly violent methods. TANU president Julius Nyerere convinced the delegates that TANU should participate, which was passed by a conference vote of 37 to 23.[8] By accepting the government's terms, TANU ensured a constitutional path to independence – one delegate present at the Tabora conference considered this 'the moment when Tanganyika as a nation was born'.[9]

Also born at this moment was TANU's first African-led opposition party, the Tanganyika African National Congress (ANC). The party was initially created as a personal vehicle for an ambitious TANU organizer, Zuberi Mwinyisheikh Manga Mtemvu. Mtemvu had enjoyed a successful bureaucratic career as a police sub-inspector, social development worker, and literacy teacher when Nyerere persuaded him to quit government and become TANU's first organizing secretary in 1954.[10] As party secretary, Mtemvu proved effective in navigating the party and its supporters through legal and bureaucratic obstacles laid down by the colonial government.[11] Knowing that Mtemvu vehemently opposed participation in multi-racial elections, Nyerere had persuaded him to stay behind in Dar es Salaam, on the grounds that a high-ranking official had to remain to run the headquarters while the conference took place in Tabora. The day after the delegates voted to participate in multi-racial elections, Mtemvu telephoned Nyerere to announce his resignation from TANU and the commencement of an opposition party.[12]

Mtemvu had good reason to believe his new party might succeed. Most TANU delegates initially opposed Nyerere's plan to participate in the elections. On 6 January 1958, two weeks before the Tabora conference convened and the same day that the Mwanza delegation declared tripartite voting *haramu* (forbidden),[13] Mtemvu received encouragement from Hassan Suleiman to form a new party. Suleiman and his mentor, Ali

Ponda, had formed an important African Association branch in Dodoma during the 1940s and joined TANU upon its formation in 1954. The two left the organization the following year after being pushed aside and publicly humiliated by a representative from national headquarters, and joined the UTP in fruitless protest.[14] Suleiman told Mtemvu that he had been the first to disagree with Nyerere after the Tanganyika African Association was reformed as TANU in 1954, and had continued to disagree with him and his principal financial backer, John Rupia. Confirming that 'every educated person has already lost faith in the leadership of Mr Julius', Suleiman invited Mtemvu to Central Province to establish branches for the Congress party and pledged his personal support, but warned that many potential adherents would be civil servants, who since 1953 had been banned from participating in politics.[15] This correspondence indicates that Mtemvu probably sought to exploit a rift within TANU between Nyerere's better educated generation and the older, pre-TANU generation, discomforted by Nyerere's easy co-operation with Europeans and Asians. An educated man of Nyerere's age but someone also raised in Dar es Salaam and with strong ties to the town's old African Association leadership, Mtemvu probably imagined himself as the bridge between older politicians and younger radicals who resented Nyerere's moderation and growing power. A week after receiving Suleiman's letter, Mtemvu announced that he had fifty supporters willing to join his party.[16]

Whether or not Mtemvu's threat to quit TANU and form an opposition party was a ploy to gain leverage within TANU, it was no bluff. Mtemvu demanded on 28 January that, unless TANU abandoned its moderate policy within 30 days, he would lead a group of former TANU members to form a party advocating 'Africa for Africans only'. Nyerere immediately expelled Mtemvu from TANU, and threatened to expel anyone else who joined Mtemvu's party.[17] Mtemvu announced that he was forming a political party 'not primarily to start a new party but to bring TANU nearer the masses'. He argued that Nyerere opposed UTP's multi-racialism with a tepid 'non-racialism' and only wished Tanganyika to be declared primarily an African state, but significantly not *wholly* an African state – therefore seeking to maintain minority protections. He wrote that 'TANU and the U.T.P. have different fathers but their mother is the same!' In contrast, the new party's manifesto announced that:

WE DEMAND TANGANYIKA TO BE DECLARED AS AN AFRICAN STATE AND WE SEEK SELF-GOVERNMENT NOW. PREMIERSHIP IS AN OFFICE WHICH MUST BE OCCUPIED BY AN AFRICAN. WE ADVOCATE AFRICA FOR AFRICANS ONLY.

The party sought to compete, ironically, in the upcoming multi-racial elections, to capture all the African seats, to seek responsible self-government by 1962, and to achieve complete independence shortly thereafter. The intended audience of the party's manifesto was firstly 'the Chiefs and the indigenous African people of Tanganyika'. The party refused to accept Asian district officers or magistrates, and replied to reports that the Ismaili community had opposed extreme African nationalism by stating 'we say to hell with Ismailians ... To us Greeks are much better nationality than the Ismailians.' Mtemvu's political program would scarcely develop beyond these statements of early 1958.[18]

Far fewer joined the party than Mtemvu had expected. About one-third of the TANU members whom he had placed on his list of supporters angrily denied their affiliation with Mtemvu.[19] Colonial administrators were initially ambivalent towards Mtemvu's party; they considered its possible success as either a boon to draw off the 'lunatic fringe' from TANU and moderate Nyerere's demands or, conversely, an energizer of African radicalism with which Nyerere would have to compete.[20] The Office of the Registrar denied Mtemvu registration, first as the Tanganyika African Congress in March and again as the Tanganyika African National Congress in May, but finally registered the party in June as simply 'African National Congress'.[21]

ANC held its first public meeting on 23 June 1958 at Arnautoglu Hall in Dar es Salaam, which became the regular site of its public meetings in the capital.[22] Mtemvu structured ANC in the image of TANU, his only model. He raised funds through selling membership cards, sought support from sympathetic foreign interests, and also sought to establish regional and district offices throughout Tanganyika – all strategies he had earlier pursued as TANU's organizing secretary. Congress symbols similarly followed the forms of TANU imagery: TANU's flag was green and black; the ANC's was red and black; TANU's symbol was a black disc, the ANC's was a lion; Julius Nyerere took the nickname *Mwalimu Nyerere*, Zuberi Mtemvu was *Simba Mtemvu*; TANU's slogan was *Uhuru na Kazi* (Freedom and Work), ANC's slogan was *Uhuru na Haki* (Freedom and Justice). Mtemvu tried and failed to register a youth league, and apparently considered but never formed an ANC women's league to match its TANU equivalent. Except for emphases on the term 'indigenous Africans', ANC's constitution closely mirrored that of TANU, down to its entrance and monthly fees of Shs. 2/- and -/50, respectively.[23] By May 1960, the ANC had set up branches in every region except Dodoma, but it had only registered three offices with the government by that time.[24] Over 1960 and 1961 the party registered twelve more offices throughout Tanganyika, concentrated in the Lake Victoria littoral, central, and two southern regions around Tukuyu and Mtwara/Masasi.[25]

The ANC is best known for its extremely poor electoral results. Tanganyika's first national election for the Legislative Council ('National Assembly' after 1961) occurred over two phases in September 1958 and February 1959 to elect 30 members to regional seats by a common electoral roll, restricted by income and education qualifications. Representation was multi-racial, 10 seats each for Europeans, Asians, and Africans, but Africans formed the majority of the electorate and voted TANU-approved candidates for all seats. Although the UTP won no contested seats, it did poll several thousand votes, considerably more than the ANC's 53 votes. Despite the massive increase in the electorate brought about by reduced voter qualifications in the second national election of

September 1960 – from 37,000 to 850,000 registered voters electing 21 seats reserved for Europeans and Asians and 50 open district seats – the ANC could field only three contestants who collectively polled 337 out of 16,001 votes cast in those districts.[26] Besides failing to win a single seat in the national elections, ANC did almost as poorly in the regional ones. By July 1962, Congress candidates had won only one seat out of 58 district council elections and 12 urban council elections with a total of 1,800 seats.[27]

TANU's electoral victories in 1958/59 marked the beginning of the transition from colonial rule to independence, to which Congress responded by championing multi-party democracy. Changes after the election's two phases were immediately evident – the new governor Richard Turnbull proclaimed the end of his predecessor's 'multi-racialism' with a new policy of 'non-racialism' in October 1958, and in March 1959 TANU's Youth League helped to control crowds at Legislative Council's opening while the Territorial Chiefs' Convention met at Tabora to endorse TANU's political demands.[28] Constitutional changes, particularly the reallocation of 50 of the 71 open seats in the Legislative Council to any race in December 1959, had partially offset Congress cries against *mseto* government, and necessitated new arguments.[29]

The ANC continued to attack TANU's alleged multi-racialism, but also criticized TANU's aspirations for creating a one-party dictatorship. Mtemvu defined democracy as '[t]he ability of a people to choose and dismiss a government', and declared that such a choice depended on the ability of a people to criticize government. 'Opposition', he argued, 'must have a real chance to organise, to secure information, and to gain support in public opinion, in order to be able to defeat the Government and to form the Government in its turn.'[30] Responding to rumors that Nyerere wanted a one-party state for fifteen years following independence, Mtemvu told an audience that 'Opposition is the essence of British Parliamentary democracy and if the Opposition has to survive its foundation must be laid NOW'.[31] Michael Sanga, ANC's press secretary, argued that TANU's affiliation with the Tanganyika Federation of Labour (TFL) illustrated this aim for dictatorship, as did TANU's administration of certain schools 'which indoctrinated children with political views and taught them to "glorify one leader".'[32] Mtemvu explained to the Fabian Bureau that he had broken from TANU 'primarily to see that people do not have perpetually the idea of a ONE party regime' in the hopes that Nyerere would appreciate a true parliamentary opposition.[33]

Lack of funds interrupted the most basic of party-building tasks. Shortly after its formation, a rumor spread that the ANC was partly inspired by TANU either to get the government to grant concessions to the more moderate party or as a cover for extreme and unlawful action – the basis being that Mtemvu had no money of his own and could only be financed by TANU.[34] One Indian vendor threatened legal action if Congress did not return typewriters, payment for which had fallen into arrears.[35] Mtemvu was sentenced to five weeks in jail after defaulting on a debt of Shs. 1,804/40 to another Indian vendor, which he blamed on the 'cruel politics' of Indians, particularly Legislative Council member K. L.

Jhaveri.[36] The ANC also received little support from the African press. The European-owned *Tanganyika Standard* and *Sunday News* had sympathized with the UTP, and found the ANC's positions more offensive than those of TANU. The independent weekly *Mwafrika* rarely wavered in its support of TANU and consistently ridiculed the ANC. One cartoon following the 1958 elections depicted TANU members burying coffins with the inscriptions 'UTP' and 'ANC'.[37] *Ngurumo*, another independent Swahili newspaper, asked TANU leaders to ignore Mtemvu because paying him public attention was only building up his undeserved reputation.[38] To counter these obstructions, the ANC published its own broadsheet, *Kilio cha Mwenyeji* ('Cry of the Citizen'), but its production was poor and its circulation small.[39]

Following electoral victory and responsible government in September 1960, TANU members took up important offices and used tools of the state to complement the party's own obstructions of the ANC. Mtemvu scored his lone procedural victory against the emerging conflation of party and state by obtaining the recall of a Public Relations Department voter education leaflet that displayed a prominent picture of Nyerere on its cover. Accepting Mtemvu's claim that the photograph unduly biased voting, the government suspended its distribution.[40] ANC pinned its hopes on public demonstrations and broadcasts, which the TANU government regularly rejected.[41] In February 1961, the Provincial police commissioner in Dar es Salaam rejected the ANC general secretary's request to march through Kariakoo to express sympathy with Patrice Lumumba's death.[42] The following month, the ANC was denied permission to air political advertisements on the government radio station, Voice of Tanganyika. Its chairman, TANU leader John Keto, explained that Congress was not, as it claimed, a revolutionary party, but just 'a cluster of a few unsatisfied people who claim to represent others' that had not yet earned the privilege of addressing a mass audience. Keto justified the station's decision by stating that advertisements generally had to be 'filtered', and that to build the nation it was necessary to choose those matters that could bring 'useful things' for its citizens.[43] TANU Home Affairs Minister George Kahama banned all ANC public meetings in July 1961 because Congress speakers had 'abused the privilege of public speech by indulging in abuse of personalities and by disregarding the accepted conventions of political speaking'.[44]

Frederick Esau Omido, the industrious, Kenya-born ANC press secretary who had organized the party's first viable branch in Arusha in early 1959, complained that the TANU government was censoring ANC's mail. Three weeks before independence, the government expelled Omido for activities 'likely to inflame racial animosities and have already shown themselves liable to lead to a breach of the peace'.[45] The Registrar of Societies refused to register the Congress Youth League, arguing that it was 'likely to be used for purposes prejudicial to or incompatible with the maintenance of peace, order and good government'.[46] This was a crippling blow to Congress, as TANU's Youth League played a major role in the party's success. Marijani Shabaani, ANC district chairman for Dar es

Salaam, complained that TANU Youth Leaguers in Dar es Salaam entered houses forcing people to produce their voting registration certificates so that they might be kept in safe custody in TANU offices.[47] Omido responded to a temporary ban on ANC activities by stating that TANU members – undoubtedly referring to the Youth League – had 'taken the law into their own hands and have arrested, tried and convicted people, they have drilled like soldiers with imitation rifles, have entered houses and ejected the occupiers and have stopped and searched motor-cars, etc'.[48] Mtemvu blamed his poor electoral performance on intimidation by the TANU Youth League, which he described to the United Nations as a vigilante organization that was 'arresting people, caning them and imprisoning them without authority from the government'.[49]

In the international context of Cold War clientelism, ANC had the potential to benefit from its position as an organized, registered, radically anti-colonial political party, and looked abroad for material support. China financed Mtemvu's trip to Beijing in 1960 and again in 1961, though it is unclear what direct support the party received beyond travel expenses.[50] Mtemvu also sought political prestige by personally dispensing foreign patronage. He claimed access to Chinese scholarship funds and helped at least one woman obtain a scholarship through the Soviet Afro-Asian Solidarity Committee, but procedures requiring government assent to sponsor students restricted this benefaction.[51] Mtemvu completed a four-month fund-raising tour to the United States, China, Sweden, Indonesia, the USSR and East Germany in April 1961, having garnered little financial support beyond office equipment and perhaps vehicles from East Germany.[52] To return this favor, Mtemvu condemned US peace corps workers as 'agents and spies of NATO powers'.[53] By September, Tanganyika's colonial Secretariat reported that Mtemvu's stock had fallen low because he was discredited in Peking, his principal financial hope.[54] Radio Cairo's Swahili broadcasts initially attacked the ANC after its formation, but Mtemvu appears to have received aid from Egypt's UAR government in 1960 – secured, perhaps, in part by Mtemvu's accusations that TANU was anti-Muslim – before being cut off in April 1961.[55] Other African countries offered little support. In early 1960, an ANC representative attended the All Africa Peoples' Conference in Tunis, but when the Conference convened again in Dar es Salaam at the end of the year, Congress failed to persuade participants to boycott a procession headed up by Oscar Kambona in his capacity as TANU's General Secretary.[56]

The dynamics of regional multi-party politics provided a potential source of support for the ANC, with Congress constituting a link in an incipient, East African political opposition. Congress initially supported Zanzibar's Afro-Shirazi Party out of ideological affinity – both supported the creation of a 'pure' African state – but Mtemvu fell under criticism from Afro-Shirazi leaders when he hired a Zanzibari Comorian, Kaikai Saidi Kaikai, as his publicity secretary, and developed relations with the rival Zanzibar and Pemba People's Party (ZPPP).[57] In May 1961, an ANC delegation traveled to Zanzibar to establish ties with the 'pro-Arab' Zanzibar Nationalist Party (ZNP) in the hope of soliciting funds and gaining access to its overseas connections. By this time, TANU had clearly allied with the Afro-Shirazi Party, and in the wake of racial riots in Zanzibar, the ZNP warmly received the opposition to TANU. It granted ANC £250 from a Chinese-funded account, and discussed the possibility of a 'progressive forces' conference in Kampala headed up by Mtemvu, Ali Muhsin of ZNP, Joseph Kiwanuka of the Uganda National Congress, and Oginga Odinga of the Kenya African National Union (KANU).[58] Ali Muhsin also offered Mtemvu an 'underground' route for aspiring students seeking to evade state travel controls to study in socialist countries by taking dhows to Mogadishu to board planes to Cairo.[59] Despite embarrassing contradictions in the parties' respective racial policies, Congress became a firm ally with both ZNP and ZPPP by 1962.[60] During his trip to Peking in January 1961, Mtemvu had delivered a statement on behalf of the detained Odinga, who led ANC to believe that KANU and Kenyatta agreed with ANC policy.[61] Ultimately, this regional network of opposition parties was bonded by little more than opportunism and the sharing of Chinese aid.

Mtemvu appealed to Africans' racial resentment towards Europeans and Indians for political gain, but neither more frequently nor more effectively than did several of his TANU opponents. He preferred reasoned arguments regarding the justice of a purely African polity to visceral appeals to racial hatred. In one essay, Mtemvu wrote that he understood European reluctance to support the African cause because they had never suffered the humiliation of foreign rule, but Indians had fought for their own self-rule and should sympathize with Africans seeking the same. India, Mtemvu thought, was on the Africans' side, but Indians in Tanganyika were more concerned with their own financial well-being. He explained:

> Now, what do we expect of the Indians? We have promised them that their trading is safe in this country. We have promised them all that the property they have and are likely to acquire or invest in this country is safe. We have told them that in a self-governing Tanganyika they will be elligible [sic] to vote. That is as much as a harassed colonial people can promise a foreign people.[62]

Only rarely did Mtemvu appeal for the removal of Indians, or stress how their mercantile practices exploited African producers and consumers.[63] Other Congress leaders were more direct. In a rare philosophical peroration on the meaning of nationalism, Congress Treasurer Kassimu Baina equated nation with race by arguing, through a specious but widely-circulated understanding of a Qur'anic verse, that God wanted the various nations 'to know one another', and that this mutual knowing 'empowers us to recognize what kind of nation this is. So why do we now cross the borders of God, or allow the craftiness of those people [who discount nationalism] to drag us and send us everywhere they want?'[64] Describing *uhuru* as 'an axe which we must use to get our people work', Frederick Omido told a crowd of 3,000 in Dar es Salaam that the government should stop the frequent arrests of unemployed Africans living in cities and their repatriation to the countryside, and argued that the people who really deserved arrest and repatriation were Europeans and Indians.[65]

The ANC's racial ideology attracted few supporters because racial polemicizing had become too universal to distinguish any party by 1959. Most joined Congress out of a specific disaffection with TANU, which itself was a very big tent that housed not only anti-racialists like Julius Nyerere but also members who held anti-European and particularly anti-Asian views, such as Bibi Titi Mohamed, Oscar Kambona, and countless middle-level figures who subscribed to the views of TANU's surprisingly racialist Swahili newspaper, *Uhuru*.[66] Nyerere's non-racial Tanganyikan Citizenship Bill, introduced into the National Assembly in October 1961, faced resistance from TANU renegades such as J. B. M. Mwakangale and labor leaders such as Christopher Tumbo, yet Congress failed to reap much political support from their well-publicized opposition to the unpopular bill.[67] Among the few ideologues attracted to the ANC solely for its racial policies were Tanganyikans with experience abroad. A medical student studying in Pakistan described Asians as 'treacherous' and considered those in Tanganyika as 'FOREIGNERS WITH THEIR HOME LANDS, a fact which Mr Nyerere tries to overlook', while students in Liberia lectured Mtemvu that non-African workers must now choose between African workers or the capitalist camp, for '[w]hen the day of stocktaking arrives it should present no problem to distinguish weeds from efficacious herbs'.[68] The ANC considered the issue of Africanization 'the most important the Government has to deal with' and that a purely African civil service would be 'absolutely faithful', but this differed little from the flow of TANU statements regarding the pace and scale of Africanization after independence.[69] TANU officials were sensitive to their potential vulnerability on race and criticized Nyerere privately for his close co-operation with Europeans and Asians, particularly Derek Bryceson and Amir Jamal.[70] The ANC withered in the shadows of TANU's occasional but effective racial demagoguery, and could only grow in those areas where specific grievances against TANU were growing.

Congress gained a new lease on life after independence by hitching its fortunes to disaffected peasant co-operatives and labor unions, which were beginning to view the TANU-led government in the same oppositionist terms they had earlier viewed the colonial government. Although the ANC's grim prospects continued to hurt its central leadership – five executive members resigned between February and May of 1962 – its grassroots membership had increased by 10,210 members over the same period.[71] Many of the supporters in Dar es Salaam appear to have joined Congress either because of falling out with TANU or simply to seek gainful employment.[72] Congress benefited from being the only place left to go for politicians alienated from TANU,[73] and now benefited from TANU's post-independence exhaustion and the new government's sweeping political changes, particularly in the affluent Lake Victoria littoral. In Mwanza Region, cotton producers and traders joined ANC to protest against the government's ban on an upstart co-operative that challenged the monopoly of the TANU-aligned Victoria Federation of Co-operative Unions. Mtemvu had opened branches covering nearly the whole of Lake Province by mid-1962, and ANC affiliated with Saida Waafrika Ltd., a company of cotton growers which had 40,000 registered members. Samson Masalu Motobogolo, its president, had become district chairman and ANC representative in the Kwimba District; the TANU-affiliated Kwimba District Council responded by urging an immediate ban on the ANC in the region.[74]

Equally important to the ANC resurgence after independence were the ambitions of traditional chiefs, who had been courted by the ANC since 1960 and were involuntarily retired by the TANU government during 1962. The ANC enjoyed new support where newly-installed regional commissioners deposed popular chiefs, in areas such as Shinyanga, Ulanga, Moshi, and Songea.[75] Party rhetoricians finally seized an effective issue:

> The Chiefs and our Ancestors had already laid down a foundation which we were, as sons and daughters of Africa, supposed to follow and upon which the Tanganyika Nationhood should be built. Unique and unprecedent [sic] in political history TANU chose to abandon the foundation and instead built up an artificial pillar, which is now mercilessly oppressing the indigenous Africans.[76]

The ANC was particularly surging in the West Lake Region.[77] The party appealed to both older Haya politicians ousted from TANU leadership by a younger generation, as well as a 'traditionalist' constituency of Haya chiefs and their followers, perturbed by TANU's uncompromising position towards the chiefs' future role. A regional ANC officer touring the area urged Mtemvu to 'mark that all the chiefs are in your hands and therefore you must repeatedly and with full force issue statements opposing the act of making our Traditional Chiefs as Executive Officers'.[78] ANC supporters in Bukoba presented a broom to Mtemvu, a symbol for him to 'sweep away' TANU from the area. As in Mwanza, violence erupted between Congress and TANU supporters in the West Lake town of Kamachumu, this time resulting in one death.[79] The ANC made increasingly hostile gestures by publicly burning TANU cards and emblems throughout the country between March and June 1962. Police canceled all Congress meetings in the Lake Region following the public burning of TANU cards and a picture of Julius Nyerere at a demonstration in Mwanza in June 1962.[80] Chief Francis Masanja of Kwimba, a National Assembly member with ANC sympathies, formally left TANU and joined Congress in September 1962, stating that the ANC was the only party that could uphold human rights and that TANU leaders were 'upsetting *baba kabwela* [the poor] without considering their rights'. Soon after he was rusticated for several months in the TANU stronghold of Geita.[81]

The ANC's outreach to potentially powerful allies was matched by increasingly draconian policies of the state. Congress attempted to exploit the resentment that rank-and-file laborers held towards the pro-government leadership faction of the Tanganyika Federation of Labor (TFL), the TANU-affiliated trade union umbrella organization. ANC's public relations office broached the subject by publishing a letter that asked, '[h]ow could a Labour movement be a TANU/TFL organisation whereas

TANU as Government is an employer, and so in the most open sense'. The letter continued:

> I am not opposed to the T.F.L. being in co-operation with TANU or any other Political Party in matters of National Interest as a whole, but both the Workers who form T.F.L. and the T.F.L. Leaders themselves, should watch and define to what extent T.F.L. should be part and parcel of TANU. If there is any correspondent who wants to see inactive labour movement, which has been converted into a neo-capitalist and neo-employers' Organisation, then I advise the correspondent to visit and study the machinery of T.F.L. at its Offices in the City of Dar es Salaam.[82]

Yet, as with race, socialist polemicizing was becoming too universal to distinguish ANC rhetoric from TANU rhetoric. The National Assembly introduced three crucial labor bills in June 1962 that TANU leaders justified as necessary for national development and the protection of workers' rights. These laws increased TFL's control over member unions, reduced the right to strike, and prevented civil servants from joining trade unions; member unions vociferously opposed this action.[83] The government responded to this growing if disunited challenge by further limiting civil liberties, passing the Preventive Detention Bill aimed at traitors from both within and without the country. This law authorized unlimited detention on the basis of the President's decision, provided minimal procedural protection for detainees, and expressly prevented any order made under the Act being questioned in any court.[84]

Just as a working political alliance between the ANC and disaffected trade unions seemed near, however, Mtemvu's ego derailed the merger. Christopher Tumbo, a popular and radical Railways unionist, whom government had assigned abroad as a form of exile, resigned his post as High Commissioner to Britain in August and returned to Tanganyika in the hopes of being named ANC secretary, going so far as to buy an ANC card. Renowned for his energy and selflessness, Tumbo significantly outshone Mtemvu in terms of popularity, and equaled Mtemvu's record of radical opposition to TANU. After having made overtures to Tumbo, however, Mtemvu withdrew his support at the last minute. Tumbo instead accepted the invitation to lead the People's Democratic Party (PDP), itself made up of former ANC officers, while Mtemvu apparently blocked attempts to negotiate a merger between PDP and Congress.[85] Echoing popular oppositionist sentiment, a Tumbo supporter argued that '[i]t is time that ANC and Amnut forgot their differences to join forces with P.D.P. under Mr Tumbo to safeguard the interests of the man in the Kichwele bus'.[86]

Rival egos also appear to have prevented a united opposition between ANC and the All-Muslim National Union of Tanganyika (AMNUT), the other African-led opposition party that emerged before independence. Neither wished to acknowledge its splinter-group origins; Mtemvu dismissed AMNUT as 'a baby of TANU', and AMNUT's vice-president responded by calling ANC 'a small baby of TANU'.[87] In 1960, an AMNUT committee member did help to collect money to pay Mtemvu's creditors for his release from debtors' prison, stating that 'Mtemvu was a Muslim and that there was now no difference in the policies of the two parties', and the following year an AMNUT *taarab* group joined ANC supporters to welcome Mtemvu's arrival at Dar es Salaam airport. But AMNUT disassociated itself from Mtemvu's ill-fated presidential campaign, and the ANC never appears to have reciprocated any of AMNUT's fleeting support or political overtures.[88]

On the eve of the November 1962 presidential election that pitted Nyerere against Mtemvu, ANC's party platform – establishing a Welfare State through social, educational and health facilities for the poor; organizing agricultural development and self-help schemes; and increasing agriculture, mineral, and industrial production – differed little from conventional TANU promises.[89] The ANC instead spent much of its efforts protesting against electoral violations committed by TANU and the TANU-led government. The state was playing a cat-and-mouse game with Mtemvu – advertising the fact that Nyerere was facing a viable opponent in a fair referendum on the nation's future, while denying the ANC permission to campaign in several places throughout the country and refusing party requests for radio access. Mtemvu alleged that TANU was campaigning unfairly in Dar es Salaam by placing pictures of Nyerere at polling stations and having party figures inspect these stations, while TANU Youth Leaguers coerced voters queueing to vote. In Tanga, a wooden flagpole bearing the ANC flag was chopped down the day after it was erected. Local officials in Mbeya region intimated to villagers that the ANC symbol of the lion would eat anyone who voted for Congress.[90] ANC supporters were detained after showing the ANC sign of two fingers meaning *Uhuru na Haki*; a TANU spokesman confirmed that the practice of stretching only two fingers deviated from 'standard obligations'.[91]

Mtemvu was not blind to his remote chances. Shortly before the election, he suffered a blow with the resignation of the ANC's Eastern Regional chairman, Ahmed Ibrahim, who directed his 700 followers to rejoin TANU with him. More ominously, the ANC's publicity secretary Emanuel Makaidi quit the party because Mtemvu, he believed, was not the right man to lead the party.[92] The newspaper *Mwafrika na Taifa* reported months before the election that Mtemvu himself was secretly negotiating his return to TANU through the PAFMECA secretary, Peter Koinange. The paper alleged that Mtemvu was motivated by his impending defeat, while TANU feared that disaffected TFL leaders would encourage their followers to vote ANC. Mtemvu's personal aloofness towards trade unions after August 1962 and his inexplicable support of the Preventative Detention Act suggest that this may have been so, but he nonetheless reassured supporters that there was no truth in the rumors.[93]

As the presidential election results came in, Congress organizers fled the party. Nyerere defeated Mtemvu by 1,127,652 votes to 21,311, receiving 98.1 per cent of all votes cast. In only 10 out of 50 regions did Mtemvu poll over 3 per cent of the vote.[94] After Nyerere defeated Mtemvu by 21,911 to 761 votes in Dar es Salaam, the area's regional executive committee disbanded and its secretary, Marikani Shabani, resigned from the party.[95] In a press release, TANU proclaimed that the most significant result of Nyerere's overwhelming victory was the repudiation of ANC's racialism, and interpreted the relatively low turnout as a counter-intuitive affirmation of TANU's support among the unregistered voters.[96] TANU supporters in Dar es Salaam painted a bed with the ANC's red and black colors and marched it through town as a coffin to symbolize Mtemvu's political death.[97]

In a bizarre press release immediately following his defeat, Mtemvu stated that banning a rival political party would be 'suicidal' for Tanganyika's constitutional development, but suggested that if the people had rejected the opposition, then remaining members of ANC and PDP 'must join the governing party, TANU, so as to make themselves useful in the running of the country. Past bitterness must be forgotten for the good of the country.'[98] Shortly thereafter, he stated his intention to rejoin TANU and advised all Congress members to do the same.[99] ANC's organizing secretary, Jackson Saileni, vowed that the party would carry on 'until Tanganyika gets a purely African Government'.[100] In one magnanimous and co-opting gesture, the TANU National Executive Committee (NEC) opened the party to non-African citizens and offered amnesty to party members who had been expelled for disciplinary reasons.[101] Zuberi Mtemvu officially rejoined TANU on 22 January 1963, the day after the party inducted its first non-African members, Amir Jamal and Derek Bryceson. At the ceremony, Mtemvu announced that '[t]he people of Tanganyika have shown the world that they do not need an opposition'.[102] Nyerere's landslide victory, the fortnightly *Reporter* observed, made him 'the unchallenged leader of the virtually unchallenged party which runs the country'. Five years after the Tabora conference had decided on Tanganyika's constitutional future and inspired the first African-led opposition party, Nyerere opened TANU's Annual Delegate Conference on 14 January 1963 by asking the committee to approve a resolution, passed by the NEC, calling for statutory recognition of a one-party system in Tanganyika.[103]

Despite the defection of its founder and the subsequent announcement of a one-party state, Congress carried on. Its interim president considered the day of Mtemvu's electoral failure as 'a rebirth day', emerging from five years of 'poor leadership and unorganized administrations some leaders were of hooliganic character and untrustfulness, unimpressiveness, lacking personality trustfulness [sic]'.[104] Holding the ANC together proved extremely difficult. Mtemvu announced that he had dissolved the party and the Registrar of Societies announced an official de-registration date of 24 January 1963, but the remaining 'rump' countered that only the party's convention could dissolve the ANC. Jackson Hadad Saileni, the organizing secretary since early 1962, told the remaining officers to ignore radio and newspaper reports that the ANC had come to an end, and called them to an emergency conference in Dar es Salaam on 6 December 1962, where he was elected president.[105] The 'rump' accused Mtemvu of 'doing all he can to embarrass the remaining members and leaders of the ANC' by attempting to close party headquarters at Kariakoo and buying 'support from ANC members through Beer Halls, Hotels, and by means of Cars offered [sic] by his unfortunate disciples and Stooges'.[106] The party's support in Dar es Salaam had dwindled to a core constituency of some 232 voters living in the neighborhoods of Kariakoo and Magomeni.[107]

The political strength of the ANC waned considerably after Mtemvu's defection, yet it remained the only political organization able to provide systematic criticism of the TANU government. Jackson Saileni retained Mtemvu's regional and international anti-colonial perspective, though the newssheet *Kilio cha Mwenyeji* and party circulars had a very small circulation.[108] Less articulate but more thoughtful than his predecessor, Saileni attacked resolutions passed at the Chinese-supported Afro-Asian Solidarity Conference at Moshi that called for the removal of the King of Saudi Arabia. 'To declare destruction of a people's KINGSHIP', he argued, 'is not only a deplorable interference in internal affairs but also a source of creating dislocation of peaceful co-existence in Asia, Africa, and the World over.' He also attacked Nyerere and TANU's support of violence to overthrow colonialism in Central and Southern Africa on the grounds that Nyerere's philosophy and career were based on advocating independence by peaceful means. In *Kilio cha Mwenyeji*, Saileni blamed the continuing high price and unavailability of foodstuffs in Dar es Salaam on the TANU leaders who had moved to 'Mastabei' (i.e., 'Oysterbay', the city's wealthiest area) and were selling off national reserves of maize meal to the Israeli-run state co-operative COSATA to make quick profits for themselves.[109] Reaching abroad for support, he congratulated Ronald Ngala for his *majimbo* activities in Kenya, and appealed to him for financial assistance to compete in an upcoming parliamentary by-election.

Saileni's political strategy differed little from Mtemvu's; through public assemblies and circulars he hoped to oppose the abolition of chieftaincies and the 'Mono-Party Dream', to obtain the support of Christopher Tumbo, and to campaign on the 'holy motto' of Africa for Africans. He continued to attack Nyerere as *Mwalimu wa Mseto* or 'Teacher of Multi-racialism', and protested against the rustications of Hussein and Kidaha Makwaia, Shinyanga chiefs sympathetic to the ANC.[110] The government rejected Saileni's applications for public meetings and re-registration, on the grounds that Tanganyika was now a one-party state.[111]

Saileni developed an extended critique of Nyerere's arguments for a one-party state. Only a month after independence, Nyerere described Tanganyika's fight for freedom as 'a patriotic struggle which leaves no room for differences'. He argued that Tanganyika Africans were all one class, the working class, and therefore did not need a second political party to represent their interests.[112] He later argued in a theoretical tract that, as Tanganyika lacked fundamental divisions, a multi-party system was therefore inappropriate so long as TANU membership was open to everyone. A one-party system would eventually do away with 'the present artificial distinction' between politicians and civil servants and, by extension, party and government.[113]

Drawing on a motley array of available writers such as Harold Laski, Kwame Nkrumah, Thomas Jefferson and David Kimble, Saileni responded by attacking Nyerere's proposition that in Tanganyika there had been no division within society and therefore no need to represent factions. He countered that division was in fact human nature, and to disallow the discussion of differences between TANU and ANC would only widen these differences. After offering standard rationales for the ANC's electoral losses – low voter turnout and polling booth irregularities – Saileni developed a prescient critique regarding accountability and freedom of expression in a one-party state. Separation between civil servant and politician was necessary, he argued, because politicians who took on civil service jobs could not be responsive to the will of the people that elected them in the first place. He offered the examples of TANU's abolition of chiefs, ban on strikes, and four-fold increase in school fees as examples of policies which TANU had not been elected to implement. Finally, Saileni questioned the opportunity for free expression in the emerging one-party state where TANU's activities ran ahead of the enactment of relevant laws, such as the extra-legal banning of ANC branches and routine rustications of ex-chiefs and trade union leaders.[114]

Saileni's critique is rendered more poignant in the light of how government removed him from the political stage. On 17 April 1963, three months after TANU's annual conference voted to make Tanganyika a one-party state, the government officially terminated the African National Congress, on the grounds that its newssheet, *Kilio cha Mwenyeji*, was prejudicial to the maintenance of peace and good order.[115] TANU's newly-launched English newspaper, the *Nationalist*, offered a surprisingly critical reaction:

> It is hard to follow the reasoning behind the Tanganyika Government's decision to cancel the registration as a political party of the minuscule Tanganyika African National Congress. Surely by allowing this tiny, ineffective Opposition party to exist, the overwhelming support for the Tanu government party was daily demonstrated. That such a party could have legal existence but only attract a pitiful handful of members among Tanganyika's millions, would seem the best answer to those who would detract from the achievements of President Nyerere's Tanganyika by howling 'dictatorship'.[116]

Saileni refused to recognize his party's banning and vowed to carry on. Ten days later, policemen arrived at the ANC's headquarters in Kariakoo and brought Saileni to an interview with the Director of the C.I.D. and his cousin, National Assembly member Jeremiah Saileni, who together escorted him to the Resident Magistrate's chambers. Whether out of fraternal compassion or state compulsion is unclear, but Jeremiah Saileni had applied for a court order to have his cousin committed to a mental ward for psychological evaluation because he was making foolish statements indicating that he was not in good health. The magistrate agreed to Jeremiah's requests, and Jackson Saileni was sent for fifteen days of examination at Muhimbili's Mental Holding Unit. Saileni later wrote that, as soon as he met the doctor, he 'gathered all that was behind the whole game ... [a]nd one more thing was evidently clear, that is Dr

Nyerere's Government had signed in favour of the employment of Force in dealing with Political Opponents'. He was quickly returned to the magistrate the following day and discharged as mentally fit.

Saileni later lectured newspaper reporters that his hospitalization had been a government trap to kill off the revolution because his politics were making the government tremble in fear. Press reports agreed that Saileni demonstrated his insanity by insisting that he was still the president of ANC, even though the party was officially banned.[117] Saileni was again committed to the Mental Holding Unit in July as the government continued to have him declared mentally unsound, and was again released. The doctor in charge told the British High Commissioner privately that he did not think Saileni was 'suffering from any mental defect, although the way he has been treated could quite easily push him over the edge'.[118]

Simple arrests proved more effective in executing the ban. Saileni and three supporters were arrested in May for 'assisting in the management of an unlawful society and of being a members of it'. Appearing in court in the strange costume of a conical hat over a red turban and a black cloth round his shoulders, Saileni pleaded not guilty, but all were eventually sentenced to three years jail with a two-year concurrent sentence for running a proscribed society.[119] Eight other Congress supporters were later arrested for continuing to run the party and displaying the party's flag and membership cards, and were sentenced to six months jail, though later released on appeal. Saileni was sentenced to three years, later reduced to six and finally three months.[120] By late 1963, there are no signs of further ANC activity; its cancellation was finally a fact. The former ANC rump that had formed the PDP dissolved itself after Nyerere's declaration of a one-party state in January 1963, though some members did join the People's Convention Party (PCP), formed later by Christopher Tumbo until his arrest following the 1964 mutiny. After rejoining TANU, Zuberi Mtemvu pursued an unremarkable career as a mid-level government administrator. He passed away quietly on 20 September 1999, and his funeral was attended by a number of important CCM officials.[121] In death as in life, he was immeasurably overshadowed by the death of Julius Nyerere three weeks later.

Conclusion

The ANC's direct political impact was meager. Its greatest effect was in forcing TANU to delay opening its membership to non-Africans until January 1963 – out of fear of conceding the multi-racialist charge to the ANC's political benefit.[122] The failure of Congress to compete with TANU is significant, however, because it demonstrates the mental and social distances between the ANC's bureaucratic leaders and the workers and peasants who themselves were beginning to take issue with TANU's unbridled dominance. When Congress leaders belatedly realized the potential to harness grassroots opposition, they faltered by continuing to emphasize racialist and socialist arguments that resembled too closely the anti-colonial orthodoxy long monopolized by TANU. The argument of Göran Hydén – that the ANC failed in northwest Tanganyika because 'there was simply not room for another ideology'[123] – should be understood as the failure of Congress leaders to imaginatively create ideological 'room' beyond the issue of race to attract followers with genuine objections to TANU policy. TANU could convincingly explain Mtemvu's total defeat in the 1962 presidential election as the nation's 'rejection of racialism' because he had moved too slowly and with insufficient imagination to exploit the emerging grievances other social groups held against the postcolonial state, and had phrased those multi-dimensional grievances in monochromatic racial terms.[124] Such was the success of TANU in identifying itself with the nation, and making the nation's goals those of development and socialism, that people roundly agreed that for Saileni to imagine he could oppose TANU was both an indication and a form of lunacy.

Amidst the wreckage of ANC's failure also lay non-ideological political dynamics. Dissatisfaction with TANU and the new government ran strongest in the country's wealthiest areas, such as the Lake Victoria littoral centers of Bukoba and Mwanza, and to a lesser extent Moshi and Same. In these areas, home to the earliest African marketing co-operatives, people had long understood the connection between local politics and economic development, and felt more confident to shop around and strike bargains with political entrepreneurs like Mtemvu than in poorer areas where TANU reigned uncontested. No ideology could neatly represent this bargain-hunting dynamic whereby wealthy producers supported local chiefs against powerful and unbending TANU bureaucrats. Thus ANC's propaganda was a bizarre combination of socialist and racialist polemics interspersed with attacks on state control over labor and marketing and defenses of chiefly authority. Congress could only become a viable political opposition if it could reciprocate the support of co-operatives, chiefs, and labor unions with tangible changes in state policy. With little cash, a weak party structure, and no elected offices, this was a bargain Congress could not keep. In any event, liberty for such political bargaining vanished with the TANU government's response to its greatest crisis.

There are few chronological breaks in Tanzanian history as sharp as the army mutiny of January 1964. Although TANU was clearly drifting towards authoritarian rule during 1959–63, the country's media and political culture still entertained political dissent. The mass arrests which followed the mutiny, including some 200 trade unionists, effectively collapsed the thin space within the public sphere where politicians critical of TANU and the government could communicate, however inadequately, with an audience. The mutiny, which witnessed low-level army officers controlling Dar es Salaam, Julius Nyerere going into hiding, and British soldiers finally disarming mutineers, laid bare the fragility of the post-colonial state and hastened the government's erratic drive towards eliminating formal political opposition.

Shortly after the mutiny, the government announced the dissolution of the TFL and the creation of the National Union of Tanganyika Workers

(NUTA), a state-controlled union umbrella that would represent all workers in Tanganyika. In mid-February, Nyerere convened a Presidential Commission to advise the government on turning Tanganyika into a one-party state, which was later enshrined in the 1965 Constitution. While the government shut down formal spheres of dissent, the party worked to eliminate political opposition on the ground. In the middle of 1964, TANU began to coerce civil servants and police to join the party, and Tanganyikans in several regions found themselves denied medical care or crop-selling privileges unless they could produce a TANU card. At the end of the year, TANU launched a system of ten-house cells for urban areas organized through ward development committees, increasing the party's ability to survey and ferret out political opposition.[125] Political debate outside of TANU had become unimaginable by the late 1960s. Even Oscar Kambona, who had become Nyerere's chief rival and was living in exile, accepted the premise of the one-party state. In political flyers dropped by airplane over Dar es Salaam in December 1971, Kambona demanded a contest between himself and Nyerere for Tanzania's presidency. After enumerating numerous civil liberties that he promised to restore, Kambona concluded that, 'We are not proposing a new Party. We want to keep TANU but as a REAL NATIONAL UNION for every one that LOVES TANZANIA'.[126]

TANU succeeded because, for a while at least, it could be all things to all people. Joan Wicken observed in 1958 that any widely held grievance could become TANU policy, leading to 'a number of quite incompatible utopias'.[127] Nyerere deftly managed these incompatibilities, but at the cost of inexorably constricting the meager, late-colonial civil liberties that formed the boundaries of Tanganyika's public sphere and had made TANU's success possible. If most Tanganyikans rejected the real political alternatives to TANU, a visible core supported the idea of political pluralism and were discomforted by Nyerere's deliberate conflation of party and state. A letter to *Mwafrika* summarizes this perspective:

> Many times I have read in your various issues that many people dislike the party of AMNUT and others don't even want to hear about it. But if Tanganyika accepts the course of democracy, that is to say every person or people should have their thoughts, why should we [not] have other parties? I am not a member of AMNUT or any other political party but I wish that educated people with more wisdom would explain to me its evil.[128]

Such arguments were easily dismissed amidst the national ascendancy of bureaucratic discourse and socialist rhetoric, neither of which could allow for legitimate social differences that would justify political opposition. The following letter wholly typifies this perspective:

> The objective truth is that the concept of an opposition party is a pet baby of the capitalists who have consented to exploit the workers in turn by fooling them with the so-called freedom of expression and bogus democracy. True democracy is economic democracy which is guaranteed only by a socialist mode of production based on the social ownership of the

means of production ... We do not need any opposition so long as we are socialists.[129]

Democracy in this widespread understanding meant TANU's struggle to create development and equality, something brought about by TANU alone through the management of expert bureaucrats and the removal of national enemies. This faith could last only so long as Tanzanians believed that TANU was in fact bringing development, and that capitalists were enemies in need of removal. As this faith collapsed in the 1980s, international pressure was brought to bear on Tanzania to make conventional political reforms by re-instituting multi-party democracy, which it finally did in 1992. Whether or not the survival of Tanganyika's fragile postcolonial state and the creation of an enduring national identity offset the sacrifice of civil liberties, the failure of a political opposition to transcend bureaucratic discourse and conjoin alternative discourses, continues to constrain public debate of problems old and new.

Notes

1. O'Leary to Hickman, 22 April 1963, Dominions Office (hereafter DO) 168/7/15, Public Records Office, Kew.
2. Judith Listowel, *The Making of Tanganyika* (London: Chatto & Windus, 1965), pp. 307–9.
3. In 1992, the Tanzanian National Assembly passed legislation to initiate a multiparty political system. This ended nearly thirty years of dominance by one political party on the country's mainland, the Tanganyika African National Union (TANU), renamed Chama Cha Mapinduzi (CCM) in 1977 following its amalgamation with Zanzibar's Afro-Shirazi Party. Since 14 January 1963, when TANU's National Executive Committee decided upon a one-party system (made law with the passing of the Interim Constitution on 5 July 1965), public political debate was officially inscribed within TANU.
4. These works include Listowel, *Making of Tanzania*; Henry Bienen, *Tanzania: Party transformation and economic development* (Princeton, NJ: Princeton University Press, 1970); J. Clagett Taylor, *The Political Development of Tanganyika* (Stanford, CA: Stanford University Press, 1963); and Cranford Pratt, *The Critical Phase in Tanzania, 1945–1968: Nyerere and the emergence of a socialist strategy* (Cambridge: Cambridge University Press, 1976). Although only concerned with the period up to independence, the best work on TANU and Tanganyikan nationalism remains John Iliffe, *A Modern History of Tanganyika* (Cambridge: Cambridge University Press, 1979). An important exception to the facile dismissals of ANC is Ronald Aminzade, 'The Politics of Race and Nation: Citizenship and Africanization in Tanganyika', *Political Power and Social Theory* 14 (2000), pp. 53–90.
5. Steven Feierman, *Peasant Intellectuals: Anthropology and History in Tanzania* (Madison, WI: University of Wisconsin Press, 1990), pp. 223–44.
6. TANU first shared political power with the British colonial government in July 1959 with the appointment of elected Legislative Council members to the Council of Ministers, increased its share with the attainment of responsible government in September 1960 and full internal self-government in May 1961, and took over completely with independence on 9 December 1961.
7. On Nyerere's (early) tolerance of dissent within TANU, see R. Cranford Pratt, 'The Cabinet and Presidential Leadership in Tanzania: 1960–1966', in Michael Lofchie (ed.), *The State of the Nations: Constraints on Development in Independent Africa* (Berkeley, CA: University of California Press, 1971), pp. 93–118.
8. Grattan-Bellew to Mathieson, 12 March 1958, Colonial Office (hereafter CO)

822/1362/197, Public Records Office, Kew; Iliffe, *A Modern History*, p. 557. Iliffe cites Hassan Issa, 'Safari ya Tabora', but also notes a differing conference vote figure, given by Martin Lowenkopf, of 37 to 11.

9. Elias Kisenge, quoted in Listowel, *Making of Tanzania*, p. 306.
10. Laura S. Kurtz, *Historical Dictionary of Tanzania* (Metuchen, NJ: Scarecrow Press, 1978), p. 136.
11. Mohamed Said, 'Alhaj Zuberi Mwinshehe Manga Mtemvu', *An-nuur*, 15 October 1999. Shortly after its formation on 7 July 1954, Government had denied TANU permission to hold public meetings. Mtemvu researched the question and discovered that the party could continue its political activities until the Registrar of Societies served notice that its registration was refused.
12. Mohamed Said, 'Alhaj Zuberi Mwinshehe Manga Mtemvu – 2', *An-nuur*, 22 October 1999.
13. Listowel, *Making of Tanzania*, pp. 304–7; Iliffe, *A Modern History*, p. 556.
14. G. G. Hajivayanis, A. C. Mtowa and J. Iliffe, 'The Politicians: Ali Ponda and Hassan Suleiman', in John Iliffe (ed.), *Modern Tanzanians: A volume of biographies* (Dar es Salaam: East African Publishing House, 1973), pp. 251–53.
15. Hassan Suleiman to Zuberi Mtemvu, 6 January 1958, Tanzania National Archives (hereafter TNA) 540/27/28, Dar es Salaam. Ironically, Central Province was the only region where ANC did not have a branch by May 1960. 'Dictatorship is threat to Tanganyika', *Tanganyika Standard*, 14 May 1960.
16. 'Kuiacha T.A.N.U. Hakutaleta Mabadiliko', *Zuhra*, 31 January 1958.
17. 'Threat to Split TANU', *Tanganyika Standard*, 29 January 1958; 'Mtemvu plans his party', *Tanganyika Standard*, 3 February 1958.
18. These statements are from ANC Press Release, *ca.* 30 January 1958, CO 822/1370/E2/3; and WHAT WE BELIEVE IN – OUR POLITICAL PHILOSOPHY, *ca.* 30 January 1958, CO 822/1370/E3/3. Emphases in original.
19. George Bennett, 'An Outline History of TANU', *Makerere Journal* 7 (1963), p. 25. The initial 'caretaker' committee of the party consisted of Mtemvu, J. N. Mulekwa, A. P. M. Lupindo (secretary of the Building and Construction Workers' Union), E. E. Akena (general secretary of the Dockworkers' and Stevedores' Union), G. P. Mbukwa, Kassim S. Baina, and Adam Kesabe. 'T.A.C. Asks for Registration', *Tanganyika Standard*, 12 February 1958. Mbukwa, Lupindo and Kondowy immediately denied their affiliations: letters from G. P. Mbukwa and A. P. M. Lupindo, *Tanganyika Standard*, 14 February 1958; letter from J. C. Nelson Kondowy, *Tanganyika Standard*, 17 February 1958.
20. Grattan-Bellew to Mathieson, 26 February 1958, CO 822/1370/4.
21. 'Chama Cha Mtemvu Kimekataliwa na Serikali T.A.N.U. Inaburura Kitara', *Zuhra*, 9 May 1958; General Notice No. 1520 of 1958, *Tanganyika Gazette*; GN No. 1828 of 1958, *ibid.* Mtemvu's first application was refused by the Registrar in March because the initials of 'Tanganyika African Congress' might have caused confusion with the Tanganyika Agricultural Corporation. Bennett, 'Outline history', pp. 31, 54.
22. Chipaka to Assistant Commissioner of Police, 23 June 1958, TNA 540/20/1, and other applications in this file.
23. Copy of ANC constitution in TNA 540/33; *T.A.N.U. Constitution* (Dar es Salaam, 1954).
24. 'Dictatorship is threat to Tanganyika', *Tanganyika Standard*, 14 May 1960. The registered offices include Dar es Salaam, Tanga, and Arusha. See GN No. 1828 of 1958 and GN No. 956 of 1959.
25. These offices include: Bukoba (September 1960); Miono, Msata/Bagamoyo, Katoro, and Newala (October 1960); Mtwara (December 1960); Tukuyu, Rusende, East Lake Branch, Dodoma, and Tabora (April 1961); Uyowa (June 1961). GN No. 2328 of 1960; GN No. 2688 of 1960; GN No. 3201 of 1960; GN No. 1046 of 1961; and GN No. 1414 of 1961.
26. Martin Lowenkopf, 'Tanganyika Achieves Responsible Government', *Parliamentary Affairs* 9 (1961), pp. 245–7. Hermangild Sarwat ran as an independent against TANU's candidate and won Mbulu District seat in 1960. Mtemvu attempted to recruit Sarwat to join the ANC, but Sarwat rejoined TANU shortly after the election, *Tanganyika*

Standard, 9 September 1960; Iliffe, *Modern History*, p. 570; Bienen, *Tanzania*, pp. 55–6; Mtemvu to Sanga, 30 August 1960, TNA 561/32/I/124. 12 of the 15 non-TANU candidates were independents who denied ties with ANC. G.W.Y. Hucks, 'Report on the Second General Election of Members of the Legislative Council of Tanganyika', mimeograph, 1960, p. 21. Mtemvu himself received 53 votes against TANU's 3,455 votes for Tanga Province in 1958, and 67 votes against TANU's 7,498 votes for Bagamoyo District in 1960. Taylor, *Political Development*, p. 173; *Tanganyika Standard*, 2 September 1960.

27. 'A.N.C. Does Rounds', *Tanganyika Standard*, 28 July 1962. Though complete numbers are not available, a handful did join ANC after having been elected as independents.

28. Bennett, 'Outline History', pp. 26–7.

29. The Swahili word *mseto*, literally meaning mixture or mash, became a pejorative term used to describe the colonial government's policy of multi-racialism and, in the case of ANC, to describe TANU's acceptance of the government's terms.

30. Letter from Zuberi Mtemvu, *Tanganyika Standard*, 25 November 1959.

31. Speech delivered by Mtemvu to senior boys and teachers of St. Andrew's College, Minaki, 13 September 1959, TNA 540/32/58. Emphasis in original.

32. 'TANU is Seeking a Dictatorship – ANC', *Tanganyika Standard*, 16 February 1961.

33. Mtemvu to Selwyn-Clarke, 12 March 1960, Rhodes House (hereafter RH) MSS Brit. Emp. 365 Box 121/4/155, Oxford. Emphasis in original.

34. Grattan-Bellew to Mathieson, 26 February 1958, CO 822/1370/4.

35. Director, Nanji Stores Ltd to Michael Sanga, 9 November 1960, TNA 540/17/C/13; Director, Nanji Stores Ltd to Honorary Secretary, ANC, 6 October 1961, TNA 540/17/C/151.

36. 'Mtemvu jela kwa madeni', *Mwafrika*, 24 September 1960; 'President of A.N.C. Released', *Tanganyika Standard*, 4 November 1960.

37. *Mwafrika*, 4 October 1958. Ceremonial burials of opposition party coffins were widespread. In Dodoma, TANU held a mock burial for a UTP coffin. Hajivayanis *et al.*, 'The Politicians', p. 252.

38. 'Hana Siasa', *Ngurumo*, 15 December 1960.

39. *Kilio cha Mwenyeji* was an unregistered newssheet, either 2 or 4 pages in length, published irregularly (often monthly) between 1958 and 1963 by ANC. Copies survive mainly in TNA files cited in this chapter.

40. 'Mtemvu Protests against Leaflet', *Tanganyika Standard*, 5 March 1960; newspaper clipping, TNA 540/16/61.

41. See Senior Assistant Commissioner of Police to General Secretary, ANC, 22 February 1961, TNA 540/20/no folio; 'Congress yapewa wazi habari zenu uoza', *Mwafrika*, 4 March 1961.

42. Senior Assistant Commissioner of Police to General Secretary, ANC, 22 February 1961, TNA 540/20/no folio; Mugambi to Provincial Police Commander, Dar es Salaam, 21 February 1961, TNA 540/20/no folio.

43. 'Congress yapewa wazi habari zenu uoza', *Mwafrika*, 4 March 1961. All translations from Swahili are by the author.

44. 'A.N.C. – Kahama Clarifies Ban', *Tanganyika Standard*, 12 July 1961.

45. 'Extract from Tanganyika Intelligence Report – February 1960', CO 822/2127/4; GN No. 956 of 1959, *Tanganyika Gazette*; 'Omido Claims A.N.C. Mail is Censored', *Tanganyika Standard*, 20 July 1961; Press Release 'Expulsion order against Frederick Esau Omido', Tanganyika Information Services, 14 November 1961, TNA 540/PP/3/1; *Kilio cha Mwenyeji*, December 1961, TNA 561/17/88. Omido had earlier joined the Tanganyika National Party, founded by David Stirling and very much a 'multi-racialist' party until, rather mercenary-like, he quit it to join Mtemvu's ANC. F. E. Omido to Lennox-Boyd, 4 January 1958, CO 822/1368/3. TANU's first organizing secretary, Domie Ockoshi, was also a Kenyan deported in 1954 by the Tanganyikan Government, in his case for connections with Mau Mau. Listowel, *Making of Tanzania*, p. 231, fn 2.

46. GN No. 657, *Tanganyika Gazette*, 17 March 1961; Sanga to Turnbull, 8 March 1961,

RH MSS Brit. Emp. 365 Box 121/4/160.
47. 'Big bid by A.N.C. in Poll', *Tanganyika Standard*, 23 December 1961.
48. Omido to Kahama, 21 July 1961, TNA 540/20/69. See also press release of Omido, 12 August 1960, TNA 561/17/21.
49. Statement by Zuberi Mtemvu to the Fourth Committee at its 1098th meeting, n. d. (*ca.* March 1961), TNA 540/33/no folio.
50. 'Extract from Tanganyika Intelligence Report – February 1960', CO 822/2127/4; 'Extract from Tanganyika Intelligence Report – October 1960', CO 822/2127/12; Chancery (Peking) to Far Eastern Department, Foreign Office, 14 January 1961, CO 822/2127/25.
51. 'Extract from Tanganyika Intelligence Report – April 1961', CO 822/2127/46A; Dmitry Dolidze to Zuberi Mtemvu, 21 June 1962, TNA 540/19/II/19.
52. 'I advanced Uhuru Date – Mtemvu', *Tanganyika Standard*, 25 April 1961; 'Extract from Tanganyika Intelligence Report – April 1961', CO 822/2127/46A; Mtemvu to H. Eggebreck (Berlin), 26 May 1961, TNA 561/32/I/151.
53. ANC press release, 29 June 1961, TNA 561/17/69.
54. Secretariat to J. C. Morgan, 1 September 1961, CO 822/2127/51.
55. Zuberi Mtemvu to Sheikh Ahmed, Cairo Swahili Radio Services, printed in *Tanganyika Standard*, 16 April 1958; 'A.N.C. Aid: Egyptian Talks of 'An Open Secret'', *Tanganyika Standard*, 14 March 1961; 'Extract from Tanganyika Intelligence Report – February 1960', CO 822/2127/4; 'Extract from Tanganyika Intelligence Report – April 1961', CO 822/2127/46A.
56. 'Extract from Tanganyika Intelligence Report – February 1960', CO 822/2127/4; Michael Sanga to Secretary, All Africa Peoples' Conference, Accra, 30 December 1960, TNA 540/17/C/33.
57. Moshi A. Sekibo to Mtemvu, n. d. (*ca.* early February 1960), TNA 561/32/I/no folio; Mtemvu to Sekibo, 11 February 1960, TNA 561/32/I/13; Acting General Secretary ANC to General Secretary, Afro-Shirazi Party, 22 February 1960, TNA 561/32/I/no folio. Kaikai was expelled shortly after for stealing party funds. Mtemvu to Kweigira, n. d. (*ca.* August 1960), TNA 561/32/I/123.
58. Mtemvu to Sheikh Ali Muhsin Ali, 2 June 1961, TNA 561/32/I/162; 'Extract from Tanganyika Intelligence Report – June 1961', CO 822/2127/47.
59. Mtemvu to Steven Mhando, 10 June 1961, TNA 561/32/I/165. Some Tanganyikan Muslims also used this route to reach Cairo for religious training. Francis N. Magliozzito, American Embassy Mogadishu to American Embassy Dar es Salaam, 6 August 1963, US National Archives (hereafter USNA) RG 59 Box 4057, College Park, Maryland.
60. Mtemvu to Sheikh A. R. Mohamed (ZNP), 8 January 1962, TNA 561/32/II/140; 'Hizbu yamuunga Zuberi Mtemvu', *Mwafrika na Taifa*, 6 October 1962; 'ZPPP yasaidia Mtemvu uchaguzi', *Mwafrika*, 5 October 1962. The Arab-Islamic orientation of the ZNP made it a logical ally for AMNUT. Ali Muhsin did invite AMNUT's secretary to appear before the ZNP's central committee, but cynically opted not to support AMNUT because he thought its policies divisive and did not believe Christianity posed a threat to Tanganyika's Muslims. Mohamed Said, *The Life and Times of Abdulwahid Sykes: The Untold Story of the Muslim Struggle against British Colonialism in Tanganyika* (London: Minerva Press, 1998), p. 251.
61. Chancery (Peking) to Far Eastern Department, Foreign Office, 14 January 1961, CO 822/2127/25; Chipaka to Obok, 29 April 1961, TNA 561/32/I/143; 'Extract from Tanganyika Intelligence Summary for October 1961', CO 822/2127/56; Mtemvu to Odinga, 14 December 1961, TNA 561/32/II/15.
62. 'A.N.C. Appeal to non-Africans', *Kilio cha Mwenyeji*, 7 December 1958, in RH MSS Brit. Emp. 365 Box 123/5/94.
63. See, for example, the statement by Zuberi Mtemvu at the 1157th Meeting of the Fourth Committee of the United Nations Trusteeship Council, n. d. (*ca.* October 1961), TNA 540/33.
64. Speech of Kassimu S. Baina, ANC Treasurer, 21 March 1959, TNA 540/20/19. This

(mis)reading of Qur'anic verse 49:13 was also prominent in Zanzibar. See Jonathon Glassman, 'Sorting Out the Tribes: The creation of racial identities in the colonial Zanzibar's newspaper wars', *Journal of African History* 41 (2000), p. 410.

65. Report of ANC speeches at Arnautoglu Hall, 11 June 1961, TNA 540/17C/95.

66. On Biti Titi Mohamed and Oscar Kambona's racial views, see respectively Jonathan Glassman, 'Between Two Worlds: Diasporic Imaginations and Racial Politics in Colonial Zanzibar, 1927–1957', in 'Reasserting Connections, Commonalities, and Cosmopolitanism: The Western Indian Ocean since 1800', conference held at Yale University, 3–5 November 2000, and William Duggan and John Civille, *Tanzania and Nyerere: A Study of Ujamaa and Nationhood* (New York: Orbis Books, 1976), p. 94; for middle-level party figures see Bienen, *Tanzania*, pp. 204–6; on *Uhuru* see Pritchard to Duncan Sandys, 2 March 1962, DO 892/168/14 and Pratt, *Critical Phase*, p. 113; for a general overview see James R. Brennan, 'Nation, Race and Urbanization in Dar es Salaam, Tanzania, 1916-1976' (Ph.D. thesis, Northwestern University, 2002), chapters 5 & 6. Under-estimations of TANU's robust racialism undermines not only academic treatments like Pratt, *Critical Phase*, that overstate the effect of Nyerere's anti-racialism, but also more critical writers who identify the significance of race but mistakenly understand ANC solely in those terms – see Aminzade's otherwise quite valuable article, 'The Politics of Race and Nation', cited above.

67. *Assembly Debates (Hansard)*, Tanganyika National Assembly, 10th to 20th October, 1961, cols. 309–17 and 329–33; Omido to Nsherenguzi, 20 October 1961, TNA 561/EL/60/135. The TANU government ensured that ANC would not benefit from the issue by prohibiting the party from conducting a parade through Dar es Salaam to protest the citizenship bill. Marijani Shabani to Provincial Police Commander, 20 October 1961, TNA 540/6/42; Provincial Police Commander to District Chairman, ANC, 21 October 1961, TNA 540/6/43.

68. Saleh Ali Ngawe to Zuberi Mtemvu, 31 January 1959, TNA 540/32/58; Tanganyika Students in Liberia to Zuberi Mtemvu, n. d. (*ca.* January 1961), TNA 540/17/C/42. Emphasis in original.

69. ANC circular, 21 November 1960, TNA 540/17/C/5. For TANU statements see editorials in *Uhuru*, 23 December 1961; *ibid.*, 6 January and 3 March 1962.

70. 'Extracts from Tanganyika Intelligence Summary Report – May 1959', CO 822/1363/267.

71. *Tanganyika Standard*, 29 May 1962.

72. See B.N. Kalembo to Secretary General, Tanganyika ANC, 10 January 1961, TNA 540/17/C/41, and other correspondence in this file.

73. For example, Justino Mpondo had been alienated from TANU and fought for the Newala seat in the 1960 national election as an ANC candidate, despite having been among the country's most vocal advocates of multi-racialism and UTP. J. Gus Liebnow, *Colonial Rule and Political Development in Tanzania: The Case of the Makonde* (Evanston, IL: Northwestern University Press, 1971), p. 271. I thank Andrew Burton for bringing this to my attention.

74. 'One-seat Poll for President "a Waste" – ANC', *Tanganyika Standard*, 25 April 1962; 'A.N.C. ban urged by Kwimba', *Tanganyika Standard*, 19 May 1962; G. Andrew Maguire, *Toward 'Uhuru' in Tanzania: The Politics of Participation* (Cambridge: Cambridge University Press, 1969), pp. 300–10, 338–40, 345.

75. I. K. Makwaia (Shinyanga) to Minister for Local Government, 21 September 1961, TNA 561/EL/60/133; E. Makaidi, ANC press release, 24 March 1962, TNA 561/17/81; Joseph Kimalando (ANC Moshi) to Mtemvu, 21 April 1962, TNA 561/32/II/262; Joseph Mkinga Kindamba (Songea) to Mtemvu, 12 June 1962, TNA 561/32/II/315.

76. E. Makaidi, ANC press release, n. d. (*ca.* August 1962), TNA 561/17/105.

77. In June 1962, ANC headquarters dispatched membership cards as follows: Bukoba, 30,000 cards; Moshi, 5,000; Musoma, 2,000; Mahenge, 1,000; Tukuyu, 1,000; Arusha, 1,000; East Region, 1,000; and Central Region, 1,000. J. Juma Abdallah Mpitakunza to Joseph Kindamba, 25 June 1962, TNA 561/32/II/320.

78. Clement K. Nsherenguzi to Mtemvu, 5 May 1962, TNA 561/32/II/no folio.
79. Mtemvu to W. K. Gao (Mombasa), 19 May 1962, TNA 561/32/II/297; Göran Hydén, *TANU Yajenga Nchi: Political Development in Rural Tanzania* (Lund: UNISKOL Bokförlaget Universitet och Skola, 1968), pp. 129–33; report of ANC speeches at Arnautoglu Hall, 11 June 1961, TNA 540/17C/95; Kenneth Robert Curtis, 'Capitalism fettered: state, merchant and peasant in northwestern Tanzania, 1917–1960' (Ph.D. thesis, University of Wisconsin-Madison, 1989), p. 681. Kiwanuka notes that 19 independents defeated TANU candidates in the 51-seat Bukoba District Council election in 1963, but explains this split in terms of independent Catholic teachers upset with the 'quality' of the area's largely Muslim TANU leadership. Government nullified the elections and banned the teachers from participating in politics. K. M. Kiwanuka, 'The Politics of Islam in Bukoba District' (B.A. thesis, University of Dar es Salaam, 1973), pp. 57–8. The ANC had been active in West Lake since 1960, when it successfully intervened in support of the Bahaya Coffee Planters Association to prevent a marketing monopoly by its rival, the TANU-supported Bukoba Native Coffee Co-operative Union. Mtemvu to H. Rugizibwa (Director, Bahaya Coffee Planters Association), 22 July 1960, TNA 561/32/I/135; Mtemvu to A. J. Kweigira (Provincial Chair, ANC Bukoba), 22 July 1960, TNA 561/32/I/136. See Curtis, 'Capitalism fettered', Chapter 10, for an analysis of the region's social and personality conflicts.
80. 'Time to Stop Card-burning', *Tanganyika Standard*, 14 July 1962; 'Police Cancel all A.N.C. Meetings in Lake Region', *Tanganyika Standard*, 13 June 1962; Maguire, *Towards 'Uhuru'*, p. 349. Public burnings occurred in Dar es Salaam, Mafia, Ifakara, and Mwanza, among other places. Maguire notes that other accounts state that Nyerere's picture had not yet been burned when some in the audience turned violent. This was likely the apex of ANC's support in the region; its publicity secretary, Emmanuel Makaidi, claimed a membership of 9,212 in Lake Region and 32,000 in West Lake. *Tanganyika Standard*, 13 June 1962.
81. 'Press Release, Chief Francis Masanja, MP, Bukwimba Constituency', n. d., TNA 540/PP/5/no folio; 'Chifu Masanja katoka Tanu kaingia Congress', *Mwafrika*, 25 September 1962; Maguire, *Towards 'Uhuru'*, p. 352
82. Saidi Mikuyah to Editor, *Tanganyika Standard*, n. d. (*ca.* May 1962), TNA 540/PP/4/2; published in *Tanganyika Standard*, 28 May 1962. Beneath Mikuyah's signature on this letter in TNA 540/PP/4, an ANC party file, is a note reading 'A shadowed letter c/o A.N.C'.
83. William H. Friedland, 'Co-operation, Conflict, and Conscription: TANU-TFL Relations, 1955–1964', in Jeffrey Butler and A. A. Castagno (eds), *Transition in African Politics* (New York: Praeger, 1967), p. 87; Andrew Coulson, *Tanzania: A Political Economy* (Oxford: Clarendon Press, 1982), pp. 138–40. Michael Kamaliza, former TFL president and Minister of Health and Labor when these laws passed, described the bill that mandated each trade union to join and obey TFL in this Orwellian way: 'There is no intention of the Government to control the labour movement. After all, as I said earlier, this is the workers' government. Now who should control who? We are all one, working for the betterment of our people', *Tanganyika Parliamentary Debates (Hansard)*, 5 June to 3 July 1962, col. 1060.
84. 'Detention Bill Goes Through', *Tanganyika Standard*, 28 September 1962; James Read, 'Human Rights in Tanzania', in Colin Legum and Geoffrey Mmari (eds), *Mwalimu: The Influence of Nyerere* (London: James Currey, 1995), p. 138.
85. Carter to Hickman, 11 September 1962, DO 168/5/42; Tumbo to Mtemvu, 1 October 1962, TNA 540/33/no folio; 'Rebuff for New 'Tumbo' Party', *Tanganyika Standard*, 30 August 1962; minutes of ANC ruling party, 18 November 1962, TNA 561/26/no folio. Government denied Tumbo permission to contest the 1962 presidential race as the PDP candidate. 'P.D.P. Call to Boycott Election', *Tanganyika Standard*, 22 September 1962.
86. Letter from Musa Kwikima, *Tanganyika Standard*, 17 September 1962.
87. Letter of H. S. El-Alawy, *Tanganyika Standard*, 20 August 1959.

88. 'Extract from Tanganyika Intelligence Report – October 1960', CO 822/2127/12; 'Congress na AMNUT zaungana!', *Ngurumo*, 25 April 1961; 'A.N.C. Still Alive, claims official', *Tanganyika Standard*, 20 November 1962. Personnel fluidity between ANC and AMNUT was driven by job openings – Sheikh Saleh H. Muhsin, a member of AMNUT's managing committee, joined ANC in May 1962 as party treasurer after ANC's former treasurer resigned. Mtemvu to Editor, *Sunday News*, 26 May 1962, in TNA 561/26/122.

89. 'Objects of the A.N.C'., draft, 3 October 1962, TNA 540/16/no folio.

90. 'A.N.C. Rally Banned', *Tanganyika Standard*, 27 July 1962; 'Nyerere is TANU candidate', *ibid.*, 1 August 1962; Zuberi Mtemvu, circular entitled 'Ushinde Ulio Haramu', 6 November 1962, TNA 540/PP/1/no folio; 'Bendera ya Congress imeangushwa', *Mwafrika*, 25 September 1962; Mariam K. Slater, *African Odyssey: An Anthropological Adventure* (Garden City, NY: Anchor Books, 1976), pp. 252–3.

91. 'A.N.C. Rally Banned', *Tanganyika Standard*, 27 July 1962; 'A.N.C. Refused Permission to Hold Meeting', *Tanganyika Standard*, 11 August 1962; 'A.N.C. Alleges its Voters Told: Poll for Tanu Only', *Tanganyika Standard*, 21 August 1962; *Reporter*, 1 September 1962; 'Tanu Denies 'Ballot Rigging'', *Tanganyika Standard*, 22 August 1962.

92. *Reporter*, 1 September 1962; 'Presidential Election', *Reporter*, 15 September 1962.

93. 'Congress yaungana na TANU?', *Mwafrika na Taifa*, 11 August 1962; Zuberi Mtemvu to Z. G. Kashumba, Kamachumu, 9 August 1962, TNA 540/16; 'Detention Bill goes through', *Tanganyika Standard*, 28 September 1962.

94. Results in *Tanganyika News Review*, November 1962. Mtemvu polled strongest in Same (6.64%), Ukerewe (5.12%), Bukoba (4.93%), Newala (4.67%), and Singida (4.36%).

95. 'Shake-up in A.N.C'., *Tanganyika Standard*, 6 November 1962.

96. 'Tanganyika Rejects Racialism', *Tanganyika Standard*, 10 November 1962. The TANU press release argued: 'The explanation of the paradox is quite simple. Tanu is the party to which our people had already given their mandate to govern; and in the minds of the people, it followed that Tanu's presidential candidate was therefore the leader they had already chosen. Many of them, particularly the more unsophisticated, could not see why they should be asked to re-register simply in order to repeat the choice they had already made in 1960'. 63% of registered voters voted.

97. 'Presidential Elections', *Reporter*, 10 November 1962; 'Congress ivunje chama', *Mwafrika na Taifa*, 10 November 1962.

98. Press Release, Zuberi Mtemvu, n. d. (*ca.* 16-18 November 1962), TNA 540/PP/5/no folio.

99. *Tanganyika Standard*, 19 November 1962. At a fascinating ANC party meeting on 18 November 1962, however, Mtemvu prevaricated on his suggestion that ANC members join TANU, telling them to join whichever party they wished, and only grudgingly admitted that he himself had joined TANU. Minutes in TNA 561/26/no folio.

100. Quoted in 'A.N.C. Still Alive, Claims Official', *Tanganyika Standard*, 20 November 1962.

101. 'TANU Opening its Doors to All', *Tanganyika Standard*, 28 November 1962.

102. 'Hugs All Round as Mtemvu Rejoins TANU', *Tanganyika Standard*, 23 January 1963; 'Lost Sheep Return', *Reporter*, 2 February 1963.

103. *Reporter*, 10 November 1962; press release dated 14 January 1963, DO 168/7/2; Pius Msekwa, 'The Decision to Establish a Democratic One-Party State in Tanzania: A Case Study', *Taamuli* 5/2 (1972), pp. 34–48.

104. Press release by A. J. Muyinga dated 26 November 1962, TNA 540/PD/1.

105. Saileni Press Release, 18 November 1962 TNA 540/PP/no folio; Saileni to ANC Regional/Branch Secretaries, 21 November 1962, TNA 540/PC/no folio; 'Live A.N.C. Elects New President', *Tanganyika Standard*, 11 December 1962.

106. ANC press release entitled 'High Treachery!' by Rashid Ngurupi, n. d. (*ca.* December 1962), TNA 540/PP/1/no folio.

107. See voter list in Saileni to Ngala, 22 December 1962, TNA 540/16/no folio.

108. 'A.N.C. Banned', *Reporter*, 27 April 1963.

109. ANC Press Release, The 'MAAS' (Moshi Afro-Asian Solidarity) Conference, J. H. Saileni, 16 February 1963, TNA 540/PP/1/no folio; *Kilio cha Mwenyeji*, vol. III no. I, n.

d. (*ca.* February 1963), TNA 540/PP/5/no folio. Emphasis in original.

110. Saileni to Ngala, 22 December 1962, TNA 540/16/no folio; Saileni to Regional Commissioner, Dar es Salaam, 20 February 1963, TNA 540/PP/2/34; *Kilio cha Mwenyeji*, 30 March 1963, TNA 540/PP/1/no folio.

111. Regional Commissioner, Dar es Salaam to Jackson Hadad Saileni, 6 March 1963, TNA 540/PP/2/no folio; Registrar of the High Court to J.H. Sailena [sic], 9 April 1963, TNA 540/PP/1/no folio.

112. *Reporter*, 3 February 1962.

113. Julius Nyerere, *Democracy and the Party System* (Dar es Salaam: Tanganyika Standard Ltd, 1963).

114. J. H. Saileni, 'Demokrasi Laghai ya Tanganyika – Jibu kwa Dr. Julius K. Nyerere', April 1963, TNA 540/PP/1; an English version entitled 'The Pseudo-Democracy in Tanganyika' is enclosed in Hennemeyer to Department of State, 25 April 1963, USNA RG 59 Box 4056. Frene Ginwala, then editor of the monthly *Spearhead* after her dismissal as editor of the *Nationalist*, attacked Nyerere's arguments on Marxist grounds in an editorial entitled 'No Party State?'. *Spearhead*, February 1963, enclosed in *ibid.*; Leonhart to Secretary of State, 7 May 1963, USNA RG 59 Box 4056.

115. MacRae to Hickman, 20 May 1963, DO 168/7/17.

116. 'Hammer and the Nut', *Nationalist*, 21 April 1963, enclosed in DO 168/7/15.

117. Jackson Saileni, circular entitled 'Dr Nyerere's Government Starts Employment of Force in Tanganyika Politics', 29 April 1963, TNA 540/PP/1. This account is also derived from 'Rais wa Congress ndani apimwe ubongo', *Mwafrika na Taifa*, 27 April 1963, and 'Ilikwendaje kesi ya Saileni', *Mwafrika na Taifa*, 4 May 1963.

118. MacRae to Price Jones, 4 October 1963, DO 168/5/88.

119. 'Saileni's Call for Minister Refused', *Tanganyika Standard*, 30 May 1963; MacRae to Hickman, 20 May 1963, DO 168/7/17; 'Saileni Charged', *Reporter*, 8 June 1963.

120. 'Saileni Sentenced', *Reporter*, 22 June 1963; 'Eight A.N.C. Men go to Court', *Tanganyika Standard*, 14 May 1963; 'Convicted A.N.C. Men Freed by High Court', *Tanganyika Standard*, 3 October 1963; MacRae to Price Jones, 4 October 1963, DO 168/5/88.

121. 'Zuberi Mtemvu Dies in Dar', *Daily News*, 21 September 1999; 'Mwinyi ahudhuria mazishi ya Mtemvu', *Uhuru*, 24 September 1999.

122. Listowel, *The Making of Tanganyika*, p. 309; 'New Attack on Nyerere by Mtemvu', *Tanganyika Standard*, 22 May 1961; letter of Emmanuel Makaidi, *Tanganyika Standard*, 9 May 1962.

123. Hydén, *TANU yajenga nchi*, p. 132.

124. 'Tanganyika Rejects Racialism', *Tanganyika Standard*, 10 November 1962.

125. *Kiongozi*, 1 August 1964; Gordon to Department of State, 10 October 1964, USNA RG 59 Box 2689; Gordon to Department of State, 29 December 1964, *ibid.*

126. Oscar Kambona, Pamphlet entitled 'Programme for Free Popular and Democratic Republic of Tanzania', 9 December 1971, library collection, Tanzania National Museum. Emphases in original.

127. 'Tanganyika Tightrope', *Socialist Commentary*, April 1958, p. 15; quoted in Bennett, 'Outline History', p. 26. I thank Gary Burgess for this citation.

128. Letter from J.B. Bukwe, *Mwafrika*, 9 January 1960.

129. Letter from B. Sam Kajunjumele, *Tanganyika Standard*, 16 December 1963.

Part IV

The Nation Reconsidered

Fifteen

∧∧∧∧∧∧∧∧∧∧∧∧∧∧∧∧∧∧∧∧

Engendering & Gendering
African Nationalism
Rethinking the Case of
Tanganyika (Tanzania)*

SUSAN GEIGER

The term 'origin' does not mean the process by which the existent came into being, but rather what emerges from the process of becoming, and disappearing. Origin is an eddy in the stream of becoming.[1]

From Benedict Anderson's concept of 'imagined communities' through Partha Chatterjee's 'difference nationalism' to Mahmood Mamdani's division of African nationalisms into 'mainstream' and 'radical' versions,[2] scholars have grappled with the relationship of the (variously characterized) nationalisms of the formerly colonized to the material and ideological impact of European colonization.[3]

To a large extent, African nationalism, like European nationalism, and even when studied by historians, has invariably been treated as a phase in the evolution of African politics – a story of men, their movements and parties, and struggles over power. Women among African colonized populations, while sometimes credited with supportive 'roles' in the parties, armies, or peasant protests associated with anti-colonial nationalist moments, are as often, especially in recent years, relegated to a symbolic representational place or role: protector of family, tradition and spiritual purity – a place or role said to be created and manipulated for the masculine nationalist project.[4] Even when women's 'participation' is included, the larger narrative remains one in which nationalism itself – whether perceived as evil, failed, triumphal or flawed – is frequently essentialized as a masculine political project based on men's activities and ideas.[5]

Because his overarching goal is to explicate bifurcated despotism – 'the hallmark of colonialism' – as the most important inheritance passed on to postcolonial African states, and the 'impediments to democratization' as colonial rule's 'most important institutional legacy',[6] it is perhaps not surprising that Mahmood Mamdani's provocative analysis of the continent's colonial and postcolonial history does not include a complex or nuanced treatment of African nationalism *per se*.[7] Rather, Mamdani offers unproblematic standard generalizations about African nationalism as a 'struggle of embryonic middle and working classes, the native strata in limbo, for entry into civil society', and as a post-World War II phenomenon in which 'nationalist movements successfully linked urban protest against racial exclusion in civil society to rural movements against the uncustomary powers of Native Authority chiefs'.[8] This definition fits his analysis of the bifurcated despotism of the colonial state – the racialism of colonialism in urban civil society and the tribalism of colonialism as enforced through Native Authority rule and customary law – and supports his argument for the centrality of the 'native question' and politics to the colonial enterprise. But it does not, in my view, accurately reflect African nationalism's diverse meanings and manifestations,[9] nor the continuing significance of varied paths taken to political independence.

My disagreement is not with Mamdani's characterization of post-colonial African states nor with his insight that only a politics that dismantled both despotisms could have led to democratization; rather, it is with his selective use of Tanzania's postcolonial history. However accurate in its assessment of increasingly centralized authoritarian rule by Julius Nyerere through TANU/CCM,[10] Mamdani's analysis erases, while it oversimplifies, important elements of nationalism as it emerged in the former British Trust Territory, elements that continue to shape the Tanzanian nation.

In part, this erasure seems to stem from a dichotomization or bifurcation central to his larger argument: like the colonial officers themselves, who established and then sought to rule through 'native authorities', Mamdani attaches something called 'culture' to the tribe – to the rural and bounded – even as he simultaneously acknowledges the multi-ethnic character of many presumably homogenous groups, and even though he details the complex and changing role of 'culture' in urban ethnically-based conflict involving migrant workers in South Africa.[11] Thus, in the process of challenging existing 'Africanist' scholarship on the issue of South African exceptionalism and on 'tribalism' as the primary curse of the continent, Mamdani imposes a few problematic distinctions of his own: culture, albeit fluid and changing, 'diverse and differentiated',[12] as essentially located in the realm of traditional/tribal/customary law – the realm of rural peasants or peasant migrants, who eventually resisted and struggled against the despotic power of Native Authorities; nationalism as a product of urban disaffection and the struggle against the racialized inequalities of colonial rule; and nationalist politics as the method nationalist leaders used to bring the two anti-colonial forces together. Bifurcated despotism as an overarching theme leads to a bifurcated analysis: Native Authority despotism on one side, Central Administration despotism on the other; urban civil society on this side, rural tribal society on the other; on this side, 'conservative' states, on the other, 'radical'. While this approach makes for a tidy theoretical model, it requires fixing a studiously blind eye on everything that does not fit on either side of the relevant coin. For example, classic labor migrants seem to fit, but what about other important flows of people and ideas between 'civil' and 'tribal' societies? What about the force of cultural concepts and understandings that can be traced neither to 'tribal' tradition nor its colonial foil, 'invented' tradition?

In this chapter, I look at the ways in which women activists in TANU, the Tanganyika African National Union, engendered and gendered the nationalist movement, performing and producing nationalism in Tanganyika during the critical period, 1955–61. I do so in order to revisit two interrelated issues: nationalism's origins, and the persistence of national commitment in postcolonial Tanzania. I argue that this persistence has as much to do with broad 'cultural' as with shared 'political' understandings of what it means to be Tanzanian. Moreover, it is less a product of submission to the state (as many scholars would have it) than of regular subversions, avoidances and renegotiations of the terms of engagement with authoritarian rule in postcolonial Tanzania. I also use the lens of TANU women's experience to question the intellectual evolutionary conflation of nationalism, nationalist movement, the nation and the nation-state into one thing called 'nationalism', to suggest that these 'figments' must be considered historically distinct. Finally, my interpretation of TANU women's narratives challenges theoretical positions staked out in both feminist and non-feminist terrain, including the construction of the nation and nationalism as invariably masculinist; (the modernity/ traditional masculine/feminine binary); and the related view that male African nationalists simply appropriated and 'used' women participants for their own purposes, discarding or transforming them into symbols of the new nation at will.

First, to the vexed matters of culture and tribes. To restrict something called 'culture' to the realm of the tribes of the colonial project is, in the case of Tanganyika, to ignore the relevance of one among many of the continuously invented populations central to East African history[13] – people who for various, diverse and changing reasons came at some point to identify, often in conjunction with other identities, as Swahili. I will not engage the question of Swahili origins here, although the acceptance or rejection of 'the Swahili' as African has, for obvious reasons, influenced their place in the meta-narrative of Tanzanian nationalism.[14] To understand the complex ways in which claims to Swahili identity became, over time, expressions of a national identity, we need to avoid both Tanzania's dominant nationalist narrative and literate Swahili culture's version of itself.[15] This latter version celebrates 'pure Swahili persons' – a 'people few in number ... who have gone serenely and happily on, while their invaders – various waves of outsider Africans, Arabs, Iranians, Portuguese, Germans, and British have disappeared', 'leaving behind' their 'traces' and 'vestiges'.[16] It has also framed the 'Waswahili Ni Nani?' debate which dichotomizes and poses an opposition of African and Arab by asking whether the Swahili are really one or the other, or really both and therefore neither.[17]

While Swahili literati, German officials and scholars of the East African coast argued over the nature, boundaries and constitution of Swahili culture and ethnicity, men and women – in increasing numbers, for varied reasons, and in many parts of East and East Central Africa – adopted, claimed, sometimes abandoned and variously shaped Swahili social identity. During the last quarter of the nineteenth century, it was African slaves and slave descendants who in negotiating their 'access to the institutions, cultural attributes and prestige of the freeborn coastal community' were 'the first to make widespread use of Mswahili as a term of self-identification'.[18] Although Thaddeus Sunseri has argued that women slaves saw little advantage in becoming Swahili because of the relative autonomy they experienced as agricultural laborers and as *vibarua* (persons hired out daily by their owners),[19] his argument seems to rest on a view of 'Swahiliness' as fixed rather than as an identity in the making.[20] In any case, as has been thoroughly documented for Kenya, women previously identified with other groups did indeed 'become Swahili', and in Tanganyika became active proponents of and participants in non-ortho-dox, popular versions of Islam, notably sufi mysticism and the Qadirrya brotherhood.[21] Meanwhile, in interior towns long associated with Arab ivory and slave traders like Tabora and Ujiji, Africans working indepen-dently as 'guides, porters and/or hunters' began calling themselves *Waungwana*, a term that meant 'freed men' but was synonymous with 'urban Swahili gentleman' and was expressed in the adoption of the Swahili language, as well as in aspects of dress and culture.[22]

During thirty years of German colonialism, from 1885 to the end of World War I, Swahili culture and identity became firmly associated with connecting nodes and links of armed and moral resistance, networks of communication, and centers of Islamic learning and popular religious practice. Expanding into the interior of East Africa since the early part of the nineteenth century, the Swahili language had become, by the early twentieth, the language of Islamic, mission and government-sponsored education, and most importantly, the language of popular political expression.[23] When German East Africa became a British Mandate after World War I, the British replaced most of the Swahili officials who had worked for the Germans with 'tribal' Native Authorities. But Swahili remained the most widespread political and educational language. As John Lonsdale has observed, common political languages are produced in historical process.[24] This is certainly true of Swahili, where political poetry, coded messages and the sharply satirical songs performed by organized groups were produced throughout the country by a wide range of women and men, from the most to the least cosmopolitan.[25]

In colonial Tanganyika, whatever else it meant to 'be Swahili', it meant identifying with a 'trans-tribal' African society – a society open to men and women from throughout the interior and from other parts of the coast, as well as from other parts of Africa – who 'became' Swahili through intermarriage, through mixed parentage, through choice and by birth. In a cultural milieu characterized by adherence – sometimes strict, sometimes loose – to Islam and to regular use of the Swahili language, they were workers, traders, craftsmen, domestic and civil servants and, where land was available to them, peasant farmers. Swahili women farmed, made and sold foodstuffs on the streets and in the markets, brewed beer, and participated in *ngoma* and *taarab* groups; they owned houses and rented rooms, in some cases to or as prostitutes. They were rich and they were poor. The Swahili gave their name to the most characteristic housing type in urban and peri-urban areas – not the stone house of elite coastal history, but the rectangular 'Swahili' house with three rooms off each side of a central passage way leading to a back courtyard used for cooking and washing, and behind that, to a latrine.

What is not in question, then, is that by the late colonial period people who identified as Swahili, without necessarily abandoning other affiliations, constituted substantial communities not only in the colonial capital, Dar es Salaam, but in the major towns and settlements adjacent to rural areas of the interior. Although typically subject to race-based urban colonial governance, most were neither aspiring to European – in this case, British – colonial lifestyles, nor enamoured of colonial Christianity. They were Muslim, with their own religious hierarchies and community leaders. Those (virtually all males) who were educated in Western schools and to varying degrees fluent in English, nevertheless conducted their daily affairs in what had already become Tanzania's national language, Swahili.[26]

Given the British administration's determination to fix Africans in tribes, it is hardly surprising that, as late as the 1950s, there was still no official recognition of a Swahili population. J.P. Moffett's *Handbook of Tanganyika* (2nd edition) offers telling evidence of the difficulties colonial officials were having – as late as 1958 when the second edition was published – in dealing with the instability of the 'tribal' categories.[27] Moffett's notes on three single-spaced pages of 'tribal names in Tanganyika' used for the *Handbook* (with an 'AT' placed before the name of an 'Authentic Tribe') include literally dozens of references to reclassifications (e.g. Kilindi, 'classified as Sambaa, 22,288 Kilindi wrongly shown as Nguu in the 1948 census'); new classifications (e.g. Baraguyu, 'to be classified as Kwavi in next Census'), and amalgamations (e.g., Haya 'includes Mwani, Nyambo and Ziba'). Two non-African (undoubtedly meaning 'non-native', to the British) populations were recognized: Asian, a category which included Arabs, Indians, Comorians, Somalis[28] and 'Shirazi', and European. Township populations were classified as European, Indian, Goan, Arab, Somali, Colored, Other and African. The administrative obsession with the relevance of 'tribe' to everything African not surprisingly carried into an early secret memo on the 21 'leading personalities' of the Tanganyika African Association (TAA) (TANU's precursor) and TANU. Thus, we are introduced to Abdulwahid Sykes (Zulu), Selemani Takidiri (Manyema), Warte Bertie Mwanjisi (Nyakyusa), and Julius Nyerere (Zanaki), among others.[29]

Just as it would have further complicated a situation that already perplexed British officials to acknowledge, let alone authenticate, a 'non-tribe' like the Swahili, recognizing the presence of a mobile, porous population spread throughout much of Tanganyika would have required Mamdani to consider urban-rural, rural-urban, and inter-urban interactions of African people taking place in the interstices of bifurcated colonial rule. This is not to say that people who identified as Swahili stood outside the colonial system; it is to say that they complicated it, and by extension, would complicate any theories about it. In addition, the Swahili presence in Tanganyika complicates comparisons of nationalism and nationalist movements – or even of 'radical' and 'mainstream' versions – throughout the African continent, making it as problematic to assume the validity of specific historical analogies within the continent as to accept Eurocentric ones.[30]

At the time representatives of Tanganyika African Association (TAA) branches (many of which were moribund) met in Dar es Salaam in July 1954 to transform that association into TANU and elect Julius Nyerere as president, anti-native authority and/or anti-colonial sentiment existed in many parts of the country and had in some places turned into active protests for all the reasons frequently cited.[31] When Nyerere and his male colleagues (including several notables of Dar es Salaam's Swahili community) claimed for TANU and nationalist politics the unsettled and ambiguous space opened up by the dialectical force of colonialism's post-war crisis and discontent and growing self-confidence on the part of the colonized, that space was relatively undefined and hence very much under construction. Nyerere, an astute, thoughtful, Western-educated teacher, came to leadership prepared to formulate Tanganyika's nationalist ideology. But as Benedict Anderson has pointed out, nationalism has never simply been about 'self-consciously held political ideologies', but has necessarily involved 'the large cultural systems that preceded it, out of which – as well as against which – it came into being'.[32] Referring to Tanganyika's nationalist origins, John Iliffe wrote:

> No state, especially no colonial state, creates a nation. A state creates subjects. The subjects create the nation and they bring into the process the whole of their historical experience.[33]

More recently, Frederick Cooper has pointed out that it is important to bear in mind that 'the nation was not the only unit that [African] people imagined', and that 'the predominance of the nation-state in post-1960 Africa resulted not from the exclusive focus of African imaginations on the nation but from the fact that the nation was imaginable to colonial rulers as well'.[34]

Although neither Nyerere nor other members of the TANU central committee predicted, much less planned, it this way in 1954, 'middle-aged'[35] Muslim women with little or no Western education – women with strong attachments to Dar es Salaam's trans-tribal Swahili communities – initiated and then sustained the transformation of TANU into a popular nationalist movement.[36]

Introduced and brought into the party through the mobilizing efforts of one of their own, Bibi Titi Mohamed,[37] these women were instrumental in creating and spreading the basic tenets of Tanganyika's nationalism, bringing to bear their historical experience and cultural understandings to bear on TANU politics-in-the-making.[38] While it seems likely that Nyerere and his organizing secretary Oscar Kambona were initially as surprised as the British administration when 5,000 women had joined TANU by October 1955,[39] their importance to Tanganyikan nationalism was thereby established. Through their *ngoma*, *taarab* and *lelemama* (dance/musical) groups, women both transmitted and created information about TANU and the independence movement.[40] Moreover, when in early 1956 TANU began taking its organizing campaign to the countryside, women's networks, often based in Swahili communities and especially responsive to the dynamic and charismatic leadership of Bibi Titi Mohamed, proved crucial to these efforts; and women's work – from housing and cooking for visiting TANU leaders, to selling membership cards, spreading and reporting necessary information and dancing, and joining local TANU leadership committees – became a basic component of nationalist mobilization.[41]

But why this kind of response from these African women? Like many of their fellow Tanganyikans, the women who joined TANU found Nyerere's youth, apparent humility, and dedication to a particular anti-colonial nationalist vision appealing and exciting. To them, Nyerere was not *Baba Wa Taifa* (father of the nation), the post-independence title he was later to prefer if not insist on; nor was he even Mwalimu (the respected teacher, in Islam as well as Western education), a title he was given and accepted for many years. Rather, to most women, he was *mwanangu* (my son) and, collectively, 'our son'.[42] Women, who already lived in multi-ethnic communities and participated in trans-tribal social and economic organizations, readily identified with and understood Nyerere's pragmatic insistence that in TANU neither tribe, religion nor race should constitute the basis for political discrimination or privilege. Similarly, when Nyerere spoke of *heshima* (dignity) as something that all Tanganyikans would gain with independence and an end to British domination, he borrowed a concept central to Swahili notions of personhood. In other words, basic tenets of Swahili culture and of TANU politics translated easily back and forth, producing, in many respects, an ideology of nationalism reflecting both. 'We are all Swahili!' Nyerere was fond of saying as a 'nationalist' claim.

There was, however, one aspect of TANU's nationalist ideology and Nyerere's rhetoric that had no parallel or precursor within the Swahili community, namely, that the concept of equality among people of different tribes, religions, and races should also include equality between men and women. It was this notion of equality that women seized upon to claim a right to public space and political participation.[43] Mwasaburi Ali's words were typical of those frequently expressed in interviews – that before TANU, no husband would listen to his wife's views, and that women had no right to speak their minds in front of men:

> The women had no say. We had nothing to say, and whatever we wanted to say we had to follow what [the man] said. That was why we increased our efforts ... A woman had no say even if she could do something useful ... still she was regarded as a useless person because she was a woman. That's why we put in more effort after learning the saying 'all people are equal'. We understood well what that was supposed to mean and we said, 'We shall see if all people are equal; we must co-operate if this saying is to become true'.[44]

To argue for the crucial role of women in the making of nationalism and Tanganyika's nationalist movement for independence is not to deny that TANU also gave expression, at least for a period, to the hopes of a small African middle class and a slightly larger working class struggling to enter civil society; or that it also involved linking nationalist goals to protest movements and organizations operating in the countryside. It is to acknowledge the extent to which 1950s' nationalism reflected and gave expanded agency to notions of trans-tribal community born of historical processes and human interactions that began long before the establishment in the 1920s of the first 'protonationalist' organization, TAA, and continue to this day.

If, however, Mamdani is correct, what has mattered in postcolonial Tanzania has everything to do with structure – the colonial legacy of dual despotism – and little to do with African aspirations given voice during the short period (1954–62) when a discourse of equality and dignity for all persons held sway, and before Nyerere began to consolidate all power for the party and government. But if centralized despotism is the legacy of colonialism in Tanzania, what is nationalism's legacy?

The postcolonial state's view of creating a nation – not unlike the colonial view of ruling a territory – has been clear. The nation was something to be 'forged' and controlled through government mandate: through ministries charged with establishing a 'national culture' and mobilizing women for 'economic development'; through the abolition of independent co-operatives and unions; through nationalizations of various kinds; by harnessing political debate and eliminating dissent through the establishment of one-party rule and control of the media; through forced villagization and cash-crop production. This history is also well known and echoes the familiar colonial view that 'ordinary' Tanzanians are 'backward and conservative', 'don't know what is best for them', must be told what is in their interest, and, where necessary, forced to do it.[45] As James Scott has noted with specific reference to forced villagization, it also reflects a 'softer version of authoritarian high modernism', the features of which include 'the logic of 'improvement'', and the reorganization of 'human communities to make them better objects of political control'.[46]

Nevertheless, simply to conclude that colonialism's legacy has thoroughly trumped and given the lie to popular nationalisms is to ignore discourse and ideas that continue to circulate not because of an authoritarian state, but sometimes in spite of, and sometimes in dialogue with it.[47] TANU women activists interviewed in 1984 and 1988 in Dar es Salaam, Mwanza, Moshi, Dodoma and Morogoro – most of them elderly and retired from politics, and many of them now deceased – spoke not of Nyerere's Arusha Declaration (except for Bibi Titi Mohamed, who was against it from the start) or his disastrous *ujamaa* village campaign (though there is no doubt that direct victims would have done so): rather, they reiterated the ideals of equality, dignity, non-discrimination on the basis of 'tribe' or religion that continued to inform their sense of what ought to be fundamental to personhood and to nationhood. And they spoke of community and co-operation, expanded educational opportunities for their daughters and granddaughters, and the undeniable access that women now had to the public sphere of jobs and citizenship. Their responses suggested that they remained in dialogue with TANU's successor party, CCM, and that they continued to expect CCM, through Nyerere, to 'do the right thing'.

It would be easy to dismiss this sense of a moral claim on Nyerere and the party as simple nostalgia. Nyerere's regular public recognition of their role in the independence movement had fed older TANU women's sense that they had his attention. Or to attribute it to the continuing effectiveness of Nyerere's pronouncements – an effectiveness that in many quarters was little diminished by the fact that he was no longer president or head of the party – or to multi-party politics, especially since CCM remains the government in power. Or it could be attributed to advanced age and, up until a decade ago, government control of the media to which the women might have access.

But whatever Tanzania's colonial legacy, it seems to me that it matters what brand of nationalism and of national identity continues to inform a Tanzanian concept of the nation, even as a new generation of women and men, in the tradition of subverting colonial control, seek in various ways, including cultural,[48] to resist the authoritarian state. This concept of nationhood has a complex history and multiple origins, important strains of which intersected in the lives and actions of TANU women.

Notes

* This essay was originally presented on a panel entitled 'The Nation and its Figments' at the annual meeting of the African Studies Association, 31 October 1998, Chicago, IL.

1. Walter Benjamin, cited in James Clifford, *Routes: Travel and Translation in the Late Twentieth Century* (Cambridge, MA: Harvard University Press, 1997), p. 281.

2. Benedict Anderson, *Imagined Communities: Reflections on the Origin and Spread of Nationalism* (London: Verso, 1991); Partha Chatterjee, *The Nation and its Fragments: Colonial and Postcolonial Histories* (Princeton, NJ: Princeton University Press, 1993); Mahmood Mamdani, *Citizen and Subject: Contemporary Africa and the Legacy of Late Colonialism*, Princeton, NJ: Princeton University Press, Kampala: Fountain, Cape Town: David Philip and Oxford: James Currey, 1996).

3. Meanwhile, the ferocity of upheavals in Eastern Europe in the late twentieth century has, as Partha Chatterjee observes, led a number of western scholars back to a definition of nationalism as 'A dark, elemental, unpredictable force of primordial nature' and to the attachment of familiar adjectives – 'ethnic', 'violent', 'ultra-rabid' – in order to subsume certain social and political phenomena under the rubric of nationalism: Geoff Eley and Ronald Grigor Suny (eds.), *Becoming National: a Reader* (New York: Oxford University Press, 1996).

4. See, for example, Anne McClintock, ' "No Longer in a Future Heaven": Women and Nationalism in South Africa',' *Transition* 51 (1991), pp. 104–23 and Partha Chatterjee, 'Colonialism, Nationalism and Colonized Women: the Context of India', *American Ethnologist* 16 (1989), pp. 622–33. But, for an excellent examination of the multiple positions imposed on and claimed by different segments of the population of Indian women, see M. Sinha, 'Reading Mother India: Empire, Nation, and the Female Voice', *Journal of Women's History* 6, 2 (1994), pp. 6–44.

5. In his comprehensive overview of African pre-, colonial and postcolonial history, Basil Davidson clearly sees nationalism as a fundamental precursor to 'The curse of the Nation-State', Basil Davidson, *The Black Man's Burden* (New York: Times Books, 1992).

For recent formulations of nationalism as a masculinist project in the countries under consideration, see M. Jacqui Alexander and Chandra Talpade Mohanty, *Feminist Genealogies, Colonial Legacies, Democratic Futures* (New York: Routledge, 1997), particularly the Introduction and chapters by Heng and Alexander.

6. Mamdani, *Citizen and Subject*, p. 25.

7. For the beginnings of such a general analysis, see Frederick Cooper, 'Conflict and Connection: Rethinking Colonial African History', *American Historical Review*, 99, 5 (1994), pp. 1516–45.

8. Mamdani, *Citizen and Subject*, pp. 19 and 102–3.

9. See, for example, John Lonsdale's work on Kikuyu nationalist concepts emerging out of a Kikuyu philosophy of life and the land, Steven Feierman on aspects of Shambaa nationalism in colonial Tanganyika, and Peter Pels on Luguru politics. See John Lonsdale, 'The Moral Economy of Mau Mau: Wealth, Poverty and Civic Virtue in Kikuyu Political Thought', in Bruce Berman and John Lonsdale (eds), *Unhappy Valley: Conflict in Kenya and Africa*, 2 (London: James Currey, 1992), pp. 315–468; Steven Feierman, *Peasant Intellectuals: Anthropology and History in Tanzania* (Madison, WI: University of Wisconsin Press, 1990); Peter Pels, 'The Pidginisation of Luguru Politics: Administrative Ethnography and the Paradoxes of Indirect Rule', *American Ethnologist* 23, 4 (1996), pp. 738–61. Mamdani dismisses Lonsdale's work, in particular as an argument for 'moral ethnicity', as an 'unproblematised transhistorical constant' which continues to accept tribalism as the problem in African countries. On the contrary, it seems to me that these scholars have demonstrated the ways in which particular groups at particular points in time brought to bear their own understandings of a national ethos and philosophy to broader anti-colonial nationalist movements.

10. For a recent analysis of Nyerere's disastrous 'hegemonic planning mentality', see James C. Scott, *Seeing Like a State: How Certain Schemes to Improve the Human Condition Have Failed* (New Haven, CT: Yale University Press, 1998), pp. 6 and 223–61.

11. Mamdani, *Citizen and Subject*, Chapter 7.

12. *Ibid.*, p. 226.

13. There are now dozens of important articles and books on the invention of tribes and ethnicity in Africa, and on the relative 'agency' of Africans and colonial rule in the processes and resulting groups and identities. I find especially useful Justin Willis, 'The Making of a Tribe: Bondei Identities and Histories', *Journal of African History* 33 (1992): pp. 191–208.

14. Mohamed Said, 'In Praise of Ancestors', *Africa Events* (March/April 1998) and 'Founder of a Political Movement: Abdulwahid K. Sykes (1924–1968)', *Africa Events* (September 1998).

15. In the latter case, we have the invocation of antiquity as a narrative involving a 'centuries old civilisation' with '180 cities of settlement dating from the ninth to the nineteenth centuries … on the east coast of Africa in an area stretching from the mouth of the Zambesi northward for a thousand miles and across to the Comoros and Zanzibar', Preface to Mtoro Bin Mwinyi Bakari, *The Customs of the Swahili People*, edited and translated by J.W.T. Allen (Berkeley, CA: University of California Press, 1981).

16. Bakari, *Customs of the Swahili People*, p. vii.

17. For an excellent summary of this debate, see Deborah P. Amory, "Waswahili Ni Nani?': the Politics of Swahili Identity and Culture', paper delivered at the African Studies Association Meeting, Baltimore, MD, 1990.

18. Jonathan Glassman, 'The Bondsman's New Clothes: the Contradictory Consciousness of Slave Resistance on the Swahili Coast', *Journal of African History*, 32 (1991), p. 296.

19. Thaddeus Sunseri, 'Slave Ransoming in German East Africa, 1885–1922', *International Journal of African Historical Studies*, 26, 3 (1993), pp. 481–511.

20. For a thoroughly documented history of the ways in which people on Zanzibar claimed, discarded and reclaimed different 'ethnic' identities, including Swahili, see Laura Fair, 'Pastimes and Politics: a Social History of Zanzibar's Ng'ambo Community 1890-1950' (Ph. D. diss., University of Minnesota, 1994).

21. Margaret Strobel, *Muslim Women in Mombasa, 1890-1975* (New Haven, CT: Yale

University Press, 1975); Sarah Mirza and Margaret Strobel (ed. and trans.), *Three Swahili Women: Life Histories from Mombasa, Kenya* (Bloomington, IN: Indiana University Press, 1989), Luise White, *The Comforts of Home: Prostitution in Colonial Nairobi* (Chicago, IL: University of Chicago Press, 1990); August Nimtz, *Islam and Politics in East Africa* (Minneapolis, MN: University of Minnesota Press, 1980); Sheryl McCurdy, 'Qadirrya Brotherhoods and Community Mobilization in Tabora and Ujiji, Tanganyika, 1880–1940' (unpublished paper, 1991); Christian Coulon, 'Women, Islam & Baraka', in Donal B. Cruise O'Brien and Christian Coulon (eds), *Charisma and Brotherhood in African Islam* (Oxford: Clarendon Press, 1988).

22. McCurdy, 'Qadirrya Brotherhoods'.
23. C. Pike. 'History and Imagination: Swahili Literature and Resistance to German Language Imperialism in Tanzania, 1885–1910' *International Journal of African Historical Studies*, 19, 2 (1986), pp. 201–33.
24. John Lonsdale, 'African Pasts in Africa's Future', *Canadian Journal of African Studies*, 23, 1 (1989), pp. 126-46.
25. Anne Biersteker, '"Kazi ya Ushairi": Post-War Kiswahili Poetry and the Construction of Nationalist Identities in East Africa', paper delivered at the African Studies Association Meeting, Baltimore MD, 1990.
26. For a consideration of the Swahili community in Dar es Salaam up to World War II, see David H. Anthony, 'Culture and Society in a Town in Transition: a People's History of Dar es Salaam, 1865-1939' (Ph.D. diss., University of Wisconsin, 1983).
27. J.P. Moffett, *Handbook of Tanganyika*, 2nd edn (Dar es Salaam: Government of Tanganyika, 1958). Noting that it was difficult to define a 'tribe', Moffett nevertheless did his best, and then grouped tribes into 'clusters' of people 'sharing many features in common [but] nonetheless lacking that essential feeling of unity which is the basic feature of a tribe' (p. 283). 'Over and above the "cluster"', Moffett identified 'what might well be called the ethnic group, i.e., people of common origins'. Here, the familiar distinctions were physical, linguistic and based on 'mode of living', giving us the Bushman group, the Nilotic (Negro), the Hamitic, the Nilo-Hamitic and the Bantu, along with some 'unidentifiable elements' (p. 283). With the Bantu ('a mixture between various Hamitic and Negro stocks') making up 95 per cent of Tanganyika's population, Moffett finally acknowledges that 'blending has been and is still going on throughout the territory, assisted today by modern transport and the break-down of rigid tribal boundaries' (p. 287). Nevertheless, he manages to divide the Bantu into six broad groups under which the tribes can be subsumed. All Africans who cannot be categorized within the tribes of Tanganyika are grouped as 'Africans from outside Tanganyika', of whom there are 36,152 according to the 1948 census, making them the 48th largest group if one were to place them within the 112 (not 120) named groups (pp. 295-7).
28. '[C]ounted as natives of Africa in the 1948 census, but, having successfully established their claims to be Ishaakias from the other side of the Red Sea, were counted as non-Africans in the 1952 census' (Moffett, *Handbook*, p. 302).
29. R de S. Stapledon to W.L. Gorell Barnes, Colonial Office, No. ABJ. 22. EAF 46/7/01 SECRET, PRO.
30. As Mamdani has aptly noted: 'Inasmuch as it privileges the European historical experience as its touchstone, as the historical expression of the universal, contemporary unilinear evolutionism should more concretely and appropriately be characterized as a Eurocentrism. The central tendency of such a methodological orientation is to lift a phenomenon out of context and process. The result is a history by analogy' (Mamdani, *Citizen and Subject*, p. 12).
31. These reasons included animosity towards abusive native authorities; harsh agricultural regulations and controls; the human and material costs of huge, ill-designed, and ultimately disastrous schemes for increased cash-crop production; and threatened land alienation.
32. Anderson, *Imagined Communities*, p. 12.
33. John Iliffe, *A Modern History of Tanganyika* (Cambridge: Cambridge University Press, 1979), p. 486.

34. Cooper, 'Conflict and Connection', p. 1537.
35. They were characterized as such because the women who became activists were for the most part over twenty-five years of age, had already been married and divorced at least once, and therefore considered themselves, and were considered, 'middle-aged'.
36. For a detailed account, see Susan Geiger, *TANU Women: Gender and Culture in the Making of Tanganyikan Nationalism, 1955–1965* (Portsmouth, NH: Heinemann, 1997).
37. Bibi Titi Mohamed's entry into TANU as head of the 'Women's Section' is detailed in Geiger, *TANU Women*.
38. As Prasenjit Duara argues, national identity is best understood as founded on fluid relationships, and there are many ways in which 'more traditional' and national identities resemble each other: Prasenjit Duara, 'Historicising National Identity, or Who Imagines What and When', in Eley and Suny, *Becoming National*, pp. 151–77.
39. Oscar Kambona, Organizing Secretary-General of TANU to Fabian Society, 18 October 1955, FCB Papers, 121, Rhodes House, Oxford.
40. See Johannes Fabian, *Power and Performance: Ethnographic Explorations through Proverbial Wisdom and Theater in Shaba, Zaire* (Madison, WI: University of Wisconsin Press, 1990), p. 11.
41. Susan Geiger, 'Tanganyikan Nationalism as "Women's Work": Life Histories, Collective Biography, and Changing Historiography', *Journal of African History* 37, 3 (1996), pp. 465–78.
42. Geiger, *Tanu Women*.
43. TANU had to quickly modify this equality by indicating that married women should have the permission of their husbands to participate in party activities. Several women interviewed, including Bibi Titi Mohamed, were divorced when they chose TANU as against their husbands. On the other hand, men who were TANU supporters knew TANU's position on gender equality, and it could therefore be difficult to reconcile a refusal to let their wives participate if they themselves wanted to be considered enlightened members.
44. Interview with Mwasaburi Ali, Dar es Salaam, 10 September 1984.
45. Of course, union with Zanzibar in 1964 created an additional set of problems regarding the 'nation' and 'nation-building' that have taxed party and government ingenuity and control mechanisms. See Kelly Askew, 'Performing the Nation: Swahili Musical Performance and the Production of Tanzanian National Culture' (Ph.D. dissertation, Harvard University, 1997), pp. 228–31.
46. Scott, *Seeing Like a State*, p. 224.
47. Larson argues that theories which *a priori* assume that the material domination of an elite necessarily assimilates ideological domination, do not, in all cases, 'accurately represent the ways in which ideas and practices of popular culture circulate across and around the contours of material power'. I agree. Pier M. Larson, '"Capacities and Modes of Thinking": Intellectual Engagements and Subaltern Hegemony in the Early History of Malagasy Christianity', *American Historical Review* 102, 4 (1997), pp. 968–1002.
48. See Askew, 'Performing the Nation' for a comprehensive study of the postcolonial state's top-down attempts to regulate and produce a 'Tanzanian national culture', via the Ministry of Culture, and of popular subversions, rejections and circumvention strategies that have to date prevented a state-controlled 'Tanzanian Cultural Revolution'.

Sixteen

Between the 'Global' & 'Local' Families

The Missing Link in School History Teaching in Postcolonial Tanzania

YUSUF Q. LAWI

Introduction

When this author visited the southern Tanzanian district of Mbinga on a research mission in 1990 he was struck by the alienation of local people from what the District Cultural Officer called 'cultural development'. As the research team was visiting the district to establish the profile of cultural institutions and activities it found itself watching a cultural performance in one of the best known coffee-producing villages. In the course of time it became apparent that the District Cultural Officer had arranged this performance for us with the view to ensuring that we left with a positive image of cultural development in the district. It turned out that what the Cultural Officer conceived to be a sensible cultural representation, and therefore what he, as custodian of culture in the district, had for years been toiling to develop, was a reproduction of state ideology among rural folk.

This was especially explicit in the songs sung at the performance. While in most other respects the dance maintained the crucial features of the famous Matengo *lindeku*,[1] the wording of the songs had nothing in common with any of the known local traditions. Of the three songs performed, the first recalled the war that Tanzania had fought about a decade earlier against the invading forces of Uganda's former president Idi Amin Dada, while the second dwelt on the evils of the South African apartheid policies of the day.[2] The third song amplified the familiar government campaign for increased rural cash crop production, in this case coffee. The themes and messages that came through the songs were clearly an amplification of established official discourses on government foreign policy and its strategy for local economic development.

In a sense, this performance epitomized success in nation-building, as it showed the permeation of the deepest rural settings by patriotic concerns and feelings of nationhood. While the ideal of national consciousness and unity cannot be denied, it is unfortunate that the effort towards this end in Tanzania and many other countries in the African continent has tended to ignore or conceal the concrete experiences and concerns of local communities. It is obvious that such an approach has deprived nation-building of the opportunity to benefit from the advantages of cultural diversity and local creativity. Within the local communities this strategy in nation-building seems to have forced people into the dilemma of having to split their efforts between the more authentic process of cultural creativity, which often takes place underground, and the government-engineered propagation of official ideology through public performances. The outcome, in the long term, is a clear split between people's authentic cultural creativity in private and public efforts towards cultural homogeneity.

One reckons that, far from being confined to dancing and related activities, this disparity has existed for a long time in other forms of culture propagation, not least in the school teaching of history. The type of history that has dominated school books in Tanzania since colonial days, and the manner in which this knowledge is usually transmitted in school settings, illustrate the gap that exists between remembrance of the past at the local community level and official history elaboration. As this chapter will show, official rendering of historical knowledge has, since its inception, kept a distance from local perspectives and genuine concerns emanating from the diverse communities constituting the nation. Like the 'formalized' Matengo *lindeku* of the past decade, school history has tended to construct narratives based on presumed universal principles rather than the concrete circumstances, experiences and concerns of real people in their various settings. Needless to say, the history so constructed has tended to be banal and largely irrelevant to local situations. In the following section I define the historical context for the alienation of people and their concrete experiences from official history, and attempt to illustrate the disparity between such history and genuine social concerns at the local community level.

The Context

The ascendance to dominance of formal institutions of education in Africa has meant a transfer of the responsibility for creating and transmitting knowledge. Such responsibility has increasingly moved from individual families and local communities to modern institutions of schooling and research. This is generally true for all kinds of knowledge. It is, however, uniquely so in the case of the creation and transmission of historical knowledge. One may say that in Africa, and Tanzania in particular, the basis and site for the production and articulation of historical knowledge have since colonization shifted from the 'local' to the 'universal' context. Consequently, history elaboration, once carried out entirely within and about local communities, has largely been confined to schools and other formal institutions of learning. It turns out that the knowledge transmitted through such institutionalized teaching of history has had little connection with the past experiences and current concerns of most of the learners. It can be imagined that this has had profound implications for the relevance of school History to families and local communities.

One must appreciate the long way the telling of history in African schools has come from the colonial outright denial of the very existence of history in the pre-European era to the Afrocentrism of the 1960s and early 1970s. It would be a mistake to belittle the many contributions that nationalist histories have made in restoring the agency of African peoples in their own history and in removing some of the unfounded prejudices of colonial historiography. Yet, the postcolonial teaching of history cannot be said to have come as close to the majority of people as it should. For one thing, it has tended to be universalistic or globalist in its approach and contents. Its elaboration centers on the nature and circumstances of the nations of Africa and the world at large, while seeking to establish universal explanatory principles. This has been a logical outcome of the apparently common assumption among the respective historians and educators alike, that scientific history is prompted by established methodological principles to study the past for its own sake. Lost from this perspective is the fact that people remember the past when faced by circumstances or challenges whose resolution requires that remembrance. The main argument in this contribution is that the teaching of history in Tanzania in the postcolonial period was just as much distanced from this methodological assumption as was the colonial school history.

The consequences are somewhat hidden, but not insignificant. On the one hand, the emphasis on nations and world political and social systems to the exclusion of local practical concerns and experience makes school History dull and socially irrelevant to members of local communities. On the other, from the viewpoint of the majority common people in rural and urban areas, such history defies the very nature of what would count as genuine historical knowledge: a socially prompted reconstruction of the past. Instead, the currently dominant approach embraces the false notion of history as simply a recollection of the past for its own sake.

The alienation of ordinary people from history elaboration in Africa and elsewhere in the world can be said to have come generally with the emergence of strong states and the rise of state ideologies. It is generally agreed that state-based histories everywhere in the world reconstructed the past largely from the viewpoint of the rulers. However, colonial and postcolonial school histories alienated the ordinary people in a unique and more profound way. As hinted at above, colonial school histories everywhere denied the very existence of the colonized people's past. Only the actions of the colonizers counted as history. The nationalist histories that at independence replaced colonial histories have taken many varied postures in different places. While in most cases they managed to restore the agency of the colonized people in history, they did so only in broad theoretical terms. In practice, history elaboration continued to appeal to universal principles and social laws for change, shying away from using the present situation as the point of departure in historical inquiry. All this is true for the situation in postcolonial Tanzania as it is for many other places around the continent.

This continuity is perhaps better explained in terms of the already mentioned transfer of the social responsibility for history elaboration. It would seem that, as long as that responsibility continues to rest with the globalist institution called the school, history will continue to be elaborated from perspectives other than those of the majority ordinary people. Accordingly, it will continue to be peripheral to the social concerns of the majority common people in rural and urban communities. The rationale for these assumptions will become clear as we examine below the historical context and significance of the said change in the social responsibility for history elaboration in Africa and elsewhere.

The Context and Significance of the Shift to Globalist History Elaboration

The shift of responsibility for history elaboration from the local community to globalist institutions of learning is clearly tied up with the development of history elaboration into a distinct trade, then a fully-fledged academic discipline, and finally a school subject.[3] In the long run the rise of academic History and its ascendance to dominance implied a shift of social responsibility for producing and disseminating historical knowledge from families and older generations in the local community to academic institutions and specialized experts. Local elaboration of history certainly continued despite this shift, but from now on the inspiration and main impetus for History teaching would come not from the direct concerns of the 'local family' of individuals and communities, but from elite-conceived universal concerns and aspirations. In contrast to informal elaboration of history that dominated in earlier periods, official histories naturally remembered only the past that mattered in celebrating and maintaining the *status quo*. For example, colonial histories emphasized European racial superiority to justify colonial domination. For their part, the nationalist historians highlighted the precolonial achievements of African rulers, traders and producers to enhance the legitimacy of the postcolonial state. Neither the colonial historians nor their postcolonial successors challenged the deeds of the governing regimes of their day, despite the fact that many ordinary people often did so in their own varied ways. In both colonial and nationalist African historiography the state is viewed primarily as an agent of modernization. In contrast, within their local circles, ordinary people in both epochs viewed the state and its agents sometimes as evil and sometimes as supportive of their course, depending on the specific ways in which state activity impacted on their lives.

The alienation of history elaboration from local concerns and aspirations started with the rise of specialized history telling, but it did not end there. The distance between official history telling and the practical concerns of local communities widened even more dramatically with the development of History into a fully-fledged academic discipline and, later, a school subject. The latter developments first occurred in Europe and the United States during the period from the late eighteenth century to the end of the twentieth century.[4]

Worth noting in this connection is the fact that these developments took place in the context of a broadening spectrum of occupational specialties in Europe and America, the European imperialist expansion to Asia and Africa, and the heightening of nationalism in Europe. The link between these phenomena and the ascendance of formalized history elaboration may not be apparent at first. It is, however, known that the kinds of histories taught during the period in question invariably legitimized exploitative relations within the emerging industrial society and vindicated European imperialist control over Asian and African societies. In this context, History teaching functioned more as an ideological weapon of the dominant class than an articulation of the experiences and aspirations of broader masses in the respective societies. The implication is that the emergence of academic History took elaboration of the past a step further away from the local context, in terms both of its contents and of the social responsibility for transmitting these.

The emergence of school history and academic historical scholarship in Africa and elsewhere outside industrial society is directly tied up with the process of colonial modernization. University departments of History first appeared in sub-Saharan Africa in the immediate post-World War II period. They were conceived as part of efforts to popularize and disseminate the colonial evolutionist perspective, which, among other things, emphasized the cultural and economic backwardness of Africa and the necessity of colonial agency in modernizing it. In most cases History appeared in school curricula shortly afterwards, but here, too, the inspiration came from the same notions of primitive Africa and the critical role of the modernizing mission of European colonialism. Hence, an elementary school textbook for French West Africa portrayed Africans as people who 'could not live in peace in their country', as warriors among them were inclined to burn down villages and towns, and kill the inhabitants or lead them away into slavery. In contrast, 'France chases away thieves and bandits, and ... fights against misery and famine'.

Histories such as these, written by agents of European imperialism primarily to justify colonialism, illustrate the furthest point reached in the drifting of history elaboration away from the local context. They could not have emanated from the common concerns and aspirations of the local people, nor could they have been constructed and articulated by persons who were rooted in the local context socially and politically.

It has been quite some time since the departure of formal colonialism from Africa. The relevant question to ask in connection with the present discussion is whether local communities have restored history elaboration to themselves, and whether History teaching in formal institutions of learning is now informed and driven by the concrete concerns and unfolding perspectives within the local communities. The answer, unfortunately, is not in the affirmative. There is hardly anything in view suggesting the narrowing of the rift between local concerns and history elaboration in formal institutions of learning. It is the global view that has dominated.

V. Y. Mudimbe has stated the point clearly in his *The Invention of Africa*. Perhaps his skepticism in this case has gone to the extreme. Yet, there is much relevance in his general conclusion that the epistemological frame within which knowledge about Africa is created has remained fundamentally the same since the early European ethnographies of Africa. This chapter does not intend to engage in a thorough philosophical appraisal of post-independence history elaboration in Africa. Instead, it limits itself to a brief examination of the school teaching of History in post-independence Tanzania. The aim is to illustrate the continuity of the globalist perspective, as opposed to local views of history.

History Teaching in Tanzania:
Independence to Late 1960s

One would have expected that the triumph of nationalist forces in the late 1950s and the resultant achievement of independence in 1961 would have had an immediate impact on school History curricula in general and the political content of this subject in particular. Contrary to this expectation, post-independence school History retained the old colonial contents and ideological mold well into the late 1960s. For instance, up until 1967 History teaching in secondary schools still aimed to develop 'pupils' knowledge and understanding of man and his behavior', as well as the growth of 'a spirit of tolerance' among targeted learners .

These statements of intent have several implications regarding the content of school History and the social values it intended to develop. First, they clearly imply that the object of historical inquiry and the focus of history elaboration would remain universal humanity rather than the particular experiences of the historical human beings in Tanzania and Africa. In addition, students and teachers would concern themselves primarily with universal patterns in human behavior, rather than with their specific social and political circumstances. Lastly, History teaching is conceived to have a practical value of enhancing social control, specifically by inculcating tolerance as an important social norm.

The focus on abstract humanity implied the denial of social relevance to school History in the post-independence Tanzanian situation. It meant maintaining or deepening the rift created in colonial days between history elaboration and the circumstances and concerns of people in their numerous and varied local contexts. This resolve is consistent with the implied behaviorist methodology, which, by putting emphasis on human individuals as the object of History, abstracts people from their social context. The behaviorist approach has its roots and relevance in the history of social sciences in the industrial world. However, the resolve to apply it to history in Africa means an inclination to using a theoretical frame based on experience in industrial society to understand social reality in a fundamentally different setting. This raises questions of relevance and practicability, but the more general concern in this discussion is that the prescribed contents of History would maintain the rift established during colonial days between local social circumstances and history elaboration in schools.

Such clues of continuities from the colonial past are confirmed by the type of History texts used in schools during most of the 1960s. Many of these openly reproduced the old colonial view of history in Africa. This is perhaps best illustrated by a volume entitled *History of East Africa*, edited by Roland Oliver and Gervase Mathew. Although the book was first published in 1963, its preparation had started during the British colonial period in Tanganyika. It is worthwhile noting that the book was written at the joint initiative of the colonial governments in Uganda and Tanganyika and the Colonial Social Science Research Council, and that the actual writing of the book was funded by the British Imperial Government. From this background information, one almost knows what the contents of the book would be. In brief, despite some lip service paid to African initiative, the book is explicitly Eurocentric and clearly supportive of the imperialist mission of colonial modernization. It alludes to the idea that external challenges were the motive force for history in Africa, and asserts the significance of studying the succession of colonial administrative regimes, and the various aspects of African responses to challenges posed by colonial modernization. In an attempt to suit the book to the early postcolonial political context, the authors phrased their objectives cautiously:

> ... readers of [of East African history] will want to know primarily what it has done to them. The detailed evolution of colonial policy, the personalities of the Governors and Secretaries of State, all the various aspects of external challenge, will rightly yield pride of place to the history of internal responses.[5]

Many other examples from school texts could be given to show that school history in the period in question told the same colonial story, albeit in slightly different words. This continuity of colonial contents of school History well into mid-1960s went hand in hand with the reproduction of colonial examination questions. In the early 1960s questions in public examinations at secondary school level typically demanded detailed knowledge of ancient European civilizations, reasons for Europeans' success in colonial empire building, and biographical details on important European heroes. This continuity in the nature of public examinations is hardly surprising, in the light of the fact that schools continued to use the same old colonial syllabi and textbooks.

The question, therefore, is: why this reproduction of colonial culture at a time when triumphant nationalist forces should have been in charge? The short answer is that nationalist forces were yet to gain clear control of affairs in the former colony. A bird's eye view of the economic and social arrangements obtaining at the time will shed some light on this context.

This was the time when foreign capital, mostly British, dominated the Tanganyikan economy. Microeconomic planning and implementation drew on the broader World Bank-designed three-year Development Plan (1961–4), which emphasized, among other things, that import-substitution industries should be established by foreign investors and protected by the government. This gives an important hint on the strength of the grip of global forces on the economy, clearly suggesting continuity in the dominance of imperialist initiative and control. In the sphere of education, public examinations remained under direct British Imperial control up to 1968. The role of examinations in determining the content and conduct of education cannot be overemphasized. Given these circumstances, it would have been difficult for a major change to occur in school History teaching. This is not to suggest that the continuity of colonial history during most of the first decade of the post-independence era was justifiable. It is simply to highlight its social basis.

The Late 1960s to the Present

If History teaching in the early years of Independence ignored the concerns and experience of ordinary people in their local settings because of continued overall colonial control, in the period from the late 1960s it maintained this rift for a different reason. From 1966 onwards History teaching increasingly took a nationalistic approach. The official aims for the teaching of History as well as the contents at all levels of schooling changed radically. For the first time official aims for History teaching linked the subject with nation-building and the creation of a 'new awareness of nationhood'.[6] A principal objective for History teaching became the development of a sense of pride in one's nation.

Accordingly, the contents of school History changed tremendously, culminating in a thoroughly 'Africanized' package at all levels of schooling. They became clearly nationalistic in character. '... [A] suitable History syllabus must be predominantly African in content', argued the History panel of the Institute of Education, adding that '... all non-African events contained must have been included [in the syllabus] because of their effects or connection with events in Africa'.[7] History teaching would put emphasis on the common cultural heritage of Tanzanians and Africans, and on the particularity of African political and cultural history.

In line with the 'African initiative' thesis, which had just ascended to popularity in academic circles, the new contents of school history stressed the precolonial achievements of Africans and the African agency in history from antiquity to independence. Teachers and students drew from a new set of school texts, many of them just recently published by liberal-nationalist historians. These included Kimambo and Temu's *A History of Tanzania*, B. A. Ogot and J. Kieran's *Zamani*, and Basil Davidson's *The Growth of African Civilizations*.[8]

Liberal-nationalist History thoroughly criticized the Eurocentrism of colonial History. It largely succeeded in overcoming the colonial ethnographers' and historians' prejudices in assessing African social and economic realities prior to European influence. Where colonial historians concealed or de-emphasized African people's achievements, liberal-nationalist history put the spotlight on it. In a way, it brought History teaching closer to home by illuminating African people's circumstances and experience before and after colonial conquest. More significantly, the liberal-nationalist articulations explicitly or implicitly longed for a better African posterity, and in this sense they can be said to be progressive.

Yet, despite the sharp contrasts with the hitherto dominant views, liberal-nationalist history reproduced some of the pertinent characteristics of colonial history. Among other things, it maintained the globalist perspective. In its general character, and especially in the way it was commonly taught in schools, liberal-nationalist history typically tended to remember the aspects of the past considered credible and inspiring to the younger generations of Africans. The assessment of content credibility or appropriateness was, however, based on certain universalistic assumptions. These include, among others, the assumptions that:

(i) In every epoch and everywhere history consists in gradual improvements in human civilization and well being.

(ii) All people, irrespective of geographical location and historical circumstances, share the same social, economic, and even cultural destiny.

(iii) States invariably work in the interests of all the people under their control.

(iv) History is accurate statements of facts or truths: no less, no more.

This universalistic approach to history had several significant implications for the status of History as a school subject as well as for students' understanding of the nature and function of historical knowledge. First, by taking such a universalistic view History teaching left aside or de-emphasized the aspects of past human experience that would have been most interesting and stimulating from the point of view of local people. When taught primarily to portray only ideal situations, rather than the usual combination of irregularities, crises and reversals in human experience, school History becomes unrealistic. This is true not only in the sense that it presents a wrong image of the past, but especially in that it fails to relate to the true experiences of people. Both in the colonial and the postcolonial settings, and including the post-structural adjustment era, people have often experienced history as tragedy and loss.[9] School texts with their progressive narratives do not reflect this critical reality.

Indeed, by emphasizing only the aspects of the past that academics consider ideal, school History tends to be globalist in character, ignoring issues and processes that are specific to local settings. History elaboration based on this approach becomes simply a way of talking, as opposed to an avenue for invoking past experience in understanding the present. It lacks meaning and relevance to specific communities of people in their local settings: peasant cash croppers, hospital or dock workers, herbal healers, high school students, emerging political parties – in short the local 'family' of actors and actresses.

It is noteworthy that, although the liberal-nationalist history was largely universalistic and schematic, it was at first highly popular among students, literate parents and even government bureaucrats.[10] This is perhaps not surprising, given the ideological relevance of this history to a people who had been denied identity and self-destiny for so long. Liberal-nationalist history reclaimed the African past, elevated the African personality, and presented a logic that allowed a better posterity for Africa than that envisaged by colonial history.

However, the popularity resulting from these characteristics could not have lasted long after the limitations of flag independence became apparent by the mid-1970s. In Tanzania the decline in the social status of school History probably started in the late 1960s, but beginning from the mid-1970s it became clearly evident and widespread. What we see, therefore, is the rise and decline of the popularity of school History in the period from the mid-1960s to the mid-1970s, a pattern that can be said to have coincided with the rise and decline of nationalism as a political ideology. The decline in the popularity of History as a school subject from the mid-1970s may be said to have resulted from the decline in the power of nationalism, the ideology that informed the nationalist historical discourse.

The crisis of the relevance of academic or school History was first voiced by the early critics of liberal nationalist scholarship. Scholars such as John Saul and Walter Rodney pointed out that liberal-nationalist history had lost the initiative to challenge imperialism and had failed to unveil the mechanisms for the continuing imperialist exploitation of Africa in the postcolonial era. In the long run, the academic historians' response to the crisis was a two-fold paradigmatic shift. Scholars first adopted the just emerging underdevelopment theory, which put emphasis on the concept of neo-colonialism. This theory illuminated the new forms of control and exploitation of former colonial domains by imperialist forces after the end of formal colonialism, and traced the roots of these mechanisms to Africa's contacts with Europe from medieval times to the days of direct colonial control. They pointed to the continuation of the system of unequal exchange and political corruption that characterized Europe's mercantilist and colonial relations with Africa.

At about the same time many historians in Tanzania adopted a Marxist-materialist perspective. In brief, this put emphasis on political economy as a methodological approach. It utilized concepts such as 'modes of production', 'social-economic formations' and 'class contradictions and class struggles'. One of the earliest histories to utilize these concepts and this approach was Issa Shivji's *Class Struggle in Tanzania*.[11] The Marxist-materialist historians often applied the underdevelopment paradigm in analyzing the African's postcolonial political and economic situation.

Both the underdevelopment and Marxist-materialist perspectives were almost immediately reflected in school History. This is evident in the syllabus changes that started in 1976 at all levels of schooling, including the teacher education colleges.[12] To emphasize the underdevelopment perspective, school History sought to bring home the understanding that the problems of development facing Africa in the 1970s were a result of external 'political domination, economic exploitation and cultural humiliation during the colonial rule'.[13] Along with this objective, post-1976 school History aimed to make students understand the various efforts and strategies undertaken by African countries in the struggle for liberation against colonialism and neo-colonialism. These objectives were fully reflected in the syllabus contents. In the high school syllabus, for example, the section on the post-independence period is all about two major issues in African history: the colonial legacy and its effects on Africa's economies, political systems, and cultural development and the efforts taken by postcolonial governments to redress these effects and develop their respective countries economically, politically and culturally.[14]

The Marxist-materialist approach was equally manifest in school History. The above-listed Marxist-Leninist terminology appeared in syllabus outlines and school History texts, some of which actually proclaimed materialism as the philosophical basis for history elaboration in Tanzania. A senior curriculum developer asserted that the new syllabus offered a history that was *materialist* and *scientific* in its philosophical outlook and *liberating* in its ideological and political considerations.

The combined underdevelopment and Marxist-materialist perspective, sometimes referred to as the political-economic approach, played a significant role in addressing the crisis of relevance. It illuminated the reality of neocolonialism from an Afrocentric viewpoint, and by so doing showed the limitations of the romanticism of early nationalist history. Teachers and writers, inclined to the Marxist-materialist perspective, at least paid lip service to the value of class analysis in understanding past African reality. Above all, the political-economic perspective recognized the inextricable linkage between the economic, political and ideological instances of historical reality, and so provided a broader and more comprehensive view.

Yet the political-economic approach, as often taken by school History teachers, has been just as abstract and detached from local reality as others that went before it. The typical tendency has been to present analytic frames and models rather than the actual contents of History. This has been a complete reversal of what prevailed in colonial history, where the listing of discrete and endless facts was the norm. The new approach allowed more synthesis of information and perhaps a higher level of coherence. However, by putting greater emphasis on explanatory models, History teaching ignored the equally important task of illuminating concrete processes and phenomena on the ground. Teachers have, for instance, found more comfort in listing the 'factors' that contributed to the militarization of the state in post-independence West Africa than in giving accounts of the actual processes of political transformation. The result has been the loss of the basic social function of history elaboration, namely, the articulation of how the present came into being.

One finds the best illustration of the problem at hand in the first chapter of what used to be the most elementary History textbook in the post-1976 period: the pupils' book for the fourth grade. The chapter deals with '*mifumo ya uzalishaji mali*', literally 'Systems of Production'. According to the corresponding contents, teachers were supposed to list and describe the various types of economic activities adopted by pre-colonial African societies, such as foraging, fishing, farming. This was aimed to show that Africans adopted various means and ways of procuring a livelihood. This was certainly a useful point to make. However, for a fourth grader, who did not even know what History was all about, such an abstract concept as a 'system of production' was definitely a wrong starting point. Perhaps narratives about how and why the children's own families and local community evolved and became what they are would have made a better starting point. Based on such narratives supported by illustrative drawings or pictures, teachers would have found it easier to nurture the concept of history as a process of becoming, rather than a past state of things. This way school History would have appealed to most pupils in class because of its relevance to the learners' own experiences and concerns.

This is not to say that to be relevant and appealing History has to confine its exposition and analysis to the local context. However distant (in time and space) a particular historical phenomenon can be from the learner, it is never impossible to connect it with local experience without entertaining fiction. The Berlin conference of 1884/5 becomes relevant and exciting if it is linked up, for instance, with the currently topical issue of the refugee problem in western Tanzania, or with the emerging question of who is or is not a citizen of Tanzania. The two major world wars become more meaningful when elaborated in such a way that they evoke certain memories of local events or help explain certain phenomena that are familiar and significant to the learners. History is by definition the reconstruction of significant pasts. Its teaching should always consider the significance of the contents to the intended learners.

The 1976 History syllabi have recently been replaced with revised versions at the secondary school level. At the primary school level History has been fused into the newly developed '*Maarifa ya Jamii*', or social studies. However, there is sufficient evidence showing that no fundamental changes have been made either in the contents of the history to be taught or in the manner of delivery. For one thing, the new high school syllabus states at the outset that no major alterations have been made in the 1976 version. A brief viewing of the *Maarifa ya Jamii* course would show that the topics for the history part were simply lifted from hitherto existing syllabi.[15] Judging from the syllabi outlines, one may therefore conclude that, to-date, school teaching of History in Tanzania maintains the globalist approach that has characterized History teaching in Tanzania and Africa at large since the colonial invasion.

Conclusion

This chapter started with an illustration of how the official nationalist conception of cultural development has alienated rural folk in an African setting. The foregoing discussion on the teaching of History in schools illustrates the fact that this process has been equally alienating to the bulk of rural and urban people. In both cases it was the urban-based educated and political elite who designed the cultural packages and engineered their implementation. For reasons not fully explored here, the elite-designed cultural packages, as exemplified by the case of school History teaching, have tended to be globalist in content and approach.

In the case of history teaching in particular, this approach has led to irrelevance and lack of genuine interest, precisely because globalist and progressive historical narratives fail to appeal to ordinary people's concerns in the context of heightened economic difficulties and social tension. This is especially true in the post-structuralist epoch, when the phenomenal decline in community control over resources has led to the exclusion of the bulk of the population from access to crucial means of livelihood. To these people, globalist and progressive narratives of the past would be irrelevant at best and disappointing at worst.

While the urban and educated elite have for some time managed to maintain authority over the propagation of culture in public institutions, they cannot prevent the dissidence that takes place in informal settings every day. If the District Cultural Officer in Mbinga managed to create a 'national' culture in a rural setting, he could not prevent the processes of cultural reproduction that went on silently and infinitely in informal settings, processes that reflected the genuine social concerns in the respective communities. Likewise, if the bosses of education have maintained authority over what kind of history should be generated and disseminated in formal learning institutions, they cannot be said to have managed to prevent dissidence in classroom instruction and other encounters between teachers and learners. What actually happens along the line separating authority from dissidence in culture propagation remains a subject for continuing research.

Notes

1. The Matengo are the largest ethic group in Mbinga District today, and *lindeku* is one of their best known traditional dances.
2. The war was fought during 1978/9 following a prolonged enmity between the regimes of Julius Nyerere and Idi Amin Dada, which ended up in Ugandan forces' attack and

occupation of Tanzanian territory in the north-western region of Kagera. The war culminated in the deposition of Idi Amin and the takeover of power in Uganda by a newly constituted alliance of internal forces, under the patronage of the Tanzanian state.

3. Martin Ballard (ed.), *New Developments in the Study and Teaching of History* (London: Temple Smyth, 1970), pp. 17–18; J. Minor Gwynn and John B. Chase (eds), *Curriculum Principles and Social Trends* (New York: Macmillan, 1969), pp. 18–19.

4. Ballard, *New Developments*, pp. 17–20.

5. R. Oliver and Gervase Mathew (eds), *History of East Africa* (London: Oxford University Press, 1963), p. xi.

6. Ministry of Education, 'Report of Tanzanian Syllabus in History for forms I to IV', 1967, mimeo, p. 2.

7. *Ibid.*, p. 12.

8. I. N. Kimambo and A. J. Temu (eds), *A History of Tanzania* (Nairobi: East African Publishing House, 1969); B. A. Ogot and J. Kieran, *Zamani* (Nairobi: East African Publishing House, 1968); Basil Davidsom, *The Growth of African Civilizations* (London: Longman, 1973).

9. Johannes Fabian, *Remembering the Present: Painting and Popular History in Zaire* (Berkeley, CA: University of California, 1996).

10. Yusuf Q. Lawi, 'A History of History Teaching in Post-Colonial Tanzania' (M. A. Diss., University of Dar es Salaam, 1989), pp. 72–111.

11. Issa Shivji, *Class Struggles in Tanzania* (Dar es Salaam: Tanzania Publishing House, 1976).

12. Ministry of Education, *Secondary School Syllabuses: Social Sciences* (Dar es Salaam, 1976).

13. *Ibid.*, p. 46.

14. *Ibid.*, pp. 45–7.

15. See, for example, chapter 12 of Taasisi ya Elimu Tanzania, *Maarifa ya Jamii*, book 6 (Dar es Salaam, E&D Ltd.), pp. 102–8 and compare it with History topics on colonial conquest and African resistance as presented in Ministry of Education, *Secondary School Syllabuses: Social Sciences* (Dar es Salaam, 1976).

Seventeen

Jacks-of-all-Arts
or Ustadhi?
The Poetics of Cultural Production
in Tanzania*

KELLY M. ASKEW

It was during a conversation in August 1992 with the American Cultural Attaché in Dar es Salaam that I first grew aware of a disjuncture between local and state artistic objectives in Tanzania. 1992 was a momentous year for this East African nation. After a prolonged and economically disastrous pursuit of African socialism and a long-drawn-out battle with the IMF and World Bank over the latter's demands to liberalize the economy and eliminate single-party socialism, the Tanzanian government formally installed multi-partyism. Economic liberalization had been introduced several years earlier, heralding this as a period of transition, a time of social transformation for this young nation. The Cultural Attaché listened politely as I described my research on musical performance and the development of Tanzanian national culture before offering his own opinion of the latter. His point of reference was an exhibit then on display at the National Museum of paintings by students at the *Chuo cha Sanaa cha Taifa*, the National College of Arts. 'Where else in the world', he scoffed, 'can you find a national museum displaying mediocre, uninspired paintings painted by *music* students?'

Although certainly an insensitive and condescending remark, the Attaché nevertheless inadvertently hit upon a significant point. As I discovered over the course of the next three years, there exists in Tanzania an unambiguous discontinuity in approach and intent in the training of state versus private musicians and artists. In stating this, I do not intend to further dichotomize state-society relations. On the contrary, the data I present here show an undeniable blurring of practices and agents across domains earmarked as state-directed versus those directed by local communities. In spite of this, an aesthetic disjuncture can be identified at levels of ideology and practice that pits state objectives against those of arts practitioners. Through an analysis of music production, I shall demonstrate here how this disjuncture – born of competing definitions of artistry and social responsibility, as well as overlapping layers of artistic discipline, sedimentary socialist rhetoric, and emergent capitalist ethos – poses contrastive sets of artistic ideals. Whereas local, private musical bands seek to produce *ustadhi* ('experts', 'masters', 'divas'), the official mandate of the National College of Arts in Bagamoyo is a 'broad-focus' education designed to produce generic *wasanii* ('artists', from the Kiswahili noun *sanaa* 'arts'). College graduates are expected to be skilled in *all* the arts (dance, music, theater, and visual arts) – jacks-of-all-arts, if you will – and are thus considered by the state as best suited to propagate and encourage the development of Tanzanian national culture.

A comparison of these divergent ideals, the objects they seek to construct, and the subjects committed to their perpetuation imparts understanding of political performativity in Tanzania and the cultural boundaries of the nation which, in the words of Homi Bhabha, contain 'thresholds of meaning that must be crossed, erased, and translated in the processes of cultural production'.[1] The question of who holds cultural authority in Tanzania presents a starting point for theorizing a 'poetics' (in the sense put forward by Michael Herzfeld of performed rhetoric[2]) of aesthetics. As Bhabha states, 'the image of cultural authority may be ambivalent because it is caught, uncertainly, in the act of "composing" its powerful image'.[3] It is the act of composition that is under scrutiny here. But while Bhabha posits a conflict in national narratives between 'the pedagogical' and 'the performative', wherein the performative (the liminal, the marginal, the popular) interrupts, interrogates, and evokes shifts in the pedagogical (official nationalist discourse),[4] I suggest that the pedagogical, to use his terms, is also essentially performative. Just as citizens perform their constructions of cultural identification, so too do states. The case of musical training and performance in Tanzania, during the recent years of liberalization (1992 to the present) when that state has been actively rewriting its narratives, provides compelling evidence to support this argument.

In examining cultural production in Tanzania, I necessarily begin with a historical review of the state's articulated cultural objectives and introduce its primary narrators: the Ministry of Culture[5] and the National Executive Committee of the ruling party *Chama cha Mapinduzi* (CCM). Understanding how national narratives are performed, however, requires attention to the multiple agents/agencies involved in official cultural production: the Ministry, the CCM, the National College of Arts, cultural officers at the regional and district levels, and performers in state-sponsored cultural troupes. This diverse cast of functionaries produces overlapping representations of national culture that are additionally complicated by local practices of cultural production. Two genres commonly performed in both state and local contexts – *ngoma* (traditional dance) and *taarab* (sung Swahili poetry) – constitute key sites of cultural production that highlight the aesthetic dissonance between and among national and local agents. While Bhabha's concept of national narratives offers analytic insight, it is flawed in its lack of attention to the performance of these narratives and by its corollary that state

305

agents alone do the narrating. As the data presented here clearly illustrate, Tanzanian citizens, far from posing a passive audience for state narrators, have always been actively involved in the writing and rewriting, performing and reforming of these narratives.

Cultural Production in Tanzania: Of Troupes and Officers

Following the colonial devastation of indigenous cultures and traditions (an experience eloquently attested to by such intellectuals as Frantz Fanon, Ngugi wa Thiong'o, and Wole Soyinka[6] among others), many African regimes prioritized the reconstruction of their cultures and the re-writing of their histories. Calls for the creation of national cultures abounded and in this spirit, Julius Nyerere of Tanzania founded the Ministry of National Culture and Youth with the oft-quoted remarks:

> I have...set up an entirely new Ministry: the Ministry of National Culture and Youth... because I believe that its culture is the essence and spirit of any nation. A country which lacks its own culture is no more than a collection of people without the spirit which makes them a nation. Of all the crimes of colonialism there is none worse than the attempt to make us believe we had no indigenous culture of our own; or that what we did have was worthless ....
>
> So I have set up this new Ministry to help us regain our pride in our own culture. I want it to seek out the best of the traditions and customs of all the tribes and make them part of our national culture.[7]

This rather inclusive approach towards national cultural production (even given the problematic qualification of determining 'the best' traditions and customs) paralleled an ideological environment immediately following Tanganyika's independence in 1961 that emphasized national unity.[8] Nyerere assigned the Ministry of Culture primary responsibility for ensuring the recovery, promotion and development of the nation's culture. He furthermore proclaimed it the most important ministry of his administration. Since *ngoma* was, and often still is, viewed as the purest and most authentic representation of Tanzanian custom, one of the ministry's first acts was to establish the National Dance Troupe in 1963.[9] This was not a uniquely Tanzanian approach. Within the first few years of independence, Tanzania entertained visits from the National Dance Troupe of Guinea and the National Dance Troupe of Zambia, in addition to the National Cultural Troupe of China. Cultural troupes clearly constituted symbolic markers and purveyors of national identity, and through the early creation of its own troupe, Tanzania asserted its identity as an independent nation-state.

In 1967, Nyerere inaugurated the Arusha Declaration and charted the course for Tanzania's twenty-five-year engagement with African socialism. This was an all-encompassing ideological/political/economic/

social platform characterized by rhetorical homage to a romanticized communal past, emphasis on agriculture, communal villagization, nationalization of major industries, and Africanization of upper-level positions in the economic sector. 'We must run while others walk', was Nyerere's motto, indicating full awareness of the inequities in the global economy and the efforts Tanzanians would have to exert to improve their position within it.

The radical turn towards socialism evoked a complementary shift in the poetics of cultural production. Whereas the ministry's goals in the years immediately following independence were to collect, document, and promote all indigenous arts and customs, from 1967 on a socialist template was superimposed on the process of collection: only those practices considered progressive and in keeping with socialist principles would be retained. The writings of Fanon, Bertolt Brecht, Ernst Fischer, Paolo Freire, and Augusto Boal wielded considerable influence in this process.[10] By the early 1970s, then, Tanzanian cultural production was clearly articulated as a political project, as illustrated by the following assessment of the ruling party's (then TANU – the Tanganyika African National Union) involvement in cultural activities:

> In a socialist society all art is seen as a servant of society. A tool to help man better understand and shape his society according to his collective needs. Divorcing art or the artist from society is another sin of the decadent bourgeoisie society, inseparable from the commercialisation of art, which all socialist societies have to fight...
>
> The art which, therefore, our division of Culture and its organs should promote in our rural communities, *ujamaa* villages, and urban centres is that which will help us to better understand our environment and transform it according to our needs.[11]

In his 1974 contribution to a UNESCO series on cultural policy, Louis Mbughuni, former Director of Arts and Language in the Ministry of Culture, summarized Tanzania's cultural policy in six points:

(i) a selective revival of our traditions and customs
(ii) promotion and preservation of our cultural heritage
(iii) our culture as an instrument of national development and unity
(iv) the development of our tribal cultures into one national culture
(v) the contribution of our cultures towards the development of mankind and the contribution of other cultures to our own development
(vi) the necessity of overhauling the educational systems inherited from the former colonial powers and the need for all Tanzanians to remove the influence of the colonial mentality from their minds.[12]

This list makes evident a number of relevant points: first, the intention to be *selective* in cultural recovery; second, the use of Culture (capitalized in the original text) as a tool for nationalist, by this time determinedly *socialist*, development; third, *standardization* or *homogenization* of culture vis-à-vis the desire to unify all groups into a single national culture; fourth, a stand against cultural isolation as expressed in the desire for *cultural exchange* with other (primarily other socialist) countries; and finally, *anti-colonialist* rejection of the colonial residue in education specifically but in all things more generally. Socialism provided the scales on which customs were weighed for selection or repression. It projected the development goals to be echoed through artistic production. In short, socialism determined both the object (a young nation struggling out from under the weight of an oppressive colonial past) and the objectives (a truly egalitarian, self-reliant, socialist society) of national cultural production.

In keeping with these goals, Tanzania forged relationships of economic, political and cultural exchange with various socialist countries (for example, Guinea, Zambia) but most significantly China with which it shared an agriculture-oriented socialist agenda. The senior-level visits back and forth between these two nations were many and China's material contributions to Tanzania constitute the largest aid program for any African state from a communist nation: as early as 1976, the total exceeded US$450 million.[13] When China's cultural troupe toured Tanzania soon after independence, its members suggested that talented Tanzanian youth be sent to China to be trained in acrobatics. A total of 20 youths between the ages of 12 and 14 were selected and sent to China in 1965 for four years training with the Wuhan acrobatic group.[14] An additional ten were sent in 1968 to be trained in the performance of musical accompaniment for acrobatic shows. Upon their return in 1969, these youths were organized into the National Acrobatic Troupe and gave their first public performance in February 1970. In 1974, a two-year course in drama was inaugurated at the University of Dar es Salaam and its first graduates in 1976 were collected to form the National Drama Troupe. Eventually, all three troupes were united to create the National Theater Company that performed the full variety of arts: *ngoma*, *sarakasi* (acrobatics), and *michezo ya maigizo* (drama).

On his appointment as Director of Arts and National Language, one of Louis Mbughuni's first official acts was to disband the National Theater Company in 1979. According to one of his successors, Godwin Kaduma, the Company was disbanded because 'it was misleading for people to think that [the troupe performers] were experts'.[15] In a 1997 interview, however, Mr Mbughuni indicated that the impetus for disbanding the troupe was his realization that these young people were uneducated and that some of them were getting involved in illicit activities.[16] Separated from their families at a very young age for four years of training in China and then directly channeled into ten years of performing as national artists, they had never received a primary school education and were showing the effects of having been raised by an impersonal bureaucracy. The conceptualization of Tanzanian socialism as *Ujamaa* ('familyhood') clearly remained for these young people little more than rhetoric.

In 1980, the year after he disbanded the national troupe, Mbughuni established the National College of Arts (*Chuo cha Sanaa cha Taifa*) in Bagamoyo, about an hour's drive north of Dar es Salaam. He recruited the former troupe performers to serve as the College's teaching staff, hoping that it would accomplish the dual objectives of resituating them in a productive role and extending their talents further afield so as to generate popular participation in the arts throughout the country.[17] In an interview, Mr Mbughuni explained that he established the College to accomplish three objectives:

(i) to provide skilled artists with access to formal education and in turn to resituate them as educators in a proper school setting;
(ii) to provide a diploma for students studying the arts that would there-after certify them as accredited teachers of the arts; and
(iii) to produce cultural officers for the planning and promotion of Tan-zanian arts and culture.[18]

Mbughuni's explicit goal was to provide what he termed a 'broad-focus training'. Students of the College had to follow a highly regi-mented three-year programme in which they took the same mandatory courses for the first two years in music, dance, theater and visual arts. They could select a major and a minor only in their third and final year of study and were offered six options: Theater major with a minor in either Music or Dance, Dance major with a minor in Music or Theatre, or Music major with a minor in either Theater or Dance. (Although visual arts constituted part of their mandatory coursework, students could not major or minor in it – hence, the American Cultural Attaché's dismissal of the student exhibits at the National Museum.) Specialization in any one art was hindered by design, so as to produce broadly trained students qualified to become cultural officers or members of government-sponsored cultural troupes (and little more). Nonetheless, admission to the College remains highly competitive with roughly 500 applicants per year, of whom 50 receive auditions and 15 are admitted.[19]

It appears that the rationale behind the establishment of the National College of Arts included an attempt to thwart the development of unequal status and power relations between experts and novices, a position resonant with socialist egalitarian principles. Rather than promote an artistic hierarchy in which there would be a division of artistic labor, the 'broad focus training' mandate would discourage expertise and generate generic 'artists' or *wasanii*, not particularly skilled in any one art but some-what adept in all. These state 'Jacks-of-all-arts' would be best suited then to encourage and promote all the arts wherever, as government-educated, government-employed cultural officers, they were posted. Although Tanzanian socialists typically rejected affiliation with Marxist-Leninist ideology, intellectual convergence nevertheless arises in this regard. In *The German Ideology*, Marx and Engels condemned the capitalist division of labor that relegates and reduces people to exclusive spheres of activity, 'while in communist society, where nobody has one exclusive sphere of activity but each can become accomplished in any branch he wishes, society regulates the general production and thus makes it possible for me to do one thing today and another tomorrow, to hunt in the morning, fish in the afternoon, rear cattle in the evening, criticize after dinner ... without ever becoming hunter, fisherman, shepherd or critic'.[20] Lenin similarly argued for the abolition of division of labor, advocating in its stead 'the education, training and preparation of people who will have an *all-round development*, an *all-round* training, people who *will be able to do everything*. Towards this goal communism is marching...' (emphasis in original).[21]

In the 1980s, the National College of Arts thus became the focus of ministerial efforts. It was expected and desired that the college would generate corps of new cultural officers and cultural troupes who would spread the state's approach to the performing arts throughout the country. This approach, crystallized in the training procedures of the college, promoted conformity and discipline (as embodied in perfectly synchronized movements and neatly arranged linear formations), a collective orientation (favoring group over individual performances), and frequent laudatory references to the nation, the ruling party, Tanzanian national culture, and the President. Although the national troupe was disbanded, the cultural troupe concept remained popular until recent times. Most major governmental bodies sponsored their own troupe (for example, the National Insurance Corporation, the Tanzania Prison Authority, the Tanzania Harbours Authority, Dar es Salaam Development Corporation, National Service Army, the Dar es Salaam Police Force, the Organization of Tanzanian Trade Unions – to name but a few), that – like the former national troupe – performed a variety of art forms of which *ngoma* was a necessary staple.[22] Thus, the hope that the transformation of national performers into national teachers would sacrifice one cultural troupe for the sake of creating many more throughout the country did partly come to fruition. Nyerere's insistence on *kujitegemea* ('self-reliance') as a national attribute and economic goal applied well in the case of cultural production, in that local communities could create and support cultural troupes of their own rather than depending on cultural sustenance from a potentially elitist national troupe.

But the 'local' in this case was still constituted by the state, for while troupes did increase in number throughout the country, the vast majority were affiliated with the state sector. A few private troupes emerged, but these were less common.[23] Thus, the envisioned populist involvement in cultural production as outlined by state narrators remained an unrealized goal. Yet arts continued to be performed everywhere. The country is not lacking in a vibrant performance ethic; music and dance dominate weddings, initiations, and a host of other celebratory occasions. What one finds, then, is that the forms and formulations of artistic production outlined by state policy in Tanzania failed to replace local forms and formulations; instead, a somewhat awkward co-existence emerged.

'A Shortened Arm': The Impact of Economic Crisis

Two reasons for this failure are lack of stability and inadequate funding. Despite the tremendous rhetorical investment in national culture and the performing arts, the Culture Division has been moved no less than ten times from one ministry to another – at times promoted to a full-fledged

Table 17.1 A Migrant Ministry: The Tanzanian Culture Division,
1948–Present

Dates	Swahili title	English title
1948	Idara ya Maendeleo	Development Department
1957	Wizara ya Serikali za Mitaa na Utawala	Ministry of Local Government and Administration
1959	Wizara ya Vyama vya Ushirika na Maendeleo	Ministry of Cooperative Societies and Development
December 10, 1962	Wizara ya Mila na Vijana	Ministry of National Culture and Youth
1964	Wizara ya Maendeleo na Utamaduni	Ministry of Community Development and National Culture
1967	Wizara ya Tawala za Mikoa na Maendeleo Vijijini	Ministry of Regional Administration and Rural Development
1969	Wizara ya Elimu ya Taifa	Ministry of National Education
February 11, 1974	Wizara ya Elimu ya Taifa na Utamaduni	Ministry of National Education and Culture
1975	Wizara ya Utamaduni wa Taifa na Vijana	Ministry of National Culture and Youth
1980	Wizara ya Habari na Utamaduni	Ministry of Information and Culture
1984	Ofisi ya Waziri Mkuu na Makamu wa Kwanza ya Rais	Office of the Prime Minister and First Vice President
1985	Wizara ya Maendeleo ya Jamii, Utamaduni, Vijana na Michezo	Ministry of Community Development, Culture, Youth, and Sports
1988	Wizara ya Kazi,Utamaduni na Ustawi wa Jamii	Ministry of Labor, Culture, and Social Welfare
1991	Wizara ya Elimu na Utamaduni	Ministry of Education and Culture

ministry only to be demoted back to a division or office within another ministry (see Table 17.1). This constant migration has prevented it from establishing a permanent base from which to devise and pursue its goals.[24]

Secondly, the Division has always suffered from a notable lack of economic support. It was constrained early on from pursuing its objectives by financial factors, and the situation has only worsened. Economic crisis – born of a series of factors including unfavorable terms of trade in the global economy, mismanagement, a long struggle to establish socialism, war with Uganda, and recent structural adjustment programs – has had an impact on every sector of Tanzania's economy and government. The Culture Division has been particularly hard hit. A large number of cultural officers have lost their jobs, and those that remain do not receive regular salaries. In Tanga region, where I did the bulk of my research, the telephone of the regional cultural office was disconnected in 1993 and never reconnected due to lack of payment, and the one automobile shared by all cultural officers was re-assigned to the education officers. Low morale plagues those who remain, and in the minds of many the lack of regular salaries legitimizes lack of regular work. Once when I stopped by the culture office to say hello, I found a cultural officer sitting at an empty desk knitting. By way of response to an unasked question, she explained with a somewhat bitter laugh that knitting was, after all, a cultural activity, was it not? Then she shared with me her plan to apply for one of the small development loans available to female entrepreneurs to open a tailoring shop and 'forget this business of Culture'.

In July 1998, I interviewed Emmanuel Mollel, then Acting Director of Arts and Language.[25] In a conversation that meandered around the cessation of arts competitions, the laying off of cultural district officers, and the virtual elimination of regional cultural officers (each region is now allocated one regional cultural officer – a significant drop from the original five or more), a word that cropped up again and again was *ukata* or 'lack of funds'. 'The government's arm', explained Mollel, 'has shortened'.[26]

The situation has forced significant changes in the National College of Arts curriculum. Since the government now lacks the means to support the original vision of cultural officers in every region and district, it can no longer justify a broad-focus training geared to the production of cultural officers. In 1998, for the first time, *second*-year students at the College were allowed to select a major – an option previously available only to students in their third and final year of study. This quiet decision to relinquish adherence to the broad-focus educational concept and allow for the training of specialists indicates a major shift in a state aesthetic that once downplayed expertise and individual talent.

Funding and stability are indeed key factors that help explain why official cultural production in Tanzania did not produce the desired results. But there are other elements that shed light on why the anticipated popular support for state-defined national culture failed to materialize. These relate not only to the strength of local practices but to an understanding of how knowledge is constructed, how practices are learned, how nations are imagined, and how artistry is defined. To elucidate these concerns, the following sections present comparisons of musical practices in different state and local contexts and the ideologies that inform them. State performers and cultural officers propagate the state's aesthetic preoccupations (as exemplified by the curriculum of the National College of Arts) with collective conformity, discipline, skill in multiple performance genres, standardization, and the stifling of individual talent. These performative parameters unambiguously reflect nationalist and socialist ideals. They do not, however, correspond to local conceptions of artistic production, and it is to this disjuncture between divergent aesthetic ideals that we turn next via comparisons between local and state *ngoma* performance, and between local and state *taarab* performance.

KIUBATA of Tanga: Performing State Ideology

The city of Tanga has a justifiably widespread reputation for musical talent. Several genres of music are commonly performed in Tanga, the three most popular being *ngoma*, *taarab*, and *dansi* (urban popular music). It is a city rich in music and cultural traditions due to the many migrants from all over the country and beyond who came to work on neighboring sisal plantations and earned for Tanga Region the title 'sisal capital of the world'. Older residents recall a time in the not too distant past when music served as a key marker of neighborhood boundaries, with the sounds and sights of *ngoma* performance identifying one street as ethnically distinct from another. On weekend nights, numerous, competing rhythms would fill the air as groups vied with each other to attract the largest audience to their *ngoma* which, then as now, required collaboration between specialized musicians (experts in the performance of one variety of *ngoma*) and bystanders who, with a little encouragement, start dancing.

Beyond *ngoma*, Tanga's position as a coastal Swahili city means that *taarab* is also highly popular. This genre of sung Swahili poetry derives its name from the *tarabun* (Arabic for 'ecstasy', 'joy') it evokes in the heart of the listener through its poetic meter, beautiful melodies, and metaphoric language. Typically performed during women's wedding celebrations, *taarab* is undergoing transformations in context and content as it expands beyond its traditionally female Muslim setting to new state (for example, political rallies, diplomatic functions) and capitalist (for example, paid concerts) situations that seek to profit from the genre's tremendous popularity. And then there is *dansi*, the urban dance music found in bar-halls across the country that incorporates elements from American swing and Congolese rumba as well as local *ngoma* to create a uniquely Tanzanian product.

Tanga hosts all these genres, and moreover claims musical fame in all three: in *ngoma* for being the home region of the Zigua ethnic group praised nationwide for its musical prowess, in *taarab* for being (until recently) the major performance center of *taarab* on the Tanzanian mainland[27] and home to the famous Black Star and Lucky Star musical clubs, and in *dansi* for producing two of the earliest and most popular bands of the 1950s – Jamhuri Jazz and Atomic Jazz. While the decline of the sisal industry starting in the 1970s generated the state of economic crisis that still characterizes Tanga today and provoked widespread emigration to healthier cities like Dar es Salaam, the polyglot ambience and musical significance of Tanga remain.

Finally, Tanga currently boasts two state-sponsored cultural troupes that put into practice the state aesthetic of displaying competence in multiple art forms. Sponsored by the local port authority, KIUBATA (*Kikundi cha Utamaduni Bandari Tanga* – 'Tanga Harbours Authority Cultural Troupe') was established in 1976 and performs *ngoma, michezo ya maigizo* ('drama'), *sarakasi* ('acrobatics'), *taarab,* and *dansi.* The Tanga Cement Company troupe, more simply known as *Saruji* ('cement'), is sponsored by the Tanga Cement Company, a government parastatal. Established in 1986, *Saruji* performs a similarly varied yet different repertoire of performing arts: *ngoma, sarakasi, michezo ya maigizo, mazingaombwe* ('magic acts'), and *ngonjera* (dramatized poetry, generally political in theme). *Saruji* does not perform either *taarab* or *dansi,* while KIUBATA performs neither *mazingaombwe* nor *ngonjera,* and of the two, KIUBATA is larger with some sixty performers to *Saruji*'s thirty-five.

KIUBATA is very popular in Tanga, but considerably more so in the surrounding rural areas where it provides a full-scale variety show to people short on entertainment options. In part, this represents a fulfillment of government objectives because the troupe performs state-prescribed Tanzanian Culture to many isolated audiences. But the troupe also acquired a national reputation following its performance in the 1992 National Arts and Language Competitions in Arusha where it won first prize in the *ngoma* competition.

By simple good fortune, my research with KIUBATA spanned the three months preceding and nearly three years following the 1992 national competitions, during which time I observed their training regimen and the ways in which state aesthetic principles were applied and practiced.[28] Since KIUBATA represented the whole Tanga Region in the competitions, cultural officers from the Ministry's district and regional branches regularly attended pre-competition rehearsals, their self-described role being to guide the performances and ensure that they befitted 'national interests'. Several of them had been trained at the National College of Arts, and their criticisms were of two types: *aesthetic* and *ideological*. These officials expressed an *aesthetic* concern with form, specifically with the flawless execution of straight lines and perfectly synchronized movements. The second layer of critique, however, focused on *ideological* content as embodied in dance and articulated through song.

The guidelines of the *ngoma* competition dictated that competing groups must perform a total of three *ngoma*: two from the group's home region, and one from a distant region (to inculcate national unity). Each group was limited to a total of 30 minutes of performance time that could be distributed among the three *ngoma* as it wished. A maximum of twenty performers was allowed per group (including both dancers and instrumentalists). KIUBATA had selected three of its most popular *ngoma* for the competitions. The two local *ngoma* selections, *Mbuji* and *Ukala,* both hail from the Zigua ethnic group of Handeni District in Tanga Region who, as noted earlier, are widely celebrated for their musical skill. The third selection was a *ngoma* of the Makonde ethnic group from the southern region of Mtwara.

Mbuji

The process of producing three *ngoma* for national consumption at the competitions entailed considerable negotiation. Each *ngoma* elicited different concerns, and these concerns made manifest the state aesthetic that KIUBATA emulated and sought to embody in order to win the competition. *Mbuji*, originally a dance performed in the context of Zigua puberty rituals and named for a type of rattle wrapped around the dancers' ankles, is performed by KIUBATA as a set of choreographed linear formations. Sometimes the lines of men and women face each other; at other times they face the audience. The moderate duple meter accompanying the first section of dancing is interrupted by a brief section of unaccompanied song with the lyrics 'Culture builds the country' (*'Utamaduni wajenga nchi'*). A sudden switch to a much faster tempo introduces the hip-rotating dance movement by the female dancers called *kiuno* – a movement that, by its overtly sexual implications, identifies this as a puberty or marriage dance. While the lyrics articulate Tanzanian political discourse, the choice of language further reinforces the message of national unity. Although troupe members frequently expressed their desire to reproduce this *ngoma* in as authentic a manner as possible, the song lyrics were sung in the national language of Kiswahili, not the local language of Kizigua – a choice signifying the workings of a state aesthetic.

Ukala

The second *ngoma* KIUBATA performed in the competition was *Ukala*, traditionally performed to accompany the presentation of offerings (*tambiko*) to ancestral spirits. This *ngoma* enacts a hunt. Dancers mime a protracted search for animals, the hunt, and then the slaughtering of the animal. In the second half of the performance, the successful hunters call for women to come and collect the meat and carry it back to the village. KIUBATA members said that, because this *ngoma* serves a very important didactic purpose, it justified spending twenty of their allotted thirty minutes on its performance.

This *ngoma* evolved through numerous variations and modifications during pre-competition rehearsals in a process that highlighted the self-conscious negotiations surrounding authenticity, nationalism, and cultural production. Here, the concern for authenticity overrode that of nationalism, at least in that the choice of Kizigua language prevailed. Yet, authenticity was not uniformly applied, as evidenced by the untraditional addition (this not being a dance associated with initiation or marriage ceremonies) of the erotic *kiuno* hip movement by female dancers simply for the sake of audience enjoyment.

In one particularly intense rehearsal, a dispute arose between the KIUBATA leadership and the cultural officers over the choreography and accoutrements of the male dancers. The cultural officers argued that every action should be meaningful and took issue with the use of wooden rifles rather than bows and arrows, which were thought to be

315

more appropriately 'traditional', whereas the rifle was a remnant of *ukoloni* ('colonialism') and therefore undesirable. This concern constituted an unambiguous rejection of Westernization, of 'colonialism', in favor of African traditionalism. It was subsequently agreed that the hunter would attempt to use his rifle but it would backfire and in disgust he would throw it down to take up a bow and arrow. This was not a popular decision among the dancers. They argued that achieving exact synchronization of movement would be considerably more difficult with cumbersome bows and arrows than with the fake rifles. Their argument could not, in the end, trump that of the cultural officers who insisted on the troupe's responsibility to perform and thus reaffirm Tanzania's ideological ideal – the return to a communal African past, inherently socialist and untainted by Western cultural imperialism.

There are multiple contradictions evident here. By this point in 1992, the government had officially retracted its socialist policies and announced plans for political and economic liberalization. In an attempt to dilute their embarrassment over political and economic failures, government officials sought rhetorical refuge in a steadfast insistence on the continued necessity of socialist *social* policy even while they were now implementing capitalist economic policy and democratic political reforms. As articulated by the cultural officers I knew, socialism remained the only responsible social policy for a country as ethnically diverse as Tanzania.[29]

Secondly, the cultural officers were selective in their rejection of Western elements. Rifles offended their ideological sensibilities, yet Western linear performance style, synchronized movements, and a performance format juxtaposing staged performers with a nonparticipating audience did not. A discursive shift, however, resolved the seeming discrepancy, for these latter practices were described as 'modern' rather than 'Western'. Whereas 'Western' evokes unequal power positions and imperialist agendas, the appellation 'modern' is considered culturally neutral and evaluated in a positive light. Here, the cultural officers mimicked a strategy outlined by Nyerere who, in describing the responsibilities of the newly-formed Ministry of Culture, stated:

> A nation which refuses to learn from foreign cultures is nothing but a nation of idiots and lunatics. Mankind could not progress at all if we all refused to learn from each other. But to learn from other cultures does not mean we should abandon our own. The sort of learning from which we can benefit is the kind which can help us to perfect and broaden our own culture.[30]

Hence, what James Scott calls an 'aesthetic of modernization' can be seen at work here, an aesthetic he identifies as one of the key motivational factors behind state-designed Ujamaa villages.[31]

Liungunjumu

The final *ngoma* KIUBATA performed in competition was *Liungunjumu*, a dance performed during the elaborate initiation rituals of the Makonde ethnic group, a group straddling the border between Tanzania and

Mozambique. Makonde, like Zigua, are widely lauded for *ngoma* performance; every cultural troupe I know in Tanzania has one or more Makonde *ngoma* in its repertoire.[32] In the 1940s, the sisal industry recruited large numbers of Makonde to work as laborers on the plantations, creating a number of Makonde communities in and around Tanga. At the time of my research, KIUBATA had several Makonde performers,[33] so *Liungunjumu* offered the advantage of fulfilling the foreign *ngoma* requirement without being truly foreign.

Makonde initiation rites continue to be performed quite frequently in Tanga as children come of age.[34] The number deemed sufficient to warrant the expense and energy involved in hosting an initiation varies from Makonde neighborhood to neighborhood. I was fortunate enough to attend four initiation ceremonies hosted by different neighborhoods, each of which spanned the course of several days. In one, four girls – all aged between twelve and fifteen – were initiated; in another, some sixteen boys and girls were initiated ranging in age from five to fifteen. Although I never saw *Liungunjumu* performed, there was enough uniformity of general performance principles in all the Makonde *ngoma* I witnessed to enable me to draw some conclusions about Makonde performance practice. Circle formations with drummers in the middle were the rule for every *ngoma* except for *guaride*, the dance in military formation performed by initiants as they returned from seclusion to their home community. The typical *ngoma* pattern consisted of a small (3–5) group of drummers surrounded by a circle of community members who dance the same step while individuals take turns entering the middle of the circle to demonstrate their skill. The uniform movements of those forming the circle complement the sense of spontaneity and improvization generated by those who enter the circle, sometimes in pairs or trios, with each individual striving to produce ever more elaborate dance moves before rejoining the circle.[35]

What a contrast, then, between these Makonde *ngoma* events and the rendition of *Liungunjumu* perfected by KIUBATA for competition. Strict linear formations define KIUBATA's *Liungunjumu*, the desired product being the precise execution of perfectly synchronized movements. During one rehearsal, I heard the director call out to the dancers, '*Mbona maembe?*' ('Why mangoes?'), which made little sense to me. He later explained that the feet of the dancers were sloppy in executing their formations, 'falling' without precision the way mangoes fall off the tree. Considerable painstaking effort went into the synchronization and standardization of movement, thereby denuding the *ngoma* of the spontaneity and improvization that characterize Makonde *ngoma* in local, non-state performance settings.

As the rehearsals progressed, this process of standardization characterized all three *ngoma* being prepared for competition. The performers grew adept at replicating their performances exactly, movement for movement, from one rehearsal to the next until variation and improvization were successfully eliminated. A few dance elements were included to give an impression of improvization, but in reality these were as rehearsed as the linear formations. In only one of the *ngoma* was a dancer singled out from the rest (the main hunter in *Ukala*) – the overall emphasis being undifferentiated group performance. KIUBATA's subsequent victory on 8 November 1992 as winners in the *ngoma* competition attests to a correspondence between the aesthetic standards they embodied and those sought by the competition judges and organizers. The troupe's message of cultural and national unity 'Culture builds the nation' was visually reinforced by the perfectly synchronized execution of these *ngoma*. Indeed, KIUBATA won for having successfully performed the state aesthetic ideal.

This exploration of KIUBATA's preparation for and performance in the 1992 National Competitions fills out the unidimensional perspective on state aesthetic criteria available in policy documents, because it shows how those criteria are negotiated and enacted in actual practice. KIUBATA is only one local manifestation of 'the state'. But as a group that has chosen to abide by state-defined aesthetic parameters of collective conformity, standardization, synchronization, strict discipline, and circumscription of individual improvization, it distinguishes itself from local performance events that display notably different aesthetic ideals. Whereas local *ngoma* performers tend to specialize in the performance of one or two *ngoma*, KIUBATA prides itself on a repertoire of 38 *ngoma* from a variety of ethnic groups, as well as its skill in performing other artistic genres such as drama and acrobatics. Whereas individual talent is celebrated and privileged in local *ngoma* events (for example, entering the circle of dancers in the case of Makonde *ngoma*), KIUBATA represses it and rehearses most improvization away. Whereas spontaneity and general participation mark local *ngoma* events, KIUBATA perform- ances clearly distinguish performers from audience and exercise strict discipline of movement.

We thus find the state aesthetic evidenced and reinscribed on various fronts and through various agents: (i) the competition guidelines (requiring two local and one non-local *ngoma* – a bid for national unity); (ii) enactment of these guidelines through the process of selecting winners; (iii) local cultural officers whose job is to voice state concerns; (iv) performances by state-sponsored troupes; (v) policy statements from the Ministry headquarters and speeches by state officials; and (vi) the National College of Arts whose training procedures and educational objectives sought to produce multi-talented non-specialists, generic *wasanii* designated to become cultural officers and troupe leaders in local areas. Taken together, these points illuminate how a state aesthetic is performed by the various agents committed to its perpetuation. We now shift genres to a comparison of state and local aesthetic principles in the domain of *taarab* performance.

Taarab Performance: Training Local *Ustadhi*

As a distinct genre of music and poetry, *taarab* arose along the Swahili

Coast but is now enjoyed throughout East Africa as well as in parts of the Middle East (especially in Oman and the United Arab Emirates). A distinguishing feature of *taarab* is its strict adherence to poetic structure. *Taarab* poetry follows conventions of rhyme (*vina*) and meter (*mizani*), and employs a heavy amount of metaphor and innuendo. The typical song is strophic, composed of verses (*mabeti*) sung to the same music (*muziki*) and interspersed with a common refrain ('chorus') and instrumental interlude. In *taarab* composition, it is not uncommon for these elements to be divided amongst different composers, with some excelling in poetry and others in melodies or instrumental parts. *Taarab* performance style entails a solo singer backed by a supporting chorus of three or more singers and an instrumental ensemble (in Tanga, instrumentation generally included an electric guitar, an electric bass, an electric keyboard, bongos, tambourine, clavé and, more recently, a drum-kit). Aside from the chorus, no one duplicates another's role in the group.

Contrasting with the training of College of Arts students as well as KIUBATA performers, the training of *taarab* performers in Tanga[36] entails the transformation of novice participants into full participants. In their path-breaking, practice-oriented approach to education, Jean Lave and Etienne Wenger offer a perspective on learning that is applicable to how *taarab* musicians learn to perform *taarab*.[37] Contrary to conventional wisdom, they argue, learning occurs not through the transmission of a defined body of knowledge from one person to another, but rather through shared participation in a given activity by both novices and expert practitioners. Education, or as they refer to it 'situated learning', is 'the process by which newcomers become part of a community of practice'.[38] Through active and increasing participation in the task at hand – be it college calculus or playing the guitar – learners develop into experts themselves.

In *taarab* bands, hierarchy is an indisputable fact of life. One attains status as a senior (and therefore more highly paid) musician only after moving up the ranks from devoted fan who memorizes the songs (*mshabiki*), to instrument handler (*mbebaji vyombo*), to technician who assists in setting up the instruments and equipment (*fundi mtambo*), to someone playing lighter percussion instruments (such as the tambourine or maracas) or singing back-up in the chorus, and finally, upon proving aptitude, to playing one of the primary instruments, singing solo, or composing (poetry, musical accompaniment, or both). Female musicians progress through a modified version of this ranking, skipping the instrument handler and technician stages. What I describe here as a coherent structure is in practice, however, only casually recognized as such. The titles of rank emerge only in passing reference rather than being conceptualized as a fully-fledged system. Through careful guidance from musicians recognized as masters, as *ustadhi* (a term that in Arabic and Kiswahili means 'teacher' as well as 'expert'), novice musicians learn *taarab* performance by participating and accruing increased ability. Every musician I interviewed readily identified the *ustadhi* with whom they had trained.

319

Taarab instruction and performance clearly emphasize and encourage individual talent and expertise. Audience attention is channeled towards the solo vocalist by his/her fancy attire and the fact that s/he stands while the back-up chorus is seated. This strikes a notable difference from state-directed *ngoma* performance, which – by means of matching costumes and synchronized, collective dance formations – emphasizes group uniformity and minimizes individuality. In these performances, it is generally only the lead drummer (whose rhythms direct the dance formations) and the cantor in call-and-response singing who perform singly, yet even then for only brief, temporary passages with no appreciable physical or visual separation from the group.

Thus *taarab* performance, like local *ngoma* performance but to an even greater degree, celebrates individual talent and expertise in a way utterly antithetical to state-directed *ngoma*. Moreover, those who achieve recognition as *ustadhi* (and for reasons I cannot explore here, these tend to be male) continually refine and improve upon their talent. Vocalists and guitarists alike aspire to execute successfully ever more intricate ornamental trills and embellishments on their respective instruments. Composers remain forever in search of inspiration to compose even more popular songs. Bongo players devise their own signature version of standard *taarab* rhythms and even invent new rhythms. There exists limitless potential for self-improvement and the acquisition of enhanced expertise. Artistic virtuosity is a celebrated aesthetic objective in *taarab* performance. While it would be wrong and simply untrue to posit state-directed *ngoma* performance as lacking in artistic virtuosity, it is not accorded the same amount of attention nor as clearly articulated a goal as local *taarab* performance. How does this compare with state-directed *taarab* performance? In the next section, I shall examine one government intervention in *taarab* performance and how the attempt to apply some of the same state aesthetic principles exemplified by KIUBATA met with only mixed success.

State *Taarab*: Aesthetics in Conflict

Tanzania One Theater (a.k.a. 'TOT') burst onto the Tanzanian music scene in 1992 with its hit song *Ngwinji* ('High-Class Prostitute'). This proved to have been a masterminded grand entrance, a marketing coup preceded by strategically leaked rumors that the ruling party CCM was hiding something top-secret at the Bagamoyo army base (within walking distance of the National College of Arts). Speculation in government as well as private newspapers fueled the curiosity of Dar es Salaam residents – just as intended. Yet it still came as a surprise when CCM announced on 18 August 1992 the introduction of its latest weapon for the propagation of CCM policy and the promotion of Tanzanian Culture: *Tanzania One Theater*.[39]

TOT's director, Captain John Komba, formerly director of the JWTZ (Tanzanian Defense Forces Army) choir and composer of the famous CCM praise song 'CCM Number One', explained that in July 1992 CCM decided to create a new cultural troupe, the cornerstone of which would be *taarab*. When I asked why *taarab*, he responded, 'It is loved by the people'.⁴⁰ This constituted a notable shift in official cultural policy that I explore at length elsewhere.⁴¹ On paper (even if not in practice), *taarab* had previously been declared 'non-indigenous' music and thus did not receive the same degree of government support as genres such as *ngoma*.⁴² For example, there has never been a *taarab* competition at the National Arts and Language Competitions nor was it a regular component of cultural troupe performances until the emergence of TOT.⁴³

TOT performances have typically ended with *taarab*.⁴⁴ The reason, I was told, is that if they performed it first, the audience would leave immediately afterwards since it was *taarab* that they came to see and hear. In support of this, descriptions of TOT shows that fill the 'Entertainment' sections of Tanzania's many newspapers often include statements such as, 'But it was the much-awaited taarab category that really made ... the memorable evening...',⁴⁵ and 'While both have powerful *ngoma* presentations, it is the *taarab* shows with their poetically social intrigues that many people love to listen to, watch the singers and sometimes dance to the tunes of *taarab*'.⁴⁶

That TOT constituted a major financial investment – sporting the latest in musical and PA equipment, housing and salaries for the performers, elaborate costumes, heavy publicity, and new transport buses – indicates the amount of importance CCM placed upon it.⁴⁷ Captain Komba, himself a member of the CCM National Executive Committee, was charged with the task of amassing the best *taarab* talent on the mainland and in the islands to create an unrivaled *taarab* performance group that would also – in keeping with standard cultural troupe performance practice – perform other genres such as *ngoma*, *kwaya*, and theater. He insisted to me, however, that *taarab* was the troupe's strength and attraction, and elaborated his point by describing his travels all over the nation from Zanzibar to Tanga to Mwanza to entice the best *taarab* singers, composers, and instrumentalists away from their respective bands with promises of high salaries and fame in this new state-sponsored troupe. He also confirmed that 'TOT was a response to the introduction of multipartyism for the purpose of promoting CCM'.⁴⁸

TOT reflects the conflict and contradictions between a state aesthetic stressing group uniformity and a local *taarab* aesthetic that values individual talent. Like other *taarab* groups, TOT demonstrates individual talent as evidenced by Captain Komba's country-wide search for the best *taarab* talent available. Nevertheless, subtle indicators of group uniformity exist in TOT that are absent from other groups. For instance, one of the most notable features of a TOT performance is the obvious expense lavished on costume. While *taarab* performances in general are marked by careful attention to star vocalists' apparel (for female singers, the most flamboyant dresses imaginable), TOT's back-up chorus is dressed as finely as another band's star soloists. And while other bands typically require uniforms for their male members only,

TOT invested heavily in its female members, thus creating a new and highly impressionable effect on its audiences.⁴⁹ Secondly, when TOT begins the *taarab* portion of a performance, the band performs soft instrumental music as the chorus files on to the stage in well-spaced lines (one for women, one for men) with all singers performing the same synchronized step. Only the soloists, who ascend the stage only during their solos and who dress differently from the uniformed chorus and instrumentalists, interrupt the image of group uniformity promulgated through movement and attire.

Finally, despite TOT's overt government affiliation, it does not sing party politics through *taarab*. Associated with Swahili wedding events, *taarab* songs articulate love politics more than anything else: love lost, love gained, love unrequited. Even though TOT was specifically billed as a promotion vehicle for CCM and organized principally around *taarab* performance, it does not sing about CCM while performing *taarab*. 'If we only sang CCM, people would run away', explained Captain Komba.⁵⁰ Instead, its members sing about love while raising the ante of sexual innuendo to previously unknown heights. Party praise songs, meanwhile, are reserved for the troupe's *kwaya* ('choir') performances, the genre in which Captain Komba acquired his musical, as well as political, reputation.

This contradiction exposes the unresolved conflict between state and local aesthetic principles in state-sponsored *taarab*. Previous attempts to employ *taarab* for party politics met with little success. In 1989 (before the advent of political liberalization), I attended a performance in Zanzibar of the CCM-sponsored *Culture Musical Club* held to raise awareness of local elections and promote voter registration. Not only did it not attract the normally sizable *taarab* crowd, but only half the orchestra attended the event. This may have reflected a conscious administrative decision rather than protest on the part of the musicians, but even so it would indicate that an official state occasion did not warrant the full orchestra that one normally finds at weddings and concert events. Then, when the orchestra performed a song with the refrain, 'Vote, vote, vote', nobody tipped the musicians (a reliable indication of audience lack of interest). Meanwhile on the mainland, JKT Taarab, a *taarab* orchestra sponsored by the National Service Army and housed in army barracks, has for years sung almost exclusively about love and personal relationships despite its government sponsorship and regular appearance at state events (before the arrival of TOT, that is, which has since largely displaced it).

To sum up, in this comparison of *taarab* as performed by private and state-sponsored bands, I inquire if the same state aesthetic I identified in cultural policy documents, in the National College of Arts curriculum, in the National Arts and Language Competitions guidelines, and in state-sponsored *ngoma* performance, also emerges in state-sponsored *taarab* performance. While my data show that it has not altogether replaced the dominant local *taarab* aesthetic that celebrates individuality, it nevertheless has inserted itself in suggestive ways. The two aesthetics combine relatively well in TOT performances. Elements from each are identifiable: collective conformity in attire and strict discipline of movement in the chorus co-exist and are in strong contrast with the flamboyant star qualities of the lead vocalists. One could argue that the latter's individuality is indeed enhanced by a backdrop of uniformity, and that TOT's tremendous popularity could be interpreted as a resounding public welcome for this aesthetic synthesis. On the other hand, the synthesis could be viewed as a concession, a recognition that *taarab* cannot exist within exclusive state aesthetic parameters. Were *taarab* vocalists stripped of their solos and forced to sing choruses with everyone else, dress like everyone else, and parade on to the stage along with everybody else, the performance would cease to be *taarab*. *Taarab* performance requires the privileging of one voice over others. Thus, rather than viewing TOT as an example of the state aesthetic insinuating itself into *taarab* performance, it is more useful to understand this as a compromise between two divergent, even opposing, aesthetics: a case of the state surrendering to an aesthetic it cannot defeat.

Conclusions

I began this chapter with the proposition that we rethink Homi Bhabha's description of national narratives as pedagogical and opposed to the performative acts of citizens. The ethnographic analysis offered here forces us to confront the performative aspects of national narratives. It would be unfair to claim that Bhabha makes a strict dichotomy between pedagogical states and performative citizens because his argument is more fluid than that. However, the theoretical strategy of contrasting 'the pedagogical' and 'the performative' inevitably sets up a dichotomy that invites modification. I have demonstrated here that 'the pedagogical' is necessarily performed. Another study another day might analyze instead how 'the performative' (acts of resistance, contention, compliance, etc.) often develops its own pedagogies.

Bhabha also points to the ambivalence and disjunctive nature common to most, if not all, national narratives that derive from tensions between pedagogical and performative elements.[51] The cases I present here of divergent aesthetic principles in Tanzania offer clear illustrations of this disjuncture and various ways it has been (often temporarily) resolved. But disjuncture can also arise from exterior circumstances, such as economic crisis or political transition.

Economic crisis in Tanzania has left its mark on cultural production. So too has political liberalization. Cultural offices do not have resources to support their pedagogical agenda. Cutbacks and government downsizing have forced a re-organization and re-writing of cultural efforts, including a re-conceptualization of the National College of Arts and its role in a liberalized Tanzania. Shifts in political paradigms, meanwhile, have opened up social and cultural space for the emergence of individual self-expression in state-defined parameters that had privileged collective conformity. The new right to choose between political parties, for example, corresponds with the promotion of TOT celebrity singers as part of an ideological shift away from collective ideologies.

Loren Kruger, who writes about national theaters and national identity in Britain, France, and the United States, also identifies crisis and transition as key instigators of shifts in national scripts.[52] Kruger offers the concept of 'theatrical nationhood' as both 'a cultural monument to legitimate hegemony and the site on which the excavation and perhaps the toppling of that monument might be performed'.[53] The performing arts, being of the public sphere, create spaces in which modes of political representation and perceptions of 'the people' are presented, endorsed, legitimized and debated. Kruger relates the differing artistic, social and political objectives of national theaters in France, Britain, and the United States to varying political-economic circumstances, histories and ideologies. The Great Depression, for instance, placed unavoidable restrictions on what the Federal Theater Project in late 1930s America could realistically accomplish: '...the FTP could not aspire to the prestige of the metropolitan national theaters of Europe, fitted with the 'greatest actors, writers, designers, plays, all housed in appropriately magnificent surroundings'. Instead, it took as its point of departure an acknowledgement of the national scale of the profound social and economic distress caused by the Depression and sought to realize the potential of theater to mobilize the nation as a whole to tackle the crisis: 'our strength lies in the problems of the majority that makes up our audience'.[54]

In the case of Tanzania, economic crisis and political change have similarly placed restrictions on the enactment of state cultural policy. Yet it is not merely material conditions but also popular responses from those who would be constituted as state subjects that shape and determine the relative success or failure of government interventions. As Kruger notes, 'the impact of the carefully orchestrated mass spectacle is considerable, but it has historically not obliterated the persistently mixed reactions of a variety of audiences, whose multiple responses resist unilateral absorption into the trances of power'.[55] Local aesthetic principles and priorities can pose significant obstacles to state political objectives. By examining the poetics of Tanzanian cultural production through aesthetic ideals and processes of musical training within both state-defined and locally defined parameters, we can discern the adjustment, modification, revision and accommodation that mark the processes of crafting musicians, artists, citizens and nations.

Notes

* This essay benefited from comments and criticisms received when I presented earlier drafts at the 1997 American Anthropological Association meetings and in faculty seminars at the University of California, Santa Cruz, Department of Anthropology (2004) and the University of Michigan Center for Afroamerican and African Studies

(2004). It draws heavily upon research I pursued during a three-year field period in Tanzania (Tanga, Dar es Salaam, and Zanzibar) from August 1992 to August 1995, plus several follow-up visits for a month each in 1997, 1998, and 2001. I wish to thank the Fulbright-Hays Fellowship program, the Ford Foundation, Indiana University, and the University of Michigan for their financial support. I also extend my heartfelt thanks to Julia Elyachar, James Giblin, Michael Herzfeld, Bradley Levinson, Gregory Maddox, Hudita Mustafa, Hanan Sabea, and an anonymous reviewer for their generous and thoughtful suggestions during the preparation of this essay. Full responsibility for any errors and omissions, of course, remains with me.

1. Homi Bhabha, 'Introduction: Narrating the Nation', in Homi Bhabha (ed.), *Nation and Narration* (London and New York: Routledge, 1990), p. 4.

2. Michael Herzfeld, *The Poetics of Manhood: Contest and Identity in a Cretan Mountain Village* (Princeton, NJ: Princeton University Press, 1985), and *Cultural Intimacy: Social Poetics in the Nation-State* (New York and London: Routledge, 1997).

3. Bhabha, 'Introduction', p. 3.

4. Homi Bhabha, 'DisseminNation: Time, Narrative, and the Margins of the Modern Nation', in Homi Bhabha (ed.), *Nation and Narration* (London and New York: Routledge, 1990), pp. 291–322.

5. As will be described later on, the Culture Division changed ministries multiple times beginning as the Ministry of National Culture and Youth in 1962 and passing through no less than nine different ministries or government offices before ending up in today's Ministry of Education and Culture. For the sake of simplicity, I shall refer to the 'Ministry of Culture' rather than specify each name change, to avoid unnecessary confusion.

6. Frantz Fanon, *The Wretched of the Earth* (New York: Grove Press, 1963); Ngugi wa Thiong'o, *Barrel of a Pen: Resistance to Repression in Neo-Colonial Kenya* (London: New Beacon Books, 1983); idem, *Decolonising the Mind* (London: James Currey, 1986); idem, *Moving the Centre: The Struggle for Cultural Freedoms* (London: James Currey, 1993); Wole Soyinka, 'Africa's Culture Producers', *Society* 28, no. 2 (1991), pp. 32–40.

7. Julius Nyerere, 'President's Inaugural Address – 10 December 1962', in *Freedom and Unity, Uhuru na Umoja: A Selection from Writings and Speeches, 1952–65* (Dar es Salaam: Oxford University Press, 1966), pp. 186–7.

8. Zanzibar received its independence in December 1963, underwent a bloody revolution in January 1964 and formed a union with Tanganyika in April 1964 to create the current United Republic of Tanzania.

9. For detailed analyses of *ngoma* practice throughout Tanzania, see Frank Gunderson and Gregory Barz (eds), *Mashindano!: Competitive Music Performance in Tanzania* (Dar es Salaam: Mkuki wa Nyota Press, 2000).

10. Elias Jengo, Louis A. Mbughuni, and Saadani A. Kandoro, *Falsafa ya Sanaa Tanzania* (Dar es Salaam: Baraza la Sanaa la Taifa, 1982); Amandina Lihamba, 'Politics and Theatre in Tanzania after the Arusha Declaration, 1967–1984 (Ph.D. thesis, University of Leeds, 1985); Louis Mbughuni, *The Cultural Policy of the United Republic of Tanzania* (Paris: Unesco Press, 1974); Louis Mbughuni and G. Ruhumbika, 'TANU and National Culture', in G. Ruhumbika (ed.), *Towards Ujamaa: Twenty Years of TANU Leadership* (Nairobi: East African Literature Bureau, 1974), pp. 275–87; Penina M. Mlama, *Culture and Development: The Popular Theatre Approach in Africa* (Uppsala: Nordiska Afrikainstitutet, 1991); Elias M. Songoyi, *Commercialization and Its Impact on Traditional Dances* (Trondheim: Radet for folkemusikk og folkedans, 1988 [1983]); idem, 'The Artist and the State in Tanzania. A Study of Two Singers: Kalikali and Mwinamila', (Ph.D. thesis, University of Dar es Salaam, 1988).

11. Mbughuni and Ruhumbika, 'TANU and National Culture', p. 280.

12. Mbughuni, *Cultural Policy*, p. 18.

13. This figure includes the financing, engineering and building of the TAZARA railway linking Tanzania and Zambia. See William R. Duggan and John R. Civille, *Tanzania and Nyerere: A Study of Ujamaa and Nationhood* (Maryknoll, NY: Orbis Books, 1976), pp. 153–4; George T. Yu, *China's African Policy: A Study of Tanzania* (New York: Praeger Publishers, 1975).

14. Yu, *China's African Policy*, p. 123, n. 67.
15. Godwin Kaduma, Director of Arts and National Languages, Ministry of Education and Culture, interview with author, Dar es Salaam, 26 July 1993.
16. Louis Mbughuni, former Director of Arts and Languages, telephone interview with author, 22 March 1997.
17. The Ministry had been attempting to engage Tanzanian citizens in a Tanzanian Cultural Revolution ever since China started its infamous Cultural Revolution. While we have the benefit of hindsight and can breathe a sigh of relief that the Ministry failed in this effort, it is still significant that the effort was made. For a full discussion, see Kelly M. Askew, *Performing the Nation: Swahili Music and Cultural Politics in Tanzania* (Chicago, IL: University of Chicago Press, 2002).
18. Mbughuni, telephone interview.
19. Juma Bakari, Instructor of Theater Arts, National College of Arts, interview with author, Tanga, 31 December 1992.
20. Karl Marx and Frederik Engels, *The German Ideology, Part One*, edited by C.J. Arthur (New York: International Publishers, 1970), p. 53. I am indebted to Carolyn Martin Shaw for this citation.
21. V. I. Lenin, *'Left-Wing' Communism: An Infantile Disorder* (New York: International Publishers, 1934), pp. 33–4.
22. The extent to which they pursued a socialist agenda is debatable, however, as Elias Songoyi points out. He argues that the opposite in fact occurred: that the increase in number of cultural troupes led to a commercialization of tradition wherein profit supplanted ideology as the defining principle. See Songoyi, 'Commercialization and Its Impact'.
23. One notable case is the highly popular Muunganao Cultural Troupe, established in 1980 by Norbert Chenga, then an administrator of the National Theatre Company. See Siri Lange, 'Managing Modernity: Gender, State and Nation in the Popular drama of Dar es Salaam, Tanzania" (Ph.D. thesis, University of Bergen, 2002), p. 66.
24. Askew, *Performing the Nation*, pp. 184–91.
25. Emmanuel Mollel, Acting Director of Arts and Languages, interview with author, Dar es Salaam, Tanzania, 13 July 1998.
26. 'Serikali mkono wake ulikuwa mfupi'. Mollel, interview.
27. Over the last decade, Dar es Salaam has grown to supplant Tanga in this regard.
28. For more details on KIUBATA's performance in the 1992 National Arts and Languages Competition, see Askew, *Performing the Nation*, pp. 196–223.
29. In another domain, newspaper editorials frequently attributed the peace Tanzanians enjoyed (as compared with the chaos in neighboring countries like Rwanda, Burundi, and Kenya) to Tanzanian socialism.
30. Nyerere, 'President's Inaugural Address', p. 187.
31. James C. Scott, *Seeing Like a State: How Certain Schemes to Improve the Human Condition Have Failed* (New Haven: Yale University Press, 1998), 231–55.
32. This is confirmed by Siri Lange whose research in Dar es Salaam revealed Makonde *ngoma* in the repertoire of every cultural troupe she canvassed. See Siri Lange, *From Nation-Building to Popular Culture: The Modernization of Performance in Tanzania*, Chr. Michelsen Institute Report, R 1995: 1 (Bergen, Norway: CMI, 1995), pp. 52–6.
33. Like most musical groups I knew, KIUBATA experienced a high rate of performer turnover, yet for the year I followed the group's activities closely, there were never less than three Makonde performers in the *ngoma* section of the troupe, which typically had around 25 members.
34. For more on Makonde initiation ceremonies, see Lyndon Harries, *The Initiation Rites of the Makonde Tribe* (Livingstone, Northern Rhodesia: The Rhodes-Livingstone Institute, 1944).
35. *Vinyago*, the famous masked dancers associated with Makonde ritual, follow a variation on this pattern. In their case, drummers are positioned as part of the circle formed by onlookers who do not dance but who clap their hands in accompaniment and encouragement, while the *kinyago* (sing.) dances solo in the middle.

36. Black Star Musical Club, Lucky Star Musical Club, Golden Star Musical Club, White Star Musical Club, Bandari Taarab, and Babloom Modern Taarab were the bands that existed during the period of my research.

37. Jean Lave and Etienne Wenger, *Situated Learning: Legitimate Peripheral Participation* (Cambridge: Cambridge University Press, 1991).

38. *Ibid.*, p. 29.

39. 'Cheche za TOT zatimiza mwaka', ('TOT finishes one year'), *Uhuru*, 14 August 1993, p.15.

40. Captain John Komba, Director of Tanzania One Theatre, interview with author, Tanga, 21 May 1995.

41. Askew, *Performing the Nation*.

42. Space does not allow for a thorough comparison here, but in contrast to the mainland, the Zanzibar government has always considered *taarab* its national music and supported *taarab* orchestras. The cultural troupe phenomenon never really took root there as it did on the mainland.

43. The privately owned Muungano Cultural Troupe (est. 1981), one of Dar es Salaam's most popular cultural troupes throughout the past two decades, introduced *taarab* into its repertoire not long before TOT's birth but was unusual in this respect. See Lange, *From Nation-Building to Popular Culture*.

44. On my most recent trip to Tanzania in February 2001, I discovered that TOT now ends its performances with *dansi* music. This is a strong indication that *taarab*'s popularity is decreasing and that the genre is following the fortunes of many a musical genre previously that fell out of popularity in the wake of some new musical trend.

45. 'Singers thrill fans in Dar', *Daily News*, 28 March 1994.

46. 'Muungano, TOT compete today', *Daily News*, 26 March 1994.

47. Estimates vary and precise figures are not forthcoming, but TOT's start-up costs are generally placed in the realm of Tsh. 20,000,000 (at that time, the equivalent of US$50,000).

48. Komba, interview. Some critics may want greater clarification on my referring to TOT as CCM- as well as 'state'-sponsored. While political liberalization officially ended the existence of the single-party state (wherein CCM and 'the state' were interchangeable), in fact, the strength of CCM compared to that of other parties, and its continued dominance in electoral politics, means that Tanzania effectively remains a CCM state. That is expected to change, however, as other parties gain knowledge, experience, and credibility.

49. This was not always the case. Older musicians describe how early *taarab* groups performed with everyone in uniform, male and female members alike. That performance pattern, however, changed in the 1970s to assign only male members uniforms. The existence, or lack, of uniforms holds different meanings in different contexts, and while *taarab* emerged in some places with an aesthetic of uniformed members, I would not extend to that an association with socialism or the state. I do, however, consider TOT's resuscitation of female uniforms in the 1990s a form of identification with the state aesthetic outlined here.

50. Komba, interview.

51. Bhabha, 'DisseminNation', pp. 299, 311.

52. Loren Kruger, *The National Stage: Theatre and Cultural Legitimation in England, France, and America* (Chicago and London: University of Chicago Press, 1992).

53. *Ibid.*, p. 187.

54. *Ibid.*, p. 134.

55. *Ibid.*, p. 7.

Index

bin Abubakari, Salim 120
Abyssinia 124
Achebe, Chinua 204
acrobatics 308, 314; National – Troupe 308
Adal Insaf 200
*Africa Newsletter*i 205, 208, 209
African Lakes Company 158
African National Congress 7-8, 250-66; ban on 265; Youth League 256
Africanization 259, 297-8, 307
Afrika Kwetu 203, 204
Afrocentrism 292, 293, 297-8, 300
Afro-Asian Solidarity Committee 257; Conference 264
Afro-Shirazi Party *see* Zanzibar
age-sets 73, 74, 86, 81
agriculture 73, 94-5, 151, 157, 207, 290
Aia, Ng'wana 16, 17, 28
aid 30
Alexander, Jocelyn 9
Al-Falaq 200, 201, 204-13, 223-4
Algeria 226
Ali, Mwasaburi 284
alienation, of local people 8, 290-4 *passim*, 302
All Africa Peoples' Conference 257
All Muslim National Union of Tanganyika 7-8, 250, 261-2
Alpers, Edward A. 3-4, 8, 33-54
Ameir, Khamis Abdullah 225

Amin, Idi 58, 63-6 *passim*, 290
ancestor veneration 141-2, 315
Anderson, Benedict 1, 99, 278, 283
Apindi, Ezekiel 120
Appadurai, Arjun 9
Arabs 198-9, 202, 203, 207-8, 210-12, 216-18 *passim*, 222, 224, 235, 239; Association 200-13 *passim;* East African Arab Union 210
army mutiny 252, 267
artists 8, 9, 304-24 *passim*
Arusha 5, 73-83 *passim*; Citizens' Union 80; Constitution (1948) 79; Declaration 285, 306
Asians 174, 180-2 *passim*, 184, 199, 222, 224, 282 *see also* Indians
Askew, Kelly 8, 9, 304-27
Austen, Ralph 4, 57-69
Azikiwe, Nnamdi 122

Babu, Abdulrahman Mohammed 216, 218-20 *passim*, 224-5, 227-42 *passim*
Baganda 117
Baines, D.L. 61
Bainu, Kassimu 258
Bakari, Mutoro bin Mwenye 41, 120
Bakhari, Seif 238
Banda, Hastings Kamuzu 206
Barghash, Seyyid 43, 45, 117
Al-Barwani, Sheikh Ali Muhsin 204-5, 207, 209-12 *passim*
Bayldon, Ivor 172

Bayume, Mohammed Hussein 5, 114-27 *passim*
beer drinking 94-6
Belgium 61, 226
Bell, Catherine 24
Bemba 158
Bene, Simeon 77, 78, 80
Bene/Wabene 34-48, 105-11, 128-48 *passim*
Berlin, Conference (1884/5) 301; treaty (1890) 59
Berry, Sara 72, 87
Bhabha, Homi 305-6, 323
Biringi bin Usambo 96
Bloch, M. 24
Boal, Augusto 307
boundaries, colonial 4, 57-66 *passim*, 104, 109
Bourdieu, Pierre 28
Bowles, B.D. 219
Brecht, Berthold 307
Brennan, James 7-9 *passim*, 250-76
Brett, F.W. 62
bridewealth 139, 162-3
Britain 2, 7, 8, 29, 58-61, 76-82 *passim*, 86, 89, 96, 104, 122, 140, 144, 168-79, 281, 282, 297, 324 *see ; also* colonialism; Indirect Rule; Colonial Office 168-79 *passim;* Communist Party 205, 208; in Zanzibar 199, 205-6, 212-13, 223, 226-31 *passim*
Brown, Gordon 131, 133
Brown, Ronald 200
Bryceson, Derek 259, 263
Buddu 59-60, 62, 63
Buganda 59, 62, 63
El Buhriy, Hemedi Abdallah bin Said 117
Bukoba 61, 62
Burgess, Thomas 7, 216-49
burial, royal 14, 17-20 *passim*, 24
Burton, Richard F. 38, 41
Bushiri rebellion 114, 117

Cameron, Sir Donald 62, 71, 72, 122
Cannadine, David 24
caravan traffic 150, 151
Castro, Raul 228
censorship 200-15 *passim*, 251, 256
censuses 152, 153
Central Africa 185-91 *passim*;

Federation 159, 174, 186
Césaire, Aimé 122, 124
Chama cha Mapinduzi (CCM) 1, 286, 305, 320-2 *passim*
Chalula 89, 90, 92-3
Chande, Suleimani bin Mwenye 120
Charamila, Kingalu mwana 47
Chatterjee, Partha 99, 278
Chawili, mwana Kumbang'ombe 47
chiefs 4-6 *passim*, 28, 29, 33-56, 70-7 *passim*, 82, 86-102, 104-7 *passim*, 111, 129-35, 139-46 *passim*, 152, ; 260, 267
China 223, 228, 229, 241, 257, 308
Christianity 2, 119, 120, 130, 135-9, 145, 146
Church Missionary Society 90, 96
Citizenship Bill 259
clans 3, 6, 34-8, 73, 88, 128-35 *passim*, 139, 140, 145, 146
class factors 7, 198, 201, 207, 219-22 *passim*, 300
coffee 5, 78-81 *passim*, 290
Cohen, Sir Andrew 177-8
Coleman, James S, 116
colonialism 2-5, 57-63, 70-3, 76-83, 87-9 *passim*, 93-4, 96, 103-21 *passim*, 129, 131-4, 144-6, 169-215; *passim*, 278-9, 285, 294-7 *passim*, 300; anti-6, 10, 96, 103, 104, 149, 164, 212, 218, 226, 227, 257, 283, 300, 308, 316; neo- 299, 300; post- 3, 4, 8, 57, 290-303 *passim*; pre- 3, 8, 10, 57-9 *passim*, 79, 103-13 *passim*, 140, 151, 293, 297-8, 301
Commonwealth 193
Commonwealth Development Corporation 142, 143
Comoro Islands 198
Constitution (1965) 268
Constitutional Development Committee 170
constitutional reform 170-83 *passim*, 255
Cooper, Frederick 283
co-operatives 5, 259-60, 267; Federation of - Unions 259
Cory, Hans 79, 81, 99
Council of Ministers 183, 184, 188, 191
councils, district/tribal 139, 143, 152

Crawford, Sir F. 184, 189
credit 202
Cuba 228, 229, 239
culture 6-9 *passim*, 119, 122-3, 279,
    280, 290, 291, 302-27 *passim*;
    Ministry/Division of 305, 310-12,
    316
Culwick, A.T. 105-6, 108, 131-4
    passim, 136
Culwick, G.M. 131-4 *passim*

Daily News Bulletin 199
dance 290, 291, 310; National -
    Troupe 306
dansi 313, 314
Dar es Salaam University 10, 11
Davidson, Basil 1, 298
Dawn in Zanzibar 228
death, royal 16-18 *passim*, 22-3
decolonization 149, 168, 169, 190-2
    passim
democracy, multi-party 250, 255, 269;
    one-party 252, 255
Depression 158, 324
Dernburg, Bernhard 61
descent, rules of 128
Deutsch, Jan-Georg 114
dissidence, political 2, 3, 5, 6, 8, 9,
    250-76 *passim*, 302
divorce 139
Dodoma 5, 86-102 *passim*, 168, 253
drama 308, 314; National - Troupe
    308
drunkenness 96
Dubois, W.E.B. 121
Dundaga, Kingalu mwana 38

East Africa 169, 185-93 *passim*, 281,
    318; Arab Union 210; Federation
    192
East Germany 223, 241, 257
education 149, 222-4, 291-302, 307-8
Egypt 223, 227-9 *passim*, 257;
    revolution 228
elections 160, 250; (1958-9) 169, 172,
    173, 178-83 *passim*; (1960) 191, 192,
    255; (1961 Zanzibar) 230, 231;
    (1962 presidential) 262-3, 267;
    (1963 Zanzibar) 234-5, 238; (2000)
    1, 251-4 *passim*; Post-Elections
    Committee 183, 189, 191

Emin Pasha 59, 66, 114
Engels, Friedrich 221, 309
Equiano, Olandah 125
ethnic factors 7, 198, 207, 219, 220 *see
    also* race
ethnography 14, 15, 104, 105, 128-46
    passim, 295
Eurocentrism 293-8 *passim*
Europe 294-6, 299; Eastern 228, 229
examination questions 296-7
Executive Council 170, 176, 185-7
    passim; Zanzibar 202

family 6, 128-48 *passim*
famine 97-8
Fanon, Frantz 116, 306, 307
Feierman, Steven 3, 4, 8, 10, 14-32,
    104, 163, 251
Fimbombili, mwana 36, 37
Fipa 152-8 *passim*
Fischer, Ernst 307
Foucault, Michel 6
France 294, 324
Franchise Committee 180
Freire, Paolo 307

Ganda 59, 63
Geertz, Clifford 24
Geiger, Susan 8, 278-89
gender issues 278-89
generational factors 7, 217, 219-25,
    229
genealogies 130
Germany/Germans 51, 58-61, 74-8,
    88-92 *passim*, 109, 114, 117, 120-3,
    281
Giblin, James L. 1-12, 41, 128-48
Glassman, Jonathan 203-4, 220
Goans 198
Gogo 82, 86-102, 107, 125
Gold Coast/Ghana 61, 168, 169, 193
Gorell Barnes, William 173, 174, 179,
    184
Gowers, Sir William 62
Grattan-Bellew, A.J. 175, 176, 179
Guinea 308
Gulliver, Philip 162
Gurnah, Abdulrazak 230
Gwassa, Gilbert 14, 117

Habari za Wiki 199

Hadimu 198
Hall, R. de Z. 94
Hamad, Rashid 212
hande 22
Hanga, Kassim 233, 234, 237
Al-Harthi, Abdulla Suleiman 210
al-Harthy, Sheikh Abdallah 205
Hartnoll, A.Y. 89, 93-4
Haya 59, 62, 63, 260
Heaney, L.M. 98
Hehe 131
Herbst, Jeffrey 2, 58
Herzfeld, Michael 305
Hignell, Hugh 94, 96
Himidi, Yusuf 238
Hindus 174
historians 14-32 *passim*, 115, 116
Historical Association of Tanzania 9-
    11 *passim*
historiography 2, 115, 116, 118, 120,
    122-4 *passim*, 219, 292
history 9-11 *passim*, 29, 86, 114-27
    passim, 291-302; colonial 292, 293,
    296-8 *passim*, 300; globalist 293-5,
    298-9, 302; nationalist 292-3, 297-
    300 *passim;* teaching of 8, 291, 295-
    302; tribal 103-7, 110, 11
Hizbu l'Wattan l'Riaia Sultan
    Zanzibar 212
Hobsbawm, Eric 122
Hodgkin, Thomas 116
Hofmeyr, Isabel 86
Holy Ghost Fathers 43-7 *passim*
Horner, Père Anton 35, 36, 39-46
    passim
Hutt, Bruce 131, 133
Hydèn, Göran 267

'Iajjemy, Abdallah bin Hemedi 17, 21
Ibrahim, Ahmed 262
ideology 2, 3, 7, 104, 130, 145-6, 207,
    259, 267, 283, 284, 290-4 *passim*,
    299, 306, 309, 314, 316, 323
Iliffe, John 6, 7, 9, 117, 168-97, 283
IMF 1, 304
Imperial British East Africa Company
    118
independence, winning of 168-97
    passim, 295; Zanzibar 238
Indians 198, 202, 258; Muslim
    Association 200

Indirect Rule 2, 4, 8, 29, 70-3 *passim*,
    76-7, 87-9 *passim*, 99, 104, 111,
    122, 129, 132, 135, 140, 145, 146,;
    150, 152, 156
inheritance 139
initiation rituals 116-17
installation, royal 14, 16, 18-21, 24, 26
International League for Defence of
    Ethiopia 124
International Red Locust Control
    Service 161-2
Iraqw 14
Iringa 131
iron smelting 151, 157-8
Islam 7, 119, 120, 201, 207, 208, 218,
    227, 281
Al-Ismaili, Amour Zahor 204, 205,
    210
Ismailis 253-4
Issa, Ali Sultan 225, 227-9 *passim*, 232-
    3, 237, 240, 242
Italy 124
ivory trade 33

Jamal, Amir 259, 263
bin Jamaliddini, Abdul Karim 117
James, C.R.L. 124
Japhet, Kirilu 171
Jhaveri, K.L. 255-6
jihad 201, 206-8 *passim*
Jones, Ernest 208
Juma, Mohamed 110

Kaaya clan 73
Kaaya, Leveria 121
Kaaya, Sylvanus 82
Kaduma, Godwin 308
Kagera Salient 58-66; Loop 60-2
    passim; Triangle 60, 61
Kagwa, Sir Apolo 117
Kahama, George 256
Kahemele 140
Kaijage, Frederick 14
Kaikai, Kaikai Saidi 257
Kambona, Oscar 191, 257, 268, 283
Kandoro, A.S. 121
Kapere, Mwene 154
Karasek, August 27
Karume, Abeid 216-19 *passim*, 237,
    240-2 *passim*
Kawogo, Tulalumba 136-7

Kenya 58, 63, 64, 115, 118, 119, 173, 174, 178, 184, 185, 188, 190-3 *passim*, 206, 281
Kenyatta, Jomo 121-4 *passim*, 206
Keto, John 256
Khalil, Khalil Ali 200
Kharusi, Ahmed Seif 200, 205, 209, 210
Kibasila 117
Kieran, J. 298
Kikuyu 123
Kilimanjaro 74, 118, 125
Kilindi 24, 27, 28
Kilio cha Mwenyeji 256, 264, 265
Kilombero Valley 5, 103-12 *passim*, 131
Kimambo, Isaria N. 10-11, 14, 16, 24, 29, 30, 104, 114, 116, 150, 298
Kimweri Mputa Magogo 17, 26-8 *passim*
Kingo, Mtoro Rehani 203
kingship 14-32 *passim*
Kinjala, Omari 117
Kinjikitile wa Ngwale 14, 117
kinship 129-33, 144-6 *passim*
Kisabengo 34, 38, 41, 42
Kishili 77, 81
Kisiri, Andreas 80
Kiswaga, Chief 134, 142
KIUBATA 314-18
Kiwanga, Towegale 105-10 *passim*
Kiwanuka, Joseph 258, 259
Kiyyumi, Sheikh Suleiman Abdulla 210
knowledge 2-4 *passim*, 6, 8, 14-32 *passim*, 122-4; historical 291-302
Koestler, Arthur 124
Koinange, Peter 262
Koitalel arap Samoei 117
Komba, Captain John 320-2 *passim*
Komsomol (Young Communist League) 221-2
Kongola, Ernest 91-6 *passim*
Krapf, Ludwig 118
Kruger, Loren 324
Kwalevele, John 103-11 *passim*

labor 2, 5, 149-66 *passim*, 198, 217, 259-61 *passim*, 309, 310
Lairumbi 77, 78
Laiser, Lazaros 78

Lake, F.J. 134, 136
Lake Province 182, 183
Lake Rukwa 151
land 76-80 *passim*, 82; alienation 5, 76-8 *passim*, 139, 141
Lave, Jean 319
Lawi, Yusuf Q. 8, 9, 14, 290-303
League of Nations 62
Legislative Council 169-70, 172, 174, 177, 178, 181-9 *passim*, 254, 255; (Zanzibar) 201-2, 211, 212
legitimacy, chiefly 3, 5, 6, 70, 77, 82, 129, 130, 134, 144, 146
Lemenye, Justin 121
Al-Lemki, Ahmed Mohamed Nassor 202, 204, 205, 209-10
Lemki, Mohamed Nassor 210
Lenin, V.I. 220-2, 227, 309-10
Lennox-Boyd, Alan 172-4 *passim*, 176, 177, 181, 183-91 *passim*, 206
Leonhart, William 240-1
Leshabar 75, 76
Lesian 78
Lesikale 78
liberalization, economic 1, 304, 316; political 323
Listowel, Judith 250
Lobolu, Mangi 74
local people 8, 290-3, 297-302 *passim*
Lofchie, Michael F. 201, 209, 212, 226
Lonsdale, John 281
Loti, Mdoe 17, 18, 21, 23, 29
Lugard, Lord 122
Lusinde, Job 96, 98-9
Lyttelton, Oliver 205-6

Maasai 79
MacGregor, JoAnn 9
Mackenzie, J.W.M. 178-9
Macleod, Iain 169, 190-3 *passim*
Macmillan, Harold 190
Macpherson, Sir John 173-6 *passim*, 183, 184, 189
Maddox, Gregory H. 1-12, 86-102, 106
Mafoudh, Ali 236, 241
Magana, Peter 123-4
Magram, Said bin Awadh 45
Mahenge District 103-13
Maine, Kas 115-16
Mair, Lucy 203

Makaidi, Emanuel 262
Makame, Hasnu 240
Makonde 316-18 *passim*
Makonnen, T. Ras 124
Makuka, mwana 36-7
Malecela, Yohana 96
Malinowski, Bronislaw 123
Malode, Amos 98
Mambwe 152-60 *passim*
Mamdani, Mahmood 1, 2, 87, 121,
    278-9, 282, 285
Mapanda, Abdalla 117
Mapunda, B. 92-3, 100
Maraai 74, 78
marriage 130, 136-9, 145
Mars, Jean-Price 122, 124
Marx, Karl 220, 238, 309
Marxism 219, 221, 236, 299-300, 309
Masanja, Francis 260
Masengye 74, 76
Masinde 76
Matengo 290-2
Mathew, Gervase 296
Mathieson, W.A.C. 173, 179-80
Matunda 76
Mazengo 5, 86-102
Mazinda 60
Mbegha 18, 21, 28
Mbeyela, Joseph 135, 141-4 *passim*
Mbeyela, Mtenzi 135, 142
Mbeyela, Pangamahuti 134-6 *passim*
Mbinga 290, 302
Mbogoni, Jioni 97
Mbogoni, Lawrence 7, 198-215
Mbughuni, Louis 307-9 *passim*
Meek, Charles 79
memory, landscapes of 114-27
Meru 5, 73-7, 81-3 *passim;* Citizens'
    Union 81
Mhanga, Mbwana Mkanka 16, 23
Migeyo, Ali 121
migration/migrants 5, 6, 104, 139,
    149-66 *passim*, 279; returning 162-3
missionaries 43-7 *passim*, 74, 118, 120,
    137, 157, 163
Mkasi, mwana 36, 37
Mkongwa 134-6, 140-5 *passim*
Mkongwa, Benedict 144
Mlenga, Eliasi 144
Mlenga, Reuben 143-5 *passim*
Mlolere, Johani 111

Mlolere, Mohamed 111
Mnyampala, Mathais E. 88-90 *passim*,
    96, 97, 99, 106-7, 121, 125
Mnyeji, Kadiria 234
modernity/modernization 2, 96, 99,
    100, 107, 118, 120-1, 293-6 *passim*
Moffett, J.P. 282
Mohamed, Bibi Titi 259, 283-5 *passim*
Mokgatle 125
Mollel, Emmanuel 312
Monela, Andrew 158
monogamy 136-9 *passim*
Monson, Jamie 4, 5, 103-13
Monthly Newsletter 199
Mooring, Sir George 231, 233
Moosa, Ali Shariff 212
Moyo, Hassan Nasser 233, 234, 237,
    240
Mpapai, Mohamed 103, 110
Mrima 35-8 *passim*, 41, 125
mtemi 87-94 *passim*
Mtemvu, Zuberi Mwinyisheikh Manga
    252-67 *passim*
Mudimbe, V.Y. 295
Al-Mugheiri, Sultan Ahmed 211
Al-Mugheiri, Sir Said bin Ali 210
Muhsin, Ali 204, 205, 227, 231-4
    passim, 237, 258
Mullen, Joseph 160, 163
Muloli, Rev. Miki 90, 91, 96
multi-party system 250-76 *passim*, 304,
    321
multi-racialism 7, 175, 178-83 *passim*,
    190, 203, 234, 250, 255, 266
Mumford, W. Bryant 133
music/musicians 8, 304, 310, 312-23
Muslims 1, 2, 4, 174, 201, 207, 208,
    282 *see also* Islam
Mwafrika 256, 268
Mwafrika na Taifa 262
Mwakangale, J.B.M. 259
Mwanga, Kabaka 59, 117
Mwenda, Edward 144
Mwenzo Welfare Association 162
Mwilenga, Anton 103-11 *passim*
Mwongozi 199, 200, 204, 205, 208, 209,
    226-7

bin Nasr, Muhammad 38, 44
Nasser, Col. Gamal Abdul 227
Natepe, Abdalla Said 238

Index

National Arts and Language
Competitions 314-18, 321, 322
National College of Arts 304, 305,
308-10 *passim*, 312, 318, 322, 323
National Theater Company 308
National Union of Tanganikya
Workers 267-8
nationalism 1-9, 57, 62-6 *passim*, 70,
99, 103-13 *passim*, 116, 129, 130,
139, 143, 149, 150, 162-4 *passim*,;
169, 172, 177, 181, 250, 278-89,
294, 297, 299; Zanzibari 201-3,
207, 208, 212, 218-20 *passim*, 222,
238
Nationalist 265
nationalization 241, 285, 307
N'damba 105-11 *passim*
Ndasikoi 75
Ngala, Ronald 264
Ng'ambo 198, 199
Ngoilenya 77, 79
ngoma 305, 306, 310, 313-18;
liungunjumu 316-18; *mbuji* 315; *ukala*
315-16
Ngurumo 256
Nigeria 61
Njau, Mzee Paulo 125
Njombe 6, 134-46 *passim*
Nkrumah, Kwame 122, 124, 206
non-racialism *see* Turnbull
Northern Province 179
Northern Rhodesia 153, 158, 159,
162, 174
Nugent, Paul 57-9 *passim*, 63
Nyamwanga 152-6 *passim*, 160-3
Nyasaland 174, 190, 191
Nyerere, Julius 1, 2, 7, 63, 65, 86, 96,
99, 149, 171-7 *passim*, 216, 240-1,
250-2 *passim*, 259, 262-8 ; *passim*,
279, 282-6 *passim*, 306, 310, 316
Nyereu 75, 76
Nyika 152-8 *passim*
Nyumbanitu 141-3

OAU 64, 65
Obote, Milton 63
Odhiambo, E.S. Atieno 5, 114-27
Odinga, Oginga 258
Ogot, B.A. 298
Ojike, Mboni 121
Okello, John 240

Okoth, George Samuel 120
Okoth, P. Godfrey 65
Oliver, Roland 296
Olonana 117
Oman 318
Omido, Frederick Esau 256-8 *passim*
Ondong', Asuman 120
one-party state 255, 263-6 *passim*, 268,
285, 304; (Zanzibar) 217, 218
Ongong, Mohammed 120
van Onselen, Charles 115, 116
von Oppen, Achim 114
opposition, political 7, 250-76 *passim*
Owalo, Johana 119

Padmore, George 124
Pan African Movement 121, 122, 124
Pare 16, 24, 104
patronage 7, 41, 76, 78
Patterson, Orlando 125
Pemba 1, 210, 212, 217, 239
People's Convention Party 266
People's Democratic Party 261, 266
Peters, Karl 66, 87, 118
Petterson, Don 241
Pogoro 109, 111
police 191-2, 210
political parties 2, 7-8, 250-76
politics 2, 4-8, 14-56 *passim*, 73, 76-83,
107-12, 216-76 *passim*
polygyny 130, 136-8 *passim*, 145
Ponda, Ali 252-3
Pottier, Johan 160
power 85-102, 114-20
press 198-215, 220
Preventive Detention Bill/Act 261, 262
Public Service Commission 193

Qadirrya brotherhood 281

Rabemananjara, Jacques 124
race/racism 7-8, 87, 171, 178, 219-22,
234, 257-9, 279
rain-making 3, 87, 88, 97-9 *passim*
Ranger, Terence O. 9, 116, 118, 122
Rankine, Sir John 202, 204; Plan 202,
212
Rashid, Rashid Khamis 237
Rawaito, 74, 76
Rebmann, James 118
reform,constitutional 170-83, 255;

Index

(Zanzibar) 216-17
refugees 301
regionalism 150, 163-4
regulations, public assembly 251
religion 2, 4, 7, 8, 119
resettlement 139, 141, 153
resistance 97, 104, 117, 163
Riami, Masoud M. 200
riots 201, 258, 260
Risklin, L.A. 38
ritual 3, 4, 14-32
Robertson, P.A.P. 230, 231, 237
Rodney, Walter 299
Rupia, John 253
Russia 221-2

Sabaya 75, 76
Saida Waafrika Ltd 259-60
Saileni, Jackson 263-7 *passim*
Saileni, Jeremiah 265
Saleh, Iibuni 212
Samachar 200
Sambegye 75-7 *passim*, 81
Sanga, Michael 255
Sante 75, 77, 81
Santi ya Umma 236
Santi ya Vijana 225
Saruni 75
Saul, John 299
Schmidt, Heike 114
scholarships, overseas 223, 227, 228, 231, 257
Scott, David 6
Scott, James 2, 285, 316
sedition, charges of 7, 200-12, 231-2; trials 7, 210-11, 231-2
Selassie, Haile 124
self-government 168, 187, 188, 190, 206
Senghor, Leopold Sedar 122, 124
settlers 5, 77, 82, 104, 121, 168, 169, 174, 175, 191
Seyyid Said 198, 202
Shabaani, Marijani 256-7
Shaha, Kingalu mwana 3, 34-48 *passim*
Shambaa 3, 14-32
Shekiondo, Saguti 16-17
Sheriff, Othman 240
Shirigdin, Sheikh Abdulla 210
Shivji, Issa 300
Sichone, Owen 156

SILABU 153, 154, 160, 162
Simbamwene 41
Simon, Chief 77
sisal 150-4, 158-60 *passim*, 163, 313, 316-17
slaves/trade 33, 35, 198, 202, 281
social studies 301
socialism 261, 304, 306-8 *passim*, 316; in Zanzibar 216-17, 2202, 225, 227, 230, 236, 238, 240
Societies Ordinance 176
Solf, Wilhelm 61
Solzhenitzyn, Alexander 124
songs 290
South Africa 115-16, 153, 279, 290
South Rukwa 149-66
Southern Highlands 5-6, 128-66
Soyinke, Wole 203, 306
Spear, Thomas 4, 5, 70-85
Stanley, Henry Morton 66
Steinhart, Edward I. 117
Stone Town 199, 217, 239
strikes 163, 186
students 221, 223, 227-30 *passim*, 236
von Stuemer, Willibald 60
sufism 281-2
Suleiman, Hassan 252-3
Sumlei, Sephania 80
Sunday News 256
Sunseri, Thaddeus 281
Swahili 8, 280-4
Sykes, Abulwahid 121, 282
Sykes, Daisy 121
Sykes, Kleist 121
'Systems of Production' 301

taarab 305, 313, 318-23; state 320-3
Tabora Conference, TANU 182, 186, 252
Tajo, Ameri 212
Tanga 6, 151, 153, 154, 160, 162, 163, 178, 179, 312-18
Tanga Cement Company /troupe 314
Tanganyika African Association 170-6, 253, 282, 283, 285
Tanganyika Elected Members Organization 189, 191
Tanganyika Federation of Labour 255, 260-2, 267
Tanganyika Standard 256
TANU 7, 9, 86, 96, 103, 104, 108-10

passim, 130, 139, 143-6 *passim*, 158,
162-4 *passim*, 168-97, 250-76; 279-
83, 285, 307; Tabora Conference
182, 186, 252; National Executive
192; Youth League 144, 162, 255-7
passim, 262
Tanzania One Theater 320-3
taxation 34, 80, 81, 110, 158
Temu, A.J. 298
Thiong'o, Ngugi wa 306
Thomas, H.B. 63
Tip, Tippu 120
trade 4, 5, 33, 202; slave 33, 35, 202
trade unions 163, 220-1, 237, 261,
262, 267; Federation of Progressive
- 231, 233, 237; TFL 255, 260-2
passim, 267
tradition 4, 5, 70-2 *passim*, 82-3, 86,
87, 316; neo- 5, 70-1, 76-82 *passim*
tribe/tribalism 6, 8, 87, 88, 103-7,
110-11, 122, 156, 279, 280, 282
troupes, cultural 306, 310 *see also*
individual entries
Tumbo, Christopher 259, 261, 264,
266
Tupa, *mtemi* 96
Turnbull, Sir Richard 182-92 *passim*,
255
Twala, Abdul Aziz 240
Twenty-First February 1954 209
Twining, Sir Edward 106, 152, 169-83
passim

Uganda 58-65, 184-9 *passim*, 192-3,
290
Ugogo 5, 86-102
Uhuru 259
Ujamaa 2, 8, 100, 149, 285, 308, 316
Ulanga 131
Uluguru 3, 34
Umma Party *see* Zanzibar
underdevelopment theory 299-300
Union of Tanganyika and Zanzibar 1,
2, 216, 219, 241-2
United Arab Emirates 318
United Nations 121, 171, 178, 181,
192; Trusteeship Council 177
United States 124, 219, 241-2, 294,
324; Federal Theater Project 324
United Tanganyika Party 172-4 *passim*,
180, 181, 250, 251, 254

universal suffrage 172, 173, 178
Usambara 3, 104, 118; Citizens Union
104
USSR 241
Ustadhi 305, 319-20
Uwanda 160-3

Vansina, Jan 33
Varian, R.W. 96
Versailles Peace Conference 121
villagization 285, 307
voting systems; common roll 178, 254;
tripartite 169-70, 178-82, 252

war; Cold 223; Maji Maji 114, 117,
189; Mau Mau 115, 189, 206;
Tanzania-Uganda 63-4, 290;
World I 61, 76, 114, 151, 152,
281, 301; II 77, 139, 154, 168,
199, 301
Wanda 154-6 *passim*
Watson, William 159, 160
Waziri 47
weddings, church 136
Wenger, Etienne 319
West Africa 168, 169, 173, 174, 294,
301
West Africa 122
West Lake Region 260
Westermann, Dietrich 114, 123, 124
White, Paul 90-1
White Fathers 163
Wicken, Joan 268
Willis, Roy 157
Wilson, President Woodrow 121
witchcraft 77, 78, 161
women 26-7, 128, 133, 138, 139, 164,
278, 280-1, 283-6 *passim*
World Bank 297, 304
Wright, Marcia 5-6, 149-66

Yngstrom, Ingrid 93, 100
YOU *see* Zanzibar
youth 7, 128, 149, 154, 159, 218, 221-
42 *passim*

Zambia 149, 156, 159, 162, 308
ZANEWS 228, 231, 235-7 *passim*
Zanzibar 1, 7, 33, 41, 43, 117, 198-
249 *see also* Arabs; Asians; All -
Students Association 229; Arab